DATE DUE

JAN 03 2006	JAN 26 2016	
	JUN 11 2018	
FEB 09 2006		
FEB 24 2006		
MAR 01 2006		
MAR 29 2006		
APR 20 2006		
APR 16 2007		
JUN 09 2007		
JUL 07 2011		
MAR 08 2012		
JAN 05 2013		

DISCARDED

GAYLORD | | | PRINTED IN U.S.A.

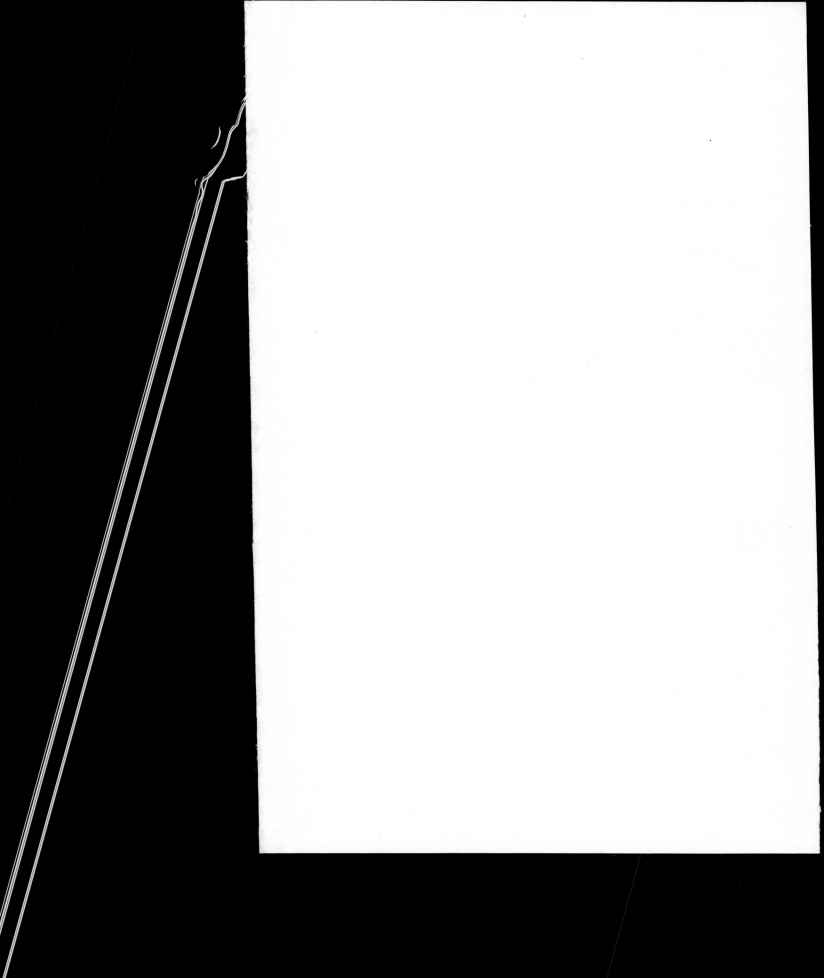

Also by Richard Slotkin

*Regeneration Through Violence: The Mythology
of the American Frontier, 1600–1860*

*The Fatal Environment: The Myth of the Frontier
in the Age of Industrialization, 1800–1890*

*Gunfighter Nation: The Myth of the Frontier
in Twentieth-Century America*

*So Dreadfull a Judgment: Puritan Responses to
King Philip's War, 1676–1677*, with James K. Folsom

The Crater

The Return of Henry Starr

Abe: A Novel of the Young Lincoln

Lost Battalions

LOST

BATTALIONS

The Great War and the Crisis
of American Nationality

RICHARD SLOTKIN

A JOHN MACRAE BOOK

HENRY HOLT AND COMPANY ▪ NEW YORK

Henry Holt and Company, LLC
Publishers since 1866
175 Fifth Avenue
New York, New York 10010
www.henryholt.com

Henry Holt® and ⬛® are registered trademarks
of Henry Holt and Company, LLC.

Distributed in Canada by H. B. Fenn and Company Ltd.

Library of Congress Cataloging-in-Publication Data

Slotkin, Richard, 1942–
    Lost battalions : the Great War and the crisis of American nationality /
Richard Slotkin.—1st ed.
        p.   cm.
    Includes bibliographical references and index.
    ISBN-13: 978-0-8050-4124-8
    ISBN-10: 0-8050-4124-9
        1. United States. Army. Infantry Regiment, 369th—History.   2. United
States. Army—Recruiting, enlistment, etc.   3. World War, 1914–1918—
Regimental histories—United States.   4. World War, 1914–1918—
Participation, African American.   5. African-American soldiers—History—
20th century.   6. United States. Army—African American troops—History—
20th century.   7. Minorities—United States.   8. United States—Ethnic
relations.   I. Title.

    D570.33369th .S58   2005
    940.4'0089'96073—dc22   2005046312

Henry Holt books are available for special promotions and
premiums. For details contact: Director, Special Markets.

First Edition 2005

Designed by Victoria Hartman

Maps by James Sinclair

Printed in the United States of America

10   9   8   7   6   5   4   3   2   1

Dedicated to my father,

Herman Slotkin—

different war, same fight

War is the health of the state.

—Randolph Bourne

Yeah, fighting a war to fix something works about as good
as going to a whorehouse to get rid of a clap.

—Norman Mailer, *The Naked and the Dead*

You can't break eggs without making an omelette
—That's what they tell the eggs.

—Randall Jarrell, "A War"

CONTENTS

ILLUSTRATIONS AND MAPS

Maps

Illustrations

Lost Battalions

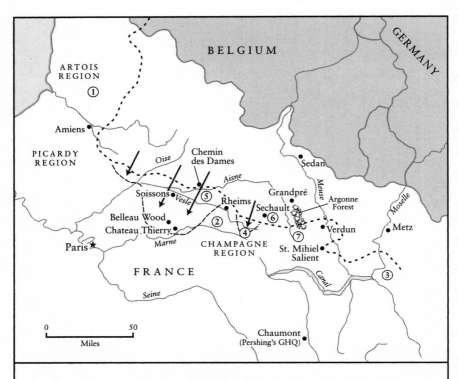

The 369th Infantry and 77th Division on the Western Front

① 77th trains with British in Picardy, May 1918   - - - - - Front lines, April 1918

② 369th fights in Champagne sector, May 1918   —— Front lines, July 1918

③ 77th trains with French in Lorraine, June–July 1918   ← German offensives

④ 369th fights in "Bastille Day" offensive, July 1918

⑤ 77th in Vesle-Aisne fighting, August–September, 1918

⑥ 369th in Grand Offensive, September 25–October 1, 1918

⑦ 77th in the Argonne, September 25–October 8, 1918

Safe for Democracy: The Lost Battalion and the Harlem Hell Fighters

> The world must be made safe for democracy. . . . To such a task we can dedicate our lives and our fortunes, everything that we are and everything that we have.
>
> —*Woodrow Wilson, Address to Congress (April 2, 1917)*

On Monday April 2, 1917, President Woodrow Wilson summoned Congress into joint session to hear his call for a declaration of war against the German empire. For two and a half years he had resisted with determination all pressures for the United States to intervene in Europe's Great War, in the hope that American diplomacy and economic influence could bring about a negotiated "peace without victory." But pressure for U.S. entry had become intolerably great. A chain of political and economic decisions bound the United States to the Allies despite our official neutrality. The nation's leaders were convinced that if the United States did not now decisively intervene, it would lose its power to influence the ordering of the post-war world.

That decision committed the United States to full participation in the worldwide competition of the Great Powers, and broke the political tradition that had restricted overseas engagements to the Caribbean and the Pacific. To fight the war the United States would disrupt and transform its political institutions, licensing Washington to regulate every aspect of civil life from the purchase of consumer goods to the expression of opinion. Opposition to the war was considerable, the risk of social disorder serious, victory by no means assured. To win the public to his cause, Wilson framed U.S. war aims as the defense of ideals at once universal and distinctly American: to make the world "safe for democracy" and create a League of Nations to govern the world of nations as our own civil institutions governed the citizens of the republic.

Wilson's dream of a new world order was the culminating expression of a vision of American power that had captivated the nation's intellectual and political elites for thirty-five years—the so-called Progressive Era of American political history. In that time the United States had developed into the world's leading industrial power. Its population, its productive capacity, its technology, its wealth, and its military potential had grown with astonishing speed. Rapid change produced social disruption. But the success with which the nation had overcome the destruction of the Civil War and mastered the technology and organizational problems of industrial mass production inspired a generation of leaders with a heroic vision: the belief that a combination of scientific method and the will to action would enable enlightened leaders to rationally control the future course of development. That belief was shared by both the captains of industry who had created the gigantic corporations and trusts, and the Progressive reformers who wanted to regulate them. The pragmatist philosopher William James expressed their creed succinctly: the world is "essentially a theater for heroism. In heroism, we feel, life's supreme mystery is hidden."[1]

The leading opinion makers of the Progressive Era conceived of war as an expression of that heroic vision. Even James, who abhorred violence, believed that to sustain both social solidarity and the dynamism of the quest for progress, a "moral equivalent of war" was required: "something heroic" that could rouse men's idealism and public spirit as war does, but without the violence and destruction. At the other extreme, nationalist Progressives like Theodore Roosevelt saw war as a positive good, the means by which "the great fighting races" spread their superior civilization to the "red wastes" of savagery and barbarism. "Aggressive fighting for the right," Roosevelt wrote, "is the noblest sport the world affords."[2] The Progressives who organized the nation's war effort in 1917 believed the quest for world power could go hand in glove with the labor of perfecting American democracy at home, because the war itself would mobilize and unite public opinion, and vest those in command with authority to get things done.

Events would prove their vision of war an illusion. Governing elites had the power to unleash war, but could not control the violent forces of nationalism, racism, and class conflict that shaped its course. The stress of war would pry apart the fault lines in American society, and reveal that the democracy for which the world was to be made safe had not resolved the most fundamental issues of its own national organization: Who counts as "American," and what civil rights must citizenship guarantee?

There were two regiments whose presence among the American Expeditionary Forces in France symbolized this unresolved dilemma. The 308th Infantry was part of the AEF's 77th Division; the 369th Infantry was on loan to the French Fourth Army's 161st Division. Both regiments were raised in New York, the city whose cultural complexity and power would shape the form American society would take in the twentieth century. They would fight their greatest battles within twenty miles of each other, as part of the all-out Allied offensive that broke the German army's will to resist.

The 77th was a unique outfit: sometimes known as the "Melting Pot" Division, because its ranks were filled with "hyphenated Americans" from the Lower East Side, Chinatown, and Little Italy, Red Hook and Flatbush in Brooklyn, the tenements of Harlem and the Bronx. It was said that its men spoke forty-two different languages, not including English. In their ranks were "all [the] races and creeds" of the great metropolis,

> men who had only recently been subjected to the pogroms of Russia, gunmen and gangsters . . . Italians, Chinamen, the Jews and the Irish, a heterogenous mass, truly representative both of the varied human flotsam and the sturdy American manhood which comprise the civil population of New York City.[3]

The division had fought with awkward courage in the battles of August and September, and its assignment in the great offensive was critical and exceptionally difficult: to protect the AEF's left flank and take by assault the heavily fortified Argonne Forest. But it was only the chance of their location and the haste with which the campaign was planned that forced Pershing's staff to rely on them. The army still did not entirely trust the men of this division. It was not simply that they were draftees and inadequately trained: that was true of most divisions in the AEF. These men were suspect because of who they were and what they represented: "hyphenated Americans" at a moment when nothing less than "100% Americanism" seemed an adequate standard of patriotism and loyalty. Many were first- or second-generation immigrants, and traced their ancestry to countries with which the United States was now at war.

Beneath the question of loyalty was a more insidious doubt. Most of the men in the 77th belonged to ethnic groups that had come to the United States in the great waves of immigration after 1881: Italians, Jews from every country and province in eastern Europe, Poles and Russians, Romanians, Slovaks, Greeks, Serbs, Lithuanians, and Chinese who came despite the various state and federal laws intended to exclude them. They represented peoples or cultures that seemed utterly alien in customs, religion, language, and physical appearance to native-born American Whites, and even to the assimilated immigrants who had come to the United States in the large migrations of 1848–65. In a society that had always been most critically divided by the color line, differences in that degree were inevitably likened to the racial differences dividing Negroes and Indians from Whites. In 1907—the year in which Ellis Island processed the largest number of immigrants in American history—an official report of the United States Commission on Immigration declared that these new immigrants belonged to "races" whose inherited and biologically fixed characteristics made them unfit for American citizenship. They were said to lack the "basic qualities [of] . . . intelligence, manliness, cooperation," without which "democracy is futile." While the men of the Melting Pot Division were fighting to make the world safe for democracy, powerful parties back home were questioning whether democracy was safe when entrusted to their kind of people and developing plans for restricting their presence in American life.

The other New York City outfit could have given the hyphenated Americans of the 77th an earful on the consequences of being marked as racially different. Unfortunately, that conversation could not happen: in war they served in different armies, in peace they inhabited different worlds. The 369th Infantry was an African-American regiment attached to the 161st Division of the French Fourth Army, with which the 308th

Infantry was supposed to maintain liaison. It was formerly the 15th Regiment of the New York National Guard, known to its hometown as the "Old Fifteenth" and to history as the Harlem Hell Fighters. Its enlisted men and noncommissioned officers had been recruited for the most part in the five boroughs. They had been elevator operators and salesmen, redcaps and shopowners, ironworkers, ballplayers, hatmakers, house painters, boxers, small-time gangsters, farmers. Among them were world-class musicians who would introduce France to American jazz and a quiet pious foundryman from the rural Catskills who would become a famous painter. Some were lifelong New Yorkers, but many were "immigrants" who had fled the Jim Crow South. Among their small cadre of Black officers were a noted civil rights lawyer and the world-famous jazz musician James Reese Europe, who also commanded a company in the line. Their White officers were scions of some of the nation's oldest and most prominent families. Colonel Hayward was handsome and famous enough to be portrayed by James Montgomery Flagg on the cover of the *Saturday Evening Post*. Hamilton Fish Jr. was the great-grandson of Grant's secretary of state, and would become a leader of the isolationist Republicans in the 1930s.

If the immigrants of the 77th Division were objects of suspicion, the Black men of the 369th were subject to something worse: a prejudice so deep and cruel it could justify the segregation, degradation, and lynch-mob violence of Jim Crow; so ingrained that every offer made in proof of the Black man's humanity provoked not only rejection but "personal disrespect and mockery . . . ridicule and systematic humiliation . . . distortion of fact and wanton license of fancy . . . the all-pervading desire to inculcate disdain for everything black, from Toussaint to the devil."[4]

These men had had to fight for the right to fight for their country: overcoming the reluctance of White politicians to authorize a Negro regiment, the violent antagonism of the Jim Crow town in which they had to train, the War Department's unwillingness to accept them for federal service, and finally the refusal of AEF commanders to use them as anything but labor troops. During the German spring offensive, when the French were begging for American units to shore up their lines, Pershing loaned the 369th to the French. The loan became a gift, and the *"enfants perdus"* found a home in the French Fourth Army commanded by General Gouraud. The French accepted them as Americans, without any marked distinction as to race—in itself a liberating experience. The men had been in combat almost continuously since April, learning their trade, taking losses. Now they were qualified to go in with Gouraud's storm battalions, not quite as expert as French veterans who had been fighting for three years, but more proficient than the vast majority of White troops in the AEF.

The presence in the battle line of the Black 369th and the "Melting Pot" 308th Infantry symbolized a crisis stage in a social and cultural conflict that was as vital to the future of American democracy and nationality as the decision to go to war. The exigencies of total war required that all the country's available manpower be mobilized, and this could hardly be done without including African-Americans and "hyphenated Americans." In 1917 roughly one-eighth of the population were African-American, and one-third of the population were either foreign-born or the child of a foreign-born parent. Many in the press and the political leadership feared that these alien or alienated groups would be indifferent or hostile to the war effort. Immigrants from Germany and Austria-Hungary might actually sympathize with the enemy; African-Americans might be subverted by enemy agents playing upon their grievances. In the anxious weeks following the declaration of war stern measures were proposed to compel these peoples to prove their loyalty or go to jail.[5]

But the War Department and army command knew—and the political and journalistic leadership would soon recognize—that in an open society it was impossible to build an effective army on the basis of coercion alone. A systematic effort would have to be undertaken to win the hearts and minds of the alien and the alienated, to awaken in them that intense identification with the nation that is the foundation of military morale. By a variety of means, and through several agencies, the nation's social and political leaders reached out to the leadership of the minority communities: heads of civic and civil rights organizations, religious leaders, newspaper editors, artists and writers. They worked out a set of useful understandings (and equally useful misunderstandings), some embodied in formal agreements and others left implied or suggested, which together amounted to a new social bargain between the government and its racial and ethnic minorities. If the minority communities demonstrated their Americanism by buying war bonds and sending their young men into the service, and if those young men served loyally and effectively on the battle line, then the government would support them in their quest for equal citizenship and acceptance.

The terms of that bargain were displayed in the vast outpouring of propaganda with which the government appealed for popular support of the war, the draft, and the purchase of bonds to finance the war. They were spelled out in the military primers and instruction manuals with which all soldiers were supplied, and elaborated in the curriculum of the training camps. For all that, what the government would actually do to fulfill its part of the bargain was implied rather than formally stated. Indeed, with respect to Blacks the War Department explicitly said it would not make the war the occasion for solving the "so-called race problem." Nonetheless, leaders of the minority communities affirmed their belief in the bargain, and urged their people to register for the draft and subscribe to the Liberty Loan; and Blacks and "hyphenated Americans" responded by buying bonds, and by enlisting and serving in numbers exceeding their share of the general population.

They believed in the bargain because it matched so precisely the expectations and desires aroused by America's promise of liberty and justice for all. Moreover, the government demonstrated its good faith by adjusting the terms of military service to meet the special needs of minority communities. Special cultural and religious facilities would be provided, and assurance given that in the army their young men would not be subject to discrimination or unfair treatment in the assignment of tasks or the making of promotions. More than that, the government conceived of the new training camps as gigantic "universities" for educating Americans of every region, race, and creed in the fundamentals of an American national ideology. The war curriculum would acknowledge that Negroes, Jews, Irish, German-Americans, Poles, and the rest had contributed to this national history, and were entitled to place their own heroes—Frederick Douglass, Haym Salomon, Thomas Meagher, Carl Schurz, Christopher Columbus, Thaddeus Kosciusko—in the national pantheon with Washington, Lincoln, and Daniel Boone.

Under the pressure of world war Americans were working out a new understanding of American nationality. The project played out on the large stage of national and international politics, and in the pages of the mass-circulation newspapers and magazines that shaped public opinion. It was also enacted in microcosm within the ranks of regiments like the Harlem Hell Fighters and the "Melting Pot" 308th Infantry. The social structure of these outfits mirrored the division of cultural power in the larger society. Officers and men had to work out, face-to-face and within the framework of military discipline, the means by which to deal with their own differences and prejudices, to live (if it were possible) on terms of intimacy with each other, and to establish bonds of trust that would bear the extreme stress and terror of a life-or-death struggle.

The officers who commanded companies and platoons represented the nation's social, intellectual, and political elite: sons of the newly rich and of old American families, Ivy League–educated, lawyers and professional men, members of the Harvard, Century, and Racquet clubs, graduates of the elite Plattsburgh officers' training camp. They shared a strong ideological and personal attachment to the ideas and the mythical figure of Theodore Roosevelt: the cowboy-president who had led the Rough Riders' charge up San Juan Hill in 1898 and won the Nobel Peace Prize six years later; the Progressive reformer who had made himself the personification of "America Militant" in his two-year campaign for "Preparedness" and for war against Germany. At times they felt like missionaries to some alien and uncivil tribe, whose language and manners were uncouth and incomprehensible. But they made the effort of outreach, hoping to teach their dialect-speaking Negroes, their immigrant "Izzies and Witzers and Tonies" to talk and think like real Americans: that is, like themselves—as if there were only one style in which to express the patriotism that enables men to fight and win their nation's wars.

The men in the ranks had their own agendas, their own ways of organizing the life of the units in which they served. Before they were soldiers they were New Yorkers, "born in the briar patch" of the mean streets. The mishmash of cultures and classes, which their officers thought strange and un-American, was their native environment, the America they inhabited. Their patriotism was expressed in the edgy and skeptical idiom of people used to living on the margins of the good American life. They would make their own original contribution to the process by which their melange of peoples was transformed into military units marked by high morale and intense solidarity. They would teach their officers, as well as learn from them, how to be American.

In the end, the men of both regiments would more than keep their part of the social bargain. On September 26, 1918, the Hell Fighters began five days of continual assault against entrenched German positions, taking hundreds of prisoners, storming fortified Bellevue Ridge and capturing the town of Sechault at a terrible cost in dead and wounded. They would hold the town against German counterattacks that threatened to turn Sechault into a modern Alamo, and when the last German attack was beaten back they still had morale enough for one last drive against German positions dug into a dense woodland. But by then their casualties were so high that they had, in effect, been destroyed as a fighting force. On October 1 the French withdrew them from the line and awarded the entire regiment the Croix de Guerre.

At the same time some twenty miles east of Sechault the 308th and its brigade-mate 307th Infantry had plunged into an ordeal of blind combat in the heavy woods and marshland of the Argonne. On October 2 the survivors of two battalions of the 308th and a company of the 307th would break through the German lines, only to be cut off and surrounded at Charlevaux Mill. They were commanded by two alumni of Harvard and Plattsburgh: Major Charles Whittlesey, a gangly Wall Street lawyer and sometime Socialist in wire-rimmed spectacles; and George McMurtry, son of a steel trust robber baron and veteran of Roosevelt's Rough Riders. Their men were the city's riffraff, Jews, Italians, Chinese, Poles, Irish, and whatnot, plus raw replacements just thrown into the melting pot: cowboys, Mexicans, and Indians from the West; IWW miners from Butte; Swedes and Norwegians from Minnesota. They held out through five days of starvation and combat, survived a friendly-fire bombardment and a flamethrower attack, while the division fought desperately to break through to them. When they were relieved fewer than two hundred of more than seven hundred men who had started the fight were able to leave the field on their own legs. Four won Medals of Honor, and a score of Distinguished Service Crosses were also awarded. The newspapers made Whittlesey's command legendary as the "Lost Battalion."

But the acceptance and equality for which the soldiers and their people had bargained and fought would not be forthcoming. On the home front the pressures of war produced a powerful political reaction which, under the banner of "100% Americanism," reaffirmed the supremacy of the White and native-born, and gave official sanction to discrimination against Blacks, Jews, and other "new immigrants." Nor did the veterans find that permanent place in the national myth they had fought to earn. The deeds of the Harlem Hell Fighters were at first overshadowed by those of the Lost Battalion, then erased as part of a systematic campaign to use the supposed "failure" of Negro troops to justify the perpetuation of Jim Crow. The Lost Battalion was better remembered, but the value of their heroism was diminished by a consensus that saw the war itself as a wasteful failure, and ultimately their fame was eclipsed by events of the greater world war of 1939–45.

Thus both were, in a double sense, "Lost Battalions." They fought their last stands cut off and alone, and their stories have similarly been lost to memory and public myth. The loss was and is a serious one, for the men and their communities, and for the nation as a whole. The myths of a nation or a community are the stories that embody the memory of their peoples' collective past. The story of the Lost Battalion and the Harlem Hell Fighters is worth recovering, if only as an act of historical justice to their veterans. But it is also worth recovering for the sake of justice itself: it is one of those stories that reminds us just how difficult it has been for America to live up to the promises of liberty and justice for all that were made at the nation's birth—just how resistant Americans as a people have been to the moral demands of the democracy they profess.

The story of *Lost Battalions* is also worth telling for the light it sheds on a critical moment in American history, and on the processes that produce social and political change. In following their story we can see how the grand structures of policy and political thought play upon the people and culture of the streets and the trenches; and how ideas arising from the streets and trenches can, in turn, affect the rationales and usages of high politics. The career of the Old Fifteenth engaged its Black soldiers in direct confrontation with the Jim Crow South; its deployment to France exposed its men to a new and liberating understanding of themselves as Americans. The men of the 77th Division and their communities were Americanized and politicized by their experience, which would contribute to their emergence in the 1930s as pillars of the New Deal coalition. Although isolationism and intolerance triumphed in the aftermath of the war, the mobilization of 1917–18 was only the opening engagement in a fifty-year struggle to answer the two fundamental issues of American nationality: Were Americans willing to become a genuinely democratic multicultural and multiracial society; and would such a society be willing and able to support the nation's assumption of a Great Power role?

To understand the political forces and ideas that shaped this struggle, we must look first at the political and intellectual arguments over the modernization of the American nation-state at the turn of the century— arguments dominated by the ideas and the personal appeal of Theodore Roosevelt.

2

"The Great Composite American":
Theodore Roosevelt and American Nationalism,
1880–1917

> A life of slothful ease, a life of that peace which springs merely from
> lack either of desire or of power to strive after great things, is as little
> worthy of a nation as of an individual. I ask only what every self-
> respecting American demands from himself and from his sons shall
> be demanded of the American nation as a whole.
>
> —*Theodore Roosevelt, "The Strenuous Life" (1899)*

The Great War of 1914–18 was the culmination of two and a
half centuries of political struggle and social change, which produced
the modern nation-state. Centralized government was one feature of the
new state system, but strong monarchies and well-run empires had existed before. What made the nation-state a revolutionary innovation was
the cultural basis of its politics: where monarchies and empires were held
together by dynastic ties and military force, nation-state governments
claimed legitimacy as representatives of the political will and unique
character of a particular people, rooted in native soil.

The nation is not a family, clan, or tribe, not the face-to-face community in which one is born and reared. We have to be taught to think of
ourselves as constituents of "We, the People," who own the nation and
belong to it. No modern nation-state has possessed from the start an ethnically homogeneous population. Within the territories ruled by European states a variety of ethnic and religious communities had long existed,

whose history, customs, and allegiances predated the nation-state. For their political creation to be viable, nationalist leaders had to imagine and propagate the idea of "the People" as a "fictive ethnicity," an identity whose claims overrode loyalty to clan, class, or sect, strong enough to sustain the nation's solidarity against rival states. The first critical element in this new culture of nationality is the creation of a national history, or rather historical myth, which treats the tangled and complex web of pre-national ethnic and political relations as simply and necessarily a prelude to the realization of national identity. The national myth explains and justifies the state's territorial boundaries, its form of government, and its ways of defining citizenship, by rooting them in an imagined and/or invented past. Propagated through a national educational system and mass media, the myth provides the People with the illusion of a common past.[1]

The national myth allows the nation's various clans and sects and ethnicities to imagine themselves as kindred in a single lineage—a "race" bound together not only by the ties of civil citizenship, but by "blood." Imagining nationality as an attribute of race allows nationalists to define relatively sharply the boundary between those who belong to the nation and those who are excluded from it. Defining Great Britain as "Anglo-Saxon" or Germany as "the state of the German people" asserts an organic and exclusive right to control the nation's territory and limit admission to the rights of citizenship.

Thus the idea of *nationality* combined two concepts of social belonging: a *racial* concept, which limited belonging to those who shared a common "lineage" or "blood," and a *civic* concept, which recognized as qualified citizens all residents willing to affiliate with the state, obey its laws, serve it in war, and adapt to certain basic elements of the prevalent culture (language, marriage customs, etc.). The proportional weight given to racial and civic standards varied from nation to nation and time to time. The civic model was particularly strong in the United States, Great Britain, and France, where political and economic liberalism were strongest. Emphasizing civil qualifications for citizenship allowed these nations to more readily attract, assimilate, and win the allegiance of immigrants and ethnic minorities. Yet there remained a real distinction between such minorities and those who shared the putative national ancestry: as in the distinction between the "Anglo-Saxon" or "Briton" and the British citizen of Celtic ancestry; or between the racial Frenchman or German and the Jewish citizen of those states. Civil toleration of minorities did not compromise the principle that the nation truly belongs to those born to its original "racial" stock. In times of social or political crisis even the most civic-minded nations could revert to racialist nationalism, as happened in France at the time of the Dreyfus case in the 1890s.

The Problem of American Nationality

The institutional structure and ideological principles of American nationality were produced by a history radically different from that of the European nation-states. The United States began as a group of colonial settlements, which grew and prospered by expanding into the undeveloped lands to the west. Settler-state conditions fostered the "Jeffersonian" tradition of limited and divided government. Given the nation's vast reserve of undeveloped land and natural resources, and the energies of a rapidly increasing and mobile population, economic growth could be fostered by granting wide freedom of action to pioneers and entrepreneurs and considerable autonomy to local governments. The European pattern of close partnership between central governments and big business was not reproduced in the United States, where the state's regulatory powers were weak and ideological tradition disapproved of government-sponsored monopolies.

Settler-state conditions also shaped the concept of American nationality. Westward expansion and economic growth required a steady and rapid increase of population, which could only be achieved by encouraging European immigration and forcibly importing slaves from Africa. Individual colonies initially imposed sharp restrictions on who could become freeholders, but exclusions tended to erode over time. One of the legacies of the colonial settler-states to the American Republic was a civic concept of citizenship, open to the naturalization of foreigners; but it co-existed with a "racial" or exclusive ideal of nationality, which barred Blacks and Native Americans. The policy of open immigration was continued (despite occasional bursts of nativism) throughout the nineteenth century, because westward expansion continued and intensified the settler-state pattern of development.

It was therefore impossible for American nationalists to follow the British and German pattern of basing their national myth on a story of evolution from a single primitive tribal root. Settlers came from so many different nationality groups that any appeal to a pre-American past would be divisive rather than unifying; and the Revolution made severance from the European past an essential part of national ideology. Instead of defining themselves by reference to a common origin, Americans defined themselves against a common enemy. Continued expansion into Indian country could only be justified if Native Americans (later Mexicans) were treated as aliens, incapable of assimilation to the body politic; and the use of African slave labor could only be justified if Africans as a people were excluded from citizenship. Thus the central paradox of American nationality, the conflict around which national politics would develop, was its official commitment to an ideology of civic nationality—most clearly embodied in the Declaration of Independence—while at the same time its social practice excluded from citizenship rights all those who fell on the dark side of the color line. (Women were excluded as well, but this exclusion was not peculiar to the United States.) America before the Civil War was a "White Republic," which recognized no significant distinctions of rights or privilege among different kinds and classes of White men, but which excluded almost all non-Whites from citizenship.[2]

The Civil War and Reconstruction forced a painful confrontation with the paradoxes of national ideology, but did not resolve them. The war abolished slavery, but left intact the beliefs and social practices that had sustained the White Republic. The central government was strengthened, but the only aspect of sovereignty lost by the states was the questionable right of secession. Their power to regulate social life and decide who should count as a political citizen remained intact, as the South would prove by its systematic disenfranchisement of African-Americans, its toleration of lynching and its "Jim Crow" segregation laws (1880–1915). Thus the nation entered the postwar period of rapid social and economic change with its primary ideological dilemmas unresolved: To what uses can the power of the state legitimately be put, and how should national citizenship and political participation be defined and limited?

The industrialization and nationalization of the economy after 1865 produced social and economic disruptions that challenged the premises and politics of the Jeffersonian tradition. The belief that democracy was fostered by an unregulated competitive economy assumed the prevalence of small to medium-size businesses and a high degree of social mobility. Industrialization and the enlarged resources of finance capital concentrated ownership and economic power in a few large corporations and trusts, narrowing the range in which small proprietors could operate freely. Industrialization also created a large class of wage-dependent workers, concentrated in large cities and industrial towns. Their prospects for upward mobility were limited, and their economic security precarious because of the extreme volatility of the business cycle. It began to seem that the United States (like the Old World) was developing a permanent "proletariat," and with it the potential for social revolution. Fear of a proletarian uprising was intensified by changes in the nation's culture and demography: industrialization fostered large new waves of immigration by workers and peasants from Europe and Asia.

American intellectuals, journalists, and politicians interpreted these changes by the light of a tradition that saw *race* as the basis of significant human differences. Hitherto the American concept of race had differed from the European in one crucial respect: its function was not to make distinctions among Whites of different nationalities, but to signify likeness to (or difference from) a Negro or an Indian, the only classes excluded categorically from American citizenship. As labor-capital conflicts intensified, and the numbers of White immigrants grew, the cultural differences of the immigrants began to seem more threatening—more like the differences that made the political demands of Negroes and Indians dangerous to the civil peace of the White Republic. As early as 1869 Charles Francis Adams Jr. viewed with alarm the development of three race-defined "proletariats": Asian in the West, where Chinese laborers were being imported to build railroads; Celtic in the North, where Irish laborers were flocking to the new factories; and African in the South. Adams rated all three races inferior to native-born Whites in intelligence, morality, and general fitness for citizenship, and thought it necessary to protect American democracy by restricting their voting rights. In 1877, after four years of economic depression and strikes by industrial workers, the *Nation* magazine, noted for its liberal views, identified the new working classes as people "to whom American political and social ideals appeal but faintly, if at all, and who carry in their very blood traditions which give universal suffrage an air of menace to many of the things which civilized men hold most dear."[3] At the same time, Southern

Whites were using that same rationale to deprive freed Negroes of civil rights.

Both the Adams article and the *Nation* editorial appeared *before* the first great waves of "new immigrants" began to arrive. Between 1881 and 1914, a succession of massive immigrations filled the cities of the East and Midwest with aliens from parts of Europe not before represented in the population. They included large numbers of eastern European Jews from Poland, the Russian "Pale of Settlement," and from the Slavic provinces of Austria-Hungary, as well as the Slavic nationalities themselves, Poles, Serbs, Croats, Romanians, Czechs, Russians, Ukrainians. Southern Italy also sent large numbers of immigrants. On the West Coast, despite the Exclusion Acts of 1882 and 1892 there was still significant immigration from China and Japan. Most of the new immigrants did not speak English, and unlike earlier German immigrants most did not come from the cities or middle classes, but from preindustrial peasant societies. They would have had a difficult time acculturating under the most favorable circumstances, and it was harder in the new industrial economy to earn and save enough to better one's condition in the American manner. Thus for native-born Americans, and even for assimilated immigrants of earlier waves, the new immigrants were marked by an extreme cultural foreignness, chronic poverty, a seeming inability to live or think like "regular Americans." Their growing numbers and concentration in critical urban centers gave them the strength to distort American politics and infiltrate American culture with alien ways and values. Nightmare statistical extrapolations suggested that they might soon replace the native-born as the majority of the population.[4]

The turn of the century therefore saw the development of the most powerful nativist movement in U.S. history. The most influential of the nativist organizations was the Immigration Restriction League (IRL), organized in 1894 by upper-class Bostonians. Its publicists drew on the natural and social sciences to develop a new theory of race difference, which placed as much emphasis on the distinctions between different White or European groups as had been placed on the differences between Whites and non-Whites. Its central tenet was that true American nationality is defined by descent from "a single race, with substantially the same social and political instincts, the same standards of conduct and morals, the same industrial capability." Like Negroes and Indians, the new immigrants

> are beaten men from beaten races; representing the worst failures in the struggle for existence. . . . They have none of the ideas and aptitudes which fit men to take up readily and easily the problem of self-care and self-government, such as belong to those who are descended from the tribes that met under the oak-trees of old Germany to make laws and choose chieftains.

As a young man Harvard President A. Lawrence Lowell had criticized the South's imposition of Jim Crow—"thrusting out one race from the body politic"—as a violation of democratic principle. Now as spokesman for the IRL he believed that "Indians, Negroes, Chinese, Jews, and *Americans* cannot all be free in the same society." Either the un-American races must be expelled from political society (or prevented from entering), or the society itself must cease to be free.[5] The unresolved contradiction between civic and racial definitions of nationality thus threatened to subvert the basic American principles of civil liberties and political democracy.

The social and economic disruptions of 1880–1900 provoked a set of political and social movements, characterized as "progressive," which aimed at reforming civic culture and rationalizing economic life. These movements drew intellectual and administrative leadership from the educated middle and upper-middle classes of native-born or well-assimilated Whites: classes whose traditional social status and moral authority had been undermined by the commercialization of American society and the dominance of the newly rich by massive immigration and by a popular culture based on mass media.[6]

Theodore Roosevelt shared with Progressive reformers the sense that the concentration of wealth threatened to corrupt and destroy the republican system bequeathed by the Founding Fathers and vindicated by the war for the Union. But he was also alarmed by the growth of radicalism in the labor movement. The political traditions and cultural values that had hitherto governed American life were inadequate to check these tendencies: they privileged the pursuit of private interest as a moral and social good, and discouraged reform based on state action. What Roosevelt offered was a new ideology, in which an idealized vision of nationality would provide an overarching value, transcending the opposed interests of contending classes and harmonizing the disparate visions of corporate moguls and reformers. That national ideology, which he would call "Americanism," offered an alternative to the polarities of laissez-faire capitalism on the right and socialism on the left. But if the promise of that ideology was to be realized, Americans would have to learn to think of themselves as members of a single national family, rather than members of some particular section or class.

Roosevelt linked this ideological program to a revised and updated version of national mythology, which he promulgated through his copious writings as historian, his popular articles on subjects ranging from big-game hunting to the theory of evolution, and his political articles and speeches. And he impressed on the public mind both the ideological program and the myth through his highly publicized adventures as Western rancher and big-game hunter, his acts of military and political derring-do, his powerful speeches, and his inimitable platform presence. He became for many people the personification of his nation, "the great composite American . . . a man's man, a hero's hero, and an American's American."[7]

He looked to history for a usable past, which would explain the current impasse of regressive and progressive tendencies in American society and offer clues to the kinds of action that might break the deadlock. There were a number of historical themes on which he might have drawn: the epic of the Revolution, the prophetic character of the Founding Fathers, the tragedy and redemptive sacrifice of the Civil War. But the Revolution and Civil War evoked specters of social overturn and sectional disunity, hardly desirable amid the age's class warfare and racial strife; and the Constitution of the Founders had not provided the state with means to cope with the new economy. On the other hand, the myth of the frontier centered American history on a grand *national* project, with the expansion and progress of civilization as its goal; and its opponents were racially alien enemies, not constituents of American society. In the twenty years between his graduation from Harvard and his ascension to the presidency he published dozens of articles, wrote the multivolume history *Winning of the West* (1885–94), and delivered and published scores of public addresses, in which he developed his version of the national myth. He traced the racial origins of the American people from the warlike, freedom-loving Teutonic tribes, especially those "picked" strains that settled the British Isles. In the American wilderness this racial "stock" was further culled and strengthened by continual warfare against the native races—the wilderness serving as a Darwinian laboratory for perfecting the racial and national type. Like his younger contemporary, the historian Frederick Jackson Turner, Roosevelt believed American politics and society were now in crisis because the "frontier" had ceased to exist, and no comparably *national* project had appeared in its place.

Roosevelt found his moral equivalent of the frontier in the quest for an overseas empire in Asia and Latin America. After using his position as assistant navy secretary to promote the Spanish-American War (1898), Roosevelt raised a volunteer cavalry regiment to fight in Cuba—and used his personal celebrity and press connections to attract Western cowboys and wealthy Ivy Leaguers to its ranks and to publicize it as the perfect microcosm of an idealized America. The newspapers soon made it famous as the "Rough Riders," a name borrowed from the premier act of Buffalo Bill's Wild West Show, perhaps the most influential show business enterprise of the time and a popular-culture celebration of the frontier myth. Roosevelt would lead his regiment and the Black troopers of the Tenth Cavalry in a gallant charge up Cuba's Kettle Hill, misidentified then and forever after as "San Juan Hill," then parlayed his victory into a spectacular political rise: governor of New York, vice president for McKinley in 1900, successor to the presidency after McKinley's assassination in 1901.

He used his campaigns to preach his new Gospel of Progressive Nationalism, and establish himself as its heroic personification. He wanted first to arouse the nation's economic and intellectual elite to assume the responsibilities of power and to assert broad national and public interests in the political arena. To them he would "preach not the doctrine of ignoble ease, but the doctrine of the strenuous life, the life of toil and effort, labor and strife." They must recover the virility and warrior spirit that had belonged to their "fathers," who had conquered the wilderness and built the great corporations. A virilized leadership class would in turn regenerate the manhood of the nation. "As it is with the individual, so it is with the nation. . . . I ask only what every self-respecting American demands from himself and from his sons shall be demanded of the American nation as a whole." Men who *refuse* the call of the Strenuous

Life risk becoming personally unsexed; a people that declines the call of world power may become racially degenerate and effeminate, and like the Chinese "go down before other nations which have not lost the manly and adventurous qualities." Since there were no more Indians to fight, the only task demanding a comparably strenuous life was that of making the United States one of the imperial great powers of the earth. Frontier expansion taught Americans that the advance of civilization is "due solely to the power of the mighty civilized races which have not lost the fighting instinct, and which by their expansion are gradually bringing peace to the red wastes where the barbarian peoples of the world hold sway."[8]

For Roosevelt, war was the primary function of the nation. The national territory was established by wars of conquest and subordination, and maintained by military preparedness for national defense. But in the industrial era, and especially in a democratic society, national solidarity also required the state to ensure a substantial measure of social justice to all its citizens. Unless the state took positive action to ameliorate the differences between rich and poor, employer and worker, class conflict would retard economic progress, diminish patriotism, and weaken the state militarily. Roosevelt's nationalist vision therefore implied a social bargain: the president would energetically pursue a domestic reform agenda, a "moral equivalent of war" designed to reconcile the interest of labor and capital; in exchange, the mass of the people would support his pursuit of an activist foreign policy by rallying behind his diplomatic initiatives and taxing themselves to increase military preparedness.

Roosevelt's nationalism envisioned the perfect identification of a singular "American people" with their uniquely American nation-state. Although he paid lip service to a civic model of citizenship, his understanding of nationality was based on the traditional confusion of nationality with tribal or racial kinship. He found in the biological sciences (and pseudoscience) of his time affirmation of his assumption that each nation was constituted by a distinct people, with a unique physiology and distinctive psychology or racial personality—and confirmation of his presumption that some races were inherently weaker and less progressive than others.[9]

Although he saw America as essentially a White man's nation, Roosevelt recognized that it had a racially mixed population, which must somehow be assimilated to a unitary American nationality. African-Americans posed the problem in the starkest terms: if racial difference was primary and permanent, Black people could never be fully qualified Americans. To square his racial beliefs with the values of civil democracy, Roosevelt took the position that races might improve their inherited potential over time. To foster such improvement, he advocated the "Great Rule of Righteousness": *individuals* of every race must be given a fair chance to succeed, and meet the Strenuous Life standard of Americanism. However, Roosevelt believed such improvement would take a hundred or more generations, and in the interim policy must recognize the real *inequalities* between races. In a letter to his friend Owen Wister, Southern-born author of the classic western novel *The Virginian,* Roosevelt denied that the Negro race was *incapable* of improvement. However, "I entirely agree with you that as a race and in the mass they are altogether inferior to the whites," and he acknowledged the Negro's "unfitness generally to exercise" the right to vote.[10]

It was a question with Roosevelt whether the supposed racial disabilities that belonged to Negroes and Chinese should also be attributed to the nominally White "races" of the new immigration from eastern and southern Europe. The chief theorists of the IRL, Madison Grant and Henry Fairfield Osborn, were among Roosevelt's closest friends and intellectual companions, and their political leader, Senator Henry Cabot Lodge, was one of his closest associates. Roosevelt's concerns were perhaps best expressed by John R. Commons, the Progressive labor historian and sociologist whose *Races and Immigrants in American Life* (1907) was prepared for Roosevelt's own Commission on Immigration.[11] Older White immigrant stocks from northern Europe had been able to *amalgamate* with native stocks, blending both socially and biologically into a harmonious hybridity, a single national "family." They were able to do so because they shared three essential traits "which underlie democracy—intelligence, manliness, cooperation. If they are lacking, democracy is futile." However, the new immigrants were capable only of *assimilation* to American conditions. They might adapt their behavior, manners, and habits of work to American standards, but could never truly enter into the spirit or collective psychology of American nationality:

> Race differences are established in the very blood and physical constitution. . . . Races may change their religions, their forms of government, their mode of industry, and their languages, but underneath all these

changes they may continue their physical, mental, and moral capacities and incapacities.

The experience of Reconstruction showed the danger of extending civil rights to an unqualified race. To protect White society from Negroes, southerners had been forced to deprive Blacks of civil rights through the Jim Crow laws. Now the nation as a whole would have to choose between closing the immigration door and "despotizing our institutions"—that is, taking civil rights away from racially unqualified Whites.[12] But if Negroes and "new immigrants" could not be trusted with the right to vote, how could they be relied upon to fight for the American nation in time of war? That form of the question was critical for Roosevelt, for whom war making was the fundamental task of the state and warlikeness the central characteristic of a dominant race. It remained unresolved at the end of his presidency.

Roosevelt's terms in the White House demonstrated the potential power of his new approach to national government but also revealed its limitations. His personal popularity allowed him to intervene successfully in labor-capital disputes and block particular attempts at extending corporate monopolies. But he failed to establish a reliable public or political consensus for government regulation of big business. The public enjoyed his bold diplomacy and use of naval power to establish American hegemony in the Caribbean, without accepting his goal (or the expense) of aggressively competing with the Great Powers. His handpicked successor, William H. Taft, abandoned both his reforms and his foreign policy agenda. So in 1912 Roosevelt tried to displace Taft as Republican nominee and, when he failed, bolted the GOP to head the Progressive or "Bull Moose" Party. His platform, "The New Nationalism," offered a more radical systematic statement of his political theory. Washington must become the center of a broad-reaching regulatory regime, "the most efficient instrument for the uplift of our people as a whole." He was opposed on the right by Taft and the conservative Republicans, and on the left by the Socialist Party, headed by labor leader Eugene V. Debs. But the election went to Democrat Woodrow Wilson, a more moderate Progressive whose "New Freedom" was leery of the government's power to regulate: "I do not want a government that will take care of me. I want a government that will make other men take their hands off so I can take care of myself."

For Roosevelt the 1912 election had been a heroic battle between forces of light and darkness with the future at stake:

> We fight in honorable fashion for the good of mankind; fearless of the future; unheeding of our individual fates; with unflinching hearts and undimmed eyes; we stand at Armageddon, and we battle for the Lord.[13]

He had tried and failed to turn a debate over domestic reform into a moral equivalent of war. Two years later, with a real Armageddon in the offing, he would offer himself again as a heroic alternative to the unwarlike Woodrow Wilson.

The Gospel of Preparedness:
Roosevelt vs. Wilson, 1914–1917

The outbreak of the European war in August 1914 shocked American political leaders. Like their European counterparts they had supposed that the complex economic relations that bound the Great Powers to one another made the cost of war literally prohibitive. A similar calculation led them to suppose that the war itself must be brief. Yet after less than a year of war all such predictions were vitiated. The Great Powers had accepted the terms of total war, committed all their financial and industrial resources to the continuous raising and resupplying of multimillion-man armies, and developed modes of warfare aimed at destroying the economic viability of enemy societies. The Entente, or Allied forces (primarily Britain, France, Russia, and Italy), enforced a strict blockade against the Central Powers (Germany, Austria-Hungary, Turkey, and Bulgaria). The Germans responded by using naval forces, especially submarines, to attack all vessels carrying goods to Entente ports.

The American economy was enmeshed in the struggle from the start. Production and profits grew as the United States supplied the insatiable demands of Europe's embattled armies and beleaguered civilians. American banks expanded in wealth and power, as the United States became the primary source of world credit. Americans enjoyed the prosperity derived from the war, but were not eager to share the sacrifice. Ties of culture and historical reminiscence made most sympathetic to Britain and

France; and those feelings were reinforced by disgust at the Germans' invasion of neutral Belgium, their brutal treatment of civilians (exaggerated by brilliant British propaganda), the submarine campaign, and the bullying rhetoric of the Kaiser's officials. But distaste for Prussian excesses was offset by the grievance of Britain's blockade, and by the anti-British sentiments of the large Irish- and German-American minorities. If most trade and financial backing went to the Entente, there was also (at least initially) significant investment and trade with Germany.

There was also a powerful antimilitarist strain in national political culture: a fear of standing armies and centralized power that went back to 1776, and accounted for the parsimonious support of the small regular army. Randolph Bourne's aphorism, "War is the health of the State," was a slogan of the antiwar Left, but expressed a consensus view of the dire effects of mobilization on republican government. Fear of centralization was particularly strong in the South, Wilson's birthplace and the base of the Democratic Party, which remembered and resented the aggrandizement of national power that resulted from the Civil War. William Jennings Bryan, the Democrats' perennial presidential candidate and leader of its populist wing, had opposed the imperialist seizure of the Philippines and was adamant against U.S. intervention in Europe. He was Wilson's secretary of state.

There was no national constituency for war, and Wilson had no wish to create one. In 1915 the most popular song in America was "I Didn't Raise My Boy to Be a Soldier."

> I didn't raise my boy to be a soldier
> I brought him up to be my darling boy
> Who dares to place some musket on his shoulder
> To shoot some other mother's pride and joy
> Let nations arbitrate their future troubles
> It's time to lay the sword and gun away
> There'd be no wars today if mothers all would say,
> "I didn't raise my boy to be a soldier."

The president hoped that a neutral United States could use its economic power to mediate a negotiated peace. He expected that the belligerent statesmen and their peoples would soon recognize that the costs of continuing the war could never be repaid by the fruits of victory. In this he misread both the passions and the economics of war: after a year the costs in blood and treasure and grief were already so great that only victory could justify them. Wilson's diplomacy was also hampered by his commitment to the odd view that as a neutral the United States was barred from arming itself against the threat of war. This compelled him to minimize the need for preparedness in his addresses to the American people and to make only small, reluctant, and ultimately inadequate moves to strengthen the armed forces. Since neither side had reason to fear U.S. military intervention, neither was compelled to respect U.S. demands or accept offers of mediation.[14]

On the other hand, Wilson was obliged to respond to encroachments by the belligerents on American rights and interests. Each inescapable response effectively engaged the nation more closely with the conflict. The pattern was set by Wilson's response to the German sinking of the passenger liner *Lusitania* in May 1915 with the loss of more than a hundred American lives, many of them women and children. The public outcry was fierce. Wilson demanded that Germany end unrestricted submarine warfare, implying that the United States might declare war if it refused. The president's diplomatic rejoinder fell far short of an ultimatum, but even so it aroused strong opposition in the president's own party, and led Secretary of State Bryan to resign from the cabinet.

In contrast, Roosevelt was free to be straightforward and passionate in advocating war. He was a warhawk by temperament and principle, for whom readiness to fight was the test of personal, racial, and national greatness. If war was indeed "the health of the state," so much the better for realizing the regulatory policies of the "New Nationalism." A generation of Progressives had tried, with limited success, to discover that "moral equivalent of war," that great but peaceful national project that would unify the country's varied peoples and interests in selfless devotion to public good. The Great War was not a "moral equivalent," it was the thing itself, and just war, in Roosevelt's view, was the quintessence rather than the antithesis of morality: "War, like peace, is properly a means to an end [which is] righteousness. . . . Righteousness when triumphant may bring peace; but peace may not bring righteousness."

Roosevelt honored the people's reluctance by presenting preparedness as a preventive measure. As late as January 1917 he was saying, "I advocate military preparedness not for the sake of war, but for the sake of safeguarding this nation against war, so long as that is possible, and of guaranteeing its honor and safety if war should nevertheless come." But he was far readier than Wilson to see affronts to national honor in the tone of German diplomacy, and saw the sinking of the *Lusitania* as an atrocity demanding immediate retribution. "This is one of those rare times that come only at long intervals in a nation's history, where the action taken determines the basis of life of the generations that follow." He launched a full-throated campaign for military preparedness, which implicitly welcomed the prospect of American intervention. Seeking to broaden support for his cause, he distanced himself from the Progressive Party and sought rapprochement with the regular Republicans.

For Roosevelt the Gospel of Nationalism had been utterly absorbed by the Gospel of Preparedness, which he would preach till the end of his life. His ideal of nationality had always been that of a racially and culturally homogeneous society, responding to challenges as if it were a single Rooseveltian personality. That an American could be divided in mind and passion about avenging the *Lusitania* was, for him, a sign of personal or racial degeneracy. "As it is with the individual, so it is with the nation." It followed that Wilson's unwillingness to defend his or the nation's honor was a symptom of personal degeneracy. He ridiculed Wilson's pious assertion that "there is such a thing as a man being too proud to fight." The statement exposed his "abject cowardice and weakness. . . . As for shame, he has none, and if anyone kicks him, he brushes his clothes, and utters some lofty sentence."[15]

Roosevelt would reach out first to the audience he had addressed in "The Strenuous Life," the nation's social, cultural, and economic elite. If he could win their commitment to Preparedness, the American masses might be won to the cause by their example. His call to arms resonated with a generation of young men between the ages of twenty-five and forty, who had in some sense grown up with his words and example always before them, to show what a man and an American ought to be. The nation was their responsibility, and if her honor was imperiled it was up to them to set the people an example. A few signed up for noncombatant service in volunteer ambulance units; some rebuked their country's passivity by enlisting in the British, Canadian, or French armies.

Alan Seeger was an American poet living in Paris when war broke out; descended from an old and prosperous New England family, he had

gone to good prep schools, graduated Harvard in the class of 1910 with
Walter Lippmann and T. S. Eliot. With Lippmann he founded a Socialist
club, which protested university policies and petitioned the legislature on
behalf of labor: for Seeger a belief had no meaning unless one was willing to act upon it. The war was a challenge to civilization and his own
manhood—he had a "moral obligation" to take part, was shamed by his
country's refusal to assume *its* moral obligations. He enlisted in the
French Foreign Legion, saw action on the Western Front, and wrote his
best remembered poem, "I Have a Rendezvous with Death," after surviving the failed Champagne offensive in the fall of 1915:

> I have a rendezvous with Death
> At some disputed barricade,
> When Spring comes back with rustling shade
> And apple-blossoms fill the air.

At about that time he also wrote "A Message to America," in which he
condemned his countrymen for their lack of manhood, honor, and public
spirit, and condemned President Wilson for making the nation the
"laughing-stock" of Europe by "turn[ing] the other cheek." If Americans would redeem their character they must follow a different leader:

> You have a leader who knows—the man
> Most fit to be called American,
> A prophet that once in generations
> Is given to point to erring nations
> Brighter ideals toward which to press
> And lead them out of the wilderness.
> . . . .
> As for myself I know right well
> I would go through fire and shot and shell
> And face new perils and make my bed
> In new privations, if ROOSEVELT led.

He would validate that pledge, dying of wounds suffered when his regiment stormed the village of Belloye-en-Santerre, July 4, 1916.[16]

Roosevelt believed that the manly and militant spirit that moved
Seeger was widely shared in young men of his class and generation. To
arouse and cultivate that spirit Roosevelt joined with ex–Rough Rider

(now Army Chief of Staff) General Leonard Wood to create a volunteer officer training program at Plattsburgh, New York.

The Plattsburgh Movement:
Mobilizing the "Sons of Roosevelt"

The Plattsburgh idea was conceived before the war as part of the program for enlarging and modernizing the army that was developed by Major General and Chief of Staff Leonard Wood. He had graduated from Harvard Medical School and joined the army in 1885 as a contract surgeon. But he had a gift and an appetite for command, and abandoned medicine to become a line officer, winning a Congressional Medal of Honor for his role in the capture of the Apache chief Geronimo. In 1898 Roosevelt enticed him to serve as the first colonel of the Rough Riders. He trained the regiment—and Lieutenant Colonel Roosevelt—before leaving for higher command. He earned praise as military governor in occupied Cuba in 1899 and later (appointed by now-President Roosevelt) of the rebellious Moro Province in the Philippines. Like Roosevelt he was strong-willed and opinionated, which sometimes put him at odds with his superiors. He also had a certain charisma, "more like a football captain than a military martinet," and counted among his followers many of the army's best younger officers, like Douglas MacArthur, George Patton, and James Harbord.[17]

As chief of staff, Wood began the process of transforming what was essentially a frontier constabulary into a modern European-style army, with a general staff and war college. He actively promoted universal military service as the foundation of national military organization, which would provide the government with manpower for an army of European scale. The army would become "a great mill," or university, educating vast numbers of young men, realizing Roosevelt's vision of class conflict reconciled through national service. It would also (in Wood's words) "heat up the melting pot" and hasten the Americanization of the immigrants. Among the activities he sponsored was a summer camp for businessmen interested in becoming reserve officers.[18]

The outbreak of war in Europe added credibility to Wood's proposal for universal military service, but his often intemperate advocacy of preparedness, which echoed Roosevelt's, hurt his cause with the Wilson administration. Then the *Lusitania* was torpedoed and American opinion was shocked out of its complacency. The desire to avenge drowned women and children was not strong enough to make Americans want war, but calls for preparedness offered an appealing symbolic response. The Harvard Club of New York was a hub of preparedness agitation. Roosevelt and Wood were members, as were Roosevelt's ex-secretary of war Elihu Root, Root's law partner Grenville Clark, and the young Franklin D. Roosevelt (assistant navy secretary in Wilson's cabinet). In May 1915 a group of fifteen lawyers and businessmen met at the club and proposed a new military training movement, to be based on Wood's Business Men's Camp. In addition to Root and Clark, the leadership included Theodore Roosevelt Jr.; Crawford Blagden, a prominent New York banker; and Hamilton Fish Jr., Harvard classmate of Alan Seeger, a Roosevelt supporter and scion of one of the nation's oldest families. Wood was enthusiastic, and Theodore Roosevelt and financier Martin Schiff contributed to the start-up. Despite the personal hostility between Wood and Wilson, the administration authorized the project and agreed to detail instructors, and Bernard Baruch (Wilson's financial advisor) contributed to the funding. Plattsburgh was chosen for the first camp, and though the program itself was formally named the Military Training Camps Association, "Plattsburgh" became the nickname of the movement. The first season was a great success, and additional camps were established in the Midwest and West in the summer of 1916.

The project was mocked by its critics as summer camp for members of the Social Register, an exaggeration to which there was some truth. The requirement that enlistees pay their own expenses eliminated most wage earners from participation. Outreach and recruitment were selective, and targeted "our kind of people." Grenville Clark boasted that "the whole table at Delmonico's" had signed up. Recruiting was done through personal contacts with university presidents, Harvard alums, and clubmen in major cities. The *New York Times* put an appeal for Southern enlistees on its sports pages, presumably the section preferred by Dixie's sporting elite. But the selectivity and elite aura of the first Plattsburgh encampment became a major source of the movement's appeal. "All the best families seem to have been drafted into the machine-gun platoon. . . . Socially it is already a tremendous success, as people like myself are already going around apologizing for not being there."

Wood said he doubted whether there had "ever assembled in a camp of instruction . . . as highly intelligent a body of men or one more thoroughly representative of all that is best in our citizenry." Three of Roosevelt's sons attended, along with a fifty-five-year-old ex-cabinet officer, a congressman, New York's police commissioner, some veterans of the Rough Riders and French Foreign Legion, Henry James's namesake and nephew, and Willard Straight—the Morgan banker who, as a diplomat, had developed the strategy of "dollar diplomacy." Straight was a friend of the Progressive editor Herbert Croly and a financial backer of his magazine; his influence helped attract favorable attention in the *New Republic* and other Progressive journals.

The men who turned out each summer for the encampments were, for the most part, exactly the sort to whom Roosevelt had addressed "The Strenuous Life": children of the social, economic, and cultural elite, sons of old families or of the newly rich, well-educated (predominantly Ivy League), born or resident in the Northeast. They were athletes and sportsmen, lawyers and bankers, successful in private life but feeling a strong obligation to serve their country, moved by a mixture of idealism and desire for power and prestige, morally serious, sometimes self-righteous—just like their spiritual father. Their credo was well stated by one of their number, in words borrowed from James but equally expressive of Roosevelt's worldview: "The world is 'essentially a theater for heroism.'"

The camp regimen involved considerable gunplay: marksmanship was the sine qua non of the hunter, the pioneer, and the soldier. Recruits received elementary training in infantry tactics and the use of machine guns and mortars, and a thorough indoctrination in Roosevelt-style nationalism. Attention was paid to the "blue nose" side of Progressivism: "social hygiene," "clean living," chastity, resistance to all forms of sensual indulgence. Unlike the training offered by ROTC and the National Guard, which emphasized mastery of the regulations, the *Plattsburgh Manual* (1917) stressed preparation for war, and indeed for the attack. Its concept of command was heroic. "History shows that victory goes more often to him who attacks," and that the "principle of the attack" is to deliver "a smashing, terrific blow . . . at the right place, at the right time." The virtues of the good officer were precisely those enjoined by "The Strenuous Life": vigor, virility, the skills of a frontier hunter, and dominating individualism. Attackers must be heroic in body and in mind.

"A soldier has little business in attacking or defending . . . unless he is an athlete . . . a good shot," a good reader of terrain. The young lawyers and brokers were invited to apply the principles that made them successful as civilians: "Initiative in war is no less valuable than in business life." The officer leading the attack must know his mission, send men "skilled in woodcraft" to scout the ground, "siz[e] up the case." But in planning he is to be utterly self-reliant and avoid any display of uncertainty to the men in his charge. "Don't ask advice from anyone. . . . Having come to a decision, stick to it, right or wrong."[19]

The Plattsburgh movement reinforced ideological commitment among the core constituency for intervention, the educated classes of the Northeast. It also succeeded in preparing a cadre of citizen-officers for eventual company and battalion command. However, the usefulness of Plattsburgh to the cause of preparedness was compromised by the antagonism between Roosevelt and Wood on one side and Wilson on the other. Wood had invited Wilson, Roosevelt, and a group of political leaders to visit the inaugural encampment in August 1915. Only Roosevelt accepted, and he arrived on August 25, dressed in his Rough Rider uniform and primed for battle, filled with contempt for Wilson ("this infernal skunk in the White House"). Though he did not name Wilson, no one misunderstood his attack on those who "treat elocution as a substitute for action [and] rely on high-sounding words unbacked by deeds," whose "mind . . . dwells only in the realm of shadow and shame." As the Preparedness debate became more intense, he would poison his critique of Wilson's policies with personal attacks, sexual innuendo, and suggestions of racial degeneracy. Wilson's policies were "folly, wickedness, and poltroonery," "absurd and wicked," even "ignoble and degrading," and would end in "national emasculation." If the nation followed Wilson's example, it "would Chinafy the country and would reduce us to the impotence of Spain."

Roosevelt's intemperate language and personal attacks served only to harden the president's determination to resist any substantial form of military preparation. Wilson would win the 1916 election with the slogan "He Kept Us Out of War," and as late as February 1917 was still speaking of the European war as one "with which we have nothing to do . . . whose causes cannot touch us." But Wilson's victory was a hollow one. Roosevelt had been right in thinking that U.S. entry was inevitable, given the great interests at stake. In January 1917 Germany resumed unrestricted submarine warfare, defying the president to make good his 1915 threat to go to war upon that cause. Thanks to his successful resistance to preparedness, Wilson would take the nation into war before public opinion was fully mobilized, before the armed forces had been increased, before his government had constructed the facilities for mustering, training, and equipping a citizen army of millions.[20]

Wilson would give the war its defining slogan: "To make the world safe for democracy." He would tell Americans their enemy was "not the German people" but the malevolent autocracy that ruled them; urge Americans to fight without hating the enemy, to take a reasoned approach to the choices they would face. But war is aggression and violence, and the Great War was limitless violence on a colossal scale, fought for ultimate objectives. As the war intensified, as the cost in lives began to mount, as the risks the United States had undertaken became clear, Wilson's appeal to cool reason would become less consonant with public emotions than Roosevelt's themes of righteous rage and vindicated manhood. That was especially true for the men whose task it was to suffer and inflict violence in Mr. Wilson's war.

In December 1916 Roosevelt set political and personal antipathy aside and appealed to Wilson for permission to raise a volunteer division that could be quickly deployed to France. With a former president in command, the division would be a powerful symbol of American commitment, sustaining Allied morale until the American Expeditionary Force was ready.[21] When Wilson turned down this attempt to relive his Rough Rider triumph, Roosevelt threw himself into the mobilization effort, stumping the country and filling the columns of newspapers and magazines with calls for volunteers, for Liberty Loan subscriptions—and for vigilante actions against any person or group whose words or actions smacked of "disloyalty," whether it be criticizing Allied war aims or conducting the music of German composers. Unable to go himself, he sent four sons to serve in France.

So it was Roosevelt who came to symbolize the martial spirit of the AEF. Those officers who had been through Plattsburgh were Roosevelt men by conviction. But the enlisted men too had a special feeling for TR. Laurence Stallings, who was both a veteran and a chronicler of the AEF, wrote of the soldiers' response to the death of Quentin, youngest of Roosevelt's sons:

So many Doughboys . . . turned aside to pray at Quentin's grave that commanders placed a *cordon sanitaire* around it, for German guns were still ranging. . . . There was something special about this grave; perhaps they sensed that they were all sons of Teddy Roosevelt.

If Roosevelt was responsible for crying up this war at least he had sent his own sons to fight alongside them. They knew he would have come himself if Wilson had not refused him.

French civilians, who had not yet learned to call their allies "Yanks," greeted the first American troops with cries of "Vive les Teddies."[22]

3

No Black in the Rainbow: The Origin
of the Harlem Hell Fighters, 1911–1917

> If this is *our* country, this is *our* war.
>
> —W. E. B. *DuBois,* The Crisis *(1917)*

The Great War provoked a crisis in the way American leaders thought about the nation's racial and ethnic diversity. If the theory of racial nationalism was right, then the new immigrants and the "colored" minorities constituted a permanent and unremediable defect in the body politic. They would make poor citizens and bad soldiers, and might be susceptible to subversion by radical agitators or foreign agents. If that were the case, the United States would find it extraordinarily difficult, if not impossible, to maintain the internal unity and muster the manpower and morale needed to contend with the other Great Powers.

But beneath its pretense of scientific analysis, the racial theory of nationality had always been a rationalization of the existing social order and its political imperatives. For most of the nineteenth century, the equation of "American democracy" with White manhood suffrage had been socially expedient and capable of generating a military force large enough to fight the border wars of westward expansion. Northern victory in the Civil War had required the use of Black troops, and the consequent expansion of civil rights. The United States could not raise an army large enough to win the war in Europe without the willing and effective participation of its racial and ethnic minorities.

During the two years from the sinking of the *Lusitania* to the American declaration of war, there was a radical change in the way the nation's political leaders approached Blacks and "hyphenated Americans." Their first, almost reflexive response, was to mistrust them, and demand harshly coercive measures to compel their loyalty, or keep their disloyalty in bounds. The "crimes of the hyphenates" became a major theme for both parties in the 1916 campaign, and a popular song told them, "If you don't like your Uncle Sammy / Then go back to your home o'er the sea." But once war was declared, and the reality of the nation's manpower needs was realized, those same leaders would embrace the principles of civil nationalism, and offer a new social bargain that would redefine the relationship of ethnic and racial minorities to the American nation.

Roosevelt condemned "hyphenism" as a form of treason. Immigrants who retain any feelings whatever of attachment to a native land "are as truly the foes of this country as if they . . . made active war against it. This is not a figure of speech or a hyperbolic statement. . . . The hyphen is incompatible with patriotism." In 1916 Roosevelt helped organize the Vigilantes, "an organization of writers working for preparedness," most with Progressive associations, who used their prestige and rhetorical skills to whip up public sentiment against any and all expressions of "disloyalty." They would not only produce reams of eloquent anti-German propaganda, but use vigilante methods to drive Germans and German works from American theaters, concert halls, universities, and libraries. Although the onus of antihyphenism fell primarily on German-Americans, Jews also came under suspicion. The most thoroughly Americanized element of the Jewish community were of German origin, and the recent immigrants from eastern Europe hated the Russian czar. Sir Cecil Spring-Rice, British ambassador to the United States and a Roosevelt confidant, told Secretary of State Bryan that he "didn't believe there was a man in the country not a German or a Jew who could advocate" the German cause.[1]

Fears of German subversion and race mixing merged with older, more traditional fears of a racial uprising among non-Whites and the foreign-born proletariats of the city. In 1915 D. W. Griffith caused a cultural and political sensation with the release of his epic and epoch-making historical film *Birth of a Nation*, which represented Negroes as a race of semi-human brutes, and praised lynch law and the violence of the KKK for preserving White civilization. Although the film's specific reference was to the Civil War, Griffith's vivid depiction of the trench warfare of 1864 reminded audiences of newsreel and photographic images of the Western Front. Screen images and editorial title cards underlined the moral horror and futility of war, echoing Wilson's pleas for neutrality. The implied analogy suggested that the European conflict be seen as a civil war of the White or (in Griffith's words) "Aryan races," which could only benefit the barbaric "Colored races" held in subjection by White powers. That view of the conflict was already being propagated by some of the Immigration Restriction League's theoreticians, including the eugenicist David Starr Jordan and the sociologist T. L. Stoddard.[2]

Fantasies of race war gained credibility from events along the Mexican border. In 1915 the revolutionary leader Pancho Villa raided Columbus, New Mexico, prompting a call-up of the National Guard and the mounting of a punitive expedition into northern Mexico. At about the same time the Rio Grande valley was agitated by civil disorders between Anglo landlords and Mexican-American tenant farmers, whose resistance to a patronal system took heart and some advice from revolutionaries in Mexico. The governor of Texas mobilized the National Guard and Texas Rangers, and local magnates hired "special deputies," who terrorized Mexican-American communities. In reaction a small group of Mexican-American anarchists promulgated the "Plan de San Diego," which called for a general uprising of non-Whites in the border states. Mexican-Americans, Native Americans, Negroes, and Japanese would form a "Liberating Army of Races," to fight for "Equality and Independence," abolish "racial hatred," and create "a new society based on 'universal love'" by exterminating all White males over the age of sixteen. The plot never got beyond the ill-advised proclamation, but its themes resonated with long-standing anxieties. The defense of the southwestern border and Indian frontier relied on African-American regulars, and there was a history of mutual suspicion and violence between Black soldiers and local communities that enforced Jim Crow. There had been an armed confrontation between Black regulars and Whites in Brownsville, Texas, in 1906, and the summer of 1917 would see similar conflicts in Waco and Houston.[3]

The inclusion of Japanese in the Liberating Army of Races chimed with a scare campaign by William Randolph Hearst, the great press baron. Hearst believed the nation's primary interests were centered in the Pacific basin and Latin America, rather than Europe, and he warned that if the United States engaged in Europe, Japan would combine with Mexico to foment a race war and stab Uncle Sam in the back. He even produced a sensational movie, *Patria* (1916), which dramatized the plot. The idea seemed implausible, since Japan was on the Allied side, busily picking off Germany's Chinese and Pacific island possessions. But the fantasy gained credibility with the interception and exposure of the "Zimmermann Telegram," in which the German Foreign Office proposed a military alliance under which Mexico (perhaps with Japanese help) would invade and reclaim Texas, New Mexico, and Arizona.[4]

The declaration of war pushed these anxieties to the crisis point. Southern congressmen feared that if Blacks were drafted en masse in five or six years the "entire negro population" of the South "will have been trained to arms," prepared and disposed for armed resistance to Jim Crow. The New York papers reported rumors of "a black rebellion through the South," organized by German and perhaps Japanese agents: Negroes were to "rise, free themselves of the white man's bondage, seize Texas and turn it into a black republic" in which "Mexicans and Japanese" (but not Whites) "were to have equal rights with the Negro." On the other hand, if Blacks were exempted from the draft they might rise up in a South denuded of White manpower. The *New York Sun* entertained similar fears about immigrants, condemning "the apparent injustice of stripping the land of American youths to furnish a fighting force in Europe while leaving millions of aliens at home to enjoy the rewards of peaceful industry." Senator Lodge demanded that resident noncitizens be drafted, because it would be dangerous to draft the native-born and leave the foreign-born in control of America's cities and factories. The *New York Times* saw immigrants as a distinctly dangerous class, and advocated conscription as "a long and sorely needed means of disciplining a certain insolent foreign element in this nation." Henry Ford thought the nation had been too tolerant of ethnic difference: "These men of many nations . . . must be taught American ways, the English language and the right way to live."[5]

Anxiety about the loyalty of the minorities masked deeper concerns about the willingness of the American people as a whole to bear the sacrifices the war would demand. Roosevelt Progressives were for war, and it had strong backing in the northeastern states; but in other regions support was reluctant, and there was significant opposition in the South and Midwest. The Social Democratic parties of the European belligerents supported their national war efforts; but the American Socialist Party, which polled a million votes for Eugene Debs in the last election, opposed the war. Wilson owed his position as commander in chief to the antiwar majority that had elected him only five months earlier, and in April 1917 "I Didn't Raise My Boy to Be a Soldier" was still the most popular song in America. In the end some twenty-four million men would be registered for the draft. But upward of two and a half million refused to register—roughly one in ten of eligible draftees, and 338,000 draftees refused to present themselves for induction, some 30 percent of those selected by the draft boards.[6]

The War Department knew, and the political and journalistic leadership would soon recognize, that in an open society it was impossible to build an effective mass army on the basis of coercion alone. A systematic effort would have to be undertaken to awaken in ordinary Americans a more intense and effective identification with the nation than they had ever been taught to feel. And particular efforts would have to be made to win the hearts and minds of America's racial and ethnic minorities.

War as Progressivism by Other Means

To head the Committee on Public Information (CPI) Wilson appointed George Creel—a western newspaperman, a Progressive in politics, the advertising genius who had shaped publicity for the president's 1916 campaign. CPI was charged with marshaling public opinion to support the war, the draft, and the president. It produced pamphlets, posters, and parades, supplied textbooks for soldiers in training, and manuals to teach teachers that the war was the logical and predestined culmination of American history. Its work was supplemented by the "Four-Minute Men," a national speakers' bureau organized by a group of Chicago businessmen. As the name indicated, they were prepared to address any audience anywhere on short notice, with simple but strongly worded appeals for the draft or Liberty Loans. CPI and other agencies supplied them with printed bulletins, offering guidance as to which issues might be most timely or crucial, what rumors or defeatist tendencies needed refutation. Their work was supported by a bevy of patriotic organizations, including Roosevelt's "Vigilantes" and the American Protective League, both of which specialized in anti-German and antisubversive agitation. A more positive approach was developed by the National Security League, an odd alliance of corporatist conservatives and nationalist Progressives whose spokesmen defined American war aims as the realization of Progressive goals by military means.[7]

The standard of Americanism defined by Roosevelt and John R. Commons required the "amalgamation" of all ethnic differences, the extirpation of the hyphen as the sign of treason. Now Princeton historian Robert McNutt McElroy described the United States as a "vast, polyglot community," in which the patriot's task is to discover the "common ideals which have transformed men and women of all these races, and kindreds, and tongues, into our nation." The basis of American nationality cannot be blood or lineage, or any "provincial patriotism. Its fundamentals of citizenship must transcend race, and its ideals must be so high that ancient animosities and hereditary loyalties cannot compete with them." They must appeal to a law "higher than race loyalty, and transcend[ing] mere ethnic prejudices . . . more binding than the call of a common ancestry." McElroy therefore explicitly rejects the idea that American culture is essentially and exclusively Anglo-Saxon or, in Roosevelt's formulation, Anglo-Teutonic in its character. By making the national war effort a struggle for universal rights, "The President has placed our intervention . . . upon a plane of idealism to which every citizen, of whatever race, may rally, without losing hold upon the best traditions of the land from which his forefathers have come." By this standard, a hyphenated cultural identity is not a disqualification for full acceptance as an American. Herbert Myrick pitched the same message in simpler terms in *Fifteen Little War Stories*, a set of vignettes that turned the ideas of McElroy and S. S. Menken into little fables: "The flower of youth—rich and poor, learned and ignorant, high and low— . . . black men, yellow men, white men, from all quarters of the globe, are fighting side by side to free the world from the Hun peril. / That's the patriotism of equality!"[8]

It is easy, after the fact, to dismiss all this as the usual hot air of American politics supercharged by the forced draft of military crisis. Some of it was hypocritical, and much of it wishful self-delusion. Nevertheless, the official ideologists of America's Great War were establishing a curriculum for soldiers and civilians, a course of education in "Americanism" that would guide the public's understanding of the process of nationalization, socialization, and militarization that the war was imposing on them—a curriculum that would create a climate of expectation for civilians and soldiers alike, about the kind of nation that would come out of the war. For an essentially conservative set of men they were setting the bar extremely high. They were offering the nation's racial and ethnic minorities a new version of the American social bargain: acknowledgment of their civic equality and acceptance as full-fledged Americans, in exchange for loyal service in battle.

"If this is our country, this is our war": The Black Man's Wager

The first test of the new wartime social bargain would be its application to African-Americans. The difference between Black and White had been the most fundamental social and political distinction from the time of the first settlements. All other social differences, whether of class or ethnicity, were interpreted by reference to this fundamental distinction. The African-American response to the war, and the government's treatment of Black soldiers, would show whether or not the war would be a plastic moment in the shaping of race relations.

Perhaps because his nationalism was so bound up with ideas of race, Theodore Roosevelt was one of the first political leaders to appreciate the significance of African-Americans for the war effort. He had composed the Rough Riders of 1898 to symbolize the reconciliation of rich and working-class cowboys, of Yankees and Southerners in a unified American nationality. The "Roosevelt Division" of 1917 would have extended the reconciliation to Black and White. His plans called for one of his infantry brigades to be made up of African-Americans, and for Lieutenant Colonel Charles Young to command a regiment or a brigade. His choice of Young was especially significant. Roosevelt had known him since 1903, and rated his abilities very high. He was the senior African-American officer in the regular army, with a distinguished record in both combat and staff assignments. Young was also a formidable military intellectual, a close friend of DuBois, and the author of *The Military Morale of Nations and Races* (1912), a remarkably prescient study of the cultural sources of military power. Though Young accepted the premises of Roosevelt's preferred theories of racial personality, his book also demonstrated that nations are not biological tribes but social "composites" united by a "soul force," an ideology or system of beliefs. A nation's military morale reflects the strength with which its people believe in and identify with their national ideology. Racial groups like Jews and Negroes, who withered under oppression, had displayed martial virtues when fighting for a country that respects their dignity and grants them civil rights. Thus the key to raising an effective mass army from among a polyglot American people was to link patriotic service with fulfillment of the democratic promise of equal rights and fair play for all: an enlarged version of the social bargain that was the core of Roosevelt's Progressive nationalism.[9]

Roosevelt's challenge to the color line would be nullified by Wilson's refusal to authorize a Roosevelt Division. Instead, the symbolic weight that might have been carried by Charles Young and his Black volunteers would be borne by the 15th Regiment, New York National Guard.

The regiment that would become the Harlem Hell Fighters was the product of a civic and political movement in New York's African-American community, centered in the new and growing neighborhoods of Harlem. The district northeast of Central Park was home to Jews and Italians as well as African-Americans, but Black Harlem rapidly grew in size and importance in the years before the Great War. It had a working- and middle-class population and was developing as a cultural capital, providing a home to Black-owned newspapers and entertainment venues, and to religious, civic, and political organizations, some of them national in scope. Every major civil rights organization had a headquarters there, from the conservative and accommodationist followers of Booker T. Washington's "Tuskegee Machine," through the more militant NAACP to radical socialist and Black nationalist movements. After 1914 the population was swelled by migrants from the South and the West Indies, seeking employment in war industries. Harlem's newspaper, *The Age*, defended their right to emigrate, but worried that the new arrivals would lower standards of living and culture and bring the race into disrepute. In "San Juan Hill," a lower-class district on Harlem's west side, intergroup relations were edgy and often hostile. Irvin Cobb, the Southern novelist who would cover Black soldiers as war correspondent of the *Saturday Evening Post*, believed that Negroes named the district to honor Theodore Roosevelt and the Tenth Cavalry (Colored) for their heroic charge in "the Yanko-Spanko war." San Juan Hill was in fact "one of the most congested areas in America's most populous city," and its name was "a parody on the neighborhood interracial battles that took place on the steep upgrade."[10]

Still, African-Americans found New York a relatively welcoming city. The range of jobs open to them was wider than in the South; discrimination was not enforceable by law. The poet, journalist, and civil rights leader James Weldon Johnson would later describe the Harlem of 1917 as "well along the road of development and prosperity":

> There was plenty of work, with a choice of jobs, and there was plenty of money. The community was beginning to feel conscious of its growing size and strength. It had entirely rid itself of the sense of apology for its existence.

The proposal to form a Negro National Guard regiment was a sign of that emerging sense of communal self-worth. Militia service—the duty and right to participate in the common defense—was a hallmark of full citizenship, and New York's Black community had been trying to win approval for such a regiment since 1847. In 1911 the Equity Congress, a bipartisan organization of African-American leaders in the city, decided to put Harlem's economic resources and political influence behind a petition for a new regiment. The Congress backed its proposal by privately financing the initial recruitment of troops and hiring Charles W. Fillmore as provisional colonel. Fillmore was an attorney, a Treasury Department official, and an experienced militia officer. A photograph taken in 1917 or 1918 shows a light-skinned man in his fifties, of distinguished appearance, with gray hair and goatee. He was something of a militant in racial matters, but in good standing with the Republican Party. By year's end he had completed his staff and begun recruiting.[11]

In the meantime Louis Cuvillier, a White assemblyman elected with the help of African-American votes, sponsored legislation to authorize the regiment and appropriate funds for equipment and an armory. Governor Dix blocked the bill, fearing it would alienate White voters. After the election of 1912 new proposals were put forward by a Progressive Party state senator and a Democratic assemblyman, but in 1913 the adjutant general of the state decided to authorize only a single company on a provisional basis. Worse, the organizational plan was amended to ensure that all field officers, and most if not all company officers, would be White.

But the idea of a Black regiment was controversial, and the Equity Congress initiative made little progress until the "Preparedness" campaign of 1916 led a prominent White Republican named William Hayward to advocate for the Negro regiment—on condition that he be appointed colonel. Hayward was the son of a U.S. senator from Nebraska, and had commanded a National Guard regiment in that state before moving to New York City, where he practiced law and entered politics. He was a glamorous figure, pictured as the *beau idéal* of the American soldier by artist James Montgomery Flagg on the cover of the *Saturday Evening Post*. He was "progressive" in the large sense of being interested in political reform, but supported Governor Charles Whitman against Roosevelt in the political struggle for control of the state party. Whitman backed the regiment as a way of stealing Roosevelt's thunder on Preparedness, and outbidding him for the support of Negro voters. However, the bill he sponsored required that all new officers appointed to the regiment be White.[12]

The Harlem leadership accepted Hayward's appointment as a compromise necessary to achieve their goal. What made it acceptable was Hayward's insistence that the few Black officers already enlisted in the provisional company keep their commissions, and his commitment to seek appointments for other qualified Black men as company-level officers when circumstances permitted. They may also have considered that having White field officers would make the regiment more acceptable for combat service if and when the United States decided to go to war. It was well known that regular army commanders were unwilling to integrate all-Negro units with their field forces, for fear that circumstances might compel White majors and captains to take orders from a Negro colonel.[13]

So on June 6, 1916, Whitman appointed Hayward colonel of a 15th New York National Guard Regiment, and recruiting began on July 15. Woodell Pickering was appointed lieutenant colonel and wealthy socialite Lorillard Spencer major and adjutant. The senior captain was Arthur Little, already in his forties, a White officer whose Guard service dated from 1891. For the sake of the regiment, Charles Fillmore accepted demotion from colonel commanding to captain of B Company, though he was "heartbroken" and perhaps resentful. But the men gave Fillmore his due, nicknaming him "father of the regiment." The *Age* celebrated with a banner head: "Union League Give Flags to 15th Regiment / Stand of Colors from Aristocratic Club," and thanked Hayward for the "enthusiasm and energy" that had made the regiment possible. The flag featured a coiled rattlesnake, and the 15th would sometimes be called the "Rattlesnake Regiment." The *Age* declared the event a victory over "a Democratic, Negro-hating Congress," and a "prejudiced President," who had refused "to provide for a single colored regiment" in the expanded regular army.[14]

Since the State of New York would do little or nothing for the regiment, the regiment's sponsors reached out to well-disposed Whites for charitable contributions. Their most potent recruiting agent was the regimental band, led by Lieutenant James Reese Europe, well known in the city as a musician and entertainment entrepreneur. Europe was the child of Black middle-class parents, born in Mobile, Alabama, in 1880, raised and educated in Washington, D.C. Though not a college graduate he had a broad musical education, had toured and studied in England and on the Continent before settling in New York. During his early years there (1904–10) the emerging theater district around Broadway was being systematically segregated. Europe played ragtime for Black audiences in the small segregated clubs and theaters of New York, and for White audiences in hotel ballrooms. He continued his study of music performance, composition, and theory at various conservatories, founded and led a series of small orchestras that played in the city, and toured widely. He was also a show business entrepreneur, who created and took on the road all-Black musical comedies—ambitious productions that overtaxed the resources of the segregated small-town theaters they were forced to play. One of his first was a military comedy, *The Shoo-fly Regiment* (1906–7), which capitalized on the popularity of the Spanish-American War. *Shoo-fly Regiment* was followed by a string of successes on New York stages and in touring companies. In 1914 he was hired as musical director by British-born "society dancers" Vernon and Irene Castle, and developed a series of musical plays and revues that made the Castles—and Jim Europe—leading figures in New York show business.[15]

At the Marshall Hotel, a Harlem meeting place for theater people, Europe led discussions of the role of the arts in improving the condition of the race. He saw the creation of a distinctly African-American music as part of the larger struggle to achieve a coherent racial identity and overcome the "double consciousness" produced by American racism, which compelled African-Americans to subject their every achievement to the judgment of inimical and uncomprehending Whites. "In my opinion there never was any such music as 'ragtime,'" he wrote. It was "rather a fun name given to Negro rhythm by our Caucasian brother musicians," who distorted its "primal Negro rhythmical element," reducing ragtime to something not much better than the minstrel show "coon song." As a critic, Europe asserted that powerful and distinctive rhythms were the core of African-American music. As a musician he set out to remake ragtime as jazz, emphasizing the percussion section and assigning it the dominant role in his band.[16]

Europe was also engaged in community affairs and the political struggle for civil rights. The orchestras he led to fame were not just business enterprises but devices for wedging open a segregated culture to Black music and musicians. He organized a Colored Musicians Union, which made him an important figure in the city's labor-management politics. So it was in character for him to offer his services to Harlem's Own Regiment. He enlisted as a line officer, but the regiment's White sponsors seized on his celebrity, appointed him bandmaster, and featured his musical performances at the dinners and soirées to which potential supporters were invited. He was a successful fund-raiser and an advertisement for the regiment as its commanders lobbied the legislature for funds to arm and equip their recruits. The catch was that the regiment became identified with its band. Europe's success helped the regiment on its way to combat-readiness, but obscured the difference between the 15th as a fighting outfit and an entertainment enterprise.[17]

The regiment, dubbed the "Old Fifteenth," became a symbol of community pride. On at least one occasion "a group of Harlem's 'best people'—ministers, newspaper editors, civil rights spokesmen, businessmen—strutted proudly along" beside the troops. The Reverend Charles Martin listed the "colored regiment [that] has lately been organized" with the other markers of racial achievement on display in Harlem: "beautiful churches," Negro physicians and surgeons, bookstores and libraries—Negroes have "even invaded the golf links," and "some of our ladies own and drive their own automobiles." But even Martin was compelled to note the irony that "the colored man is marching under the flag that often fails to protect him when alive but honors him when dead." The community's leaders had chosen to accept that irony and work within it in order to achieve an important civic and political goal. But the Harlem street was skeptical. The state provided none of the physical necessities normally supplied to a National Guard regiment. The 15th had no armory in which to assemble and drill, no uniforms or kit, no weapons. When the troops paraded their best-uniformed men, the few with rifles were put on the outside of the formation to mask the defects of dress and armament. A Black man in the street noted, "It was amusing to see a group of colored soldiers marching through 134th Street with broomsticks on their shoulders."

At the head of the parade on a big white horse rode Bert Williams, the Negro vaudeville comedian, smiling and waving. Whites who watched the show snickered at the spectacle of "darkies playing soldiers." The papers compared the Old Fifteenth to "the Mulligan Guards," the ragtag Irish unit from Edward Harrigan's long-running Broadway comedy. It was as if the military pretensions of the race had been brought out to be publicly mocked. It did not ease the pain that Williams was as qualified as any man to ride that horse: he was a commissioned captain in the California National Guard.[18]

For African-Americans a confusion of that sort had profound, even fatal consequences for their hopes of achieving civil equality. As W. E. B. DuBois had written in *Souls of Black Folk* (1903), the Negro in America faces "a world which yields him no true self-consciousness" but only a "double-consciousness"—the effect of always "looking at oneself through the eyes of others, of measuring one's soul by the tape of a world that looks on with amused contempt and pity." Every aspect of life had to be conceived as a performance for a skeptical and even ill-disposed White audience. It was not enough for them to *be* soldiers—their performance as soldiers must offer no occasion whatever for denigration or ridicule.[19]

The outbreak of war sharpened the irony and raised the stakes of compromise. For African-Americans the war raised a fundamental question: Should Black Americans fight to defend a nation that treated them as pariahs? As a company of the 15th marched by "with the easy swing of veteran soldiers to the music of their magnificent band . . . the spell . . . was broken by a young man standing on the sidewalk who said, 'They'll not take me out to make a target of me and bring me back to Jim Crow me.'" A man in a Harlem barbershop was unmoved by the call to arms: "The Germans ain't done nothin' to me, and if they have, I forgive 'em." A draftee from Brooklyn wrote to the secretary of war that he would "go forth to battle, not as a patriotic soldier eager to defend a flag that defends me and mine, but as a prisoner of war, shackled to a gun that shall spit fire in defense of a humanity that does not include me."[20]

Even moderate leaders thought the time right for hard bargaining. Adam Clayton Powell Sr., minister of Harlem's Abyssinian Baptist

Church, called on community leaders to demand some concrete demonstration of the government's willingness to redress Black grievances as a prior condition for Black enlistment: "This is the proper time for us to make a special request for our constitutional rights as American citizens. The ten million colored people in this country were never so badly needed as now." But their bargaining position was problematic. If they opposed the war, or showed reluctance to support it, they would gain nothing of substance and might lose a good deal. White patriots would think of Negroes as slackers, yet Black men could still be compelled to serve. As they considered this prospect, established community leaders, across the spectrum from Tuskegee accommodationists to NAACP militants, were ineluctably drawn to the view that African-Americans must assume a positive role in the war effort, even in the absence of specific promises that their grievances would be redressed. As Powell put it, "Volunteered service in such a time as this constitutes . . . the strongest argument and the noblest appeal for political and economic rights which colored men could present to the nation after the war is over." In return for loyalty the Black man would receive "opportunity . . . advancement . . . usefulness"—everything for which Booker T. Washington had hoped. "The Duty of the Hour," said James Weldon Johnson, was for "the members of the race in New York [to] enlist in the Fifteenth Regiment and thus receive all the honors and credit due those who act at once for the defense of their country."[21]

Their support for Black enlistment was reinforced when Southern congressmen came out in strident opposition to the recruitment and combat training of large numbers of Negroes, especially at Southern cantonments. If Jim Crow was against the drafting of Black men, should not Black men be for the draft?[22]

Wilson and the Democrats relied upon the electoral and congressional votes of the "Solid South," but the War Department was desperate to find manpower for an army of millions. Major General Tasker Bliss, assistant to the army chief of staff, told Secretary of War Newton Baker that "Negroes seem to take naturally to military service," and that with "the snap of a finger" the government could have all the colored soldiers it required—enough to form three or four combat divisions. The mass conscription of Negroes was essential to the war effort: exemption of Blacks from the draft would cause deep resentment among Whites, and there was no way to train the numbers required without using Southern training sites.[23]

The leaders of the Tuskegee Machine understood the situation and knew how to turn it to advantage. In March, Emmett Scott, who had been Booker T. Washington's secretary and political agent, approached the War Department with an offer to rally Negro support for the draft and the Liberty Loan, and to work on his own side of the color line to keep the peace. Secretary Baker had been a reform mayor of Cleveland, and recognized the advantage of having an official spokesman for the Black community in his department. After verifying Scott's political bonafides with Dr. Robert Moton, Washington's successor as president of Tuskegee, Baker hired him as "Special Assistant for Negro Affairs." Baker warned Scott that there was "no intention on the part of the War Department to undertake to settle at this time the so-called race question." Soldiers training in Jim Crow states would be bound by Jim Crow laws, in camp as well as out. But Scott and other Black leaders believed that the necessities of war would make the race question unavoidable. It was impossible to train large numbers of Blacks without sending some to Southern cantonments, thereby exposing Jim Crow to local stress and the embarassment of national attention. On a deeper level, it was impossible to raise and deploy a national army without challenging the fundamental assumption of American racism: the belief that Blacks lacked the soldierly virtues—the attributes of manhood—that were the prime requisites for full citizenship and civic equality. Although Scott was an accommodationist, his presence in the War Department gave the Black community a representative with access to the secretary, who would get what benefits he could for African-Americans. Black leaders in the South followed Scott's lead. The chairman of the Four-Minute Men in Birmingham, Alabama, reported that Black leaders "are full of patriotism and enthusiasm and ready and anxious to do something for their Government—'MY Government,' as one of their speakers proudly said." This in a state where the Black speaker was forbidden to vote or sit on a jury.[24]

The NAACP, led by W. E. B. DuBois, took a more militant approach. The organization had been antiwar on principle, but DuBois and his colleague Joel Spingarn also came to see the war as a unique chance for black Americans to prove themselves equal to "The Strenuous Life" standard. However, to achieve that goal they had not only to convince

Black people to support the war, they had to convince the government to use Black troops in combat and allow Black officers to command men in battle. The army command was resistant to both policies, and southern congressmen were actively opposed to it. Spingarn, a Jewish Progressive and member of the NAACP directorate, proposed the creation of a Black officers' training camp, and won the support of his friend and neighbor Leonard Wood, father of the Plattsburgh movement. DuBois was skeptical of the plan, which implied acceptance of a racially segregated army and defense of a Jim Crow nation. But an exchange of letters with his friend Charles Young convinced DuBois that Spingarn was "right in practice" though wrong in theory. The choice was "between the insult of a separate camp and the irreparable injury of strengthening the present custom of putting no black men in positions of authority." Likewise, it was acceptable for Black troops to serve in segregated regiments, because then their achievements would have to be accepted as signs of racial quality.[25]

DuBois and Spingarn were opposed by more radical Black leaders like Hubert Harrison and the Socialists Chandler Owen and A. Philip Randolph. Isaiah Butts of the NAACP admonished his colleagues that consent to a Jim Crow camp would mark Negroes as unmanly and hence "unworthy of American citizenship." DuBois met such objections by casting his acquiescence in a tone of defiance. If he urged Black citizens to "join heartily in this fight . . . to labor in all ways by hand and thought," he did so "despite our deep sympathy with the reasonable and deep-seated feeling of revolt among Negroes at the persistent insult and discrimination to which they are subjected, and to which they will be subjected even when they do their patriotic duty." The "Colored man" would *demand* certain specific rights even as he agreed to enlist: "the right to serve . . . on the battlefield, . . . the right of our best men to lead troops of their own race in battle." The Negro would expect fulfillment of his long-standing demand for social justice: "an immediate end to lynching," abolition of Jim Crow cars and segregated housing ordinances, votes for all men—and women—and "equal civil rights in all public institutions and movements." By serving in battle the manhood of the race would be roused to resistance and trained to make resistance effective: "If we fight we'll learn the fighting game and cease to be so 'aisily lynched.' " Finally, if Black men served in and supported the war, they would establish an undeniable claim to full acceptance as Americans: "If this is *our* country," DuBois wrote, "then this is *our* war. We must fight it with every ounce of blood and treasure."[26]

DuBois had, in effect, signed on to the War Progressives' "social bargain," whose terms he stated explicitly and succinctly: "First your Country, then your Rights!" He had broken with Booker T. Washington because the Tuskegee Machine was willing to surrender the demand for civil rights in exchange for a chance to prove the Black man's value to the productive economy. If DuBois was willing to accommodate segregation now, it was because he believed that war offered a radically different kind of opportunity, a chance to demonstrate that the Negro was (in Roosevelt's phrase) one of the great fighting races, and that the "Talented Tenth" or the educated elite of Black men could exercise responsible and effective command in war.

But the "bargain" was entirely one-sided: Black leadership bound itself to advocate the war, Black civilians bound themselves to serve, but the Wilson administration bound itself to nothing whatever—not even a promise of future negotiations.[27]

The officers and men of the 15th New York had to live the terms of that bargain, and its contradictions gave the regiment's collective personality its peculiar mixture of pride and grievance.

"The ability of the Negro to command": The Officers of the 15th New York

William Hayward's first task as colonel was to recruit the regiment up to its authorized training strength of 2,002 officers and men, to qualify the unit for federal service. Between April and June 1917 the Old Fifteenth became the first New York National Guard regiment to reach that goal. It was a remarkable achievement, especially considering the reluctance of many in the community to fight for a Jim Crow nation. Hayward and Harlem's community leaders conducted a vigorous recruiting campaign, which succeeded in promoting the regiment as an expression of race and community pride. Theaters and dance halls and churches served as recruiting stations and temporary sites for drilling. Some two hundred army veterans were engaged in helping recruit the regiment. An attempt was made to give each battalion a distinctive neighborhood identity: the First was recruited from Harlem and San Juan Hill, the Second from the

Williamsburg section of Brooklyn, the Third from upper Manhattan and the Bronx. Selective Service spurred enlistments, compelling men to choose between joining a hometown regiment or being conscripted.

Yet despite this success, the Old Fifteenth was treated as a poor relation of the New York National Guard. Since they had no armory of their own, it was impossible to assemble the whole regiment for drill and exercise. They had the lowest priority for equipment and training. It was a major achievement when, on May 13, Hayward won them a stint at Camp Whitman near Peekskill. For the first time the entire regiment was assembled in one place, and they paraded down Fifth Avenue to the railroad station. James Europe's band played "Onward Christian Soldiers" with a jazz beat, jagged drumming driving the march down from Harlem. But after only two weeks of close-order drill and target practice they returned to New York, where their elements were dispersed among various auditoriums and dance halls around the city, and to guard details protecting bridges, tunnels, and "alien property" seized from German nationals.[28]

Any regiment treated in this way would have had morale problems. For the 15th the situation was complicated by the color line that divided Hayward and his White officers from their Black colleagues and enlisted men.

Hayward recognized that the "Black officer" question was central to the problem of attracting Black men to enlist in the regiment. Roosevelt had become a hero when the *Age* reported his offer of a regimental command to Charles Young. It showed America's hero-president had "confidence in the ability of the Negro to command." John Jamieson, a sergeant in the 15th New York, thought Colonel Roosevelt was "amongst the stoutest supporters of the colored race . . . a firm believer in equality," who would "do everything in his power to get a square deal for the colored race. He said that the colored people should not only get the material things, but also the same respect that is given the white people in aiding them to maintain their dignity."[29]

Hayward did what he could to increase his cadre of Black officers. He had retained the small group of Black officers who had commanded during the unit's provisional phase, and publicized his desire to appoint more as soon as the increase in enlistments permitted. To encourage applications he issued a statement promising that the "color line will not be drawn in this regiment and as rapidly as COLORED MEN CAN AND DO QUALIFY . . . they will be COMMISSIONED AS OFFICERS." The response was disappointing, as were the personal approaches he made to several of the "leading colored professional and business men of Greater New York." As Hayward told the editor of the *Age*, a number of promising candidates had withdrawn their applications, because word in the community said that "no 'highbrows' [were] wanted in the regiment." The editor endorsed Hayward's good faith, and criticized his own people for not seizing the opportunity. But few additional enlistments were forthcoming, and Hayward could not wait for Black candidates to appear. The regiment was due to be inspected, and if he failed to complete its table of organization it would be disqualified for federal service. To fulfill the regiment's larger purpose he had to sacrifice the plan for a thoroughly integrated officer cadre and settle for a combination in which Whites predominated.[30]

Officer recruitment may have been affected by rumors that the Militia Bureau would limit the number of Black officers appointed to the 15th and the ranks to which they might be promoted. Ambitious men may have thought their chances for promotion better if they went through the new officer training camp in Des Moines, Iowa, and served in the 92nd Division. But the rumor that "highbrow" Negroes were not welcome in the Old Fifteenth may have reflected a conflict that troubled other African-American regiments, a perverse by-product of "double-consciousness": working-class Black soldiers sometimes resented being commanded by men no whiter than themselves. Or it may have reflected the tensions between Fillmore and the original Black officers, and the White men who had displaced them.

The historian Gail Buckley has observed that "white officers of black troops generally came in three types: noblesse oblige liberals, ambitious younger officers, and superannuated patriots." Colonel Hayward, Major Lorillard Spencer, and Captain (soon to be Major) Arthur Little were older men, wealthy, highly educated, and experienced National Guard officers. They also conformed in a general way to the "Sons of Roosevelt" model: Ivy League, athletic, military, progressive in politics (though not necessarily Roosevelt partisans). The White officers Hayward recruited to fill out his table of organization were younger versions of the same type: Plattsburgh alums, Ivy Leaguers from Harvard, Yale, and Princeton, scions of wealthy New York families. Many of them deliberately sought service in a "Colored" regiment, following the tradition of leading New York and New England families like the Jameses and the Shaws, whose sons had officered Black regiments in the Civil War. Lt. Richardson Pratt of Glen Cove, Long Island, grandson of a founder of the great Standard Oil trust, left his job with Standard Oil to enlist, and brought with him enough Black fellow townsmen to make up two rifle squads.[31]

The most notable recruit was young Hamilton Fish Jr., the heir of one of America's great political families. An ancestor had served in Washington's army; his great-grandfather had been Grant's secretary of state. His father, Hamilton Fish Sr., and uncle Nicholas Fish had expanded the family's already considerable wealth running railroads during the Gilded Age. Nicholas's son, also named Hamilton Fish, had left the life of a high-society rowdy to enlist in Roosevelt's Rough Riders and died in battle at Las Guasimas. Hamilton Fish Jr. was raised in luxurious surroundings in New York and Geneva, educated at a series of prestigious private schools, and graduated from Harvard in the 1910 class with T. S. Eliot, Walter Lippmann, and Alan Seeger.

As a young man he was spoiled, competitive to a fault, occasionally a bully, often reckless, not much engaged by academics but a star at debate and as an athlete. The family was close to Theodore Roosevelt politically and socially, and young Fish followed TR's prescriptions for the Strenuous Life. He was an avid hunter, and with a classmate in the summer of 1909 made an adventurous foray into the Alaskan wilderness—earning money for the trip by working in a mine alongside members of the IWW. TR had said that football, of all sports, fostered "in-reared manliness," and, at Harvard, Fish was an all-American, playing offense and defense as captain of a strong varsity team.

Pride in his family heritage could make Fish arrogant, but it also gave him a strong and genuine sense of obligation to public service. With his father he supported Roosevelt and the Progressive Party in 1912, and in 1914 was elected state assemblyman. He was not a warhawk, distrusted the British and wanted to keep the country free of entanglement in European affairs, but supported preparedness as a way of deterring German provocations. He helped found the Plattsburgh movement, attended the summer encampments of 1915 and 1916, and helped TR found the "Junior Patriotic League," which raised money to pay the expenses for less well-to-do enrollees. When it became plain the country would enter the war he pulled strings to get a commission in the regulars. When the army refused him he turned to the 15th, the only New York regiment that had not completed its table of organization. Governor Whitman and Hayward seem to have made him sweat for having bolted the party, but ultimately commissioned him as lieutenant and soon promoted him to captain.[32]

Fish was the model of the "ambitious younger officer," but he had solid credentials as a supporter of Negro rights. According to one biographer, "Had it been left to Fish, the armed forces would have been integrated in 1917." Although the 15th was not his first choice, Fish believed in the mission of race betterment that the regiment symbolized. He had strong support from the small Black community in his home district, and (like Pratt) recruited among them for his own company. Private Layton thought Fish the best of the White officers, "gentle . . . understanding . . . proud of the men."[33]

The White officers' Black colleagues were for the most part men of comparable education and social standing. Charles Fillmore had an impressive record as a public official and field-grade militia officer. James Europe was a cultural celebrity, a figure familiar to New York society. George Lacy had been an officer in the all-Black 8th Illinois. Chaplain William H. Brooks was a well-known minister, and also an activist, a severe critic of Roosevelt's handling of the so-called Brownsville Raid. Another Chaplain was Benjamin C. Robeson, then prominent in his own right, now remembered as the brother of Paul Robeson, renowned as singer, actor, and activist after the war. Vertner Tandy was "a prominent architect and founder of Alpha Phi Alpha fraternity." After the war he would design and build the regimental armory in Harlem. Vergil Parks had been a trooper in the Tenth Cavalry and helped promote the regiment among army veterans in the city.[34]

The most important addition to the cadre of Black officers was Napoleon Bonaparte Marshall, a distinguished and wealthy forty-one-year-old lawyer. As a Negro he would have been excluded from Plattsburgh, but in other respects his background was that of a "Son of Roosevelt." He was a graduate of Exeter, Howard University, and Harvard Law (class of '97), where he had starred in track, and had practiced law in Boston and later on Wall Street, where he was a popular member of the Harvard Club. His wife, Harriet Gibbs, was the daughter of a prominent Black political leader and had impressive credentials as a musician, philanthropist, and educator.[35]

Marshall was a political activist who opposed the imperialist policies of the McKinley-Roosevelt ticket in 1900 and challenged Booker T. Washington's "suicidal policy of political self-effacement for the race." Like DuBois, he saw imperialism and Jim Crow as related aspects of the politics of white racialism, and warned that the nationalization of American life was not undermining Jim Crow but nationalizing it:

> Back of and under a solid South is steadily forming along the color line in opposition to us . . . a virtually solid country, regardless of sections or party affiliations. . . . Scratch the skin of Republican leaders like Hanna, Lodge, Roosevelt and McKinley and you will find race prejudice close underneath, an invincible belief on their part in the divine right of the Anglo-Saxon to govern the republic and to subjugate darker races to his despotic rule.

He also saw the race problem as a subset of the larger struggle between the masters of capital and the working classes. The country was in danger of being ruled by "an almost omnipotent plutocracy . . . an imperium in imperio under the constitution," and the attack on Negro citizenship was just the prelude to an attack on "the rights of the whole people" and "the principle of equality itself, of popular suffrage in general."[36]

In 1906 Marshall was chief attorney for the Black regulars accused of mutiny in the Brownsville Raid. He and his colleagues developed strong exculpating evidence, which was ignored or overridden by the court-martial and President Roosevelt. (Some sixty-five years later, that same evidence would be used to reverse the verdicts and win posthumous acquittal for the soldiers.) Marshall joined the Democratic Party in New York City and became a strong supporter of Woodrow Wilson. Nevertheless, he shared Roosevelt's belief that war was the supreme test of a race or nation, and that Blacks must seize the chance to fight. Like TR, he offered to raise his own regiment: "This I believe constituted the first offer of services in the World War of any colored citizen in the United States, as it was over a year before the declaration of war." Wilson ignored the proposal.

As the 15th's judge advocate he was able to moderate tensions between White officers and Black soldiers unused to discipline and suspicious of Whites. In May 1917, when Harlem's response to the war seemed tepid, Hayward sent him out to "harangue" crowds on street corners and to speak between the acts to audiences at the Lafayette Theater. When he appeared on the stage in uniform, applause gave way to "a bedlam of protests and catcalls. . . . And rising clear and sonorous above the din I [heard] a voice from the gallery shouting: 'What Has That Uniform Ever Got You?' " Marshall answered that in his opinion "any man who was not willing to fight for his country was not worthy to be one of its citizens." The *New York Tribune* credited Marshall as "a patriot," but characterized the audience response as a "near riot." Marshall thought that an exaggeration: his people had good reason to question the value of service and the uniform, and justified anger to express. Marshall persuaded some of them that joining the 15th was a way to turn anger into positive action.[37]

The mix of socially prominent men, political figures, and ex-soldiers was typical of National Guard regiments. Only the racial composition of the groups distinguished them. The regiment was successful because these two groups were able to work harmoniously, despite the raw feelings left by the politics that had shaped the regiment's organization. This must have required some effort to achieve. We don't know how much, because the history of the regiment was written by a White officer, Major Little, who was at some pains to represent the 15th as a band of brothers.

White and Black officers worked closely, but did not mix socially as a rule. Napoleon Marshall had many White friends at the Harvard Club, but his only friend in the regiment was Major Lorillard Spencer. Hamilton Fish considered James Europe "a high type of person," and they occasionally met for dinner; but as Fish remembered it, theirs was almost the only such friendship among the officers.[38] There may have been some feeling among the Black officers that their White colleagues considered them social inferiors, political tokens rather than competent colleagues. For their part, the White officers might have expected that the Blacks would harbor resentment at the takeover of their regiment, and be ready to see any differences between them as the result of prejudice.

Some such mix of mutual suspicion underlay a sharp exchange between Captains Arthur Little (acting as Hayward's adjutant) and Charles Fillmore of Company B. In August 1917, Fillmore reported a serious infestation of vermin at two posts under his command and requested help from headquarters with the words, "I insist that something be done at once." Little found that expression offensive and rebuked Fillmore: "Attention is called to the Army Regulations . . . which prohibit the use of admonitory language from subordinate officers to superior officers." He then advised Fillmore on methods for getting rid of lice and bedbugs.

Fillmore was stung by this officious response. He was older than Little, his senior in experience and in prior rank (he had served as a major in 1898 and had been temporarily colonel of the 15th). He replied that there was "no intention on my part to be admonitory"; he had simply been emphasizing the urgency of the matter. He also implied that Little's advice was patronizing and irrelevant. As an officer of many years' experience, "I am fully advised by this time how to handle the spread of lice" and would have done so already "if I had the necessary supplies." Little was oblivious to the difficulty of Fillmore's situation: reduced to company command in a regiment he had been hired to lead simply to accommodate White prejudices. He dismissed Fillmore as one of those colored men who saw "racial prejudice . . . in every development that did not operate to their advancement or personal satisfaction."[39]

In other Black regiments acerbities of this kind tended to grow with time, producing serious conflicts among the officers and diminishing unit morale. That did not happen in the 15th New York. Much of the credit belongs to Hayward. He made it clear to White officers seeking positions in the regiment that they must be prepared to "meet men according to their rank as soldiers [and] if [they] intended to take a narrower attitude [they] had better stay out."[40] Though all the field officers were White, at the company level there were White lieutenants serving under Negro captains. With the strong support of the African-American press and Harlem's political and cultural leadership, Hayward and his colleagues were able to attract hundreds of Black men from communities throughout the region to enlist in "Harlem's Own."

"To be a somebody . . .": The Enlisted Men

The regiment drew recruits from African-American communities throughout the metropolitan area and adjacent states and from a variety of social and cultural backgrounds: porters, teachers, salesmen, displaced farmers, semiskilled workers, postmen, craftsmen, small businessmen, hustlers, entertainers—even a street-corner "Bolshevic" [*sic*] who was paddled by the sergeants for trying to stir discontent in the ranks. The agitator was the exception. Young Black men were as susceptible to war fever as Whites: an emotion that mixed anti-German feeling, patriotic enthusiasm, and the wish to be in on the adventure and excitement. John Graham, who worked as a shipping clerk on upper Broadway, said without irony: "Being a lover of Democracy and Liberty, I decided to join up." The White officer at the Brooklyn recruiting station reported, "Many men who had been unmoved by the recruiting speeches of our best spellbinders responded with a rush to the rumor that . . . the colored Infantry was to be the first to go" to war. Enlistment was also a family affair. Seven Fowler and four Davis brothers enlisted, including fifteen-year-old Hannibal "Spats" Davis, who lied about his age: "To be a somebody you had to belong to the Fifteenth Infantry. So to be somebody I joined up."

The regiment was rich in celebrities. James Europe and Napoleon Marshall were of course major figures in Harlem, the chaplains were well-known preachers, and there were community notables even in the ranks. Spotswood Poles was the star centerfielder for the New York Lincoln Giants, a Negro League baseball team that played at Harlem's Olympic Field. He was a superb hitter and fielder, fast enough on the bases to be nicknamed the "black Ty Cobb," skilled enough to hit Major League pitching in the interracial exhibition games that were sometimes played. "Kid" Cotton had been a trainer for Jack Johnson, the Black heavyweight champion who had fought off a succession of "Great White Hopes" until his defeat in 1915. Johnson's punch was legendary: doughboy slang would refer to German heavy artillery shells as "Jack Johnsons." Valdo Shita was (or claimed to be) a Zulu warrior, who had fought with the British in the Boer War and on the Western Front.[41]

A different sort of celebrity was Sergeant Bayard, namesake of the French Chevalier Bayard, the knight *sans peur et sans reproche*, in this case fearless but hardly irreproachable. "He is said to have been tried three times for murder" and acquitted "upon the grounds of self-defense." So terrible was his reputation as a street fighter that "the police of Harlem have a special unit called the Bayard Squad" whose duty "is to attend all the colored balls and concerts or other assemblies of fashion, and trail or tail Bayard and his cronies" to forestall violence. Yet Captain Little found Bayard to be "a wonderful soldier and leader of men, very quiet and gentlemanly in manner and speech, and well educated." (Little was particularly taken with men who represented the raffish criminal side of Harlem life. When the key to a box of important records was lost, Little was happy to make use of the services of Corporal Hall of C Company, who "in civil life is a burglar.")[42]

The most celebrated enlisted men were Europe's bandsmen, who included some of the best and best-known brass players and drummers in the country. Most prominent among them was twenty-seven-year-old Noble Sissle, Indiana-born, the son of a Methodist minister and a schoolteacher. As a boy he worked odd jobs, picked up a high school and college education by bits and pieces, always drawn to show business. A meeting with James Europe gave him his opportunity to perform, singing and playing the "bandolin"—a hybrid of mandolin, banjo, and snare drum. In 1915 he met Eubie Blake, a jazz pianist and a composer of genius, and the two began a song- and musical-comedy writing partnership (Blake the music, Sissle the lyrics) that would bring them extraordinary fame and popularity after Sissle's return from service.[43]

Most in the regiment came from working-class and middle-class families. Charles Conick had worked as a stenographer for the U.S. attorney in New York. Frederick Williams had left the South at age eighteen to get away from Jim Crow and had worked at a little bit of everything in Harlem, shined shoes, was a cook, ran an elevator. "I had to fight like hell to save my life" and get by. He signed up before the war and drilled at the Lafayette Dance Hall. Needham Roberts grew up in Trenton, New Jersey, "a northern outpost of the old Confederacy," son of the minister of the African Methodist Episcopal Zion Church in Mount Holly. He attended the segregated Lincoln Elementary School with its "leaky water pipes and drafty windows" and dropped out to work as a bellhop at the Hotel Windsor and clerk in a drugstore. In 1916 he tried to enlist in the navy but was turned down as underage. When war was declared he was determined to get into it with the regiment whose fame was trumpeted in the city's Black newspapers. His father gave him money and sent him downtown to pay their poll tax, and he used it for a ticket to New York, where he stayed with two older brothers. Before they caught on he had signed up with the 15th New York, lying about his age. There seems to have been some confusion about the spelling of his first name: the army and the newspapers gave it as "Needham," though in civilian life it was often spelled "Neadom."[44]

Henry Johnson was a porter in Albany's Union Station, who took the train down to enlist: there was a war on, and he wanted to get into it with the one outfit that belonged to a Black community. He was a "sweet, unassuming boy," small and wiry, who had come up from North Carolina, found work with the New York Central, rented a house in a mixed Black and Italian district near his work. Shortly after enlisting he married a minister's daughter named Edna Jackson, and their son Herman was born while he was in the service. His brother-in-law Charles Jackson, who shared his house, enlisted with him. [45]

Melville Miller of Brooklyn was drafted after war was declared. His older brother had already been drafted, and the rules allowed his mother to withhold her second son. But everybody was going to war, and Miller was determined to join the 15th. He got a doctor's note, which somehow overrode his mother's refusal to sign away his exemption. William Layton was another underage and undersized Harlem kid, who scarfed a meal of bananas and milk to make the weight for enlistment. His ancestors had escaped from slavery; his grandfather was a veteran of the Civil War. Told that the 15th was at full strength and could not accept any more enlistments, Layton dug in his heels. He refused to enlist in the 24th Infantry, which would not be sent to France because of its anti–Jim Crow "riot" in Houston. He joined the 15th in time to train with it in Spartanburg.[46]

Then there was Horace Pippin. On the surface he was like many of the recruits, tall, quiet, deeply religious, a barely literate country boy who had moved to the city to better himself doing semiskilled industrial work. He was a little older than most. Born in West Chester, Pennsylvania, on Washington's Birthday, 1888, he never knew his father and was one of three children raised by Harriet Pippin, who may not have been his birth mother. When he was three the family moved to Goshen, New York, in the Catskills, where Horace and his sisters studied in a segregated one-room schoolhouse. "When I was seven I began to get into trouble." Instead of copying spelling words in his notebook he'd draw a picture of the thing the word referred to. The teacher would keep him after school to redo the work, and he'd get a beating when he went home "regardless what I were kept in for." He won a box of crayons from a magazine contest ("[Draw] me and win a prize"), made colored pictures of Bible scenes on doilies for a class display, and was proud when a woman bought them—and embarrassed when she came back to complain that the pictures came off in the wash. When he was ten his mother moved to Middletown, New York, and went into private service. Horace was hired out for farmwork when he was fourteen. The farmer offered to send the boy to art school, but his mother got sick and he had to find better-paying work to support her: heaver in a coal yard, clerk in a feed store, porter at the St. Elmo Hotel for seven years.

His mother died in 1911, and he left the Catskills to find work in the city. He packed furniture for shipping at the Fidelity Storage House in Paterson, New Jersey, for four years, then found work at the American Brakeshoe Company: a step up, he learned to be a molder, a skilled worker—nonunion of course, no Blacks allowed in the metal trades. In March 1917, with war imminent, he crossed the river on the Hoboken Ferry and enlisted in the 15th New York. His boss told him his job would be there when he got back—he was respected as a workman. Among the gear he packed was a notebook, pencils, and a set of crayons. He still liked to respond to things by making small pictures, but kept his practice secret. It would take the experience of war, and rehabilitation from a terrible wound, for him to recognize his desire to become an artist and begin the work that would make him an important American painter.[47]

For African-American men in the greater New York region the 15th offered an attractive way to serve, among people from one's own community, in a unit with assembly points right in town. Selective Service added to these positive inducements the fear that if you didn't get into the 15th, you would probably be conscripted and sent among strangers. Even so, volunteer enlistments did not come in fast enough to allow the regiment to reach the minimum combat strength of 3,000 to 3,600 men, and the number was made up by drafted men. But the tone of the regiment was set by the volunteers who had chosen Harlem's Own Regiment and identified with it, and the draftees shared the feeling that the 15th was "theirs." When the regiment was redesignated as the 369th U.S. Infantry after it arrived in France, drafted men and volunteers alike were aggrieved. The "three hundreds" were used to identify National Army regiments—the "Old Fifteenth" thought of itself as a volunteer National Guard outfit even after it ceased to be one. It was a sign of their unit pride, their esprit de corps.

That unity had not been easy to achieve.

Military Training and the "Americanization" of the Negro

The officers' primary mission was to school their men in the discipline
and techniques of soldiering. Black and White, they brought to the task
the presumptions of Progressivism: leadership and authority are vested in
an intellectual and moral elite, and the people ought to be willing followers and pupils eager for instruction. Arthur Little's is the fullest account
we have of this training, and his approach was that of the "noblesse
oblige liberal." His goodwill is unmistakable, but so is his sense of being
modestly but entirely superior to the African-Americans with whom he
deals. He saw himself and his colleagues as colonial administrators trying
to civilize a primitive people. The first recruits reminded him of "Rem-
ington's pictures of Cuban Reconcentrados, published in *Harper's
Weekly* during the years 1896 to 1898." The sight of the men bathing
naked in a pond caused "a number of us to exclaim—"With Henry M.
Stanley, in Darkest Africa!" He saw Negroes as a people governed by un-
reasoning emotion and brute strength, and believed he must be consistently authoritative in his manners and action: "If mental strength was to
govern brute strength, there must be no apparent doubt of its superiority
upon the part of the advocate of mentality."[48]

Little mistrusted the culture from which his soldiers came. At the recruiting station in Brooklyn, he was appalled by the emotionalism and
the forwardness of the Black women who crowded in with their men.
Some pleaded, in what seemed to him a crude and heavy dialect, for their
men to be let out of their enlistment: " 'Doan take mah bebby erway ter
war ter git shot!' . . . 'Ef yoo all takes him erway me an' mah fo' chillen
will stave, cuz I cain't do no washin' now till after mah bebby is bone.' "
Others were willing to let their men go, but "wanted to cry a little with
the captain over the farewell." Some wanted the captain to see their boys
didn't get wet feet and catch cold; others wanted the captain to make
sure a spendthrift husband sent his pay home. One woman, "the daughter of well-to-do parents" who had married a husband "too good-
looking for her peace of mind," told Little the man was living with
another woman and "contributes nothing to my support." She hoped
Little would put him in the front line to "win fame or death, and my
baby . . . will be able to speak with pride of its father."

For Little, the scene seems to show that Black men are lacking virility and not quite adult, because they let "their women folks do the talking" and treat them like wayward children. From the Black perspective these displays signified nothing of the kind. African-American culture allowed the women a freedom of emotional expression that would have been repressed among Little's set, for decorum's sake. The feelings voiced by the women (and acknowledged by the silence of their men) were just those that would have played through the minds of any set of mothers, sisters, or wives sending husbands, fathers, brothers, and sons to war: fearful of the outcome even as they acknowledge the necessity, wishing to snatch the men back even as they let them go, seeing them one moment as brave men and in the next as the vulnerable children they so recently were. "Baby" can be a term of affection between adults. But Little saw all this as proof that his troops were "bebbies" who had to be taught to be men.

The enlisted men were used to such attitudes in White people and had developed ways of resisting or deflecting their demoralizing tendencies through a subtle kind of mockery. Their handling of the military salute was a case in point. To Captain Little's pleased surprise, "Our men accepted the principle of the salute more readily than any other principle of a soldier's training. They seemed to love to salute. They would walk out of their way to approach officers so as to find an excuse to salute." So astonishing was the regiment's love of saluting that "it was dubbed *The Saluting Fifteenth*" (a name "intended as a compliment"). Visitors came to the camp just to enjoy the spectacle.

Saluting was a highly charged issue in the new citizen-army. The War Department believed, with reason, that free-born White Americans resented the compulsion to salute as a form of social degradation, a coerced acknowledgment that some other free-born White American was one's superior. *The Home Reading Course for Citizen-Soldiers* therefore provided an elaborate history, which argued the salute was not a mark of subservience, but a privilege of the soldier that was denied to civilians. The soldier was admonished to salute his superior—and look him squarely in the eye. This elaborate rationalization evaded the uncomfortable fact that in the military the free-born individual is in fact made distinctly and ineluctably subordinate to a class of men no better than himself (and sometimes worse).[49]

The African-American soldiers of the 15th New York were familiar with that sort of paradox. Those who had lived in the South had had to observe the manners of Jim Crow, which required demeaning and subservient forms of salute every day of their lives: to yield the sidewalk to a passing White man, to bow the head when addressed, and never to look the White man straight in the eyes. Now they were in the army, fighting for a chance to fight and die for a country that named them niggers and treated them like niggers. So they not only saluted, they went out of their way to salute, saluted indiscriminately, ignoring or mocking the fine gradations of rank the salute was supposed to support. Nor did they follow the prescribed form. They "adopted a style of military salute all their own," first raising the right hand "smartly to the visor of the cap," then "bow[ing] very low in the most approved style of cordiality of a Saratoga Springs hotel headwaiter, and murmur[ing], 'Mawnin' Suh—mawnin.' " It is possible they were merely ignorant of the proper forms and peculiarly resistant to learning them; or that, as Little explains, they had been trained in subservient manners by their work as "Pullman porters and waiters . . . and theatre doormen." But porters, headwaiters, and doormen are not sharecroppers or hod carriers. They had some dignity within their community, and could aspire to a lower-middle-class standard of living, with amenities at home and education for their children; and their work allowed them to observe the full range of American manners. Perhaps their excessive salute was a way of satirizing the form while nominally following it, accepting orders while signifying their independence of mind with regard to the overmastering ideological and political power of the army. One is reminded of the injunction given to the narrator of Ralph Ellison's *Invisible Man* (1953) by his grandfather: "I want you to overcome 'em with yeses, undermine 'em with grins, agree 'em to death and destruction."[50]

Of course, the men of the 15th were not saluting their officers to destroy or undermine them. The bargain that they and their community leaders had made required them to find their way to civil equality and dignity through effective service to the regiment. That meant they had to learn from their officers, Black or White, and follow their leadership in battle. The elaborate, unique salute of the 15th was both a mockery and a mark of pride—a gesture embodying the double-consciousness of the people who invented it.

In some companies defiance took more overt forms. Company F was considered the hardest to manage, its ranks filled with Brooklyn hard cases who cultivated a reputation for recalcitrance. Their captain, a former high school principal and attorney named John Holley Clark Jr., recalled a rumor that went around the company to the effect that sergeants who pushed too hard were likely to get shot. After that, "if there was a shot fired and you didn't know where the shot came from, someone would turn to another and say, 'What was that sergeant's name?' "[51]

In the end officers and men were able to work through their tensions and differences. Black officers used their position to ease rather than exacerbate relations between the men and their White officers.[52] The officers earned the respect and allegiance of the troops by doing their job as drillmasters and organizers. They displayed their fairness in promoting private soldiers to corporal and sergeant. They encouraged close ties with the community: in the early days, when the companies had to train in dance halls or on streets in Harlem and Brooklyn, company officers invited the neighborhood to cheer and kibitz at the close-order drill.[53]

An outbreak of racial violence in East St. Louis in July 1917 gave Hayward and his colleagues a chance to prove that good faith. Southern Blacks had come to East St. Louis in search of better jobs and had been used as strikebreakers in the heavily unionized town. Democratic politicians played up fears that Black voters would throw control of the city to Republican and antilabor interests. There was sporadic violence and drive-by shootings through May and June. When a group of Blacks mistakenly fired on a car full of city police on July 1, there was a massive outbreak of White mob violence. Over three days at least 125 Negroes were killed, many mutilated or burned to death, and the Negro quarter was torched. There was widespread condemnation of the riot. Robert McElroy told the National Security League that he "dread[ed] the use which Germany will be able, legitimately, to make of that incident." But conservative Democrats saw the riot as the necessary response of White communities threatened with Black political "domination." And there were many voices, liberal as well as conservative, who mitigated the offense as arising from the inevitable and perhaps legitimate resentment of White communities facing Negro intrusions.[54]

In New York, events took a dramatic turn at a mass meeting in Carnegie Hall, which had been called to honor a delegation from the Russian revolutionary government of Alexander Kerensky. The meeting was organized by Captain Fish of the 15th New York, at the request of Mayor John Purroy Mitchel (who had been with Fish at Plattsburgh). Theodore Roosevelt spoke first in praise of Kerensky's effort to establish democratic government in Russia. Then AFL president Samuel Gompers took the podium and "launched into a bitter attack on the Negro strike-breakers at East St. Louis," implicitly blaming the Blacks for the riot. Roosevelt rushed up and "shook his fist in the labor leader's face." He shouted that he had heard the same excuses "advanced in behalf of the Russian autocracy for pogroms of Jews. Not for a moment shall I acquiesce in any apology for the murder of women and children in our own country." He then stood defiantly as the audience dissolved in "pandemonium."[55]

Roosevelt followed up by becoming a prominent supporter of the 15th New York and its civilian auxiliaries. But his militant stand was controversial in a White community more sympathetic to the plight of White labor and the wounded pride of "our Southern friends" than to Negro grievances. The *New York Times* reported the incident under the headline, "Roosevelt and Gompers Row at Russian Meeting," and its editorial blasted Roosevelt as "The Spoiled Child" whose temper tantrum violated decorum and offended foreign visitors.[56]

The regiment's officers, White as well as Black, kept their men's trust by consistently demonstrating their commitment to them and to the cause the regiment embodied. On July 3, with East St. Louis on the front pages, a "race riot" was reported in the San Juan Hill district, involving "Negro Guardsmen" and some two thousand civilians. Several soldiers of the 15th (fifteen by one account) had been standing about and skylarking when a White policeman decided to arrest some of them for loitering. The troops resisted, more police were called—officers Kavanaugh, Kelly, and Huben, two Irishmen and a "Dutchman"—and one man was arrested. The *Times* at first played up the "riot" as a sign of political unrest and disloyalty in Harlem, noting that the incident followed a provocative speech by Hubert Harrison at the Liberty League, which "Urge[d] Negroes to Get Arms" and defend themselves against abuse. At that point Hayward stepped in, made a swift inquiry, and informed the *Times* that in his view the policeman had accosted his men for no good reason—his troops had been "within their rights." In an interview with the editor of the *Age* he called the 15th "a picked regiment of the very best, self-respecting, law-abiding Negroes." The *Times* quoted his words and dropped the "riot." Hayward's reputation in Harlem and regimental morale were boosted by this proof of that Hayward was willing to take his men's part in a public controversy. Private Layton rated the colonel "basically okay," and believed "he loved those fellas, street boys you could say."[57]

For civilian Harlem, Hayward's and Roosevelt's gestures did not outweigh this evidence that White America cared little for the victims of East St. Louis or the grievances of African-Americans. Community leaders organized a "Silent Protest Parade" on July 28, in which ten thousand marchers, led by children and women dressed in white, "paraded down Fifth Avenue to the sound of muffled drums." Though the marchers were silent, they carried banners that asked, "Mother, Do Lynchers Go to Heaven?" and challenged the administration to make good on its pretensions to be the worldwide defender of democracy: "Mr. President, Why Not Make America Safe for Democracy?" "Patriotism and Loyalty Presuppose Protection and Liberty." The marchers' manifesto memorialized "our butchered dead" as "honest toilers who were removing the reproach of laziness and thriftlessness hurled at the entire race. They died proving our worthiness to live."[58]

What was said retrospectively of the victims of the mob applied prospectively to the soldiers of the 15th New York: they too were willing to die to remove from the race the reproach of a lack of courage and soldierly virtues. Would White Americans show any more respect for their sacrifice than it showed for the dead workers of East St. Louis?

Through the summer and into the fall, Hayward had to struggle to keep the regiment together, get it equipped, and win time for it to train at Camp Whitman. Companies were continually detached for guard and construction duties across southern New York and New Jersey. One battalion "pioneered" the building of Camp Dix. Another provided military police for the National Army's 77th Division assembling at Camp Upton on Long Island, where mosquitoes were so thick that if you wiped your hands across your government-issue mosquito mask you'd get "a handful of mosquitos." They clashed with White construction workers who resented having their papers checked by Black MPs. There was a gunfight down at the railroad yards, and one major brawl that drew headlines, "Negro Troops Clash with White Men." For their part, the Black troops were dismayed to see newly drafted Whites training for combat, while they—who had been in the service for months—had had less than five weeks' regimental drill. Perhaps the War Department intended to follow the advice of regular officers, who thought Black regiments fit only for garrison duty or labor battalions. In August the New York National Guard regiments were assigned a training depot, and paraded down Fifth Avenue to the troop trains—but the 15th were not allowed to go with them.

That summer's experience of disappointment and discrimination heightened the identification of officers and men with the regiment and with each other. The emotional tone of that solidarity mixed pride with a sense of grievance: "The 15th Heavy Foot was the self-made regiment of the American Army . . . without traditions, without education, and without friends." No West Point officer appeared to instruct it, its equipment was shoddy and late to arrive, it had no armory in which to assemble, its training was curtailed and continually disrupted. But instead of buckling under discrimination, the regiment made its own way, just like the hero of a Horatio Alger success story—or Booker T. Washington struggling "up from slavery."[59]

"The self-made regiment": what Hayward and the Harlem sponsors wanted was a regiment capable of winning a place for Black men in the American national mythology. Conformity to the Horatio Alger/"Up from Slavery" myth was important, proof that Negroes could acquire the values and virtues of middle-class Americans. But Hayward, Fish, and Little had begun to imagine the Old Fifteenth (and themselves) as heroes in the more potent Rooseveltian mythology of conquering Indian fighters and race warriors. Fish told newspaper reporters that the 15th New York would be the Rough Riders of the war. He would repeat that assertion in interviews and in letters from France, which he had his father publish in the *Times*. Little remembered how all the officers were possessed by the idea: "We developed a terrific *Esprit de Corps*, and went about our work with heads up and chests out, assuring each other that our regiment was undoubtedly the most talked of regiment of the American Army, the natural successor, in the World War, to the picturesqueness, in the Spanish War, of the Rough Riders."[60]

Like the Rough Riders, they represented a social experiment, a possible model for a modern democratic society in which old lines of distinction—class and section then, race now—would be replaced by a patriotic meritocracy. As for the officers, San Juan Hill had catapulted Roosevelt into the governorship, the vice presidency, the presidency. Perhaps a battlefield success for the 15th would do the same for its politician-officers. If their appeals produced no immediate results, their political influence was strong enough that they were never denied a hearing. Hayward and Fish used their press connections to keep the 15th in the public eye. Fish had connections in the movie business, which he exploited. The symbolism of the regiment seemed to them so potent, so perfectly consonant with the wartime ideology of democracy and fair play, that it could only be a matter of time and publicity until they were recognized and put to use.[61]

Behind the scenes Hayward was using all his influence in Albany and at the War Department to attach his regiment to a division already slated for combat in France. The 27th Division, composed of New York National Guard units, was a logical choice. But Hayward's imagination ran along lines similar to those that had led Theodore Roosevelt to propose the inclusion of Black regiments in his "Roosevelt Division." He wanted the 15th incorporated with the 42nd "Rainbow" Division. That outfit had already been made a symbol of national unity, mingling units from two-thirds of the states, brigading the Irishmen of New York's own "Fighting 69th" with the Alabama regiment whose Confederate ancestor had shot it out with the 69th at Fredericksburg. What better fulfillment of the Rainbow's ideological mission than to include the descendants of slaves, masters, and liberators under a single banner? As Herbert Myrick had written, "Black men, yellow men, white men, from all quarters of the globe, are fighting side by side to free the world from the Hun peril. / That's the patriotism of equality!"

Both proposals made sense, and the "Rainbow" idea was brilliant. But General O'Ryan, commander of the New York National Guard, turned down Hayward's application for attachment to the 27th Division, and Governor Whitman declined to push the matter. The commander of the 42nd Division is said to have told Hayward, "Black is not one of the colors of the rainbow."[62]

Developments at the War Department that fall proved more favorable. Emmett Scott's hand was strengthened by the administration's desire to placate Black opinion after East St. Louis, and he had DuBois's support as well. The War Department finally granted Hayward's wish to have the 15th train with the other New York National Guard units. The catch was that they would train at Camp Wadsworth in Spartanburg, South Carolina, the Jim Crow heartland.

On October 7 the Fifteenth's guard detail at Camp Upton on Long Island turned over military police duties to the embryonic 77th Division. The *New York Sun* took notice of their departure: "Negro Battalion to Vanish," no more "chocolate boys" at Upton—as if that were a bit of good news. As they waited to board the train at the depot, mobs of pasty-faced tenement draftees from Manhattan and Brooklyn scrambled out of the coaches. One gang carried a poster that identified them as "Harlem's Hun Hammerers."[63]

Neighbors.

4

"The Jews and Wops, the Dutch and Irish Cops": Recruiting the Melting Pot Division, July–December 1917

> Take a look at me, I'm a Yankee thru and thru,
> I was born on July the Fourth in Ninety-Two.
> And I'll march away with a feather in my hat,
> For I'm joining the army, What do you think of that?
> And I don't know where I'm going but I'm on my way,
> For I belong to the Reg-u-lars, I'm proud to say,
> And I'll do my duty-uty night or day,
> I don't know where I'm going but I'm on my way!
>
> —*George Fairman, "I Don't Know Where*
> *I'm Going But I'm on My Way" (1917)*

Camp Upton was built near the town of Yaphank, Long Island, in a "wilderness of sand and scrub oak and famous for nothing but our great national bird, the mosquito." It dissolved in "universal mud" when it rained, while "in dry weather walls of dust swept [it] from end to end." Crews had labored mightily, but there still weren't barracks enough for the thirty thousand men the camp would have to handle, and construction was hampered because the recruits kept stealing the building materials for firewood.

The officers arrived in the dog days of late August and September, "grop[ing] their way among a myriad of sweating workmen, teams, wagons, motor trucks, jitneys, lumber piles, stables, shanties; over fresh broken roads, felled trees, stumps, brush and sticky mud" to find the unpainted shack assigned as their quarters. There was a dearth of blankets and bedding, and "colored workmen" who had engrossed the supply of iron cots sold them beds at exorbitant prices. Most of the officers were Plattsburgh alums or "ninety-day wonders" from the army's jerry-built officer training camps, ignorant of army procedures. Their first inkling of the roles they were to play came when they discovered their names "dangling from a sort of family tree" on a table of organization posted at headquarters. Initial assignments were subject to continual reshuffling as individual personalities and special skills were revealed.

Down at the depot trains arrived hauling cars full of conscripts. The men had received no instructions about what to bring with them or what to expect. Damon Runyon had observed them with wry amusement straggling up Fifth Avenue from the assembly hall to the train station, dressed in everything from Sabbath finery and "Palm Beach Suits" to workmen's overalls while a band blared "Over There!" "Some were late of the Hudson Dusters . . . [others] from the ornate houses on Park and Madison. . . . More were from the Lower East Side, Broad and Harlem, Broadway and the Bronx." There were "Chinamen from Mott Street . . . Japs and Italians, all jabbering in their own language." They piled off the train at Yaphank, some with valises and others with nothing but the clothes on their backs. They "stood about eyeing [the officers] with expectant curiosity, with friendly amusement, with critical displeasure, or with apathy, according to their nationality or mood—with any and every emotion save military respect." Gruff regular sergeants tried to sort them out, while "nervous young officers, fresh from Plattsburgh, fluttered about."[1]

The 77th was a New York outfit, and the great majority of the city's population was either foreign-born or first-generation American.

> The recruits represented all races and creeds—men who had only recently been subjected to the pogroms of Russia, gunmen and gangsters, a type peculiar to New York City, Italians, Chinamen, the Jews and the Irish, a heterogenous mass.[2]

The papers variously nicknamed it the "Metropolitan," the "Times Square," the "Statue of Liberty," and the "Melting Pot" Division. But the melting pot moniker was premature. It had yet to be demonstrated that the constituents of the city's heterogenous mass were capable of living in peace among themselves, let alone amalgamating into a single and *American* people. They would have to be Americanized and prepared for combat at the same time.

There was hardly time to do either job properly. The week after Wilson's eloquent call to arms, Congress and the press awoke to the reality that the nation was utterly unready to fight. Despite legislation adopted the preceding year, nothing had been done to shift industry to war production. The greatest industrial nation in the world would send its troops into action without any of the finished goods of war—trucks, tanks, artillery, machine guns, airplanes. These would be supplied by the French and British, while America supplied raw materials—and raw recruits. In 1916 Congress had increased the authorized strength of army and National Guard to 225,000, but Britain had lost that many men in a week's fighting along the Somme. An army of millions had to be created from scratch, with urgent speed.

The necessity of rapid mass mobilization forced the Wilson administration to resort immediately to conscription. The regular army (with the Marine Corps) and the National Guard would combine conscripts with a core of voluntary enlistees in a ratio of two or three to one. In addition the "National Army" was created, whose ranks would be filled entirely by draftees. It would be the largest of the three elements of the American Expeditionary Force, mustering seventeen divisions, as against sixteen National Guard and eight regular divisions. Thus the nation's ability to play a decisive role in the Great War would depend on the successful performance of units mostly composed of conscripts.[3]

Captain (later Major) Julius Adler of the 77th described the National Army as an "experiment . . . to determine whether the natural assets of initiative, alertness, courage and determination could be matched against the iron discipline of a great war machine." But the natural assets of his recruits were doubtful. These were the peoples whose racial aptitude for American citizenship had been questioned by President Roosevelt's Commission on Immigration. Their life in the slums, their work in the sweatshops, hardly prepared them to live the Strenuous Life. "To stamp the fundamental principles of military discipline on such men was a gigantic task."[4]

And their loyalty was suspect. Immigrants from Germany and Austria-Hungary might have lingering loyalties to their homelands, and they had reason to fear they would have to face their kindred in battle. In 1915 Russian Jews in Cincinnati had tried to raise a regiment for service against the czar, and the Socialist Party leader Morris Hillquit had declared that a German defeat of Russia would be a victory for socialism. Of the new immigrant groups only the Italians came from a country aligned with the Allies. Misunderstandings were inevitable, and under the conditions dangerous. When a German-American conscript gave out cigars on the anniversary of the sinking of the *Lusitania* he was hauled in for questioning. It turned out he was celebrating some family event, and had no idea when the *Lusitania* had been sunk.[5] That was well enough. But the sinking was a watershed event for the Plattsburghers, the Great War equivalent of "Remember the Alamo!" What sort of patriotism could be expected of a man who did not remember the *Lusitania*?

The city's immigrant workers were also known for the militancy of their unionism and their attraction to socialism. The metropolitan area had just come through a decade of labor turmoil, marked by violent strikes and lockouts. The 1915 Paterson, New Jersey, strike drew the leadership of the Socialist Party and the IWW to New York, and engaged the sympathies and energies of the city's intellectual and cultural elite, which staged a huge pageant for the strikers at Madison Square Garden. The strike of the shirtwaist makers in 1909–10 united Jewish and Italian "working girls" and set off a wave of organizing drives that culminated in an abortive General Strike in 1916. A politics oriented toward labor and driven by Socialists and militant women—these were hardly consonant with American traditions. And the laboring classes of New York were also feared as "dangerous classes." Crime was rife on the mean streets, and ethnic gangs ruled organized criminal enterprises. There were old Irish gangs like the Hudson Dusters, Gopleens, and Five Pointers, and newer ones like the Jewish "Eastmans," the Sicilian "Black Hand," and several Chinese "Tongs," which corrupted officials or shot it out for control of neighborhoods and rackets.[6]

Was it possible to create from such diverse and even dissident elements a new democratic army, large enough to contest a world war and loyal enough to see it through? One of the primary tasks of the 77th Division's officers would be (in General Wood's phrase) to "heat up the melting pot" by using military training to instill "100% Americanism" in the polyglot mass.

Gentlemen and Officers

The generals and field officers assigned to the 77th Division were regular army veterans who had learned their trade as agents of Theodore Roosevelt's military imperialism. If they had any experience of labor unions it was as antagonists. As professionals they were skeptical of the Plattsburghers' skills, but respected them as men of the same social class. What they expected of their hyphenate cloakmakers, shopkeepers, gangsters, and firemen may be imagined. *The U.S. Army Manual of Instruction for Medical Advisory Boards* informed them that "the foreign born, and especially Jews, are more apt to malinger than the native-born."[7]

Major General Franklin Bell, who was in charge during the division's training, had commanded in the Philippines during the height of the war there. His policy of forcing peasants into "reconcentration camps" contributed to a civilian death toll that Bell himself estimated at a quarter of a million. George Duncan was Bell's deputy and successor, and would command during the division's first months of combat: he had fought in Cuba and headed the Philippine Scouts. Robert Alexander, who would command the division in the Argonne, was a "mustang" who had enlisted as a private and risen through the ranks. He saw service against the Sioux during the Ghost Dance troubles (1890–1), fought in Cuba, and commanded troops in the military interventions that broke the Pullman strike (1894) and the Colorado coalfield strikes of 1902–3. He served under Brigadier General Jacob Smith in Samar and Leyte in 1901–2, in a series of campaigns marked by atrocities and massacres.[8]

The division's cadre of company officers was dominated by Plattsburgh alums—the figurative "Sons of Roosevelt," well-born, Ivy League–educated, virile, vigorous sportsmen and hunters, physically fit, and used to the outdoors. A French military observer noted, with amused surprise, that "the officer corps is drawn almost entirely from the rich, cultured bourgeoisie." The New York papers often mentioned them as men well-known in business, political, and social circles. These were the men who would do the difficult, face-to-face work of training the melting pot draftees to be soldiers: teaching them the "School of the

Soldier"—the fundamentals of discipline, camp hygiene, physical conditioning, drill, use of weapons; teaching them how to think and work and function effectively as members of a military unit—first the squad, then the platoon, the company, the battalion, the regiment, and ultimately the division.[9]

Crawford Blagden was from a prominent banking family, a football star who had led Harvard to victory over Yale in 1901. He had organized the Harvard Club meetings that led to the first Plattsburgh encampment and would command a company in the 307th Infantry. James A. Roosevelt, a cousin of TR, Harvard '05 and Plattsburgh '17, would command the divisional supply train. Gordon Schenck was a Yale man, class of 1913. Philip Mills (Harvard '14) was the son of a regular army general and a French mother, a wealthy lawyer who had served in a volunteer ambulance unit in France, "powerful of frame and deep of voice, full of jest, the very figure of an ideal soldier." W. Kerr Rainsford was an architect, the son of the Episcopal rector of St. George's Church in New York City, Harvard '04, an avid sailor, athlete, and hunter. George McMurtry Jr., Harvard '99 and veteran of the Rough Riders, dark-haired and solidly built, "bustling, breezy, and busy," would command E Company of the 308th Infantry. Charles Whittlesey (Harvard Law and Wall Street) was tapped for staff duty: "tall, lank, serious, bespectacled. He listens judiciously or talks quietly in the same level tones which he will never lose in the face of danger and despair."[10]

The worlds of entertainment and professional sports were also represented. Edward Harrigan was the son of a famous Irish vaudevillian, creator of the comic "Mulligan Guards"—the man celebrated and imitated in George M. Cohan's signature song: "H, A, double-R I, G—A—N spells *Harrigan*. / Proud of all the Irish blood that's in me . . ." The vaudeville money paid young Harrigan's way through Harvard and Plattsburgh. He would command a company in the 308th. Captain Edward L. Grant of the 307th had made a living playing third base for John McGraw's New York Giants, but he was also a graduate of Harvard and Plattsburgh. As if to mark the difference between Manhattan and working-class Brooklyn, pitcher Leon Cadore of the Brooklyn Robins (later the Dodgers) lacked the Ivy League/Plattsburgh credentials, entered the 77th as an enlisted man and would have to earn his commission in the wartime Officer Training Camps (OTC). He would see active service with the 15th New York/369th Infantry.[11]

These men brought to their task not only the physique but the values of the Strenuous Life: a personal identification of their own honor with the honor of their country. Rainsford had been studying art history in Paris when war broke out. Like Alan Seeger he felt personally shamed by Wilson's neutrality, and volunteered for the American Ambulance Service, taking it on himself to do what his country feared to attempt. Philip Mills had joined the Norton Ambulance Service for similar reasons, and was on the verge of joining Seeger in the Foreign Legion when the United States finally entered the war. L. Wardlaw Miles was the son of a Confederate army doctor, and so something of an exception at Plattsburgh. At forty-four he was also older than most, married with three children when the United States entered the war. He had graduated from Johns Hopkins in 1894, completed medical studies, then decided to pursue his interest in literature. He received a Ph.D. from Johns Hopkins in 1903, taught German language and literature in prep school, and was an assistant professor of English at Princeton when the war broke out. He signed up for Plattsburgh in 1915 and 1916 because "the neutral and unprepared position of our country became embarrassing"—to him, personally. In 1917 he resigned his professorship to attend the last Plattsburgh encampment and enlist in the National Army. He would end the war as a captain, a Medal of Honor winner, and historian of the 308th Infantry.[12]

Julius Ochs Adler was Jewish by birth and religion, but in every other way fit the Plattsburgh template: Princeton '14, Plattsburgh '15 and '16, and heir apparent to the *New York Times*, owned by his uncle Adolph Ochs. The family's wealth and social standing was two generations old. His grandfather, Julius Ochs, came to the United States from Germany in 1845, settled in Knoxville, prospered, served as an officer in the Union army during the Civil War. When his fortune was wiped out by a depression in 1867, his oldest son took a job as a newsboy in Chattanooga. By age nineteen Adolph Ochs owned the paper, and in three years made it the most important one in the region. He was prominent in the city's social elite, and in 1883 married a daughter of Rabbi Stephen Wise, founder of Reform Judaism and the preeminent figure in the American Jewish community. In 1896 he moved to New York, bought the *New York Times*, and set out to make it the national paper of record.

Julius Adler was the son of Adolph's sister Ada, was raised in Adolph's house, and as the only male child of his generation was called "Son" and identified as Adolph's successor. He attended an elite prep school and Princeton, from which he graduated in 1914. The family's celebratory trip to Europe coincided with the outbreak of war, and they fled for home on the liner *Lusitania*. The sinking of that ship the following year made the *Times* an advocate of preparedness, and moved Adler to sign up for Plattsburgh. Like many of his fellow Ivy Leaguers, he was an athlete, "broad-shouldered and barrel-chested," used to the outdoors, and did well in training. If there was a difference it was that as a Jew his standing as a "Son of Roosevelt" was subject to question. His uncle Adolph Ochs was a wealthy, respected figure in New York society, but would not allow his name to be put forward at the Century Club for fear of rejection. He kept aloof from "Jewish" causes and organizations, and the editorial policy of the *Times* eschewed any position that might make it appear a "Jewish newspaper." When war came he worried, with reason, that the family's German origins would make them suspect. Adolph's brother George changed the family name from Ochs to "Oakes." Despite the *Times*'s advocacy of preparedness, its mere suggestion that the United States receive a 1917 Austrian peace overture produced a backlash. It required assiduous editorializing, and Julius Adler's sterling combat record, to fully restore the *Times*'s reputation. In July 1917 Adler was assigned as a senior instructor to the 77th Division at Camp Upton. He would win a Distinguished Service Cross for valor and end the war as a major and historian of the 77th Division.[13]

Charles W. Whittlesey, who would command the Lost Battalion, was a more complex character. In most ways he fit the "Son of Roosevelt" profile: Harvard Law and Wall Street, well-born and well-read, physically fit, with a strong sense of moral idealism. But in 1912 he did not vote for either Roosevelt or Wilson, preferring Eugene Debs and the Socialist Party. He was a late and reluctant convert to preparedness, and never accepted the morality of the war in which he would distinguish himself.[14]

Whittlesey could trace his ancestry to the Puritan colonists, and Whittleseys had served in all the nation's wars since the Pequot War of 1637. He was born in the Midwest, but moved to Pittsfield, Massachussetts, where his father worked as a business executive. His family was prosperous, but not wealthy. Whittlesey went to Williams College, class of 1905, where his roommate and close friend was Max Eastman, the minister's son who would become one of the leading figures of the literary and political Left.

Whittlesey was an attractive figure, "towering like a cliff over a brook," lean, bespectacled, with a manner that was "sharp-edged, impersonal, and unsentimental." He was an ROTC cadet, had gifts of leadership, perhaps something of the Roosevelt style—"seemed more than the rest of us, in the lightning speed and intemperate force of his judgments, designed for fame." Yet he was also "contemptuous" of celebrity and "of all those values that loom so large to the ambitious." He wrote for and edited the college literary magazine, yearbook, and newspaper, but (unlike Eastman) his tastes ran to the classical rather than the romantic. His favorite poem was Milton's sonnet that begins, "Lawrence, of virtuous father virtuous son"—a tribute to Puritan rectitude and filial piety. He could be a wonderful companion and conversationalist, "loved speculation and friendship; classic beauty; a jest; an argument; a convivial evening." But he also had an odd coolness or reserve, a need to distance himself from suffering or exhibitions of vulnerability. His sister-in-law would describe him as "a man of finely wrought nerves, which he always kept under control. It was his suppressed, nervous temperament that made him stand out among men." His classmates gave him two different nicknames: the affectionate "Chick" for his sociability and "The Count" for his mysterious but somehow attractive reserve.

Whittlesey and Eastman belonged to an intensely intellectual circle, which pursued a variety of enthusiasms in reading, art, sexuality, and politics. Their intellectual curiosity was driven by an intense moral seriousness, a search for ideas around which to organize a Strenuous Life. They found socialism attractive, though it troubled them that socialists considered patriotism "a virtue of the childhood of the race." Whittlesey told a classmate that he was thinking of becoming a missionary, though he knew "hardly anything" of the Christian religion. "Well, why do you want to be a missionary?" Whittlesey answered, "I want to do something that I *don't* want to do." For Whittlesey the height of moral strenuousness, the test of character and virtue, was to push yourself beyond the bounds that your own nature sets.[15]

Law and banking were typical careers for the Whittleseys, and Charles would fulfill the virtuous father's expectation of the virtuous son. He graduated Harvard Law in 1908 and opened a partnership with his best friend, John Bayard Pruyn, a descendant of one of New York's old Dutch families, with offices at 2 Rector Street in the heart of the financial district. He settled into a "bachelors' boardinghouse" at 136

East 44th Street, just east of the Times Square theater district and the "Uptown Bohemia" where performers and artists lived. Whittlesey was a popular and convivial member of the Harvard and Williams clubs, easygoing, with a "keen eye for the ridiculous" and a gift for storytelling; an avid sports fan, he would travel anywhere in the Northeast to catch a good college football game. He was best man at Pruyn's wedding, but his sister-in-law described him as "a confirmed bachelor," never "married or engaged to be married." A longtime friend remembered, "In the ten years or more that I [knew] him, I never heard him mention the name of a woman." There is no evidence of his having had an ongoing intimate relationship with any person. He also spent time in Greenwich Village with his college chum Max Eastman. The Village was a crossroads in which "bohemian" intellectuals and artists, refugees from the best schools and the upper middle class, socialized with workingmen from the waterfront and garment districts to the west and the immigrant neighborhoods of the Lower East Side, Little Italy, and Chinatown.[16]

The Greenwich Village community of intellectuals and artistic bohemians allied themselves with the cause of the workers and the socialist movement, organized pageants and relief programs to aid strikers, published essays and investigative reports in mainstream journals. Max Eastman was prominent among them. In 1912 he became editor of the *Masses*, a pioneering effort of the avant-garde Left; he supported the IWW strike in Lawrence and the "coal war" in West Virginia. In 1912 the *Masses* endorsed the Socialist candidate for president, declaring "every vote cast for Eugene V. Debs is a vote for revolutionary socialism and the class struggle."

Whittlesey was one of Eastman's converts. This was, on the surface, a revolutionary turn in the moral development of the ex-ROTC cadet and Wall Street lawyer. But for the man whose moral yearnings were expressed in the wish "to do something that I don't want to do," the possibility of having to suffer as a missionary for an embattled faith might have actually been an attraction. Eastman's socialism was a kind of secular Christianity: Christ was a virile prophet of the revolutionary spirit, willing to undertake the world's work. Eastman expected to find the same kind of "joy of struggle" in the cause of socialism that the missionary found in the cause of Jesus. Moreover, Eastman's socialism had strong affinities with the "Strenuous Life" Progressivism with which Whittlesey was imbued:

> The socialist doctrine appeals to three major motives: the love of liberty, the yearning for brotherhood or human solidarity, and the wish to plan and organize things in a rational manner. There is also the religious motive, the desire of God's orphans to believe in something beyond reality.

Although the *Masses* opposed preparedness, Eastman praised Teddy Roosevelt in Roosevelt's own terms, calling him "the only entirely male citizen in a nation of mollycoddles and college sissies."[17]

When war broke out in 1914 the *Masses* opposed it as a thing immoral in itself, and as an instrument for exploiting the working classes. Whittlesey's antiwar principles were deeply held. He was a classicist in taste, a man of the Enlightenment: reason not passion, kindness not cruelty ought to govern human affairs, and war was the essence of cruelty and unreason. But the sinking of the *Lusitania* in May 1915 forced him to reconsider. It symbolized for him, as for others of his generation, the inhumanity and immorality of the German war effort, which negated everything Whittlesey believed in. War against such a power could not be dismissed as misguided patriotism or the dirty work of capitalists. His younger brother Elisha dropped out of Harvard to serve in a volunteer ambulance service. If war came to the United States, a man of Whittlesey's heritage and social position had a positive duty to serve his country. Whittleseys had served in every American conflict since the Pequot War.[18]

"I want to do something that I *don't* want to do."

In 1915 Charles Whittlesey, "of virtuous father virtuous son," socialist and pacifist by conviction but born to the Strenuous Life, signed up for a course at Plattsburgh, returned for another in 1916 and again in 1917. In the fall of that year he was commissioned and assigned to the 77th Division at Camp Upton, Long Island.

Mobilizing the Melting Pot

Officers' mess in the 77th Division was an extension of the Harvard/Racquet Club circle, which was good for the morale of the lieutenants and captains, but potentially an impediment to the development of an effective infantry unit. As one observer sardonically noted, "The problem with this outfit . . . is that all the officers come from below Fulton Street and all the men from above it."[19]

The racial background and tenement socialization of their soldiers gave them pause. These were "men unused to the sturdy activity of outdoor life; men who had had little chance for that physical development which enables them to endure great privation, fatigue and suffering; men who had no knowledge of woodcraft and the use of firearms, and in consequence were lacking in the principles of self-preservation and the confidence which comes from such knowledge." The Plattsburghers thought their men "probably experienced no patriotic thrill" at the prospect of fighting for America or the cause of world democracy. They were puzzled that the men seemed so willing "to prepare for a war of which so many could not know the meaning."[20]

All of the men were draftees, yet their presence in uniform was testimony to something like a volunteer spirit. Only declarant aliens (those who had filed for citizenship) were liable for the draft. The Selective Service Act of 1917 exempted three other classes of resident aliens: diplomatic personnel; "nondeclarant aliens," who had not filed for naturalization; and "enemy aliens," which included foreign-born residents from all of the other categories. Jews who had emigrated from Germany or Austria-Hungary, Poles from Austrian Galicia, Italians from the Tyrol, were technically "enemy aliens." Since it was easy to enter and reenter the United States, and since most old country governments forbade dual citizenship, many immigrants remained "nondeclarant."

Although they could have claimed legal exemption from the draft, the vast majority of nondeclarant and enemy aliens registered, and accepted induction when called up. Though fear of internment or deportation may have influenced their choices, for many it reflected a positive decision to seek American nationality and fight to defend their adopted nation. Like young men all over the country they were also moved by the public excitement, the parades and posters and extravagant propaganda by which the government roused enthusiasm for a war so few Americans had wanted. But the war also forced to the surface the conflicts of culture and loyalty that separated the new immigrants from the White native-born mainstream of American culture.[21]

The new immigrant communities were separated from the social mainstream by the combination of social prejudice and discrimination, poverty, and differences of language and culture. The language barrier tended to erode as immigrant children picked up English. But the size of the post-1881 immigrations created and sustained a large base for cultural institutions—especially newspapers and theaters—using the immigrants' native languages. The eastern European Jews were a non-Christian people in an overwhelmingly Christian nation, and their preference for Orthodox Judaism put them at odds with the assimilated German-Jewish community. Russian and Greek Orthodox Christians were put off by the distinctly Protestant tone of American Christianity. Roman Catholic Italians and Poles felt the antipapist strain in American religious culture, and were alienated by the predominantly Irish-American hierarchy.

Most Jewish and Italian first- and second-generation immigrants toiled in the lowest-paid segment of the working class, as day laborers and garment workers. The tenements in which they lived were crowded and unsanitary. A 1908 census of the Lower East Side indicated that only 25 percent of the residents slept two to a room; half slept three or four to a room; and 25 percent shared sleeping space with five or more persons. A typical tenement had, at best, two bathrooms per floor; many had backyard privies, although a 1901 reform (not well enforced) required water closets for each apartment. The overcrowded quarters stank of coal smoke, stale food, and fecal matter.

These communities were profoundly ambivalent about the meaning, the possibility, and the desirability of Americanization. The surrender of one's own culture and the adoption of another is always accompanied by the guilt of betrayal; and where the adopted culture has presented itself as "superior," there is also a feeling of humiliation in the process. Such a change would alienate immigrant communities from their kindred in the old country, could even alienate immigrant parents from Americanized children. Yet to resist Americanization was to remain a stranger, always marginal, always liable to persecution or expulsion. In all of the immigrant communities there were organizations working for the economic and social betterment and the successful Americanization of their people, led by men and women who had successfully assimilated and prospered as Americans. Politicians and reformers consulted these organizations, and they became semiofficial mediators between their communities and American officialdom. Within their communities they were the primary advocates and agents of Americanization, and as such the focus of all the fears and resentments caused by the process.[22]

The Chinese were the most segregated of these communities, marked by difference of skin color and by their non-European culture and religion. Their unique isolation is suggested by a passage in an 1898 citizenship primer:

> A citizen may be of any color, may be born in any other country, or may be a Christian, a Hebrew, a Mohammedan, a Confucian or a follower of any other religion, or of no religion; so long as he obeys the laws, no matter what his color, his nationality, or his religion, he is entitled to all the rights which citizenship confers (except the Chinese, who are excluded by the act of Congress of 1882).

Like Europeans, Chinese men immigrated to earn money that could be sent to families in the old country. Some also sought a permanent home to which they could bring wives and children. The Exclusion Acts prevented all but a few previously naturalized Chinese from bringing wives from China, and made reentry problematic even for long-term residents and naturalized citizens. Chinese who wished or needed to stay were cut off from homeland, family, and even the possibility of marriage and family life. Chinatown had a preponderance of unmarried men, which was a source of instability and profound unhappiness within the community, and a cause for the growth of prostitution. The Chinatown chamber of commerce and church-based organizations acted as Americanizing agents, and in 1917 tried to win friends for the community by supporting the Liberty Loan and encouraging draft registration. Since the Exclusion Act had kept young men out and limited the natural increase of the population only a handful of Chinese were eligible, but those few "eagerly signed up to show their patriotism."[23]

For Italians, willingness to Americanize depended on whether or not an immigrant planned to return to Italy—as many did. Most were peasants from rural southern Italy, and their limited education reinforced their linguistic isolation and their status as low-wage workers. They preferred to live in close-knit neighborhoods centered on churches (with Italian priests), and parochial rather than public education. Nonetheless, Italian-American children learned English rapidly, and second-generation and long-term immigrants were able to balance Italian cultural affiliations with American nationality in a hyphenated identity. The Society for the Protection of the Italian Immigrants worked with the padrones—the wealthy businessmen who brought their countrymen in as contract laborers—to reform abusive and exploitive practices and better the condition of the workers. Italians were in principle more supportive of the war than other new immigrants. Italy was engaged on the Allied side, and the community's pride was invested in the success of the Italian armies. On the other hand, most Italians in America had been happy to escape their country's conscription from 1915 to 1917, and preferred to serve (if they must) in the American army.

As the largest of the new immigrant constituencies, the Jewish community's responses to the war were closely watched. Jewish ambivalence toward Americanization had religious and political dimensions. Orthodox Jews and socialists agreed that America was a land devoted to greedy materialism, which was corrupted socialist idealism and tempted the Orthodox to apostasy. Yet it was also clear that for the vast majority of Jewish immigrants America must be a permanent home. Only the most devoted socialists dreamed of returing to a revolutionized Russia, and before 1917 the return to Zion seemed to most an improbable fantasy. There was therefore a countervailing commitment among Jewish immigrants to the achievement of full integration with American society, reflected in the high levels of attendance at English and citizenship classes at night schools and settlement houses. Immigrant parents hoped their children would succeed as Americans, and at the same time feared the consequences.[24]

Numerous civic and religious organizations served the Jewish neighborhood and earned the community an enviable reputation for "taking care of its own." The largest national organization, the American Jewish Congress (AJC), sponsored a variety of educational, health, and social services, worked to redistribute immigrants outside the large cities, and lobbied against discrimination. In New York City the Kehillah, a consortium of religious and secular organizations, tried to coordinate a range of social services and provide a central forum for the development and expression of community views on city politics. One of its departments, the Committee for the Protection of the Good Name of the Immigrants, was a precursor of B'nai B'rith's Anti-Defamation League, responding to anti-immigrant remarks by public officials and challenging acts of discrimination.

For Jews and Italians labor struggles became an expression of resistance to American working conditions and a means to Americanization. In 1909 a federation of Jewish unions, the United Hebrew Trades (UHT), organized a series of strikes that touched every trade in the city and won major concessions, especially in the garment trades, which employed half of the working-class Jewish population and a substantial number of Italian women. The clothing workers' union and other unions in the UHT were not products of the American labor movement, as represented by the American Federation of Labor (AFL). Rather, they followed the traditions of self-help organizations like the hometown societies, or *landsmannschaften,* developing programs of social insurance, education, and cooperative housing for their members. They were also strongly inclined toward socialism. Between 1900 and 1917, the Socialist Party became the strongest political organization on the Lower East Side. Working in both the labor and the political arenas, Jewish Socialists were able to improve living standards in their community through "legislation, inspection, and unionization." The party's and the community's greatest political triumph came in 1914, when the Lower East Side elected Meyer London to Congress, and reelected him in 1916. Thus the Jewish immigrant community entered the mainstream of American politics by espousing an ideology at odds with the dominant ideology of market capitalism.[25]

Political influence was accompanied by increasing cultural prominence. By 1917 Jews constituted something more than a quarter of the city's population. Their cultural and political influence was felt throughout the city, which produced resentful reaction among some native-born Whites. In January 1917 Harold Ardsley wrote an article complaining of the "everlasting Hebraism" of the New York cultural scene. The *American Hebrew* responded with a sharp rebuke: Jews were contributing to American culture, and their success simply indicated that Americans valued their work.[26]

From 1914 to 1917 antiwar sentiment was strong among both the assimilated and well-off German-Jewish leadership and the socialist, working-class eastern Europeans. However, they opposed the war for different reasons. German-Jewish banker Jacob Schiff had strong cultural and commercial ties to Germany. The Socialist settlement-house pioneer Lillian Wald opposed war on moral grounds, the eastern European Orthodox and Hasidic communities on religious grounds. The Marxist parties, the Jewish *Bund,* the IWWs and anarchists (all represented on the Lower East Side) opposed the war as a struggle between imperialist powers for the benefit of their capitalists. The American Socialist Party split into pro- and antiwar factions, but the two best-known Jewish Socialists,

Morris Hillquit and Victor Berger, followed Eugene Debs in opposing U.S. entry. Hillquit wrote the party declaration that called on "workers of all countries to refuse support to their governments." Some "peace Progressives" among the German-Jewish community joined the Socialists in opposition. On the other hand, New York's Socialist congressman Meyer London thought Hillquit's platform too extreme, dangerous to the party's future and the Jewish community as well—an anxiety he shared with the conservative German-Jewish leadership.

The Russian Revolution of February 1917, and the Balfour Declaration calling for a Jewish homeland in Palestine, shifted the balance toward acceptance of war. The *American Hebrew* greeted the Russian Revolution as a "New Passover" that would bring Yiddish Jewry out of the house of bondage. As Jacob Schiff frankly declared, "Had we been called upon to show our Americanism under conditions that existed in Russia two months ago, we no doubt would have followed the call of duty, but . . . with a heavy heart." The eastern European communities celebrated Russia's February Revolution and General Allenby's advance on Jerusalem. It now appeared that patriotic service in the American war effort would address two of the primary concerns of American Jews: the persecution of Jews in eastern Europe and the creation of a national homeland in Palestine. Abraham Cahan, editor of the Socialist *Forverts* (*Forward*), the leading Yiddish newspaper on the Lower East Side, kept his criticism of war measures within the bounds of loyal opposition. The nephew of anarchist leader and antiwar activist Emma Goldman, concert violinist David Hochstein, concealed his tuberculosis, "waived exemption and volunteered for the army."[27]

The *American Hebrew*, which reflected the views of the AJC, adopted the Strenuous Life version of Americanism as the standard for Jews to emulate. Rabbi Joseph Silverman thought that Americans in general, and Jews in particular, "must be trained to be heroic." Each man must "become a moral hero," renounce pleasures that are "enervating and degrading," and "recover lost vigor." Rabbi Samuel Schulman told his congregation "not to be sad if the names of your sons are drawn," but to "teach our sons to think life cheap when their country demands their honorable service." Rabbi Stephen Wise hailed the first day of registration as "the burial, without hope of resurrection, of hyphenism, and . . . the birth of a united and indivisible country." Wise had opposed the war on moral grounds before April 1917—now he would support Wilson's policy of using American power to achieve a just peace.[28]

In adopting the Roosevelt standard of nationality, the German-Jewish leadership also inherited the Progressive confusion about race. Despite their formal commitment to a civic definition of Americanism and Judaism, articles and editorials in the *American Hebrew* often spoke of the "Jewish race" and urged the sort of race-improving measures recommended by the eugenicists. The emergence of a strong Zionist movement in America brought this confusion to a head. The racial and national identity claimed by Zionists undermined the claims to civic nationality made by the Americanizers. But as Rooseveltians, those same Americanizers saw Zionism as a heroic and patriotic endeavor that displayed "Jewish character"—that is, *racial* character—in a positive light. Thus Harry Friedenwald summoned Jews to "Israel's Cause" in the language of "The Strenuous Life," demanding they abandon "selfish and petty concerns" and prove they are not "fainthearted weaklings" but "scions of a great ancestry."[29]

At street level these confusions were conditions to be lived with rather than contradictions to be resolved by rigorous logic. Abe Krotoshinsky had run away from the *shtetl* of Plotzk in Russian Poland "to escape military service," and because "I hated Russia, its government, its people, and particularly its cruel and unhuman treatment of Jews."[30] He arrived in New York in 1912 and "walked the streets . . . somewhat in a daze, not understanding the language, and my mind awhirl with the greatness, the hustle, the brightness, the confusion, the things of beauty and the things of ugliness which all go to make up a great city." A photo taken shortly after his enlistment shows a wiry man with a lean face, a long narrow wedge of a nose, a serious expression. He found work as a barber, which brought him into "intimate contact with a great variety of people [and] . . . intensified and hastened [the] process of [my] Americanization."

> Soon the newness wore away, and what was left was a comfortable, happy feeling. Here I was conscious of a freedom which I had never known in Russia. I could feel it in everything, and everything was sweet and precious to me. . . . [America] has given us freedom and an equal chance, which is the only thing, and no more, that a Jew has ever wanted or wants. This is a tolerant and a good country. America, my

adopted land, was always more precious to me than the land of my birth, in which I considered myself an alien and an outsider.

But he was also aware that native-born Americans and older, assimilated immigrants regarded him as an outsider. He captures this double-consciousness in the way he remembers his new, Americanized self walking the streets in which he now felt at home: " 'This is a great land; it is *my* land' was the thought that beat against my head even as the big Irish cop good-humoredly watched me for the strange figure I must have represented." His love for the new land is poignant, his desire to belong genuine. But the Irish cop, the *big* Irish cop, keeps his eye on him—with good humor, to be sure, but still with the surveillance appropriate to a native inspecting an interloper. Relations between the Irish and Jews were often hostile—there would be several incidents that summer in which Irish cops abused Jews waiting to register for the draft.[31] So along with his dream of being at home in America, Krotoshinsky also dreamed of living in a Jewish country, where his belonging would be presumed: "It was one of my day-dreams to be able some day to establish myself in Palestine."

The 77th Division was exceptional in having to integrate such a rich mix of ethnicities, but every division in the AEF faced similar problems. Like a large-scale Rainbow Division the AEF was supposed to be a national army composed of units with strong local identities. But it was impossible to maintain community-specific units in divisions that mustered between 25,000 and 28,000 of all ranks. As the pace of mobilization increased, as specialists were shifted between divisions, and especially after losses in battle, the local character of all units was compromised. When the 82nd Division (Alabama/Tennessee) was completed with recruits from the Northeast, Alvin York—the Tennessee mountaineer who would become one of the war's heroes—found himself "throwed in with a lot of Greeks Italians and New York Jews." In the platoon that Sergeant York would lead to glory were men named Parsons, Sacina, Donohue, Sok, Konotski, Dymowski, and Mazzi. Living in regional isolation, conceiving the nation as an enlarged version of the only community he knew, York had not imagined such men existed, let alone that they might be as American as he. The regulars, Plattsburgh alums, and "ninety-day wonders" were better educated and had a wider experience of the world. Nonetheless, they shared the astonishment of discovering, on arrival in camp, that "America" was not the coherent national community they imagined it to be. As York's experience of the nation was segregated by regional isolation and lack of schooling, theirs was segregated by class and culture.[32]

How was such an army to be imbued with a sense of unit pride and *national* identity as intense as the community-centered loyalties that had sent Civil War regiments cheering into the hell of combat? Bringing strangers together at random was as likely to produce culture shock and xenophobia as a sense of American brotherhood. The papers applauded the Rainbow Division reconciliation of the New York 69th and the Alabama regiment it had battled at Fredericksburg. But what Father Duffy called "a small family row at Camp Mills" was actually a brawl in which an Alabaman was killed.[33]

Secretary of War Newton Baker brought the best of Progressive thinking to bear on the question. He was an odd choice for secretary, though appropriate for Wilson in his "too proud to fight" mode: a Quaker, a student of Professor Wilson's at Johns Hopkins, and mayor of Cleveland. But he learned quickly, was a reasonably good administrator, and his political experience made him adept at managing relations between the military and civilian interest groups.

Baker created a new "Military Morale Subsection" within the larger Military Intelligence Division (MID) and assigned it the task of continuously assessing the effects of training and leadership methods of soldier morale. MID would also undertake surveillance to find and sternly repress disloyalty. He also established the Committee on Training Camp Activities (CTCA), headed by Raymond Fosdick, a New York political reformer and brother of liberal theologian Harry Emerson Fosdick. The core problem was the incomplete nationalization of American life. The CTCA would develop a training curriculum, including literacy classes and courses in U.S. history and politics, which would for many draftees be their first experience of public education. Its ambition was to transform the "thousands of Izzies, Witzers, Johnnies, Mikes and Tonies" in "the great Melting Pot" of Camp Upton into idealized types of Anglo-American manhood, "virile yet virginal," immune to sexual temptation and the Demon Rum, "broad-shouldered, deep-chested, square-jawed," full of that "distinctive American" spirit called "pep": " 'Pep' will win the war. Let's cultivate it."[34]

During that first summer of war, while the training camps were being formed, a complex process of negotiation was taking place between community leaders, government officials, and the army. The government sought the cooperation of community leaders to persuade their constituents to register for Selective Service and support the war effort by subscribing to the Liberty Loan. Community leaders in turn sought recognition and respect for the cultural difference of their people, in the army and in the larger society. One of the most important organizations was the Jewish Welfare Board (JWB), formed by a consortium to lobby for the recruitment of Jewish military chaplains and the provision of religious and social services for Jewish soldiers in the cantonments. Though still a small minority, measured against the Irish or the African-Americans, Jews represented a significant share of the population (3 percent), and an even greater share of those in military service (4 to 5 percent). Their importance was enhanced by the fact that the 77th Division would be the first in the National Army to be sent overseas, and between 30 and 40 percent of its enlisted men were Jewish. Secretary of War Baker set a precedent by accepting most of the JWB's requests and authorizing its agents to deal directly with the commander of Camp Upton. A Hebrew prayer book was prepared for use by military chaplains, and Rabbi Voorsanger of San Francisco became senior chaplain of the division. (He would win a DSC for tending the wounded under fire.) A Kosher restaurant was set up off-base as an alternative to the mess hall. It was also agreed that if Jewish soldiers should be killed in service the army would bury them under the Star of David instead of the cross.[35]

Other groups achieved similar recognition. The Knights of Columbus received permission to provide religious and social services for Catholic soldiers, particularly those of Italian origin. The Polish Falcons played a similar role, as did organizations representing the Armenian, Czech (Bohemian), Slovak, Slovene, Serb, Croat, and other Balkan groups. When Italian soldiers complained of the prevalent use of "wop" and "dago" as terms of insult, efforts were made (well intentioned but doomed) to make the soldiers stop. The War Department also formally prohibited calling Negro soldiers "niggers" and "coons," which had some effect on the language used by White officers training Blacks at Des Moines. It does not seem to have affected the rank and file.[36]

Over time, this process of accommodation transformed the Army's way of dealing with immigrant soldiers. Under the aegis of a newly created Foreign Soldier Service, "Soldier after soldier is turned out fit and eager to fight for liberty under the Stars and Stripes, mindful of the traditions of his race and the land of his nativity and conscious of the principles for which he is fighting." Implicit in these developments was a new form of the social bargain between the nation and its adopted children: Americanization did not require conformity to a single cultural standard—both sides of the "hyphen" were acceptable, so long as the citizen was loyal.[37]

It would be an exaggeration to say that Camp Upton was a multiculturalist utopia from which ethnic prejudice was systematically eliminated. Nonetheless, it is the case that of all the major institutions that shaped the life of the nation—schools and universities, government, corporations—the wartime army may have been the one most willing to acknowledge and accept ethnic difference as an inescapable element of national identity. The government backed its invitation to citizenship by easing naturalization rules, and the men took up the offer. Some 12,000 individuals were naturalized while at Upton, nearly all of whom belonged to the 77th Division. Depending on how one estimates the number of men who passed through Upton, that figure suggests that 15 to 20 percent of the division may have been naturalized while in the service.[38]

Court-martial records are a suggestive indicator of the division's morale and state of discipline. The records of the AEF's judge advocate general's office show that some 911 cases were brought to trial during the 77th Division's term of service, approximately two-thirds of which resulted in convictions (mostly for offenses such as "insolence," disobeying orders, disrespect to noncoms or officers, etc.). During a much shorter period of time the 27th Division held over 5,000 courts-martial, nearly all of which ended in conviction; and figures for the 26th Division (New England National Guard) are comparable. The low rate of courts-martial, coupled with the 77th's good performance in combat, suggests that officers were able to maintain discipline among their armed civilians without excessive insistence on strict conformity to "the book."

The burden of testimony by surviving veterans is that, on the whole, the 77th Division treated them fairly. This is not to say that the experience was happy, or that the recruits were not subjected to injustices, petty tyrannies, bigotries, and abuse; rather, that it was not too bad when measured against their civilian experience and their expectations of military life. Private Morris Gutentag of the 308th described his experience as "positive," and attributed it to the strong leadership provided by "Reserve" (that is, Plattsburgh-trained) officers, which enabled men of many different ethnic groups to work together.[39]

"The Soul of the Group":
The Art and Politics of Company Command

The officers approached their problematic charges with an ambivalent mixture of suspicion and expectation. They might share Roosevelt's skepticism about the soldierly potential of Russian Jews and "effeminate" Chinese, but they were also morally committed to the idea that (as Charles Young had written) "the military virtues can be cultivated" and that with proper training *any* of the nation's constituent peoples could achieve the "civic and military courage, patriotism, and the vigor, strength and sturdiness of American manhood." Roosevelt himself gave them their cue in "Factories of Good Citizenship," a newspaper column on Camp Upton. "I have just seen a party of drafted men from the East Side of New York City start for Camp Upton," he wrote, "with a band playing, an American flag flying," one man dressed as Uncle Sam leading in chains another dressed as Kaiser Bill.

> A captain at this camp, a Plattsburgh man, told me that his company of East Side New Yorkers showed all the intelligence and desire to learn which the fine young graduates at Plattsburgh have shown. . . . Another captain told me that one of his men, a young Jew, had come to him and said that at first East Siders had hated coming, not knowing what was ahead of them, but now they felt they were in a University of American citizenship.[40]

The officers saw training as a way for immigrants to relive the American historical myth, from frontier past to industrial present. Frank Tiebout and Julius Adler looked at the sprawling cantonment and were reminded of the Wild West: "Had Bret Harte accompanied [our] advance guard he might have thought himself in one of the western mining camps. . . . Civilian guards, singularly reminiscent of the old West—lean, bronzed and gaunt, arrayed in broad-brimmed hats . . . rode about on decrepit mares . . . [and] packed guns in true Western fashion." The first part of their task was to train their polyglot troops into men fit for the strenuous life: to teach them how to live outdoors, improve their physical conditioning and fitness. General Pershing believed the rifle was "a distinctly American weapon"—celebrated in American myth as the weapon of Boone and Crockett and Buffalo Bill. Adler boasted that after "the men were initiated into the mysteries of the rifle . . . the results confirmed the late Colonel Roosevelt's statement that the American youth is a born shot." Pershing's infantry would be taught to "Rely on the Rifle as of Old," a tactic pleasing to the Germans who relied on barbed wire and machine guns.[41]

But they would have to take their men beyond frontier individualism, train them in teamwork and subordination. For two generations, analysts of the American economy had drawn the analogy between the new corporations and military organizations, between battle captains and "captains of industry." The point of the analogy was to rationalize the subordination of labor to capital, to accept that the old free days of mobility were over—that striking or jumping from job to job for higher pay were akin to mutiny and desertion. Now that analogy was to be made literal. Adler saw the recruits as representative of America's working people, a mix of "laboring classes" and "dangerous classes," of headworkers and handworkers. It would be the task of the company officers to apply modern theories of management in the military workplace, to teach these individualists "to bow down before the military God, *Authority*," to make Upton a "melting pot" in which they would become "amalgamated" with the corporate machine.[42]

The U.S. Army version of scientific management was not up to corporate standards. The United States had not only to raise and train two million troops in a year, it had to create from scratch all the administrative and command structures of a modern army. U.S. forces had been organized as regiments: each roughly two or three thousand men, trained in a single arm of combat. The basic unit of force on the Western Front was the division, a coordinated combination of infantry, machine-gun, and artillery regiments plus a bevy of specialized units; and the conduct of large operations required groupings of dozens of divisions into corps and armies. American officers had no experience in division-scale operations, and their problems were compounded by the decision to make AEF divisions twice the size of Allied counterparts (25–28,000 men). Their tactical doctrine and equipment were obsolete. It is a tribute to the professionalism and adaptability of the officer corps that the army was able to put over fifty divisions in the field in less than eighteen months. But the effectiveness of the AEF was compromised, first to last, by tactical blunders and breakdowns in basic organization, because skills that should have been practiced in training had to be learned in combat.[43]

The "arsenal of democracy" did not have on hand, and could not rapidly produce, enough of the standard issue Springfield rifles to equip all divisions. What was worse, the American army was almost entirely lacking in modern automatic weapons and would have to purchase most of its machine guns and automatic rifles from the Allies. This meant that troops could not learn the essentials of automatic weapons use until they arrived in France.[44]

Neither the Guard nor the regulars had sufficient numbers of trained experts around whom to organize the more highly specialized units (e.g., gas warfare and machine guns) and did not know how to put their hands on those they did have. As a consequence divisional and even company-level training was continually disrupted by transfers of specialists—mechanics for the motor pool, machinists for weapons repair, German speakers for intelligence, and so on. Because the 77th was organized early, and drew on the most concentrated manpower pool in the country, it also experienced wholesale transfers of enlisted personnel to fill out the ranks of divisions forming in less densely populated regions. All of this impeded their training and—what was more vital from the company officers' point of view—delayed the moment when the conscripts might begin to identify with their unit and their comrades.

Training was also complicated by the intense press scrutiny that followed the 77th Division right from its awkward beginning. Upton was a short train ride from Manhattan, and the city's English-language papers sent teams of correspondents out to report on the "Izzies, Witzers, Johnnies, Mikes and Tonies." Like the Plattsburgh officers, they were not sure how seriously to take their melting pot division. Unlike the officers of the 77th, the papers could get as much benefit from displays of haplessness as from demonstrations of competence. The people of the tenements, the Yids and Wops and Chinamen and Polacks, had been for a generation the subjects of mocking portrayals on vaudeville stages and in the columns of the press. The stories written in September and October of 1917 generally represent the immigrant soldiers as a spectacle or sideshow to amuse an audience of "real Americans." The *New York Sun* reporter, adopting the persona of Sergeant Flaherty ("a real American"), ridiculed an "Eyetalian" named Piazza, who would rather eat than work: "He's a furriner—and furriners are always great of eatin' away from home like that." The *Herald* and *Sun* reported on a Filipino recruit, reputedly a headhunter who was "after [the] Kaiser's Head." He did a war dance, grunting and barking "Woof! Wo-o-o-offf!! . . . You couldn't see the likes o' that nowhere for less'n 10 cents."[45]

The officers of the 77th shared many of the biases displayed in the papers. Charles Whittlesey was as well disposed in principle as any of the officers, yet he found the "foreign-ness" of his men off-putting. His first impression of Private Herschkowitz was that the Jewish soldier was "the worst possible material from which to make soldier-stuff . . . thick-set, stupid looking, extremely foreign." But he was willing to see his prejudices disproved—he would remember Herschkowitz as one of the bravest and most effective soldiers in the outfit. Frank Tiebout liked his Irishmen, but didn't think much of his Italians and Jews. He expected them to whine and wangle their way out of service, and issued a preemptive warning: "I want no pathetic telegrams [from your families]. . . . I don't care to hear that Solomon Levinsky has to be present Saturday morning, at the winding up of his pants business." For Tiebout all Jews are "pants-pressers," and all pants-pressers Jews. Rainsford sniffed that the 308th was recruited "very largely from the East Side of the city" and took a jaundiced view of their character: "And oh, the pathos of those poor Italians, and Slavs, and Jews—Americans all—who came to their company commanders with the letters from their sick wives, uncared for, and often about to be ejected from their pitiful homes." He also questioned their understanding and acceptance of American war aims. "Some of German parentage . . . were excusably unwilling to face their relatives with a rifle." For the rest, "What could it mean to the late worker in the East-side sweat-shop that Messine Ridge was retaken by the Germans?"[46]

Enlisted men (especially New Yorkers) are quick to spot the signs of dislike or prejudice in a platoon or company officer. Success in company command required an open-minded approach to cultural differences—and an awareness of the problem of publicity. Captain Philip Mills (Harvard '14, Plattsburgh '17) displayed both in his handling of the "Bearded Soldier." Private Isidore Bednash (the name is spelled various ways) was an Orthodox Jew who reported to camp with a beard of biblical proportions, "a great beard—long, fuzzy, and innocent of all tonsorial attacks." The Orthodox insistence that a man not trim his beard was confronted with army regulations requiring the shaving of facial hair. In order to inform Private Bednash of the requirement, it was first necessary to communicate with him—a problem, because while he could speak four languages, none of them happened to be English. The ranks were canvassed and produced as translator Private Havas, who spoke English, French, German, Arabic, Turkish, Russian, and Greek. But the fun was just beginning. Through Havas, Bednash informed his officers that he had been living on a diet of bread and sardines, since kosher laws forbade him to eat any of the meat or prepared foods from the camp kitchens. (He purchased the sardines at an off-base store—the kosher restaurant was not yet in place.) He also admitted that he was not twenty-seven years old, as his records said, but actually thirty-three—too old to be drafted. The discrepancy had been created at Ellis Island, when he had been unable to make himself understood by the immigration officers. But Bednash made no claim of exemption. On the contrary, he wanted above all else to be allowed to stay in the army. "Do I like this business of being a soldier of the United States? . . . It is a much better business than working in a sweatshop sewing coats and pants from morning until late at night. There is more sunlight and fresh air and happiness here." He didn't mind the bread and sardine diet. After all, "poor people in Europe have still less."

The newspapers could amuse their readers by playing the Bearded Soldier for laughs, for patriotic propaganda, or some combination of the two. The *New York World*'s reporter saw him as a demonstration that military service could transform the stoop-shouldered, fearful, money-grubbing Jew of the ghetto into an American whose "shoulders were straight as becomes a soldier's freedom." The *Sun* suspected Bednash chose army life to escape work: "Was it not well for an operator . . . used to working fourteen hours a day on cheap ladies' wear to be out in the big open air and play and think and stroke his beard?" Mills had to find a way to balance enforcement of regulations with respect for the men he would command. He chose to accept Bednash's declaration that he wished to serve, scanned his copy of army regulations for some way to accommodate the Bearded Soldier—and found a rule that permitted beards if they were neatly trimmed.[47]

Mills's attitude was widely if not universally shared by other Plattsburghers. Rainsford was surprised to discover that for all their foreignness, their lack of fitness and education, his troops were genuinely willing to serve and to be trained. Those weeping Italians, Slavs, and Jews he had complained about seldom asked for anything more than a brief leave to deal with some real emergency, or aid for dependents left unprovided for. When he looked into their cases, Rainsford found that many if not most were entitled to exemption, which "they should have had by right, but of which they had been defrauded by some Local Board, more concerned over the safety of its native sons than over the rights of its foreign-born residents." Instead of resenting nativist discrimination, Rainsford's soldiers usually declined to seek the discharge to which they were entitled. Although they sometimes gave their officers a hard time, they never showed "any apparent unwillingness . . . to serve, nor conscious wish to defy authority." To Rainsford, "They were lovable men, probably because nearly all men become lovable when the relations between them are right, and are long continued." Even Tiebout admitted that "the men were ready, willing, and ambitious to become good soldiers."[48]

Mills was an officer with the human touch. One of his recruits learned that his mother was dying and asked to be allowed to visit her. There were strict limits on granting passes to enlisted men and no trains scheduled to run that night. So Mills detailed the man to accompany him, drove the man into town, waited for him to visit his dying mother, then drove him back to Upton in time for reveille. But there was more to commanding a company than being a good man. At college and at Plattsburgh, Mills and his colleagues had been imbued with the Progressive theory of heroic leadership, which Roosevelt had mythologized and military professionals had reduced to a manual of practice. The national hero embodies the spirit or soul of his people at the highest pitch of quality. On a lower scale the company commander's goal is to embody "the soul of the group," so that his random collection of soldiers will see him as the heroic or idealized version of their own aspirations and personalities, and follow him into danger as if obeying the promptings of their own better selves. The officers must model as well as enforce the proper approach to soldiering. They must lead by "example, by exhortation, by appeals to the highest and best in [the people], by encouragement, by reproof, by praise." And, "having come to a decision, [the officer must] stick to it, right or wrong." It was all right to let your men see that you too were learning how to soldier, but in giving orders or setting the unit's tone it was necessary to repress all weakness or self-doubt: "Faith in himself, faith in his cause, faith in the ones led, are prime requisites. . . . Faith! Faith! Faith! This quality enthusiastically urged will accomplish miracles."[49]

George McMurtry was one of the most successful at company command. He was an attractive figure, with dark hair, a muscular build, and athletic carriage, "bustling, breezy, and busy, yet full of his own humorous ways . . . as cheery and cool as he was competent and capable." His father was Irish-born, a self-made millionaire in steel-plate manufacturing. In 1893–94 McMurtry Sr.'s Apollo, Pennsylvania, plant was the target of a unionizing drive. Like most of his class, he was the sort of manager who thought he could decide what was best for his workers a lot better than they could decide for themselves. So he built a new factory across the river in Vandergrift and hired Frederick Law Olmsted to build him a model company town, embodying the best modern thinking about urban design and public hygiene—and allowed only nonunion workers to settle there. The industry journal *Iron Age* (1901) described Vandergrift as a "paradise"; Apollo and its unions withered and died. When his company merged with US Steel in 1901, the trust used Vandergrift's favorable image as cover for its policy of using such worker towns to increase corporate control of their employees' lives.

His son and namesake was a sportsman and athlete, a polo player of note, Harvard '99. In 1898 he took leave to enlist as a trooper in Troop D of the First U.S. Volunteer Cavalry, Roosevelt's Rough Riders; he charged Kettle Hill, was honorably discharged, returned to Harvard, and graduated with his class. After law school he joined a Wall Street brokerage and succeeded his father as a corporate director. He belonged to the city's social elite, was a member of the best clubs: Harvard, Knickerbocker, Tennis, Racquet. Like his former colonel he deplored the nation's lack of preparedness; he thought he bore a personal responsibility to rectify matters so he signed up for Plattsburgh in 1916 and 1917.[50]

McMurtry used his wealth to make life easier for his men and provide his company with the accouterments of an elite force. It was a leadership technique he learned in the Rough Riders, whose monied officers and enlisted men had provided the troops with special weapons and amenities. "No one will ever forget [McMurtry's] company barracks . . . with its cement incinerator, gray painted walls, elaborately constructed gun rack, bronze fire gong, and ever-polished windows and doors." If there was anything to celebrate, McMurtry supplied the refreshments. He identified with his men: "His pride in [his company] became unbounded; his joy in its successes limitless; his gloom at its failures heartbreaking." His men reciprocated by thinking of themselves as McMurtry's boys.[51]

Charles Whittlesey never formed that kind of bond with the men. His principles were more democratic than anything Roosevelt would have espoused—he had, after all, voted Socialist in 1912. But neither his temperament nor his position allowed him to make the personal connection with the men that McMurtry achieved. He was an awkward odd figure in uniform—"a stork on stilts," long legs wrapped tight in puttees, thin and a little stooping, his eyes enlarged by rimless glasses. He was also shy and reserved in public, a bred-in-the-bone Yankee Puritan in a crowd of New Yorkers. Like the classmates who had dubbed him "The Count," the divisional staff saw in him the authority and organizing ability required for higher command. He was promoted to captain almost immediately and assigned to staff duties at regimental headquarters, where his executive skills were in demand. Whittlesey was unhappy with his role: he wanted to prepare troops to fight under his own command, but he "accepted the situation philosophically, as he accepted most situations."

He was at his best among his fellow officers in private settings, at his clubs in the city or in the officers' mess. To Miles he was "the outstanding figure of the 308th Infantry . . . Puritan, patriot, gentleman and idealist, wise and daring leader, genial and tender friend. . . . By his officers he was respected and beloved more than any man in the Regiment." His style, as reflected in his letters, was breezy, a little glib, self-deprecating, and humorous. Writing to Miles of an episode in France, Whittlesey could go on at length about how "dear old Lieutenant Colonel Smith had bought a lot of grape marmalade," and how lovely the poplars were, and the good inn and wine his brother had recommended. It is easy to imagine him talking just that way in the great room of the Harvard or the Williams Club. Yet his official action reports were accurate, concise, and unsparing in their criticism of error or incompetence, whether his own or others'. "That he was a strict disciplinarian, no one familiar with his ancestry and character would doubt, but he was human as well as conscientious." But if he was the agent of "the military God, *Authority*," he remained "a bold individualist too, never afraid to dispute wrongly employed authority," particularly where treatment of the enlisted men was concerned. The men of the 308th saw Whittlesey mainly as a taskmaster, passing down strictures from regiment and division, "a kind of drill-sergeant with brass on his shoulders." They dubbed him "Galloping Charlie," laughing off his officious authority by mocking his gangly parade-ground stride.[52]

Yet he would stand up for the men in a way no other officer would. That fall the Wilson administration was pressing a national campaign for public subscriptions to the Liberty Loan, the bond program through which the war was being financed. Government speakers recruited and trained by the Committee on Public Information (CPI) held mass rallies that urged bond purchases as the litmus test of loyalty and Americanism. Even among the native-born, those who did not buy bonds with sufficient enthusiasm were liable for persecution, on the ground that "A Bond Slacker Is a Kaiser Backer." For hyphenates the question was, "Are you 100% American? . . . Prove It! Buy U.S. Government Bonds."[53]

Speeches by Four-Minute Men promoting bond purchases were part of the morale regimen at Camp Upton, but results were disappointing. So the commanders of the 77th Division decided that the "Boys at Yaphank" must not only "Buy Liberty Bonds," they must outsubscribe the rest of the National Army. In October 1917 orders came down that enlisted men would be required to spend part of their meager and oft-delayed pay to buy Liberty Bonds. The demand itself implied that the army had doubts about the sincerity of their patriotism, despite the fact that they had put on the uniform and were readying themselves to fight. Jews in particular were held suspect. The *New York Tribune* declared that socialism was simply a "racial" movement among Germans and Russian Jews, implied that "Morris Hillquit, of Riga," was a congenital traitor, and condemned Abraham Cahan as "The Upside-Down Oracle Who Spread Judaized Hearstism on the East Side." That implication was made explicit when General Bell barred Morris Hillquit, a Jewish Socialist and candidate for mayor, from speaking to his constituents at Upton, on the presumption that Hillquit was disloyal.[54]

The task of raising soldier subscriptions fell, predictably, on the Plattsburghers who commanded companies and platoons. How some of them went about it is suggested by a story in the *Sun*. A captain named Sproule formally assembles his company and speaks at length urging them to buy bonds. He appeals to patriotism, love of democracy, President Wilson's Fourteen Points, tempering his vocabulary to the presumably low educational level and imperfect English of his hearers. He suggests that "the American people" are watching them as if from a distance—the *American* people, the genuine natives of the soldiers' imperfectly adopted country— and "nothing will please the American people so much right now as to know you are willing to bet on your own game." But the troops remain unresponsive, and we are to imagine the American people growing displeased. Captain Sproule becomes more stern and insistent: "Now don't you think you must buy a bond?" When the troops still stand mute he orders that "everyone who can afford to buy one or ten bonds should put his name down right now." At this the men respond, and the *Sun* reporter records the quaint and appealing foreign accents in which they affiliate themselves with the national cause: " 'I betta fifty dollar on United States,' one dark-eyed son of the sunny slopes of southern Italy cried' . . . 'I tink I buys one bon',' [said] an East Sider." The reader is left to guess why they did not immediately respond to Sproule's appeal. Was it their poor English? Or had it required his direct order to compel them to contribute?[55]

Most of the 77th's officers seem to have handled the Liberty Loan campaign more or less like Captain Sproule, but at least one of their number objected. Charles Whittlesey "bitterly opposed making poverty-stricken men subscribe to Liberty Loans." Even in uniform Whittlesey retained his socialist sympathy for the working classes, asserted his trust in the uncompelled patriotism of the men, and resented (on their behalf) the indignity of the compulsory loan. Wardlaw Miles remembered the moment as symbolic of Whittlesey's independence of mind and willingness to stand up to authority. But if his colleagues admired his independence, they did not follow his lead.[56]

Americanization and the Play of Ethnicity

If it was hard for officers and men to understand each other because they came from different social worlds, it was no less difficult for the men to understand each other, for though they shared the same social space they came from different tribes. Jack Herschowitz from Bessarabia spoke Yiddish and Romanian and (perhaps) Russian. Agel Geanekos spoke Greek, Bonaventura Pistoria and Catino Carnebucci the Italian of southern Italy. John Karaulinas came from Lithuania, Anthony Hiduck from somewhere in the debatable Balkans. Henry Chinn and Sing Kee were drafted out of the hermetic ghetto of Chinatown. Beyond the purely linguistic difficulties, there would be problems in establishing the basic understandings of how to live and work at close quarters among young men from an incredible variety of cultural backgrounds. Stanislaw Kozikowski was a Polish-American machinist, Abe Krotoshinsky a Jewish barber from Poland, not yet a citizen of the nation whose uniform he wore. Even if the two could speak Polish as well as English, given bitter Polish-Jewish relations in the old country, how would they talk to each other?

> Among its gamblers could be found Chinese from Mott Street playing fan-tan, Jewish boys from Allen Street in stuss games, Italian boys from east of Union Square playing piquet.[57]

Ethnic difference and class conflict ran the city streets in tandem. The labor battles that had marked city life for a decade had pitted immigrant workers, chiefly Italian and Jewish, against a police force that was predominantly Irish.

Their officers found the babel of languages and cultures off-putting, because their concept of a healthy community was one in which a single culture prevailed and class distinctions were well understood. But what was alien to the Plattsburghers was home truth to the city men, for whom community meant ethnic mixing and the continual disruption of class lines by shifts of economic fortune. Before they were soldiers they were New Yorkers, and their high morale and willingness to serve was due in some part to the sense that they represented the pride and self-worth of their mishmash community. A private writing to his parents was proud to say, "Our guys come from all over New York. Flatbush, Canarsie, Richmond Hill, Yorkville, Park Avenue, The Bowery . . ." Corporal Hussey boasted that E Company included "men from all parts of the Greater City . . . the lawyer, the clerk, the storekeeper, the tradesman, and the artist, representing not alone the American born, but the citizen representative of nearly every country in the Old World." Abe Krotoshinsky remembered that he "made good chums in the army. The men in the ranks were all mixed. There was a feeling of brotherhood and comradeship. Race and color lines were broken as we tried to make life livable and pleasant."[58] Most of the veterans of the 77th Division seem to have felt the same way, and the combat morale of the division suggests that its components did develop that unit pride and identity that is essential to an effective infantry command. But "race and color lines" were not transformed into "brotherhood and comradeship" easily or without conflict. The men had to work out their own ways of living with their differences.

The ethnic or racial joke is one of the most revealing elements in the repertoire of cultural devices by which one group marks its superiority to another or excludes a particular group from the social equality. A community of equals is established among those who join in the laughter; and the belonging that unites the jokers is emphasized by the exclusion and demeaning of the butt of the joke, the object of ridicule. Captain

Tiebout took an indulgent view of his "wild Irishmen" when they played practical jokes on Jews, making a fool of "poor old Simon," a Jewish barber, by rigging his cot so it would collapse with himself in it. For Tiebout the funniest part is poor old Simon complaining in his comical accent that the Irishmen are a " 'geng uff loifers.' . . . Thus ended, as in a score of barracks, a perfect day."[59] Tiebout's pleasure in his "wild Irishmen" reflects an attitude typical of the 77th's officers: the Irish, once the most despised of immigrants, were now the most Americanized, still differentiated by their "racial" propensity for whiskey and brawling, but generally up to the Strenuous Life standard.

If there was a difference between that kind of joking and outright bullying it was, perhaps, in the eye of the beholder. A soldier of the 77th named Sher wrote to the *Forward* that "there was no lack of anti-Semites among the Christian boys" in his company, and their prejudice was expressed in the minutiae of daily experience. The barracks had one steam iron and the men had to take turns using it to prepare their uniforms for inspection. The Jewish boys would "stand and wait our next," but

> each time another *shaygetz* [Gentile] comes over, takes the iron, and that's it. And if you demand justice, ask how can you do this, what about who's next, he shows you his fist; and go do him something, go fight for such a little thing like ironing a shirt. . . . It's a lost cause.

Yet if the Jews wanted to establish the principle that there were limits to the sort of verbal and physical abuse they would take, they had to fight over just such little things.

One benefit of growing up on the mean streets of the Lower East Side was that there were likely to be a number of "tough Jews" in every company. Sher had a friend who knew how to deal with such situations: a proud Jew—an "ardent nationalist" and a socialist as well, "a faithful admirer of Yiddish and Yiddish literature," a good-natured and patient fellow who could take a joke, but who also had "broad strong shoulders and a hand that knew how to deliver a blow." He was "short, thickly and compactly built, with an alabaster, clear-white skin . . . and hair thick as sheep's wool," and had learned to box at the Maccabee Club on the Lower East Side. "[He] was a source of pride for us, the 'green' Jewish boys." There was a *shaygetz* named Truslow, "intelligent and well-mannered" but "an embittered anti-Semite. . . . A pious, ardent Catholic

[who] fully believed that the Jews had crucified Jesus, and for that, even now, he . . . was their sworn enemy." He was "too respectable" to simply insult the Jews, but would start "theoretical debates" which allowed him to "shoot his poisoned arrows. . . . Jews are traitors to the land where they live. Jews are cowards. . . . No way a Jew would know how to fight. You run away like mice." The proud Jew stepped in and challenged Truslow to wrestle: in "the blink of an eye" he seized Truslow in "the grip of his iron arms . . . bent him over, lifted him up, and threw him to the ground" where he remained groaning in pain, "spread out like a *shmatah* [a miserable rag]."

Sher's friend was waiting his turn for the iron when an Irishman named Krinley pushed in: "A short ugly soul, dregs of the dregs. If he had any assignment in the company, it was to make fun of Jews." When Sher's friend demanded his "next," Krinley shook his fist, "Next my eye. Get out of here." The proud Jew stepped up to Krinley and "coldly, calmly, and dispassionately" punched the Irishman so hard in the eye that Krinley "did a somersault, howled, and crept away into a corner."[60]

For men reared in the Progressive tradition, simple equality was not the most important attribute of a modern democratic society. An industrial economy differentiated the mass of workingmen from the intellectual elite that possessed the ability to command and control the work of others. It was possible for a Tiebout to imagine that Jewish pants-pressers and Italian fruit peddlers might make decent riflemen, much harder to imagine the presser as a platoon or company officer, let alone a battalion commander. The divisional command was suspicious of the city troops from the first and never wholly abandoned its initial prejudices. Promotions of corporals and sergeants from the ranks were made slowly and reluctantly, and only when it proved impossible to transfer a sufficient number of noncoms from the regulars. Standing orders required that an officer be always present, "whether at the fairly simple tasks of filling a bedsack, or at an inconsequential gathering of any sort." Even Tiebout, who was skeptical about the martial aptitude of Jews and Italians, thought this practice hurt the division when it went into combat.[61]

However, the prejudice of the high command was offset by the daily demonstration of trust by most of the company officers. The lieutenants and captains who knew the men best urged the appointment of noncoms from the ranks and insisted that they be allowed to exercise command authority over squads and sections. Though this plea would not be fully heeded until after the division experienced combat, the soldiers came to see their officers as men who kept the pledge of trust in exchange for loyalty. For their part, the officers recognized some of their troops as men capable of command responsibility. Three who earned particular admiration were Sergeants Ben Kaufman, Harold Kaplan, and Herman Bergasse of the 308th, all of whom would rise to "top-kick," or first sergeant, of their companies. Bergasse was a "Dutchman" who excelled as regimental mess sergeant and later as a front-line platoon commander for E Company. Kaplan was another tough Jew, a Brooklyn-born fighter rather than a "pants-presser," who might have wound up breaking heads like Gyp the Blood or Gurrah Shapiro. He chose instead to do his brawling with boxing gloves and his killing with the U.S. Marines, with whom he had seen action during the 1914 occupation of Veracruz. He would be top-kick of A Company.

Kaufman's parents had arrived in the 1880s with the first wave of eastern European Jewish immigration, driven out by the pogroms that swept their region in the wake of the czar's assassination. The Kaufmans settled on a small farm near Buffalo, aided by one of the charities dedicated to creating a new class of Jewish-American farmers. Ben was born in 1894 and spent his first eight years working the land. But Kaufman's father was in chronic ill health, and in 1902 they moved to a small apartment in Brooklyn, where his father managed a livery stable and his mother worked as a janitor. It was a tough neighborhood, "remote and scraggly . . . a melting-pot . . . of Italians, Negroes, Germans and Irish, [and] Ben, undersized, undernourished, soon learned to take care of himself." Scuffling and playing street baseball, he developed into a strong and athletic adolescent, smart enough to succeed in school but often in trouble for fighting. He won a scholarship to Syracuse University to study engineering, but the field "offered few opportunities to one of his faith," and he dropped out. For a year or two he worked at dead-end jobs in construction and sales, and played professional baseball at the minor league level.[62]

He was an odd mix of qualities: committed to the Jewish-American dream of success and assimilation through education and the professions but also a tough angry kid, a street fighter, and a hard drinker who occasionally went on binges. When war was declared in 1917 he was drafted. The army channeled and disciplined his anger. He gave up drinking and became regimental boxing champion in his weight class. He was smart, athletic, with his two years of college, an ethnic complement to the Plattsburghers, and made first sergeant before the regiment got to France.

Soldiers from other ethnic groups were also promoted to positions of responsibility. Sing Kee, a Chinese soldier in the 306th, would arrive in France as a corporal and communications specialist in the headquarters company and end the war as color sergeant. Among the sergeants listed on the honor rolls in the divisional and company histories are Kelly (Irish), Cieslinksi (Polish), Del Duca (Italian), and Leumann (German). Individuals emerged from the double anonymity of uniform and ethnic label. Some impressed their officers and fellow soldiers with their personalities or particular skills. In the 308th, Al Summer, the Cockney, and Anthony Anastasia were agile and smart enough to earn assignments as battalion scouts. Omer Richards, the French-Canadian, was given charge of the carrier pigeons—the only communications link between front-line and headquarters in the absence of a portable wireless system. Phil Cepaglia, the little jut-jawed Bronx-Sicilian, would be tapped as a runner, a dangerous and responsible job. Abe Krotoshinsky earned the same assignment with the 307th.

The men also drew on the resources of popular culture for devices that allowed them simultaneously to act out and defuse social and ethnic tensions. The CTCA tried to restrict camp entertainment to uplifting speeches by political dignitaries and noted evangelists, and performances suited to the taste of middlebrow WASPs. Appearances by popular vaudevillians, entertainers, and dance bands (especially Negro jazz bands) were forbidden or discouraged. But New York was the entertainment capital of the nation, its stages high and low were dominated by ethnic performers. Broadway insisted on its right to entertain "our boys," and the boys themselves demanded it.

The most popular entertainments were those generated by the men in the ranks. There were professional comics and song-and-dance men among them, but as New Yorkers they were all steeped in the conventions and routines of vaudeville, minstrel shows, and burlesque; and the street culture of the city was rich in variations on the Jewish joke, the Polish joke, the comic Chinaman, and so on. Their unofficial anthem was a "famous and touching lullaby" written by Corporal John Mullin of Company E:

Oh the army, the army, the democratic army,
    They clothe you and they feed you
Because the army needs you. Hash for breakfast,
    Beans for dinner, stew for supper-time.
Thirty dollars every month, deducting twenty-nine.
    Oh the army, the army, the democratic army,
All the Jews and Wops, the Dutch and Irish Cops,
    They're all in the army now.

For this number, bands of singers, some mixed and some representing a single ethnicity, were each assigned a particular part of the song. "Sergeant MacWhinney, Mess Sergeant Kessler, and Lieutenant Jerry Mullin 'starred' in the first five lines . . . assisted in the grand finale by Goldberg, Ginsberg, and Perlberg holding up the Jewish end; Del Duca, Patrissi, and Carucci as Italian tenors, with Schmidt and Leumann carrying the air for the land of Dikes and Canals, supported by the heavy bassos Curley, Fallace, and Sargeant, Erin's representatives of 'New York's Best.'" The historian concludes his description of the occasion by reminding his reader that "Company E was a fighting company as well as a singing one; Jack Curry, the popular sergeant, Corporals Leumann and Del Duca, as well as Cook Luchansky, always brought home the 'bacon' in the boxing contests in the camp."[63]

All this play with ethnic identities used the comic acknowledgment of difference, the deflection of hostility into humor or athletic competition, to negotiate terms of mutual acceptance and prevent ethnic difference from fragmenting unit solidarity. That did not mean that old grievances were entirely forgotten. When Morris Gutentag of the 308th's Company C was asked, some forty-odd years later, to recall the divisional anthem, he remembered the chorus as "the Jews and the wops and the *dirty* Irish cops." Nor did it mean that the terms of acceptance were those of perfect equality. In fact, the ethnic jokes and fables told by the officers and men of the 77th Division suggest that they interpreted the process of Americanization by using a sliding scale of "racial" reference, in which the Irish were the immigrant "race" that comes closest to meeting the White American standard. The newer, more suspect ethnics in the division gain approval by their gradual approach to the standard set by the Irish, who acted as symbolic mediators on their behalf, ushering them into the anterooms of Americanization.[64]

But if the Irish defined the "top" of the evolutionary sequence that could transform immigrants into Americans, there was also a bottom line that defined the nether limits of Americanization: the color line. One of the highlights of the Upton experience was the "circus" staged in February 1918, toward the end of their training. The division's singers sang, the dancers danced, the comics put on clown makeup and funny hats. Some costumed themselves as animals—horses, elephants, lions, tigers— and marched in a mock parade. Others dressed up as sideshow freaks. The most popular of these was " 'Bachi Galoop' transformed into a negro," who "offered his head as a target—three balls for a nickel." The Italian, introduced by a mocking version of his last name, in turn disguises himself as a Negro and so becomes a legitimate target of mock assault—the racial masquerading of the minstrel show "carried on by other means."[65]

Likeness to the Negro (or the Indian) was the sign that native-born Americans always used to declare a new immigrant group beyond the pale of equal citizenship. In the first days at Upton, when the ethnic soldiers were homesick and hapless in their new surroundings, they took comfort in mocking the Black troopers of the 15th New York who had been assigned to guard them, "who being indistinguishable from the darkness had you at a considerable disadvantage when they were at the delivering end of a bayonet." Jokes about the Irish and the Jews could sometimes have the effect of assimilating each group to the other. Jokes about Negroes always marked them as apart in spirit from the willing soldiers of the 77th, as well as militarily inept.[66]

Of all the men at Upton the Chinese fell closest to that color line. The fact that they were integrated with White soldiers is actually quite remarkable and flies in the face of the passions and the legal proscriptions that isolated Asian-Americans. We can imagine them receiving the kind of hostile treatment accorded the Jews, or worse; but the unit histories make almost no mention of their presence. Only Sing Kee and Henry Chinn—a winner of the DSC and a member of the Lost Battalion—are mentioned, and only for their role in the fighting. Whatever their position in the division's racial hierarchy, their presence marked an important distinction: they might not be White, but they were not classed with the Blacks.

Of the White immigrants, the Jews were closest to the edge of the color line (with the southern Italians a close second). Just how near the edge the Jews were is attested by Charles Young, who sees the Jew as

Tiebout and Miles see the Irishman: as the proper model for aspiring races to emulate. The Jew is the best model for the Negro, because both "races" were *made* weak and unmilitary by generations of oppression. In the United States, where Jews are accepted as full citizens of the Republic—that is, as *White* citizens of the Republic—they have proved willing and effective soldiers. As it is for the Jew, so it may be for the Negro: "The Negro race in America—and, indeed, all oppressed peoples—can afford to take a lesson from the Jews." Jewish socialists reciprocated this recognition of fellowship. The *Forward* supported African-American civil rights leaders and initiatives, and consistently spoke of anti-Black riots and lynchings as *pogroms*, equating them with the anti-Jewish violence promoted by the czars and by Russian reactionaries. A perceptive reporter for the *Forward* captured the essential viciousness of Jim Crow when he explained to his readers that in the South the Black man is always a "nigger," and that "the word 'nigger' must be said in a despising voice, as though he were an ugly creature, a frog instead of a person."[67]

In this symbolic proximity of Negroes and Jews we may perceive the beginnings of the later alliance between these two groups in the civil rights movements of the 1930s and 1948–68. But for the half-naturalized soldiers of the 77th Division, likeness to Negroes was grounds for anxiety rather than fellow feeling. To be like a Negro was to lose one's hopes of full equality and acceptance. The enjoyment of civil equality was understood as an attribute of "Whiteness." A Jewish soldier told his parents that "Jews especially . . . ought to be among the first to offer their sons for service" to the United States. They "have been in bondage or slaves in every country in the world," but in the United States "they have been treated like white people ought to be."[68]

5

The Politics of Ridicule:
The 15th New York Goes to War,
October 1917–May 1918

Pickaninny cute in his khaki suit
Wanted to join the kiddies playing soldier, as a new recruit;
Because his skin was brown,
The white kids turned him down;
So he ran home crying to his Mammy, saddest little kid in town.

—*Sidney D. Mitchell and Archie Gottler,*
"Mammy's Chocolate Soldier" (1918)

Throwing balls at an Italian disguised as a Negro might be a bonding ritual for "the Jews and Wops, the Dutch and Irish cops." But for African-Americans the "African Dodger Booth," a regular feature at fairs and carnivals, was one of those everyday rituals of humiliation by which White people kept them personally and collectively abject. A Negro man, sometimes in "African" costume, would serve as a target for thrown balls, his ability to "dodge" restrained by a collar or tether. It was so common an abuse that the NAACP had it on a watch list and protested every occurrence that came to its attention.

At the heart of the American idea of civil equality is the assumption that the individual is entitled, self-evidently and *by nature*, to dignity and respect. It is this entitlement that compels his fellow citizens, his government, and the laws of the nation to treat his suits, petitions, appeals for justice with due seriousness. But slavery had created, and Jim Crow had perpetuated, the identification of citizen-dignity with racial "Whiteness." The concept was embedded in the American idiom. When a midwestern draftee wanted to characterize the good treatment he and his buddies were receiving, he told an interviewer for the magazine *Outlook*, "the people of Atlanta treat us white." When Theodore Roosevelt wanted to express his contempt for Germany's barbaric war making, he remarked that he had met the Kaiser before the war, "when he was a white man." That "niggers" could be routinely ridiculed was something most White Americans took for granted, a self-evident fact, and each new act of ridicule reinforced the assumption that everything about Negroes, including their pretension to civil equality and human dignity, was inherently laughable.[1]

The mission of the 15th New York was to replace the public image of the Black man as racial clown, inevitable butt and victim, with something heroic. In this context, their assignment to a training camp in South Carolina seemed likely—was perhaps even intended—to put that mission in peril. A man of soldierly quality is one who will resent an insult to his person or dignity, and defend himself. But if the men of the 15th resented and resisted the normal humiliations of Jim Crow, they were likely to be met with violence by local Whites; and if that occurred, they were damned whatever they did. Any association with racial violence, however innocent, would put an end to their hopes. But if the men were compelled to accept abuse without retaliating, their morale—their trust in their officers, their willingness to fight—would be degraded. Moreover, passivity would would confirm the stereotype of Negroes as "serfs and sycophants," and as an *Age* editorial noted, "such do not win battles."[2]

Abuse was not only likely, it had been officially promised. Mayor Floyd of Spartanburg sent a menacing letter to the New York papers. He expected that "with their northern ideas about race equality" the Negroes of the 15th "will probably expect to be treated like white men. I can say right here that they will not be treated as anything except negroes. We shall treat them exactly as we treat our resident negroes. This thing is like waving a red flag in the face of a bull." The *New York Times* reported that the Jim Crow shops in Spartanburg were so dingy and poorly stocked that it seemed likely the 15th's soldiers would want to shop in White stores. A White citizen was quoted as saying that if they did "they'll be knocked down." To make matters worse, the day the regiment left Camp Upton the *New York Tribune* reported "South

Alarmed by Threat of Negro Uprising." Spartanburg itself had passed through a couple of race-riot scares that spring, allegedly fomented by IWW organizers to scare away the Black laborers constructing Camp Wadsworth. The local chamber of commerce declared, "The most tragic consequences . . . would follow the introduction of the New York Negro with his Northern ideas into the community life of Spartanburg."[3]

"Tragic consequences" had very particular connotations in the South. On August 24 a Negro in nearby York had been lynched for "seditious utterance." Even more ominous was the lynching of a Negro farmer named Crawford by a mob in Abbeville, not far from Spartanburg. The lynching had occurred in October 1916, but the story was being replayed in the New York papers in the spring and summer of 1918 because indictments were being considered and the authorities were going through the usual post-lynching routine of cover-up and denial.

Anthony Crawford had been a respectable and prosperous Black farmer who "embodied everything that Booker T. Washington held to be virtuous in a Negro." He had haggled with a White businessman over the price of his cotton. When the merchant threatened him with an ax handle he backed away to avoid punishment. A mob gathered but he was saved by the police, who arrested him for "impudence." The store manager and the president of a local bank declared that he "deserved a thrashing" for being "insolent to a white man." When Crawford, free on bail, went to the gin to pick up his cotton, a mob attacked him. Crawford defended himself, injuring one of the Whites with a hammer. The mob kicked out his teeth and beat him unconscious, but he was again saved from death by the police. He remarked to his jailers, "I thought I was a good citizen." That night the mob was allowed into the jail. They threw Crawford down three flights of stairs, mutilated him, stomped on his face, threw a noose around his neck, and dragged him through the streets of the Negro quarter as a warning to others, strung him up on a pine tree, and took target practice with his body. Crawford's family was given three weeks to get out of town. The coroner's jury found he had died at the hands of persons unknown.

The New York Age quoted liberally from the Southern press to show that it was precisely Crawford's respectability, his implicit self-respect, that had aroused the mob and "justified" his murder. The mores of White supremacy required that the "lowest white man" be above a "rich Negro." The Age's September 6 editorial on Crawford was a warning to the

15th: "It is only when the Negro appears . . . as a man who respects himself and demands respect that he becomes obnoxious."[4]

The manners and customs of Jim Crow required the African-American not only to bear ridicule but to adopt the sensibility of his persecutor: to accept the humiliating *mockery* of himself, *as* himself. Any protest, the display merely of self-respect, the least "sauciness" in glance or manner made the Negro liable for the worst punishment the local White citizenry could conceive. In 1916 there had been fifty-one known lynchings of Blacks, in 1917 there would be forty-eight—not counting the dead of the race riots in Waco, Memphis, and East Saint Louis.

Spartanburg: Jim Europe vs. Jim Crow

Spartanburg, South Carolina, was very much a "New South" city. It was the cultural and commercial hub of its region, with two colleges, good railroad connections, and several textile mills in the surrounding countryside. Its business leaders were "go-getters" who sought investment by northern capitalists, and when mobilization began they sold the army on establishing Camp Wadsworth near their city. But to achieve their goals it was necessary that Spartanburg gain and keep a reputation for civil peace. There had been only two officially recorded lynchings in Spartanburg County proper between 1880 and 1900. But the racial situation had become increasingly explosive since the turn of the century. The development of textile mills brought with it a steadily intensifying labor-management struggle over wages and workplace control, which disrupted the race-based unity of South Carolina Whites. Blacks had already been disenfranchised by the state constitution. Between 1895 and 1916 the conservatives attempted to set literacy and property tests for all voters in the state Democratic primary, which would have effectively disenfranchised poor Whites as well. The poorer White farmers and mill workers supported a populist faction of the Democratic Party, led by Ben Tillman and Cole Blease, who appealed to the Negrophobia of their constituents as well as their class resentments. The contest was particularly bitter in Spartanburg. Mill workers howled agreement when Blease told them the mill owners were trying "to place you cotton-mill men and you farmers on the same basis as a free negro!"[5]

The Spartanburg city fathers had reason to fear that the arrival of more than two thousand armed northern Negroes would set off the hair-trigger tensions between townsmen and mill workers. Even if the Blacks were well behaved and well spoken, their dignity, their "respectability" could be taken as a provocation in itself. So the very people who, in other circumstances, might have been supportive of "decent, respectable Colored men" had felt it necessary to take the lead in opposing the arrival of the 15th New York, and to threaten violence if it came anyway.

Colonel Hayward and his officers were on notice to be prepared for trouble. The War Department had instructed officials in charge of camp activities that "the Race segregation system will be carefully observed" wherever local law or custom requires it. The colonel was a politician: he dealt with the problem by negotiating agreements, first with his own men and then with the conservative leadership of Spartanburg.

Shortly after arrival, Hayward assembled the regiment and explained his view of their situation: they must promise to follow the customs of the community when off the base, and refrain from retaliation when—as they should expect—they were insulted or even physically abused by White citizens. He made clear his own awareness of the injustice of Jim Crow, and endorsed the legitimate sense of grievance his men felt. But he also tried to mitigate that sense of grievance by explaining, even rationalizing, the attitudes of Spartanburg's Whites. He reminded the men of the anti-Jim Crow "riot" by the 24th Infantry in Houston, and suggested that that discreditable episode lay behind the protest made by Spartanburg's mayor. He told them that the "unfriendly attitude" of local Whites was to be "excuse[d] upon the grounds of ignorance and misunderstanding," but offered a curious explanation for their errors:

> Southern people did not appreciate the fact that the colored man of New York was a different man [from] the colored man of the South—different in education, different in social, business, and community status, different in his bearing a sense of responsibility and obligation to civilization.[6]

This in effect rationalized prejudice by accepting the Whites' view of Southern Negroes as inferior in social and moral development—and by implication, deserving of subjection.

If this problematic appeal passed muster with the soldiers of the 15th, it was because many of them shared (in some measure) Hayward's values. Even W. E. B. DuBois had declared himself willing to accept "so much of this strange prejudice as is founded on just homage to civilization, culture, righteousness, and progress." Hayward offered his men a flattering portrayal of their own character, addressed them as men of superior personal and social development, a "Talented Tenth" of sorts, more advanced than Southern Negroes and in a sense superior to Southern Whites as well: their intellectual appreciation of the basis of prejudice allowed them to tolerate it from a position of moral superiority. He also implied that the entire regiment—not only its Talented Tenth, but its porters, waiters, janitors, and hod carriers—belonged to the great American middle class. Hence they had no need to challenge Jim Crow exclusions. Simple "self-respect" would tell them to refuse to shop in stores that did not want their trade. He reminded them that their larger mission depended upon their winning the goodwill of White officials. Only if they bore themselves well, first in South Carolina and then in war, could they "win from the whole world respect for the colored race, with an advance in the elimination of existing prejudices to follow." To make that demonstration clear, "See to it . . . that if violence occurs, if blows are struck, that all of the violence and all of the blows are on one side, and that that side is not our side. If by wrong, disorder is to occur, make sure and doubly sure, that none of the wrong is on our side."

The men were also moved by the fact that, instead of simply issuing orders, Hayward had asked for their free and informed consent. In so doing he had offered an extraordinary recognition of their citizenship. It was a departure from military norms and was remarkably successful as a practical means of averting trouble and of building the regiment's sense of solidarity and unit pride. When Hayward asked the regiment's assent, "a sea of hands shot up over that sea of heads—and the meeting was dismissed." Hayward made sure that the larger community knew of his action. He was in close touch with A. F. Moore, the editor of the *Age*, and the paper approved the meeting and Hayward's policy as helpful to their hope that the "Fifteenth Regiment May Soon See Active Service in France."[7]

Hayward next made a personal appeal for support to Spartanburg's "better classes." Hayward and Hamilton Fish, as representatives of the corresponding class of Northern good families, met several times with local magnates and officials to ask them to check or restrain their citizens, and offered assurances that their soldiers would behave like good Washingtonians, eschewing assertions of social equality, proving their value by steady service. Spartanburg's notables tried to be accommodating.

They had, after all, asked the army to build the camp to bring more money into town, and a scandal might ruin their prospects. When Hayward suggested that the regimental band give an open-air concert in the city's largest public square, the offer was accepted. The idea was well considered: Negroes were acceptable as public entertainers for White audiences, and James Europe's band had begun to acquire national celebrity. But the concert also exposed the band to a crowd of unfriendly White men. Hayward's White officers circulated in the audience, wearing overcoats to hide the regimental numerals on their collars. "If disorder had started . . . every colored soldier present would have been able to find at least one officer's face that he knew. And our men, with their own trusted officers leading them, would never (and never did) go wrong." Although the officers in mufti overheard some disturbing sentiments, the concert was a success. Local businessmen invited the White officers to join the country club. They were seconded by "the well-to-do colored citizens," who invited the soldiers to their church socials. It was a perfect example of the Progressives' elite-centered approach to reform.[8]

What was left out of Hayward's calculations was the home truth that Progressives and Washingtonians refused to see: that for a Negro to act in a dignified and self-respecting manner, and to succeed in proving his economic or social value, was in itself an insult and a threat to White supremacy—as the Crawford lynching so bloodily proved. The elites spoke only for themselves, and those who shared their interests. The ordinary White citizens of Spartanburg defended their racial dignity by keeping up a drumfire of insults and provocations against the 15th. The situation was exactly parallel on the other side of the color line. Black officers set an example of peaceful accommodation. Captain Marshall, the Harvard man and lawyer, was ordered off a streetcar after he had paid his fare. "He knew his rights. He was by no means lacking in appreciation of the wrongs of his race. But [he] had volunteered to help lick Germany, not to force a social or racial American revolution."

While Black enlisted men tried to keep their bargain with Hayward, they also showed their temper and willingness to defend their dignity. Little tells the story of a soldier of the 15th who was thrown into the gutter by a gang of Whites, offended because he had used the sidewalk. He responded: "Ah dun promise mah Kunnel dat ah woo'den' stra'k back ef yoo all er-goes ter licken me." Little represents the soldier as speaking in Southern dialect, suggesting he had migrated to New York and been transformed by fair treatment and military training into a man neither abjectly subservient nor reflexively defiant. (To make sure the White reader gets the point, Little adds that the soldier later proved himself in combat.) Although Southern rednecks are not won over by this display, Northern Whites *are*. Among the crowd were White New Yorkers from the "Kid Glove" 7th New York—a regiment noted since the 1850s for its elite membership. As the Negro soldier "shuffled off," a "clean-cut youngster in Seventh Regiment uniform" shouted, "Well, I didn't prom- ise my Colonel to keep my hands off you bullies!" With a companion he waded in and "knocked the town toughs into the gutter from which their victim had arisen." In Little's hands, the incident has the force of a para- ble: under Progressive tutelage the Negro learns discipline; his good be- havior earns the respect of the "better classes" of Whites, who defend him from his "cracker" tormentors. The good Negro rises from the gut- ter, and the redneck is dropped in his place.

The gutter incident looks different when viewed from the perspectives of the Black enlisted man and the Spartanburg Whites. The Black soldier had told a crowd of angry Whites that the only reason he did not strike back in self-defense was that his Colonel had ordered him not to. In that time and place, such a speech was defiant and "saucy"—poor Crawford had been tormented and murdered for a much milder display of self- respect. The Black soldier obeyed the letter of Hayward's orders, but still showed enough pride and resentment to test the edge of White tolerance. That temper was widely shared in the regiment. Enlistment in the 15th New York had appealed to Black men because it offered an opportunity to vindicate their dignity and manhood; to deny both for the ostensible sake of the regiment was more paradox than they could stand. Within days of their arrival, their responses to Jim Crow became more explicitly defiant. When local Whites posted "No Niggers Allowed" on a barracks wall, a guard tore it down. When a second sign appeared, two hundred Black sol- diers in battle gear marched to the building to destroy that sign as well.

During their second week in Spartanburg, a White truck driver spread a rumor in camp that "two colored soldiers had gotten into a fight with a policeman in town; and . . . had been hanged in the yard of Police Headquarters." The soldiers were willing to endure some degree of in- sult and abuse for the cause of the race, but the killing of a fellow soldier could not be tolerated, whether the killer was German or South Carolin- ian. Next morning a platoon of forty or fifty men (led by their noncoms) drew arms and ammunition and marched in formation into downtown Spartanburg "with pent up grievance and wrongs (some real, some fancied) bursting their hearts—marching upon that town—to kill." Another forty or so were intercepted as they assembled in the mess hall. Colonel Hayward was alerted and raced to town in an automobile hoping to "save the regiment from disgrace . . . [and] the population of that town from destruction." At the far end of the main street he found the men, "standing at ease in column of squads . . . in perfect order." When they saw him they presented arms in salute. The leader told Hayward that the men "had been . . . under perfect discipline," had threatened no one; only stood there, under arms, for the town to notice. A detail had been sent to the police station to "make inquiries." At the jail Hayward discovered that the rumored lynching had never occurred, and that the two-man detail had been allowed to look through the jail, because the sheriffs assumed they were military police. Hayward returned to find that a crowd had gathered to gawk at his platoon standing in formation. But when he marched them off ("Those men never drilled better in their lives") the crowd merely applauded.

Hayward and Little believed that the town never knew what was afoot, and they saw to it that the incident remained secret, to save the regiment from disgrace. However, it would be surprising if local Blacks, and eventually Whites, had not heard some rumor of it—heartening to the former, dismaying to the latter. The soldiers themselves were satisfied that they had displayed a willingness to confront lynchers; proud also that they had maintained discipline during the confrontation, in spite of the absence of White officers. The fact that those officers did not punish what was in effect a mutiny signaled that the officers appreciated both the spirit that made them disobey and the discipline that kept them in hand. Little thought his troops had shown the requisite characteristics of Rooseveltian heroism: a willingness to resent insult and defend one's honor, disciplined by perfect moral restraint.

Then on October 20 Spartanburg gave James Europe his chance at heroism. Lieutenant Europe, drum major Noble Sissle, and about seventy-five other soldiers and band members were standing in the street, waiting for transportation to an evening church service. Europe asked a passing White man where he could buy a New York paper. The man told him he could get one at a nearby hotel: it was a Whites-only establishment, but "colored people here in town go there for papers," and two

Black soldiers had bought papers earlier that day. Europe told "Siss" to "get every paper that has the word 'New York' on it. I never knew how sweet New York was until I landed here."

The hotel lobby was full of White soldiers. Sissle exchanged greetings with "a Jewish boy from New York." Relations between White and Black New Yorkers had warmed up. Since the "gutter" incident there had been other occasions on which White New York Guardsmen sided with their Black fellow townsmen against abusive Carolinians. Perhaps they sympathized because, as Yankees in Dixie, they also experienced antagonism from the local people. Perhaps the difference between soldier and civilian was beginning to seem more important than differences among soldiers wearing the same uniform. Perhaps the liberal propaganda of *The Home Reading Course* and other publications was having some effect. Whatever the cause, White soldiers from two other National Guard units visited shopkeepers in town to tell them that if they did not change their Jim Crow policies they might as well close shop, for the White soldiers would boycott them. "[The] colored soldiers are all right. They're fighting with us for our country. They're our buddies. And we won't buy from men who treat them unfairly." Years later, veterans of the 15th would remember that support with pleasure.

In the hotel, the desk clerk served Sissle politely. But at the door he was struck suddenly from behind, his hat knocked off, and a White man was in his face hollering "Say, nigger, don't you know enough to take your hat off[?]" Sissle was small, slight, and wore spectacles; the White man, proprietor of the hotel, large and angry. Sissle had served his apprenticeship in city saloons and clubs; he would not brawl with the bouncer but would not suffer in silence either. He could see well enough that every other soldier in the lobby was wearing a hat, and as he picked his up he told the man off for abusing a United States soldier, and that this was a "government hat" he had knocked to the floor. The man went for Sissle again, cursing and kicking at him till he was outside. No one from the 15th had seen the scuffle, and as he walked away from it Sissle was deciding not to tell them—he didn't want to cause any scandals for the regiment.

But the White soldiers in the hotel now took a hand, yelling at the proprietor, "Let's kill the so and so, and pull his dirty old hotel about his ears." The Jewish soldier ran up the street, told the men from the 15th what was happening, then ran with them back to the hotel. As they barged through the door Lieutenant Europe caught up with them, and called out in "a voice of command . . . heard above all other voices . . . 'ATTEN . . . TION!'" The habit of discipline made the men of the 15th stop, and there was enough authority in Europe's voice to bring the Whites to obedience as well. They left the hotel on his orders, quietly. As they did, the proprietor cursed Europe, "whose brave action had probably saved his property and his life."

> For a moment Jim Europe's eye held that of the man who was insulting him. There was no sign of fear in the glance of the negro. . . . Then, with quiet dignity, he turned his back and walked into the street.

Europe had managed to avoid a scandalous incident without backing down in the eyes of his own troops and the Whites in the hotel. Sissle, who was an eyewitness, saw Europe's manner as defiant—staring into a White man's eyes was a breach of racial manners in that place, and a challenge to the hotel keeper. He had exercised *command:* he had showed he not only had the power to control himself but the ability to lead others. In a sense he was the first of the regiment's officers, Black or White, to show that ability under threat of attack. For Little, the incident showed James Europe as the embodiment of his race's Rooseveltian potential: "The officer who had quelled that riot by the power and majesty of command was a black man, a full-blooded negro."[9]

But his heroism was not the kind that makes a soldier famous. In fact, it was absolutely necessary that the incident be hushed up, because any association with a racial "incident" in the South would kill the regiment's chances for a front-line assignment. The incident was not reported until August of the following year, when the theater columnist of the *Age* referred to it.

The White officers, no less than their Black troopers, were caught in the double-bind of racial politics. Their silence in the face of discrimination could be read as acquiescence, but any protest would mark them as unreliable malcontents. No other minority labored under disabilities so debilitating and complex. At about the same time as the Europe-Sissle incident a Jewish private in the National Guard named Otto Gottschalk was physically abused by his company commander (Captain Sullivan) and three noncoms. Gottschalk complained to the regimental commander, and to the Kehillah—the consortium of New York City religious and civic leaders that tried to provide organized leadership for the community. The "Committee for the Protection of the Good Name of the Immigrants" investigated, found that Sullivan had also been using his position to prevent Jews from enlisting in the National Guard, and saw Sullivan court-martialed.[10] Though Jews were subjected to discrimination and abuse, the customs and politics of the country permitted community leaders to organize public protests and take political action, without fearing that Jewish soldiers as a group would be degraded by being forbidden to participate in combat.

Fighting for a Chance to Fight

Hayward's strategy for keeping the peace did win some points for his regiment and for African-American troops in general. South Carolina authorities eventually admitted that Negro soldiers were well behaved and said they would welcome more of them. There was no public scandal as a result of the Sissle incident, though word of it did reach New York and may have reached the War Department. After barely two weeks at Camp Wadsworth the regiment was ordered north to prepare to ship out for France. Hamilton Fish claimed it was his personal pull with Assistant Secretary of the Navy Franklin D. Roosevelt that got the regiment out of Spartanburg. That seems questionable. The move was so sudden as to suggest the War Department wanted to get them out of town before they caused more trouble. Although the news was welcome, it did not really resolve the question whether they would be used as labor or as combat troops. Counting their two brief stints at Camp Whitman in the spring and summer they had had less than eight weeks' training all told—far less than the bare minimum of four to five months' combat training thought necessary for the National Army troops.

Before they left there was another racial confrontation, which did get into the papers. The 15th was billeted at Camp Mills on Long Island, next to the 167th Infantry—the Alabama National Guard regiment brigaded with the Fighting 69th in the Rainbow Division. The 167th had already made its racial feelings known in the neighborhood. Some of its soldiers had beaten and deliberately blinded a Black man who had been seated in their car on the Long Island Rail Road. At Mills there were confrontations between individuals and small groups from the two regiments. The Alabamans put up "Whites Only" signs which the men of the 15th tore down. One morning Hamilton Fish heard a rumor that the Alabamans intended to attack his company that night. (By one account the rumor was just a practical joke by the playful Irishmen of the Fighting 69th.) Once again they faced a Hobson's choice: if they did nothing there would be a "bloody massacre," if they resisted there would be a scandal. Either way, the affair could destroy their chance of getting into combat.

Hayward ordered that no ammunition be issued to the men, for fear of what might happen. But Fish had always been an aggressive character. He borrowed ammunition from a White New York regiment, and said, as Private William Layton remembered it, "If we were attacked we should shoot." There are several versions of what happened next. As Fish later told it, he and his men were roused that night by an unexplained bugle call. Fish went stumbling through the dark to forestall the expected attack, his service automatic in hand, and ran into a group of Alabama officers out on the same errand. Fish convinced them that if their men did attack the camp, whether armed or not, they would be shot by the regiment's trained marksmen. The Southerners agreed to rein in their men, and their colonel wrote a note of apology to Hayward.

The stories that were current in the regiment, and reported by the New York papers, were more dramatic. Captain Fish had gone to the Southern camp to confront the Alabama officers, accompanied by his fellow Harvardian, African-American Captain Napoleon Marshall, and by Private "Kid" Cotton, formerly the trainer of heavyweight champ Jack Johnson. There he had either personally whipped five Alabamans, or issued a challenge: he would fight "any man of equal rank," and " 'Kid' Cotton . . . offered to take on any five privates." When the fracas was over, the 15th was said to have marched out of camp "led by its band." The early editions of some city newspapers treated the story as a North-South confrontation in which Fish and the Negroes outfaced the Sons of the Confederacy. Joseph Pulitzer's sensationalist New York World put the headline on page 1: "Alabama Troops Clash with Negro Soldiers in Camp / Fearing General Attack . . . They Fall in With Bayonets Fixed." The paper quoted Fish's boast that "my men have shown that they possess wonderful self-control. There is no community that is not rendered safer after the arrival of the Fifteenth." The New York American, published by Pulitzer's rival in yellow journalism William Randolph Hearst, was less friendly to African-Americans in or out of uniform. It offered a longer tale of "twenty-four hours of terror" under the headline "Negroes Moved at Camp Mills / Troops Withdrawn Following Threatened Clash with Men of Alabama Regiment." There had been "a dozen encounters Friday night." Colonel Hayward was quoted praising the restraint and discipline of his men. However, by noon the regiment's publicity (and antipublicity) team had weighed in. The afternoon edition of the *Times* reported "No Race Riot in Camp," despite the "sensational stories in some New York morning newspapers." The other papers dropped the story, which allowed the army to "forget" the incident and avoid trouble with both Southerners and Negroes.[11]

Nevertheless, the incident got just enough publicity to make the men feel they had vindicated their "manhood," and that the home folks knew and approved. It gave a boost to their morale, their sense of solidarity with their officers and each other. For Sergeant Jamieson it was one of the memorable events of the war, and the roles played by Captains Fish and Marshall and Kid Cotton acquired a legendary gloss. Whether or not Fish actually offered to fight "any officer who thinks he knows how to scrap," Fish's men believed him capable of it. Sergeant Jamieson said it "showed his real love for the colored soldier." Private Fred Williams admired Fish's toughness—Williams who had said he had "to fight like hell to save my life" first in the South and then in Harlem. William Layton rated Fish high, because he "liked music," was "proud of the men," and did not disapprove of them retaliating when insulted or attacked by Whites.

But the army still would not promise to use them in combat, and the way in which it sent the regiment to France confirmed their worst suspicions. It took them forty days and forty nights to get "over there." Twice they were turned back when the wheezing old hulk they were given for a troopship caught fire and sprang a leak. Only Hayward's "impassioned" pleading and the skill of some marine metalworkers convinced the captain that the ship could be repaired enough to keep up with the next convoy. With all the delays their departure still had the appearance of haste, of the wish to see the troublesome outfit gone. The government even neglected to formally take the regiment into federal service, so it landed in France as the 15th New York, carrying state as well as national colors— the only regiment in the AEF to do so. Despite all this, the men were in good spirits. Horace Pippin's account of their departure has a jaunty tone:—"the good old U.S.A." was in trouble, and the Old Fifteenth would help her out.[12]

They landed in France in a snowstorm on New Year's Day 1918. The officers expected the 15th would be attached to a French or British brigade for advanced combat training close to the front. Instead they were packed into boxcars and sent to Saint-Nazaire to serve as a labor battalion. Horace Pippin, the ex-ironworker who liked to draw in his spare time, remembered it "was growing colder and our overcoats were not much use to us that night. You see the boxcars were so packed that no one could lay down." The regiment was put to work building railroads and dock facilities for the eventual landing of the main body of the AEF. In two months "we laid about five hundred miles of rail . . . went to bed in the dark and got up in the dark, only the moon showing."

The regiment's unit pride and solidarity remained strong. But as in Spartanburg, its response to mistreatment was resentment and, ultimately, resistance. There was intense hostility between White American troops stationed in and around Saint-Nazaire and the Black labor battalions quartered in the area. Private Layton remembered a series of racial murders, lynchings in effect, U.S. Marines "killing black soldiers one by one." Soldiers from the 15th responded in kind, "When a black was found dead they killed a white soldier." Layton's recollections were more than seventy years old when they were recorded, and his account is impossible to verify. Rumors of such incidents were rife in the AEF and in Black newspapers during and after the war, and it is possible Layton's memory merged hearsay with actual remembrance. A Senate investigation in 1923 heard testimony and saw some evidence indicating that a large number of Black troops had been executed by summary courts-martial in violation of sanctioned procedure, and that many Blacks had been hanged or lynched out of hand. But the committee adjourned without reaching any conclusions. Whatever the literal truth of the matter, Layton's story reflects the intensity of resentment within the regiment, and (given its pride) the potential for violence with White American troops. As in Spartanburg, if the men defended themselves, the regiment would be discredited; if officers prevented the men from defending themselves, morale would collapse. Their appeals to the authorities were ignored or mocked.[13]

The officers went to work to get the regiment reassigned. As before, their methods were a mix of public relations and political pressure. Fish drew on all his connections in politics and the media to focus attention on the regiment. With some of the other White officers he arranged to have many of the regiment's activities filmed for newsreels and news photos. He wrote letters to his father, which Hamilton Fish Sr. arranged to have published in the *New York Times* and other important papers. These letters were political documents disguised as personal communication. Fish mended fences with Governor Whitman and echoed Roosevelt's pleasure in hearing that "the nation had shaken off its shackles and destroyed the maggots of pacifism." He also repeated his boast that the regiment "would be as well known as the Rough Riders were."[14]

Colonel Hayward kept up a continuous correspondence with Moore of the *Age* and Emmett Scott, who were in a position to advocate for the regiment and publicize its achievements. But he needed to get his story into the White press as well. He used his social and political connections to bring visiting celebrities and correspondents to his headquarters, where they were invariably impressed by the good order, hygiene, and morale of the Negro soldiers. A letter from the Broadway actor E.H. Sothern was published in the *New York Herald*: he was happy to be able to say that "there was no doubt of the genuine affection and regard these colored soldiers had for their officers." Hayward also made good use of Lieutenant Europe and the regimental band. Their performances had won support for the Old Fifteenth at the start; their concerts in Spartanburg had ameliorated some of the racial hostility there. Now Hayward got permission for Europe to take the band on a tour of France, as a contribution to the *amitié des nations*. The tour was a triumph, not only for Europe and the 15th, but for the reputation of American culture in France. There were some initial misunderstandings: the French failed to recognize Europe's highly syncopated version of "The Marseillaise" and the bandsmen misunderstood the audience's shrill whistles as catcalls, when they were in fact the highest form of applause. Europe's concerts introduced French audiences to jazz, inaugurating a national enthusiasm that persists to this day. More than that: he made the case that the most distinctively *American* music is *African-American* music. Europe's success also helped Hayward make his case. Thirty-seven days into the tour, their host announced with regret, "Tomorrow, these men, who . . . have given us so much pleasure, proceed to the front lines."[15]

Thus the regiment won the opportunity to prove itself. But their enemies had so limited the regiment's training that it would enter the line with less preparation than any front-line unit in the AEF. Their stateside training amounted to less than eight weeks of close- and extended-order drill, a little shooting practice, plus "various night school and correspondence classes." In France they had used no instrument more lethal than shovels, or in the case of the band, trombones. As Hayward later declared, "It is not an exaggeration to say that the men of the regiment never saw their rifles except by candle light, or . . . on the Sabbath Day, from December 27 to March 12 when [the regiment] was turned over to the French Army as an American combat unit." The officers had had no advanced training in infantry tactics, nor in gas defense, nor in the use of machine guns, the most important weapon on the battlefield. Bandleader James Europe was pressed into service as commander of one machine-gun company; Napoleon Marshall, the forty-two-year-old judge advocate, commanded the other till he was appointed gas officer.[16]

On Patrol in No-Man's-Land

Although they were going to a quiet sector, the 15th New York came into the line just at the great crisis of the war on the Western Front. On March 21 the great German spring offensive opened with a massive assault against the British in Flanders.[17]

The stalemate of trench warfare had persisted for three years because of the inability of attacking units to retain tactical mobility after achieving their initial penetrations. Horse cavalry and tanks had a theoretical potential to exploit a breakthrough, but the heavy churning of the battlefield by artillery limited their usefulness. Infantry making an assault were typically exhausted by their initial advance and inclined to spread laterally in captured trenches, for protection from artillery and to secure their flanks from counterattacks. To break the stalemate the Germans employed new tactics developed on the Eastern Front. They brought an unprecedented concentration of artillery to bear on the British Fifth Army front. Prior to emplacement, every gun was registered by firing behind the lines. Since they did not have to fire ranging shots, the bombardment would take the British completely by surprise. To exploit the break blasted open by the artillery they prepared an elite force of "storm troops," whose training emphasized infiltration of weak points in the line and continual forward movement by "spearheads," leaving it to conventional infantry to mop up and secure their gains. The *Stosstruppen* were equipped with light machine guns and flamethrowers, supplemented by mortars when beyond the range of artillery support. The German assault plan worked to perfection. Behind the massive bombardment the storm troop spearheads fractured the British lines, smashed the Fifth Army, and threatened a decisive breakthrough into open country.

In this crisis, General Pershing offered the Allies the use of his few available units: three regular divisions, the Guardsmen of the 42nd, and the 15th New York. Before these units could be deployed the crisis in Flanders ended with the temporary exhaustion of the German offensive, and Pershing reclaimed his White divisions. But he made his Negro regiment a permanent gift to the French.

The 15th New York was now belatedly adopted into federal service, the state colors were cased, and the outfit renamed the 369th Infantry. They were assigned to the French 16th Division for combat training in the "zone of advance." Hayward wrote to a friend that the regiment were now " '*enfants perdus*' and glad of it." He told a French colonel that Pershing had "simply put the black orphan in a basket, set it on the doorstep, pulled the bell, and went away." The Frenchman replied, "Weelcome, leetle black babbie." Hayward concluded, "The French are wonderful—wonderful—wonderful," though he never gave up hope that the regiment would ultimately join the AEF.

James Europe left the band in the hands of Noble Sissle and took up his duties as commander of Company I, Third Battalion. He was grieved to learn that Vernon Castle had died: "My one real and true friend," who had left Broadway in 1915 to serve in the British army. But the prospect of action put him in a heroic mood. He told Sissle that now he was just an underling, who "must ONLY TAKE orders . . . my hands are tied and fast but if the war does not end me first sure as God made man I will be on top and so far on top that it will be impossible to pull me down." As they marched out the band played the national anthems of the United States and France, Sousa's "Stars and Stripes Forever," then swung into the ragtime "Army Blues," which set the troops and townspeople cheering and laughing. Closer to the front things looked grim. Maffrecourt, where they had their headquarters—"Mapherycoat" to Horace Pippin—was "toaren up bad." Pippin could tell that their forward position, Herypont (or "Hairypoint"), had been "a nice layed out town," but now it was a wreck. Old men and women stumbled out of the ruins, tears running down their faces: misery or gratitude, it was hard to tell.[18]

There were inconveniences attached to their assignment. There was a language barrier to overcome. The regiment had to be reequipped with French rifles, ammunition, packs, and helmets. The new gas masks were an improvement: the troops said they were easier to fit over their soft noses. The French helmet had style, a raised crest on top, a medallion in front above its small projecting brim. But wearing it set the men further apart from their fellow Americans, who wore the British-style helmet with its shallow crown and flared brim. Only after the 369th had made its reputation fighting with the French did that helmet become a badge of distinction and earn adoption as the identifying symbol on the 93rd Division's shoulder patch. Rations were also a problem. Americans did not consider *la soupe* equivalent to a meal. The French ration of two quarts of red wine per day was welcome, but Americans tended to drink it all at once, which made them unfit for service till they sobered up. The men were given extra sugar in its place—officers retained the wine ration.

The consequences of the change in weaponry were more serious. The regiment had trained with the big American Springfield rifles and the long, heavy American bayonet. Switching to the French Lebel rifle required retraining in both marksmanship and bayonet drill. The Lebels were outdated weapons, useless at long range, and their magazine clips held only three bullets as against the Springfield's five. The French relied on artillery rather than riflery to suppress enemy fire, and their infantry tactics emphasized closing in to work with the bayonet. For the first time the Old Fifteenth were taught how to use mortars, grenades, heavy machine guns, and the Chauchat or "sho-sho." The Chauchat was a light machine gun or "auto-rifle," similar in size and function to the "tommy gun" of World War II, usually fired handheld but sometimes with a bipod—an absolutely essential weapon for close-in fighting by troops assaulting or defending trenches. Some of the best soldiers in the 369th and the 77th Division made their reputations with it, but as a weapon it was ugly, cranky, and unreliable. It looked as if it had been "stamped, pressed, screwed, and generally botched together" from scrap, which in a way it had been. The French designed and produced it on the cheap. Its barrel was made of ordinary industrial steel tubing, incapable of withstanding for very long the stress of automatic firing. Its pistol grip was roughened wood, its forward grip a round wooden handle, something like the pull-chain handle of a crapper. When it fired, the entire barrel and bolt assembly recoiled, then sprang forward, a rock-and-roll effect that made it impossible to hold aim for more than one or two shots. It used a semi-circular magazine, which had to be attached fore and aft and had a tendency to jam.

But despite initial misgivings and inconveniences, the French connection proved a transforming experience for African-American soldiers and officers. The practical lessons in trench warfare were priceless, far more valuable than the close-order drill and rifle-range lessons of their too-brief training in the United States. They learned how to deal with vermin and excrement; how to recognize incoming and outgoing artillery fire, and distinguish the kind of explosives that might be coming your way; how to recognize the moment when the bombardment has lifted, the moment to leave the sheltering dugout to man the trenches against infantry attack.

They also learned gas discipline, perhaps the hardest self-defense measure to master. In 1918 the Germans were using three kinds of gas: non-lethal tear gas and the deadly phosgene and mustard gases. Phosgene is a by-product of chloroform, corrosive to skin, eyes, and lungs, and capable of damaging the central nervous system. Mustard gas was the more deadly, an odorless poison gas lethal even in small amounts. It blistered skin on contact, attacked mucous membranes in the eyes causing blindness, and in the bronchial tubes caused internal bleeding, extreme pain, and death by suffocation after weeks of prolonged suffering. The gas also lingered unless dispersed by wind and could be absorbed in the soil and reactivated several weeks after initial deployment. It was much slower-acting than phosgene, but its effects were so horrible that troops subjected to it were likely to become demoralized, flee, or surrender in hopes of getting medical attention. A gas bombardment was heralded by the distinctive *plop* of shells whose smaller explosive charge was designed only to disperse the gas.

Troops were taught to recognize gas by its smell. According to one guidance, tear gas smelled "just about like new mown hay," while the deadly mustard and phosgene gases smelled like "mustard, garlic, burnt chocolate." Good gas discipline meant that the soldier always had his mask handy, always sealed his dugout against gas, knew when to wear the mask and when to take it off, and above all did not panic. "Don't you ever run. It's when you are out of breath that you are more likely to get caught" by a gas barrage. Mustard and phosgene clung to whatever surfaces they touched and tended to pool in low breaks in the ground. No food was to be eaten or water drunk from an area hit by gas, and before taking shelter in a poisoned shell hole the doughboy was instructed to spray it with chloride of lime—if he happened to be carrying any and was not being shot at or shelled at the time.

It was the responsibility of officers and noncoms to enforce gas discipline, to keep the men from exposing themselves in their panic. Conversely, if the officers judged that the attack consisted *only* of tear gas, then their responsibility was to compel the men to take off their masks, overcoming their terror of mustard and phosgene. To prove that it was safe, the officers would have to take off their masks and breathe whatever it was that fumed and fogged the air around them. Few American officers received any stateside training in gas warfare, and the history of the AEF would be marked by ineffective use of gas as an offensive weapon and inadequate response to German gas attacks. The officers of the 369th went into combat with less training than any regimental cadre in the American army, so their ignorance of gas was complete. Napoleon Marshall was appointed regimental gas officer on the strength of his high intelligence, and perhaps his linguistic skills: to help him meet his new responsibility the French simply handed him a stack of their army manuals.[19]

The French taught officers and men alike; exposed them to bombardment; led them in small groups on patrols into the no-man's-land between the trenches. Lieutenant Europe volunteered to accompany a French patrol that was going out to raid the German trenches for prisoners. He wrote the story of his adventures to his friend Sissle back at the regimental depot with the band, treating the whole thing as an elaborate joke. Claimed he only went because he'd talked too much to some French officers about his eagerness for combat—there was no heroic posing between two hip New Yorkers.

Armed only with a French automatic pistol "the size of a cap gun," Europe followed the lieutenant commanding the patrol out of the trenches, "stumbling in the intense darkness." They paused at the jump-off point. "I noticed how beautiful the night was. Every star seemed as bright as a shining silver light. It seemed they were mockingly winking their eyes at me, and how I wished I could change places with them."

They crawled through a gap in their own wire and wormed their way through shell-torn ground to the edge of the enemy's wire where a previous patrol had cut an opening. One soldier crawled ahead, unreeling a white tape to mark the shortest route back to a shell hole in which they could take shelter. Friendly artillery let go behind them, shells whizzing overhead "like a thousand pheasants" and burst forty yards ahead, pounding the enemy trenches while Europe and the patrol hugged the ground with shrapnel "hizzing" all around them. The bombardment shifted away—the officer commanding the patrol brought the men to a crouch, then led them single file through the cut wire, waved them into a skirmish line on the other side, and led their rush into the German trench.

Europe was experiencing the expert coordination of artillery and infantry in staging a tactical assault—a method that had taken the French three years to learn and which even veteran American divisions would not master until the last weeks of the war. As the artillery shifted its aim to bombard the German reserves, the French troops worked their way up and down the trench line, bombing the dugouts with grenades. A green flare above their own lines was the recall. They had plenty of German paperwork for Intelligence, some souvenirs but no prisoners. One wounded man on an improvised stretcher was groaning, "Aw, Aw." They scrambled back down the tape line and across no-man's-land chased by a German counterbarrage. "Don't tell me Frenchmen can't run," Europe wrote "Siss"—and added that as for himself, it was a case of "don't know where I am going, but I'm on my way!" Europe was the first African-American officer to be under fire in the Great War.

After three days of direct tutelage, the French turned the trenches over to the Americans: a mark of trust, though the sector was peaceful and they were still supervised by the French divisional and brigade staff. After ten days in the trenches they were relieved and given ten days to recuperate in the rear. Europe liberated a piano and tried turning some of his experiences into songs. In later years Sissle could recall only one, " 'Everything reminds me of you' . . . a beautiful melody" and lyrics that invoked all the things that would run through the mind of a soldier in the intervals of combat.[20]

Most American troops who fought for any time under French command came away with feelings of intense antipathy for their commanders and sometimes the nation as well. For the Black troops of the 369th the experience was overwhelmingly positive. France's definition of citizenship officially followed the civic model and since their revolution had been open to the naturalization of liberal and Francophilic foreigners. There was probably more hostility to Jews—perceived by some as a racial tribe of significant power, living in but alien to the French nation—than to Blacks. French officers and noncoms formed close personal friendships with their African-American counterparts. Colonel Hayward wrote to Emmett Scott that two of his Negro officers had been invited to dine regularly at the French officers' mess, and that "the poilus and my boys are great chums." The French had already shown their enthusiasm for African-American music. Black troops returned the liking; they picked up the French word for the enemy, "*Boche,*" and translated it into a hybrid epithet, "Bush-Germans," a phrase invoking the contemptuous "bush nigger" leveled against tribal Africans or backwoods Negroes by Black Americans as well as White.

The commander of the French Fourth Army, General Gouraud, set the tone. He had a superb combat record, which gave him great moral authority; and his service in France's African colonies had given him "a high opinion of African troops." The French military regarded African-American troops as having the potential to equal their own Senegalese colonials in ferocity. However, they did not regard African-Americans as racial primitives, but rather as "Senegalese" improved by being reared in an advanced society—more literate, better acquainted with modern weapons and machinery. Some French officers thought the American Africans better than Senegalese in their ability to tolerate artillery bombardment and less prone to neglect firing their rifles in their zeal to close with the bayonet. Colonel Hayward found this idea congenial. Writing to Emmett Scott, he asserted that two of the great questions "of gravest importance to our country and your race" had now been answered in the affirmative. The first was, would Black Americans get along well with French soldiers and civilians? The second, "Will the American negro stand up under the terrible shell fire of this war . . . and thus prove his superiority, spiritually and intellectually, to all the black men of Africa and Asia, who have failed under these conditions and whose use must be limited to attack or for shock troops?" What is interesting here is the stress Hayward (and presumably Scott) place on proving the superiority of African-Americans to pure Africans in *modern* warfare. For Progressives, Black or White, it was crucial to prove that the Negro could display qualities of race superiority, proof of membership in the "great fighting races" whose imperial power spread "civilization" among the barbarous colored peoples of the world. It is therefore worth noting that Hayward's assertions about the French-colonial troops were wrong in two respects: the Senegalese were indeed capable of defending against shell fire, which is why they were classed as shock troops; and their supposed preference for the bayonet over aimed fire merely reflected their uncritical acceptance of French tactical doctrine.

French civilians tended to consider the African-Americans as "Yanks," welcomed them (or suspected them) as they would have any American soldiers, and fraternized liberally. The army and the CTCA were obsessed with the dangers of sexual temptation and venereal disease and adopted stringent rules to limit and control relations between American troops and French civilians. With African-American troops this generalized anxiety had a more specific focus: fear that promiscuous French women would undermine the central tenet of Jim Crow, which treated intercourse between a Black man and a White woman as the ultimate and fatal taboo. In the first quarter of 1918, when the 369th was one of the few Black units in France, these concerns had not yet risen to a level that required official notice. But as more Black labor battalions and combat regiments began to arrive in the spring and summer of 1918, headquarters would address the issue and intervene emphatically.[21]

The contrast between the attractiveness of French civilian society and the boredom, filth, and danger of the trenches challenged discipline in the 369th. Enlisted men seized any excuse to leave the lines and go "roaming all over the surrounding country." In "Hairypoint," Horace Pippin, as corporal of the Guard, shot a man trying to sneak out of camp and into the town. Dodging details and scrounging food and wine might be standard operating procedure for labor battalions, but not for combat troops. The French divisional commander complained and threatened to take the 369th out of the line. Hayward shifted Napoleon Marshall's assignment again, appointing him acting provost marshal and sending him out on "a splendid chestnut sorrel standing sixteen hands high" to round up the stragglers. Marshall single-handedly "corrall[ed] the A.W.O.L.'s" and "I soon had discipline restored. I shall always remember the complete obedience which the boys of the 'Fighting Fifteenth' gave me."[22]

Jim Europe and his comrades found the regiment's connection with the French liberating, because it immersed the men in a society apparently blind to the difference of color. That "double-consciousness" and division of spirit of which DuBois had spoken dissolved in the gaze of people who saw them simply as Black Americans—as if those two terms were perfectly and naturally consistent with each other. Even their own officers had not been so unconditional in their acceptance. The French would give them the chance to fight that their own army begrudged them. Their transfer to the French was a liberation rather than an exile. As James Europe wrote to the editor of the *Age*, "Their broad minds are free from prejudice . . . [and] despite the desperate efforts of some people, the French simply cannot be taught to comprehend that despicable thing called prejudice. . . . 'Vive la France' should be the song of every black American over here and over there." Europe supposed that, seeing how readily the White people of France could accept the equality and the Americanness of Blacks, African-Americans would learn to see the prejudices of their White countrymen as absurd and arbitrary, rather than normative and natural.[23]

Nevertheless, it was their White countrymen who had the power to give or withhold political and social rights, their White countrymen to whom the proof of their quality must be made. Even with Whites of goodwill, the impulse of racial ridicule was always just below the surface. A pair of articles published that spring in the *Outlook* magazine illustrate the phenomenon. The *Outlook* was an important national organ of Christian Progressivism, edited by Lyman Abbott, a leader of the Social Gospel movement and a Roosevelt supporter. Editor and magazine were fairly liberal on racial issues: supported Booker T. Washington's approach to the amelioration of Jim Crow, supported a federal antilynching statute and federal financing of Negro education, both advanced positions for White liberals in the early part of the century. It was in keeping with these liberal views that the magazine published a long article on the 367th Infantry, composed of Negro draftees from the New York area, training at Camp Upton for service with the 92nd Division. " 'The Buffaloes' A First-Class Colored Fighting Regiment" was written by a Negro lieutenant, Osceola E. McKaine, with an introduction by Colonel James A. Moss, the Louisiana-born regular who commanded the 367th. Moss had served with Negro regulars for eighteen years and believed they were racially suited to military life, willing to trust a good leader who offered them a "square deal. . . . If properly trained and instructed, the colored man makes as good a soldier as the world has ever seen." McKaine's part of the article shows how Moss's theories worked in practice. White officers worked alongside their troops on a range of tasks; social events were integrated. Lectures on the military history of the Negro race were added to the CTCA agenda of "Americanism" indoctrination, to appeal to racial as well as national pride and offer a pantheon of Black heroes as models for emulation.

On the other hand, two months earlier the *Outlook* had published an even longer piece that treated the whole business as blackface comedy. Lieutenant Charles C. Lynde, an officer training recruits for the 92nd Division, entitled his article "Mobilizing 'Rastus' "—lumping his soldiers together under a name associated with minstrel show "coon" caricatures. Lynde extends the joke by giving his recruits still more ridiculous names, like "Potassium Acetate" and "Anathema Maranatha Johnson," and mocking their apparently congenital ignorance, their inability to grasp the meaning or method of White culture and language, and above all for their absurd *pretentiousness* in thinking they can do all of the things Whites do.[24]

What display of virtues could annihilate that image? The Booker T. Washington theory held that earnestness, deference, and economic usefulness would earn respect. But in a modern competitive society Washingtonian passivity wins nothing but second- or third-class status in the marketplace and nothing whatever in the muster, the polling place, or the legislature. The wartime social bargain accepted by both Tuskegee and the NAACP proposed that patriotic loyalty and the display of soldierly qualities would do the trick. Yet the army and the administration had done everything it could to limit the opportunities for Black men to make that proof. The ban against Black field officers deprived them of the chance to show they could command in battle at a high level. It had taken all the political skill and influence of the 15th New York's officers and supporters just to win them the chance to show their quality as private soldiers. It was left to the enlisted men of the regiment to make the only kind of proof available to Black men, to establish the manhood of the Negro in terms no one could mistake.

The Battle of Henry Johnson:
"Another Way to Spell 'American' "

After the German offensives in Flanders in April and March there was a
lull. The Allied high command expected either a second stroke in Flanders or an assault against the French in the Champagne region. There
were continual adjustments to the line and redistribution of forces, probing attacks and raids to discover the enemy's intentions and deployments.
The 369th was serving with the French Fourth Army in Champagne, east
of Rheims, on the edge of the Argonne Forest. As a mark of its progress
in training, the regiment was given responsibility for a section of the
front in the "Afrique" sector (so called because it was defended by
French-colonial troops). It was a more active sector than their first; their
training would be more advanced and more costly in lives.

The "Oregon Forest" (as Horace Pippin called it) was a dark and
gloomy place. Its outlying edges had been crudely cleared by shell fire,
but the core of the forest was untouched. The weather was miserable.
Pippin remembered it as dark and rainy almost all the time. "We took to
them lonely, cooty, muddy trenches," water seeping everywhere, you
went to bed wet and woke up the same. At night "you could not see
your hands before you. . . . In the Day time it were Dark, even, we could
not see anyone comeing, but you could hear them." Clothes and hair
were infested with lice, known as "cooties" or "seam-squirrels," impossible to exterminate or escape. They were under what seemed like constant bombardment, which snapped big oak trees like "pipestems"
around them and interdicted the forest path up which their provisions
had to come. "All we could hear were the shells. They would burst all
the time." Suffering bombardment was harder, Pippin felt, than going
"over the top." Every time he left his dugout he found himself thinking,
"They will shore get us this time." The tension was unremitting. Every
bombardment might be the prelude to a heavy infantry attack. You had
not only to endure the pounding, but to be ready when it lifted to grab
your rifle and gas mask and man the trenches. The expected assault always impended, but never materialized. Still, if it had come, the regiment would have been prepared for it. "I never seen the time the 15th
N.Y. inf. were not ready. They were always ready. Ready to go and they
did go to the last man."

Pippin himself was achieving recognition by his comrades and superiors as a cool and competent soldier, able to handle serious responsibilities. He was promoted to corporal and given command of a squad. At twenty-nine he was older than most of the men and known as a good Christian. He was keeping a journal of his and Company K's experiences, illustrated with pages of sketches in black and colored pencil. His sketches of the Argonne are done in shades of gray and black, shadowy men crouched in a black bar of trench, heavy shattered trunks of trees in the place where "the Germans gave us plenty of gas." The war, and the life of the regiment, "brought out all of all the art in me."

It also brought out a bleaker gift, the ability to kill his fellow man. A sniper was picking men off from a post somewhere out in no-man's-land. Pippin judged he must be up a tree, because he could shoot down into the front-line trench. With a buddy Pippin studied the terrain, looked for any change that might give a clue to the enemy's movements. After a day or two, the displacement of a post they had been watching gave them the hint they wanted. In that area there was a low, brush-covered hill with a few trees on it where the sniper might be hiding. Rain forced Pippin to postpone his attack, "but at last I could began to see the out lines of the trees down the viley then my days work began and I were ready for it." Before first light Pippin slipped out of the trench, across the open ground, and into a thicket within short range of the trees. His buddy trained the glasses on the trees; he'd spot the sniper if Pippin started him. Waiting for mess call, the sniper's favored time with the men moving around, Pippin had begun to daydream a little when he heard the distinctive crack of the sniper's rifle and saw leaves move in a tree just a few yards away. He leveled his rifle and fired where he guessed the sniper was. Heard the rustle of his fall, but he didn't know for sure he'd hit him till he got back to the trench: his buddy had seen the sniper drop. Pippin went back to his sodden dugout and slept through supper and breakfast: utterly drained.[25]

The trenches here were not continuous. The French had fortified a series of strongpoints, fighting positions consisting of short entrenchments around a dugout artillery shelter, which they linked by a chain of small-unit "combat groups." It was easy to cut the wire and infiltrate this front, and the Germans had been active in raiding. On their first night in the lines Little positioned three platoon-size combat groups in front of his main line to ambush any raiding parties the Germans might send over. Random bursts of firing and illuminating flares kept them on edge, but they waited in vain. The following night, May 13–14, they set three more ambushes at different points in the line. But the Germans had scouted them well, and at 2:30 A.M. a large raiding party slipped through at the very spot where Little's platoons had waited the night before. The first alarm came with the firing of a flare and a cry of "Corporal of the Guard!" from Combat Groups 28 and 29—a pair of isolated posts fifty or sixty yards behind Little's ambush position. CG 28 was manned by a half-platoon, but the enemy had struck CG 29, which was held by only four soldiers and a corporal.

The five soldiers in CG 29 had been on duty for three days and nights without relief, without fresh water or rations, and three of them were down in the underground bunker, "dead asleep from hunger and tire." Two privates remained on watch. One was Henry Johnson, the slender redcap from Albany. The other was Needham Roberts, the seventeen-year-old ex-bellhop who had run off to join the regiment with his family's unpaid poll tax in his pants. Roberts had developed into a good soldier: Captain MacClinton used him as a runner between his two platoons on a night raid across no-man's-land, and he had done this responsible job under artillery fire.[26]

Roberts and Johnson both heard the sound of cutters at work on their wire. As soon as they fired their alarm flare, the German raiders (probably about twenty men) began hurling "potato masher" grenades into the position. Roberts and Johnson were immediately wounded by the explosions, the corporal and the two men off-watch were trapped in the dugout by falling earth and timbers. From the bottom of their trench Roberts saw heads pop up over the parapet, and he banged away with his Lebel rifle, hitting two men (he thought). The Germans fired down on him and kept throwing grenades, and Roberts was hit several times, by shrapnel and one explosive bullet in the shoulder. He was too hurt to stand, but propped himself up and flipped hand grenades to Johnson, who hurled them blindly over the parapet, hollering all the while for the "Corporal of the Guard!"

But the Germans were right on top of them, firing into the entrenchment. Johnson returned fire, revealing his position. German gunfire homed on him, one shot "clipped" his head, another stung his lip, another hurt his hand, and then he took a couple of bullets in the side and another that smashed his left foot. But he was going on adrenaline, temporarily immune to the pain. Roberts crawled toward the dugout, too bled-out to fight. Johnson shoved a new clip into his rifle—and it jammed. Somehow he had kept one of the clips for his old Springfield, and the American clip jammed the French rifle.

German soldiers jumped into the trench and attacked Johnson hand-to-hand. They had obviously been instructed to bring back a prisoner. Johnson saw "there was nothing to do but use my rifle as a club and jump into them." He "banged them on the dome and the side and everywhere I could land until the butt of my rifle busted. . . . They knocked me around considerable and whanged me on the head, but I always managed to get back on my feet." A raider armed with a Lüger, whom Johnson believed was an officer, rushed Johnson, who swung his rifle like a baseball bat and clubbed the man to the ground.

Freed of attackers, Johnson turned to help his buddy Roberts and saw that a pair of Germans were trying to drag him off as a prisoner. Like a number of other men in the regiment, Johnson carried a "bolo knife," a heavy double-edged weapon some nine inches long. Johnson dropped his empty rifle, drew his bolo, and jumped on one of the Germans, striking him with such force that the bolo was driven through the top of the man's skull. The second German fled. But the German with the Lüger had roused himself, and he blazed away at Johnson, hitting him a couple of times. Johnson dropped to his knees with a cry, pretending to be badly wounded. When the German came close to finish him off, Johnson sprang to his feet and rammed the bolo into the German's body, ripping upward until the man was "disemboweled." According to Johnson, the man cursed him in "good New York talk: 'That black——got me.'" By now the rest of the raiders were scrambling back through the gap in the American wire, carrying their wounded with them. Johnson heaved a few grenades to chase them along. The CG 28 relief came at daylight to find Johnson and Roberts seriously wounded and rescue the men trapped in the dugout. They counted five bodies (one an officer) around the post and tracked the German retreat by following the "pools of blood" left behind when the Germans dragged off their wounded and dead. Hayward later wrote to Mrs. Johnson that the two soldiers had inflicted as many as a dozen casualties: "We feel certain that one of the enemy was killed by rifle fire, two by your husband's bolo, and one by grenades thrown by Private Roberts, and several others grievously wounded." Press reports converted this to the killing or wounding of more than thirty Germans.

Captain Little rushed to see them as they were carried off to the hospital. On the way he learned some details of the action and found both Roberts and Johnson conscious and coherent, able to confirm what he had heard. Johnson told Little not to worry about him, as he'd "ben *shot* befo'." Little immediately recognized the fight as a superb opportunity to publicize the regiment's achievement. Some days after the fight he wrote an official report recommending Roberts and Johnson for the Croix de Guerre, the French army's award for valor. As he was finishing Colonel Hayward arrived with three prominent journalists he had persuaded to come visit his men. These were Lincoln Eyre of the *New York World*, Martin Green of the *Evening World*, and Irvin Cobb of the *Saturday Evening Post*. The correspondents were at first reluctant to follow Little out to the scene of the action. But after reading Little's report, Cobb exclaimed, "You win, Little! . . . You played your hand well." The three were impressed by the effort it took simply to get to the front, and overwhelmed by the evidence of carnage at CG 29. Cobb asked whether Johnson had been trained for trench warfare, and Little told him the men had received barely a week's training. " 'Well,' said Irvin Cobb, 'I've been thinking. It seems to me that the performance of that young man was truly remarkable. Why, if he had had the normal training that our men at home are getting today, I believe that by tomorrow night Henry would have been storming Potsdam!' "[27]

It took a week for the story to clear censorship and reach the States. On May 21 the *World* gave a front-page spread to Eyre's account of "The Battle of Henry Johnson." Thomas M. Johnson, who had visited the scene after Eyre, published an extended and colorful account in the *Sun*. The other New York papers and the national magazines reprinted or paraphrased Eyre's and Johnson's stories and spread the "Battle of Henry Johnson" across the country. Ham Fish's prophecy had been vindicated: the "Old Fifteenth" was for the moment the most famous regiment in the American army.

The news of Johnson's exploit reached the States at a strategic moment. It had been more than a year since the declaration of war, and only now were small numbers of American troops beginning to appear in combat. Action was restricted to minor skirmishes by units learning their trade in quiet sectors. The story of the first U.S. casualties, suffered by a unit training with the British, made martyr celebrities of two enlisted men from the Midwest. Thereafter AEF censorship forbade certified correspondents to identify specific units or the men in them. Thus reporters could not develop tales of personal heroism to characterize the first heavy engagements of American troops, at Seicheprey and Cantigny. But AEF censorship did not apply to American units in French service. The regiment's officers had taken full advantage of the situation and made the public aware of the regiment's increasingly active career through letters and interviews published in the *Age*, the *Crisis*, and some New York dailies.[28]

All of that preparation bore fruit on May 21, when the "Battle of Henry Johnson" hit the front pages of nearly every New York daily. Only Hearst's *American* refused to cover the story—a reflection of its publisher's strong commitment to color-line racism. Eyre's story in the *World* and Johnson's in the *Sun* provided a blow-by-blow account of the way Johnson dispatched German after German, despite his wounds. Eyre noted that Roberts and Johnson were not draftees: "They were recruited voluntarily a year before we declared war, yet they [deleted by censor] to go into action." The deleted phrase would have criticized the army for its reluctance to allow these eager volunteers to get into combat. The *Herald* backed its version with a front-page line-cut captioned "Two First-Class Americans," which showed Henry Johnson clutching his bolo on a heap of dead Germans. The staid and (where Negroes were concerned) skeptical *Times* led with a smaller item on page 6, quoting the commander of the AEF as authority for believing that Negro troops in an unspecified action had offered "a notable instance of bravery and devotion." But in an editorial on May 22 the *Times* joined the cheering for "Privates Bill and Needham." The editorial began with a quote from Mrs. Henry Johnson (who called her husband Bill): "Bill ain't big, nor nothin' like that . . . but oh, boy, he can go some." Then followed an acknowledgment that the "tepid enthusiasm" Whites had shown when the 15th New York was created was now more than vindicated: "It was an excellent thing, after all," to have organized a Negro Guard regiment. Colonel Hayward was quoted, declaring his troops were all "clean, brave men, fearing nothing." The editorial concluded with a recital of the martial deeds of earlier Negro regiments as an indication of the valor of Negroes as a race. The *Literary Digest*, which had been a leader in shaping pro-war opinion since 1915, headlined their reprint of Eyre's story on Henry Johnson: "Bush Germans Better Watch that Chocolate Front." Johnson became an important symbol for both military recruitment and the Liberty Loan campaign. An advertisement posted in New York's trolley cars admonished riders, "Sgt. Johnson licked a dozen Germans. How many Victory Stamps have you licked today?"

These stories enlarged the little outpost skirmish to legendary proportions. As legend, the tale of Black heroism was available to serve larger ideological purposes. At a meeting held at the Harlem Casino to "Honor Negro War Heroes," Mrs. Henry Johnson and the parents of Needham Roberts received the ultimate accolade: a letter from Theodore Roosevelt (invited, but unable to attend) declaring that the two Negroes "have shown themselves to be of the heroic type." The phrasing is significant: by "type," Roosevelt means something like "genus." The Battle of Henry Johnson is not merely an anecdote of valor, but proof that Negroes as a race can produce individuals capable of meeting the Strenuous Life standard and reproducing their own *heroic* character. In a letter to Johnson's wife, written shortly after the fight and later published, Colonel Hayward makes a little parable of antihyphenism out of Johnson's killing of the German who cursed him in English. The curse proves that

> he was undoubtedly one of the so-called German-Americans who came to our country, not to become a good citizen, but to partake of its plenty and bounty and then return to fight for the Kaiser and help enslave the world.

Johnson's celebrity also lent itself to baser uses. A confidence man was able to bilk a Brooklyn AME congregation of $31 by pretending to be the hero of the hour.[29]

The African-American press was eager to read the story as evidence of racial valor, and as a symbol of their successful fulfillment of their part of the social bargain. With the award of "the Two War Crosses," said the *Age*, "the Negro has vindicated his character as a fighting man." It quoted the praise of Johnson's fight in Southern newspapers as proof that even enemies of the race were now on the way to being convinced. But the Black press also called attention to the fact that the violent oppression and abuse of Negroes had not been diminished by this evidence, but seemed actually to have grown worse. James Weldon Johnson wrote a column contrasting two headlines that a New York paper had juxtaposed without comment: "Two Negroes Whip 24 Germans" and "Mob Lynches Negro and His Wife." The lynching referred to was one of the most atrocious in the long catalogue of Jim Crow horrors. A White farmer in Valdosta, Georgia, was killed by a gunshot fired into his home. His wife accused a Black man named Sidney Johnson of the crime, grounds unspecified. A mob went looking for Johnson, and when they failed to find him took revenge by killing several Black men chosen at random. Among these was Haynes Turner, whose wife, Mary, was eight months pregnant. Mary Turner protested vehemently and threatened to take the matter to law. The sheriff put her in protective custody, then turned her over to a mob that stripped her, hung her by her ankles, soaked her with gasoline, and set her ablaze. While she was still alive and screaming, a White man split her belly with his knife; the near-term baby fell to the ground, uttered a cry, and was stomped to death. Women and children were among the large crowd. The *Atlanta Constitution* explained that Mrs. Turner had "made unwise re-marks" and "the people were angered by . . . her attitude." The Turner lynching was one of sixty-three committed that year.

Initially none of the White papers in New York remarked on the coin-cidence of the Turner lynching and the Battle of Henry Johnson. But as the story sank in, and as the all-Black 92nd Division prepared to enter the fighting, some papers and magazines began to point up the contra-diction between "the world made safe for democracy" and the mistreat-ment of Black citizens. The *Outlook* came out strongly for the NAACP's antilynching statute and condemned Southern mobs as implicitly pro-German: the army's ranks are full of Henry Johnsons, and "it is treason to the country to do anything that will take the heart out of these men."[30]

DuBois used Johnson's victory and the press reaction as evidence that his acceptance of the social bargain had been a wise decision. The *Crisis* covered the Harlem meeting at which Roberts and Johnson were honored and reprinted a long interview from the *Times* with an unnamed Black lieutenant from the "Ole [Fifteenth]." The lieutenant explicitly affirms that he and his Negro soldiers are fighting to keep their part of the bargain:

> Now is our opportunity to prove what we can do. If we can't fight and die in this war just as bravely as white men, then we don't deserve equality with white men. . . . But if we can do things at the front; if we can make ourselves felt; if we can make America really proud of the Ole —th . . . then it will be the biggest possible step toward our equal-ization as citizens. The whole [regiment number censored] has the same spirit.

The lieutenant added that their taste of a "new equality" in their treatment by the French had increased their appetite for civil equality at home.

Both the *Age* and the *Crisis* measure the importance of the Battle of Henry Johnson by the way it registered on *Southern* opinion. Particular note was taken of a Richmond newspaper's use of Henry Johnson to rebuke a recent lynching, and the *Chattanooga Times's* assertion that "the Negro citizen is making golden opinions for himself."[31] If Southern Whites could be convinced of Negro equality, then the cause of civil rights was won. In light of that hope, perhaps the most significant contribution to the emerging legend of Henry Johnson and the "Old Fifteenth" was made by Irvin Cobb of the *Saturday Evening Post*.

Cobb was a popular and respected Southern writer, known for his wry depictions of small-town Southern life. One of his trademarks was the use of heavily stereotyped Negro characters, with distorted speech and ridiculous ways of reasoning. In "Hark! From the Tombs," published in the *Saturday Evening Post* in April 1917, he tells a tale of Negro hijinks in the big city, featuring members of a ludicrous fraternal order called "The Afro American Order of Supreme Kings of the Universe," who have goofy names like "Smooth Crumbaugh." Cobb's standing among literary Progressives was high, as attested by his being invited to join the Vigilantes.[32] Progressives of every political strain saw the "better classes" of the White South as the keys to any useful reform of race relations and Cobb was the perfect embodiment of that class.

Cobb went to France to cover the arrival of American troops and stayed through the beginning of the German summer offensives. He sent back a series of articles that were published in the *Saturday Evening Post* in the first nine months of 1918, and later collected in book form under the title *The Glory of the Coming* (1918). Hayward and Little knew that winning a man like Cobb to their cause would be a major victory on their "second front." They staged a band concert for him and a battalion drill, with everyone on his best behavior. That actually required some effort, because many of the enlisted men were familiar with Cobb's work and regarded it as damaging to the race. Some hoped he might change his mind if what he saw on the visit pleased him, and the band did its best to charm him. But most of the enlisted men considered him incorrigible and ignored or greeted him coldly. One man said, "Well, if he gets back alive . . . it will be because he's standing beside the colonel."[33]

Cobb was impressed by the order and discipline of the troops, but what made a convert of him was his tour of Henry Johnson's battlefield. The stages of that conversion can actually be followed through the series of articles that traced his tour from the port of entry to the front lines.

He begins with the presumption that ridiculing Negroes is a normal and natural expression of America's national personality. Young dough-boys become very solemn as they debark in France and sense "the responsibility intrusted to them as armed representatives of their own country's honor." However, once they become acclimated their characteristically American "irreverence" reasserts itself, directed upward against "things stately and traditional," and also downward against Negroes. Much of their humor involves the mockery of "a certain . . . Afro-American [type of] individuality." Cobb then tells a dialect joke currently making the rounds, in which a Negro soldier takes out a life insurance policy. When a comrade asks why he'd do such a thing when he has no one to leave the money to, the Negro says that the policy is to insure he doesn't get killed: "W'y, you pore ign'ant fool, does you s'pose w'en Gin'el Pershing finds out he's got a ten-thousand-dollar nigger in dis man's Army dat he's gwine take any chances on losin' all dat money by sendin' me up to do Front whar de trouble is?"[34]

Cobb's next stop on the way to the front brings him to a recently arrived Black regiment, probably the 371st Infantry, which was raised in the South and had White officers. Cobb treats them with the sort of genial ridicule he employed as a novelist. The Blacks speak a heavy dialect, are ignorant and credulous, vain about false distinctions—as in the case of the former Harlem elevator boy who calls himself an "indoor chauffeur." When the colonel asks them what they will do if the Germans attack, the man answers, we "may not stick by you but we'll . . . spread de word all over France 'at de Germans is comin'!" But having done his version of "feets don't fail me now," Cobb shows that war has transformed the Negro as well. Neither the "indoor chauffeur" nor any of "black and brown mates showed the white feather or the yellow streak. . . . Those to whom the test came stayed and fought, and it was the Germans who went away."[35]

Farther up the road Cobb meets a different kind of Negro, the Northern volunteers of the 369th. They are (to Cobb's eye) lighter-skinned than the Southern Blacks, suggesting they had more White "blood." They were city men not rural folk, they "wore their uniforms with a smartened pride . . . were jaunty and alert and prompt in their movements" and eager for a "whack at the foe." In style and manner they are closer to the White soldiers first seen at the landing dock than to their Southern race-fellows back up the road. Of course, they are still amusing to Cobb, who sees his visit as "two days of a superior variety of continuous blackface vaudeville."

But when Cobb is taken to the scene of Henry Johnson's fight, hears the tale and sees the evidence of his valor, and is assured by Hayward that all his troops are "like that buddy with the bolo," Cobb reconsiders the prejudices he has always held, even regrets the language used to voice them:

> I am of the opinion—and I make the assertion with all the better grace, I think, seeing that I am a Southerner with all of the Southerner's inherited and acquired prejudices . . . that as a result of what our black soldiers are going to do . . . a word that has been uttered billions of times in our country, sometimes in derision, sometimes in hate, sometimes in all kindliness—but which I am sure never fell on black ears but it left behind a sting for the heart—is going to have a new meaning for us, South and North too, and that hereafter n-i-g-g-e-r will be merely another way of spelling the word American.

Cobb then reads a soldier's letter that praises the French for ignoring the "colour-line business. They treat us so good the only time I ever knows I'm coloured is when I looks in the glass." But instead of rebuking the thought he agrees, "Yes, most assuredly n-i-g-g-e-r is going to have a different meaning when this war ends."[36]

The transformation of Cobb's view of Negroes was impressive testimony to the validity of the social bargain DuBois and the Harlem leadership had accepted. He had cut straight to the heart of American racial thinking by acknowledging that *nigger* was the word that expressed most people's perception of Negroes or Colored People. The War Department had tried in vain to "Ban . . . the Use of 'Nigger' and 'Coon' in [the] United States Army," as it had tried to ban "dago" and "wop." "Nigger": that word spoken or merely thought every time a White person looked at a Black, either in derision, in hate, or in a contemptuous kindliness; that word which, however used, left a sting in the heart. If the war was to transform Americans' understanding of who "the Negro" was, all of the connotations and implications, all of the symbolized history of abjection contained in the word *nigger* would have to be utterly purged.

The terms of the social bargain specified that they be purged in blood, and Henry Johnson had paid the first installment.[37]

But the Henry Johnson story played into a culture that presumed that Blacks were socially inadequate until proven otherwise. That presumption even affected the way in which the *Crisis* responded to the battle. On the same page of the August 1918 issue that reprinted the letter from the lieutenant of the Old Fifteenth, DuBois published a letter from Isobel Field—a White Progressive now, like Irvin Cobb, associated with the Vigilantes—which describes the regiment's success in an odd and disturbing way. First she uses the proven valor of the Negro regiment to denigrate the Americanism of immigrant soldiers, echoing Hayward's letter to Mrs. Johnson and the theme James Weldon Johnson had sounded during the Hillquit campaign: "When this war broke out the nation was stunned to find itself split asunder by a number of hyphens; but the Negro stood together with the original stocks that landed at Plymouth Rock and Jamestown."

Field also echoes Cobb's notion that the success of the 15th has effected a transformation in the standard "nigger" stereotype, but in language that forcibly reiterates that stereotype. She describes the victory of the 15th New York as the death knell of a figure she calls "Mistah Johnston, the Darktown Coon," a characteristic type of Negro who loves vain display and prefers Saturday night hoopla to doing the work of the world. Johnson's fight has replaced him with a "young warrior . . . trained and alert." The magazine's juxtaposition of the Black lieutenant's interview with Field's letter suggests that DuBois accepts this "death" as fulfillment of the lieutenant's dream. But in Field's symbolism, it is not the White stereotype of "niggers" that has died; rather, it is the Darktown Coon, who represents for her the ridiculous aspect of Negro character.[38]

That same reflex of ridicule compromises the terms of praise lavished on Henry Johnson and the 369th Infantry. Lincoln Eyre's original story, printed in the *World* and reprinted in other dailies and in *Literary Digest,* refers to Johnson and Roberts as a couple of "coffee creams"—a comic way of referring to their color, suggesting they are not full-blooded Negroes. (*Literary Digest* had run a story in September 1917, "Evolution of a Superior Race," suggesting that mulattoes were superior to and distinct from Negroes, and might well be qualified for full citizenship.) Reporter Thomas Johnson also suggested that Henry Johnson appeared to be a "mulatto," but a reporter who saw him at the regiment's homecoming parade found him "blacker than most." The blackness of the first African-American war hero seemed to depend upon the eye and the ideological agenda of the White beholder. Eyre's account of Johnson's and Roberts's knife fight ends with his portrayal of another soldier in the regiment, in terms suggestive of an African "savage": "a little chap, his ebony skin beaded with sweat," honing his bolo knife and testing the blade on his tongue, all the while "croon[ing] a low-pitched chant in a language all his own."[39]

The same *New York Times* editorial that praised "Bill and Needham" and the military record of the Negro also observed in passing that Henry Johnson had grabbed his bolo knife because it was "handier than a razor"—the razor being the weapon of choice classically attributed to Blacks in minstrel shows. "Come out tonight," Mr. Bones invites his fellow darkies, " 'cause there's gonna be a fight, / There'll be razors flying through the air." The point was reiterated in a brief story highlighted by a "box" on page 1, "American Colored Troops Excel at Killing Germans." No event is referred to. The point of the "box" is the bald assertion that Negro troops prefer to close with the bayonet, because of their "partiality for the

TWO FIRST CLASS AMERICANS!

This cartoon, with the above title, was drawn by Mr. W. A. Rogers, the famous cartoonist of the New York Herald, in celebration of the exploit of Henry Johnson and Needham Roberts, the first two American soldiers to win the Croix de Guerre.— Copyright, 1918, by New York Herald Co.

razor." In an editorial cartoon a Black soldier holding a razor "high-jumps" into a trench and asks a terrified Hun, "Hair cut or shave[?]"[40]

The terms in which Henry Johnson's heroism was praised suggested that the African-American as hero retained the essential qualities of the Negro as "nigger." The line-cut on the front page of the *New York Herald*, designed to emphasize and glorify the initial account of "The Battle of Henry Johnson," captured the idea perfectly. Henry Johnson stands ankle-deep among the dead, a blood-dripping knife in his hand. His frowning mouth is white in his Black face—he is at one and the same time a "first-class American" hero and a blackface minstrel.[41]

With due respect to Irvin Cobb's good intentions, there was no way to read "nigger" as just another way to spell "American." The essence of the term was its designation of a being without dignity or honor, an always appropriate object of contempt and ridicule. In the *Ziegfield Follies* that summer Eddie Cantor sang in blackface "When the Boys from Dixie Eat Melon on the Rhine," about the great day "when they play that Memphis blues / They will use a lot of shoes / And fill them full of Darky gin / They'll rag their way right to Berlin." But the best-loved song about Negro troops was "Mammy's Chocolate Soldier":

> Come lay your kinkey head on Mammy's shoulder,
> Don't you cry you're Mammy's chocolate soldier!
> And a soldier can't be crying, even though he thinks he's dying,
> ... Though your skin is dark as night,
> I know your little pickaninny heart is white."[42]

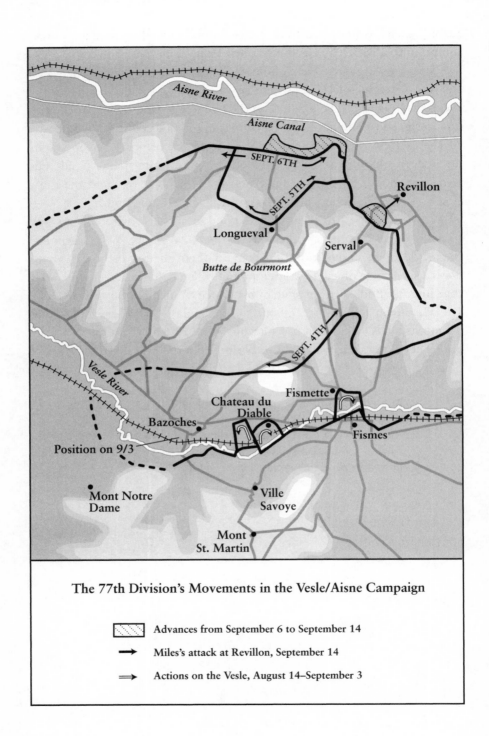

The 77th Division's Movements in the Vesle/Aisne Campaign

Advances from September 6 to September 14

Miles's attack at Revillon, September 14

Actions on the Vesle, August 14–September 3

6

The Slamming of Great Doors: Entering the
World of Combat, May–September 1918

Where do we go from here, boys, where do we go from here?
Anywhere from Harlem to a Jersey City pier . . .
Oh joy! Oh boy! Where do we go from here?

—*Howard Johnson and Percy Wenrich,*
"Where Do We Go from Here?" (1917)

After his visit to the 369th Irvin Cobb traveled north to visit American troops training with the British in Flanders and Picardy. He was particularly interested in the newly arrived 77th Division, the "Melting Pot" boys from New York. Cobb believed the war was ultimately about "the making-over of nations," and through it the United States was becoming, for the first time, a single nation and people. He had already endorsed the idea that "n-i-g-g-e-r" might be just another way to spell "American." Now he would see if war was making Americans out of Jewish tailors, Italian pushcart peddlers, and Chinese coolies.

Cobb was impressed. Military training had actually transformed the physical nature of the immigrants, the shape and stance of their bodies, and thereby altered the "racial" character those bodies carried:

I saw them when they first landed at Camp Upton, furtive, frightened, slow-footed, slack-shouldered, underfed, apprehensive—a huddle of unhappy aliens, speaking in alien tongues, and knowing little of the cause for which they must fight, and possibly caring less. I saw them again three months later. . . . The stoop was beginning to come out of their spines, the shamble out of their gait. They had learned to hold their heads up; had learned to look every man in the eye and tell him to go elsewhere, with a capital H.

Where once they had been a disintegrative presence in the social body, they were now imbued with an informed acceptance of law and social order.

> They knew now that discipline was not punishment, and that the salute was not a mark of servility, but evidence of mutual self-respect between officer and man. They wore their uniforms with pride. The flag meant something to them and the war meant something to them. Three short, hard months of training had transformed them from a rabble into soldier stuff; from a street mob into the makings of an army; from strangers into Americans. . . . For swagger, for smartness in the drill, for cockiness in the billet, for good-humor on the march, and for dash and spunk and deviltry in the fighting into which just lately they have been sent, our Army can show no better and no more gallant warriors.[1]

Cobb was not mistaken about their morale. Their experience of army life had so far been positive. The indoctrination to which they had been subjected made them aware, in many cases for the first time, of the historical myths and political ideologies of the American nation. As their training taught them new skills—above all, the use of force—they associated their new awareness of nationality with personal empowerment. New hopes and ambitions were awakened. For some, aspiration was overtly social or political: the desire to prove themselves and their people worthy of Americanization or the patriotic commitment to the government's war aims. For others, it was more personal: the desire to "get along" or even "get ahead" in the army, to take advantage of its promise to reward merit with promotion. Letters from home and articles in the newspapers reinforced the sense that their personal achievements served the vital interests of the impoverished or embattled home communities from which they came.

They had been disappointed that their embarkation for France (at the end of March 1918) had to be made in secret—and dealt with the disappointment by leaking word to family and friends. So when they arrived in the gray predawn at the Long Island City ferry slip there were crowds on hand, anxiously scanning the ranks and calling out last farewells. The ferryboats shuttled them under the arch of Brooklyn Bridge to the transports that waited at the Battery docks. A last look around the harbor at the Statue of Liberty and the Wall Street towers, then the men were sent belowdecks. Few of them would see the windows of lower Manhattan "alive with fluttering handkerchiefs" as the ships got under way, but they could all hear the whistles and hoots as the ships in the harbor saluted them. From this moment the division would only be visible to its home folks in brief flashes that slipped through the deliberate obscurity of army censorship.

Officers were permitted to stay on deck, and Lieutenant Wardlaw Miles would remember how "high overhead in the sun of early spring the Statue of Liberty looked down on the ships carrying thousands of men each of whose equipment bore her stamped image," gold in a blue field, the division's badge. Among those thousands "so widely differing in race, fortune, and desires" were many for whom the first sight of that statue had marked their arrival in the New World. For thousands of those thousands it would be the last they saw of America.

Lieutenant Miles and his brother officers were educated men whose commitment to American war aims was principled and well informed. As "Sons of Roosevelt" they also made a mystique of war, seeing in it not merely "the health of the state," but the ultimate expression and vindication of a people's health, its capacity for the Strenuous Life. Miles had been moved by William James's vision of life as a theater for heroism and by his call for a "moral equivalent of war" to transform modern society: "something heroic that will speak to men as war does, and yet will be as compatible with their spiritual selves as war has proved itself to be incompatible." But Miles believed with Roosevelt that "aggressive fighting for the right is the noblest sport the world affords." What Miles's spiritual self desired was "the Real Thing," and his prayer was, "May I play a man's part in it."[2]

The prayer was sincere, but the Progressive vision of war was mistaken. War is not a noble sport, a level playing field for the exercise of intelligent purpose, but a pit in which cross-purposes clash. Force in war, no matter how massive and well directed, is always deflected and deranged by counterforce, by the friction of movement across the ground, by the weariness of men and the defects of equipment. Between purpose and execution falls the horror and confusion of battle, the lag between what the front line sees and what headquarters knows, the difference between map and terrain, ignorance and blind chance, the inertia of men and things, sudden unexpected ruptures of morale, the seizure of unforeseen opportunity by men beyond reach of their commanders.

Combat soldiers learn this truth before statesmen and remember the lesson longer. Unlike the men in Washington, or even the generals at AEF headquarters in Chaumont, the front-line troops had to live and die by the mismatch between what orders say and what combat requires, between imagined purposes and the actual work of combat. Whatever intentions they began with, once they entered the zone of combat their sense of purpose—indeed, their whole personality—was subjected to an immediate horrible persistent friction. The experience of combat would change them, "Americanize" them, in ways not anticipated by *The Home Reading Course for Citizen Soldiers*. They would become naturalized citizens of the world of infantry combat, "amalgamated" (to use Commons's word) to the community of their comrades, devotees of a loyalty more specific and imperative and all-embracing than "100% Americanism." They would learn to rely upon their own experience and understanding of events, instead of deferring to the nostrums with which they had been indoctrinated. Those who survived would have an unshakable belief that their claim of American identity was proved beyond question and would hold to that belief despite the wave of reactionary ethnic and race prejudice that would greet them on their return.[3]

"Good Morning, Mister Zip-Zip-Zip": The 77th Division Learns Its Trade, April–August 1918

> We come from ev'ry quarter, from North, South, East and West,
> To clear the way to freedom for the land we love the best.
> We've left our occupations and homes, so far and dear,
> But when the going's rather rough we raise this song of cheer:
> Good morning, Mister Zip-Zip-Zip,
> With your hair cut just as short as mine,
> Good morning, Mister Zip-Zip-Zip,
> You're surely looking fine.

It took more than a month to convoy the several elements of the division "over there." At full strength the 77th would muster some 27,000 officers and men, distributed among four infantry regiments, two machine-gun battalions, a field artillery brigade, and a supply train. Once it got to France it would also deploy a variety of attached artillery units and an airplane squadron. Infantry and machine gunners were organized in two brigades, which at 6,500 men each contained most of the division's strength. The 153rd Brigade consisted of the 305th and 306th Infantry and the 305th Machine Gun Battalion; the 307th and 308th Infantry and the 306th Machine Gun Battalion composed the 154th Brigade. In action these units might be joined by elements of the 302nd Trench Mortar Battery, and would be supported by two batteries of French 75-mm guns and a battery of 155-mm cannons of the Field Artillery Brigade.[4]

The infantry and machine-gun battalions arrived by various routes at Camp de Souge in northern France. A kind of giddy excitement at being off the transports and in the country of war made it seem as if they were "entering a circus. 'The greatest show on earth.' . . . a minor Coney Island." The walls of the town were adorned with "flaring pictures of American movie stars [with] captions in French." The strangeness of their circumstances was disconcerting. They had gone from toast of the town in New York to a set of rubes and rookies in France.

They took comfort in the fact that there were others still more ludicrously out of place. Their camp was pitched "near the segregation barracks of the Chinese coolies," imported by the British and French to do heavy labor on the docks. (Black conscripts would do the same work for the Americans.) At first the coolies "seemed merely Chinamen," the kind one poked fun at on any given day in Manhattan, "who stole other people's clothes, and with whom it was possible to make strange deals for worthless trinkets." But soon they became "the chief source of amusement in the camp . . . the great clown department of [the] circus" that was Camp de Souge. While the troops labored and drilled under discipline, they might see "one of these men, with a shovel in one hand, an umbrella in the other, trying to make a half-hour's job last all day." The contrast reminded them—at least those who were not themselves Chinese-American—of their racial and cultural superiority. Their "coolie" jokes repeated the rough play with ethnic stereotypes that had characterized their Camp Upton theatricals. The big laugh in Company A was that two German-American (a.k.a. "Dutch") privates, Herzog and Eppler, recognized "their brothers" among the coolies: a joke that made light of all the war propaganda that identified Germans with the "Huns" who had swept out of Asia to destroy Roman civilization. But racial mockery rationalized more abusive forms of play:

The only time [the coolies] moved faster than a shuffling walk was when one of the many trucks whizzed through camp. Then it was the delight of the driver not to let them off, but to speed up while a very much frightened Chinese flapped from the tail-gate like an old shirt. . . . [they] scratched and screamed for a place in a truck.[5]

As soon as it was assembled the division was ordered to the British front in Flanders. This was the area that had been assaulted in the first two German offensives of the spring, the second of which had just been stopped, and rumors of their movement reached the press just as the Germans opened their third offensive on the French front along the Chemin des Dames. Some New York papers reported the 77th was being thrown into a breach at the critical moment. In fact, they were going to a quiet sector to learn the ins and outs of trench warfare.[6]

They entrained in box cars marked "*Hommes 40—Chevaux 8,*" a disconcerting equation of men with livestock. When the cars were fully loaded some joker would tell them to close up and make room for the horses. They exchanged the Springfields on which they had trained for British Enfield rifles, then marched to the front through little Flemish villages, noticing the "foreign" architecture, the red roofs of the small houses, and the quaint peasant costumes. Only after an interval did they realize that nearly all those who turned out to watch them pass were old men, women, and children. It was a peculiar feature of the Great War that behind the front, often quite close to the lines, the towns and countryside were untouched by violence. Poplar-lined roads drew them past "spring blossoms, peaceful fields of green" toward the "far-off, muffled, ominous sound like the slamming of great doors" that spoke of the front, "The Thing Itself."

Once in the zone of combat the landscape turned hellish. The stabilization of the trench lines from 1914 to the spring of 1918 had confined destruction to a wide belt of land between the Allied trenches and the German fallback positions on the "Hindenburg Line." Within that zone the destruction was absolute and catastrophic. Continual artillery and gas bombardment had blistered the vegetation and reduced forests to stumps. In the no-man's-land between the lines the topsoil had been blasted off, and the undersoil was a moonscape boiled and cratered with overlapping shell holes.

The British 39th Division had been badly shot up in the recent offensives. They were glad to be in a quiet sector and to see fresh American troops preparing to take their place in line. A British observer found the Americans had an "exceptionally high level of intelligence among the rank and file," were "less repressed by discipline," and "more original" in expressing themselves than the British. The officers hit it off immediately, "fraternized in the actual meaning of the word." They were men from essentially the same social class, educated on similar lines.[7]

The doughboys (with the exception of the Irish) got along with their British counterparts. They griped about English rifles and grenades and British rations that, among other unwanted variations, featured tea instead of coffee. They felt aggrieved not to be allowed the Tommies' daily tot of rum—temperance enthusiasts were strong in the Committee on Training Camp Activities (CTCA) and were trying to sell the whole country on Prohibition. They learned the basics of trench warfare, not just the tactics but the facts of life: how to stave off trench foot (or acquire it as a ticket off the line), how to police your shirt and trouser seams for "cooties." They learned the first verses of the soldiers' anthem:

> Mademoiselle from Armentières, parley-voo!
> Mademoiselle from Armentières, parley-voo!
> Mademoiselle from Armentières,
> She hasn't been fucked in forty years,
> Hinky dinky parley-voo![8]

They began adding their own improvisations to the interminable sequence of verses:

> Mademoiselle from Orléans, parley-voo!
> Mademoiselle from Orléans, parley-voo!
> Mademoiselle from Orléans,
> She made me sell my Liberty Bonds.
> Hinky dinky parley-voo!

American platoons went into line along with British units, to learn by watching and doing. German snipers taught them to keep their heads down.

> Good morning, Mister Zip-Zip-Zip,
> With your hair cut just as short as mine . . .

Particular emphasis was placed on training officers and noncoms so they in turn could train their men. Small groups of Americans were attached to British units for outposts and raids across no-man's-land. Captain Mills proved particularly skilled at reconaissance and earned the highest praise from the commander of the British battalion to which he was attached. Sergeant Kaplan, the ex-marine boxing champ, liked the action so much he dodged orders returning him to his unit in the rear. Technically he was AWOL, but no one wanted to rebuke such displays of fighting spirit. Although patrols were dangerous, the only fatalities were Privates Belen and Schiesser, killed in one of the desultory bombardments with which the Germans harassed this front. They were the first National Army casualties of the war and so a source of honor to the 308th.

> Ashes to ashes, and dust to dust,
> If the Camels don't get you, the Fatimas must,
> Good morning, Mister Zip-Zip-Zip,
> With your hair cut just as short as
> With your hair cut just as short as
> With your hair cut just as short as mine.

At the beginning of June, with the new German offensive in the Champagne bearing down on the Marne, they were ordered to the Lorraine front, a quiet sector west of Verdun, for further tutelage by the French 61st Division. They exchanged their Enfields for Springfields, British rations for "honest American white bread, beef, bacon, and potatoes," and boarded another set of *Hommes 40—Chevaux 8* boxcars. Although there were fewer cultural affinities, the men got along better with the French than with the British. The French put less emphasis on spit-and-polish, were less formal in manner at all ranks, which harmonized with the democratic manners of the slightly militarized civilians of the 77th.[9]

Baccarat was a more active sector than Flanders. The terrain had been fought over in 1914; the towns behind the front were ruined by shell fire. Instead of poplar-lined avenues, the 308th marched up a road "camouflaged with dirty yellow cloth" to shield it from bombardment. They were immediately sent to relieve units of the Rainbow Division, which had completed training and was going into the fighting in Champagne. On the night of June 21 the 308th, marching in single file up the road, passed the men of New York's own Fighting 69th (now the 165th Infantry) coming

down. Father Duffy of the 69th remembered it as "Old Home Day," the
New Yorkers greeting each other, "Anybody here from Greenwich Village? . . . Any of you guys from Tremont?" One youngster in the 308th
hollered for his brother in the 69th and the two broke ranks to grab and
swear at each other "for lack of other words" to express themselves.
There was a virtuoso display of New York attitude. The veterans needled
the rookies, "sometimes good-humored, sometimes with a sting in it":
"Look out for the Heinies or you'll be eating sauerkraut." The rookies
answered they were "going up to finish the job that you fellows couldn't
do." The Guardsmen sneered that they "was over here killin' Dutchmen
before they pulled your names out of the hat." The draftees replied that
at least they did not have to "get drunk to join the army." From time to
time each column would start singing, "East Side, West Side, all around
the town . . ."

By midnight the three battalions of the 308th had effected the exchange of positions, and occupied their own section of a front line trench
sector. Lieutenant Miles was satisfied: "At last! *This* is the Real Thing."[10]

Their positions here were similar to those the 369th had occupied at
the time of the "Battle of Henry Johnson." Rather than a continuous line
of entrenchments, they manned a system of strongpoints connected by
communication trenches or gullies giving cover from gunfire. Half of the
sector was held by the two regiments of the 154th Brigade, the 308th and
307th, each with one battalion in line, one in support, one in reserve.
Headquarters for the front-line battalion of the 308th were established in
the Pink Chateau, a two-story stucco residence whose brilliant facade
had never been marred by shot. Rumor had it that the Kaiser had ordered
it spared from some obscure motive of honor or romance. The battalion
was linked by wire to the company command posts, and each "CP" communicated with two forward positions called *Points d'Appui*, or PAs,
which formed the main line of resistance. Forward of these were the CGs,
a series of miniature strongpoints that served as outposts, raiding bases,
and a first line of defense. Since they were still under tutelage, American
units shared the position with French units. In the CPs and PAs, American
and French platoons were mixed, and command shared with the Americans as junior partners. In the outer line of CGs French units alternated
with Americans. In the 308th's sector two American platoons held the
first two CGs, French platoons the next two, and so on. The French were
given charge of the most vulnerable position, on the far right.[11]

For two days the sector was quiet except for the odd shell. But the Germans were aware that a new, presumably raw American division was in the lines, and they planned a heavy local attack to take advantage. The 35th *Landwehr* (the German equivalent of a National Guard division) was reinforced with a battalion of specially trained storm troopers, a flamethrower unit, and six aircraft. Those odd shells that had been dropping in the lines were ranging shots, by which the Germans registered their guns. At 3 A.M. on June 24 they hit the 154th Brigade with a heavy barrage of high explosive and gas, the shells pouring in all at once without prelude, everything from "light stuff" up to heavy 155-mm cannons. Every third shell contained mustard gas, which seared and blistered exposed skin, eyes, the mucous membranes of nose and throat. The Pink Chateau was blasted by five direct hits (so much for the Kaiser's protection). Blankets over the doors were supposed to shield the telephonists in the cellar from gas, but the constant coming and going compromised that protection and the cellar soon reeked of corrosive fumes. The half-wrecked village of Badonviller, at the center of the forward battalion's position, was reduced to shattered walls and piles of smoking debris stained with puddles of mustard gas. The bombardment soon isolated battalion command, cutting the wires to the advanced posts and those connecting to regiment and brigade. Signalmen went out into the storm to patch the lines, but the task was impossible. Runners reported the left of the line secure. In the center the Machine Gun Company and Company B had been heavily gassed. The men would remember how the gas shells came in with "a sort of gurgling and hissing in flight, . . . exploding with a softer detonation than high explosives." American gas discipline actually proved better than that of their French tutors. They were sickened, but able to hold.

But reports from the right were terrifying. A breathless runner informed battalion that C Company was wiped out: "Trenches all gone. Men all gone. Everything all gone."

The report was just short of the truth. The Germans had followed up the barrage with a heavy assault by infantry and broke into the French-American positions in strength. The French platoons holding the GC at the extreme right of the line were indeed wiped out. The American platoon to their left, led by Lieutenant John Flood, had been hit hard by the artillery and by aerial bombs dropped by circling German aircraft. One corner of Flood's position was hit by a 250-pound bomb that blew "a gaping shell crater twelve feet across and fifteen feet deep." Flood's platoon considered itself a crack outfit, the best drilled in the 308th. Under bombardment they stayed hunkered in their dugout as they had been taught. When the barrage lifted Flood gave the word and they jumped to their firing positions in the trench. There were about fifty of them, armed with rifles, Chauchat auto-rifles, and grenades. They still wore their gas masks—a mistake, but not their fault since they were following a routine laid down by the French. Despite that handicap they met the German infantry assault with heavy and accurate fire to the front.

Combat brings tunnel vision, especially to raw troops, an extreme focus on what is immediately in front, the targets, the need to keep firing. While the first wave of Germans went to ground in front of the platoon, others worked around the flanks of the strongpoint. Flood spotted the move, was picking his way through the broken trenches out to the flank with a sergeant and his orderly when a party of Germans appeared at a turn in the trench. Flood fired his pistol twice, hit two men, then ducked behind the turn as the Germans hurled a flurry of potato-masher grenades. One exploded between Flood's feet and put him "out of it." The sergeant and orderly were hit at the same time. Racco Rocco, "a young Italian who could hardly speak a word of English," tried to rescue them but was mortally wounded by another well-thrown grenade.

Deprived of their commanders, the platoon fought through the ruins of the strongpoint, rifles against grenades, even some hand-to-hand fighting with bayonets (as their comrades discovered next day when they looked things over). In the end the position fell, half the platoon killed or wounded, twenty men taken prisoner.

The platoon to the left of Flood's was commanded by former English professor Wardlaw Miles. Since their position threatened the flank of the Germans attacking Flood's platoon, Miles's post was hit with an especially heavy bombardment of high explosives and gas that killed or wounded forty of his fifty men. But he was clear-headed enough to mark the attack on Flood and to anticipate an attack on his own position from the right. He shifted his men's fire to check that threat; and as the Germans dropped another barrage to cover their withdrawal "walked along the parapet . . . encouraging his men by his coolness and bravery."

Although the 308th suffered a defeat and heavy losses, the Badonviller raid did not lower morale. The men believed they had proved their courage under bombardment and attack. Flood's platoon had been outnumbered by perhaps as many as three to one; had stood up to the bombardment and fought to the last, taking a heavy toll of the enemy. Miles's platoon had held its ground, and his display of courage would earn him a Distinguished Service Cross and promotion to captain. When all the details of Flood's fight became known, he too would receive the DSC. When Miles thought about the action he decided:

> No better platoon than Lieutenant Flood's could have been picked on which to try the effect of battle upon our conscript army. It was about the most cosmopolitan platoon of the most cosmopolitan company that came out of the melting pot of New York. It comprised Irish, Italians, East Side Jews, Russians, Scandinavians, and even a few native Americans, but they all acted as one would wish Americans to act in such a crisis.

That was exactly what the Melting Pot Division had come over to prove.

Still, not all officers were as ready as Miles to see their men as *Americans*. Tiebout, for one, was still amused and contemptuous of his Italian and Jewish soldiers, and made invidious comparisons between them and the Irish. He found the latter "staunch" and gallant in combat, which they seemed to enjoy, while the Jews and Italians kept making comical errors and seemed not to understand what was happening on the battlefield. During that first severe bombardment, "one swarthy little Italian, horrified and indignant," complained to a noncom, "Gee, Corp, dey shoota da redda hot bullets!" In contrast, when Corporal Kelly was wounded "he still wore his Irish smile" and was cool enough to dictate a farewell note to his dad: "Somewhere in France. To Mr. Kelly of Buffalo. Died Happy. Dennis." Then after a hearty laugh with the boys (as Tiebout remembered it), he was carried off to hospital where he died.[12]

For most of June the Baccarat justified its reputation as a "quiet" sector. The rookies adapted to life in the trenches, practiced raiding and patrolling. They became skilled in the use of machine guns and weapons developed for fighting in the confined and bunkered space of the trenches, especially the claptrap Chauchat auto-rifle and grenades or "bombs." Their officers worked to learn the difficult technique of coordinating artillery and mortars with infantry attack, without which successful offensive action was nearly impossible. This was the greatest weakness of the newly modernized American army, and until the method was perfected the AEF would suffer thousands of unnecessary casualties.

There were no more major attacks, but the division suffered a continual drain of men, some lost to snipers, shell fire and gas, raiding parties, more to the diseases and accidents of trench life. The trenches were chronically wet and vermin-ridden, and men who served in them for any length of time suffered from fleas and lice and the illnesses they carried. Periodic delousing baths proved useless. Trenches and foxholes (or funk holes, as they were called) acted as catch basins, and soldiers who spent long spells in them developed "trench foot" or "immersion foot": painful swelling and a liability to sores and infection, which could (if untreated) lead to gangrene and amputation. Diarrhea was chronic from a variety of causes, ranging from infection to unsanitary food preparation. It was a life of extreme monotony and discomfort pervaded by constant anxiety, an unending watchful waiting for the sudden eruption of murderous violence.

Some of the more ardent spirits chafed under this regimen. Captain Mills of G Company, 308th Infantry, thought he could capture the hill in his front from which German gunfire dominated the American line. Mills was the Plattsburgh alum who had so impressed the British with his skill at reconaissance—the same man who had shown such care for his men at Upton and handled the "Bearded Soldier" affair so well. He made a careful study of the maps, explored the terrain on nightly patrols, and developed a plan for storming the place with a fast-moving strike force. While his project was being considered he continued training his men in the use of the *tromblon*, a new weapon supplied by the French that fired rifle-grenades. He fired two bombs by way of demonstration. The third exploded in the *tromblon*, killing Mills outright and wounding two of his men.[13]

By the middle of July the 77th had learned its job well enough so that tutelage by the French could be dispensed with, and the Baccarat sector was left in their charge. Division command decided to set the tone for this new phase by hitting the enemy early and hard. On the morning of July 21 a platoon of B Company of the 307th, led by Captain Barrett, mustered in the front-line trenches. Division had ordered a heavy raid against undermanned German positions opposite the left of the American line. There was to be no artillery preparation for the raid, which Barrett was ordered to conduct "in broad daylight—presupposing a thinly held enemy line and surprise." The German wire had been cut by artillery bombardment and by engineer details sent out the previous night.

Barrett was a Plattsburgh alum, a slim pale young man who wore round eyeglasses and a bold mustache. He was one of the few Southerners in the club, proud of his heritage. In his breast pocket he carried a small silk Confederate flag "to fly from the first enemy trench captured." This was his first real exercise of combat command. Barrett and his men passed their own wire and slipped through a belt of thick woods that screened the left of the regiment's position, crossed several hundred yards of exposed ground, and got into the enemy wire, using heavy long-arm wire cutters to snip the last barriers before the German line. Then Barrett signaled his men to file out to the right, silently, preparatory to a rush. At that moment the silence was pierced by "the clear notes of a German bugle." To Lieutenant Rainsford, watching from the American trenches, it was like "the clarion blare of trumpets, when the curtain rose on an old-world pageant."

It was no pageant. B Company had walked into a trap. The enemy were veterans, perhaps warned by the cutting of their wire the night before, and their trench line was neither undermanned nor taken by surprise. "A line of German infantry rose up in a trench in front; enfilading machine guns opened up on either flank, and . . . auto-rifles fired from the trees in rear," where German troops had infiltrated behind the Americans. Barrett and his men hit the dirt and fired back, but their position was hopeless.

In his first trial by combat Captain Barrett had erred, and the error would destroy his men and himself. Division erred too, its intelligence assessment wrong and its tactical plan inept, but none of that could matter to Barrett. He had accepted the assignment as given, made no request for modification of his orders. He was the man in charge on the ground, and he had put his men in the way of destruction. Rather than be shot down or surrender ignominiously, he tried to redeem disaster with gallantry. His only surviving lieutenant and about a third of the original force were ordered to cut their way back through the wire. To cover their retreat, "to the undying credit of Captain Barrett . . . he ordered and led a charge . . . [with] the remainder of the force, against hopeless odds."

> Poor, brave, beloved Captain Barrett, with his little silk Confederate flag folded in his breast pocket . . . never was the flag of the Lost Cause more gallantly borne, nor to more utter disaster. Of that charging line not one man came back, the captain reeling from a wound and staggering on to death, and of those taken prisoner only one was unwounded.

Out of fifty-two men Barrett had taken into action seventeen were killed, sixteen captured. Rainsford blamed the green division staff, which sent Barrett out without adequate artillery preparation or support. In fact, staff's errors were so egregious that a rumor went around that Barrett must have misread his orders, the weak eyes behind those round spectacles seeing "2:30 P.M." when "2:30 A.M." was meant. There was no truth to the rumor, but its existence registers the moral impact of the action, which had the potential to injure the men's confidence in their commanders.[14]

On August 4 the division was relieved, and allowed a five-day break before their assignment to the Champagne sector, where they would face intense combat against first-rate German troops. It was unfortunate the break was not longer. Aside from their need to recuperate, officers and men needed time to consider and assess the lessons they had learned on the job and make necessary changes in organization and tactics. Still, even this brief respite gave them perspective on their experience. Though they had taken losses and endured more than a month of misery, fear, illness, and boredom, their morale was not seriously impaired. If anything, it had been strengthened. This is not to say that every man had proved himself in battle. Some broke under the strain; the division had its quota of shell shock and battle fatigue cases. Some men malingered or goldbricked, some tried to get out of combat with self-inflicted wounds, and some deserted. But in the aggregate, by all the measures the army knew, the 77th came out of Baccarat at a higher level of combat effectiveness than when it went in. If its morale was deflated from the unrealistic levels of rookie expectation, it had a more solid basis. As individuals the men had acquired the skills needed to survive life in the trenches and be effective in combat. As members of platoons and companies, they had learned how to work together, discovered which men and units could be counted on in a crisis.

Most of their officers had proved competent enough for the ordinary tasks of command. Their understanding of tactics and weapons was still rudimentary, well below the skill level of veteran British and French officers; but they could be trusted to look out for their men's welfare and to keep their heads in a fight. The trust their men gave them was not uncritical. It incorporated a real understanding of just how limited a man's powers were once the shells started dropping, accepted that even the best officer could screw up fatally and get you killed. That understanding was expressed in the sardonic gripes about top-kicks and "shoulder-straps" that peppered their conversations and their correspondence.

> The officers get all the steak, parley-voo!
> The officers get all the steak, parley-voo!
> The officers get all the steak,
> And all we get is the belly-ache.
> Hinky dinky parley-voo!

They would follow their leaders (if they did), not because they thought them heroes or military geniuses, nor because they were "regular guys," but because they trusted them just far enough.

Battle deaths and demonstrations of ability brought new men forward. Miles, Rainsford, and Tiebout were given company commands; McMurtry got temporary command of a battalion. Charles Whittlesey was appointed operations officer for the 308th. He had the ability to understand the complex ways in which an action could develop and to envision ways of coordinating the efforts of different units. He also displayed a remarkable coolness under artillery fire, continuing to "scribble in [his] field message book" when others were "cowering in funk holes." New corporals and buck sergeants were tapped from the ranks of private soldiers, their names as ethnically varied as a ship's manifest at Ellis Island: Greenstein, Kee, Riley, Blohm, Del Duca, and so on. Sergeants Kaplan, Kaufman, and Bergasse got an extra stripe and wider responsibilities. Kaufman was twice recommended for officer training—the army had promised promotions for men of merit, Gentile or Jew. But winning a commission meant transfer to another outfit. Sergeant Kaufman wanted to stay with Company K, "advancement" be damned. It was the unit that mattered now, not the family or community back home, not the old men in Washington wondering whether Jews would make good officers.[15]

The troops also received letters and newspapers from home, which gave them a glimpse of how their labors fit into the larger patterns of the war and, more important, what the people back home thought of what they had done. The American press had been covering the war as comprehensively as it could, given the difficulties of communication and the censorship enforced by Pershing's GHQ. Of particular interest to the New York papers were the activities of the 27th "New York National Guard" Division, serving with the British armies in the north; the 42nd

Rainbow Division, because of the presence of the "Fighting 69th"; and the 77th, in which most of the city's National Army men and Plattsburgh gentry were serving.

Army censorship forbade correspondents mentioning specific units, so the Lower East Side had to deduce the safe arrival of its sons by a Talmudic decoding of dispatches. The army released the names and units of men killed or wounded for publication in hometown papers, and reporters were allowed to interview men in the hospital. So it was possible to figure out which units had been where and what they had been doing by stringing these tiny personal stories together. Reporters also circumvented censorship by using certain familiar references to identify particular outfits. Among the regiments of the 27th Division were the old 7th New York, whose members had once been drawn from the city's social elite; and the former 14th Brooklyn, a working-class outfit that had won its laurels at Antietam, Fredericksburg, and Gettysburg. A reference to "kid gloves" or "Brooklyn boys" would identify these units to any editor familiar with the city's military lore, and the editor could take it from there. A reference to "Upton men" usually identified the 77th Division, though many other units passed through Upton. Reports of the fighting in the Baccarat sector appeared in the New York papers in June and July. On July 1 the *New York Times* editorial hailed the 77th as "New York's Own Division," representative of all its racial, cultural, and social variety, proof that a polyglot society could also be patriotic:

> The city men, the fifty nationalities from the tenements and Fifth Avenue, peddlers, longshoremen, newsies, teamsters—yes, and loafers, rich and hard-up, from clubs and saloon corners—lawyers and tradesmen, clerks and capitalists, the Four Hundred and the riffraff, college men and illiterates, the dandies and the unwashed, good, bad, and indifferent, all that mob and conglomeration . . . that strode, trudged, and slouched into Camp Upton . . . were transformed into as fine a looking body of men as ever shouldered arms.

A more sober, and (if the troops had known of it) equally gratifying assessment of their performance came from the enemy. A Leutnant von Buy of the German army, who had questioned POWs from the 77th, reported, "Only a few of the men are genuine Americans by ancestry, the majority is of German, Dutch, or Italian parentage; but these half-Americans . . . consider themselves unhesitatingly as genuine sons of America."[16]

What the troops thought of themselves is hard to know. They would certainly have been gratified by the good press their actions received and by praise in letters from home. But they had just escaped from a period of total immersion in the world of combat, so utterly unlike the world of home as to seem like life on another planet—an alien ecology in which destruction is production, and life revolves around the omnipresence of death, which must be feared and resisted and inflicted. In that world home and its values, the nation and its ideals and purposes, exist as memories of another age or state of being, becoming increasingly ghostlike, with the power of haunting, but never quite materializing.

> [Soldiers] may hold fast in memory to their civilian existence . . . and stubbornly resist . . . the encroachments of the violent and the irrational. They may write home to their parents and sweethearts that they are unchanged, and they may even be convinced of it. But the soldier who has yielded himself to the fortunes of war, has sought to kill and to escape being killed, or who has even lived long enough in the disordered landscape of battle, is no longer what he was.[17]

In place of kin and country, soldiers are bonded to the unit in which they serve, the men with whom they share an utter and mutual dependence for physical and psychological survival. This sense of attachment to the unit can be liberating and enlarging, enabling them to establish powerful bonds of comradeship with men and types of men they might never have met in civilian life, freeing them from the behavioral constraints of civilian life to live by different rules, which sanctify the destruction of lives and property. In intervals of rest and relief, they may revert temporarily to their civilian selves. But if they know, as these men did, that they will soon have to return to the trenches, such reversion has to be kept within strict limits. If you think of yourself as your mother's child, your lover's lover, the risks you take in the line are unacceptable, a cruelty to those you love. If you see yourself as a buddy to your buddies, shirking combat seems harder than taking your chances with the rest.[18]

While the division rested and trained near the red-roofed Vosges town of Rozelieures, the soldiers speculated on where the army would send them next. Rumors ran the gamut from prophecies of imminent action in France to a transfer to the Mexican border, perhaps to fend off a "Liberating Army of Races." These rumors all presumed that the men of the 77th were special and very much in the public eye. Among the favorites were the one that said the division "will never see action," because it was full of important men and "the nation can't afford to lose them," and one that declared:

> This Division . . . is in for a lot of action. It has political influence behind it. It contains a host of men prominent in the business, political, and social circles of the nation's greatest city. They are all anxious to make a name for themselves and get tons of glory. We are going to a hot sector, you bet!

Which rumor reflected optimism and which pessimism is not easy for an outsider to judge.

> Where do we go from here, boys, where do we go from here?
> Slip a pill to Kaiser Bill and make him shed a tear;
> And when we see the enemy we'll shoot 'em in the rear,
> Oh joy! Oh boy!
> Where do we go from here?"[19]

"God Damn, Let's Go!": The Hell Fighters in the Champagne-Marne Sector, June–August 1918

While the 77th was completing its education in the Baccarat, the 369th was heavily engaged as part of the French Fourth Army opposing the third of General Ludendorff's great spring offensives. At the end of May, shortly after the Battle of Henry Johnson, the Germans staged a massive attack in the Champagne sector, smashing the French lines along the ridge of the Chemin des Dames north and west of the cathedral city of Rheims.

> Three German officers crossed the Rhine, parley-voo!
> Three German officers crossed the Rhine, parley-voo!
> Three German officers crossed the Rhine
> To fuck the women and drink the wine,
> Hinky dinky parley-voo!

The French divisions here were not organized for defense in depth, and their morale had not fully recovered from the mutinies that followed the failed Nivelle offensives a year before. Many units broke, and the victorious Germans drove them south and west across a series of river valleys carrying tributaries of the Seine—the Aisne with its canal, the Vesle, and the Ourcq—carving a deep broad bulge into the French lines. By the first week in June the German offensive had driven the French back to the Marne River, the last defensive barrier before Paris, less than seventy miles away.

In this emergency, Pershing released the four all-White divisions then in France to fight under French command to stem the German advance. The First and Third were regular army divisions, the Second mixed a regular army and a marine infantry brigade. The Fourth was the Rainbow Division, recently relieved in the Baccarat by the 77th. In the first week of June the impetus of the German advance was checked along the Marne by a series of furious counterattacks. In one of these the Second Division and its Marine Brigade earned immortality for the bloody assault on Belleau Wood.

The German high command paused and reorganized its forces for one last supreme offensive stroke, by which they hoped to break the Allied front and compel a peace settlement on favorable terms. They would attack on either side of Rheims, which was the tip of a narrow salient jabbed into the eastern shoulder of the German bulge.

East of Rheims General Gouraud's Fourth Army held the line, its ranks bolstered by the Rainbow Division and the 369th Infantry. The Old Fifteenth had made great progress since the Battle of Henry Johnson. Hayward was periodically entrusted with command of his sector, which gave him control of French units as well as his own. On June 6, as part of the 16th Division, the 369th advanced against German forces that had pulled back into the outskirts of the Argonne Forest. A battalion of the 369th was in the front line, Hayward himself up with Fish's Company K, leading by example when they came under heavy fire from German machine guns. The French general commanding the assault appeared out of the smoke, waving his arms to catch Hayward's attention: German fire was too hot, the Americans must "Retire! Retire!" Hayward, "with his hat knocked off," shouted back: "My men never retire. They go forward or they die!" Heroic words—they seem too pat to have been spoken on a battlefield. But then, Hayward and others in the 369th felt themselves to be under perpetual scrutiny by the press. Perhaps, like Colonel Robert Shaw of the Civil War's 54th Massachusetts, Hayward had such words ready, knowing they would be expected of him. In any case, the troops proceeded to validate the colonel's boast. Sergeant John Jamieson remembered that Hayward "tore off the 'eagles'" that marked his rank, "grasped a gun from a soldier, and darted out ahead of the rest of Company K" to lead a "suicidal" rush at the German positions. Hayward was hit in the leg, his second in command Lieutenant Colonel Pickering and six other men went down with wounds, but the Germans picked up and left.

At about that time the enlisted men found their own battle cry, less showy than Hayward's but no less eloquent. Artillery was thundering on the horizon, the men held in reserve were waiting to go forward, when someone said, "God damn, let's go!" Others took it up and overnight it became their slogan.[20]

They held the line in the forest when the Germans counterattacked, driving back the French troops in the forward posts. Company K was the reserve, and Corporal Pippin's platoon commander ordered him to take charge of the rear guard. It was a responsible and difficult duty. Pippin's squad had to stand steady while retreating French troops ran back through their line, resisting panic, holding fire until they were sure the last friendly troops had cleared their front, then checking the German pursuit. Pippin got the job done and brought his squad off in good order.[21]

Combat apprenticeship built them up and wore them down. Their confidence and morale rose with each success that proved their growing efficiency, while the continual stress and steady drain of hurts and losses ate away at their combat power and emotional reserves. The regiment had been understrength before combat attrition began. They started to receive large numbers of replacements to restore their losses and bring them closer to the desired combat strength of 3,100 to 3,500 officers and men. But the new men were draftees who had been serving in labor battalions where they were demoralized by bad treatment. Hardly any had received infantry training or weapons instruction. They did not belong to the community that had created the regiment and sustained it through its early trials; had no basis of comradeship with the enlisted veterans other than skin color; had no reason to trust their White officers. Hayward and his French division commander complained to Pershing about the quality of the replacements, to no avail.

Below the surface there was also discontent among the more ambitious officers and NCOs, several of whom requested transfers in June and

July. The regiment's early successes had given their credentials a bright luster, but their possibilities for advancement were limited. The 369th was isolated among the French. Promotion for company officers was therefore highly unlikely except by the death or incapacitation of the five field-grade officers (and not guaranteed even then). Among those considering transfer was one of the regiment's stars, Hamilton Fish. On July 2 Fish wrote to General Mark Hershey of the 78th Division, asking him to use his influence to get Fish transferred to the 78th. "I have not ask[ed] for a transfer but would like very much to serve with you if it can be arrange[d]. I am confident that if you can find a place for me and speak to the Adjutant General that I would be transferred immediately." He was not dissatisfied with his men or the regiment, praised both strongly to Hershey, but felt his path to advancement was blocked while he remained with the 369th.

Black officers like Fillmore, and perhaps Lacey and Marshall as well, may have thought Hayward favored Whites for battalion command. Mistrust of that sort was possible because racial mores limited social contacts between White and Black officers. The "friendship" of Ham Fish and James Europe was exceptional and hardly intimate. Personality conflicts also played a role. Relations between Fillmore and his battalion commander, Arthur Little, had been strained from the start. Now Little was slated for promotion to major while Fillmore was to remain a captain. In Little's defense, it should be noted that one of the other Black officers, Lieutenant Lacey, asked for a transfer because of personal problems between himself and Captain Fillmore, who was apparently not an easy man to get along with.[22]

The 369th was no longer the only Black combat outfit in France, and this opened opportunities for Black officers and noncoms seeking advancement. Three other regiments of the 93rd Division, to which the 369th nominally belonged, were already on the scene. These were the 370th Infantry, formerly the 8th Illinois National Guard; the 372nd Infantry, a sort of Black "Rainbow" composed of Guard units from various states and the District of Columbia; and the 371st, which was recruited from Black draftees in Georgia, Alabama, and South Carolina. The 92nd Division was arriving in France and would soon be going up to the front for a training stint. Although all division and brigade commanders were White, the 370th was officered and staffed entirely by

Black men, from colonel on down; and both the 372nd and the regiments of the 92nd Division had Negro officers of field grade (major, lieutenant colonel, colonel). There might also be positions available in field artillery and other specialized regiments and on the division and brigade staffs. Fillmore believed his age and experience qualified him for a staff job.

Two of the regiment's top sergeants also asked for transfers. Henry Cheatham and Benedict Cheeseman had been recommended for field commissions by their company commanders, but Hayward told them "it is not considered good policy to make any more colored officers in this regiment." He also refused to endorse their transfers. Cheatham was a veteran of the 24th Infantry who had served in the Philippines and risen to the rank of sergeant major in the regulars. His father had been born a slave, but obtained an education and served two terms as a congressman from North Carolina before the adoption of a Jim Crow constitution deprived his people of the ballot. Cheatham wrote to his father, asking him to use his influence to get him and his friend Cheeseman transferred. In other regiments noncoms and even privates in considerable numbers had been sent to the States for officer training. "A certain colored colonel," probably Denison of the 8th Illinois/370th Infantry, "made FORTY such appointments [but] not a man from this 'dear regiment' has been sent":

> And yet we are calmly assured that, though there is no question as to our merit, we may not be advanced because the "policy" decrees otherwise. And this "policy" has been so devoutly followed that . . . TWENTY-NINE young reservists [officers] were requisitioned for and obtained. They were white, of course, and they are here with us now. "It is a laugh."

In the end Cheatham would get his transfer and a lieutenant's commission; Cheeseman would remain a sergeant in the 369th.[23]

Hayward was certainly to blame for holding Cheatham and Cheeseman back, but he had good reason. He could ill afford to lose experienced sergeants at a time when the regiment was getting replacements, new officers, and a more demanding combat assignment. Nevertheless, Hayward was lying when he told the press that his noncoms had refused promotion, because "they'd rather be sergeants in the 15th than lieutenants or captains in other regiments." (He added that the men were "splendid material" for officers—did not want it thought that Black men were unqualified for higher command.) But the "policy" Cheatham resented was not Hayward's. The army had originally resisted acceptance of the 15th New York because it had both White and Black company commanders. Politics and the emergency of the German offensives had forced GHQ to take them as they were. The army preferred that in each regiment the division of ranks and roles should conform to the principle of racial segregation: company officers in a Black regiment must be Whites-only or Blacks-only. There were plans afoot to replace *all* the 369th's Black officers with Whites.[24]

In the end the opportunities for promotion outside the regiment proved illusory. The 93rd would never complete its divisional organization—never acquire the necessary field artillery, supply train, and other specialized units. Its truncated administrative staff would oversee four infantry regiments, serving with three different French divisions in the Fourth Army. GHQ also decided that no Negro officers would be appointed to field rank, and that those already holding that rank would be relieved and returned to the States. But in July 1918 it would have appeared to ambitious Black officers and noncoms of the 369th that their "dear regiment" had become a personal dead end. Their discontent was overridden by the promise of a major battle, in which they would be given a chance to win real distinction for themselves and their regiment.

One-armed Gouraud was a superb combat commander and an intelligent military professional who understood the tactical problems of trench warfare and could predict the likely course of the next German offensive. Without compromising security, he shared his understanding of the coming battle with subordinates down to battalion level, so that the soldiers would understand their role in the strategic design. Gouraud explained that the Germans would have to make one more attempt to break the Allied front on the Marne, that the Fourth Army would bear the brunt of the assault east of Rheims, and that they should expect theirs to be the "decisive" battle of the war. He even predicted the Germans would strike on Bastille Day, July 14. He laid out a defense in depth designed to break the German shock troops and prepared a powerful counterattack, mandating specialized training for each unit to learn its part in the action. As soon as the Germans began their preliminary bombardment, troops in the forward trenches would be largely withdrawn, leaving behind a sacrifice line of small units to break the momentum of the German infantry assault—then retreat, if any survived. The reserves would be marshaled in a well-concealed second line, from which they would mount a smashing counterattack when the critical moment arrived. Gouraud planned to use his American troops, the Rainbow Division and the 369th, to stiffen his French divisions for the counterattack. They were fresher than his poilus, and still had the élan that had been beaten out of the French veterans. The 42nd formed the center of the Fourth Army reserve line and would lead the counterattack there. The 369th was assigned to the 161st Division and placed in the second line so that Gouraud "could hold us at his personal disposition" and accord the regiment "the honor of making the counter attack, and winning distinction." The assignment was a sign to the 369th of its high standing with the army commander. The 161st was a crack assault division, which included the mountain-fighting Chasseurs Alpins and a Moroccan regiment known for its bayonet work. With the counterattack in view, the 369th was trained in the difficult techniques of "Advance by Infiltration."

The officers, Black and White, remained mindful of the regiment's larger mission even as they went into action. The "one anxiety" they expressed, the "one point upon which we *all* wanted assurance to complete our happiness," was "how soon the great news could be known at home." The men seemed eager to get into it, "God Damn, Let's Go!" Colonel Hayward was in hospital with a leg wound, but showed up at the command post on crutches, determined to lead his men in what he believed would be the decisive battle of the war. Captain Fish and part of his company volunteered for duty in the sacrifice line; Little's battalion sent two squads for the same mission, all volunteers. Fish understood clearly what that duty would entail and wrote his father on the eve of battle, "I do not believe there is any chance of any of us surviving the first push." He told his father he had been assigned the post, not wishing to confess he had volunteered for a suicide mission.[25]

The German assault began, as Gouraud anticipated, on July 14. Most of the sacrifice posts (including those from the 369th) were able to do their job and pull back before they were wiped out. After a day of intense combat the Germans stalled in front of Gouraud's reserve line. They were lambasted by French artillery and responded in kind. "All through the night of July 15–16 hell was at work." German artillery hit the 369th with high explosives and air bursts of shrapnel, from which their shallow field trenches offered little protection. Elements of the regiment were holding a section of the lines in front of Gouraud's right wing when German troops tried a second attack behind a rolling barrage on July 16.

French troops in the first line poured back through the 369th, which held its ground. Then the barrage rolled onto them. Intensive artillery bombardment was one of the worst ordeals suffered by troops on the Western Front: a continual assault of sound, the banshee scream or express-train roar of incoming shells, then the blasts of explosions rocking the ground. Veterans testified that prolonged intense bombardment made you feel like you were falling apart, utterly beyond help, your mind scattering away from your nerveless body. Driven in on themselves, individuals became disoriented and psychologically distraught, unable to function, incapable of pulling themselves together to resist an attack. In the terrible isolation and disconnection such a barrage produces, with men being "killed and wounded by an unseen enemy" against whom their rifles were useless, the 369th held its ground. Planes circling over the advancing Germans served as range markers for the French artillery that broke up the attack. Losses were light, only four men killed, but two of the bodies were so macerated by high explosives that Napoleon Marshall and Hamilton Fish could only identify them by recognizing one man's watch and another's notebook.

The German attack had driven French troops of the 161st Division out of their trenches north of the town of Minaucourt, and on the night of July 17 the 369th was ordered up to join a division-strength counterattack to retake the position. Far off to the north and west, on the right shoulder of the German salient, a French-American force under General Mangin was poised to hit the German flank at Soissons. It was the beginning of a five-day battle that would break the back of Ludendorff's last offensive and compel him to begin a long retreat to the Aisne.

The 369th was utterly exhausted and had to assemble at night, which added to the confusion and sense of disorientation. Little's First Battalion was caught in a traffic jam on a road that ran along high ground, silhouetting men and vehicles against the skyline. In daylight the road was pounded by German artillery. If the enemy had chosen to fire the guns it had registered on the road, losses would have been "hideous." Little hoped his men were ignorant of their peril, but was not sure. The danger set his "heart and mind" racing "with trip-hammer fury" as he waited "momentarily for panic to break loose." Little prayed for deliverance, as he had "at my mother's knee,"and the barrage remained unfired. That night the officers cheered the men with news of French-American victories on the first day at Soissons. But the Germans hit them with a heavy raid in the darkness, coming in behind a rolling barrage. It was broken up by a camouflaged two-piece machine-gun section commanded by Lieutenant Shaw, who rolled from gun to gun to keep his head below the bursts of shrapnel from the German shelling. The raiders fell back into the cratered ground to regroup, and two Black enlisted men, Sergeant Robert Collins and Private Howard Gaillard, jumped over the parapet and staged a two-man counterattack, Gaillard firing his Chauchat "from the hip" into the huddled Germans, Collins snaking forward to fire his rifle "point blank." Collins later told an interviewer, "I thought their shells had messed us up a good deal. But man you should have seen what we done to them." Privates Gaillard and Brown, Lieutenant Shaw, and Sergeant Collins all won the Croix de Guerre. There were headlines in the *Sun* as well as the *Age*: "American Negro Troops Put Germans to Flight Near Verdun."

Next morning the whistles shrilled along the trench line and the troops clambered over the parapets to make their first regimental combat assault. They went into the cratered ground between the trench lines, running, dropping, creeping ahead—then up and running again to get through the German shelling, a two-kilometer advance under fire. Every dip and roll of the terrain was "full of gas and smoke from exploding shells or from the previous night's bombardment." You could not help breathing in the "sickly sweet" poisonous fumes, whose effects were debilitating. For raw troops such an assault is an extreme ordeal, the confusion due to inexperience compounded by the terrifying and disorienting effect of the rain of high explosives, the ground-shaking detonations and blinding smoke. Henry Johnson's brother-in-law Charles Jackson had his right foot blown off by a shell, one of fourteen killed and fifty-one wounded. The 369th retook the trench line of the 161st, and to their left the 42nd Division and the rest of the Fourth Army counterattacked successfully—the Germans falling back to well-entrenched positions.[26]

The regiment's success sent morale sky-high and completed that integration of individual and collective identity that is called "unit pride." It was after this battle that word began to spread that the Germans referred to the Black Americans as "hell fighters," and the regiment proudly adopted that as its nickname. But the primary unit with which the men identified was the company. Horace Pippin described these feelings as well as anyone ever has. He was a corporal in Ham Fish's K Company, a well cared-for, high-morale outfit:

> That Co. K. I liked and I stayed with it all throu the Big War. I did not care for any otheres, for every man in the Co. were a man. And ther were not one of them that did not look to his Maker to bring him throu. his hird fight. All the [same] it were hird to do in that place to do Gods Will. But we did the best we could. I did not care what or where I went at. I ask God to help me, and he ded so. And that is the way I cam throu that tirebell, and that Hell place, for the houl intir batel feel were hell, so it were no place for any human been to be, for one night.[27]

The horrible paradox of unit pride is that it compels the men who feel it to destroy the thing they love. The trust that binds them to one another is the understanding that every man will do his duty, that none will shirk and expose the rest to destruction. But their duty is to go in harm's way, which in turn ensures that this community of precious comrades will inevitably, by ones and twos and dozens, suffer losses, terrible wounds, death. While the unit is learning its trade, proving its members, testing its unity, even suffering and loss can contribute to a growing sense of strength, competence, and well-being. But inevitably, as the unit *uses* its strength in battle, "that tirebell, and that Hell place," the losses accumulate; defeats and blunders, grief and anger, and exhaustion take their toll. The same actions that in the beginning built them up as men and companies, in the end wear them down and destroy their ability to go on fighting.

One night the battalion of which K company was a part had to effect a relief of front-line units under artillery fire. The road they had to follow was blocked by wrecked vehicles and interdicted by German shelling. As they went forward through the fields the German gunners found the company and broke them up. Pippin was "sad and mad all at the same time" to see men "laying all over the feel and Road men that I knew." Among them was one he considered his buddy: "I looked to see if I could Do him any good [but] he were Done for." Around him men were panicking, dropping to the ground instead of moving forward to get out of the fall of shells. "I called to them, come on," rallied a few squads of disorganized men and led them up the road, past a ruined church to the entrenchments. He looked around—not a single man of his beloved K Company was with him. But he was a corporal, and when the German infantry attacked in the lee of their barrage Pippin got the men with him up on the fire-step to shoot the German infantry back into the ground. Later, when the battalion regrouped, the losses to his unit struck him hard: "[When I] seen what were left of my plattoon I yet say to myself some times, how did I ever do it that were the trien time." They slept two nights on sodden stacks of wheat dragged in from the fields.[28]

They would get no rest after Minaucourt. Gouraud wanted to press the Germans hard, keep the enemy retreating. Little and First Battalion were sent to relieve the Moroccans in front of the German positions on a hill named Butte du Mesnil. The other two battalions were assigned to a different French command two miles away in a straight line and much further by road. Corporal White remembered that "shells were bursting all along the roads, killing men, horses, and blowing up wagons. As we moved towards the front we could hear nothing but our comrades lying on the ground crying, 'Help me, boys.' "[29]

The French planned a climactic assault on the butte, a complex operation that involved the coordination of four regiments and the 161st Division artillery, augmented by additional battalions drawn from other divisions. On July 20 Little's battalion was assigned to seize and hold a position on the left of the division. The Marson road, which they would have to take, appeared to be exposed to enemy shell fire from the north. In fact, the road itself was protected from artillery by high ground that ran along its northern edge. But for the soldiers, its seeming vulnerability was confirmed by a barrage of gas shells, which flew over and exploded in the swamp that bordered the road on the south, sending clouds of poison gas billowing out onto the road. Gas is a terrifying weapon, and its effect is to isolate the soldier inside the choking obscurity and blinkered sight of his gas mask, making him prone to disorientation and panic. Little and his officers recognized the fumes as nonlethal tear gas and were certain that as long as the men stayed on the road they were safe from direct shell fire. But "the men didn't know that, and it was extremely difficult, under the circumstances of confusion and darkness and mask wearing, to make the men understand. . . . Our greatest danger that night lay in the possibility of panic." It was the first real gas attack for many of them; for the replacements it was their first action, and "a considerable percentage of officers and men suffered from loss of morale." In their ignorance they "yielded to various forms of extravagances in expressions of distress . . . choking and crying," crawling into dugouts and "waiting to die." Rumors spread that their movement was to be abandoned—the sure prelude to a stampede. "To meet this state of near-panic . . . a few officers adopted the plan of removing masks . . . while giving orders, so that the men would be under the reassurance or the fear (or whatever it is) of the personality that makes some men obey other men." Many officers and noncoms who removed their masks were partially or wholly disabled by the effects of the gas.[30]

One of those who displayed that mystical power of personality was Charles Fillmore, the gray-haired veteran who had once been colonel of the regiment. "During the scenes of semi-panic along the Marson road Captain Fillmore, with marked calmness and courage and persistency moved among the troops," and in organizing the movement into the trenches acted not only as captain but "lieutenant, sergeant, and corporal, as well." Little found his help "inestimable" and his example "inspiriting," and after the battle recommended him for the Croix de Guerre. Though Little had mishandled their relationship back in training, he now praised Fillmore's battlefield performance in the terms Progressives reserved for "leaders of men." Unfortunately he said nothing of this to Fillmore, who had already asked for a transfer. The two were not reconciled until the end of the war, when Fillmore learned that Little had cited him for gallantry.

For the next four weeks the 369th defended its section of the Fourth Army line under continual bombardment from German guns on the high ground of Butte du Mesnil. The troops were subjected to a steady rain of high explosives and gas shells, punctuated by periods of intense shelling that sometimes portended a local infantry attack. The Germans laid so much gas on their sector that the lingering clouds looked like a pervasive ground fog. In the intervals between heavy bombardments the troops were subjected to harassing fire, directed against their lines of supply as well as the trenches themselves. "Them Germans would shell one man as well as they would one hundred," Corporal Pippin complained. Major Little called it "sniping with 155s." Pippin was a strong character, who believed it was important that he show no weakness to his men and tried always to look for the "good p[a]rt" of events. But even he found himself thinking "they will shore get us this time" whenever he left his dugout. He admitted that the constant shelling was harder to endure than the prospect of going "over the top." Prolonged tension and fear, sleeplessness, hunger, and thirst, wore them down.[31]

The morale situation was complicated by the fact that the regiment's three battalions were separated from each other and assigned to different French regiments, where they manned positions either in the front line or in the first line of reserves, always within range of German gunnery. The troops can be forgiven for suspecting that French commanders were using them up to spare the lives of their countrymen. Sergeant Jamieson recalled, "It was while holding the sector opposite Butte du Mesnil that we heard that the chief of staff of the Germans had offered a prize for every black soldier captured." Pippin remembered his unit staying in the line twenty days out of the thirty they spent in the zone of advance—ten of those without relief, hunkered down under constant bombardment, shells, gas, rain, with only intermittent deliveries of water and fresh rations. When relief finally came the men were so weak and stiff they could hardly move. There was no relief from the infestation of lice—they stung Jamieson to poetry, a ballad for cooties set to a popular tune:

> They ran wild simply wild over me,
> They're as reckless as reckless can be,
> No matter where I'm at, when I take off my hat,
> There are little ones, and big ones, you could pick them off like that,
> Oh how they bit, oh, how they bite all over me,
> They made me just as sore as I could be.

Private Turpin stepped out of their dugout to get some water and was torn apart by a shell, decapitated, his blood spattering Jamieson. Another one of his buddies was blown up by a shell from a "minnie waffle" (*Minenwerfer*). "We were forced to shovel this poor boy up, as the pieces of his remains were too small to put together."[32]

Pippin spent every night in front of the lines, in charge of a three-man listening post. The duty was lonely and extremely hazardous. "The listening post is a sacrifice concern. . . . The runner comes and gets your report at midnight and returns to the main trench. After that there is no more correspondence regardless." If a German raiding party hit the post, the men could expect neither support nor rescue. During the day there were other duties: repairing the trench after bombardment, bringing up rations, re-laying telephone wire between the posts. Pippin spent twenty days in the line and ten off that month and went weeks without being able to take off his boots. Once after a wire-laying detail he was so tired and hungry, so eager to get back in time for mess, that he didn't stay under cover and was nearly killed when a German plane dropped out of the clouds and strafed him. Back in his dugout he collapsed on his sodden bunk: "I lit another Cigarette, my mind were not with me at that time, it were home of the U.S." He hadn't had a letter in months. When he'd got that one, "I did not know what to do for I were so glad to get it I could not speak. . . . It were so short that I red it over and over so after I got thrue the litter all I could red it by hirt and not miss a wird of it."

So in his exhaustion he'd close his eyes, silently rehearse the letter he knew "by heart" and "burn a smoke" while he slumped in his bunk with the water dripping on him. He couldn't keep doing this: "I say no man can do it agan. He may have the well. But his b[o]dy can not stand it." He craved cigarettes, his only comfort, spent hours planning how to get some. In the notebooks Pippin wrote after the war, it was always raining, cold, and dark, whether he was writing about July in the Argonne or September under Butte du Mesnil. That was how he remembered the war: "We stayed there two days and every one of them looked like night time." The men wore sodden blankets over heads and shoulders, they had no overcoats. "I seen rain but not like this."[33]

Some troops slide into a sort of dull lethargy under such conditions or become so resentful they barely obey orders. Others may become demoralized and incapable of effective action. But some are roused to anger by it all, anger building and looking for a chance to cut loose. There were enough of the last type in the 369th to maintain its fighting edge. So when those endlessly impending attacks finally materialized, when the enemy came out from behind the shell bursts and gas fog to where you could hit him hard and hurt him back, any number of men were ready to visit all the grievances of their lives on the enemy. Sergeant William Butler—in civilian life an elevator operator or "indoor chauffeur"—is a case in point. During one particularly heavy nighttime raid, German infantry overran parts of the regiment's outpost line. Butler and the lieutenant commanding his platoon rallied their men and staged a successful ambush. The officer called out to draw the Germans in his direction; then Butler jumped out of a funk hole on their flank and opened up with a Chauchat, fighting the weapon's full-barrel recoil and tendency to jam, laying down steady and accurate fire on the raiders. As the Germans fell or fled, Butler pursued them, single-handedly killing four, capturing a German officer and rescuing the five Americans captured in the outpost, chasing twenty or more Germans right back to their own lines. "I guess I just ran amuck," he later explained. He was awarded the Croix de Guerre.[34]

Corporal Pippin preferred not to wait for the Germans. When his "looey" asked him to assemble a volunteer squad for a raid—"I w[a]nt you with me, Corp."—"I were glad myself to get the chance."[35] They were to cross no-man's-land to the German outpost line and capture prisoners. This was a deadly dangerous business: the need to make captures meant you couldn't shoot first. As Pippin put it, it was a case of "get them or they get us." Pippin chose eight from his squad (all twelve had volunteered); another noncom assembled a second detail. Pippin couldn't sleep in the interval between evening mess and their midnight assembly. "The Big Guns were on the go all the time." He noticed how the new men in his company ducked every time a shell hit—at that rate they'd be ducking all day. He didn't mind shelling anymore; he had gotten used to it. He sat and smoked while the others looked at him as if it were the "last time," but his way was to show no fear, to *have* no fear, to think only about the "good part."

The night was rainy and cold, water "like a river" in the trenches, a good night for a patrol to the other side. They crept out into a "boyau," a shallow communication trench snaking out from the main line. There was a machine-gun nest that obervers had marked in an old wrecked house, and the lieutenant had briefed the noncoms how the men were to get there. As they crouched at the end of the boyau a random shell knocked them down, "and the [pieces] of shell sang its deadly song to us." Then a machine gun opened up, firing blind, but it "swept the top" of the boyau and sent slugs into the back wall. The soldier next to Pippin muttered, "That Mr. Germen has got the right dop[e] on us all right." They went out one by one, scurrying humped over from shell hole to shell hole, circling broken tangles of "bobwire." The Germans were leery on this rainy night and shot flares up into the dark, bright bursts whose light was a net dropped to catch and kill the patrol. An old wrecked house "looked like a letter V in the night."

They split, one squad working straight ahead, Pippin's squad around the right flank, to "where the Door use to be." The house was empty, they pushed on.

A machine gun opened up. Pippin looked for the brightening of newly turned dirt that would mark the nest, spotted it. They split up again, to come in on the gunner from two sides. Pippin saw him, one man with a light machine gun looking the wrong way when two of the soldiers jumped him and slapped a gun to his head. They had one prisoner— three of their own men had been killed getting him. They wanted more. The Germans would be sending a regular relief for this outpost, especially since he'd been heard to fire. So the Americans found shell holes near the boyau that linked the German's outpost to his lines, and sat down in them to wait. Sitting there in the rain waiting for the Germans to show up was "the hardest part of the job." Shells kept dropping and detonating, flares kept going up. Their clothes were soaked through, they huddled and flattened themselves, "st[u]ck to the shell hole like a sirpen [serpent]." Machine guns still probed for the raiders in the dark, bullets zipped like "bees" over their heads.

Finally they heard a "funny" sound, voices. Then a signal like an owl hooting in the dark. A five-man patrol came down the boyau, hooting for their outpost. The Americans swarmed them, scuffling—knives—left two dead and had four prisoners to take back. As they dodged back toward their lines the German machine guns opened up again, and they had to crawl under their own wire to get back in. "The bullets were hiteing all a round our heads and would play in the bobwair[,] it sound like birds Chepeing."

Back at last in his dugout Pippin lost the nervous elation that had carried him. He was suddenly depressed. Rain, gas, shells, hunger, death— no letter from home to remind him of who he used to be. But he'd felt this way before, back in the Argonne. That time he went to sleep, and "that bad feleing all went a way from me." Maybe a sleep now would do the same.

Lieutenant James Europe was put in command of the regimental machine guns. At the start of the second week in front of Butte du Mesnil Germans hit his position with a poison-gas bombardment. The unit's gas discipline held, but Europe got a dose that damaged his lungs and sent him to a hospital a short distance behind the lines. Sissle went to visit him and was horrified by the strangled wheezing and blinded eyes of the gas victims in the hospital. Europe was racked by "dry-hacking painful coughs," but he greeted Sissle with a grin and showed him the draft of a song he'd written while lying in bed. "On Patrol in No Man's Land" would become a hit back in the States, and Europe's band would make a recording of it. It's an upbeat, jaggedly syncopated, early jazz tune:

> What's the time? Nine? Fall in line
> Alright boys, now take it slow
> Are you ready? Steady!
> Very good, Eddie
> Over the top let's go!
> Quiet, lie it, else you'll start a riot
> Keep your proper distance, follow 'long
> Cover, brother, when you see me hover
> Obey my orders and you won't go wrong.

"Obey my orders"—the words not only of a Black man fighting but a Black man commanding. Europe still saw himself as a line officer, a man who would win a position in American society not simply as an entertainer, but as an officer of the Great War. While he was at it he would also give Americans something to sing besides "When the Boys from Dixie Eat Melon on the Rhine" and "Nigger War Bride Blues."[36]

The assault on Butte du Mesnil, and the defense after, would have tested the solidarity of any unit. In battle officers ask their men to do things that are inherently unreasonable under the best construction: get yourself killed so we can get past this machine-gun nest. But for the soldiers of the 369th the stress of combat was augmented by the stress of racial feeling: the sense, justified by long experience, that most of the bad things that happen to Black people happen because White people want it that way. They had been segregated within their own army from the start, then segregated from it by assignment to the French. Then in the midst of the July fighting, Pershing's headquarters ordered all of the Black officers in the 369th transferred and replaced by Whites. These transfers were not responsive to the officers' own requests: Fillmore went to the 370th Infantry, not to division staff, and Lacey (who had tried to get away from Fillmore) went with him, along with Lieutenant Reid.

Others went to the 371st. Napoleon Marshall was sent out of the division entirely, to the 365th Infantry of the 92nd Division. Sergeant Major Cheatham got his bars and a transfer to the 370th.[37]

The regiment was in combat when the order came down, disrupting its most fundamental relations at a moment of high stress. Hayward protested strongly, to no avail. All the men in the line knew was that Black officers who had been with them from the start, suffering through the indignities of Spartanburg and railroad building at Saint-Nazaire, were gone, replaced by White strangers. They were unaware that some Black officers had been seeking transfers; they knew nothing of the change in army policy the transfer signaled. For them the mass transfer-out of Black officers, during the worst of the fighting on the butte, simply bespoke the army's uncaring attitude toward *this* Black regiment (the only one in the world that really mattered).

The egregious loss of their Black officers was underlined by the deeper losses of comrades killed and wounded. The regiment held its lines under the German guns on Butte du Mesnil and took a beating. Little's First Battalion was especially hard hit. In one forty-five-minute barrage their lines were raked by 9,000 shells, the sort of bombardment that could break morale. In addition, the divisional command insisted on active patrolling along the front to keep tabs on the enemy's condition and anticipate further attacks. Little protested the assignment. Headquarters maps, showing fairly simple contour lines, bore no resemblance to the complex and broken ground in his front. The Germans knew the ground well and had covered most lines of approach with registered artillery or sighted machine guns. Patrols sent out on successive nights were driven back with losses. The patrol on the third night drew machine-gun fire and returned "without gaining any information and without evidence . . . of having made a zealous effort to accomplish its mission." This was a warning sign of deteriorating morale. Little ordered the same personnel out for a patrol the following night, and "the result of that fourth patrol was demoralizing. No sooner had the enemy opened fire than a number of our men fell into a state of panic, threw away their rifles, and fled." Although half the men and all the officers stood their ground, the rout was ominous, a sign the men no longer trusted their commanders. "Rumors . . . came to me that mutterings were being indulged in to the effect it was a pity officers of high rank couldn't be made to go upon some of these dirty missions." Little proposed taking out a patrol composed of equal numbers of officers and men, but before the plan could be executed his battalion was finally relieved.

The cause of the breakdown may simply have been the stress of extended combat. The 369th had been in the line and under fire for 130 days with only brief interludes of rest, the last two weeks in intense combat. In such circumstances, any troops would begin to doubt whether the orders they received were justified by military logic or were rather the product of minds enjoying privilege and safety, out of touch with the realities of the front. Where the line between officers and men was also a color line, these suspicions inevitably took on a racial tinge: harsh or mistaken orders must be the product of malice, not of simple error or misunderstanding.

The morale of the 369th ultimately withstood these tensions because of its unique character. Its solidarity was based upon loyalty to its original mission to "prove" and "win" the equality of the Negro race, now powerfully augmented by the intense sense of obligation that binds soldiers to their unit and their comrades. That sense of obligation is especially strong among men who have been given some responsibility for others, as officers, sergeants, and corporals. This is not to say that every combat soldier in the army or every officer and noncom felt this way, or lived up to this imperative. But in both the 369th and the 77th Division there were many instances of men who refused to leave the line even when badly wounded, who "deserted" from hospitals to rejoin their unit at the front or refused assignments that would have put them out of range of German guns.[38]

That sense of obligation imposed a difficult choice on Lieutenant James Europe after his recovery from gassing. Colonel Hayward had appealed to Army Headquarters for Europe to be made an exception to the mass transfer of Black officers. Without its legendary leader the most famous band in the AEF would lose half its effectiveness as the army's goodwill ambassador and morale booster. The exception was allowed, on condition that Europe cease to serve as a line officer. Europe took his role as a combat officer seriously. He felt a strong obligation to the men he commanded and the race he believed he represented; and both of these were bound up with the ambitions he had for himself, which he shared with Noble Sissle. He was tired of taking orders, of having his hands "tied and fast" as a Black man perpetually under the thumb of Whites. If he could win promotion to higher command as a line officer, all that would change: "If the war does not end me first sure as God made man I will be on top and so far on top that it will be impossible to pull me down."[39] Now he had to choose between his ambition and his loyalty. If he chose to stay with the regiment, he would have to forfeit his combat role; if he retained line command he would have to leave the regiment. With some reluctance he finally accepted the bandmaster appointment, which at least allowed him to stay with the 369th, the regiment he had helped organize, Harlem's Own.

"Like Boxers with Their Hands Tied": The 77th Division in the Aisne-Marne Offensive, August 1918

The battles of July 15–20 stopped the German offensive, broke its right flank, and compelled Ludendorff's armies to begin a systematic withdrawal to the line of the Aisne River. The German success in breaking out of the stable trench lines of 1914–17 had created an opportunity for the renewal of mobile warfare, a chance to strike the retreating Germans, break them, and win a decisive victory. But the divisions of Gouraud's army east of Rheims and the striking force that had broken the German flank at Soissons were exhausted by intense combat. Fresh divisions had to be thrown into the pursuit, and the biggest and freshest were the American divisions that had just completed their brief tours of battlefield training. For the new offensive in the Champagne, French forces were strengthened by the regular Fourth Division, and four National Guard divisions, the 26th "Yankee" Division, 28th Pennsylvania, 32nd Michigan-Wisconsin, and 42nd "Rainbow." These divisions pressed assaults with enthusiasm, but their tactics were awkward, their organization unpracticed. And the veteran divisions opposing them had not in fact been broken or demoralized. The German generals prepared a series of defensive lines along the river barriers they had crossed with such relative ease in May and June: the Ourcq, the Vesle, and the Aisne. At each of these rear guards checked pursuing French and American divisions with heavy losses. From July 18 to August 6 the Allied offensive recovered about two-thirds of the "bulge," driving from the Marne, to the Ourcq, to the Vesle. The Fourth Division forced a crossing of the Vesle between the towns of Fismes and Bazoches but was brought to a stand under the high ground on the north bank of the river. By the first week in August all of these divisions (except the 28th) were fought out and had to be relieved. The offensive ground to a halt while new divisions were brought up to replace them.

One of these was the 77th. During the second week of August they were shifted north and west by train (*Hommes 40—Chevaux 8*) to a station twenty miles south of Château-Thierry, then boarded trucks to go north to the headquarters town of Fer-en-Tardenois, some ten air miles behind the center of the Allied lines south of the Vesle. They would be the first National Army division to participate in a major offensive on the Western Front. Their drivers were "skillful brown Annamite[s]," as Miles called them, or "little brown devils," as Tiebout had it: drafted by the French out of the colony later called Vietnam. The soldiers showed more respect to these Asians than to the "coolies" back in Camp de Souge, because their work was next door to combat and they were good at it.

The road was jammed with long lines of trucks that rocked in the ruts and ground gears as they left the hardpack to get around shell holes. The country along the roadside was not the untouched farmland they had seen on the march to Flanders. It had been just that pretty two months earlier, before the German offensives rolled over it one way going and the other coming back. Now it was plowed up by shell fire and vehicle tracks, houses and barns wrecked, towns reduced to stands of fractured walls among heaps of debris. Trampled wheat fields marked where the Second Division marines made their great attack into Belleau Wood. In the farmyards "unexploded gas shells lay in dangerous profusion," along with "regularly stacked shells which the enemy had not had time to carry away." Sharp-eyed foragers found a welcome store of the bottled mineral water with which German troops had been supplied. They camped in a woods "full of dead horses and . . . Huns." The night was "so dense and black that a hand could not be seen before the face," and the whole forest "reeked of horrid ghastly smells," rotting corpses of men and horses, heavy drifts of gas lingering in rifts of the ground. From up ahead the concussion of continual shell fire made the atmosphere shudder.

They approached the front through the rear areas of the fighting divisions, past field hospitals filled with wounded.

Friend, did you ever smell a field hospital—after it had stood all day under a blistering summer sun—with newly turned mounds all about—
where the burial squads had stowed the festering dead of a rapidly
retreating enemy—where this year's barrages have burrowed into the
tortured countryside and spewed the half-rotten contents of last year's
graves—where the sweaty, unwashed smell of sick and wounded men is
strangely blended with the odor of disinfectants and chemicals—where
the blazing sun has warmed the newly clustered graves until they almost seem to breathe?[40]

The 77th was to relieve the Fourth Division and part of the 28th,
which had been forced to halt by German entrenchments on the far side
of the Vesle. The American divisions had got just far enough to put themselves and their relief in a horrible tactical position. American artillery
was well placed behind the "red line," the main line of resistance on high
ground south of the river around the town of Mont St. Martin. But relief
troops had to cross a mile of open ground between Mont St. Martin and
the shattered hamlet of Ville Savoye, perched on the edge of the bench
above the floodplain. A steep road dropped through Ville Savoye and ran
for another mile across open fields to the muddy, sluggish Vesle, bordered with shattered willows. Every step of this journey was exposed to
observation and artillery fire, as well as aerial bombardment and strafing,
which made it exceptionally hard and costly to support the front line—
which was itself exposed to German artillery fire and infantry assault,
with high ground in front and an unfordable river at its back.[41]

Relieving another unit on the front lines was a difficult and risky operation under the best of circumstances. Two units rather than one are in
range of enemy artillery, and an alert and aggressive enemy can mount an
infantry assault while the troops are in motion and the defense not well
established. The difficulties are compounded when the sector involved
has been in active and intense combat, because the trench lines are likely
to be sketchy and incomplete. Being in close contact, the enemy has a
better chance to smell out the moment of exchange and plan his attack or
bombardment; and since he has already registered his artillery to fire on
the support and communication trenches, even a barrage leveled blindly
in the dark has a good chance of causing casualties and disrupting the relief. That was exactly the situation faced by the 77th, which had never
before had to effect a relief under fire. Fourth Division officers warned
their colleagues in the 77th that the front line there was "mere holes in

the ground" and was under constant shelling by shrapnel and high explosive, with gas in the intervals.

The first attempt was made on the night of August 11 by the 153rd Brigade (305th and 306th Infantry). The officers were unfamiliar with the ground—the abstract image on their maps lost its meaning as they stumbled forward into the dark, "by devious shell-torn roads and lanes, through woods and muddy fields . . . past a battery of naval guns whose sudden belching almost blew the wits out of us." They descended the steep slope into "wretched" shell-wracked Ville Savoye. They had not even reached the river crossing, and already their ranks were a "hopeless jumble." As their columns "buckled and filled" in the road the Germans began shelling, first high explosive, then "the pungent odors of mustard gas—to some it smelled like crushed onions" poisoned the darkness. The 305th's battalions became separated in the dark and there was a mad scramble to reestablish contact. The companies that managed to get across before dawn spread thin to hold the lines till the rest could join them, which would take another day and night.

The 308th had a worse time of it. It was ordered up on August 12 to replace units of the Fourth Division on the right of the 305th. But the front lines were so sketchy and fluid that no one was sure of the precise positions they were to occupy. Corps and Army headquarters were basing their orders on completely erroneous accounts of landscape features and troop dispositions. The 308th dug funk holes in the red line along the southern high ground and waited their turn on the miserable road through Ville Savoye, under shell fire much of the time, taking casualties. American batteries answered, and the artillery fire went on without pause hour after hour. The regiment's Second Battalion was heavily shelled as it crossed the open ground between Mont St. Martin and Ville Savoye. Those who reached that town found its ruins "and the whole of the river valley drenched with gas." In the dark, on unfamiliar ground, their gas masks reduced them to near-blindness. Led by Captain McMurtry, E Company found the road to Ville Savoye jammed with "the continuous traffic of ammunition trucks, ambulances, and ration wagons going and coming, [a] dense turmoil of traffic and humanity" alongside which they marched in a column of twos. German shells began dropping on the chaos, "cries of 'First Aid' were heard," and the column took cover off the road, Sergeant Greenstein killed, another sergeant and two privates wounded. They worked their way down to the river and reached the lines exhausted, disoriented, and diminished by casualties. The other companies of the regiment went through similar ordeals on succeeding nights. Worst hit was Company H, which began the relief on August 12 with 196 men and completed it on the fifteenth with 6, all the rest being gas or wound casualties. It would take three nights for the 308th to complete the relief.[42]

They now found themselves in an impossible position. The high command thought of their outpost line beyond the Vesle as a "bridgehead," which they were to hold at all costs as the springboard for a renewed attempt to break up the German retreat. In fact, "there was no road leading to a bridge nor any bridge nor the remnants of any." The Americans had dropped a large beam salvaged from a wrecked house across the stream at one point: troops had to cross it single file. On the far side the American lines ran along a railroad embankment that paralleled the river, but the Germans overlooked them from the high ground, which began a half-mile from the riverbank and rose in a series of benches to the crest, on which sat the well-named Chateau du Diable. The stream at their backs was thirty feet wide and six to eight feet deep, "full of barbed wire and . . . unfordable." Colonel Averill, who had commanded the 308th since Upton, reported the facts to headquarters and asked to be allowed to "rectify" his line by withdrawing the troops on the far bank. He was relieved of command. Pershing and his generals were showing their determination by being quick to sack officers who seemed to lack the offensive spirit.

For the men in the Vesle lines, offense was impossible and defense extraordinarily difficult. As Captain Lewis of the 308th wrote, they were like "boxers with hands tied behind their backs":

> They could neither advance nor fall back to improve their positions. Their orders were to stick right there. And they obeyed orders and stuck. To anyone who is at all familiar with military fundamentals . . . such a predicament constitutes the most severe and nerve-wracking test for recruit divisions made of up troops freshly arrived from the so-called quiet sectors.

They would spend the next month fighting along the Vesle, attacking the Germans on the high ground, beaten back with loss every time. "Our Intelligence Section by careful observation reported at least thirty-seven machine-gun nests in the town of Bazoches," which was only one of the German strongpoints. They were also subject to continual bombardment and gas attacks. The ground to their rear on the south side of the Vesle was flat and exposed, so reserve positions were established well back from the front, on and below the steep south-side bench in the shattered hamlets of St. Thibault and Ville Savoye. The latter town was headquarters for whichever battalion of the 308th was in the lines. Its main street ran from the top to the foot of the bench, all of it exposed to enemy fire from across the river. This was the route used by the battalion runners, who were the primary communication link between front line and headquarters. Attempts to connect the positions by telephone wire were frustrated by German bombardments, which cut wires strung across the flat ground between bench and river. Behind and above the bench the village of Mont St. Martin was headquarters for the supporting battalion. Mont Notre-Dame, similarly situated to the west, centered the reserve positions for the regiment on the left of the 308th. Everything forward of those villages, and much of the ground to their rear, was vulnerable to shell fire from German batteries well behind their infantry line on the northern bench, and "they kept up a constant bombardment of gas and high explosives. The Vesle Sector was never free from gas during the entire time we spent in that precarious place."[43]

The line of the river was marked by groves of shattered willows, trunks cracked off at heights of eight to ten feet by air bursts. On either side of the river was a belt of swampy bottomland a quarter of a mile wide. The muddy stream could be crossed only by swimming or by improvised foot bridges, vulnerable to German fire. If the Germans were to mount a successful counterattack the forward units might be trapped against the stream. The troops on the far side of the Vesle lived in conditions that represented the worst of the Western Front. Exposed as they were to German fire, they had to hunker down in their trenches and funk holes and stay put. Washing was out of the question. You got filthier by the minute, and lousier—cooties swarming in hair and armpits and crotch and infesting the seams of the uniform. If a man had to relieve himself he had to wait till dark to do it away from his trench or funk hole; if he couldn't wait—and diarrhea was endemic to trench life—he fouled his own nest and lived with it, and the man who relieved him lived with it too. The trenches they occupied had been improvised under attack and "improved" under fire. They were in the river's floodplain, where the water table was high. Water seeped into them from the ground and accumulated in the September rains. Troops stood, sat, ate, slept in the wet, unable to dry or change their socks for a week, their feet swollen and painful with trench foot so that their hasty scrambles between dugout and firing line were hobbling and crippled.

Hot food was impossible, even cold rations could reach them only by running the gauntlet of German artillery. The army rewarded them with an issue of fresh beef, "delivered under shell fire to the ruined church in Mont St. Martin." But kitchen smoke, even in the reserve area, drew artillery fire—they couldn't cook the meat and it hung in the church till it rotted and had to be buried.[44]

They suffered intense artillery bombardments: mind-numbing sense-shattering barrages of high explosive, tearing mutilations of white-hot shrapnel. But gas claimed the largest share of victims, and to Miles "the never ceasing menace and presence of gas was in a way more hateful than high explosive itself." The enemy used chlorine and phosgene, "the latter a vile and sweetish stench," and mustard gas, distinguished by its odor "of rare, ripe onions." The ground they occupied had been heavily fought over, and the air was full of the stench of the unburied dead, cows, horses, and humans. In some places it was a heavy livid stink, so strong it almost had a color; in others it was a pervasive breathing of rot, a continual reminder of how easily one's own precious incomparable body could be made into meat. They smelled it as they bolted the cold rations that managed to reach them in the lines, cans of corned beef whose taste was so vile they called it "monkey meat." Each of the frequent bombardments they suffered renewed the stench, churning the old dead out of the ground and making new dead. They saw dead men and men killed and wounded every day—most of the wounds resulting from artillery fire, high explosive, and shrapnel that tore men to pieces, inflicted horrible dismemberments and mutilations. "Battle . . . if it is sufficiently severe, intense, and long in duration . . . will ultimately break everyone committed to it."[45]

Their morale, their ability to function as soldiers and maintain coherence of mind and feeling, was steadily worn down to "just the accumulated blur, and the hurting vagueness of too long in the lines, the everlasting alertness, the noise and fear, the cell-by-cell exhaustion, the thinning of the ranks around you as day follows nameless day. And the constant march into eternity of your own small quota of chances for survival." What made the experience bearable was the tunnel vision imposed by the omnipresent strain and fear, which cut them off from normal feelings.

That, and the support of belonging to the unit, the intense feeling of mutual dependence that bound the men of squad, platoon, and company to each other and, by extension, their organization.

Even the isolating terror and helplessness felt under artillery bombardment were easier to bear when "in company with others." The sense that others suffered along with you, were there to support you with whatever comfort might be found, were loyal to you, personally—so that you were assured that, if you were wounded under fire, there would be someone willing to risk his own life to bring you back, or (a cold but real comfort) recover your body for a burial as decent as willing men could manage. That knowledge imposed the same burden on you, to risk everything you were or hoped to be to save the man next to you, six months ago a stranger and now closer than most blood kin. Like James Europe of the 369th they felt uneasy, obscurely guilty even, when a minor injury or illness, a chance for promotion or a rear-area assignment took them away while their own squad or platoon remained in action. Ben Kaufman of the 308th repeatedly turned down nominations for officer training to stay with his unit. Some even found themselves becoming horribly at home in the war's environment of deprivation and imminent danger: "They get an itch for the old miserable life—a disgusting, illogical yearning to be back again in the place they hated."[46]

The experience of combat immerses the soldier in a world whose fundamental conditions, language, temporal rhythms, functions of life are utterly foreign to the "normal" life that produced him. In adapting to that world his personality, his thought processes, his emotions and body awareness are transformed in ways that alienate him from his civilian self. To survive psychologically, he must become inured to the omnipresence of death, numb to the horror of seeing loved friends killed or maimed.

> As in a polar expedition . . . life is simply one continual watch against the menace of death—it has transformed us into unthinking animals in order to give us the weapon of instinct—it has reinforced us with dullness, so that we do not go to pieces before the horror, which would overwhelm us if we had clear conscious thought—it has awakened in us the sense of comradeship, so that we escape the abyss of solitude—it has lent us the indifference of wild creatures, so that in spite of all we preserve the positive in every moment, and store it up as a reserve against the onslaught of nothingness. Thus we live a closed, hard existence of the utmost superficiality, and rarely does an incident strike out a spark.

But the alienation is (for most men) conditional, not permanent. The soldier too has a double consciousness. Within the shell of that saving numbness he is aware that his old vulnerable "home" self survives, so his adaptation is unstable, unsafe, the numbness laced with poisonous anxiety: "Unexpectedly a flame of grievous and terrible yearning flares up. Those are the dangerous moments. They show us that the adjustment is only artificial, that [our indifference] is not simple rest but the sharpest struggle for rest." Once the pressure of combat is relieved, repressed feeling could strike a shattering blow. Ernie Pyle, the great front-line correspondent of World War II, experienced this cycle of numbing and terrible reawakening.

> My emotions seemed dead and crusty when presented with the tangibles of war. I found I could look on rows of fresh graves without a lump in my throat. Somehow I could look on mutilated bodies without flinching or feeling deeply. It was only when I sat alone away from it all or lay awake at night in my bedroll re-creating what I had seen . . . that at last the enormity of all those newly dead struck like a living nightmare.[47]

Each man assimilated the ordeal as he could, repressing or compartmentalizing memory, or "socializing" the memories by putting them in play among the others who had shared the experience, transforming horror and fear into sardonic humor. The vile rations were "monkey meat," lice were "seam squirrels," a wound serious enough to cripple but not kill was a "blighty," a million-dollar wound, a ticket home. They gave joke names to the different types of artillery shells whose shrieking approach and detonation racked mind and body to the breaking point. For short-range bombardments the Germans used 77-mm howitzers whose shells were called "whizz-bangs" because "the noise of the exploding shell is almost coincident with the shrill whistle that announces its coming."

> Here was a course in the ethics of high-explosive society. When a whizz-bang makes an afternoon call, it whistles first, then knocks; and the best manner in which to receive it is by lying prone. . . . The acquaintance of other fast company was made. Herr Whizzbang brought along his "lady-friend," Minnie Werfer, whose custom it was first to burst into the most uncouth of caterwaulings, and then into splinters.

The *Minenwerfer* (mine-thrower) was a heavy trench mortar that fired powerful shells in arcing trajectories that could reach men protected from direct fire. They called these shells "Iron Mermaids" because of the fish-like tails that stabilized their flight. "They are peculiarly disconcerting, as they come through the air with a wailing sob-like whistle, something like a mixture of a locomotive whistle and siren, and they are hard to 'judge.' " The Germans also hit them with heavier guns firing at long-range, eight- and ten-inch howitzers and rifled cannon whose big high-explosive shells were variously dubbed "Tons-of-Coal," "G.I. Cans," "Whimpering Willies," or "Jack Johnsons"—in tribute to the knock-out punch of the celebrated (and hated) Negro heavyweight champion.

Battalions took turns occupying the front and reserve positions. Typically the 308th would have one battalion manning Ville Savoye and its sector of the Vesle lines, a second battalion in the reserve line, and the third farther back recovering from its stint across the Vesle. Each battalion relief had to be accomplished under fire and entailed losses. For the 306th, fighting to the left of the 308th, there was only one path runners and relief parties could use. Second Battalion's cadre of runners and carriers was decimated as they ran the gauntlet of German fire between headquarters and the forward positions several times each day. During one relief the enemy hit village and road with a heavy bombardment, the village itself absorbing thirty shells a minute, high explosive mixed with gas. The last man left to man the communications center was the Chinese-American soldier, Sing Kee. Although he too had been "badly gassed and was ordered evacuated," he refused relief and for twenty-four hours "stuck on the job and kept up communication with his battalion until too weak to move." Captain Adler believed "it was only one more evidence of the fact that in the cosmopolitan composition of the Division lay its strength." Sing Kee would receive the Distinguished Service Cross and be promoted to color sergeant, the highest rank attained by a Chinese-American in the AEF.[48]

Losses mounted steadily. The shattered houses of Ville Savoye, Mont St. Martin, and the rest offered little protection. Even divisional headquarters had to be relocated to a cave, in which officers and enlisted men huddled in democratic squalor. On August 21 the First Battalion of the 308th headquartered in Ville Savoye also decided to move into a cave. To the west, across the Vesle, the 306th was attacking those thirty-seven machine-gun posts in the village of Bazoches and taking heavy losses. At ten that night, as a group of officers took the air at the cave mouth, the Germans fired a harassing barrage. A direct hit by high explosive killed four officers and wounded two, among them the battalion's gas officer and the artillery liaison. Captain Belvedere Brooks, Wardlaw Miles's dearest friend, was one of the dead. "None among [us] is better to look upon than Bel Brooks with his fair hair and clear blue eyes." Miles took over his company. Also killed were two enlisted men, "names unknown."[49]

That same day regimental headquarters at Chéry Chartreuve took "a direct hit by a combination high explosive and gas shell," which broke through the ceiling and burst in the room occupied by the operations and intelligence staff. Captain Whittlesey had just finished dictating a field order to Corporal Harry Goodman, a Jewish lawyer from Brooklyn who had formerly worked for the State Department. The room was filled with blinding, choking gas in which the living crawled and groped to escape. Whittlesey saw Goodman dragging himself along the floor toward the dugout in which the telephone switchboard was located. Not until Whittlesey got to him did he see that Goodman's leg had been nearly severed from his body by a shard of shrapnel that had struck him in the groin. First-aid men did what they could, but he died at the field hospital. Half a dozen men in Whittlesey's section were wounded or incapacitated by gas.

That night the Germans followed up their repulse of the 306th with a heavy counterattack on the American lines beyond the river. At 3:30 A.M. they hit the Second Battalion of the 306th and Companies I and K of Third Battalion 308th with high explosive—no gas, because their own infantry came storming in as the barrage lifted.[50] The 308th's lines ran along the low railroad embankment parallel to the river. Company K held its positions hard, Sergeant Ben Kaufman moving from hole to hole to coordinate the fire of his platoons. One attacker got into the position and was killed by Private Spinella, who "first used the butt of his Chauchat" to disable the German, then "finished" him with his own bayonet. At the boundary between I and K a *Flammenwerfer* broke through to K Company headquarters and shot a jet of "liquid fire" into the shelter where Private Van Duzer was on liaison duty, desperately trying to contact Battalion HQ over the unreliable phone system. Van Duzer fled the dugout sheathed in flames, and was saved by Private Rosenthal of I Company, who threw him into a pool of water. Van Duzer, his face and body blistering from severe burns, "without helmet or gas mask," hauled himself out of the water and made his way to Captain Frothingham of K to report that I Company was "badly cut up

[and] there's a dozen Dutchmen in the woods back of you!" The Germans had sent infiltrating parties behind the company's exposed right flank into the ravaged trees along the riverbank. Frothingham ordered Van Duzer wrapped in "endless thicknesses of gauze" and sent to the rear, then pulled his flank platoons back to anchor their position on the Vesle itself. (The party escorting Van Duzer managed to capture a German patrol, thanks to one of their number who was able to negotiate the surrender in German.)

On the left I Company had been hit by four companies of troops from a Baden regiment, led by flamethrowers. Machine gunners had come forward with the infantry, and they blazed away at troops by the "bright yellow light of the [flame] projectors [that] illuminated the surroundings."[51] Lieutenant Langstaff found that German troops had infiltrated the woods behind his main position along the railroad embankment and were also attacking his forward posts "in overwhelming numbers." One platoon was split, its survivors driven back on the supports. Langstaff later wrote:

> Many a brave deed was done that day. Acting Corporal Stein, a New York ladies' hat manufacturer, saved his platoon . . . by rushing out alone to an extreme flank with a Chauchat and putting out of commission a Boche machine gun that was about to enfilade [our] line. Private Bologna, a New York bootblack, covered the retirement of Sergeant Riley's post, turning and firing his Chauchat from the shoulder, mowing down a file of Germans pursuing his detail along a narrow pathway. Private Comarelli, a day laborer, insisted on keeping up fire from the path over my dugout, although four little red spots on his buttocks showed that a machine-gun bullet had threaded its way in and out of him four times. Only rough handling could get him up to have his wounds dressed.

Langstaff's own striker, "Private Arzano, a candy-maker at home," went with another private to rescue some wounded crying for help. The other man was killed and Arzano badly wounded, but after being treated to ward off infection he refused to leave the line "till he had killed a couple of Huns." Sergeants Carter and Riley suckered a German platoon into an ambush and wiped it out.

Elsewhere things went badly. The platoon that anchored I Company's right was "overwhelmed and captured" entirely, except for "smiling little [Private] Connell [who] had been overlooked under the dirt of a caved-in trench" and returned alone to tell the tale. Supports were slow in coming, the Germans had broken their connection with K Company, the platoons on both flanks were being pressed back to the river. Sergeant Blohm, a German Jew whose two brothers were serving in the Kaiser's army, was cut off on the river bank with Private Catalano, who was wounded. Blohm used belts to wrap a bundle of driftwood into a makeshift raft, and with Catalano clinging and himself swimming, towed and hauled it across the Vesle.[52]

Lieutenant Langstaff pulled his men back from the railroad embankment into the woods along the river. Here the German attack was finally repulsed and the *Flammenwerfer* operators killed, many "by their own hands through getting the nozzles of their machines entangled in the heavy underbrush of the swamp." The flamethrower was an effective weapon, both for its actual power to destroy troops fighting from shelter and for the fear it inspired. But it was often as lethal to the user as the target, and doughboys repaid the terror they inspired by killing any operator who tried to surrender.

As the German infantry pulled back, their artillery covered them with the usual mix of shell fire and gas. On the right, where K Company had also been driven into the willows, Sergeant Kaufman was out of his funk hole making sure the company's lines were intact. A shell smashed into the position, wounding soldiers in one hole and collapsing its walls on top of them. Kaufman had to take off his mask to supervise the rescue and got a dose of gas that temporarily blinded him. But he refused to leave his men, groped through the ruined woods from hole to hole, avoiding officers and aid men until late in the day, when he was found out and ordered to the rear.[53]

Back at Ville Savoye the reserves had also taken casualties from the bombardment. The Third Battalion's supports went forward, reinforced by Captain Harvey's A Company. But the situation was still desperate, and the plan made by 154th Brigade commander General Evan Johnson was a nonstarter. It called for a battalion assault using "bombs." Captain Breckinridge, whose battalion was to make the attack, had only four hundred exhausted men to do a job that required a thousand fresh ones, and hardly any grenades. For once a line officer's protest was heeded, perhaps because Johnson knew Breckinridge personally and trusted him. But Johnson was overruled by higher commanders, who characteristically ignored protests from field officers, however well founded. The back and forth went on late into the night while I and K were bloodied along the riverbank, and in the end the commander of the 308th had to say, "Tell Breckinridge to do the best he can."

Breckinridge had three understrength companies to work with. Company A under Captain Harvey was at the river, ready to cross. Companies B and C worked forward to the river, some squads becoming lost in the woods and darkness. Captain Miles and B Company were to lead the relief. The covering barrage was delayed an hour, and Miles hurried through the dark to forestall his lead platoon's attack. All wasted effort: the barrage never materialized, and the lead platoon made its attack anyway, there were brothers *dying* on the other side. They plunged into the river, losing men and weapons to the mud and moving water. In the misty woods ahead they thought they saw Americans—hailed them—and were cut down by the fire of a large force of German troops. Of forty-five men who began the attack, only six survived—the rest were killed, wounded, or captured. Meanwhile, most of C Company under Lieutenant Sheridan managed to join forces with Harvey's A Company on the riverbank. Harvey ordered an attack to retake the railroad embankment. "Well," said Sheridan, "I expect this is going to be a real Irish Wake." His men waded across the river and fought their way through the woods nearly back to the railroad line, where Sheridan fell mortally wounded by a machine gun. Losses were so heavy that Captain Harvey had to pull both companies back across the river. It was daylight now, and they saw new companies coming forward, taking casualties from whizz-bangs and machine guns as they crossed open ground. "By nightfall practically all of the ground had been regained and our outpost line was nearly back in its original position."

They tried to push it further out, but got nowhere. They remained in the same lines for two more weeks, suffering the same bombardments, bloodying German raiding parties and being bloodied by them, sending out their own raiders and making local attacks that were always repulsed with loss but at terrible cost. Losses were particularly heavy among the best officers and noncoms, the ones who were always in the line with their troops and characteristically "led from the front." These were the men whose skills in organizing an action and maintaining morale were most critical to the unit's ability to function. Although other men would prove themselves and earn promotion from the ranks, the combination of giftedness and experience could not be infinitely replicated or replaced. Among the casualties were men who had been beloved characters since Upton: "Jack Curry, the popular sergeant" and boxing champ, severely wounded; Private Patrissi and Sergeant Kessler, who sang "The Jews and Wops, the Dutch and Irish cops," wounded and gassed; Corporal Flynn, ex-vaudevillian and Upton stage manager, wounded. The cost of this fighting, which left the 308th's position essentially unchanged, was high—1,400 killed and wounded, about 11 percent of the division's rifle companies.[54]

Their experiences increasingly alienated them from everything that did not belong to their squads, companies, and regiments. Orders sent down by the high command struck them, and their officers, as weirdly out of touch with reality, and therefore as arbitrary and even cruel. The alienation was inevitable. For division, corps, and army HQ, knowledge of what was happening on the ground was necessarily mediated by the abstractions of tactical doctrine and strategy, the paperwork of maps and logistical tables and unit-strength reports that are supposed to represent the ground and the strength available to take and hold it. Even the best headquarters makes mistakes, and the staffs commanding the American divisions and armies in France were too new at their jobs to be very good at them. For the men at the front every misconceived order, every rejection by headquarters of recommendations made by the officers on the ground, suggested—proved—the high command was out of touch, didn't know, didn't care whether K Company of the 308th or the 369th—to its men the most precious community in the world—spent its lives uselessly, for objectives whose value, if any, was invisible to the men who died for them.[55]

It went on like that until September 3. For days there had been rumors, carried by German POWs snaked out of their outposts by raiders, that the enemy was preparing to withdraw. The Germans leveled a heavy barrage on September 2—it was cover for their rear guards. The Second Battalion of the 308th went up and over the vacated positions on the high ground as observation balloons rose behind American lines to search out the enemy's line of retreat. After a month of frustration the 77th could get up on its legs and move again, ordered to pursue the enemy and break him as he fled.

But the enemy was still not fleeing. From the start of their retreat in

July, the Germans had planned for a staged withdrawal, rear guards holding and slowing the Allied counterattack, followed by a pullback to new positions already prepared for defense. The last and strongest of these were dug in along the line of the Aisne River and its canal, a pair of water barriers wider and more formidable than the muddy little Vesle.

Pursuit is a difficult business for inexperienced troops, and especially for officers who have never had to coordinate the rapid movement of masses of men and equipment over unknown and devious roads to pin down and destroy an enemy whose numbers, position, and disposition are unknown—a veteran enemy, whose movement is not improvised but carefully planned. The pursuing battalions and regiments lost touch with one another, ran into pockets of heavy resistance. The men dropped their packs and pressed on, with the 306th on the left, the 308th in the center, and the 307th on the right. A pair of villages defended by rear guards held up the two flanking regiments, but the 308th pressed on until its lead battalion ran into an ambush as it crossed a steep-sided ravine. The front line of M company seemed to "fade" as the German machine guns opened up. A pair of German airplanes dived out of the clouds and strafed the troops as they pulled back. Nonetheless, they had hit a weak spot in the German lines, and the next day they pushed through it, following orders that told them to go on without regard to anything happening on their flanks. The 308th advanced until they had seized a section of high ground called Butte de Bourmont, where stiffening German resistance stopped them well short of the Aisne. They held the butte for a day while isolated from the rest of the division. When the others came into line they found themselves in the same sort of stalemate they had known on the Vesle: holding an advanced position under fire against an enemy well entrenched and in good order on high ground. They were trapped in a cycle of horror and frustration, doomed to repeat the same terrible ordeal of suffering death and futility from which they had just escaped.

Closing with the Enemy: September 2–16, 1918

Black and White, the soldiers of the 369th Regiment and the 77th Division had entered an ever-narrowing tunnel, in which their concerns steadily drew inward until the only remaining purpose was to survive yourself, and for your buddies to survive—forgetting the Fourteen Points and making the "world safe for democracy," forgetting the NAACP and the Society for Protecting the Good Name of the Immigrants, no longer taking to heart the praise or blame of the *New York American* or the *Age*, the *Journal, Tribune, World*, or *Times*, the *Crisis*, the *Outlook*, the *Literary Digest*, or the *American Hebrew*—valuing only the opinions of the other men in the platoon, on whom your own life and dignity absolutely depend, that they should think well of your deeds, that together you do nothing to be ashamed of.

They were trapped in a terrible irony. To refuse to fight would be to betray the beloved community of platoon or company; to keep fighting is to consent to the deaths of the comrades who make up the company. The only way to break the trap is to win the war—only victory will end the stream of cruel and stupid orders from GHQ, only victory can simultaneously fulfill the unit's mission and spare its comrades. Combat soldiers have to do more than inure themselves to their own suffering, to the sight of their own dead. They have to be able to kill, and to persist in killing, to think of killing as the necessary and most effective means to their greatest end—which is to survive the battle and the war. Ernie Pyle noticed that the difference between combat troops and everyone else was the casual and workshop manner in which they talked about killing. It was no longer something extraordinary or terrible.

> To the fighting soldier that phase of the war was behind. It was left behind after his first battle. His blood was up. He was fighting for his life. . . . He wanted to kill individually or in vast numbers. He wanted to see the Germans overrun, mangled, butchered . . . spoke excitedly of seeing great heaps of dead . . . in that one respect the front-line soldier differed from all the rest of us. . . . We wanted terribly yet only academically for the war to be over. The front-line soldier wanted it to be terminated by the physical process of his destroying enough Germans to end it. He was truly at war. The rest of us, no matter how hard we worked, were not.[56]

It was acquisition of this willingness to kill that marked the soldiers of the 369th and the 77th Division as fit to participate in the "Big Push." They had made the psychological transition from their normal belief that taking human life was sinful, to a new professional outlook where killing was a craft.

Thousands of youths who never suspected the presence of such an impulse in themselves have learned in military life the mad excitement of destroying. The appetite is one that requires cultivation in the environment of disorder and deprivation common to life at the front. It usually marks the great difference between green troops and veterans.

It enables the soldier to do more than fight in defense of himself and his buddies. It enables him to "step over the line that separates self-defense from fighting for its own sake," to put himself and his buddies at risk for the sake of destroying the enemy. "Generals often name it 'the will to close with the enemy,'" and it is the vital necessity of troops who must lead a great offensive.[57]

It was the quality Sergeant Butler of the 369th had displayed when he bushwhacked that German raiding party and chased them back to their trenches, killing all the way—Butler, the "indoor chauffeur" who used to say a respectful "Good morning" to the White passengers stepping into the elevator he drove. "I must have run amuck," he had said, wonderingly. Until that moment he had not believed himself capable of doing such a thing. Now he knew he could—and would.

L. Wardlaw Miles—the once and future professor of literature, whose students would remember his love of poetry, the way he urged them to "taste poetry on the tip of the tongue"—would achieve that state of mind in front of the town of Revillon. For ten days the regiment had fought it out on the slopes below the town. The men suffered from diarrhea. They were nearly without food or water for the first three days, until Captain James Roosevelt could bring the supply train forward. The high command, unwilling to admit that the chance to break a retreating enemy was lost, ordered the division to crack the German front at Revillon by assault. They tried it several times between September 7 and 13 and lost heavily every time. In Miles's battalion on Butte de Bourmont not a single captain was left alive, most companies had but a single officer left, and some were commanded by sergeants. Miles had commanded his company as a lieutenant since his friend and mentor Bel Brooks had been killed on the Vesle. He had been offered a promotion if he would return to the States for an advanced training course—he had refused in order to remain with Company B, and on the thirteenth he was promoted captain within the regiment. Another attack on Revillon was ordered for the next day and he volunteered to lead it.[58]

He had no reason to expect success after so many attacks had failed, but if he did not try then everyone he cared about in the regiment would certainly have to stay in this deathtrap. He planned things as well as he knew how. "At dawn our machine-gun barrage screamed overhead with a peculiar and prolonged intensity." The assault troops waited through most of that day in a quarry and a marshy wood below the butte. Late in the afternoon, with the sun in the eyes of the German gunners, Miles took his assault force over the top and into the open, leading the first wave in person. The Germans opened with their own machine guns—there was no artillery support for Miles—and his men began to drop. His lieutenant and a sergeant were killed as they reached the enemy wire entanglements, and Miles was hit before he threw himself at the foot of the wire and began chopping into it with the long-handled wire cutters, some beside him doing the same while others simply threw themselves onto the wire, pressing it down with their bodies so the next wave could pass over them. As Miles worked the cutters he was hit again, shot in both arms, one leg shattered by machine-gun bullets, but the shock of wounding is terrific and adrenaline dulls any nerves but those you need to fight or flee, so he refused to be evacuated. As long as he was still able to function he was going to take his men into that trench, and as his second wave came through he ordered two men to put him on a blanket and carry him forward, into the trench from which they had driven the Germans, bombing them out of their revetments, clearing the trench with Chauchats and trench-sweeper shotguns.

That trench was only eighteen inches deep, a "straitjacket" which offered little protection from German mortars and machine guns, but the survivors held it against a counterattack that night. Miles finally lost consciousness and was carried to the rear, to a field hospital where his leg was amputated. He would be awarded the Congressional Medal of Honor. The men he left behind would be decimated by an all-day bombardment on the fifteenth, then driven out by a German counterattack. But Sergeant Norwat, on whom command of the survivors devolved, rallied the remnant, "drove out the Germans for the last time" and retook the trench.

For all that, the Germans still held Revillon. But at least the town was no longer the 77th's problem. On September 16 they were relieved by elements of an Italian division, and sent to the rear to rest and recover.[59]

At nearly the same time, on the far side of Rheims below Butte du Mesnil, Corporal Horace Pippin was also displaying a disposition to close with the enemy. He had responded to the trials of battle by becoming increasingly aggressive, taking the lead in sniper hunts and trench raids. Now, on September 12, his battalion was ordered to make one more try to capture the butte. The French would lay down a preparatory bombardment. Pippin's company would advance behind a rolling barrage, through a swamp, and over a wooden footbridge, then attack and capture a small hill, from which the next wave of the assault on the butte could be staged. At one in the morning artillery lined up "hub to hub" and opened fire on the Germans, who answered with a heavy barrage of their own. The whole first line seemed to Pippin to dissolve into "the sea of shells craters" that stretched across no-man's-land. Then the barrage "raised and we went over the top once more." It took most of the morning to work their way through the swamp, but by noon they had taken the hillock. It was bare of cover on top, flailed by machine-gun and artillery fire from Germans on higher ground. "That afternoon we got in a crossfire of machine gun that took away about all of my platoon[,] it only left four on hirt." It was sure death for the survivors to stay there, but to escape they'd have to "cross the swamp with machine guns sitteing by." German artillery was heaving shells into the swamp—they would "dive in the mud and . . . birst. After that you could get a team of horses in the hole and bury them." Pippin began crawling from man to man, to prepare them for retreat. The first man he got to was hit, said, "I'm done," and rolled over. "I creeped away, then the Bullets were hieting in front of me and would throw dirt in my face." But he got to each of the three survivors, and on his signal they got up and made a run for the swamp.

In the swamp they met I Company coming forward. Sure now that the remnant of his platoon was safe, and with fresh troops preparing to attack the hill, Pippin decided to go and get payback from the machine gunner that had "cleaned out the first platoon." While I Company moved against the hill, Pippin sneaked out to the flank, worked his way through brush and rocks till he got an angle on the machine gunner. One shot avenged his dead buddies. "I'm a good shoot," Pippin wrote: for once he was simply satisfied with his work. I Company went on to take the hill, and over the next two days took a further objective—a ruined town several hundred yards closer to the butte. The battalion took five hundred prisoners and fourteen machine guns. "We only hell the line that night," and after three days without food were relieved.[60]

On September 15 the 369th Regiment was marched to the rear for a brief spell of rest and the receipt of replacements. The 77th Division was relieved at Revillon on the sixteenth, tramping to the rear through the wreckage left in the wake of their advance from the Vesle. Their respite would not be long. Forces were already being assembled for a colossal Allied offensive, millions of men and thousands of guns massing along the whole length of the Western Front, from the Swiss border to the North Sea. The hard-fought decimated companies of the 369th and the 77th Division, which had been in action continuously for most of the summer, would be asked to lead the assault. The rest areas to which they marched after being relieved would be the base camps from which they would march to attack the German lines in and around the Argonne Forest.

An observer might have marked as the difference between them the crested silhouettes of the French helmets worn by the Blacks and the low-crowned British helmets of the Whites. Other differences, of skin color and kit, would have been obscured by the unwashed filth of the place from which both had just come, which was in its essentials the same place.

> The men are walking. . . . Their walk is slow, for they are dead weary, as you can tell even when looking at them from behind. Every line and sag of their bodies speaks of their inhuman exhaustion. . . . They have fought hard, eaten little, washed none, and slept hardly at all. Their nights have been violent with attack, fright, butchery, and their days sleepless and miserable with the crash of artillery. . . .
>
> Their feet seem to sink into the ground from the overload they are bearing.
>
> They don't slouch. It is the terrible deliberation of each step that spells out their appalling tiredness. Their faces are black and unshaven. They are young men, but the grime and whiskers and exhaustion make them look middle-aged.
>
> In their eyes as they pass is not hatred, not excitement, not despair, not even the tonic of their victory—there is just the simple expression of being here as though they had been doing this forever, and nothing else.
>
> The line moves on, but it never ends. All afternoon men keep coming round the hill and vanishing eventually over the horizon. It is one long tired line of antlike men.

There is an agony in your heart and you almost feel ashamed to
look at them. They are just guys from Broadway and Main Street, but
you wouldn't remember them. They are too far away now. They are too
tired.[61]

The description is Ernie Pyle's and belongs to a different war, but is
probably as true a picture of the 1918 doughboys as it was of the "God-
damned Infantry" in 1943 Tunisia.

With this difference: the troops Pyle described had been four days and
nights in the line. At the time of its relief the 369th had been in combat
for two months with hardly a break, and nearly two weeks of continuous intense combat on the butte. The 308th Regiment of the 77th Division had been under fire for a month in the Baccarat sector and intensely
engaged along the Vesle and in the pursuit to the Aisne from August 12
to September 14, with only a week's rest. It had fought in front of Revillon for eleven consecutive days, either assaulting or fending off counterattacks, with intense bombardments in the intervals. Both regiments had
been drained by the steady wastage of trench warfare—snipers, bombardments, disease. The 77th lost 4,700 men between the Vesle and the Aisne,
the vast majority of them from the rifle and machine-gun companies—
about 17 percent of the division's initial strength. The 308th lost 128
killed and more than twice that many wounded out of an initial strength
of about 3,200. The 369th had seen as much combat, but was not quite
as badly damaged—Gouraud handled both attack and defense more economically than his American counterparts. Even so it had lost 200 men
out of about 3,000 in its ranks.[62] Casualties in both outfits were particularly heavy among junior officers and noncoms, the very men whose skill
and personality had formed the unit's original solidarity. New men
stepped up to take their places, some already part of the unit, others
strangers, "ninety-day wonders" fresh out of OTC. In the 369th this
problem was compounded by racial politics, which had removed the regiment's Black line officers for reasons that smacked of race prejudice.

Their experiences had transformed the men and the units in which
they fought. What built them up as soldiers broke them down as men, and
vice versa. Captain Lewis caught something of this paradox in his reflections on the sufferings of the 308th, although he emphasizes the positive:
"At the very time of discouragement when they feared that they were

being shattered as fighting units, they were, although they did not guess it, finding themselves." From the perspective of divisional and army command, they had learned, at acceptable cost, to be competent soldiers. They had "cracked their helmets against the real thing—modern warfare" and emerged "with their mettle tempered and their morale strengthened." At least some of the Sons of Roosevelt who commanded them were ready to grant them their highest accolade, metaphorically amalgamating them to the "American stock": "The fibre of the heroic American stuff which stood the final acid test in the Argonne was toughened by subjection to terrible stress on the Vesle. . . . They approached its banks as recruit divisions. A month later these same troops were chosen as veteran divisions to participate in the drive through the Argonne. They had arrived."

The veterans of the AEF recognized their arrival, and their peculiar identity, by giving them their own verse in the endless anthem of the Western Front:

> Oh, the Seventy-seventh went over the top, parley-voo!
> Oh, the Seventy-seventh went over the top, parley-voo!
> Oh, the Seventy-seventh went over the top
> A sous lieutenant, a Jew and a Wop,
> Hinky dinky parley-voo![63]

That was honor of a kind the infantry could appreciate.

7

Home Fires Burning: Political and Racial Reaction, Summer 1918

> The problem in defense is how far you can go without destroying
> from within what you are trying to defend from without.
>
> —*Dwight D. Eisenhower*

War might be, as Clausewitz said, politics continued by other means; but once war is engaged, the means are no longer subordinate to the political ends. The purposes of the war-making nation are implacably transformed by the very measures and actions used to achieve them: limited war aims become demands for unconditional surrender; limitless ambitions collapse in compromise and demoralization. All other values recede before the necessity of averting defeat. Pro-war Progressives had seen U.S. engagement in Europe as the seizing of a "plastic" juncture in American and world history. A nation united in purpose, following voluntarily the commands of an intelligent leadership, would assert its mastery over the forces of modernization. But a war to make the world safe for democracy could not be won without the use of measures and the rousing of passions that would alter the nation's understanding of "safety" and "democracy." The armed defense of America and American principles would put the nation and those principles at risk.

Woodrow Wilson is said to have told reporter Frank Cobb, "Once lead this people into war . . . and they'll forget there was ever such a thing as tolerance. To fight you must be brutal and ruthless and the spirit of ruthless brutality will enter into the very fibre of our national life, infecting Congress, the courts, the policeman on the beat, the man in the street." In his call to war Wilson tried to set rational limits to that intolerance, by declaring that our quarrel was with the German government and its ideology: "We have no quarrel with the German people. . . . It was not upon their impulse that their government acted in entering this war. It was not with their previous knowledge or approval." But Wilson misconceived the character of the German war effort and the political dynamics of warfare among advanced nation-states. War was certainly initiated by diplomatic and military actions of the Kaiser's government. However, those actions were supported, and the declaration of war accepted with tremendous enthusiasm, even by liberal and socialist parties in the Reichstag. The pattern was the same in all the warring states. It was not upon some spontaneous impulse of the people that the United States went to war. The Wilson administration made the decisions; the people and their representatives accepted and cheered the event.[1]

Roosevelt might have erred in explaining Germany's willingness to fight an increasingly brutal war as the by-product of racial character, but he correctly understood that Germany's power to sustain the costs of total war rested on the nationalism of popular masses—and that the United States would have to muster a similar degree of nationalism if it was to defeat Germany. War demands passionate engagement, the awakening of a desire to kill and destroy, a desire so powerful that masses of men and women will accept deprivation, loss of loved ones, and personal death in order to satisfy it. Before the public would embrace the kill-or-be-killed demands of war, it had to be made to feel an intense fear of the enemy and rage against the cause of that fear. Wilson preferred to represent the war as a battle of principles. But if a difference of ideas was to define the bounds of deep enmity, then certain ideas must be marked as dangerous and outlawed; and in a political struggle ideas cannot be separated from the persons who hold them. Soldiers at the front were required to kill Germans, not German ideas; a feeling close to hatred would make the killing more acceptable. Civilians would have to be brought to feel a comparable rage against "enemies" closer to home. As Yale president Ralph Barton Perry pointed out, "You cannot expect to incite people to the emotional level at which they willingly give their lives or the lives of their sons, and at the same time have them view with cool magnanimity the indifference or obstructiveness of their neighbors."

Wilson himself gave the public its cue for intolerance, warning those who opposed his policies, "Woe to the man or group of men that seeks to stand in our way in this day of high resolution," and Congress gave him authority to make good the threat. The Trading with the Enemy and Espionage Acts gave the executive broad powers to suppress publications deemed subversive. Postmaster General Burleson used his authority to ban or threaten to ban newspapers and magazines critical of the war; agents of the Justice Department's Investigations Bureau (forerunner of the FBI), the Treasury Department, and the Military Intelligence Division (MID) conducted surveillance of individuals and groups who were, or were supposed to be, antiwar or pro-German. That category came to include not only those who opposed the war, but those whose support was considered tepid.[2]

As the campaign of repression proceeded, competing interest groups attempted to exploit it, and so increased its range and power. Labor leaders and industrial magnates sought advantage by accusing each other of, respectively, retarding the war effort and profiteering. Spokesmen for minority communities tried to advance their group's interests by contrasting their loyalty with the failings of others, while advocates of immigration restriction and Jim Crow used the climate of fear to advance their policy agendas. Vigilante action against supposed dissidents was encouraged by the government, which blended with the ongoing social violence between employers and workers in the West and Blacks and Whites in the South.

From Ideological Difference to Racial Enmity: Germans Become Huns

As long as the enemy, the object of fear and hostility, could be defined as the Kaiser's regime and the ideology of militarism, German-Americans could prove their loyalty in purely civic terms by obeying American law and consenting to conscription. But the theory of nationality prevalent among the political and cultural elites and mass culture held that national politics and culture were expressions of racial character. It followed that the German nation—that is, the people and their *Kultur*—were the enemy;

and any German-American who retained any shred of feeling for either was "pro-German," anti-American, un-American.

By the summer of 1917 high school and college curricula were being purged of courses in German language, culture, and history, libraries were dumping books by German authors, German artists and musicians were driven from galleries and concert stages. Theodore Roosevelt and the Vigilantes took a prominent part in these operations. Professor Dunlap of Johns Hopkins declared German a "barbarous tongue." Committee on Public Information pamphlets argued that the German language was structured to inevitably produce the evil philosophies of Nietzsche and Bernhardi and a *Kultur* of militarism and slavish obedience to authority. Guy Empey, an American writer wounded while serving with the British in 1915–16, wanted German culture and language eradicated in the United States:

> If a man *cannot* speak English, and can speak only German, that man must be an enemy of the United States, because he does not understand this wonderful democracy of ours. . . . I say . . . wipe out the German language in the United States, wipe out the German newspapers, and make this America for Americans.[3]

Vigilante Ray Stannard Baker was appalled by the rage and hatred expressed by his friends and colleagues. Even "dear gentle John Burroughs," the naturalist and disciple of Walt Whitman, "is reported in the paper this morning as wanting to wipe out ruthlessly all things German. Half the ministers in the country are in the same mood . . . skewering all Germans on bayonets and then twisting the bayonets." Frederick Tupper, writing in the liberal magazine the *Nation*, viewed the purge with ironic detachment. He reminded readers of Mark Twain's quip that he "would rather decline two drinks than one German adjective," and remarked that between Prohibition and anti-Germanism "apparently the American of the future will have little opportunity of exercising either mournful privilege." But even Tupper acknowledged that "to be a strong, united nation, we must be a one-language people."[4]

Roosevelt and the men of his generation had glorified the Teutonic peoples as the root race of White America, models of the warlike, heroic spirit Roosevelt hoped to instill in his countrymen. It was not a

myth he abandoned easily. In 1914 his criticism of the German invasion of neutral Belgium had been tempered by his disdain of the "effeminacy" that had entrusted that nation's fate to paper treaties rather
than strength of arms. He expressed respect for the Germans' "honorable fear" that their "civilization would be wiped out if they did not
strike"; accepted the premise that the "iron law of self-preservation"
was higher than treaty law; had "nothing but . . . praise and admiration [for] a stern, virile and masterful people [and] hearty respect for
their patriotism and far-seeing devotion." But once he had decided that
war with Germany was a national necessity, it became critical to distinguish the "evil" militarism of the Prussians from the virtuous militarism of American patriots.

By the logic of racial nationalism, that difference would have to reside
in some fundamental moral defect in the German race, which made them
more like the traditional enemies of American civilization—the non-White
"barbarians" of the world, Native Americans, Asians, and Negroes—and
to racially unassimilable aliens like the Jews. The identification of Germans
with "Huns" suggested an Oriental rather than a Caucasian racial heritage
for modern Prussians. Professor Henry Fairfield Osborn, holder of the
Chair of Evolution at Columbia University and a leader in the Immigration
Restriction League, drew on racial pseudoscience to explain "Prussian Ferocity in War." He used the "cephalic index," which classified races according to the size and shape of the skull, to show that Prussians had the
round skull typical of Asiatic races, whereas true Teutons were "long-
headed." Osborn traced "the Blood of the German Leaders" to the "Wild
Tartars" and "Most Ancient Savages" of the steppes. Genuine Teutons
had a "gentle" racial disposition and were therefore still acceptable as the
root race of White America, but the Prussian *Kultur* had exploited and distorted that gentleness into slavish obedience to authority. The German
army's apparent taste for sadistic cruelty and amoral disregard for civilized
laws and customs reflected the "natural" disposition of a ruling race that
was closer in spirit to the Apache or the Mongol than the Anglo-Saxon.[5]

The source of Osborn's idea was probably an older theory that had
been used to explain the difference between the Jews of Germany and
western Europe and the Yiddish-speaking Jews of eastern Europe. The
supposed inferiority of the latter was explained as a consequence of their
Asiatic origins in the vanished Khazar peoples of Asiatic Russia. The

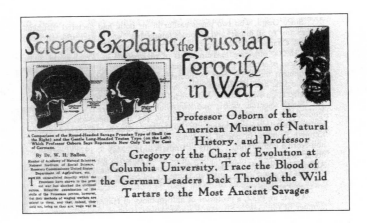

association was not fortuitous. Irvin Cobb and other Vigilante writers noted the tendency of German nationalist philosophers to represent themselves as "a Peculiar and Chosen People," which in effect likens them to Jews. Cobb—whose stock in trade as a writer was the racial stereotyping of Negroes—also described German "racial traits" as an unstable mix of extreme "docility" and a latent savagery that transforms them from decent men to monsters at a "flick of the thumb"—the combination typically attributed to Negro men. The association of Germans with Negroes was vividly realized in posters and cartoons that pictured apelike men hulking over pale, helpless women. These images resonated with the iconographic traditions of American racialism, derived from the history of Indian wars and Jim Crow. As "Huns" the Germans were akin to Indian-like Asiatic barbarians; as apes, they recalled the mythical Negro rapist, whose menace justified the rage of the lynch mob.[6]

If Germans were a racial enemy, they (and any group associated with them) became liable for the kind of treatment sanctioned for use against Indians and Negroes: persecution and humiliation by vigilantes, mob violence, repression by special deputies and police, biased judicial proceedings, excessive prison sentences under abusive conditions. The first to feel the force of this association were those who opposed or criticized the war on ideological grounds. But the racial animosity roused by the anti-German campaign eventually rebounded against those groups whose racial difference provided the analogies that defined the racial Hun: Asians, Jews, and Blacks.[7]

Shadow Huns and Unhung Traitors:
The Nationalization of Vigilantism

In this, as in so much else, Theodore Roosevelt set the tone. The *New York Tribune* and *Sun* praised "the infallible instinct of Theodore Roosevelt [which] has given a name for all the shapes of treachery that squeak and gibber in the American streets." Those who were reluctant to enter the war, like William Randolph Hearst and Senator LaFollette, were "Shadow Huns" and "Ghost Dancers" (an allusion to the last of the Indian wars). Implicit in Roosevelt's condemnation was the suggestion that official force and unofficial mob violence be visited on these subversive beings: "The Hun within our gates masquerades in many disguises; he is our dangerous enemy; and he should be hunted down without mercy." Nearly all the New York dailies reported favorably on the activities and opinions of Roosevelt's cultural Vigilantes, and on the violence of western vigilantes and Justice Department officials against the IWW.[8]

The administration's treatment of conscientious objectors was a scandal among civil libertarians, but Roosevelt thought the government "altogether too weak." The citizen has no civil right to withhold full support from the state: "No man has any right to remain in a free country like ours if he refuses, whether conscientiously or unconscientiously, to do the duties of peace and of war which are necessary if it is to be kept free." Conscientious objectors should be drafted for noncombatant service, "and if they refuse . . . treat them as criminals and imprison them at hard labor." Better yet, assign them to labor battalions behind the front "where association with soldiers might have a missionary effect on them and cause them to forget their present base creed and rise to worthy levels in an atmosphere of self-sacrifice and of service and struggle for great ideals." If that should fail, let the government intern them as "alien enemies and send them permanently out of the country as soon as possible." Although immigrants were cited as the source of most disloyalty, Roosevelt intended his punishment regime for citizens as well as aliens:

> Every man ought to love his country. If he does not love his country and is not eager to serve her, he is a worthless creature and should be contemptuously thrown out of the country when possible, and at any rate debarred from all rights of citizenship in the country.[9]

In their different styles, both Wilson and Roosevelt were asserting a radical new principle in American government: that the requirements of national security can trump constitutional protections of civil liberties, and even nullify American citizenship. Their ideas were given effect by the new apparatus of surveillance and repression created by the administration. But official repression was substantially augmented by an appeal to the more traditional community-based forms of surveillance and repression, which manifested themselves in *vigilantism*—the use of extralegal violence by local elites to maintain social order.[10]

Roosevelt had always glorified vigilantism as a spontaneous and heroic expression of American racial character. As a historian, Wilson had rationalized the vigilantism of the KKK as a necessary counter to Black Reconstruction. Now his administration encouraged vigilantism by sponsoring and assisting local organizations. The policy was in effect an application of his "New Freedom" principles to social control in wartime: it limited the the central government's authority by engaging private enterprise in the tasks of surveillance and repression.

In the West, war vigilantism was simply the continuation of the decades-long struggle between the Western Federation of Miners and IWW on one side, and employer-organized vigilantes and detective forces on the other. Like other unions, including those in the conservative AFL, the IWW tried to take advantage of the wartime combination of scarce labor and high demand, and launched organizing drives in the iron and copper mines, among loggers and migrant harvesters in the West. In Butte, Montana, vigilantes encouraged by federal operatives tortured and lynched Frank Little, who was leading the organizing drive in the iron mines. Vigilantes backed by "special deputies" hired by the owners also attacked IWW strikers in the Maine lumber camps. Vigilantes and state law enforcement rounded up IWW strikers in the Bisbee, Arizona, copper mines and "deported" them. The Supreme Court refused to hear the IWW's appeal for prosecution of the Bisbee vigilantes. Arkansas Wobblies caught trying to organize Black sharecroppers were taken out of jail, whipped, tarred, and feathered. William Fitts, a Justice Department prosecutor, affirmed, "Fear is the only force to keep the wretches in order."[11]

As the war progressed, vigilantism became a national movement, in which figures of national prestige and prominence advocated and sanctioned the actions of local organizations and mobs. The tone was set by Roosevelt's Vigilantes, the organization of Progressive writers and political leaders who systematically propagandized for a "hard war" against Germany and repression of dissenters at home. They were active in the drive to purge the schools, libraries, and concert stages of German, Germans, and German art. Even the progressive *New Republic*, which deplored violations of civil liberties, noted that vigilante activities were not the work of mobs but of the "better elements" of society and defended them against English critics: "Our English friends should remember that there were domiciled in America thousands of aliens who were friendly to Germany" and that our socialist and peace parties were "practically controlled by Germans."[12]

Among the larger organizations engaged in these activities were former "Preparedness" groups like the National Security League (NSL), the Council of National Defense, and the American Defense Society. The latter had a hundred-man "Vigilante Patrol" whose mission was to stop "seditious street oratory." Local organizations proliferated, adopting names whose style reflected the conventions of fraternal orders and vigilance movements: the Liberty League, Knights of Liberty, American Rights League, All-Allied Anti-German League, Anti-Yellow-Dog League, American Anti-Anarchy Association, Boy Spies of America, Sedition Slammers, and the Terrible Threateners. The American Protective League (APL) was one of the largest organizations, with chapters in six hundred cities and a membership that rose from an initial hundred thousand to a quarter of a million by the summer of 1918. Its members were "leading men in their communities . . . bankers . . . railroad men . . . the choice citizens of their particular locality." In addition to rallies and parades they sponsored nonlethal mob action against the foreign-born and those identified as slackers, a category that included anyone who did not subscribe a sufficient sum to the Liberty Loan. Vigilantes knocked on the doors of foreign-born residents to demand tax returns as proof they had contributed; if neither return nor contribution was forthcoming, the house might be trashed, painted yellow, or the residents expelled. With the consent of the Justice Department, APL members acted as a "secret service," ferreting out "traitors" by breaking into homes, intercepting and reading mail, and the like. The *Literary Digest* endorsed their call for neighbors to turn in neighbors, and children to turn in parents who expressed antigovernment ideas.[13]

By the spring of 1918 mob violence was becoming an embarassment. The president spoke against it, although his Justice Department continued to support the APL and other organizations responsible for the violence. Wilson's cabinet reasoned that loyal mobs were taking the law in their hands because the law itself was not stern enough. The administration therefore proposed the Sedition Act, which authorized the government to punish dissent of any kind, including the use of "contemptuous and slurring language about the President." A minister was jailed for calling Wilson a "damned old hypocrite" and a "wooden-headed son of a bitch." Since slurring the president was Roosevelt's stock in trade, he protested; but the act was not aimed at him, and it passed in May 1918. It had no effect on the vigilantes, who simply took it as a sign of approval.[14]

Social and cultural elites, North and South, licensed the mobs by passive acceptance or active advocacy. As the *New Republic* noted, the prevalence of mob violence was "notorious,"

> Yet they meet with comparatively little reprobation or even notice from the newspapers or from great public speakers. There is no indication that the great majority of those people who do most to mould public opinion in this country are particularly shocked at the presence of mob violence and other evidences of collective moral disintegration.

Roosevelt used all his powers to mark those opposed to or critical of the war as recreant to both race and nation and as legitimate targets of popular violence. He told the Harvard Club that pacifists and antiwar socialists were "sexless creatures," that opposition to the war was "veiled treason." Police action alone was insufficient: TR wanted the people to take the law into their own hands. All those who refused to affirm "one allegiance, one flag, one language," must be treated as "half-hidden traitors" and "hunted down without mercy." Elihu Root, who had been Roosevelt's secretary of war, told the Union League, "There are men walking about the streets of this city tonight who ought to be taken out at sunrise tomorrow and shot for treason." It is conceivable that Roosevelt and Root were merely indulging rhetorical excess. But TR had always regarded vigilante movements as a signature of the racial and spiritual unity of a community. In any case, as a historian of the West he knew what the consequences of such speeches were likely to be.[15]

The vigilante theme was echoed in national mass media. Guy Empey called for a war of extermination against Germans and German sympathizers in the United States. In a July 1918 article in *McClure's* magazine he dismissed Wilson's notion that America was fighting Kaiserism: "*We are at war with Germany, the German people, and everything connected with Germany.*" American soldiers would take care of "that baby-killing, crucifying Kaiser, and his idiotic son." The "Real Enemy . . . the German that we have to watch and exterminate is the one that wears the American flag in the lapel of his coat," while impeding the war effort, spreading "snake-like" antiwar propaganda, and advocating a negotiated peace. What makes this enemy so dangerous is that he isn't "German" at all: he is the man "who has lived next door to you for twenty years, and broken bread at your table."

> Constitute yourself a secret-service agent, and if at any time you hear a remark against our Government . . . no matter how trivial or unimportant it may seem to you, either arrest the person or report to your nearest police station. . . . Quick action will follow . . . and that German is going to disappear. Perhaps after the war we will see him again; perhaps we won't. Let us hope we won't, for the United States will be well rid of a parasite.

If anyone took offense at these proposals, whether of "German blood" or not, "they are not one hundred per cent Americans. They must be pro-German," and deserving of the most extreme punishment:

Mark my words, before this war is over they are going to be put where
they belong—in an internment camp, behind barbed wire, with an
American soldier . . . with a fixed bayonet watching their every move.
But if I had my way I would line them up against a wall in front of a fir-
ing squad, and shoot them as traitors and enemies of the United States of
America.[16]

Empey's best-selling novel was titled *Over the Top*, and the phrase
aptly describes his polemics. But the rhetorical excesses of Roosevelt and
Empey contributed to a broader agreement among political and social
leaders that vigilante and mob actions were necessary and justified. U.S.
Attorney General Gregory set the tone, using the standard tropes of vigilante rhetoric in his promise of swift action against slackers and antiwar
activists: "May God have mercy on them, for they need expect none
from an outraged people and an avenging Government," and Secretary
of the Treasury McAdoo declared that talk of peace must be "silenced."
An editorial cartoon in the *New York Herald* approvingly showed eight
bodies hanging from a tree limb, identified as saboteurs, seditionists,
spies, and IWWs. At the local level the language was more extreme. A
Muncie, Indiana, paper editorialized that pacifists "must be effectually
muzzled or exterminated, preferably the latter. . . . They should be tried
by court-martial and shot with their backs against a wall." Local vigilantes and mobs understood this as encouragement to act on their impulses. After a trial exonerated members of a midwestern lynch mob, the
local paper reported, "Having lynched [one] undesirable resident and escaped without unpleasant consequences, Madison County is ready for
the next. . . . If a deserving victim should happen along there are other
trees and plenty of unused rope." In Iowa the operation of vigilante
"courts" was justified by public officials on the ground that "the American people have a power—a God-given power, a power higher and
greater than the Constitution or law . . . to save the Government, to save
the flag, to save the law itself from destruction." A Seattle editorialist
sarcastically advised his readers, "If you don't like your neighbor, shoot
him! . . . Then declare he made seditious or pro-German statements."[17]

What had begun as a campaign against "pro-Germans" expanded,
through a systematic use of guilt-by-association, to include the violent
repression of all forms of dissent. As the number and kind of identified
"enemies" increased, as their unsuspected presence was "unmasked"

everywhere from local neighborhoods to the editorial boards of re-spected journals to the halls of Congress, the menace actually appeared to be growing, and the fears that justified repression were augmented. The catalogue of pro-Germans and Shadow Huns expanded to include "Bolsheviks," Socialists, IWWs, anarchists, dissident reform movements like the agrarian Non-Partisan League of the northern plains, and paci-fists. In the spring of 1918 Roosevelt and his allies extended the definition of pro-Germanism to cover those who preferred a negotiated settlement to unconditional surrender and a victory peace. Alfred Brooks, profes-sor of fine arts at Indiana University, told the NSL that the hesitancy with which some liberal-minded "Americans" accepted war—their failure to leap instinctively to arms when the *Lusitania* was sunk—marked them as something less than "100% American" in spirit or nature. Their not-quite-American character now expresses itself in the cow-ardly insistence that "we should forgive our enemies" and negotiate a fair-minded peace. "While, no doubt, some of these are not actually traitors, all of them are such potentially, and, therefore, not to be trusted. . . . Let all such learn to await, and, when it comes, meet a trai-tor's fate." By Brooks's definition, even Wilson and his party were traitors—hesitant to avenge the *Lusitania*, advocates of a peace with-out indemnities.[18]

Roosevelt certainly thought Wilson's promulgation of the Fourteen Points, with its call for a negotiated peace and a League of Nations, was treason to American national interests. "We are not internationalists," Roosevelt cried, "we are American nationalists." He also saw clear evi-dence of "the only half-secret alliance between these [Bolshevik or leftist] leaders and certain high Democratic politicians." He wanted to "stamp them out." Liberal apologists for the IWW and the Bolsheviks are like those "make-believe social reformers who have sought to excuse a brute who raped a little girl on the ground that social conditions made him what he was." The analogy invokes the standard common formula for rationalizing the lynching of Blacks, and it suggests that, for Roosevelt, Shadow Huns, Bolsheviks, and Negro rapists had become metaphors for each other—and all were legitimate targets of vigilante vengeance. Oth-ers shared his sentiments. In June 1918 the *Atlanta Constitution* warned all slackers and enemy sympathizers on notice that the Loyalty Commit-tee intended to "put the fear of God in your souls or wring the life from

your detestable bodies. . . . The hemp and torch are ready and waiting."
Threats hitherto reserved for Negroes accused of rape could now be
made against even moderately dissident Whites.[19]

Racism Ratified: The Army IQ Tests

If political enmity and disloyalty were attributes of an alien racial or national character, it followed that all groups that were not "100% American" must be suspected of a *liability* to disloyalty, and preemptively
deprived of civil rights. In a judicial opinion published as an article in the
Outlook, Judge Charles F. Amidon—noted for his past defense of civil
liberties—rejected the idea of "America, the Melting Pot" as a delusion
that "appealed to our vanity." War has taught us that the only acceptable
standard of Americanism is that of perfect 100% amalgamation. Civil
naturalization is insufficient. The would-be citizen must undergo something akin to religious conversion: the German immigrant must "put
away your German soul" and "earnestly set about growing an American
soul." Even naturalized citizens who "cherish foreign ideals" should be
deported: "If it is necessary, we will cancel every certificate of citizenship
in these United States. The Federal Government has power to deal with
that subject, and it is going to deal with it." The standard was not literally a racial standard, and both Amidon and Roosevelt thought it "wicked
and . . . un-American to deny the loyal American, of whatever origin,
the full benefit of his allegiance."[20] But 100% Americanism left so little
leeway for ideological, let alone cultural difference, that its practical effect was to mark imperfectly amalgamated ethnic minorities as racial
aliens.

The crisis of mobilizing for war had temporarily empowered the advocates of civil nationality and opened American ideology to a new social bargain and the vision of a multiracial democracy. Once the war
was engaged, the pressures and anxieties generated by the conflict produced a reversion to racial nationalism in its most virulent form. But the
bargain *had* been made; promises that had stirred the patriotism of
African-Americans and hyphenates, and sent their young men to battle
in France, could not be left unsaid. Nor could the reality of their suffering, death, and heroism in battle simply be erased. If the nation's politi-

cal and cultural leaders wished to reestablish the authority of the White/Anglo-Teutonic standard, they would have to systematically discredit the democratic principles behind the new social bargain and establish beyond cavil the racial inferiority of Negroes, Jews, Italians, and the rest.

The anti-immigration movement and the political advocates of Jim Crow exploited the public's fear of subversion to advance their political agendas. The Immigration Restriction League (IRL) in particular was well connected to the Vigilantes, the APL, and nativists within the administration. They won an important victory in 1917, when Congress overrode a presidential veto of a law requiring new immigrants to pass a literacy test. The vote was purely symbolic, since immigration was cut off by the war, and the IRL doubted whether the test would seriously reduce the number of immigrants. But the override suggested that restriction enjoyed broad support and was indicative of a reversion to racial nationalism among the nation's political and cultural leadership.

In the fall of 1917 the government provided the IRL with an unprecedented opportunity to win official acceptance of its racial theories. As part of its commitment to scientific management, the War Department asked the Committee for Psychology of the National Research Council to develop and administer tests of the skills and competencies of the masses of men pouring into the training camps. The council recommended use of the Stanford-Binet test of "general intelligence." After a trial run in October–November 1917, the army authorized administration of the test in all cantonments, and between April and November 1918 more than 1.7 million men were tested.

The version of Stanford-Binet used by the U.S. Army had been developed by Lewis Terman of Stanford University. It was based on the test of "general intelligence" developed in France by Alfred Binet (1903), which was designed to assess the problem-solving skills of individuals. Binet explicitly denied that the test measured hereditary intellectual endowment for the individual tested and believed it had no validity in assessing groups of individuals, however defined. Rather, he saw the test as a way of assessing how well students were being taught, which would suggest ways of improving the schools. Terman was a convinced eugenicist, who believed heredity was the absolute determinant of human development and that groups identified as "races" in the common idiom constituted genuinely distinct genetic units. He promoted his English version of the Binet test as an instrument for proving that these so-called races were inherently unequal in mental capacity.

The racial assumptions behind Terman's IQ test ought to have been familiar to the administration that hired him, because they had been the subject of a major controversy before the war. In 1912 Henry H. Goddard, like Terman a eugenicist and advocate of immigration restriction, had administered a version of the Binet test, in English, to immigrants at Ellis Island. Since those tested had limited mastery of the language, the results confirmed his assumption that Jews, Italians, Poles, and other new immigrants were not equal in endowment to American "Nordics." He interpreted low test scores as proof that 83 percent of all Jews were "feeble-minded" and that this necessarily hereditary condition was shared in much the same degree by other "new immigrants." Terman's revision of Binet's test was based on assumptions derived from Goddard's work, which enjoyed a popular vogue until 1915, when a group of Chicago politicians took the test and earned scores that classed them as "morons." However gratifying to the political satirist, Goddard's findings were manifestly absurd. Even at its lowest Chicago politics required polemical and mathematical skills of no mean order. The findings not only insulted Chicago's rulers but outraged the presumptions of American democracy by suggesting that voters and their representatives were mentally inferior. Amid the wave of criticism, psychologist Robert M. Yerkes defended Goddard and his test results at that year's meeting of the American Psychological Association, accepting even the radically antidemocratic implications of the Chicago tests. Yerkes was chosen to organize the army's testing program, and he adopted Terman's system in its entirety.

The procedures used to administer and evaluate the army IQ tests were deeply flawed. Tests were given to large groups, not individuals, and the conditions under which the tests were taken varied widely from segregated camps in the rural South to suburban camps in the Northeast. Tests were scored by enlisted men unqualified for the job, and the scoring system was not the numerical ratio called for in the protocol but a "letter grade" system that corresponded to value-loaded terms like "superior" and "inferior." Success in answering the questions depended on the subject's recognition of terms and figures from professional baseball and football, medicine, commercial trademarks, and advertising slogans—

information familiar to English-speaking middle-class urban Whites, but likely to be unfamiliar to non-English speakers and to Blacks and Whites from rural districts. For example:

2. *Five hundred* is played with

           rackets   pins   cards   dice

7. *Christie Mathewson* is famous as a

        writer   artist   baseball player   comedian

22. The *mimeograph* is a kind of

        typewriter   copying machine   phonograph

Failure to answer such questions was interpreted, not as a deficit of cultural experience or schooling, but as evidence of hereditary mental defect.

The results appeared to confirm the testers' presumption that Negroes and immigrants were mentally "subnormal." What was more shocking was their finding that the average intelligence of *White* Americans was also subnormal. As scientific critics pointed out, that finding was absurd on its face: the average intelligence of a population cannot, by definition, be "below average." Terman and Yerkes had adopted an *absolute* measure of "IQ," which corresponded to the score achieved by an average White American middle-class English speaker. Moreover, even if the scores were accepted, the results did not support the interpretation that Jews were "feeble-minded" or Negroes inferior to Whites. Jews and Northern Negroes consistently scored higher than Southern "Nordics." Nevertheless, the tests were widely accepted as an authoritative basis on which to classify the several "races" of Americans and as confirmation of the view that class differences within the White race were also the product of heredity. The academic credentials of the testers, backed by the sheer size and mass of the statistical base the army provided, gave them an insuperable advantage in public debate. But their influence was also enhanced by the fact that their "findings" corresponded to assumptions about race and class difference that had been widely held before the war.

The interpretation of the army IQ tests by Yerkes, Terman, and their colleagues would provide the IRL with the "scientific" proof it needed to win the postwar political argument over immigration restriction. In the meantime, newspapers and magazines began the process of popularizing the results of the IQ tests by reporting preliminary findings in the summer and fall of 1918. Dr. Frederick Peterson, "an alienist of note," reported to the National Education Association the disturbing finding that 30 percent of drafted men were unfit for service because of mental or physical defects. A eugenic catastrophe was in prospect: "We are sending the best we have to foreign battlefields . . . and retaining the 30 per cent of imperfect citizens to leaven the race of tomorrow." Since under our democracy a "moron" can be elected governor, "it may be easily imagined how the smaller offices in our legislatures, county boards, and city councils overflow with the inferior and the unfit." The *Literary Digest* reprinted his speech. Less well publicized were the reports that suggested the congenital inferiority of particular races—the conditions that had produced the social bargain between government and minorities still obtained. But Terman, Yerkes, and their colleagues would make those findings public once the war was concluded and the fight for immigration restriction began in earnest. The gist of their position was summarized by one of their number, Charles Brigham, in 1923:

> In a very definite way, the results which we obtain by interpreting the Army data by means of the race hypothesis support Mr. Madison Grant's hypothesis of the superiority of the Nordic type. Our figures would rather tend to disprove the popular belief that the Jew is highly intelligent. . . . Our results showing the marked inferiority of the negro are corroborated by practically all of the investigators who have used psychological tests on white and negro groups.[21]

The shift in elite opinion toward a reaffirmation of racialism was reflected in war propaganda. The July 4 bulletin of the Four-Minute Men, "The Meaning of America," offered the thoughts of sociologist Herbert Spencer as a "fresh viewpoint" on the war's significance. Spencer was the elder statesman of social Darwinism, a strict hereditarian who believed that class differences were the result of biological superiority and weakness. His statement seemed to affirm the principles of the social bargain: the "hyphen" of transitional nationality had been "changed to vapor in the melting pot" of war to produce "a wonderful amalgamation of races within America. . . . [Henceforth] no American may owe a secret heart allegiance to some foreign country. This is home." But in explaining the biological basis of this transformation, Spencer makes it clear that not all the races of the melting pot could successfully hybridize with Americans: "It is to be inferred from biological truths that the eventual mixture of the allied varieties of the Aryan race will produce a more powerful type of man than has hitherto existed." The melting pot he envisioned was to be restricted to Aryans or Nordics. Jews, Latins, and Negroes need not apply.[22]

Hoping for Headlines: Confidence and Concern in the Minority Communities

Despite the vigilante attacks on foreigners and "Reds," and in ignorance of the significance the IQ tests would acquire, the immigrant communities of New York remained confident that the social bargain of 1917 was being kept. The APL and other patriotic organizations harassed slackers in the city, but by national standards vigilantism in New York was mild and did not operate in the large ghettoes of Little Italy and the Lower East Side. German- and Irish-Americans were more frequently the objects of such violence, but even so, in July 1918 the Friends of Irish Freedom held an indignation meeting, praised LaFollette, and damned the Vigilantes and the "vocal Volcano of Oyster Bay." They were not molested.

Community newspapers kept the city's Jews and Italians apprised of the continuing debate over postwar immigration restriction in Congress. They were also aware of the demagogic attacks on hyphenated loyalty being made by Roosevelt and his allies. But they heeded as well the assurance that real loyalty would be recognized, that (as Roosevelt said) it was "un-American to deny the loyal American, of whatever origin, the full benefit of his allegiance." The *Literary Digest*, which was delighted to publish the fulminations of the literary Vigilantes, also ran an ongoing feature called "Education in Americanism," which reviewed the history of each racial-ethnic group and noted its success in becoming American and serving the war effort. For Columbus Day it not only celebrated the Italians, it reminded the reader, "We are all immigrants . . . [who] came as travelers and have become citizens. . . . We are a nation of immigrants. Other nationalities are born, Americans are made." Although each immigrant group has moved to realize its Americanism, each has also added a bit of its own culture to make America "a Treasury of Traditions."[23]

The Jews, at least, believed that their community leaders and political representatives, and non-Jewish allies from the settlement house movement, were well placed to defend their interests. Bernard Baruch sat at the president's right hand, and Louis Brandeis was a Supreme

Court justice. There were Jewish Socialists like Meyer London and Victor Berger in Congress, Jews on the city council and in legislative assemblies. Morris Hillquit was still despised outside the city, but Abraham Cahan and the *Forward* had regained respectability—Cahan would accompany Woodrow Wilson on his journey to Versailles. Lillian Wald defended the racial heredity of the immigrants in the pages of the *Times*. Frances Kellor, founder of the Committee for Immigrants in America and an exponent of Americanization, was engaged in developing a "War Americanization Plan" for the Federal Bureau of Education. She worked with the Committee of Public Information, the Loyalty Leagues, and the National Security League to make them aware of immigrant concerns and reassure them of immigrant loyalties, and to soften their rhetoric on the subject of hyphenism. Unfortunately, her labors had the effect of masking the steady drift of these organizations toward an anti-immigrant position.[24]

Anxiety about the status of American Jews was reawakened by the fallout from the Bolshevik Revolution. Native-born Americans and German-American Jews had always been put off by the apparent leftist predilections of the eastern European Jews. Most of the Lower East Side celebrated the Bolshevik triumph as both a victory of socialism and a promise of rescue for Russian Jews oppressed under the czars. Some expressed a wish to return and share in the redemption of their people in the Russian homeland, and a few acted on that impulse. But for the Wilson administration, the Roosevelt Progressives, and the Republicans alike, Bolshevism was a radical and anarchistic offshoot of Kaiserism, which menaced the West with the threat of an underclass revolution. The association of eastern European Jews with Russian Bolshevism would prove far more damaging to their status than earlier attacks on their supposed "pro-Germanism." The government's anti-Red campaign began in February 1918 with the secret indictment of Victor Berger and his arrest the following month in the midst of his congressional campaign.

As the ethnic group most closely identified with Russia and socialism, eastern European Jews were placed at the intersection of three currents in the rising tide of American fear: fear of rebellion by the underclass, fear of demographic pollution through immigration, and fear of subversion by an enemy power. The question of Jewish loyalty was also complicated by the rise of Zionism, given new impetus by the Balfour Declaration of 1917, which promised British support for a Jewish homeland in Palestine. To the extent that Jews were recognized as a distinct nationality, their racial difference was affirmed and their eligibility for Americanization became questionable.[25]

There were many reasons for Jewish anxiety in the summer of 1918, but all could be dispelled by the successes of the Melting Pot Division. If the boys in the 77th proved their valor in battle, the community's place in America would be secure. Reports of the fighting in the Baccarat appeared in the New York papers in June and July, and the *Times* editorial hailed the 77th as "New York's Own Division," representative of all its racial, cultural, and social variety, proof that a polyglot society could also be patriotic:

> The city men, the fifty nationalities from the tenements and Fifth Avenue, peddlers, longshoremen, newsies, teamsters—yes, and loafers, rich and hard-up, from clubs and saloon corners—lawyers and tradesmen, clerks and capitalists, the Four Hundred and the riffraff, college men and illiterates, the dandies and the unwashed, good, bad, and indifferent, all that mob and conglomeration . . . that strode, trudged, and slouched into Camp Upton . . . were transformed into as fine a looking body of men as ever shouldered arms.

The army also released the citations associated with the awarding of medals, and such reports reinforced confidence in the melting pot and the social bargain. The *Sun* reported that Private Kavanagh, now in the hospital, had killed eight Germans in bayonet fighting. Tom Johnson's dispatch in the *Times* told how Sing Kee of Bayard Street in Chinatown had "stood firm" with Captain Adler and Privates Duff, Foy, and Finurane—a Chinese, a Jew, and three Irishmen. Particular notice was taken of killed and wounded officers who had been prominent in New York society. The news of Bel Brooks's death was published weeks after the event, in fortuitous association with news of the German retreat: "New York Boys Win Honors on Vesle" was the headline in the *Sun*, "New Yorkers Lead Chase from Vesle / Yankees Make Brilliant Coup, Rout Enemy South of the Aisne"—this was the New York papers' version of the division's lurching advance from the Vesle and its enforced halt on the Butte de Bourmont.[26]

Community leaders were not mistaken in thinking such stories had a good effect on their standing. In the spring of 1918, Madison Grant of the IRL tried to win Roosevelt's support for cutting off further Jewish immigration, on the grounds that they would degrade the nation and the Nordic race. Grant was a friend and fellow member of the Boone and

Crockett Club, and Roosevelt shared his affinity for eugenics, but the war had changed his mind about Jews. While it was true that "the great bulk of the Jewish population, especially the immigrants from Russia and Poland, are of weak physique, and have not yet gotten far enough away from their centuries of oppression and degradation," there were plenty of Jews who had worked at hard manual labor or "taken to boxing, wrestling, and the like," who were proving to be "excellent material" for soldiers. "The Maccabbee or fighting Jewish type" was an excellent one, and well displayed in the AEF—if "men of the Jewish race" would emulate that model, Jewish immigration might not be a bad thing.[27]

The effect of these stories about the 77th Division was to boost the confidence of the Jewish community in its Americanism. The German-Jewish leadership began a project to raise a billion-dollar relief fund for the aid of Jewish communities being ravaged by the Russian civil war. They thought of it as a Jewish counterpart to Wilson's war and his Fourteen Points and saw themselves acting as *Americans*, projecting "American system, energy, and resourcefulness," as well as "American millions," into the "Greatest Humanitarian Work in History." As for the Lower East Side Jews, in their pride and enthusiasm they assumed that their passions for Socialism, Zionism, and Americanism involved no contradiction whatsoever. Their confidence is reflected in Yiddish popular songs like "*A grus fun di trentshes*" (Greetings from the Trenches). The first verse praises the boys who "fight with spirit, courage and blood" and identify themselves proudly as "Sammies," an early nickname for the doughboys. The second looks beyond the war to that "bit of hope" and "ray of happiness" that seemed to promise "we might get / Our land back," in Israel:

> In every land a Yiddish legion is being founded.
> They will go and fight for the home
> Of our nation.[28]

The songwriter would not have imagined such sentiments could be seen as a treasonous violation of Roosevelt's one country, one flag, one language rule.

African-American communities were more aware of their vulnerability to a renewed enthusiasm for race discrimination—not because their leaders were better informed than Louis Marshall and Abraham Cahan, but because the war had made little substantial change in the racial iso-lation, defamation, and victimization that had shaped their community life since 1865. They were the only native-born group to be subjected to the kind of mob violence experienced by German-Americans, pacifists, and Wobblies. But the lynching of Blacks for lapses in patriotism was dif-ficult to distinguish from lynchings for the usual reasons: accusations of rape, bad racial manners, resistance to or verbal defiance of the will of the White community.

The NAACP tallied 92 lynchings of African-Americans during the war, all of which occurred in the South; the *Crisis* put the number at 110. The riot deaths from East St. Louis, Waco, and Houston were not in-cluded in either count. Few of these lynchings were related to campaigns against slackers. Such violence added to the long-standing grievances of the community, but did not require African-Americans to give up the hopes and expectations they had invested in the wartime social bargain. Indeed, in the summer of 1918 African-American leaders finally won from a reluctant President Wilson a public recognition of both their ser-vice and their entitlement to better treatment after the war: "With thou-sands of your sons in the camps and in France, out of this conflict you must expect nothing less than the enjoyment of full citizenship rights—the same as are enjoyed by every other citizen."[29]

Things were bad in the way they had always been bad. Some things were better now: the pay for war work, the willingness of employers to fill vacant spots on the factory floor with Negroes. News from the bat-tlefield was everything that could be hoped. Thus the shocking coinci-dence that juxtaposed news of Henry Johnson's battle with the horrifying details of the Mary Turner lynching did not lead Black edito-rialists or their readers to despair. Henry Johnson's heroic disembowel-ing of the "Bush Germans" could be seen as a promise that success in war would give African-Americans the power to break the moral author-ity and physical power of lynch mobs, like the one that had tortured Mary Turner.

Thanks to the "Battle of Henry Johnson," the 369th had attracted the attention of the press when few American units were in action, and the regiment's isolation actually proved a benefit, enabling reporters filing on the 369th to evade army censorship and provide vivid and personalized accounts of the fighting. When the front page of the *New York Times* bannered the mustering of "270,000 Americans" for the great July "counterblow" against the Germans, the only units identified in the sub-heads were the "Rainbow [Division] and Negro Regiment," both fighting with the French. Sweet revenge for Hayward: black might not be "one of the colors of the Rainbow," but for the moment, at least, it was equally vivid in the public eye.[30]

Perhaps the most gratifying news was the recognition being accorded to both the regiment and individual soldiers for heroism in battle. On August 31 a banner headline in the *Age* reported Sergeant Butler's single-handed charge on the German trenches. The article reprinted a dispatch by Lincoln Eyre, which had been published with similar éclat in Joseph Pulitzer's *New York World*. Elements of the standard comic treatment of Black soldiers lingered in the story. Butler's civilian employment as an elevator operator is given the pretentious title "indoor chauffeur," and when he springs his ambush Eyre has Butler shouting, "Look out you Bush-Germans, I'm comin'!" White reporters were so taken with the linguistic misunderstanding of "Bush-Germans" that they attributed it to Black troops whenever possible. Nonetheless, this kind of coverage was a sign that the labor and suffering and courage of Black troops were indeed being noticed and appreciated by White America.[31]

While praise for the soldiers was gratifying, for Black readers the most important question was whether or not these military achievements were making Whites more willing to address their grievances: to end discrimination in hiring and housing, to take action against Southern lynch mobs, and to extend civil rights to the subjects of Jim Crow. The evidence was generally favorable. The *Age* took notice of Irvin Cobb's article on Henry Johnson, recently published in the *Saturday Evening Post*, as a sign that even the hearts of Southern racists could be changed by achievements on the battlefield. James Weldon Johnson was a bit more skeptical, noting that Cobb still attributed a ridiculous dialect to Negroes and reduced their culture to the love of "watermelon and possum." But he acknowledged that Cobb had been careful to distinguish the men of the Old Fifteenth from Southern Negroes and had given full credit to their martial prowess—a very good thing, considering that the *Saturday Evening Post* had four or five million readers.[32]

The *Outlook* now condemned lynching as "a danger to national safety and to success in the war" and suggested that lynchers be treated with the kind of extralegal rigor accorded to slackers and pro-Germans—charged under the Sedition Act and sent before military tribunals rather than civilian courts. "It is treason to the country to do anything that will take the heart out of these men and make them feel that they have no country. Is there anything that would be more likely to do that than to allow Negroes at home to be murdered by mobs?" The editor was of the opinion that his position would be supported by the majority of Southern people, and in proof cited a statement by the Tennessee Conference of Charities and Correction: "The lynching of men of one blood or race by those of another . . . strikes at the very root of our National solidarity and efficiency." In "Negroes Under War Conditions" the magazine praised the "Buffaloes" of the 367th and the fighters of the 369th for earning in France "a hearing such as they have not always had heretofore." It quoted a Southern officer as saying, "I can never again think of Negroes as I used to think."[33]

Good news from the front always had a double meaning for African-Americans. It boosted their pride and self-confidence in asserting their grievances and claiming their rights, but at the same time reminded them of the disadvantages and injustices under which they were compelled to act. James Weldon Johnson reminded his readers that, justly or not, effective military service was an absolutely necessary precondition for the Negro's acceptance as an equal citizen. Lester Walton of the *Age* was pleased that "the Old Fifteenth" was being featured in newsreels at New York movie theaters. But Walton complained that most portrayals of Negroes in movies about the war still showed the Black man as a "clown" and a coward: "AT NO TIME HAS THE COLORED SOLDIER BEEN SHOWN AS A MAN." Still, signs of progress were strong. In October 1918 the *World* reported an interracial brawl in which Blacks were the aggressors. In the past, such incidents would be used as proof of the Negro's lawless character; now the *World* reporter simply remarked that the brawlers were not like "our Buffaloes," the Black soldiers of the 367th. The *Herald* made a powerfully significant suggestion when it headlined a story on a German peace initiative, "Germany 'Offers' Peace to the Ku-Klux Kaiser's Enemies." The story itself has nothing to do with African-Americans. The headline simply assumes that Ku-Klux-ism and Kaiserism are essentially the same, both evil and un-American.[34]

Through the summer of 1918 W. E. B. DuBois believed that the bargain he had made was being kept, and he began looking ahead to the international conferences that would remake the world order once the war was over. His colleague Joel Spingarn shared his confidence. He had won an appointment to the Military Intelligence Division (MID), and took it as a mark of confidence that he was invited to join the surveillance of less reliable reformers. He felt himself "a real American" as never before and planned to use his position in MID to win support for an antilynching bill. On his recommendation DuBois applied for a captaincy in MID and reaffirmed his part of the social bargain in an editorial that called for Black Americans to "close ranks" with the nation. This was "the crisis of the world," and "we of the colored race have no ordinary interest in the outcome." A German victory would end the hopes of colored races for justice and equality. "Let us, while the war lasts, forget our special griev- ances and close ranks shoulder to shoulder with our white fellow citi- zens. . . . We make no ordinary sacrifice, but we make it gladly and willingly with our eyes lifted to the hills."[35]

But the bargain was already unraveling, as its unforeseen consequences for segregation and White privilege became manifest. White Southerners had recognized from the start that training of Black soldiers for national defense would undermine the ideological basis of Jim Crow. They re- sponded to the presence of Black troops by intensifying the rigor of local segregation ordinances and tolerating an escalation of mob violence against defiant or "uppity" Black civilians and Blacks in uniform. Black troops stationed at Southern cantonments were routinely subjected to hu- miliation and even physical assault by White troops and civilians. A Vicks- burg paper declared that "no nigger" would be allowed to wear in the streets "a uniform that a white man was bound to honor," and a Black of- ficer who did was assaulted and run out of town.[36] Outside the South, the reaction developed more slowly, but in a similar direction. The increased integration of industry, which African-American leaders saw as proof the bargain was succeeding, was perceived by White workers in Northern and Midwestern cities as a threat to their jobs, their social status, and the racial exclusivity of their neighborhoods. The rhetoric of rising expectations, which was energized by the battlefield successes of Black troops, suggested that still more radical and menacing changes would be demanded, unless Negroes could somehow be put back in their "proper" place.

The Wilson administration had begun working to limit the potential for further radical change. Those African-American leaders who contin- ued to stress the injustice and abuse being suffered by their people be- came targets of surveillance by the Investigations Bureau of the Justice Department and the Military Intelligence Division. MID considered that support for the war was critically low in most Black communities. A. Philip Randolph's Harlem Socialists opposed the war, supported Irish independence (anathema to our British ally), and expressed sympathy for both the IWW and the Bolshevik Revolution. With Hubert Harrison, Randolph continued to score DuBois's support of the war as a "surrender of life, liberty, and manhood" and to demand that Blacks put their own rights and interests first. Randolph and Chandler Owen were stalked by MID agents when they traveled to speak in the Midwest, but no arrest warrants were issued, because MID believed they could only be pawns of White radicals rather than organizers in their own right.[37]

As fear of pro-Germanism spread to include all forms of dissent, civil rights militants who supported the war also came under suspicion. Spingarn's superiors at MID had begun to suspect him of sedition because he was a Jew. Prejudice against Jews was traditional in the army. Line officers had to suspend such prejudices when dealing with their Jewish soldiers, and many had their attitudes transformed by the performance of Jews under their command. But the staff remained suspicious of Jewish patriotism, and in July 1918 their prejudices were confirmed by reports from anti-Bolshevik Russian and Polish officers that attributed Communist success in Russia to an international Jewish conspiracy. These informants sent MID a copy of the *Protocols of the Elders of Zion*, an anti-Semitic fabrication composed in the previous century and disseminated by the czarist police, which MID accepted as valid intelligence. Now Spingarn was doubly suspect, first because he was a Jew, and second because he had recommended DuBois for a captaincy. DuBois was already a target of surveillance by MID, his tough criticism of the administration's failure to act against lynch mobs and its toleration of Jim Crow outweighing his strong endorsement of Black enlistment. DuBois's application to MID was rejected, Spingarn was buried in meaningless paperwork, and the proposed antilynching bill was rejected.[38]

The shift of attitude that transformed Spingarn and DuBois from patriots to suspects was not visible to the public. But as the primary instrument of state power, the army was a more sensitive register of ideological shifts among the political leadership. The effects of the racial reaction would be felt immediately by the Black troops of the 92nd and 93rd Divisions as they prepared for their roles in the climactic offensive of the Great War.

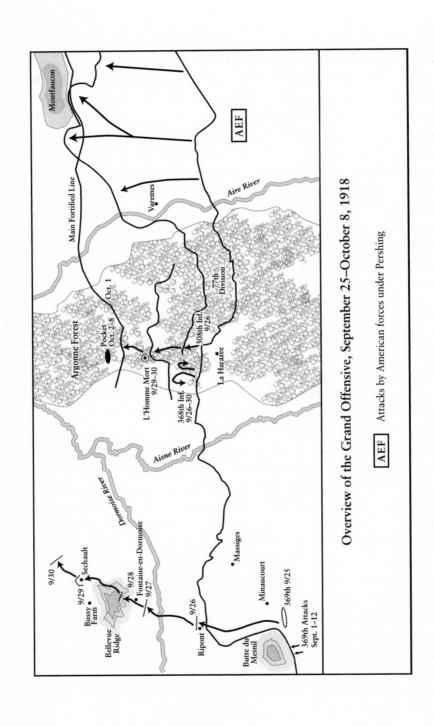

Overview of the Grand Offensive, September 25–October 8, 1918

AEF   Attacks by American forces under Pershing

8

"Tout le Monde à la Bataille!": The Allied Offensive Begins, September 12–27, 1918

> "Good-morning, good-morning!" the General said
> When we met him last week on our way to the line.
> Now the soldiers he smiled at are most of 'em dead,
> And we're cursing his staff for incompetent swine.
> "He's a cheery old card," grunted Harry to Jack
> As they slogged up to Arras with rifle and pack.
> . . . .
> But he did for them both by his plan of attack.
>
> —*Siegfried Sassoon, "The General" (1917)*

The decision to commit the AEF to battle in the Meuse-Argonne sector was driven by a combination of political and military considerations. Ludendorff's spring and summer offensives had broken the stalemate that had lasted since 1914, and in the process taught his enemies how to break through entrenched positions. The defeat of those offensives had cost Germany most of its assault troops. All conscription classes through 1919 had been called up, and the last reserves were already in the line. For the first time since the fall of Russia the year before, the Allies had numerical superiority on the Western Front. They could bring 3.5 million men into line against perhaps 2.3 million Germans, of whom only 600,000 were still rated as assault troops.

The Allied governments were confident Germany could now be defeated, though they doubted final victory could be won until 1919. The entire Western Front had been placed under the command of the French

General Ferdinand Foch, who planned a grand offensive from Verdun to the North Sea: *"Tout le monde à la bataille."* By hitting in strength at several widely separated points he would dissipate the German reserves; eventually one of his armies would hit a weak spot and break through. The offensive might be decisive, though it seemed more likely to result in a German withdrawal from France and make possible an offensive into Germany the following year. The British and French were also drawing the last of their manpower reserves, but American manpower constituted a reserve so large it more than replaced the defeated Russians and the buried conscript classes of 1914–18. In the long term—say by summer 1919—Americans would comprise more than half the Allied forces, and as the strongest power in the alliance the United States could be arbiter of the peace. The prospect was not entirely pleasing to the other Allies. However, at the moment Americans amounted only to a third of the Allied armies, the most energetic but not the most skilled component.

At the end of August Foch met with Pershing, ostensibly to discuss deployment of the AEF as a national army. Instead Foch proposed dispersing the American divisions among French and British formations, on the grounds that the troops were still raw and that Pershing's GHQ could not manage a large field army. Pershing was furious. From the beginning of U.S. engagement, Wilson and Pershing had insisted, as a fundamental principle of American policy, that the AEF must fight as a distinct national army. American influence over the ultimate peace settlement depended upon the unmistakable demonstration that the American army had been decisive in producing victory. Pershing had allowed his divisions to serve under foreign command for training purposes and to meet the emergency of the Ludendorff offensives. But the emergency was past, and so was the AEF's apprenticeship. Pershing told Foch he would refuse to send his troops into action rather than see them parceled out to foreign armies. Foch challenged him: Did the American refuse to fight? Would he abandon his allies in the supreme crisis? Pershing answered that he would fight wherever Foch wanted him, so long as he commanded an *American* army.

This was probably the result Foch was angling for. He was now free to assign the Americans a sector that would use their awkward strength profitably, while the veteran British and French forces struck the decisive blows. He gave Pershing the choice of mounting his offensive in the Champagne or the Meuse-Argonne sector, and Pershing chose the latter.

The AEF's assignment was to take charge of the Verdun sector, stage an offensive to eliminate the St. Mihiel Salient (September 12–16), then join in the grand assault on September 25 by attacking between the heights of the Meuse River and the Argonne Forest.

Pershing chose the Meuse-Argonne because it was convenient to his base of supply and because it appeared to offer some strategic advantages. The German invasion had carved an L-shaped salient into northeastern France, the vertical leg of which ran roughly north-south from the North Sea to the vicinity of Compiègne, then west-east to Verdun, after which the lines curved south again close to the prewar border. The Meuse-Argonne fronted the south-facing leg of the *L*: it was effectively on the flank of the main German armies, and the flank attack was a classic route to decisive battlefield victory. To Pershing it seemed that if his assault succeeded, he could roll up the German line from south to north. The German lines in the Meuse-Argonne were very strong, but defended by second-rate troops. Pershing counted on surprise, superior numbers, and morale to achieve a quick breakthrough. The character of the opposition and the mix of woodland and open terrain seemed ideally suited for exploitation by the open-warfare tactics in which his men had been trained. The strategic rail hub of Sedan lay in the path of the American advance. Its capture would compel a German retreat and have tremendous symbolic significance: it was at Sedan that the Prussians destroyed the armies of Napoleon III and created the German empire.[1]

The French commanders, Foch and Pétain, made a colder calculation of American chances. Surprise, numbers, and élan notwithstanding, they did not think Pershing could achieve anything decisive in the Meuse-Argonne. French armies had bloodied themselves for a year against those lines, gaining nothing. The Germans would recognize the threat of a flank attack and reinforce heavily. Pétain believed it would take Pershing till winter just to capture his first day's objective, the heights of Montfaucon. Foch's strategic calculations anticipated nothing more from the AEF than an effective holding attack, which would draw German reinforcements away from sectors where truly decisive action was possible, on the British front in the north or the French in the center. If Pershing himself expected more, so much the better: he would attack with the greater energy. To keep him up to the mark Foch would continually goad him with the threat of an Allied takeover of the AEF.

Pershing's own calculations were wrong in nearly every respect. It was true the German lines were held by only five understrength divisions of second-rate troops. Against them the Americans could send nine divisions on the first day—divisions twice the size of their European counterparts—with more to follow. The initial advantage in troop strength was calculated as high as eight to one, with a comparable edge in artillery. However, these advantages were offset by the terrain and the high quality of the German entrenchments, which had been perfected over a two-year period. The sector as a whole was too narrow for Pershing's purposes, compressing his superior numbers and canalizing their lines of advance instead of compelling the Germans to spread their inadequate numbers to defend a broad front. There would be few opportunities for his preferred tactics of maneuver. Instead, his men would have to make frontal assaults, their heavy concentration of manpower making them terribly easy to kill.

The sector had been relatively quiet since 1916, the year in which a million French and German troops slaughtered one another around Verdun, sanctifying the name of that fortress-city for Frenchmen and turning the region into a corpse mine, its underground chambers packed with human bones like veins of ore. From AEF observation posts northwest of Verdun the terrain between the Argonne Forest on the left flank and the Meuse River on the right appeared fairly open. Montfaucon in the center of the sector rose in a gradual slope only 250 feet above the plain. But Montfaucon was heavily fortified and within range of support by German artillery firing from flanking positions on the high ground westward in the Argonne and the eastern heights beyond the Meuse. Neither of these flank positions could be assailed by U.S. infantry until substantial advances had been made in the center. The Germans had line-of-sight observation and gunfire over 80 percent of the battlefield. It was from Montfaucon that German commanders had supervised the murderous assaults on Verdun, clearly visible fifteen miles away, well behind what were now the American lines. "In 1918, with artillery at a peak of accuracy, the sector was effectively a shooting gallery."

Montfaucon was merely the central strongpoint in the first line of a defense-in-depth. In front of it were lightly manned sacrifice lines, designed to delay and derange the first assault. Behind it were a series of fortified lines, named for figures from Wagnerian opera, set along ridges of high ground: the *Giselher Stellung*; the *Kriemhilde Stellung* on Romagne Heights, the strongest natural position in the region; and the *Freya*

Stellung on the Barricourt Heights. Any advance would shift the balance of artillery power, bringing American troops closer to the German guns and farther from their own. Von Gallwitz, commanding German forces in the sector, could take advantage of the rail network behind his lines to bring in reinforcements. He had twelve divisions in reserve, six of which could move into the Meuse-Argonne on one day's notice, effectively doubling his forces there. These divisions were seriously understrength, but the troops were not as demoralized as intelligence thought and were far better supplied than the Americans believed. Advancing doughboys would find well-engineered bunkers well supplied with food, even luxury items like brandy, wine, and cigars.

Morale was a strategic consideration at this point in the Great War. Most Allied commanders now recognized that under prevailing conditions decisive battlefield victory was impossible. A Great Power could only be defeated by breaking the morale of its army and the powerful interests and mass of popular support that sustained it. The collapse of Russia had come from within, and Germany's allies were showing the same symptoms. Pershing believed the spirit of his men was high enough to offset their limited training. All observers agreed that American troops had remarkably high morale and attacked with a verve not seen on the Western Front since 1915. As Laurence Stallings put it, "The Yankees went into the business as if to a clambake."

The dark side of the picture was that American officers had not learned the lesson the Allies acquired at such terrible cost: against entrenched troops using machine guns and supported by artillery, frontal assaults by riflemen produce ruinous casualties and no results. A successful assault required systematic and coordinated artillery support and the use of tanks to effect a breakthrough. For clearing trenches, attacking troops needed training in teamwork among grenadiers, riflemen, Chauchat and light machine gunners, and the mobile one-pounder infantry cannons used for breaking into pillboxes. Wilson's refusal to prepare for war until war was declared meant American soldiers arrived at the front without having seen, let alone mastered, these weapons. The artillery used by the Americans was borrowed from the Allies; there was little time to train gunners in the skills of forward observation, liaison, and timing that were required to make artillery effective in support of attacking infantry. The problem was compounded by Pershing's insistence that the rifle, which he called the characteristically "American" weapon, be the focus of tactical doctrine. Thanks to Pershing's training regimen, and Wilson's failure to prepare for war, the American infantryman would go up against artillery and machine guns with nothing but "raw courage, enthusiasm, inexperience, guts, some support from his auxiliary arms, and his own blood."

Pershing's acceptance of the plan to clear the St. Mihiel Salient before shifting forces to the Meuse-Argonne imposed additional liabilities on the AEF. The Salient was a triangular intrusion in the Allied lines east of Verdun, which threatened the rail lines that fed the armies in that area. It was an objective limited enough for Pershing's staff to manage with relative ease. But the timetable Pershing accepted required his army—which had never acted as a unified command—to conduct its first major offensive on a rigid timetable; then turn around and, in no more than the ten days allotted by Foch, shift 800,000 men and four thousand guns between two fronts, and launch a second and greater offensive west of Verdun. All of this had to be organized by staff officers inexperienced in operations beyond the corps level, using transport borrowed from the French (who would need the best they had to move their own troops) over a road network that was unfamiliar and utterly inadequate. The Americans would also discover that autumn in this part of France was a season of "rain, rain, rain" that turned the unpaved roads and farm tracks to soupy mud. Pershing's brilliant chief of staff, George C. Marshall, succeeded in bringing the AEF's divisions into line on time despite chaotic traffic jams. But the lines of supply that would have to feed men and matériel into the front lines were a muddle, barely adequate to support a limited advance let alone the rapid breakthrough Pershing desired.

The short time between the two offensives also meant that Pershing's best combat units—the ones he needed to break the German lines in the Salient—would not be available to spearhead the Meuse-Argonne assault. Of the nine divisions that would attack on September 26, only the Fourth was regular army. Four were National Guard divisions, and four National Army. Only three divisions—the Fourth, the 28th (NG) and the 77th (NA) had had any considerable experience of combat. Of the others, the 35th (NG) had had a brief taste of action, but the 37th (NG), the 91st, and the 79th (NA) had no combat experience whatever. The tight timetable, the limitations of the road network, and inadequacy of transport meant that divisions had to go into line at whichever place they could reach most easily. Thus the least experienced National Army divisions were entrusted with the primary day-one mission: to capture Montfaucon, the ridge that dominated the center of the front.

The 77th was assigned to the extreme left of Pershing's army, its mission to clear the enemy out of the dense thickets and tangled ravines of the Argonne Forest. Its right flank would be covered by the advance of the two other divisions of I Corps, both National Guard outfits, the Pennsylvanians of the 28th (which had fought beside them on the Vesle), and the relatively green 35th from Kansas and Missouri—one of whose field artillery batteries was commanded by Captain Harry S. Truman. But protection of its left flank was entrusted to the French Fourth Army, commanded by General Gouraud. It was a matter of deep concern to General Alexander, commanding the 77th, that they would have to depend on a foreign army for the close flank support their advance in the Argonne required. It did not comfort him that the corps reserve was the 92nd Division, which consisted of Negro troops and was completely untried in battle.

The understrength French division covering the terrain between Gouraud's main assault force and the 77th was not expected to mount an assault, but to advance in rough concert with Gouraud's Ninth Corps and the 77th Division, maintain liaison, and prevent the Germans from slipping between them to counterattack against their flanks. Gouraud's main force would drive toward the German strongpoint of Blanc Mont, the towns of Sechault and Monthois, and the rail junction of Challerange. Three Negro regiments of the 93rd (Provisional) Division would spearhead the drive against Monthois/Sechault: the 371st and 372nd serving with the French 157th Division, and the 369th as part of the 161st. The 370th was attached to another division on the left of Gouraud's front. The jump-off point for the 369th was perhaps twenty miles west of the 77th Division's position facing the Argonne Forest.

Replacements: September 16–24

The soldiers who slogged wearily into their camps after the bloody fighting of August and September had only the dimmest knowledge of what was going on back in the States. Newspapers and mail from home reached them at irregular intervals, delayed by passage through military censorship. They were in any case so locked into the world of their squads and companies that even the gravest domestic issues in a month-old copy of the *New York Herald* or *Age* would have seemed unreal. All they cared about was how soon the war was likely to end, and the "khaki telegraph" was more current than anything that came through the mails. Rumors of a coming offensive were rife but vague. They expected a decent spell of rest before going into the line again.

They would be disappointed. The 369th had eight days grace between its relief under Butte du Mesnil and its deployment for the grand offensive on the night of September 25. The 77th had only four days from its relief in front of Revillon to its deployment to the Argonne on September 21. In the brief period allotted to them they had to heal wounds and cure illnesses, replace and refurbish arms and equipment, train for the new tasks that the offensive would demand. They also had to absorb the large number of replacements brought in to offset the losses they had suffered in the summer's battles. But soldiers in a unit are not interchangeable parts of a machine. Something qualitative is lost with the death or wounding of the original personnel, especially the noncoms and junior officers who have led the unit in training and combat. Well-organized units can assimilate a small steady stream of trained replacements. But these units had been poorly trained to begin with, and the AEF's replacement system compelled them to integrate large numbers of new troops who were woefully undertrained.

It had been intended that each AEF division should draw replacements from its own depots, preserving regional ties as an aid to unit solidarity. But the need for replacements was so urgent that the system was abandoned. As soon as the 41st Division arrived in France it was cannibalized to feed divisions in the line, and the same happened to other late-arriving outfits. As losses mounted individuals and small groups were hauled out of training units, shipped to Europe among strangers, and dropped into replacement depots where they were more or less neglected until someone snatched them up and shipped them to the front.

The experiences of Ralph John and John Nell were typical. Both were cowboys, from South Dakota and Colorado respectively, drafted and sent to local camps for induction, then sent from camp to camp, receiving only perfunctory infantry training and a little close order drill. John had only two sessions on the rifle range before shipping out. Both men went to France as part of a bunch rather than a unit and on arrival were assigned to a temporary company. One night Nell's group were ordered out at three in the morning for what they supposed was a hike. Instead they were loaded on box cars, *Hommes 40—Chevaux 8*, and railroaded into the dark without explanation or rations. Expecting a trip of no more than a day, they spent three shunting their way across France, their only food some potatoes they stole from broken sacks in an adjacent boxcar. They arrived at the 77th Division at three in the morning and were split up among various companies. Private John was with a different bunch, slated for Fourth Division, but he caught the measles and was left behind. The hospital released him while he was still covered with lesions, and after two practice sessions in bayonet fighting he too was packed in a boxcar and shipped to the 77th.[2]

The new additions to the 307th and 308th Infantry came from every part of the country, especially the heartlands of the West and Midwest. Albert Kaempfer, Arthur Hicks, and James Rainwater (a Native American) had been miners in Butte, Montana—drafted as part of the government's plan to break the IWW and the mining unions' hold on the region. Bob Yoder, Ted Tollefson, Olaf Swanson, Olaf Nilson, and Haakon Rossum were Scandinavian-Americans from Minnesota, where there had been battles between patriot vigilantes and socialists, pacifists, and farmers of the radical, populist Non-Partisan League. Nell and John were cowboys, Robert Dodd a Paiute Indian who had graduated from a Midwestern "Indian College." George Newcom was a Kansas rancher, William Christensen a Danish immigrant from Colorado. Frank Martinez and Alfred Rodriquez were from the Southwest, Rodriquez a Mexican-American, and Martinez listed as an Indian. They too were from an area swept by vigilantism against labor unions (as in the Bisbee "deportations") and "foreign" workers, in their region Mexicans.[3]

Contact with these new men might have offered a source of news about what was happening at home—if anyone in the division had been interested. But for men immersed in the world of combat, such news was irrelevant, and rookies regarded with only slightly less disdain than civilians. What was most needful was to integrate the new men into their squads and platoons, and see to it that they knew enough about soldiering to keep up their end in the coming battles. On this score, the replacements looked to be more of a liability than an aid. Some had used firearms in civilian life, and Bob Yoder was a marksman. But for the most part they were "entirely unbroke to the matter of war."

Some had been less than a month in France; some had been in the service about forty days, most of which they had spent in travel. . . . Many of the new men had no reserve rations and there was no way to get them. Men took the jump-off into the Argonne battle who did not know how to use a hand grenade or work the magazines of their rifles.

It was AEF folklore that sergeants charged five bucks to teach them to load, aim, and shoot, and that most lessons were given right before the offensive began. They had had no practice whatever in the basic techniques of assaulting and defending entrenchments, let alone the more difficult skills of battalion-strength assault. Some arrived without such essential equipment as overcoats or gas masks. Some had not been issued rifles. They also brought with them the viral agent that was causing an epidemic of influenza back in the States, which would eventually become a worldwide pandemic.[4]

The problem of integrating replacements was compounded by the fact that, despite its experience of heavy combat, the 77th was inadequately trained. The division had supposedly spent eight months training at Camp Upton, but organizational problems wasted the month of September and in November nearly a fifth of the troops on hand were distributed to other divisions and replaced by new men. Training was broken by another wave of transfers in January and February, 4,500 out and a different 4,500 in. As a result the 77th had been "unable to complete unit training at a level higher than rifle company" while in the States and had to learn the rest through trial and error in combat. Most battalion and company officers were courageous and could keep their troops in hand under fire. The experiences of the summer had transformed the soldiers into veterans, who would not panic when in difficulty, knew the fundamentals of infantry combat, and could compensate to some extent for the failings of green officers. But they had never learned how to conduct a scout or the "storm trooper" techniques of assault by infiltration they would need to achieve a breakthrough. They were utterly unprepared for the special conditions of forest warfare they would confront in the Argonne—that gloomy woodland where Horace Pippin said it rained all the time, and it was so dark under the trees at night "you could not see your hands before you."[5]

Their effectiveness in division-scale operations had been impaired by frequent changes in the top command. Major General Bell had commanded them through their training, but was relieved for health reasons.

Major General Duncan led the division through July and August, only to be replaced by Major General Robert Alexander during the fighting along the Vesle. Each of these changes entailed an upheaval in the organization at a time when it was imperative for divisional staff to be perfecting the methods of administration, unit coordination, and liaison that they would need in combat.

In the 308th the replacement of Colonel Averill by Colonel Austin Prescott hurt morale. Charles Whittlesey was not one to complain, but he wrote to Miles (who was recovering in the hospital) that officers returning from leave got an unpleasant "jolt" when they saw what Prescott "had been doing to everyone's spirits." "Dear old Lieutenant Colonel Smith"—the term of affection was Whittlesey's heroic epithet for the man—was doing what he could to "eas[e] things off." Smith was a regular who got along well with his Plattsburgh juniors and showed his care for the men under him by the same sort of consideration that had marked Captains Mills and McMurtry. While they were resting after the Vesle fighting, Smith "bought a lot of grape marmalade at his own risk" and sold it to the men at cost. Among men starved for anything to vary their diet of hardtack and monkey meat, it was a gesture of real kindness. (The officers dined on rabbits one day, duck another—the fruits of Lieutenant Hass's skill as a hunter.)

The division had suffered heavy losses among the men best qualified to lead troops in combat: the company commanders, lieutenants, and top sergeants. Some could be replaced from within the division. Herman Bergasse, who had earned a superb reputation as mess sergeant, had been pressed into line service and done well along the Aisne. Supply sergeant Lawrence Osborne was given a platoon after Company B was decimated on the Vesle. "Zip" Cepaglia earned corporal's stripes and promotion from company to battalion runner.[6]

In the reshuffling Whittlesey was promoted to major and given the line command he had always wanted. But though he had been with the division from its birth, his former staff position had distanced him from the men of the rifle companies he would command, and his reserve made that distance hard to bridge. As battalion commander he was somewhat closer to the troops, but not as intimate a part of their lives as company commanders were. Battalions were "largely theoretical" units, the elements of which did not train together and were liable to be reshuffled under the exigencies of combat. The men of the 308th Infantry called

Whittlesey "Galloping Charlie," mocking his gangly stride as a way of bringing a distant and officious figure down to earth and expressing their disdain for all that smacked of the staff and parade ground. They would measure his performance in command of First Battalion against the standard of grit and common sense set by captains like Miles and McMurtry.[7]

The division also had to assimilate a large number of replacement officers, some of them "ninety-day wonders" out of the officers' training camps, others men who, for a variety of reasons, had been transferred out of other commands. They had, on average, less training and combat experience than the officers they replaced, and as newcomers did not automatically enjoy the confidence of their colleagues or their men. Among them were White officers transferred out of the Negro 92nd Division. Most were grateful to be assigned to a White outfit, but their credentials would have been suspect. Everyone knew, or thought they knew, that the Negro division was second-rate.

All officers were issued *Training Memorandum No. 1*, which included "Questions for a Battalion Commander to Ask Himself Prior to Taking Over and While Occupying a Portion of the Front Line." There were thirty-three such questions, "of a soul-searching nature, suggestive of an almost morbidly meticulous introspection." What is the condition of the enemy wire? What routes of egress through our own wire may be used? The section for junior officers had a more "devotional" tone: "Questions a Platoon Leader Should Ask Himself on Taking Over a Trench and At Frequent Intervals Thereafter": "Have I caused organizations to take their assigned places at night, and is my liaison between all such groups and individuals complete?" Does each man understand what he must do if the position is attacked? Has each man been prepared for the part he must play in the assault? The manuals had no advice to offer on how the 308th Regiment was to assess the skills and incompetencies of 1,250 replacement troops (roughly one-third of its total strength), integrate them into their platoons, assign them places and tasks in less than forty-eight hours. It was the evening of September 24. At 5 A.M. on the day after tomorrow, ready or not they would go over the top and into the Argonne Forest.[8]

For the 369th Infantry and the other Black regiments in France, the problems of integrating replacements and preparing for battle were compounded by fallout from the racial reaction back in the States. The battlefield success of the 369th and the other three regiments of the 93rd Division had had consequences that were unforeseen and unwanted by the U.S. Army. The presence of Black field officers in the 370th and 372nd challenged the army's presumption that Negroes were not to be trusted with commands larger than a company, and the integrated officer cadre of the 369th violated the principle of segregation. GHQ was also deeply concerned that the warm and equal treatment accorded these troops by White-skinned French men and women would undermine the social and sexual taboos on which the authority of Jim Crow depended.

In the summer of 1918 the army took positive action to re-create the American color line in France. In July GHQ disrupted the organization of the 93rd Division's four infantry regiments with a wholesale transfer of officers. The measure was intended to eliminate all field-grade Black officers from combat units and to segregate the junior officer ranks within each regiment, eliminating the anomaly (which had always existed in the 369th) of having Whites and Blacks of equal rank in the same unit. This was followed in August by issued instructions (titled "Secret Information"), which in effect ordered French soldiers and civilians to act in accordance with the manners and customs of Jim Crow.

From the first arrival of Black labor troops in France, American commanders had tried to induce in the French a proper respect for the color line. They told French authorities that Negroes were racially backward and prone to larceny and rape. The French paid little attention, as their friendly reception of Black combat troops showed, but the 369th was aware that American military authorities were trying to discourage such openness: James Europe mentioned it in a letter to the *Age* on July 28.

On August 14, Colonel Linard, a French liaison officer at AEF headquarters, issued the "Secret Information Concerning Black American Troops," which carried the imprimatur of Pershing's staff. Linard told his compatriots it was useless to argue the issue of prejudice with the Americans. Their opinion of Negroes was fixed and unanimous. They had adopted strict racial separation specifically to prevent "mongrelization." No such fear existed in France, where there were few Negroes, but it was essential that Frenchmen understand that to Americans, displays of interracial friendship were deeply offensive. White Americans feared such experiences would encourage "intolerable pretensions to equality," which would pose a danger to America's civil peace when the troops came home:

> Although a citizen of the United States, the black man is regarded by the white American as an inferior being with whom relations of business or service only are possible. The black is constantly being censured for his want of intelligence and discretion, his lack of civic and professional conscience, and for his tendency toward undue familiarity. The vices of the Negro are a constant menace to the American who has to repress them sternly.

It was vital, therefore, that French soldiers and civilians beware of "spoiling the Negroes." Social relations with civilians must be restricted: "Americans become greatly incensed at any public display of intimacy between white women and black men." Black troops serving with the French should not be too highly praised, especially to White Americans. French officers must repress any impulse to befriend Black counterparts:

> We may be courteous and amiable . . . but we cannot deal with them on the same plane with white American officers without deeply offending the latter. We must not eat with them, must not shake hands or seek to talk or meet with them outside the requirements of military service.[9]

So much for the army as the place above all others in which a man might rise according to his labor and his merit. So much too for "n-i-g-g-e-r" as just another way to spell "American." The men in charge of the AEF were determined to see that the original definition was protected from French subversion, and the French taught to understand "nigger" exactly as Americans did. They did not entirely succeed with the French. Generals like Gouraud continued to praise Black units who served effectively and to award them the Croix de Guerre, and when after the war the National Assembly was told of the Secret Information, it treated the matter as a scandal.

Linard's memorandum was "Secret" because so frank a confession of an illiberal prejudice would embarrass the Americans by revealing their pretense of racial toleration as sheer hypocrisy. But its wide distribution to civil and military officials guaranteed exposure in the press, and Harlem got word of it within the month. For the troops in France its effects were palpable and immediate. By the end of September, when the 369th were enjoying a brief rest before the great offensive, French and American authorities had effectively made "all of France . . . off-limits to the black man, including, more often than not, the YMCA 'huts' " that were supposed to provide social and sutlers' services to the troops. In the 369th, and in other regiments whose commanders were opposed to Jim Crow, White officers found ways to mitigate application of the rules when French civil authorities seemed inclined to ignore them. They showed their resentment of the post-Linard regime by an increasing insistence, in letters and press interviews, that their Black soldiers were decent, clean, and well behaved—an implicit refutation of the assumptions behind the Secret Information.

On the other hand, there were outfits in which the officers agreed with the spirit of the instruction and enforced them to the letter. On August 31 Lieutenant Ernest Samusson, the 371st Regiment's intelligence officer, formally requested civilian authorities near their camp to "take steps to co-operate toward the prevention of these harmful relationships [i.e., between French women and Black men] by enlightening the residents concerning the gravity of the situation and by warning them of the inevitable results." Samusson implied that if the French permitted fraternization their wives and daughters might be sexually assaulted. But Samusson's greater concern was not for the French, but for those "American towns, the population of which will be affected later when the troops return to the United States." An experience of "undue social mixing" in France would undo the lifelong lessons inculcated by Jim Crow.[10]

The new policies had the potential to undermine morale by reminding Black troops they were fighting for a Jim Crow nation. The reshuffling of Black officers in the 93rd Division directly affected the combat effectiveness of its four infantry regiments.

The 371st Infantry weathered these trials with the least difficulty. It was raised from draftees in the South and officered by Whites, most of whom came from the same region. Jim Crow shaped the conditions under which the regiment was assembled, and the issue of Black leadership was never allowed to arise. Monroe Mason and Arthur Furr, the African-American soldiers who wrote the history of the 371st and 372nd Infantry, characterized the officers' treatment of their men as paternalistic and oppressive, but were compelled to admit that the men of the 371st did not feel this as a Northern Negro would: "Accustomed to the whip-and-lash method of living, [they] meekly submitted." The troops may also have felt they were enjoying what any southerner would regard as an extraordinary *privilege* for Black men, the right to bear arms in combat. Since it was already organized on segregationist principles, the 371st was not disrupted by officer transfers, and developed into a good combat unit.[11]

The 370th was one of only two regiments with Black field officers, the only one commanded by a Black man. As the Eighth Illinois, its traditions reached back to the Civil War and were marked by the militant assertion of community and race pride: when asked, "Where are the white Officers?' . . . 'There's not one in the Regiment' was our proud reply." On July 4, 1918, the 370th learned that Colonel Denison was being replaced. Chaplain William Bradden told a colleague, "It's all up with us, that for which we left home and loved ones is about to be taken from us; once that white Colonel gets in command it's goodbye to all spade officers." Denison's relief was not wholly unwarranted. The regiment's training tour with the French had not gone well. As in many White National Guard regiments, commissions were granted to men of social and political prominence, and the officer cadre of the Eighth had become more like "a big social club of fellow race-men" than a military establishment. But the fairness of Denison's relief was questioned because it was part of a general policy of dismissing Black field officers regardless of merit. Denison was replaced by Colonel T. A. Roberts, for Bradden "the arch enemy, vilifier and traducer of the Negro soldier, who delighted to sign his private mail as coming from 'The White Hope in a Black Regiment.'" Enlisted men greeted Roberts with shouts of "Blue eyes ain't our Colonel." In this troubled condition the regiment was ordered into combat.[12]

Bradden and his colleagues may have done Roberts an injustice. He kept most of the company officers in place and told GHQ his men were "excellent material." If they had fallen short it was because the army had failed to support them, and "the same would apply to a white outfit." Under Roberts the 370th became a solid combat unit.[13]

The 372nd was also a Guard outfit, but its components came from several states and lacked the Eighth Illinois's tradition and unit solidarity. Colonel Glengie Young "steeped [himself] in machinations" to get rid of the regiment's two Black majors, and "partly admitted that color prejudice was the reason." This set the tone for his White officers. "A feeling of disdain and disgust was justly aroused both in the negro officers and the men, and smouldered day after day, only to be aggravated by some other disagreeable event." On July 5 it was rumored that the Whites were intriguing to remove all "Colored officers." Three Black officers protested, were arrested for insubordination and charged with trying "to create a propaganda . . . among all colored units in France." Pershing showed his disdain for political colonels by replacing Young with a regular, Colonel Herschel Tupes—who was, if anything, more committed to Jim Crow than his predecessor. Tupes formally segregated officers' mess and forbade Negro officers to visit the civilian cafés frequented by Whites. He asked that all his Negro officers be transferred out, primarily because "the racial distinctions which are recognized" in civilian and military life "present a formidable barrier to that feeling of comradeship which is essential to mutual confidence and esprit de corps." He also claimed that "with a few exceptions" Negro officers "neglect the welfare of their men and . . . perform their duties in a perfunctory manner. They are lacking in initiative also."

On August 18, with the regiment preparing to go into the line, Tupes began sending Black officers before an elimination board. The enlisted men staged a "demonstration of silence and contempt . . . held their own secret meetings and not a word leaked out as to what they had in their minds." Mutiny was averted when departing Black officers "admonished them to keep up the morale they had already attained" so they might "vindicate themselves from the stigma" put upon the race by the "organized perfidy" of the elimination board. Some of these officers were allowed to stay with the regiment when it returned to the front. The 372nd performed well, but there were rumors that some White officers were shot by their own men under cover of the fighting.[14]

The Old Fifteenth had started with good commanders and high morale, though it received less stateside training than any regiment in the AEF. It had also seen more combat and suffered more casualties than the other regiments in the 93rd Division and therefore had a larger number of replacements to assimilate. Because of the haste with which it had been shipped out, it had never entirely filled its ranks to the standard minimum of 3,500 troops. Its combat casualties of 200 killed and wounded fell most heavily on the rifle platoons, and many more men had been lost to noncombat causes, disease, accident, air attack, or bombardment while in reserve. Little reported that after the July 18–21 offensive

40 percent of his battalion was made up of replacements, all of whom arrived untrained and in some respects unfit for service. But the replacements the regiment received on the eve of their last and greatest battle
were worse than useless. Drawn from labor battalions in France and replacement depots in the States, they were demoralized by bad treatment
and had received little if any training. Unlike the veterans they had no
shared memory of Harlem and Spartanburg and Camp Mills, nor of
Bastille Day and Butte du Mesnil. They were strangers cast unwillingly
and without preparation into an alien society, to be menaced continually
by the threat of violent death.[15]

To complicate matters the regiment also had to assimilate the untried
White officers sent as replacements for Fillmore, Napoleon Marshall,
and the rest. It was probably an officer new to the regiment who ordered
Horace Pippin to destroy (for security reasons) the journal-sketchbook
he had kept since enlisting. Pippin obeyed, though it must have cost him
a great deal. But just as he had learned by heart the words of his one
scrap of mail from home, those images of terror and fear were "burned"
into his mind in ways he believed he would not forget and might some-
day reconstruct—if he managed to survive the coming battle with eyes
and mind and skill of hand intact.[16]

The 369th was fortunate in that most of the new officers were competent. During the August and September fighting some had had a
chance to earn, and show that they valued, the respect of their men.
Among these were medical officer George F. Shiels, Lieutenant George
Robb, and a New York City celebrity, Leon "Josh" Cadore, better
known as a pitcher for the Brooklyn Robins. Cadore had originally belonged to the 77th Division, but stayed behind at Upton for training as a
machine-gun officer. He wound up in the replacement pool, which assigned him as a first lieutenant to Company G of the 369th.[17]

Georgia-born Second Lieutenant Emmett Cochran was a more dubious addition, and his mishandling of a disciplinary incident had fatal
consequences. On August 21 Major Spencer received word that a detail
from F Company, on guard in the village of Dommartin, had got its
hands on some champagne and gone riotously drunk. Spencer ordered
Cochran to take a squad from F and arrest the detail. He warned
Cochran to be careful: F Company had a reputation as tough and difficult to discipline—they were the ones rumored to have shot at sergeants who rode them too hard. But Spencer ordered Cochran to go

unarmed: "I don't think you will have any trouble, but if you do, get you a club and club them good alongside of the head." But Cochran kept his automatic strapped on his belt; he loaded six men in the back of a wooden horse-cart, sat himself next to the driver, and set off for Dommartin.

The report of a "riot" was exaggerated. The five soldiers on the detail were veterans who had been with the regiment from the start, had good combat records, and were considered trustworthy. Champagne made some of them loud, but Sergeant Emmanuel had them under control—he had disarmed Private Shields and given his rifle to Private Walter Whittaker, a steady married man from Freeport, Long Island. Whittaker was a clerk, with a box of papers to lug around, so he unloaded and slung both rifles. When Cochran and his horse-cart approached the position, Emmanuel stepped into the road and challenged them, as orders required him to do. Cochran ordered the driver to keep going, straight at the sergeant. Whittaker, standing at the roadside, yelled at Cochran to halt. Neither man knew why Cochran was there, and Cochran made no announcement of his orders or intentions. Whittaker dropped the box of papers and ran to grab the horse before it ran his sergeant down. Cochran jumped off the cart, drew his pistol, leveled it at Whittaker, and ordered him to disarm. The private obediently unslung one rifle and laid it on the ground. As he moved to set the second beside it Cochran fired, shooting Whittaker in the belly. Whittaker straightened and stared at Cochran. "Well, Lieutenant . . . you have shot me. I was carrying out my orders, and you have shot a good man." The two stood facing each other in silence till Whittaker dropped to his knees. "Boys . . . if I die tell all the people a good man is gone." Cochran threatened to kill anyone who moved, but he was shocked, unable to think what to do next. After about twenty minutes he finally explained his mission and ordered Whittaker taken to a hospital, where he died. Cochran was acquitted by a court-martial, which ruled he had had reason to think his life was in danger. Whether the shooting was racially motivated or was simply the fearful response of an inexperienced officer, its effect was the same: "a good man . . . gone" and the solidarity of the command threatened.[18]

In spite of all this, the 369th and its brother regiments of the 93rd Division were able to maintain their morale because experience had taught them that in combat all considerations other than survival were secondary. The veterans were held together by the memory of what they had been through together and the certainty that they were in for more of it in the near future. They would continue to follow their officers because they had learned exactly how far they could trust them, as commanders and as White men—without illusions in either case. It helped that the departing Black officers urged the men to remember and abide by the terms of the original bargain. For the raw replacements, demoralized and aggrieved by their treatment as labor troops, utterly untrained and never integrated into the solidarity of their units, that trust had never existed. When the action started the fear of the law that held them in the ranks would be overwhelmed by the terror of being helpless and alienated under the endless bludgeoning of artillery and the flail of machine-gun fire.

Those same demoralizing forces played upon the untried and poorly trained troops of the 92nd Division, which lacked the resources to cope with them. The division was commanded by Major General Charles Ballou, who had also presided over the Des Moines camp for Black officer trainees. He had led Negro troops in the Old Army, and African-American leaders considered him relatively friendly. He certainly had a personal interest in seeing that Des Moines and the 92nd Division were successful and was aware that many White officers in his command "were rabidly hostile to the idea of a colored officer, and . . . will never give the Negro the square deal that is his just due." Ballou tried to mitigate the effects of these prejudices, but he had also to defer to them. He could not choose his White officers as Hayward had done and was obliged to respect the War Department's orders that protests against the "so-called race problem" not be accommodated. He also shared the general belief that few if any Blacks could qualify to be field officers, that they required intense supervision by White superiors if they were to succeed, and that Black troops were reluctant to take orders from Black officers—they preferred to rely on the proven superiority of Whites.

Although the technical training was as good (and as bad) as that in other officer-training venues, Des Moines taught all the wrong lessons about building unit pride and morale, and these were carried over to the 92nd Division. The officer cadre was split into three antagonistic camps: educated Blacks, semiliterate Black noncoms from the regulars, and White regular officers. The noncoms resented their educated Black colleagues, who had not earned their bars by hard service and whose manners assumed an entitlement to be treated like White officers and gentlemen. The "Talented Tenth" looked down on the ex-sergeants, not only because they were uneducated but because they seemed (to a civilian) unduly subservient to White officers. The "Tenth" also had reason to think that the Whites liked to put them in their place by favoring their former noncoms and otherwise humiliating the college men. A postwar investigation led by Lieutenant General Bullard found that, except for Ballou, none of the ranking officers of the division believed Negroes were capable of commanding soldiers in battle. "Not one of them believed that the 92nd Division would ever be worth anything as soldiers. Every one of them would have given anything to be transferred to any other duty. It was the most pitiful case of discouragement that I have ever seen among soldiers."[19]

To change the situation in positive ways required a stronger hand than Ballou's and a determination to alter rather than accommodate the mind-set of bigoted officers. Hayward had set the tone in recruiting White officers for the 369th and Colonel James A. Moss did the same for the 92nd Division's 367th Infantry.[20] But in the rest of the 92nd Division mutual suspicion and bad faith undermined relationships between the company officers and their men, and between Black junior officers and White field officers and commanders. Enlisted men are quick to pick up divided counsel among their officers and to take advantage of it, evading the hardships and arbitrary injustices of army life by playing their White major against their Black captain, their "Old Regular" lieutenant against the "dickity" Des Moines captain. The net effect was to make a self-fulfilling prophecy of the belief that Black soldiers would not follow Black officers—not universally, but often enough to affect the morale and effectiveness of many units in the 92nd Division.[21]

In July, while the 92nd Division was undergoing its combat training, Private Sidney Wilson of the 368th Infantry wrote an angry and defiant letter to the Tennessee draft board that had sent him to France:

> It afoads to the soldier boys wich you have sint so far away from home a great deal of pledger to write you a few lines to let you know that you low-down Mother Fuckers can put a gun in our hands but who is able to take it out? We may go to France but I want to let you know that it will not be over with untill we straiten up this state. We feel like we have nothing to do with this war, so if you all thinks it, just wait till

> Uncle Sam puts a gun in the niggers hands and you will be sorry of it, because we have colored luetinan up here, and thay is planning against this country everday. So all we wants now is the ammanition, then you can all look out, for we is coming.[22]

There is a certain pleasure, at this distance, in hearing Private Wilson tell his Jim Crow draft board exactly what he thinks of them; and you have the feeling that whatever else it has done, the U.S. Army has given him a sense of his and his people's potential power, which he might be able to turn into productive militancy after the war. But what it says about the 92nd Division's morale and readiness for combat is not hopeful at all. This soldier does not believe in the war he is to fight, does not identify with the army or even the division in which he serves. He is angry, aggrieved, alienated, trusts his Black lieutenant and perhaps his squad but no one else, and the only people he wants to shoot are White Americans 4,000 miles away from the Argonne Forest.

The mishandling and mistreatment of the 92nd Division and the poisonous psychology that made those things possible would have a direct and immediate impact on the Allied grand offensive that was being prepared. The Division's 368th Infantry in particular would be thrust without preparation into a critical position linking the left flank of the 77th Division with the supporting elements of Gouraud's Fourth Army. What happened to it during the first few days of the Meuse-Argonne offensive would affect the fates of both the Lost Battalion of the 308th and the Harlem Hell Fighters of the 369th.

Moving Up: September 25–26

On the night of September 25–26, 1918, the last of the guns were being hauled into place, the final troop dispositions made along the lines. There were a quarter of a million men in Pershing's front line, 400,000 in reserve, 2,700 artillery pieces registered on targets in his front. With Gouraud's Fourth Army they represented about a third of the three and a half million troops lining the Allied trenches all the way from the Belgian coast to the Swiss border. Pershing and Gouraud would open the attack along the southern face of the wedge that German advances had carved out of northeastern France. The following day the British in Artois would attack toward Cambrai, and the day after a British-Belgian force in Flanders at the northern end of the line would support them with an assault on the Germans' extreme right. On September 29 a British army with French support would smash at the German center.[23]

In the 77th Division camps Private Nell, just arrived from the replacement depot, had raked up a nice pile of dry leaves to soften the floor of his pup tent, anticipating a week-long stay, when his company commander blew his whistle and ordered them to fall in. They were to stack their tents and full packs under an oak tree and prepare to march with mess kits, canteens, rifles, and ammunition only. "Speaking in a heavy, choking voice," he told them they were going up to the front at midnight, prepared to go "over the top" at first light. "If one of your buddies, or friends, or even relatives, if you have any in the company, gets shot or wounded, do not stop to help him or to apply first aid, as every fighting man is needed. . . . Now I want to impress on your minds and you to remember, anyone caught lagging behind will be considered a straggler and a yellow coward and even a deserter. A man of this type, a straggler, is shown no sympathy." He also told them the woods they were in was the Argonne Forest, if that meant anything.

The supply sergeant and his men started passing out ammunition, grenades, and other gear, "about half enough of everything." No rations were issued, and no arrangements made to bring them up. The supply sergeant reported that three of the men who had drawn ammo had no rifles. "Where are your rifles? Did you lose them?" "No sir; we have never had any issued to us."

"Questions a Platoon Leader Should Ask Himself on Taking Over a Trench and at Frequent Intervals Thereafter": *What do I do with riflemen who have no rifles?*

The lieutenant shrugged, told them to go over the top as they were. Someone was bound to get killed or wounded and they could pick up his rifle. Apparently it was permissible to stop for that purpose without being thought a slacker.[24]

Officers were assigned to scout the terrain over which the first wave would pass, and they went out disguised in French uniforms so the Germans would think the French still manned the sector. Major Whittlesey led the 77th Division scouting party, which included Lieutenants Whiting, Schenck, and Lewis. The French officers got a good laugh at their expense—all the borrowed overcoats were the same small size, which fit

Whiting and Schenck but looked ridiculous on Whittlesey and Lewis, both over six feet tall. They scouted down into the valley of a small creek, then through the ruins of a town that to Whittlesey "looked as though it had been destroyed in the Middle Ages." There were mossy caved-in trenches there, "like a relic from some earlier war," a position designed for a regiment occupied by an exhausted French company. They saw what they could, which wasn't much, just the first bit of ground to be crossed before they hit the forest.

While Whittlesey's men waited to move up they were put to digging trenches, for which they blamed Colonel Prescott—a regular army stickler who thought idleness bad for troops, never mind how hard they would be used. Whittlesey thought it a waste of their energy on the eve of battle to dig "silly trenches, that never would or could see war." He was pressed for time to get his replacements ready—was still teaching them how to use hand grenades and load the magazines of their rifles when someone came from division with a stack of "some new-fangled rifle grenade affair—very complicated with a tail"—the sort of contraption that had killed Captain Mills. Whittlesey simply refused to issue them. The troops were told to leave shelter halves, blankets, overcoats, and rain gear behind; they would only be in the line a few days. It would be weeks before they saw their packs again.[25]

The left flank of the 77th, which was held by the 308th, was the subject of some anxiety. The boundary between two units is always vulnerable, whether in assault or defense, whether the line falls between companies of a regiment or armies of allied nations. It is the line where command responsibility divides, where—given the always dubious connection between the general's map and the lieutenant's terrain—vital positions may be disregarded, enemy penetrations go unobserved. Liaison is extremely difficult across such a boundary, especially when it falls between two armies from different national organizations. Here the problem was complicated by the fact that the 77th had to maneuver in the tangles of the Argonne, where it would be difficult to maintain contact between its own units let alone those under different command on its flank. As a National Army division the 77th had the least training, the fewest experienced staff officers, of any division in I Corps' line. Its division commander had only been appointed a month earlier.

So when Gouraud asked Pershing for another American regiment to shore up his right flank and maintain liaison with the 77th, Pershing was willing to oblige. It was September 25; the fight was to begin at dawn tomorrow. The only reserve force convenient to Gouraud's positions was the 92nd Division. The French would not object to the assignment of Black troops, even if Pershing considered them second-rate. Fourth Army was already home to the 93rd Division, and very happy with them.

General Liggett, commanding I Corps, selected the 368th Infantry for the task. His choice was never explained, but cannot have been based on its performance. Along with the rest of the 92nd Division it had served the briefest of apprenticeships with the French in quiet sectors and had not been tested in heavy fighting. The division commander, General Ballou, ought to have been aware that the 368th was not a well-run outfit. Its brigade-mate, the 367th Infantry, recruited and trained in the New York area and commanded by Colonel Moss, had come out of training with good morale and would be rated the best in the division. Perhaps Liggett and Ballou preferred to retain the stronger unit for their own use. If so, it was false economy.

The 368th made a night march behind the lines and took over a two-mile section of the French front, facing German troops entrenched behind tangles of barbed wire in a wooded outlier of the great Argonne Forest to their right. Their officers studied the ground through field glasses. They had no time to scout, their maps were inadequate, and they were short of wire cutters. Orders were to attack at first light on the 26th.

What Private Sidney Wilson thought of the situation we do not know. What he thought about those "mother fuckers" on the Memphis draft board can be guessed.

West of the 368th, the Hell Fighters had been trucked out of their rest area to Somme-Bionne, a small village well south of the front line. There Hayward was given his assignment and briefed on the battle plan. He understood that there would be a frontal assault along the whole line, that rapid advance was expected, that Fourth Army was to move in time with the AEF, and that the spearheads of their two attacks were to join in Grandpré at the northern extremity of the Argonne. "It was all made very clear." Gouraud's method was to inform his commanders and troops as fully as possible about his intentions, so that they could follow them intelligently. Obsessed with the need for secrecy and surprise, the AEF gave no such briefing to regimental commanders.

The 369th assembled after dark on September 25 and marched along the road that ran from Somme-Bionne to Minaucourt, east of the Butte du Mesnil where they had suffered through August and September. Hamilton Fish was away on a staff training course, but he pulled strings to get leave and showed up at Hayward's headquarters, willing to be used wherever he might be needed. Hayward gave the battalions their orders. Third Battalion under Major Lorillard Spencer and Second Battalion under Captain Frederick Cobb would go in with the first assault wave, flanked by French infantry on one side and the Moroccans on the other. They would hit the German line at the village of Ripont, break it if they could, then advance toward the high wooded ridge called Bellevue Signal, the town of Sechault, and the vital railroad junction of Challerange beyond. Little with First Battalion would form the reserve.

Little's battalion started out at the rear of the column. The highway was so jammed with traffic that the only way to reach their jump-off position was to march cross-country. Little had had the foresight to order Lieutenant Seibel to scout the ground earlier. Now with Seibel guiding them the battalion picked their way across woodlots and pastures, marched down farm lanes and across fields, "the stars . . . our guide-posts, and the only sounds to break the stillness . . . the occasional clatterings of tin cups or canteens carelessly used by some hapless soldier due for instant correction of violent language from his non-commissioned immediate superior." They reached their assigned positions with twenty minutes to spare. The great bombardment was slated to begin eighty minutes later, at 11 P.M. Sergeant Hannibal Davis remembered that Little spoke to them "like a father," told them that "a million men would go over the top with us."

Horace Pippin was in the front line with K Company. He stared into the dark and suddenly a picture of his home came into his head: "i could see it right in front of me. i wonder if i will see it again." Then he wished he had a letter from home he could pull out and read, "how happy i would be," but he hadn't had a letter in a long time. He lit a last cigarette and passed it around. Then the French guns cut loose, the Germans answered, and it was hold on where you were and pray you lived to see the morning. And if you did, you'd have to get up and go over the top and make your run at the German wire.[26]

Over the Top: The Meuse-Argonne Offensive Begins, September 26–27

Night of September 25–26, 1918: pitch-black and a heavy fog over the 77th Division's sector of the lines. In the dark you could hear the incessant rustle and clank as the assault troops shuffled down the muddy twists of the communication trenches and filed out along the trench lines from which they would jump off at dawn.

The Germans dropped harassing fire out of the darkness. The rookie Ralph John was tramping down a deep communication trench when without warning "the trench blew up. And such a mess!" Instinct took over, and John dropped into a defensive stance, "crouched on my knees with my gun down in firing position. . . . But there was no enemy in sight, nothing but blackness pierced by the screams and moans of those all but torn to pieces." He helped roll a large rock off his buddy—" 'Is that you Reuben?' and Reuben replied, 'What is left of me.' "[27]

The troops took shelter under the brow of the front-line trenches or, if they were lucky, in damp dugouts. "It was pitch dark and we just sat around, listening to the big shells going over." Off west in the dark they could hear the thud and rumble of the Fourth Army's guns blasting the German lines. From the sound a veteran could judge the distance as fifteen to twenty miles away. Their own guns were silent. General Pershing had rejected the French plan of an all-night inundation of shell fire in favor of a short three-hour bombardment to preserve the element of surprise on which he was counting heavily. The men in the trenches had heard such plans before, counted on nothing but the guys next to them. The damp chill crawled inside their shirts.

Ahead of them was a belt of blasted ground that had once been woods, now a cemetery of dead standing trunks snapped off by airbursts. The ground between the trunks was churned and cratered with shell holes. The far slope in the last light had seemed to be covered with a mat of withered gorse, which was in fact the German wire, curled, bunched, twisted, and heaped in great masses. When it had been laid in

1915 it had shimmered a steely blue in the sun. Now it was rusted and ingrown with vines and shrubbery, forest and fortification melded into a semiorganic conglomerate. Behind the wire were the trenches of the German sacrifice line, and behind these the looming black of the Argonne, by report the densest woodland in western Europe, which the enemy had been fortifying for three years with trench lines, pillboxes, cleared corridors slanting through the trees to open fields of fire for hidden machine guns. The division's orders were to clear the forest in less than a week.

Finally at two in the morning the American guns cut loose, and the men huddled in the trenches heard the express-train roar and whoosh of their own heavy stuff going over and then the crump and rumble of explosions invisible behind the wall of fog like "the collision of a million express trains." The ground quivered and the air shuddered with waves of concussion. It went on for three hours, while the troops shivered in the bitter cold of pre-dawn. Then the barrage lifted—the thick fog around them was suffused with milky light—the whistles shrilled and they clambered up over the parapets and began to stumble forward as the rolling barrage began, blasting the fog and chewing the ground a hundred yards ahead of the skirmish line, the men stumbling over the churned earth and around the dead standing stumps of the murdered forest as they tried to keep pace with it. If the barrage was well aimed and well timed it would carve paths for them through the dense integument of old rusty wire and woody vines that masked the German front, it would keep the machine gunners' heads down till they were close enough to bomb them, maybe it would even destroy the Germans in their dugouts, and for once in this war give the boys a walk-over.

But it was hard to keep the green troops from bunching at the wire gaps, from drawing close together for comfort in the fog. The ground was broken and cratered, which made it hard to keep up with the barrage, and men tended to congregate in the seeming safety of low ground. With vision restricted to 100 feet, each company felt itself isolated from the rest of the battalion. Now here came the Germans' return shell fire, heavy, killing bursts erupting in the blind fog, from guns previously registered on the ground in front of their sacrifice trenches. And gas shells blending their poisonous fumes with the mist. "It was almost as if the infantry was asked to go over the top blindfolded." The rolling barrage jumped forward 100 meters every 45 minutes. But though opposition was light from the German sacrifice line, the difficulties of visibility and terrain held the infantry to a much slower pace, and the barrage soon ran so far ahead of them as to be useless.[28]

The division went forward with all four regiments in line, one battalion leading, a second in support, the third in reserve. But liaison between these components became tenuous as soon as they entered the fog and the forest. Kerr Rainsford of the 307th found himself and two runners "adrift in a blind world of whiteness and noise, groping over something like the surface of the moon."

> One literally could not see two yards, and everywhere the ground rose in pinnacles and ridges, or descended into bottomless chasms, half filled with rusted tangles of wire. Deep, half-ruined trenches appeared without system or sequence, usually impossible of crossing, bare splintered trees, occasional derelict skeletons of men, thickets of gorse and everywhere the piles of rusted wire. It looked as though it had taken root there . . . and it was so heavy that only the longest-handled cutters would bite through it.[29]

The German positions were well designed for defense. Ralph John's squad of Company A never saw them till they heard the "Pop Pop! Pop!" of the machine guns. But only the weakest troops had been left to man the sacrifice line, and as soon as the Americans lobbed grenades against their bunker they surrendered, three young boys and three old men who looked "around seventy years of age and had great long whiskers . . . tickled to death to get out alive." It was the terrain that made their advance nightmarish. The ground was muddy and slick, the barbed wire everywhere. Private John was able to step the wire down, because the army had given him size ten hobnailed boots—two sizes too large for his feet. (He would pay for that advantage with flat feet and broken arches, so painful they would disrupt his sleep for the rest of his life.)

Communication between units was nearly impossible, and even within units it was difficult. Rainsford complained, "It was never possible to pass an order down a column or single file. A Polack or some limited intelligence would invariably intervene as a non-conductor." In Whittlesey's First Battalion, companies and even platoons lost touch with each other as they entered the forest proper, soldiers hollering, "Hello— who are you?" "Where in hell is C Company?" It was lucky the Germans had pulled back to lines deeper in the woods, though even so the companies took casualties from snipers, machine-gun nests, and rear guards.

Whittlesey dropped runner-posts as he advanced to maintain contact with headquarters, but the runners got lost and Lieutenant Colonel Smith had to come forward to find out where everyone had gone. Still, Whittlesey managed to get his men up to their designated objective line—only to discover that it ran through an indefensible tract of swampy marshland. He pulled them back to better ground, dug in, and sent back for orders.

They barely reached their objective, advancing a mile and a quarter. Casualties were light, but the disorder and confusion of the advance worried everyone. Not only had they lost liaison with the 28th Division on the right and the 368th Infantry—the Negro regiment serving with the French—on their left; the support and reserve battalions of the regiment were out of touch with the front line, with each other, and with headquarters. They had to wonder whether this day's performance measured up to GHQ's expectations, and they could be certain tomorrow's fighting would be much harder. The night was "rainy, cold, and uncomfortable"; they had "little food and no overcoats or blankets." But they found bottles of mineral water in some of the German dugouts, so as Whittlesey said, "It might have been worse."[30]

Just how much worse it could have been was learned as word got around about what had happened to the rest of I Corps, and to V Corps in the center opposite Montfaucon.

The Argonne held the fog much longer than the open country through which the rest of the army had to advance. By 9:30 A.M. the sun had burned it off, and it became possible for forward observers and observation balloons to see what was going on. Across the whole front the troops had gone through the sacrifice line in a rush. On the right III Corps seized its objectives, securing the right flank. But everywhere else the army had been brought to a halt by the Germans' first line of resistance. Already the defects of training, equipment, and command were beginning to show.

In the center V Corps' two green National Army divisions, the 91st and 79th, stumbled in their attack on the vital high ground of Montfaucon. Theirs was the most important mission on that first day, and they were the divisions least prepared to accomplish it. Neither had received adequate training in the States, and their field shakedown had been brief. Over half the men in the 79th had joined the division after May 25. This meant that half their officers, noncoms, and soldiers had received little or no training beyond platoon and company level and did not know how to coordinate the actions of their units. The higher levels of command were not much better prepared: many senior officers at regiment and brigade level had been replaced in August.

The 79th went through the sacrifice line in fairly good order, although the forward phone lines were broken early on and there were delays due to the shell-scarred terrain and the troops' tendency to yell "Gas!" at every drift of ground mist. Their skittishness was understandable, since many did not have masks, and those who did had not been taught how to use them. The real trouble began after the mist burned off and they butted up against the entrenchments below Montfaucon. As soon as they struck strong resistance the troops became confused, unable to advance but too full of bravado to retreat. They " 'mill[ed] about,' remaining in the killing zone, taking no action to silence the fire" of the German machine guns. They had, perhaps, mastered that "characteristically American weapon," the rifle, but nothing else, and in these circumstances their courage and mastery of Pershing's rifle tactics were liabilities.

> The Americans were not using their grenades! Many had none: either they had failed to draw any or they had dropped the ones they were issued. In the close-in fighting they could not see targets for direct rifle fire. They did not think either to lob grenades at hidden machine gun nests or to call for supporting fire from their trench mortars.[31]

Artillery would have helped, but the rolling barrage had gone on ahead of the advance, the gunners keeping to their timetable while the infantry fell behind. Division headquarters could not establish contact with the artillery to adjust its fire. The two regiments of the 79th's assault brigade lost touch with each other and with brigade headquarters. The division lost contact with corps and army headquarters. The lead regiment, the 313th, clawed its way up the slopes of an outlying foothill of Montfaucon, trying to knock out pillboxes and machine-gun nests with riflemen alone—getting it done at terrible and pointless cost. The colonel commanding kept asking for artillery, tanks, infantry support. The lone Tank Brigade, commanded by Colonel George S. Patton, had gone forward in support of the attack, but its light French-made machines were put out of action by German batteries, churned-up terrain, and mechanical failure, and Patton himself was wounded. The other regiment in the 79th's assault brigade, the 314th, was disorganized when the division's second brigade, pressing forward to help, plowed into their ranks producing a mishmash of "troops, commanders, equipment, wounded, and supply parties." The 314th extricated itself and went forward, hit a line of machine guns, was pinned down and left hanging on without orders. The supporting artillery tried to move forward and got stuck in the mud.

V Corps headquarters in front of Montfaucon had no idea what was happening at the front. They sent GHQ a report which, when plotted on their maps, indicated Montfaucon had been taken. In fact, the 79th was pinned down under the heights; its component regiments had taken heavy losses and were out of contact with one another and with supporting artillery. When V Corps discovered the truth, late in the evening, it sent peremptory orders to advance and seize the heights first thing in the morning. It characterized this as "exploitation" of a breakthrough.[32]

The Germans had a more accurate understanding of what had happened. They had bloodied and halted the Americans' first rush using only sacrifice troops and heavy machine guns. They reserved their heaviest artillery fire—they would let the Americans pour their masses into the killing ground before playing that card.

To the left of V Corps, the 35th and 28th National Guard Divisions of I Corps launched their drive up the valley of the Aire River, which ran south-north alongside the Argonne Forest. They had some tanks to help them and drove ahead with the inexperienced 35th taking heavy casualties as they approached the fortified line of the *Kriemhilde Stellung*. They were well short of their day-one objectives and badly hurt. With all its blundering and misdirection, the 77th had been the only division in I or V Corps to reach its objectives. But its task tomorrow would be much harder, the woods thicker and the resistance stiffer as they came up against the Germans' main line.

It took till 1 P.M. the next day, September 27, to get the advance restarted. The forest looked worse in the clear light of day than it had in the fog.

> It was a bleak, cruel country of white clay and rock and blasted skeletons of trees, gashed into unnumerable trenches, and seared with rusted acres of wire, rising steeply into claw-like ridges and descending into haunted ravines, white as leprosy in the midst of that green forest, a country that had died long ago, and in pain.[33]

The air was heavy with "the odor of stagnant, muddy pools, hiding beneath treacherous carpets of tangled wire grass," an odor reminiscent (to the troops) of rotting corpses which was "more depressing than the lack of vision." The woods got thicker, and as they worked their way through the trees Whittlesey's battalion butted up against a line of entrenchments that the enemy had planned to defend in strength. The Germans laid down interlocking webs of machine-gun fire from concealed positions, and their mortar batteries lobbed shells onto the American positions.

Company A's experience was representative. It started with 205 officers and men and by evening was reduced to one officer and 145 riflemen. The rookie Ralph John remembered continually slogging ahead, and "I didn't think anything of stepping over dead bodies of men with whom I had started out or wading through a pool of blood, but now something comes up in my throat. . . . I can just see them drop . . . look at them and hear what they said and their requests for help. But we had to go on and leave them lay. . . . I don't know who felt the worse." John slipped in the muck, fell in a trench, and dislocated his "trick" knee; popped it back into place and caught up with his squad, using a stick and his rifle as crutches. "I didn't want to go back to the hospital for treatment for something like this." He had already accepted the principle that loyalty to his unit transcended all other values.

Second battalion under McMurtry came to Whittlesey's support, and together they worked around the flanks of the German position and forward in small rushes till their own rifles and grenades could be brought to bear. Artillery support was not effective in thick woods, and liaison with regimental and division commanders had broken down. Losses were serious and fell most heavily on the officers, noncoms, and veteran infantrymen who naturally took the lead in battle. With all this, the division managed to advance only 800 yards.

At 4 P.M. with the action at its height, Colonel Prescott, the regular army stickler whose judgment Whittlesey mistrusted, suddenly asked to be relieved of command. Not many were sorry to see him go. The regiment's historian, English professor Wardlaw Miles, marked his departure with a footnote that reads: "*Hamlet*, Act I, Scene 1, line 8." The line is, "For this relief much thanks." But Prescott's departure left regimental command in disarray till his replacement, "dear old Lieutenant Colonel Smith," could be located on the firing line and brought back to headquarters.

Orders for September 28 called for the capture of a small hill with a cemetery on its top, identified on the maps as L'Homme Mort. The officers

and men of the supply train struggled to bring rations forward and succeeded in supplying a meal of "cold cabbage, beef, and bread," but the
noise they made gave their positions away and brought down a barrage
from German one-pounder cannons. It was rainy and cold. "I sat on
muddy stairs of an old German dugout, trying to keep warm by smoking
cigarettes. A weird night."[34]

> Ashes to ashes, dust to dust,
> If the Camels don't get you the Fatimas must.

9

The Last Long Mile: The Hell Fighters at Bellevue Ridge and Sechault, September 26–October 1, 1918

> Oh, it's not the pack that you carry on your back,
> Nor the Springfield on your shoulder,
> Nor the five-inch crust of Khaki-colored dust
> That makes you feel your limbs are growing older,
> And it's not the hike on the hard turnpike,
> That wipes a-way your smile,
> Nor the socks of sister's that raise the blooming blisters,
> It's the   last   long   mile.
>
> *—Emil Breitenfeld, "The Last Long Mile" (1917)*

Fifteen miles to the west of the Argonne the 369th Infantry had gone into action with the Fourth Army. Two battalions of the 369th went over the top in the foggy pre-dawn of September 26 along with the rest of the 161st Division, acting as the support element behind a front line composed of one French and one "Black" Moroccan regiment. "The furious Africans plunged onward waving their arms and huge knives with fiendish glee. . . . The American blacks advanced in a more scientific manner," in wave formation from shell hole to shell hole. When a space opened between the two front-line regiments, the Third Battalion "on its own initiative" moved forward oblique left and "closed this gap."[1]

They were qualified storm troops now, trained to advance by infiltration and in all the techniques of trench combat. They had at last been

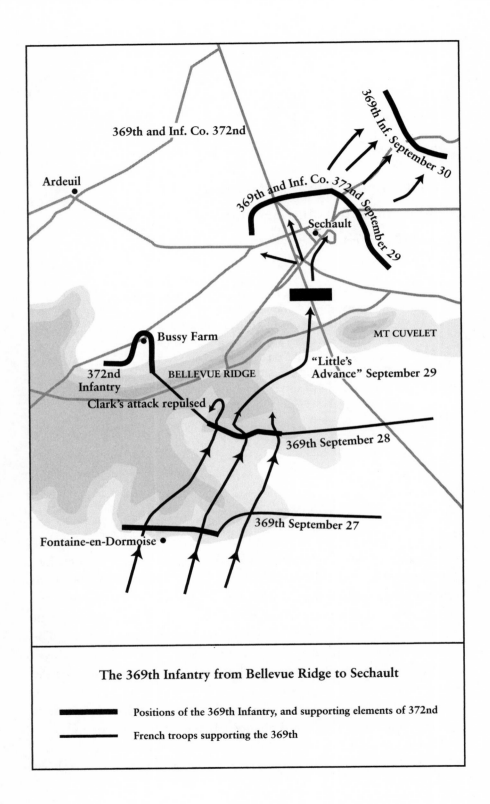

The 369th Infantry from Bellevue Ridge to Sechault

▬▬▬▬ Positions of the 369th Infantry, and supporting elements of 372nd

──── French troops supporting the 369th

reequipped with American helmets and overcoats, which distinguished them from their French comrades and marked them as Americans in a way that increased their unit pride. But they were fortunate to be going into battle with the French. Gouraud's army was well organized and well practiced, with experienced leadership in all ranks of the assault divisions. Their rolling barrage was adjusted to the pace of the infantry advance and was as effective as it could be in clearing the way through the German wire.

Third Battalion passed through the wrecked hamlet of Ripont from which the Germans had fled. Then Cobb's Second Battalion leapfrogged them and raced across the Dormoise River on three narrow footbridges. As Cobb's men overran a German trench, fifteen of the enemy burst from a dugout and there was a wild brawl of hand-to-hand fighting. A German knocked out Private Scott's teeth with his rifle butt; Scott went down but the German's bayonet thrust just ripped his uniform. "It didn't cut me but it felt cold." Scott pulled his bolo, got inside the German's reach, and "got my strokes in."

Third Battalion came up on their right and were ambushed by German machine gunners as they started to ford the swampy stream. Major Spencer was a portly man and made a big target walking calmly up and down, demonstrating a proper carelessness toward danger to the men splashing across the stream under fire. A machine gun ripped up his leg. Captain Shaw of his machine-gun company was angered by what he saw as grandstanding: "Larry Spencer, the ass, was hit the first day needlessly." Lieutenant Shethar carried Spencer to an aid station; both would win DSCs but the battalion lost their services as the action was just beginning. Hayward sent Captain L'Esperance to take Spencer's place, disappointing Fish. By 8 A.M. the battalions were digging in beyond the small stream of La Dormoise.[2]

Their losses breaking the first line had been acceptable. Orders called for the French 163rd Infantry and the two battalions of the 369th to continue the advance the next day. At noon they went over the top again with a rolling barrage ahead of them, moving into the broken terrain that crested far ahead on the heights of Bellevue dark with trees. There were German spotters up there, marking their approach and calling in fire from artillery in their main line of resistance. The Hell Fighters advanced with painful slowness, taking losses.

On the right Corporal Pippin's K Company was out front of Third

Battalion, dodging forward from hole to hole. "I were in shell holes that were smokeing, and they were hot." The Germans had this ground well covered. Shell fire was constant, and there seemed to be machine guns everywhere, firing out of trees and clumps of bushes and wrecked houses, "any thing they could get a machine gun in." Rumor had it that the Germans had put everything into the fight, "wimen as well as men" behind the machine guns. The irregular terrain and artillery fire broke up the advancing lines into smaller units, separated men from officers and noncoms. The constant whip and zing of bullets, detonation of shells, the accelerating maddening pressure of imminent death broke the morale of some of the replacements; they huddled into the ground, unwilling to move, or actually broke for the rear.[3]

The area had been sown with snipers and machine-gun nests to punish and disrupt the Allied advance—you couldn't spot them till they'd had their shot at you—and they had to be taken out one at a time. One of these machine gunners drove Pippin and a buddy to ground in a shell hole. They had got separated from K Company and were toiling forward on their own. The German was firing from the protection of a boulder, and the way to get him was for each man to work out toward a flank. The German might spot one and take a shot, but when he did the other man would locate and put him out of action. His buddy crawled off to the left. Pippin peeked out far enough to spot a series of shell holes he might use. Then he broke cover and began to dodge forward. At the second or third jump the German "let me have it," a short burst whose first bullet "cliped my neck," second and third broke his shoulder and right arm. Pippin dropped into a hole, no pain yet, just the shock of the wounding and an instant disordered attentiveness to himself alone in his body. He knew he was hurt, but felt so suddenly intensely hungry and thirsty that he immediately checked his pockets and found "I had nothing to eait yet and i only had a little water in my canteen." Then he remembered his hurts and "began to plug up my wounds." While he was doing that his buddy appeared at the top of the shell hole. He had got the machine gunner. He jumped in with Pippin and gave him first aid. But orders were to keep moving, not stay behind with the wounded. He told Pippin he'd be back, then disappeared and "I never seen him [again]."

Pippin could hear and feel German shells falling all around, but there was nothing in the top of his hole but sky, and then later sun. He guessed he had been four hours in the hole when the French "sweepers" came by, following the advance and recovering the wounded. One of them looked down into Pippin's hole—Pippin tried to cry a warning about snipers, but was too weak to make a sound and in the next instant there was a bullet's impact and the Frenchman tumbled into the hole on top of him, stone dead. "So I had to take him. I were glad to get his water and all so bread. I took my left hand and got some coffee, after some hird time getting it from him. After that I felt good and I trided to get up a gain. But I were to weak." His right arm seemed to be paralyzed and the pain started then. He drifted in and out of consciousness as the afternoon wasted away.[4]

K Company went on without him. Ahead of them was another patch of swampy ground, and as the company approached, machine guns hidden in the brush behind it ripped into them and brought them to a stand. German artillery began to search them out. This area had been worked over with gas shells, the poison lingered in the swamp muck, and now it came alive again as shell fire churned the stagnant pools.

Some men broke in these conditions, others were driven to rage, bravado, and a willed defiance of death. Private Elmer McCowan, runner for Company K, carried dispatches between Hayward's command post and the front line. As he started one trip, his company commander "hollered to bring him back a can of coffee. He was joking but I didn't know it." McCowan made the run, delivered his messages, and picked up a can of coffee along with the reply. On the way back, as he dodged from hole to hole so many bullets came zipping around him that "it seemed the whole war was turned on me." He saw a shell hole and "dented it another six feet when I plunged into it." Then it was duck and dodge forward through the bullets again, and this time one put a hole in the coffee can, which his captain should not have asked him to fetch in the first place and he might get killed because of it, but he was into it now, so he plugged the hole with his finger and held the damn thing up "to show the Germans they were fooled." When they hit it twice more he put in another finger, jammed his lucky rabbit's foot in the third hole, and ran back to his company with the bullets "picking at my clothes." McCowan was in an exalted state of mind, daring the Germans to kill him, and he kept it up the rest of the day, making several forays "out into no-man's-land" to bring back the wounded until he inhaled a disabling dose of the gas drifting up from the swamp. "Even then he refused to go to the rear, and went out again for a wounded soldier. All this under fire." He would be awarded the DSC.

K Company kept trying to advance, riflemen and machine gunners firing to pin the Germans while a couple of squads worked out to flank the position. Then an assault squad crawled forward from the main line, drawing fire till the flankers hurled their grenades, and when you heard them booming you got up and rushed the machine guns. Repeat till the whole series of nests was carried. Of fifty-eight men who attacked the swamp position only eight came out unwounded.

The noon attack was followed by assaults at 3:30 and 5 P.M., but the battalions made no further headway. Nonetheless, in two days of fighting they had captured the village of Ripont, taken 125 POWs, 25 machine guns, and two artillery pieces, and advanced four kilometers under intense fire. After the easy start the costs had mounted steeply. Third Battalion jumped off with twenty officers and 700 men, and ended the day with seven officers and 150 men—enough for one under-strength rifle company. The battalion commander and his adjutant were both badly wounded.

As evening fell they held their lines under heavy shelling. Captain Cobb's battalion was being hit hard by German mortars in an entrenched position off their flank. Lieutenant Charley Dean, commanding a machine-gun platoon, thought he could clear them out; he led his men into the German wire and they began cutting their way through. When they were well into the wire, hidden machine guns opened a crossfire and massacred them. Cobb had to shift position, which gave the staff trouble when they tried to organize the next day's assault. No one could do anything about Dean's platoon. They didn't get to them until the regiment was relieved four days later, when they found them "all together in perfect alignment, with faces toward the enemy and with bodies hanging in the wire, all present— . . . dead!"

A cold rain began to fall at dark and lasted all night.[5]

OUT IN HIS hole in the ground, Horace Pippin was weak and cold, in severe pain from the wound in his neck and the shattered bones, violated nerves and muscles of his right arm. He tried to work the blanket roll off the body of the Frenchman, "my dead comrad[e] . . . But that I could not do, and could not get him off me." He fell asleep like that, the dead man his only shelter from the soaking rain. Along toward first light he heard the voices of another group of sweepers, and though he was too weak to call out these men did a thorough job of searching the shell holes. They came down for him, lifted the dead man off his chest, lifted Pippin himself up and put him on a stretcher, carried him joltingly across the battlefield and left him at an aid station, still out there in the falling cold rain but now with a blanket over him. He lay untended among dozens of wounded French and Moroccan soldiers, dozing in fits, wakened every now and again by the calling voices and tramping feet of French reinforcements going up into the line.

Later still some German POWs picked up his stretcher and put it in an ambulance, which took him to a field hospital where he once again was set down without shelter. He still had one of his pens with him and used it to print his name and serial number on his shirt. After a while some orderlies came out, gave him some dope, and the last thing he remembered was them putting him on an operating table and the white-faced French doctors looking down at him.[6]

The 369th Takes Bellevue Ridge, September 27–28

Meanwhile Hayward was concentrating the battalions of the 369th to renew the attack. Their objective was the high ridge of Bellevue Signal Station, and the 369th would form the center of the assault. It took most of September 27 to concentrate the infantry battalions and move the artillery forward to support the advance.

Little's First Battalion had been in reserve, occupying the same entrenchments they had suffered in back in August, a place full of horrible memories, not to mention the usual disgusting relics of old battles. Now the battalion moved up along with the divisional artillery, which was displacing forward to provide a covering barrage of the new advance. Moving the guns over the "mutilated surfaces" of the battlefield was a colossal labor, horses straining in the traces and men pushing the mired wheels "through the thick, sticky mud of Champagne, over trenches and dugouts, through broken wire, over dead bodies of horses and human beings, up the steep inclines of small mountains."[7] The French army had lost a good deal of its élan in four years of futile assaults, but had learned the value of close artillery support and perfected the routines for moving guns on the battlefield. For lack of this expertise, the American 79th Division attacking Montfaucon and the 35th attacking in the valley of the Aire River would experience a day of defeat and crippling casualties.[8]

The steep ridge was sown with machine-gun nests, and the men of Second and Third Battalions wormed forward on their bellies. Captain Clark and twenty F Company hard cases worked their way to the top of a small prominence that enfiladed the Germans on the crest: a line of machine guns in a grassy field, with officers walking "coolly" from gun to gun. Before Clark's men could open fire they were spotted, their position swept by fire from below and from other machine-gun batteries on the ridgetop. Clark backed his men off and down the hill. Lieutenant Parish stopped by a barbed-wire barricade to bind up a soldier's wounded hand, but German guns were firing from every angle, and "one after another the whole line was hit." Parish left the man hanging in the wire, dead. They took shelter in a shell hole and tried to fight back, but every man who exposed himself to shoot was hit. When Clark spotted a German party working around their flank he pulled his men out and took them back to their start line. Other companies had similar experiences.

Casualties were piling up in the regimental field hospital, the wounded bleeding to death as the two overworked medical officers did what they could, the dead dropped outside "like so many sacks of oats." "Spats" Davis of First Battalion saw a "particularly salty, hardheaded" sergeant from Second weeping with anger and grief. His platoon had been wiped out. He had gone back with stretcher bearers looking for survivors, but the whole detail were killed by a shell burst.

But the German line on the crest of Bellevue ridge was not continuous, as Clark's abortive foray showed. The rifle platoons of the 369th and the French 163rd Infantry kept up the pressure in front, infiltrating gaps in the line. In the dark, Second Battalion rushed the crest, raked by the German rear guard as it pulled out. The 369th and 163rd Regiments moved up to occupy the high ground.

It rained again that night. Orders for the 28th were to continue the attack, to take and hold the town of Sechault in the plain below them. Hayward's part of the assault would be difficult to plan and execute. His Second and Third Battalions were just about used up. He would have to bring Little's First Battalion forward, use it to relieve the 163rd on Bellevue Signal, then send it across the flats and into the town with whatever support the other battalions could give it. Staff officers worked through the night to reestablish lines of communication with forward companies, so that the next day's maneuvers could be concerted. Their efforts were matched by line officers who had learned from the French that in battle "liaison is more important even than ammunition."[9]

To the east of the Fourth Army, the AEF was learning that lesson the hard way.

Crisis of Morale: The Stalled Offensive and the Disgrace of the 92nd Division, September 28–30

The battle on Pershing's front was not going well. The 79th and 91st Divisions continued to claw their way up Montfaucon, crippled by their limited training, faulty logistics, communications breakdowns, and inability to effectively coordinate artillery and infantry. Similar problems and heavy concentrations of well-sited artillery firing out of the Argonne stopped the 35th and 28th Divisions in the Aire valley. The 77th lurched forward a mere 800 meters into the Argonne, at high cost in casualties. These advances all fell well short of the objectives called for in Pershing's overly sanguine battle plan, but what troubled GHQ most was that the battle seemed to have slipped out of their control.

Some of their problems were due to the inadequate communications technology of 1918. There was no such thing as mobile wireless radio communication, and hardwired telephone nets were cut as soon as shells started falling. Front-line units communicated with headquarters by means of human runners or carrier pigeons, not much of an improvement over the methods used by Napoleon. However, much of the blame belonged to GHQ itself, which had chosen its ground badly and accepted a timetable that deprived it of the services of its best shock troops. Instead of a breakthrough followed by a battle of exploitation and maneuver, the AEF had to fight a battle of attrition, and "an offensive strategy based on the attrition of an enemy in strong defenses is really no strategy at all."

The high command's trust in its division commanders was shaken, and the feeling was mutual. But GHQ could act on its mistrust, and as early as the 27th of September it began to summarily relieve officers who questioned orders or failed to carry them out, never mind the reasons.

General Johnson of the 79th was sacked for failing to renew the attack on the 27th, though he and his men had done better than ought to have been expected. Rumors of Pershing's displeasure ran through the army on the khaki grapevine, every division commander whose men failed to reach their objectives—and nearly all had come up short—felt his head might be next on the block.[10]

For the "poor bloody infantry," the situation threatened to crack the morale that enabled them to fight. They could bear losses if these appeared to be in service of a successful or a necessary operation. But they could see for themselves the disarray that attended every assault, the breakdowns in communication and resupply, and the confusion of their field officers. If orders time and again seem to have no relation to the terrain or the situation, the soldier has to ask whether the men at the top know what they are doing. If a man sends you up one time to take a pillbox without artillery, one-pounders, or grenades, he might have made a mistake in judgment, or he may have been so green he didn't know the right way. But if he sends you up a second time, and a third, and does no better for you in the way of support, then that man is an idiot or worse: an officer who makes his reputation with the bodies of his men.[11]

On September 28, the third day of the offensive, signs of a crisis in morale began to appear, and on the next day some units began to break down. The 91st Division made some gains but had to give them up when units on their flank were driven back. The 79th Division finally succeeded in taking Montfaucon, but the Germans simply executed their planned withdrawal to their next fortified line. The 79th was wrecked and had to be relieved. In the Aire valley the 35th Division took extremely heavy losses advancing to Exermont—it never did get its artillery support straightened out. A German counterattack on September 29 drove them back in disarray, and there was no choice but to pull that division out of the line as well.

The 77th Division was stuck in the mud, struggling to move forward in the jungle of the Argonne. Here all difficulties were compounded by the dense woods, which impeded communications and broke liaison at every level. It was difficult to correlate the undifferentiated wall of trees with precise map locations, which made accurate artillery spotting almost impossible. There were so many "shorts" that the troops began to fear their own guns. If an American unit was being hit by its own artillery it had to send a runner to battalion, half a mile back in the woods;

then battalion could phone regiment (if its lines had not been cut by German shelling), "who in turn would take it up with the artillery; and the artillery would quite likely reply that the infantry were mistaking enemy fire for their own." To make matters worse, artillery and infantry used different methods for specifying coordinates. But then, as Captain Rainsford of the 307th admitted, most of the infantry officers could not properly read their maps:

> Many a company commander or liaison officer was entirely capable of waving a vague finger over a valley marked on the map, while stating that the troops in question were "on that hill"; and, if pressed to be more precise, he would give as their coordinates figures which represented a point neither in the valley to which he was pointing nor on the hill on which they were.

The rank and file knew the men in charge were not up to their jobs. Sergeant Stephen Murphy of the 307th "noted that his company officers were learning the hard way, by getting men killed." If you can't trust your artillery or your officers, your unit is walking the edge of breakdown.[12]

Through the battles of summer, American commanders had told their troops they must never retreat, because the Germans must be convinced that American morale was unbreakable—that the massive reinforcements being rushed to France were not mere cannon fodder, but troops whose determination was equal to their own. But on the fourth day of the Meuse-Argonne offensive the AEF had been fought to a standstill, so wounded by second-rank German troops and so poorly organized for battle that it had to suffer its units to make local retreats and stand on the defensive until it could reorganize. It was a blow to the morale of the high command, and Pershing responded by relieving those officers, from generals down, who seemed unable to make their units perform to expectation. He was also judging whole divisions, like the 35th and 91st, as lacking in the morale required for battle service. That was a warning to the enlisted men that the units of which they were personally so proud were in danger of public disgrace. To be deemed unfit to fight, to be identified as one of a group lacking in the "military morale" that drives "the great fighting races," was a nightmare prospect. It cast you out of the company of the Sons of Roosevelt and dropped you among the lesser breeds. That point was made in the most unmistakable terms by Pershing's handling of the Negro 92nd Division.

Most of that division had been held behind the front as a reserve for I Corps in the Argonne. But one of its regiments, the 368th, was loaned to the French to provide liaison between the right flank of Fourth Army and the 308th Infantry on the left of the 77th Division. To maintain liaison between two advancing forces belonging to different national armies requires a high level of expertise in the commanders and staffs of the units involved and a command structure in which intelligence flows swiftly and accurately from line to headquarters. The troops have to be well trained enough to maintain their organization and advance in pace with the flanking units, to find and hold positions chosen not for their own safety and defense but to serve the needs of the units on their flanks. The officers and men of the 368th had none of the qualifications for such a task. Though they would be working with the French, few of the officers could speak that language. Their White and Black officers were divided against each other by racial antipathies and mutual mistrust, their enlisted ranks uncertain whether their officers could be relied on to take care of them on the battlefield. And the terrain in which they had to operate would have made their task close to impossible even for a better-trained and better-run outfit.

The 368th had arrived on the line on the night of September 25, in the dark, with no time to scout the ground before them. At the last minute they were also informed that, instead of only providing liaison, they were also to participate in the French division's assault. The next morning their Second Battalion went over the top and into the fog, and like the White troops of the 77th became disorganized and disoriented. By 2:30 P.M. they had lost contact with the French troops to their left and the 308th Infantry on their right. They had not been given any artillery support, which left the German wire in front of them uncut. Although the sacrifice line was lightly held, they could only approach it by searching out the lanes cut through the wire for the use of German patrols. In following these they were canalized into three divergent lines of advance. The White battalion commander followed one of these with two companies, but lost touch with the other two. It was getting dark when they finally reached the German line of resistance—only a light rearguard fire. The battalion commander felt he was out on a limb, sent back a request to be relieved, and when it was denied had his two companies break contact and dig in. The Black officers leading the other two elements, cut off from each other and unable to locate their commander, withdrew on their own initiative. Under similar conditions, elements of the more experienced 369th and 308th held their ground, trusting that headquarters would search them out and their comrades come up to support them. The 368th was an isolated unit in a foreign army, and its ranks were riddled with mistrust.

At 3:45 A.M. on September 27 the regiment's Second and Third Battalions were ordered to advance in conjunction with the French, and promised artillery support—which never materialized. The battalions went forward against light resistance, but were delayed and scattered by the huge muddle and disorder of the enemy entrenchments and the woods through which they moved. Although Third Battalion, on the left, successfully attacked the lightly held trenches in its front, the commander of the Second lost touch with his own companies and with the 308th attacking on his right. He began to think his troops were "breaking," though they may simply have been disoriented, as he was. He pulled the battalion back to its starting line and was relieved forthwith. (This was the day on which Whittlesey's men advanced only 800 yards, at heavy cost; on which the 369th clambered and shot its way up Bellevue Ridge.)

The next day, September 28, everything fell apart. On the right Whittlesey's First Battalion of the 308th was pushing ahead to the cemetery called L'Homme Mort. It was vital that the 368th advance to prevent Germans from swinging in behind Whittlesey and cutting him off. Third Battalion went forward, but the Second under its new commander was too disorganized. Between 11:25 A.M. and 12:30 P.M. regimental headquarters issued increasingly frantic orders for it to advance. In this crisis the racial prejudice that had plagued the regiment from the start produced a breakdown in command. Lieutenant Howard Long, a Black staff officer at Second Battalion headquarters, observed, "Many of the field officers seemed far more concerned with reminding their Negro subordinates that they were Negroes than they were with having an effective unit that would perform well in combat." With headquarters bickering and no one exercising command, Second Battalion's companies went up piecemeal, became confused and demoralized, and turned back—all but one company that advanced, but was unable to maintain liaison with the 308th.

Meanwhile the Third Battalion of the 368th advanced until it hit resistance. Neither the White battalion commander nor the White field officers assisting him were able to organize a battalion-scale attack. The company commanders (Black) tried this and that, but without much energy or effect, except that their maneuvers caused the battalion's elements to lose contact with one another. The battalion commander sent L Company to attack, but when German fire intensified, it broke and "withdrew in disorder." Three other companies pushed forward, one ahead and two in support. But then confusing orders caused parts of the supporting companies to pull back. Given the regiment's inexperience and culture of mistrust, there was no overcoming such a blunder. With the exception of the advance company, the whole battalion began to pull out, and as it did so lost all cohesion and, in effect, "broke and ran" not only to their starting line but well behind it.

The 368th was relieved on the night of September 28, but the commander of First Battalion evaded the order, hoping for a chance to redeem his and the outfit's reputation. His battalion would make some successful local attacks on September 29 and 30, but whatever proofs of valor its men gave were undermined by a White officer who claimed he had had to drive his Black officers and men into battle at gunpoint.[13]

After the war there would be an investigation of what had gone wrong with the 368th, which would be enlarged into a debate over whether or not Negroes as a race were fit to serve as combat officers and soldiers in a modern war. The course of that investigation was prefigured in the immediate recriminations among White and Black officers in the 92nd Division: the Whites blaming the failure on the incompetence and cowardice of Black company officers, the Blacks (and some White officers) blaming the White regimental commander and his field officers, who had failed to organize coherent movements and maintain internal liaison. What Pershing and GHQ did was a clear statement of how the high command would interpret the case and deal with the future status of Blacks in the military. On September 29 the entire 92nd Division was taken out of combat and shipped to a quiet sector. GHQ degraded the whole division for the failure of one of its regiments, and the army's postwar investigations would cite the presumed failure of the division to justify degrading the role of African-Americans in the military.

The disgrace of the 92nd Division was general knowledge throughout the army within twenty-four hours. It was now perfectly clear that any division that had to be taken out of combat for lack of "fighting morale" would be in the same class as the Negroes.

L'Homme Mort: Whittlesey's First Last Stand, September 28–30

The failure of the 368th to maintain liaison with the left of the 308th Infantry gave the Germans an opportunity to infiltrate and outflank the 77th Division's advance in the Argonne. On the morning of September 28 First and Second Battalions under Whittlesey and McMurtry moved forward through abandoned German positions, until in the early afternoon they struck a new line of resistance. The woods were too thick to permit the use of one-pounders or Stokes mortars, so the infantry had to break the line with machine guns, rifles, Chauchats, and grenades. They took losses from snipers and from their own mistakes. A bag of bombs carried by Private Murray somehow exploded, blowing him to pieces. Casualties mounted, especially among officers and platoon leaders. Lieutenant Whiting, commanding Company A, was mortally wounded. As they carried him to the rear he clutched Whittlesey's hand: "Oh, Whit, I don't want to leave the men." Herman Bergasse, the ex-mess sergeant, took over the unit.[14]

It was an "Indian war" of raids and ambushes. The Americans worked their way through the trees and brush as platoons, watching and listening intensely, never able to find the enemy till the sudden *pt-pt-pt* of a machine gun, a couple of men hit, falling, crying out, the bullets "chirping like the quick sweet notes of the meadowlark," then stopping abruptly. The Germans fired in short bursts to hinder discovery of their positions. So the platoon leader would crawl ahead looking for telltale signs in the "turmoil of the undergrowth": a clump of leaves faced wrong-side out indicating cut brush, a light blue haze of gun smoke hovering in front of what might be a twig but is in fact a gun muzzle. Then he would send his "gangs" crawling out left and right, set his Chauchat auto-rifle men to pin the Germans down till the flankers got in position. Then a flurry of bombs, the shriek of wounded, perhaps a surrender—the Germans were not prone to last-ditch struggles.[15]

The stress was compounded by shortages of food and water. Although

Captain James Roosevelt did his best to keep supplies coming forward, units in the ever-moving front line were seldom relieved long enough to enjoy a meal and a rest, or even to receive a full resupply. For Private John, "Hot food or coffee was something I could remember I had had long ago"; he lived on "hard tack and corned willy" and filled his canteen with puddle water. Once a German ambush drove him facedown in a place where there were bushes heavy with large wild blackberries. He was so hungry that he got to his knees to pick them, "Pop! Pop! Pop! went a machine gun, but he didn't get me."

As evening came down on the twenty-eighth, elements of Whittlesey's two battalions managed to break through part of the German line and seize a piece of open high ground that offered real advantages as the jump-off for a breakthrough attempt. They passed through the cemetery identified as L'Homme Mort and dug in on a bald hill just beyond it. But the reserve battalion had had to halt and reorganize, and there was no sign of the French on their left. (The 368th was coming apart among the woods and German entrenchments.) Whittlesey knew what was expected of a battalion leader. He had his men dig in and used his line of runner-posts to tell headquarters where he was and what he needed: mostly food, water, and Chauchat ammunition. The men, who'd had no fresh water for four days, except what rainwater they could catch in their helmets, "are very tired but in good spirits."

It rained hard that night, water filling the funk holes and trench lines the men dug. In the darkness the Germans infiltrated infantry and machine guns behind Whittlesey's position and cut his line of runner-posts. Whittlesey sent out patrols to all points of the compass "and found Boches each way, and also in the rear." In some places the enemy worked forward and began firing directly on the American position. Whittlesey and his company commanders responded aggressively, sending squads to knock out the most dangerous machine-gun nests, capturing a mortally wounded officer who provided intelligence on the numbers they faced. They reformed their position, entrenching as a hollow square of companies, facing all ways.

Whittlesey had been regimental operations officer and understood that his role as commander of the front line was to advise headquarters on the best methods of aiding him. His messages, sent back now by carrier pigeon, showed his grasp of the situation. His men could fight back toward the regiment, clearing out the infiltrators, but "we understand our mission is to advance"—that was everyone's mission, as decreed by Pershing—and he thought it better to keep his men concentrated for forward movement. "Can line of communication not be kept open from the rear? We have been unable to send back detail for rations and ammunition, both of which we need very badly."[16]

Lieutenant Colonel Smith made the attempt early next morning with Third Battalion, which was seriously understrength because of its losses on the Vesle. Smith sent staff officers to scour the woods for stragglers and lost detachments to beef up his relieving force. In the meantime he went forward himself, with Lieutenant Wilhelm and a small party of runners and ammunition carriers, to see if there was a way to slip supplies past the Germans. They found the path Whittlesey's runners had used—and were ambushed by a crossfire of machine guns. Smith went down with a bullet in his leg, popped away with his automatic pistol to give cover to their retreat, and was hit a second time but refused to go to the rear. "Dear old Lieutenant Colonel Smith"—Whittlesey was his friend as well as his strongest subordinate; now he was surrounded with more than half of Smith's regiment, the Germans were there in force, and the men on the bald hill might be wiped out or forced to surrender. Smith kept trying to find a way through to L'Homme Mort and the third time up a machine gunner killed him.

With no apparent help from headquarters, Whittlesey sent his adjutant, Lieutenant Arthur McKeogh, with a combat patrol of three men to clear out the machine gunners firing out of the cemetery to their rear. The patrol worked their way back in the dark, but McKeogh found the cemetery occupied in greater strength than he expected. He sent Private Quinn back with a message for Whittlesey, and with Privates John Monson and Jack Herschkowitz, the Bessarabian greenhorn, tried to worm his way through the German cordon to reopen communications with regiment. They spent a horrible night crawling through the mud past German outposts, freezing when enemy patrols walked past. At one point they blundered into a small party of the enemy, there was a quick exchange of shots, German rifles and American pistols—one German was killed and the rest ran off. Later during that nightmare crawl they found themselves in the middle of a German bivouac and had to lie there for three hours with enemy troops snoring nearby or walking about the campsite. Knowing they would be discovered as soon as dawn came, they made a break for it—Herschkowitz and Monson deliberately drawing enemy fire to allow McKeogh to complete the mission. All three managed to escape and make their separate ways back to the regiment.[17]

Quinn never made it: he was listed as missing, his body discovered after the war only when an article by McKeogh provoked a search—dead, with three dead Germans near him. McKeogh wrote a poem about him, one line of which ran: "Quinn died as game as his racial name," and Miles's history adds: "And what a race—Quinn, McKeogh, McGrady, McDermott . . . !" To the Sons of Roosevelt the Irish were the "model minority," a great fighting race. All four on the patrol—McKeogh, Quinn, Monson, and Herschkowitz—were awarded the DSC.

It took most of September 30 for the relief to reach Whittlesey's position. The 308th's own push was now aided by the French on their left, whose forces still included the First Battalion of the 368th Infantry. When the relief marched up Whittlesey felt almost jaunty: "Lt. Taylor came up with a lot of rations. . . . Looked 'Practically O.K.,' as George McMurtry put it. And everybody ate!" But he and his men were worn out, and Whittlesey's high spirits did not last. He stumbled back to regiment through "the blackest night I've ever seen . . . I had to be passed on from reserve post to post holding the hand of each successive guide." At regimental HQ they gave him some cocoa and a cigar, a brief touch of fellowship with Captain Weld—then the news that his good friend Smith had been killed. Colonel Cromwell Stacey, a regular with twenty-four years of service and two citations for gallantry, was now in charge: a good officer, but nerve-wracked by long exposure to combat command.

Stacey had orders for Whittlesey from Division: return to your battalion and prepare to attack again at daybreak. Division commander Alexander knew Pershing expected a rapid advance and that he hadn't given him what he wanted. He didn't want to be one of those commanders given the ax "pour encourager les autres." Whittlesey was to drive ahead at all costs, without regard to support from the flanks; but Division assured Brigade, which assured Regiment that the French were going to keep liaison on the left. Whittlesey doubted they could depend on the French; he had seen nothing of them in four days. His men were unfed, short of water, and dead tired after three days of hard fighting. He'd do what was ordered, but he wanted Stacey to understand the situation as it really was. Then he groped his way back to his men "with great difficulty in the darkness."[18]

"We Only Just Got Here": The Hell Fighters at Sechault, September 28–October 1

The 369th Infantry was not immune to the morale crisis that overtook nearly all of the American forces in action between September 26 and 30. Some of the raw replacements were breaking under the strain. These made up a significant part of the regiment's manpower, in some units as many as 40 percent. Those who had lived through two days of unimaginable horror were now told that instead of going to the rear to recover, they had to continue the assault. Some slipped away in the dark. Others stayed, but when their battalion rose to go over the top they ducked and ran, leaving the weight of the assault on the shoulders of the veterans.[19]

Hayward's reaction to this was a sign of his own frayed nerves and damaged body: he had gone limping into action on a partly healed broken leg, and during the attack on Bellevue Signal had caught a dose of gas. Now he raged that "large numbers of enlisted men . . . conducted themselves in the most cowardly and disgraceful manner . . . stealing away in the night, throwing away their equipment, lurking and hiding in dugouts, and in some cases traveling many, many kilometers from the battlefield." He wanted them captured, court-martialed, and shot. Their actions jeopardized everything for which he and the men in the regiment had suffered and died. These replacements were a disgrace to "the regiment, the Negro race, and the American Army." Like his veterans, Hayward now completely identified with the regiment. In his hierarchy of grievance he valued the regiment first, the Negro race second, the army third—and the humanity of deserters not at all.[20]

When combined with battle casualties, these desertions brought the 369th close to that level of loss at which most military units become ineffective. There is no day-by-day record of their losses from September 26 through 28, but by a conservative estimate combat casualties amounted to about 450 out of approximately 1,800–2,000 riflemen in Second and Third Battalions. If losses to desertion are added to that figure, it reaches the 30 percent level at which units are thought to have exhausted their combat effectiveness, and losses to desertion can be more demoralizing than combat casualties.[21]

But the 369th as a unit did not crack. The troops fought on through the night of the twenty-eighth to take and hold Bellevue Ridge. In the darkness and cold rain Little's First Battalion moved past the exhausted remnants of Third Battalion to lead the next day's attack on Sechault. If they could take and hold it they would have broken past the high ground and into a broad green plain, "dotted with farms" and groves of huge ancient oak trees, where there were fewer strong defensive positions for the Germans to entrench. On their left their 93rd Division mates, the 371st and 372nd Infantry, would strike out of the sharp salient they held at Bussy Farm, to the left of Bellevue Signal.

The survivors of Second Battalion would not be relieved, but held ready to support Little's advance. Captain Cobb had commanded Second Battalion through three days of intense combat, and exhaustion slowed his thinking. He stuck Captain Clark and the F Company hard cases in an exposed spot in front of his position on the right of the line, where they could protect the flank of Little's battalion when it attacked Sechault. But the attack was slow getting started, and Clark believed F Company would be hit with a barrage if they didn't go forward or back soon. He ran back to talk with Cobb, just in time to see the battalion commander blown up by a shell. Hamilton Fish was nearby, troubleshooting for headquarters. He ran to the Command Post, and "there was Cobb's body and one of his lieutenants, standing there with a blank stare in his eyes." The man was unresponsive when spoken to. When Fish ordered him to the rear, the man pulled his service automatic and waved it at Fish, then fell to the ground in a dead faint. "That poor fellow had . . . nothing left." Clark got command of the battalion.

Little's assignment was the sort a smart general would only assign to experienced officers and trustworthy organizations. He was to advance from his reserve position, relieve French troops on Bellevue Ridge, then stage his own attack in full strength on Sechault, a mile away across a flat plain open to artillery fire. After that he was to move forward another two to three miles to seize an advanced line from which a new offensive could be staged toward Challerange. From the start, Little and his subordinates had to exercise discretion and independent judgment in adjusting orders to fit the facts on the ground. This was the kind of thing less experienced officers and men simply could not do, or not do well. They tended either to follow orders regardless of circumstances or to abandon their initiatives in the face of unforeseen events. The French sent them a guide who did not, in fact, know the proper way to ascend Bellevue Ridge. As they approached the crest he ordered them to file to the right, which would have exposed them to the Germans as targets on a skyline. The Germans opened up with whizz–bangs, "as in " 'Whizz-bang!' The shell has arrived and exploded." Little stopped the advance, had his men take cover, interrogated the guide, and, when he admitted he did not know where the French troops were, sent his own "liaison group" scurrying about under fire to locate them.

Working in small groups and with great patience, the battalion effected the relief of the French "in broad daylight, under heavy fire, and with less than ten casualties." That in itself was a major accomplishment, but their day was just starting. Once the position was secure, Little sent his companies down the wooded slopes one after the other, each rifle company with a section of two machine guns attached. His attack jumped off at 3 P.M. and moved swiftly, First Battalion advancing in skirmish order. Little went last with his command and liaison group. As they passed through the woods at the foot of the ridge they captured a German artillery spotter, who had been calling in shellfire from his advanced position. His elimination may have hurt the German artillery plan: the battalion crossed the plain to the outskirts of town without severe casualties.

Little soon dissipated his cadre of runners, staff officers, and noncoms. His practice was to post a runner every 200 paces of the advance, "an expensive plan of liaison" that kept a lot of rifles out of the line. But he had taken to heart the dictum, "Liaison is more important than ammunition," knew that success would depend, in the end, on coordination of his advance elements with the resources of the rear. Little put his last remaining runner, Corporal Cooper, in charge of gathering a new liaison group—a sergeant major's job, but one the corporal was equal to. "I have always, since those days, felt for Cooper a full measure of gratitude and affection." Costly or not, Little's method worked. In the days that followed there would be no break in communications between the fighters in Sechault and their regimental HQ.

Little stayed in the rear of his advance, eschewing the role of gallant leader that less experienced men saw as an officer's chief responsibility. Little had to exercise command over a line half a mile wide and be in position to observe the direction of German counterattacks. In the event, the only opposition in Sechault and its environs came from snipers and rear-guard machine gunners, and his veteran infantry knew how to take these without requiring instructions or heroic example from their commander. So "while the men were performing deeds of heroism in undignified postures," flopping and crawling about as they cleared the enemy out of the town, Little sat in the rear "receiving and dispatching letters at a rate which would have done justice to an efficiency expert directing the campaign of a mail order house one week after the publication of its fall catalogue." Little was a publisher in civilian life and knew whereof he spoke. A German plane swooped low along the ditch in which he was sheltering, strafing them with machine guns, but hitting no one.

However, as soon as his men got in among the houses of Sechault the casualties began to mount alarmingly. As Lieutenant George Robb of D Company led his men up to the stone and brick houses of Sechault, he was hit with a burst of machine-gun fire that knocked him down, wounded him in the hand, and smashed his pistol, canteen, and binoculars. He lay stunned for a while—then rallied, picked up a rifle from a dead German, and hurried after his command; caught up and led his men into the narrow cobblestone streets of the town. Two major highways, east-west and north-south, crossed in Sechault, and three other roads radiating out of the town made it the hub of any military movement in the sector. The main crossroads was on the western edge of the town, its major feature a large half-ruined church. There was a nest of three machine guns firing down the main road past the church. Robb led his men up the street, dodging from door to alleyway, to take the nest out with grenades—getting himself a second wound from shrapnel. He refused evacuation, and took over a two-story brick house with a gang of Chauchat auto-rifle men. From their vantage point they covered the advance of C and D Companies as they moved to establish a perimeter in ditches beyond the town.

C Company had also worked its way through the town, capturing an ingeniously camouflaged "77" artillery piece, set in a ruined house and fired by remote control from a cellar a hundred feet away. Their Lieutenant Holden captured an enemy machine gun and turned it on the Germans, and they seized a grenade dump and a cache of shells. B and D Companies lost their senior lieutenants, wounded and sent to the rear.

Shortly before 5 P.M. Little saw a company advancing across the plain. It was Clark and the remnants of Second Battalion. After Cobb's death Clark had decided the battalion's position was untenable, and since it had to move either forward or back he chose to go to Little's aid. He informed regiment of his decision, and on his own initiative ordered the remnant of Second Battalion forward, actions characteristic of a smart veteran officer and a well-organized regimental command. Second Battalion was down to less than company strength, but they added 150 rifles at an opportune moment. Little sent them in to help clear the town.

The 369th were in possession of most of Sechault, but Little's command was badly cut up and out on a limb. Most of the buildings were located in a wedge of cross-streets east of the crossroads. These had to be cleared house by house. Hours after they had "taken" Sechault they were still prying snipers and machine gunners out of odd corners. The Germans seemed to be building up for a counterattack, and Little's men were far from their supports. French units were supposed to have advanced on their right, but the scouts sent out by Little could find no sign of them. The 157th Division had advanced on their left, but at an angle that diverged from Sechault. Only one lost detachment of the 372nd, twenty men under Captain Coleman, got into the town.

In the falling dark Little had his men dig trench lines on three sides of the town, leaving open only the rear or southeast side through which reinforcements and supplies would come. It was hard, slow work because the French had told them to leave their entrenching tools behind. French officers had been educated to think that troops equipped to entrench did that in preference to pressing the assault, and thus lost élan; evidently those advising the 369th had not unlearned that fatal lesson. First Battalion's own twelve machine guns, the six brought by Clark's battalion, and the captured German weapon were placed to give interlocking fire against German infantry trying to cross the plain. Headquarters were set up in a wrecked house near the ruined church in the northwest corner of town. Fallback positions were established among the houses in case their outer trench line should be driven in. Movement within their positions was perilous, since there were still snipers among the broken buildings and all the main streets were swept by German machine guns firing from the woods and fields outside the town—firing from three sides, which indicated they were all but surrounded with German infantry.

On the other hand they had plenty of ammunition and, more important, liaison back to headquarters through their runner-posts. Dr. Keenan, the regiment's senior medical officer, came forward after dark to establish a field aid station. But "our casualties were hideous and continuous." Even with the addition of the 150 men from Second Battalion and the platoon from the 372nd, Little's command amounted to fewer than 450 effectives, the equivalent of half a battalion.

At 7 P.M. Hayward sent written orders for them to hold the village and keep in touch with headquarters. Little sent his own adjutant back to Hayward to report on their condition and take charge of liaison. Hayward answered, "The high command [is] informed of your situation and will act accordingly." "That communication confirmed the growing horrible suspicion that we were alone, a mile or more in advance of the rest of the division, out in the open plain, with a long night ahead of us, and subject to being surrounded and cut off." Little had to trust the regiment and division of which he was a part to keep their promise to support him. He was old enough as a soldier to know their best efforts might not be good enough. His officers knew it too. In the dark, one of them—most likely one of those brought in during the summer purge of Black officers—came to Little to urge withdrawal: the position was "suicidal . . . we should be wiped out." Little refused: he was ordered to hold to the last. The officer then invoked the standard-issue nightmare of White officers leading Black troops: "[Little] couldn't hold the men. . . . They would run out on me." Little knew better, and told the man so. But here, under the pressure of crisis, the racial fault line had slipped and flashed its nasty grin.

Their position was a compact one, and Little's headquarters were within easy earshot of the enlisted men manning nearby firing positions. The men heard both the grim statement of their situation, and Little's expression of faith. Shortly after the unnamed officer left, Little heard "an unseen private [talking] to an invisible sergeant."

"Sergeant, does you think we-all's goin' back?"

"Hell no! We only just got here."

Little himself was now swept by an emotional reaction. He was not, after all, a professional soldier, just a civilian in uniform carried forward by his training and the momentum of events. Now he had full responsibility for the conduct of a battle, and a moment in which to stand back from the rush and consider who he was and what he had been doing. "I remember that I commenced to suffer tremendously under the strain of the situation." He questioned whether the holding of Sechault was worth the lives it would cost, of men he knew and cared for. He questioned whether he had the right to hold them there; and if he had that right, did he have the skill to do the work properly?

Little rallied when Hamilton Fish arrived at his headquarters, with a sergeant carrying great bags of bread commandeered from divisional supply. Fish volunteered to take over a section of the Sechault lines. He found Charles Peterson, his trusted first sergeant, who told him his old Company K had taken 30 percent casualties. Meanwhile Little cut the huge French loaves into shares, then summoned the platoon leaders to distribute them. It was the only food they had had for more than a day and would be their only resupply in three days of fighting for Sechault.[22]

It was a long night. After the bread was distributed, the officers had to go out and try their best in pitch darkness to establish the exact coordinates of their positions, so supporting artillery would know where to fire. At first light the company officers woke their men, and "some wag, kicking awake a delinquent group of sleepers or hiders, called out . . . *'All out for Custer's last stand!'* " Division sent orders for Little to resume the advance to the northeast, in the direction of the Rosiers Farm, and promised him a covering barrage at 7 A.M. and three French infantry regiments to attack on his flanks. Clark and the remnant of Second Battalion went house to house to clear out the last of the snipers east of the church. Little pulled all but the sacrifice squads out of his trenches, taking losses from German artillery but sparing the bulk of his assault force.

But 7 A.M. came and went, with "no sign of any French troops" and "no artillery preparation that we could discover with the naked eye." Instead Sechault was hammered by a heavy German barrage that prevented Little's survivors from assembling for the advance. As the bombardment waned the 163rd French regiment came up, passed them at the double-quick, and plunged into the line of woods in front of Rosiers Farm. Little's battalion formed up and followed, about half an hour behind. The two outfits gathered in the forest and advanced together at 8:20 A.M., the 163rd on the left, with Little's B, C, and D companies abreast from left to right. C and D were held up by a line of machine guns—Little ordered a section of his own machine gunners to work out and hit them from the flank. It was after noon now, and the advance slowed as resistance hardened. At this moment a "demure looking little colored boy" arrived from headquarters with a basket of carrier pigeons—but without the trained handlers who knew how to use them. Little blew his top. Here he had spent his strength for days maintaining the runner-posts and all the help "the department of modern methods" could spare him was "*birds*— without anybody to take care of them!" He told the runner to take the damned things back.

Little gathered D Company and a machine-gun section behind the battalion line, then leapfrogged them forward with Hamilton Fish in command. The volume of fire from behind the screen of trees began to build and scouting reports indicated Germans were gathering on the flanks of Fish's advance. Little sent Private Layton with orders for Fish to hold where he was. Layton went forward through the beginnings of a new German barrage, high explosive and gas shells, was blown off his feet by a near miss and inhaled a lungful of gas, but managed to crawl through with the message.

At 3 P.M., with German pressure increasing, Little ordered his three companies to "*creep* back three hundred yards" and asked for a barrage to cut their way for them. The losses were mounting, and the men nearing the limits of endurance. Casualties among officers were becoming critical. The commander of D, Lieutenant Seibel, and his second were both killed. Lieutenant Robb was wounded a third time, but took over the company until they could complete the withdrawal, then turned command over to a First Sergeant, the highest-ranking survivor in the company. Hayward had sent the regimental reserve, Third Battalion under Captain L'Esperance, into Sechault. But they were only 137 men and 7 officers, the equivalent of a half-strength company. There was nothing left with which to reinforce Little's attack.

For an hour Little dickered with Hayward, and Hayward with division headquarters, trying to get artillery support, to no avail. Little was at the end of his means. A conference of his officers affirmed his belief that the command was "all in." "The spirit of the survivors, however, was magnificent: It seemed to us it would be wrong to abuse that spirit." Read from a distance of seventy years, Little's words have a sentimental ring. They were in fact a clear statement of a tragic dilemma. The regiment had suffered terrible losses in its rifle companies. Little now had nearly all the regiment's infantry with him, and his effectives amounted to no more than half a battalion. All of the men had been in intense combat for three days, and those from Second and Third Battalions had been fighting since September 26, nearly six days. During that time they had not been fed (except for Fish's loaves of bread) or given fresh water. They might have held a defensive position, but were physically incapable of making another assault.

Still, Little knew that the French would be reluctant to grant them relief, and that Hayward would not want to ask for it. The great mission of the Old Fifteenth, the justification for all the sacrifices of pride, comfort, and even life that its officers and men had made, was to prove to the White world that "Colored men" had a military morale and fighting spirit that made them equal in every respect to White men. That proof, which they had been making in blood since May, had been discredited by the public disgrace of the 92nd Division. Little knew how furious Hayward himself was at the defection of so many replacements. Now he was compelled, for both military and human reasons, to ask that his troops be relieved. If he was to save the regiment's reputation he must make the request in a way that distinguished it from the appeals of incompetent or frightened officers for relief from danger and responsibility.

Little wrote out the dispatch, addressed to his liaison officer Lieutenant Langdon, and the others approved it:

> Dear Harold:
> Please say to the Col. for me that in my opinion no attempt further should be made through those woods without either tanks or full demolition of concrete pillboxes by heavy artillery.
>
> The 2nd Batt. has about 100 men and 2 officers.
> The 1st Batt. has about 300 men and 9 or 10 officers.
> The 3rd Batt. has about 137 men and 7 officers.
>
> I believe every man will obey orders to go in those woods if orders are given; but, under present conditions, they will all stay there—and the 15th N.Y. will be a memory.
>
> Our men are wonderful. Without 5% of normal food or sleep they are standing by; but great weakness is upon us all.
>
> I hope that a relief can be made.
>
> Also, that no unsupported advance by any soldiers be ordered through those woods.
>
> A. W. Little
> Major

He sent Captain Clark, commander of Second Battalion, to deliver the message and support it with his own testimony. Clark had been Hayward's secretary when he served as public service commissioner. Looking at the numbers of troops on hand Hayward would see that his regiment had lost more than half, perhaps as much as three-fourths of its effective combat strength. Taken together with their having been in intense combat for six days, Little had given Hayward reason enough to conclude his troops could do no more. But Little understood the pitilessness of military necessity, knew Hayward might feel compelled to order another attack, and so he appealed to the thing for which he knew Hayward had the deepest affection: not just "the men" but "the 15th N.Y.," Hayward's creation, which would be wiped out if he sent them forward.

Little was also writing the dispatch for the press and the historians, putting on record his assertion—a sort of deathbed testimony—that his men were "wonderful," had performed brilliantly under extreme hardship, and had the courage, moral strength, and devotion to continue to do so even when it was certain to end in their own destruction. Reading this, no one could impute to the officers and men of the Old Fifteenth the incompetence or poltroonery for which the 92nd had been disgraced. Little's closing line is beautifully designed to clinch his point: he asks that no troops be sent through those woods without artillery or tanks, evading any charge of special pleading by implying that the difficulties were insuperable for troops of any race or nation.

At 4:15 Hayward wrote back promising an artillery barrage, but "after its completion, continue your advance as before." At the stated hour "half a dozen shots" dropped into the woods, and that was the end of their barrage. Little now had no choice but to attack as ordered. He tucked Hayward's instructions into his pocket, in the hope that "the written order, when found upon me, might fall into honest hands—to place the blame for the disaster about to occur, where it belonged." Considering his close relationship to Hayward, that was a harsh thing to have thought and to have written fifteen years later. But before he could give the orders an urgent dispatch arrived, notifying Little that the 363rd Infantry was coming up to relieve him and to "sit and hold on until relief comes." Hayward had in fact been hounding Division all day to relieve his men. Little's accounting of their losses must finally have convinced the high command of what the line officers already knew: the 15th New York, 369th United States Infantry, had achieved its mission—achieved both of its missions—and had destroyed itself in the process. Their losses could never be replaced. Even the combative Hamilton Fish admitted, "We'd practically ceased to exist as a combat unit. . . . Yet, the 369th held on to the town, through forty-eight hours of machine-gun and artillery fire, repulsing every German counterattack, until we were relieved." When the last of them pulled out of Sechault they were "shell-shocked, gassed, sunk to the verge of delirium."[23]

There was still a regiment there, still a hard core of veterans who had served from the beginning. They would get more replacements and serve again in the lines, in a quiet sector of the Vosges region. The French would honor the regiment with a unit citation of the Croix de Guerre, and when they rejoined Fourth Army after the German surrender they would be accorded the distinction of being the first American regiment to cross the Rhine. But they had been raised as a combat outfit and trained for assault, and the losses they had taken meant they could not play that role any longer, not without a longer period of refitting and recruitment than events would allow.

On October 6 they returned to Minaucourt, "the place from which [the Old Fifteenth] had made its debut, some eleven or twelve days before, as an organization of shock troops, in the great victory drive of the allies."[24] But there were no American war correspondents to greet and interview them after their greatest triumph and catastrophe. An event on the I Corps front of the AEF had drawn every American newspaperman in France to the Argonne Forest. Two battalions of the 308th Infantry had broken the German lines and then been cut off by strong enemy forces. For four days the whole left wing of the AEF had been struggling in vain to break through to what the papers were calling "The Lost Battalion."

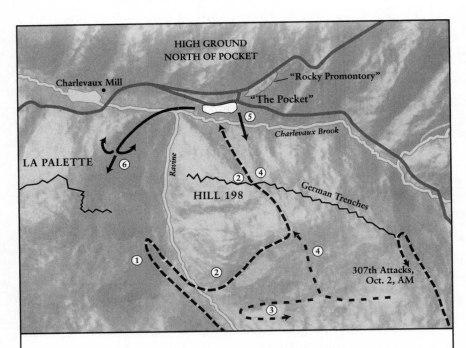

The Lost Battalion at Charlevaux Mill

① Whittlesey attacks La Palette, afternoon of October 2
② Whittlesey advances to the Pocket; Rainsford-Blagden attack Hill 198, morning of October 2
③ 3 Cos. of 307th Infantry, night of October 2–3
④ Holderman, K:307, night of October 2–3
⑤ Holderman's attack, October 3
⑥ Wilhelm and E:308 attack, October 3

10

The Lost Battalion: Whittlesey's Command at Charlevaux Mill, October 1–8, 1918

Do you remember the rats, and the stench
Of corpses rotting in front of the front-line trench—
And dawn coming, dirty-white, and chill with a hopeless rain? . . .
And the anger, the blind compassion that seized and shook you
As you peered at the doomed and haggard faces of your men?

—*Siegfried Sassoon, "Aftermath" (1919)*

On October 1, as the survivors of the 369th were gathering their dead on Bellevue Ridge, the 308th Infantry returned to the attack. Major Whittlesey and his men were badly worn. They had just been rescued after standing a three-day siege near L'Homme Mort. First and Second Battalions were down to about 850 effectives, less than the authorized strength of a single battalion. Several companies had suffered ruinous casualties. Company A had lost half its initial strength. Instead of relief it got the demoralizing honor of burying the regiment's dead.[1]

The regiment as a whole had been in combat since September 26, trying to advance through thick wooded terrain that would have taxed their strength even if it had not been defended by entrenched German infantry. It had rained off and on much of that time, the nights were bitter cold, their blankets, boots, and clothing were sodden. Most had left raincoats and overcoats behind, as ordered. They also had to carry the weight of a growing discouragement. Some of this filtered down from the higher echelons, which were aware that the campaign was not going as planned.

But the evidence was all around them: orders to carry objectives that were unreachable and sometimes unfindable, inadequate artillery support, failure to deliver supplies and equipment.

The dense forest had made communication and liaison extraordinarily difficult from the start. Heavy troop losses compounded the problem by reducing the frontage each battalion could cover. Assault commanders had to choose between spreading their front thin to maintain liaison, or concentrating for attack at the risk of exposing their flanks. Whittlesey and McMurtry had combined their two battalions in a single command and paid the price when they were cut off September 28–30. They would have to run the same risk again on October 1.

As the men prepared to renew the advance, they learned that two of their battalion commanders had been ordered away for courses at the General Staff College. GHQ expected the war to last another year and needed staff for an army twice the size of the present force. But the departure of trusted field officers in the midst of a battle was a shock to morale and to the organizational efficiency of the regiment. Since September 26 the 308th had lost two commanding officers (Prescott and Smith) and its two senior battalion commanders. The regiment was now commanded by newly appointed Colonel Stacey. Field command of its two assault battalions would be exercised by newly promoted Major Whittlesey, who had not previously commanded infantry in combat. Captain McMurtry had been offered a tour at staff college too, but turned it down because he did not want to leave the men he had trained and served with since Upton. He commanded Second Battalion, but was in effect Whittlesey's second in command. Several company and platoon officers in Whittlesey's battalions had just been transferred in from other units, two from the Negro units of the 92nd Division. They were highly suspect, an unknown quantity to their colleagues and to the men they commanded.

The attacks on October 1 did not go well. Whittlesey led the advance from his old defensive position on the bald hill east of L'Homme Mort. His men had to cross a deep wooded ravine that ran across their front, then assault German positions on La Palette, a high hill whose bare slopes were swept by the interlocked fire of German machine guns firing from strong entrenchments and concrete pillboxes. On the right, separated from La Palette by another tangled ravine, was the wooded ridge of Hill 198, which was the objective of the 307th Infantry on Whittlesey's right. Heavy woods and muddy forest paths prevented the bringing up of artillery to shell the German emplacements. The 308th's Stokes mortar battery tried to dislodge them but failed, and its commander was wounded. Whittlesey pressed the attack on La Palette and his men again took heavy casualties. Company A, which led the attack, lost twenty-three men, the company commander, his successor First Sergeant Bergasse, and *his* successor, Sergeant Anderson. By the night of October 1 they were down to fewer than thirty men, understrength for a platoon—the company had been virtually wiped out. E Company had started on September 26 with two hundred officers and men; it was down to fifty-two men and two officers.[2]

That night when Whittlesey returned to headquarters he found the atmosphere strained. Division commander Robert Alexander was putting pressure on his brigadiers, Brigadier Johnson had leaned on Colonel Stacey, and Stacey passed it along to Whittlesey with regular army brusqueness: the division must advance whatever the cost. Whittlesey was to go forward "without regard to his flanks," pressing on whether or not the French on his left or the 307th on his right could support him.

Whittlesey did not like the orders. He ought to have had at least 1,600 men in the two battalions and had barely half that many. Third Battalion, which was supposed to provide support, had never recovered the strength it lost between the Vesle and the Aisne. Experience had taught Whittlesey he could not trust the French to cover his left. His men had not been adequately fed since the twenty-sixth and had actually starved for two days on L'Homme Mort. They had been living for days in the sopping woods without rain gear or blankets, were sick and worn out. Whittlesey himself had a severe cold and dysentery—a chronic disease for combat troops, for which the only palliative was the ration issue cheese.

Stacey was sympathetic in spite of his veneer of regular army toughness. He sent Whittlesey back to the front but spoke with General Johnson, commanding the 154th Brigade, describing the condition of his command and the difficulty of advancing. Johnson had already protested to Alexander that the German positions were too strong to assault with his diminished force, but he tried again.

Alexander fired his response back early next morning, October 2: "You tell General Johnson that the 154th Brigade is holding back the French on the left and is holding back everything on the right, and that the 154th Brigade is to push forward to its objective today. By must I mean must, and by today I mean today, and not next week." When

Johnson telephoned again to say his troops were unable to advance, Alexander blew up and gave him peremptory orders for his units to attack "without regard to flanks or losses." Alexander also told Johnson the French division on his left had already made a substantial advance. If that was so, it was imperative that the 77th Division advance in concert or the Germans might outflank and defeat the French. Such a disaster would make the 77th's status as a combat outfit questionable, and it might suffer the shame of relief along with the 35th and the Negro 92nd Division.[3]

Alexander was not telling the truth: the French had *not* advanced on his right. But his responsibility was to forward the strategic designs of the high command, spending men and matériel as required to perform that task—if it was necessary to exaggerate some element of the situation to get Johnson's brigade moving, so be it. It was his job to use his men as instruments of strategy. He silenced Johnson's protests, because he knew that the closer an officer was to the front, the more likely he was to balance the lives and well-being of his men in the same scale (if not with the same weight) with the military mission.

But the strident edge in Alexander's anger reflected more than military calculation. Pershing's GHQ was desperate to rescue their great offensive from apparent failure, and it was passing that anxiety down the chain of command. Two division commanders had been sacked already, and more would follow. If his division failed Alexander would find himself in the discard pile, with plenty of company but none of it welcome. Alexander was not a West Pointer, but a "mustang" who had enlisted as a private and risen through the ranks. He had seen service against the Sioux during the Ghost Dance troubles (1890–91), had fought in Cuba, and served in Samar during one of the most vicious antiguerrilla campaigns of the Philippine Insurrection. He was a good combat officer and an intelligent military professional, who had earned prewar tours at army staff colleges. But for all that he would never be a member of the West Point club. If he failed in his part of the Argonne offensive, there would be no old boy network to protect him.

Alexander had taken over the division in August and tried to imbue it with some of his own professionalism, while carefully modulating regular army rigor to suit the manners and amateur status of his National Army officers. The instructions he issued during the fighting between the Vesle and the Aisne were sometimes teacherly, his orders strongly worded but temperate and unworried. He even seemed appreciative of the New York City style and culture of his men. Attack by infiltration required them to act in squad-size groups called "gangs," and Alexander told his men to bring the "gang spirit" of their mean streets to the task. The New Yorkers accepted this as a tribute to their toughness and thought well of Alexander.[4]

But when his division's advance was stopped with heavy losses in the first week of the Argonne offensive, his orders and admonitions took on a hectoring and anxious tone. He insisted on a ruthless commitment to advance, and reinforced his demands with shrill warnings against treason and treachery. His General Order No. 27, issued on September 28, warned the troops that some Germans were showing a "barbaric lack of faith" by pretending to surrender, then hurling grenades at the troops who came forward to accept. He ordered his men to take "extreme measures to prevent a recurrence. . . . In the heat of combat each individual man must determine for himself" whether to accept surrender. In effect, Alexander was giving his men permission to refuse quarter to the enemy.

More significant for Whittlesey were Alexander's concluding remarks, which were to govern the division's tactics through the next phase of the campaign:

> It is again impressed upon every officer and man of this command that ground once captured must under no circumstances be given up in the absence of direct, positive, and formal orders to do so emanating from these headquarters. Troops occupying ground must be supported against counterattack and all gains held. It is a favorite trick of the Boche to spread confusion . . . by calling out "Retire" or "Fall Back." If, in action, any such command is heard officers and men may be sure that it is given by an enemy. Whoever gives such a command is a traitor and it is the duty of any officer or man who is loyal to his country and who hears such an order given to shoot the offender upon the spot. WE ARE NOT GOING BACK BUT FORWARD!—ALEXANDER

It may be that Alexander's experiences fighting guerrillas in the Philippines and repressing "labor conspiracies" in the States made him especially reactive to the "treacherous" tactics inherent in the sort of sniper/ambush jungle warfare he faced in the Argonne. But Alexander's language here is that of the Vigilantes and the American Protective League: *anyone* who speaks of retreat is guilty of constructive treason, and should be shot down where he stands. The language of Alexander's dispatch was so exceptional that the newspapers picked it up and made of it a sensational addition to the Committee on Public Information's propaganda campaign against the "savage Hun." Rumors ran throughout the AEF that Alexander had ordered military police to shoot any officer or man who retreated from the line.[5]

It is doubtful that Alexander's chief subordinates took that order literally. But his rhetoric did suggest that anyone who held back the advance would be subject to the harshest possible sanctions. So rather than lose his command and his honor, Johnson passed Alexander's orders to Stacey, who reiterated them to Whittlesey at 11:30 A.M. on October 2. He was to advance with his command no later than 12:50 P.M., and "The infantry action will be pushed forward until it reaches the line of the road and the railroad generally along [map coordinate] 276.5, where the command will halt, reorganize, and establish liaison to left and right and be ready for orders for a further advance." The man who would have to make the infantry make that push thought the orders would get them all killed and accomplish nothing. Over the phone Whittlesey told Stacey that if they advanced "We'll be cut off again," as they had been at L'Homme Mort.

"You're getting panicky," Stacey told him. Given Alexander's attitude, that was as much warning as reassurance. But Stacey added Alexander's positive assurance that the French were already advancing on the left. Whittlesey could proceed with the expectation that support would appear on his open left flank. To secure his right, Whittlesey sent runners to try to contact the 307th, find out where they were and what they expected to do.

Into the Pocket: October 2–3

Brigadier General Johnson's battle plan called for Whittlesey and McMurtry to carry La Palette, then move on to a position near Charlevaux Mill. Stacey took charge of the regimental reserve, which consisted of Third Battalion and two companies (D and F) under Lieutenant Paul Knight drawn out of Whittlesey's command, which was thereby reduced to fewer than six hundred men. Should the French fail to appear in spite of Alexander's word, Knight's command would guard Whittlesey's left flank against a German blow.

Whittlesey still did not like the orders, but he was used to doing things he did not like. It was, in fact, his definition of a man's, and a gentleman's, duty in this world. "All right," he said, "I'll attack, but whether you'll hear from me again I don't know."[6]

He also kept his own counsel and took measures to protect the men who depended on him. The line officer lives and dies by the difference between the map and the terrain, and a veteran officer learns to trust only what he has seen for himself. He also learns who can be trusted to come to his aid in desperate circumstances. Maybe Alexander was telling the truth about a French advance, but Whittlesey had been fighting for five days on the extreme left flank, had seen no sign of a French advance, and had no reason to think one would materialize. He trusted the 307th on his right to make the effort, but he knew how hard it was for different commands to maintain contact in the Argonne. So he made his own arrangement with Knight and his two-company flank guard: as soon as Whittlesey reached his objective he would send a company to connect with Knight. For his part, Knight would be prepared to move in Whittlesey's direction to prevent his being cut off.

It had been a bitter cold night, its bite turned the trees all around them yellow and the ground and brush were frost-rimed at first light, the men in their damp uniforms shivering and griping through chattering teeth as they formed up. They had a little coffee and bread and waited through the morning while Whittlesey and Stacey thrashed out their orders. The regiment had not been able to renew its rations, so Whittlesey's men drew just enough for the day—a package of hard bread, a can of corned beef, a can of beans, a canteen of fresh water—and jumped off at one o'clock. A thin scouting line pushed out ahead and the rest of the two battalions crept forward in columns, each column a series of platoons in file—a formation that allowed them to snake through the tangles between them and their objective. The six hundred men in the command constituted the headquarters platoons of the two battalions, plus a medical detachment; Companies A, B, and C of First Battalion; E, G, and H of Second, under McMurtry; and four sections (nine guns) drawn from Companies C and D of the Brigade's 306th Machine-Gun Battalion. Lieutenant Teichmoller and two privates from the 305th Field Artillery were with them as forward artillery observers.[7]

Whittlesey and his headquarters company were just behind the scout line, the major himself stalking along near the front, a "tall gaunt figure, armed with an immense pair of wire cutters . . . serenely indifferent to enemy fire." As soon as they entered the forested no-man's-land they began to take losses from snipers and machine-gun nests and from the harassing fire of German artillery. But when they emerged from the brush and boulders at the base of the bare slope of La Palette, they were hit with a storm of fire from the trenches at the top and suffered about twenty casualties. E Company lost three sergeant platoon leaders, Curley, Leumann, and Del Duca. Curley had been one of the company boxing champs back in Upton, and Del Duca had sung tenor to Leumann's basso in the chorus of "The Army, The Army, The Democratic Army."[8]

Whittlesey and McMurtry reconnoitered the ground, battalion commanders doing a second lieutenant's job because their platoon officers did not have the experience to run a proper scout. There was no sign of the French, no fire from their supporting artillery. They agreed that they could not assault La Palette with their present strength and that if they stayed where they were they would suffer crippling losses from accurate enemy fire.

Whittlesey spied a narrow "chimney" or ravine running up the west side of Hill 198 on his right, which seemed to offer a route to the top of that hill out of sight of the machine gunners on La Palette. He had been careful to leave two-man runner-posts at 200-yard intervals to link him to headquarters. An exchange of messages with Stacey authorized him to try the alternate route and granted a brief covering bombardment. In giving him permission to attack Hill 198, Stacey showed his trust in Whittlesey's judgment. He had just been bawled out by Johnson (who had been raked by Alexander) for not carrying out orders as given. The new plan would put Whittlesey in the sector assigned to the 307th Infantry, and if he mismanaged it he ran the risk of friendly fire casualties.

The barrage kicked up enough smoke and dust to distract the troops on La Palette. The two battalions began to work their way up the brushy ravine to their right, a long narrow column of platoon-size snakes moving ahead in fits and starts, from cover to cover. The ravine protected them from La Palette, and the German artillery searched for them (mostly) in vain. But they began to lose men by ones and twos to sniper fire and machine-gun nests among the trees. By now fifty or sixty men had been killed or wounded, and with the persistent dropping off of runner-posts, Whittlesey's small command was rapidly shrinking. Whittlesey himself was in the lead with his scouts and at 2 P.M. located the main source of machine-gun fire. He sent a patrol from B Company out to the flank, which swept in and captured a platoon of Hessian troops. The captives were glad to be out of the war, willing to talk: they had just been plucked from a rest billet in the rear and thrown into the line to face some vague emergency.

The Americans moved more cautiously as they reached the top of 198. The entrenchments here were part of the *Giselher Stellung*, which (it was said) the Germans had been ordered to defend to the last man. But the sniper fire actually diminished, and when they reached the crest they found the beautifully engineered trenches utterly abandoned. There were signs of recent fighting, but nothing to indicate the German lines had been taken by assault. There had been no report of a breakthrough, or of a German retreat. Whittlesey checked their position carefully to verify that he was where he thought he was. He had taken meticulous observations at regular intervals during the whole course of his long march and had reported his positions regularly (and with astonishing accuracy) to headquarters. By all appearances his command had cracked the *Giselher Stellung* and achieved a major breakthrough at what now seemed remarkably light cost. But there was too much about the situation that was unaccountable. Where had the Germans gone, why had they left, and would they come back? If the Germans had been driven off, where were the troops that had done the driving? Where for that matter were the units of the 307th Infantry that were supposed to be advancing to support Whittlesey on the right? If this was a breakthrough, the Americans ought to be pouring reserves in to exploit the breach before the Germans could mount a counterattack to close it.

HILL 198 WAS unoccupied because of a series of errors and misunderstandings by American and German commanders. The ravine between Hill 198 and La Palette was also the boundary between two German army groups, and on such boundaries there is liable to be confusion as to assignments and responsibilities (as the 77th Division and the French Fourth Army had been discovering). In an adjustment of the boundary, the German division holding Hill 198 was ordered to shift position eastward, and it began pulling its garrison out before the relieving division was ready to replace them. On the morning of October 2, while Whittlesey was trying to get his orders changed, a battalion of the 307th commanded by Captain Crawford Blagden was attacking the eastern half of Hill 198. Two of his companies were stopped with heavy losses by machine gunners of the German rear guard. But his left-flank company, commanded by Kerr Rainsford, drifted westward in the dense woods and hit a part of the German line as the rear guards were abandoning it. Rainsford seized the position, but did not know how to exploit it. He was isolated on an open flank with no support at hand—and asked Blagden for orders. Blagden's units had been hard hit and had failed to get into the German trenches: Blagden ordered a retreat. When Blagden left, the Germans completed their pullout from Hill 198, but without waiting for the relieving force to arrive.[9]

The result was that when Whittlesey's command worked its way through the snipers to the crest of Hill 198 it found the trenches abandoned and no sign of either the Germans or the 307th. It was just after 5 P.M. Whittlesey notified Stacey of where he was and what he had found, and led his scouts to the reverse slope of Hill 198 to examine the terrain. Below him was the valley of Charlevaux Brook, marshy along the banks of the stream that ran its length from east to west. The ground rose steeply in heavily wooded slopes on the far side of the brook, and along its base he could see the line of the Roman road marked on his map. At the western end of the valley was the wrecked Charlevaux Mill and its millpond from which the stream ran. A second road slanted up the far slope into the trees, diverging at an angle from the Roman road. The bare top of La Palette loomed to the west—it did not seem to be under attack by the French. Clearly there was nothing to prevent Whittlesey from fulfilling his orders and planting his force directly on the objective he had been told to seize, the road junction east of Charlevaux Mill. He led the command down the steep slope, heels skidding in the mud, then across the valley floor in a somewhat disorderly rush toward the safety of the trees on the far side of the brook. Distant machine gunners on La Palette now rediscovered them; they were firing at very long range but every now and then a man would be brought down, crying he'd been hit. They dashed across a patch of foot-beaten ground, evidently a German drill field. Then there was a crude wooden bridge to cross; squads dashed across in file with bullets flailing the air and water around them.

In the falling dusk they assembled in the woods and established defenses for the night. Their purpose now was to hold until the rest of the brigade could come up to exploit this breakthrough, and in the meantime to patrol actively to front and flanks to keep the enemy at bay and establish liaison with their supports. Whittlesey and McMurtry laid out a banana-shaped perimeter some 350 yards from end to end and less than 100 yards at its deepest. The position was well chosen for defense. Whittlesey tucked his lines in close to the steep slope that rose above the northern bank of Charlevaux Brook. This would make it impossible for German artillery, firing from the north, to hit his position. They would still be vulnerable to trench mortars and to the heavy-caliber *Minenwer-fers*, which fired in a high looping trajectory, but the trees and their own funk holes would offer substantial protection. German infantry to the north and east could attack them from higher ground, but the vulnerability of the northern front of their perimeter was mitigated by being set along the embankment of the road that ran uphill. Map to the contrary, there was no rail line. The eastern flank of their position was overlooked by a high rocky promontory, from which Germans could conceivably fire and throw grenades into their position. But the position there was protected by heavy underbrush, and the terrain unsuited to an infantry attack from above.

The command post was set up in a group of funk holes at the center of the position. The remnants of A Company—seventeen men and one officer, the strength of a half-platoon—manned the southern front of the perimeter, facing Charlevaux Brook, the sector least likely to suffer a heavy assault. The right flank under the rocky promontory, and part of the northern front along the embankment, was held by Companies E and G with three machine guns, commanded by Lieutenant Wilhelm of E Company. McMurtry commanded the sector where a German counterattack appeared most likely: the left or western flank of the perimeter and the contiguous section along the embankment. He had companies B, C, and H with him, and the other six machine guns. The Chauchat autorifle men were distributed around the perimeter. In making these command arrangements Whittlesey and McMurtry discarded rank, protocol, and administrative divisions. Two of McMurtry's units were from Whittlesey's battalion. Lieutenant Cullen would serve as McMurtry's second, and Wilhelm would command a two-company mini-battalion, though both were outranked by Captain Stromee of C Company. But the lieutenants were tried and proven veterans and Stromee a newcomer—he understood and accepted the arrangement.[10]

Whittlesey had reason to be satisfied. They had taken their objective and achieved a breakthrough. Headquarters was apprised of what they had done and where they were—he had sent runners back every half hour since he began the ascent of Hill 198, with clear and accurate statements of his position and the condition of his troops. He had requested resupply with rations (his men had had one meal in twenty-four hours) and with ammunition, anticipating either a holding action or a continuation of the advance. It was a little worrisome that he had had no reply to his messages. But the doubts he had expressed to Stacey that morning seemed excessive now. The empty trenches on Hill 198 suggested the enemy was either disordered or in retreat. It was the business of regiment and brigade to seize the opportunity by pushing troops across Hill 198, cleaning up the scattered enemy troops in his rear, securing his flanks, and concentrating to further exploit the breakthrough.

The men dug their funk holes and machine-gun emplacements, replenished water from the brook, ate their rations. They set out sentries, and those off watch went to sleep, some lucky enough to have blankets or overcoats to wrap themselves in, the rest heaping quilts of dead leaves or huddling together against the damp and chill.

Just before first light Whittlesey was awakened. One of the outposts on the left flank, toward the mill, had a German prisoner. Through an interpreter Whittlesey and McMurtry learned that the man was from the 254th Hessian Reserve Regiment that had just been moved up and would (the man said) soon descend upon the Americans. Whittlesey ordered a patrol out beyond the road embankment, up the slope to the north. They reported hearing and seeing a considerable number of Germans moving through the woods and were fired on by a machine gun. It was apparent that German troops were moving to contain and perhaps eliminate the breach in their line and the men who had made it. There was no sign of either the French beyond La Palette or their own troops from beyond Hill 198, and no runners had come from headquarters to apprise Whittlesey of an impending assault or to modify his original orders. It appeared his command was about to be cut off again, just as he had predicted.

Whatever might have happened to the rest of the regiment and brigade, Whittlesey trusted that Paul Knight, whose two companies had been posted to watch his left flank, would do everything in his power to keep his part of their private pact. The advance had taken him beyond the territory Knight's units could cover, but if he could get word to Knight his friend would surely come to his support. The German technique of infiltration called for the slow accumulation of small parties of men in the targeted sector, rather than swift and massive rushes. If Knight could be brought up quickly, the infiltration of troops between Whittlesey and the rest of the division could be blocked, and the German counterattack forestalled or defeated. Whittlesey sent messages back down his chain of runner-posts to summon Knight. Then he called Lieutenant Wilhelm from his post on the right flank. He was to take his own E Company, about fifty men, and work his way back through the ravines that divided Hill 198 and La Palette till he reached the position the battalions had occupied before turning up Hill 198, where he could connect with Knight's command. Whittlesey would then be able either to strengthen his present position or concert an attack on La Palette.

While Wilhelm was getting his orders there was a hail from the sentries facing Hill 198: Captain Nelson Holderman with Company K of the 307th was coming in to reinforce them. Evidently headquarters had received his reports and was sending troops forward to exploit the breakthrough.

WHILE WHITTLESEY'S MEN were digging in on the night of October 2, Brigadier Johnson had ordered Colonel Houghton of the 307th to send his four-company reserve battalion to join Whittlesey. They were to make a night march through the woods behind Hill 198, Indian-file, one company behind the other, then wheel to the right and sweep uphill in line to seize the abandoned trenches on the crest. Once there they would be in position to protect Whittlesey's line of supply. If no counterattack developed they could combine with Whittlesey, and while the latter held fast they could sweep to their right, taking the Germans in flank and peeling back their whole line in the Argonne.[11]

An excellent plan, but it went awry in the dark tangles of the forest. It was so black on the trail that the relief battalion marched with every man holding the belt of the man in front. During a rest halt the chain broke. Holderman followed the correct line of advance, ignoring a verbal order to retreat that was passed down the line, whether German trickery or a message garbled by, as Rainsford would have said, "some Polack" they never found out. He ran into one of Whittlesey's runner-posts and got directions to the Charlevaux Mill position. Holderman told Whittlesey to expect the rest of his "lost battalion" to show up soon, which would make their position secure.

But the other companies had gone astray. Two of them marched right past Hill 198 to the foot of La Palette, and at daylight were stopped by the same intense fire that had deterred Whittlesey. Rather than search for Holderman or Hill 198 their commanders decided to go back to base for new instructions. The commander of the rear-most company also lost contact with the others during a rest stop; but unlike Holderman, he decided to stay where he was and rest his men. In the morning he took them back to the bivouac, where he was arrested for dereliction of duty.[12]

Whittlesey wanted to believe Holderman's assurance that relief was at hand, but he knew all too well how easily such certainties could evanesce and took measures to draw the strength he needed to hold his position and prepare for a continued advance. It was 7 A.M. He sent a message down the chain of runner-posts, informing Stacey of the tactical measures he had taken: calling on Knight's command to come to his support and dispatching Wilhelm to connect with Knight. He was doing what a senior officer on the front line was supposed to do, taking tactical control of the combat on his front and giving his commanders the information they needed to support him.

He gave Wilhelm his final orders, and E Company filed off through the perimeter and across the brook. McMurtry watched them go. E was his own company, the men he had commanded since Upton, who thought him the best company commander in the regiment and would follow him anywhere; their achievements had filled him with "pride . . . unbounded; his joy in [their] successes limitless; his gloom at [their] failures heartbreaking."[13] Of his original 250 fewer than fifty men remained. Meanwhile Holderman brought his company out of the woods on the north slope of Hill 198, and they took over E Company's funk holes on the right of the perimeter. The Germans began lobbing shells their way, but they flew over the protected position and fell in the brook.

At 7:30 A.M. a dispatch finally came through from Stacey. However, both the time of the message and the content were disturbing. The heading indicated it had been sent at 7 P.M., which meant it had taken all night for the chain of runner-posts to operate. That much of a lag meant that close coordination with headquarters in the coming fight would be impossible. The dispatch referred to an attack order, to be transmitted to Whittlesey by 7 A.M.—here it was 7:30 and no such order had come through. If it had been intended that they move in concert with other forces, that plan had failed. Even more disturbing was Stacey's response to Whittlesey's request for rations and ammunition. Stacey's dispatch blithely informed him that there were "plenty of rations at your P. C. [command port] of last night" and to "send for them if you want them."

There was intense activity in the command post for the next hour and a half. McMurtry dispatched patrols in every direction, to feel out enemy positions and see if they couldn't connect with the French or the rest of the 307th. Whittlesey sent a new dispatch down the chain of runner-posts acknowledging Stacey's message and asking again that rations, overcoats, and blankets be sent forward by Regiment, because "[I] don't dare send [men] back for them if we are to advance." He told Stacey he had sent E Company off toward Knight, but did not want to disperse the command any further "if we must advance again." He also reported casualties, 8 killed and 80 wounded out of the companies that remained with him. At McMurtry's suggestion a second message went out at 8:20 reporting Holderman's arrival and the positions at which Holderman believed the remainder of the 307th's relief battalion could be found. (They were not there, having returned to their bivouac.) Shortly after, another dispatch went out revising the ration requisition. All this time the German shelling continued, artillery now joined by the fire of a *Minenwerfer* that was capable of looping shells into the position. This called for more urgent communication than the runner-posts could provide. Whittlesey summoned Omer Richards the carrier pigeon specialist, a French-Canadian from upstate, and at 8:50 sent off a brief message requesting artillery support from Regiment.

Each of these messages began with the same heading: "At: 294.6–276.3." These numbers identified the position of the command by reference to the French military maps with which all units and headquarters were provided. The represented terrain was overlaid with a grid of numbered lines, which allowed the user to identify any position by a precise set of coordinates. Whittlesey had carefully observed and recorded the movement of his command from jump-off to their arrival at Charlevaux Mill, and reported his position to headquarters at half-hour intervals. Although some of his messages miscarried and there were minor errors in some of his reports, his identification of the command's position on every occasion was nearly perfect. Headquarters ought to have known where he was. Whittlesey was not one of those officers who, as Rainsford had complained, could not read maps or relate map-abstractions to the actual terrain.

The same could not be said of Lieutenant Teichmoller, the artillery forward observer sent by Division. It was his job to coordinate artillery support, and he now sent a message by carrier pigeon to his headquarters at the 305th Field Artillery. He reported they were being shelled at a "cadence" of one per minute, asking, "Give us artillery; work quickly," and giving as coordinates "Place: 294.8–275.6." These coordinates put the command half a mile south of where it actually was, and on the wrong side of Hill 198. The two positions were similar in conformation, a high ridge to the north with German positions marked on it. It is possible that, unlike Whittlesey, Teichmoller had not kept track of their march from point to point, and so based his reading on similarity of terrain and a guess at how far they had penetrated German lines.[14]

At 9:30 A.M. things started to go bad with a rush. The patrols reported no evidence of the French or the 307th, but increasing contact with small parties of Germans. Then cries from the left of the perimeter announced bad news: Lieutenants Leak and Harrington of Company E were back, with nineteen enlisted men and word of a disaster.

Lieutenant Wilhelm and E Company had somehow drifted too far to the west and kicked in a hornets' nest of snipers and machine-guns on La Palette. The German fire was intense and accurate, coming in from all sides. They were pinned down in heavy underbrush, taking casualties. Wilhelm ordered Leak and Harrington, both wounded, to return to Whittlesey with the walking wounded and a few sound men. Thirty-three men followed Wilhelm as he worked around to his left, to try to cut his way back to Knight's position south of La Palette. The woods were full of Germans, and his command broke up. Sergeant Kaplan, the ex-marine and division boxing champ, was cut off from the company with a section of his men, wounded, and taken prisoner. Wilhelm did not make it through until nightfall, wounded and with only four men.[15]

Leak and Harrington had just returned when the *Minenwerfer* finally found them. Its heavy high-explosive shells began to dump into the position, churning up huge gouts of muddy soil, turning one man's foxhole over upon him. A few minutes later the perimeter came under fire from German machine guns on the slopes of Hill 198 and other positions up the valley, their grazing fire crisscrossing the position, "chirping like a flock of canaries." There were cries for first aid where men were being hit. McMurtry's patrols came tumbling back to report machine-gun positions all around. The patrol that had gone west looking for the French never returned. The line of runner-posts had been cut.

The German infiltration was developing rapidly. Nothing could be expected from Knight unless Wilhelm managed to cut his way through, and that was now doubtful. If he didn't want his command cut off again, Whittlesey had to act from his own strength. Holderman's was the largest and freshest company: he ordered them to cross the stream, retake Hill 198, and reopen the line of runner-posts. Holderman's second, a Texan lieutenant named Thomas Pool, demurred for reasons like those Whittlesey had given Stacey. Like Stacey, Whittlesey would not relent. Holderman's company filtered down through the scrub and began to cross the stream and open ground in small rushes. They disappeared into the woods under Hill 198, and out of the trees came a rising clamor of rifle and machine-gun fire.

At 10:45 A.M. Whittlesey sent an urgent dispatch to Stacey's headquarters via carrier pigeon. He repeated his position, described the repulse of E Company and his orders to Holderman, and gave coordinates for the *Minenwerfer* and for all of the German positions his scouting patrols had discovered. With this, and the information he had sent earlier, Regiment and Brigade should be able to provide him with artillery support aimed to knock out the most dangerous enemy emplacements and to surround with a ring of protective fire the "Pocket" in which he was now trapped. If they could get troops forward fast enough and in sufficient strength, the breakthrough might yet produce important results.

DIVISION, BRIGADE, AND Regiment were trying to get help to the men in the Pocket, but the enemy and their own weakness prevented doing anything effective. Alexander believed Whittlesey's breakthrough had created an opportunity for a major victory, and he ordered both brigades to attack in strength. But on the right the 153rd Brigade ran into unbroken German troops defending well-established entrenchments and were stopped with very heavy losses. The 306th Infantry, Julius Adler's outfit, had to be pulled out of the line. Action on the 154th Brigade's front was even less effective. The 307th was leery of going up against the entrenchments that had balked them on October 2. Blagden's battalion was exhausted by its efforts that day; the three companies that had returned from the futile relief mission had been out all night, and there may have been some doubts in Colonel Houghton's mind about their commanders (he had already put one of them under arrest). The 307th patrolled and probed along its front, but made no concerted advance.

The 308th was simply too weak to accomplish anything. More than half of its combat strength was already in the Pocket with Whittlesey. It was not only responsible for the advance to Charlevaux Mill, but for protection of the division's left flank—where there was no sign of a French advance against the western slope of La Palette. Command of their remaining elements was divided between Brigadier General Johnson—who controlled the Third Battalion as "brigade reserve"—and Colonel Stacey, who commanded the regimental reserve, which at this point consisted only of Lieutenant Knight's two companies and his own headquarters troops. Knight tried to keep his promise to Whittlesey by attacking toward La Palette on the morning of October 3, but the positions there had turned back Whittlesey's much stronger force. Knight got nowhere. Johnson held Third Battalion out of action, pending developments (which did not occur) on the French side of the boundary.

The Germans had been thrown off balance by the events of October 2, especially by the errors that had emptied the position on Hill 198, and were surprised by the speed with which Whittlesey had exploited the gap. But they were old hands, and by nightfall had organized an effective response. They had no idea of the strength of Whittlesey's command, and at first believed he might be able to strike directly into their unprotected base area, just over the ridge that looked down on the northern face of the Pocket. But their command system was efficient, and they had the advantage of well-designed lateral communications behind their entrenched positions. Command of the forces facing what they called the *Amerikanernest* was assigned to the headquarters of the 76th Reserve Division. Reserve infantry units were shifted to block any advance to the north. The 122nd *Landwehr* Regiment was ordered to scout the American position from the east and infiltrate from that direction. The veteran 254th Regiment was given the heavier task of infiltrating from the west (that is, from La Palette), seizing Hill 198, and cutting the Americans off from relief.

Since the ground was familiar to them they were able to accomplish this with speed and efficiency. Infantry patrols scouted the terrain and killed or captured the men manning Whittlesey's runner-posts. The patrols were followed by squad- and platoon-size packets of infantry and machine gunners that secured the position. Some of these spotted Company E's advance and enabled the commanders on La Palette to ambush and destroy Wilhelm's command. But the Germans remained in doubt as to the size of the American force. The interrogation of POWs indicated the presence of two battalions, which implied a force of perhaps 1,200; scouting suggested a smaller force. Colonel von Sybel, the 76th Division chief of staff, decided to err on the side of caution. He sent extra machine-gun units and supplies of wire to Major Hünicken, commanding the 254th Infantry on Hill 198, and instructed him to prepare to hold the entrenchments on the crest against attacks from *two* directions: from the *Amerikanernest* to the north and from the main American position to the south. Accordingly, Hünicken packed his line atop Hill 198 with machine-gun posts at ten-meter intervals along the length of his line, to offset his lack of infantry with firepower.

By the time Holderman's Company K made its attempt on Hill 198 the Germans were already there in strength. Company K ran into carefully placed sniper and machine-gun nests, which channeled their advance into a prepared belt of barbed wire that stopped them under Hünicken's guns. The Americans kept up the firefight, rifles against machine guns, while they tried to cut through the wire; but Hünicken worked patrols around their flanks and Holderman had to give it up and get out as best he could. By noon he was back in the Pocket, dragging his wounded and leaving his dead.

The German command was now satisfied it had matters in hand. The Americans had responded predictably to their situation: vigorously, combatively, but also inexpertly. They had made two company-size attempts to break out of encirclement and failed. Now they must be kept in position by continual bombardment and harassing fire, and the probing of their position by active patrols, while Major Hünicken prepared a heavy assault on the vulnerable western flank of their perimeter.

AFTER HOLDERMAN'S RETURN, Whittlesey gathered his officers in his command post to decide what to do next. Despite Holderman's repulse, they believed it was still possible for them to recapture Hill 198 if they abandoned the Pocket and struck with the whole command. This would restore their connection to supplies and supports, and if they could defend that position they would have achieved a substantial advance and a solid position for a new American front line. But there were good reasons for them to stay where they were. They had a large number of wounded who would have to be evacuated in the rear of the attacking line, and experience taught them that such a procedure was likely to disorganize the command.

On the other hand, their present compact position was better suited for defense by a force of their size against the predictable German counterattack than any Whittlesey had seen—including Hill 198, which required a larger force to cover its extended entrenchments and was more exposed to German artillery fire. More important, this was the position Alexander had ordered them to take and hold at all costs. Those orders could not have been stated more strongly: "Ground once captured must under no circumstances be given up in the absence of direct, positive, and formal orders to do so emanating from these headquarters." No such order to retreat had been received. Those same orders also demanded that "Troops occupying ground must be supported against counterattack and all gains held." Surely Alexander would do everything in his power to sustain their seizure of this advanced position. They had every reason to believe that operations were already afoot to break through to them. Any attempt to break out should be coordinated with whatever operation Alexander had put in play.

Behind these careful calculations there was also a psychological factor, which some of them would have seen as a matter of moral obligation, others as a question of honor, or of pride, or of character. It had been drummed into these men that to retreat was to fail as a soldier and as a man—to diminish the reputation and morale of the AEF and to fall short of the heroic standard by which a Son of Roosevelt was supposed to live his life. Blagden and Rainsford lived by the same standard and had chosen to pull back rather than hang on in the zone of fear and doubt. But they had had to act quickly, under the pressure of swift events that threatened to overwhelm them. Whittlesey and his colleagues had time to deliberate their choice of action; and to do it face to face, where each man could see and judge the disposition of his fellows. None of them took literally Alexander's strident tirade about shooting as a traitor any man who gave an order to retreat. But they understood the sentiment behind his rage, and the determination of GHQ that, in this crisis of morale for the AEF, examples would be made—had already been made—men would be shamed before their fellows for failures that were in most cases beyond their power to prevent.

So they decided to fight it out where they were, and McMurtry wrote out the order that Whittlesey sent around to all the officers in the perimeter:

"Our mission is to hold this position at all costs. No falling back. Have this understood by every man in your command." The word went around and the men seemed to accept it. The veterans recognized the strength of their position, especially its immunity from the shell fire they feared above all else. If they had to fight, just as well here as elsewhere. Whether or not they shared their officers' commitment to a last-ditch struggle remained to be seen. Their chief concern was food: most had eaten the single ration they had snatched on their way to jump-off more than twenty-four hours ago. Out on the left flank Lieutenant Peabody, who commanded one of the machine-gun detachments, had a jar of jam—perhaps one of those that "dear old Lieutenant Colonel Smith" had found for them on the march up—and he invited two privates from his outfit to share it with him. Living in close quarters, under the indiscriminate peril of the Germans' harassing fire, officers and men drew closer.

One of Whittlesey's first actions after making the critical decision was to supervise the siting and digging of latrines. Troops under fire would rather shit and piss in their funk holes than risk death crawling out to a latrine. Too much of that and their entrenchments would become uninhabitable, or demoralizing to inhabit. The filth would increase the chances of the men becoming seriously ill and make them more liable to gangrene if wounded. It was one of the thousand things a good officer was supposed to take care of, but it was the sort of detail many, perhaps most, would have let slip in the stress of action. "Where will your men go to take a shit?" was not among those "Questions for a Battalion Commander to Ask Himself Prior to Taking Over and While Occupying a Portion of the Front Line."

In the early afternoon the first German infantry attack hit the right flank of the position, below the rocky promontory. There was rifle and machine-gun fire from the bluff, then a volley of bombs into the north side of the perimeter—"potato mashers" the troops called them, a can of explosives with a projecting wooden handle. The *Minenwerfer* began lobbing its heavy shells into the Pocket, and a second sharp flurry of bombs and bullets tore into the American position. Captain Holderman and his officers had been moving about, exposing themselves to fire in order to direct the defense. Now Lieutenant Griffin was shot through the shoulder, and Captain Stromee's back and shoulder were laid open by shrapnel from a bomb. These bursts of fire were followed by the shouting of orders in German and an officer calling for his men to identify themselves, followed by a long sequence of names and cries of *"Hier!"*

McMurtry ran over to the right to help Holderman, limping from a painful shrapnel wound in his leg, and recognized all this as a bluff to convince the Americans they faced overwhelming force. He also knew the German pattern in attacks of this sort: their next move would be to rush the American position using successive volleys of thrown grenades as a rolling barrage. But McMurtry believed the Germans overrated the effectiveness of their potato mashers. They were deadly enough when exploded in the confines of a trench, but in the open had more bang than bite. McMurtry and his seconds spread the word to the men in the threatened sector. They let the German attack develop, endured three waves of hurled grenades, each from closer in than the last, then opened fire at close range and paid the Germans back for their losses.

Sergeant Anderson was in command of Company A facing Charlevaux Brook—the officers all wounded or dead—and thought he saw an opportunity to throw back the Germans blocking their supply line back to Regiment. He took his twenty men forward in a skirmish line and got as far as the road when a barrage from hidden machine guns made them all jump, dive, and roll back into the brush. Private John escaped with scratches and torn clothes, Anderson with a bullet-graze that left a burn line above his eyebrows.[16]

On the German side Major Hünicken was quick to call off the attack because he too was understrength and could ill afford heavy losses. But he followed up his probing attack by opening up with machine guns all around the perimeter and directing the *Minenwerfer* to walk its shelling back and forth across the American position. They kept it up for an hour, with special attention to the left or westward flank of the position. A *Minenwerfer* shell blew up a machine gun and all its crew, a burst of machine-gun fire tore up Lieutenant Peabody's leg, and one of the men with whom he had shared his jam was wounded. Whittlesey tried to send reinforcements, a section each from H and A Companies, but half of them were wounded trying to dodge across the position and the rest had to go to ground where they were.

At dusk the fire died down, and Whittlesey sent off another pigeon with a long and urgent message. He reported his position as usual, described the German attacks, and told headquarters, "Situation on our left flank very serious." He wrote Stacey that he had not been able to reestablish his runner-posts; that he was in need of ammunition ("8000 rounds rifle am

7,500 Chauchat, 25 boxes MG, 250 offensive Grenades"); and that his casualties had been grave: in addition to the 88 killed and wounded yesterday he had lost another man killed and 60 more wounded. "Present effective strength of companies here 245. Situation serious."[17]

That evening Private Judd was killed down by the brook trying to refill canteens for the wounded. The shortage of water was becoming serious as well, and the only source of clean water was entirely exposed to German fire.

"For heaven's sake, stop it": October 4-5

> Oh the General got the Croix de Guerre, parley-voo!
> Oh the General got the Croix de Guerre, parley-voo!
> Oh the General got the Croix de Guerre
> But the son of a bitch wasn't even there,
> Hinky dinky parley-voo!

On the afternoon of October 3 General Alexander had gone to a meeting of I Corps division commanders, where they were informed that the general offensive would resume next morning. The well-blooded 42nd Division had been brought up to strengthen V Corps' drive against the German center. In I Corps the fresh 82nd Division replaced the disgraced 92nd as Corps reserve, and the 35th Division was replaced by the veteran First Division, recovered from having borne the brunt of the St. Mihiel offensive. The First Division would spearhead a new drive against the German forces in the Aire valley east of the Argonne, and the French Fourth Army would mount a fresh drive west of the Argonne. These advances would threaten the flanks of the Germans in the forest and compel them to withdraw—if the 77th kept up the pressure. Alexander had been somewhat concerned about Whittlesey's isolated command, but he believed the new offensive would achieve his relief by forcing a German withdrawal. So when he returned to his headquarters that evening, his plans for October 4 called for the 153rd Brigade on his right to do no more than pin the Germans in front of them with spoiling attacks. On his left, Johnson of the 154th Brigade would be given charge of all available reserves and instructed to drive through to Whittlesey's position, in cooperation with the French west of the forest.

The plans that seemed so solid on paper dissolved when men tried to execute them. Nominally, the assault by the 154th Brigade was to be made by elements of two regiments, the reserve units of the 308th commanded by Colonel Stacey and a battalion of the 307th commanded by a major of that regiment, under the direction of brigade commander Evan Johnson. But the 308th's reserve consisted of Lieutenant Knight's two companies—reduced from 100 to 54 men by yesterday's attack—and the woefully diminished Third Battalion. The battalion of the 307th was likewise understrength. And the command arrangements for putting these forces in action was far too elaborate for the numbers involved. There was no "brigade" for Johnson to command, only two understrength battalions. Stacey, who knew the ground and should have been in tactical control, had no authority over the 307th. Communications from the two front-line commands had to be routed back to Johnson, reconciled, then separately referred to each battalion commander, all under conditions which made the simplest communication a matter of hit or miss. But all of the field officers and generals involved were on the brink of mental and emotional exhaustion, and Stacey was about to go over the edge.

Even Colonel Eugene Houghton, who commanded the 307th, thought Alexander's plan a waste of good men, and he was as tough as any regimental commander in the army. Houghton was American-born, but had made a successful business career in Canada. He had also been a soldier of fortune in Asia, had gone through the hell of the Somme and Ypres as a private in a Canadian regiment, had been promoted from the ranks, then transferred to the AEF. He was hard enough to tell Alexander to his face exactly what he thought of the plan, in effect daring the general to relieve him. Then Houghton told his men he considered their attack a "forlorn hope" and instructed them to stop attacking if they couldn't find a gap in the German wire. He got away with it because Alexander recognized him as the best fighter among his regimental commanders.[18]

The officers and men of the 308th could not take so cynical and daring an approach to their orders. Looking back on it after the war, Julius Adler cast what they did in a chivalric light: "The one thought in the minds of every officer and every man was to fight through at all costs to Charlevaux Mill. The heart of King Richard had been thrown far into the enemy lines and a way must be won to it." The reality was more prosaic. The men trapped behind La Palette were from their own regiment, blood of their blood in the only way that now mattered. You did not leave men who belonged to you that way to die or surrender without hope of aid. So on October 4, after the artillery had delivered an inadequate barrage, the remnant of Knight's command and the skeleton Third Battalion staged a furious assault against La Palette and the left of Hill 198 while the the 307th made its pro forma drive to their right.

La Palette had always been impregnable and the drive against it was beaten down. On Hill 198 Major Hünicken had machine guns lined up every ten meters in the trenches along the crest, and the wooded slopes below had been resown with snipers and machine-gun nests. Company K of Third Battalion was working up the slope of Hill 198 when it was stopped by one of these nests. Top Sergeant Ben Kaufman was back with his company, still partly blind from the gassing he had taken on the Vesle. The doctors at the base hospital had refused to release him, but he stole a uniform and made his way through the rear area back to Company K. Technically AWOL, he was actually threatened with court-martial until regimental officers intervened. His men considered him "the best top-kick" in the AEF, and he returned their admiration with fierce loyalty. He had turned down OTC to stay with them, and with the greatest battle of the war imminent he would not be separated from them.

Now he located the nest, and with Sergeant Kruger and Privates Vanderlip and Iacoviello, crawled off to get on its flank. Another machine gun spotted the patrol and brought it under fire, scattering the men, bullets shattering Kaufman's right arm. But he had long ago acquired the will to close with the enemy: he drew his automatic with his left hand (utterly unaware he had already emptied the clip) and went for the machine gun in a zigzag rush. The German gunner had dropped him for other targets and so was taken by surprise when Kaufman burst into the rear of his position, pointed the empty pistol at him, and demanded his surrender. Kaufman made him pick up the machine gun, then walked him back down the slope. Private Iacoviello materialized in front of them just in time to take charge of the prisoner as Kaufman fainted from loss of blood. He would be one of four in the 308th to win the Medal of Honor in the Argonne, the only one not an officer.[19]

But all that valor accomplished was to increase the casualty list by 150 men and deplete their already severely diminished strength. By noon on the fourth the infantry attack had to be given over.

In lieu of further attempts, Division scheduled an artillery bombardment for 3:30 P.M. The idea was to drop a ring of fire around the Pocket, to relieve Whittlesey's men of the continual machine-gun and mortar fire that was wearing them down. Alexander ordered up a couple of planes from his 50th Aero Squadron, gave them orders to be dropped into Whittlesey's position telling him to hold on and that help was coming.

But the planes couldn't find Charlevaux Mill. And somehow the accurate coordinates Whittlesey had been sending for two days never found their way to the gunners of the 305th Field Artillery. A new man, Captain Putnam, had just assumed his duties as artillery liaison at Stacey's headquarters, and when he asked for firing coordinates a staff captain (whose name Putnam never learned) gestured to a spot on his map: 294.2–276.4. This was half a mile from the actual Pocket and corresponded neither to Whittlesey's repeated report of his position nor to the erroneous report sent earlier by Teichmoller. It may have been an instance of the kind Rainsford had complained of, an officer ill-trained in map usage gesturing confidently but ignorantly at a piece of paper.

THE TROOPS IN the Pocket could hear the sounds of battle from beyond the hills that cut them off from the rest of the regiment. The sound of Chauchat auto-rifles was unmistakable, a low-pitched *phunk-phunk* grunt different from the spitting *t-t-t* of German machine guns. They were encouraged by this proof that their comrades were trying to break through to them. It would have been better to have had some inkling of what headquarters was thinking, but the chain of runner-posts was broken and the pigeons only flew one way. At 7:25 A.M. Whittlesey used one of his three remaining birds to tell Colonel Stacey they were still at the same coordinates, were sending out patrols, and badly needed rations. He also set his men to burying the dead, policing the perimeter, digging and maintaining the latrines.

In the late morning the Germans on the rocky bluff above the right flank began throwing a grenade barrage. Whittlesey led ten volunteers from C Company to Holderman's support and the German probe went no further. But the major understood that the German tactics were well calculated to ruin his command. The forces around him were not especially strong in numbers (otherwise they would have tried to overwhelm him). But all the Germans had to do to hold his battalion in place was to pin them down with harassing fire and use repeated probes to keep his reserves hopping around the perimeter. The numbers, energy, and ammunition of his companies would be steadily eroded, the men rendered incapable of exploiting their breakthrough and subjected to steady demoralization that might end in their surrender or abandonment of the position. Hunger was beginning to make the men desperate. Private John crawled out to search the bodies of dead Germans in front of A Company's position facing Charlevaux Brook. German riflemen picked him up, firing from all sides, and he jumped back into the brush so fast he was "behind himself. . . . You may laugh at this, but if you had been there you wouldn't have had time to laugh. The bullets were close enough to clip the leaves off the trees and low brush so that they would sting the devil out of my face."

At 10:35 A.M. Whittlesey used one of his last three pigeons to send a long dispatch to Stacey: the Germans still surrounded them, the position was still being heavily shelled; four officers wounded, Lieutenant Wilhelm missing, only 235 effectives on the firing line. He explained as briefly as he could why they could not attempt to break out by attacking Hill 198: "Cover bad if we advance up the hill and very difficult to move the wounded if we change position. Situation is cutting into our strength rapidly. Men are suffering from hunger and exposure; and the wounded are in very bad condition. Cannot support be sent at once?"

Then he began another circuit of the position, ignoring the grazing fire that swept the Pocket intermittently, checking on his men, making sure the machine guns and Chauchats were properly sighted, making sure the men were using the latrines. As he worked his way around the perimeter he spoke with the men in the funk holes, showing them how sure he was that help was coming, how satisfied he felt that they could handle the situation. His runner, Private Manson, thought he was "as cool as ever" as he moved "from one to another, giving us good cheer and hope." The men had got word, probably from Richards, of the message he had sent to HQ, and appreciated that Whittlesey was doing his best for them: "We could have fought our way back at great cost, but the Major would not leave the wounded to the mercy of the Hun."[20]

Whittlesey had reported 140 wounded over the last two days, most of whom were sheltered toward the center of the perimeter in funk holes surrounding the command post. All were disabled by their wounds (walking wounded were on the perimeter), and some seriously hurt. Those who had been shot through the stomach or bowels or lungs were tormented by thirst. Others like Lieutenant Peabody had shattered limbs, and their wounds already showed signs of gangrenous infection: the blackening of flesh around the wound as muscle and skin became necrotic, the stink that told you your body had begun to rot while you were still alive, the pain of torn flesh and of nerves flaring as they died.

They needed clean water to drink and to treat their wounds. Whittlesey had sent two men down to the brook to replenish canteens, and German patrols killed them both. Whittlesey forbade further attempts, but "Zip" Cepaglia steeled himself to make a run for it, ignoring the orders. He was the runner for Second Battalion, "active as a monkey, with his nutcracker jaw and his funny Italian-Bowery accent." He zigzagged through the brush and jumped into a funk hole bringing a load of mud down with him on the man hunkered in it—and just like that the two of them, mad with the constant strain, blew their tops and popped up ready to lay into one another, when something brought them to their senses. Cepaglia picked up his clanking garland of canteens, dodged and slipped and slid down to the brook. His luck was in: the orderly Germans were taking their noonday lunch break, and he got away clean.

At 3:30 that afternoon every man in the perimeter heard from beyond Hill 198 and La Palette the distinctive bark of the French 75-mm cannons used by the American artillery, and moments later the detonations came walking toward them across Charlevaux valley, ripping up the brush on the far side of the brook and sending up big brown gouts of mud and water along the swampy stream. For a minute or two Whittlesey, McMurtry, and the rest believed headquarters was finally responding to their messages and was about to lambaste the encircling enemy with high explosive and shrapnel. Then the next round of shells took a giant step from stream to woods and suddenly the Pocket itself was being rocked by huge explosions that ripped away the cover of brush and trees and chewed up great gulps of muddy ground and of men whose names and faces you knew. Sergeant Major Ben Gaedeke was blown into atoms by a direct hit, nothing left but his empty helmet in the mud. Officers and noncoms in exposed positions were hit, the wounded were hit, Whittlesey's position gave perfect shelter from German artillery but was naked to guns firing from their own side. Private John and his buddy were buried in their funk hole by a near miss—John's one free hand, groping above the dirt, found his short-handled trench shovel, and he used it to scrape them loose. Then another shell hit and buried them again. That was "too much"—they abandoned their hole and went stumbling back, looking for a safer place. John stepped into a patch of swerving ground—three men buried under a pile of earth, "I would not have known they were there if I hadn't stepped on the leg of one of them." He dug them out, then threw himself flat and let the shrapnel whizz over his head.

Artillery bombardment was the most terrible aspect of combat on the Western Front, demoralizing even when you knew your own artillery was trying to protect you. But to be bombarded by your own artillery was the most demoralizing thing that could happen, the real effects of the shelling augmented by terrible proof that your own people were so out of touch as to be more dangerous than the enemy.

Whittlesey was away from the command post when it started, walked back through it quickly but more or less upright, calming the men by word and example. Inside he must have been frantic. He had risked the lives of all his men to fulfill the orders of the high command, and now they would be destroyed not by the enemy but through some terrible blunder by their own people. He reached his command post; he needed to get a carrier pigeon into the air right away. Pigeon specialist Richards fumbled at the door of the cage, the ground jarring from the shell fire.

And suddenly they were trapped in a hideous slapstick comedy, a joke that made them ridiculous even as it killed them. Richards's hands slipped and one of the two remaining birds flew the coop. Shells were smashing all around them, shrapnel carved a bloody line across the major's nose. He swore at Richards, who pulled himself together and carefully cradled the last bird, Cher Ami, out of the cage. Whittlesey scribbled the message that went into the clip on the bird's foot:

> At: 294.6–276.3
> Date: 4 Oct.
> To: Delaware 1 [Stacey]
> We are along the road parallel 276.4
> Our own artillery is dropping a barrage directly on us.
> For heaven's sake, stop it.

The bird fluttered up into the air, felt the buffeting of shell concussions, and took shelter on an overhanging tree limb. Richards and Whittlesey hollered at it to make it go, chucked twigs and small stones at it—the bird fluttered to a higher limb. Richards, swearing, shinnied partway up the tree, got hold of the limb, and gave it a shake. The bird took wing, the German snipers recognized it for what it was and started peening away, but Cher Ami whirred off through the woods.

Richards dropped back to the ground. Whittlesey had gone off somewhere. Richards sat there in a funk. Suddenly the major reappeared and told him to find the other pigeon specialist, Tollefson, and see if he had any pigeons. Richards crawled away. Tollefson wasn't far, but half his head had been blown off by a shell and there were no more pigeons. Richards let it go at that. He was utterly exhausted. Hungry. But he had a sack of pigeon food in his pocket, "cracked corn, split peas and birdseed," and since there were no more pigeons to feed he ate a mouthful of seeds and was grateful for them.

Meanwhile Whittlesey and the others in the command post helped the medical detachment shift the wounded to better shelter, snugged closer to the base of the slope. "Paul Andrews, the Boston Jew-boy, who had valiantly volunteered to get water . . . now lay dead with a piece of American shell in him." Through the shell bursts they made out the sound of an airplane overhead, spotted the roundels that marked it as Allied. Whittlesey sent his signalman, Corporal Larney, to lay out the white panels used to mark ground positions for air observation. Larney and another man got it done, under fire that wounded both of them—Larney in the leg, and a shot clipped off one of the other man's fingers. The shells kept falling, hurt men were screaming all over the position, and the German machine guns were chipping in with a grazing crossfire.

CHER AMI CAME to roost at brigade HQ at 4 P.M. The corporal on duty read the nightmare message and reported it instantly to Division. A motorcycle rider roared off to the artillery post. By 4:15 the barrage had lifted. All things considered it was as swift and accurate a communication as had yet been seen in that army—although it is possible the ceasefire came because the artillery had finished its fire mission.

THE GERMANS SURROUNDING the Pocket responded as if the barrage had been of their own making. As soon as it lifted they came slipping through the woods to assault the right flank, where Whittlesey and his pickup squad from C had stopped them earlier. Captain Holderman and Lieutenant Schenck led the defense, and the Germans cut the attack short when the Americans responded energetically. But they kept up heavy sniper fire. Robert Yoder, the replacement from Minnesota, volunteered to lead a three-man sniper-killer team, with Nebraska rancher George Newcom and the Native American Frank Martinez. Yoder was the 308th's answer to Sergeant York and managed to pick off three Germans in the falling dusk. The two sides shouted insults back and forth in the dark, the Germans in broken English. There were any number of fluent German speakers in the battalion, among them Max Probst (whose brother was in the Kaiser's army) and Private Speich. It was Speich who settled the duel by hurling a German word meaning "stink-experts," which silenced the enemy and made his buddies howl.[21]

Whittlesey sent Corporal Baldwin around the position to get a casualty count: eighty killed or wounded, including Captains Holderman (lightly) and Stromee seriously. In addition to the main gathering of wounded near the command post, there were now wounded men sequestered in small groups all around the position. The officers' conference that evening recognized that it had become impossible for them to change position for defense and that there was no hope of exploiting their breakthrough as envisioned in the original orders. They had no more pigeons, and therefore no way of contacting headquarters—unless runners could manage to slip through the encircling Germans and find their way back to Regiment.

The lack of food and water was wearing down their powers of resistance, and the men were becoming increasingly desperate. After dark, Holderman let his men sneak out to rifle the bodies of the German dead to see if any rations could be scavenged. They hadn't eaten since the first night in the Pocket, and their hunger was so desperate it was worth a life to slake it. Some crawled out to scoop muddy water, still reeking with the sulphur of high explosive from the shell holes left by the *Minenwerfer*. Others, against orders, sneaked off simply on the chance of finding a dead German with some bread in his pocket, and some of these were picked off. There were not a lot of these cases, but enough to show how easily their line of resistance could melt away.

The bounds of their perimeter were permeable, the main resistance line consisting of clusters of funk holes with gaps between them, and the outpost positions beyond of smaller holes more widely separated, all of these buried in the brushy undergrowth and half-shattered trunks of the forest. It was easy in these circumstances for their combat strength to dissipate and drift. Lieutenants Leak and Harrington, who had been wounded in Wilhelm's attempted breakout, had tried to shift some of the wounded in their part of the Pocket to more sheltered positions. In the confusion they moved beyond the perimeter and were captured by German patrols working forward to throw grenades.

THE BATTLE ON October 4 was the last straw for Colonel Stacey. That night he reported that his men had done all they could, were tired, disorganized, ill-equipped, and poorly trained for this kind of fighting. When Alexander and Johnson ordered him to attack again in the morning he refused: his men were "brave and loyal and willing to do anything they can"—no slackers here, no disloyal hyphenates—but they "have no instruction and no equipment, and they are now thoroughly tired and disorganized. I don't believe the General understands the shape my regiment is in. I must refuse to assume responsibility for any further attacks until we have some equipment and reinforcements." He asked to be relieved. Johnson passed his message to Alexander, who snapped back an order to relieve Stacey at once. "You should have done that without reporting to me. The responsibility for this attack is on me. I'm ordering it." Since relieving Stacey would leave a captain in command of what was left of the 308th, Johnson himself went forward to take charge. He probably knew that his command of the brigade would end with this last attempt to relieve Whittlesey. Alexander was not likely to forget Johnson's own reluctance to attack and his endorsement of Stacey's views.

IT RAINED MOST of the night of October 4–5, a chilling, soaking downpour that turned funk holes in the Pocket into sumps. The men shivered in sodden clothes. Those who had disobeyed orders and lugged their overcoats, blankets, or rain gear shared them with two or three others. The rain let up at first light, leaving the air full of a penetrating damp fog, which at least gave them some relief from snipers. There was nothing to eat. The burial detail that crawled out to deal with the men who had died overnight hacked so weakly at the rocky, root-tangled soil that Whittlesey couldn't stand it: he had McMurtry tell them to just throw dead leaves and branches over the dead.

Then Whittlesey made his regular tour of the Pocket. He bawled out a man he caught relieving himself behind a tree. Didn't he know what a latrine was for? He went around to all the wounded. Some had been lying in filth for four days, and their gangrene was advanced. "The stink was almost unbearable. Many wounded men would almost rot before they died." They had been without water most of the time, except for raindrops and the muddy stuff scooped from shell holes. The medical detachment—Privates Sirota, Bragg, and Gehris—had served them constantly, fetching what water there was, bandaging and tourniqueting. But their morphine and disinfectants were used up, and so were their bandages. They salvaged dressings from the dead, turned them bloody-side out, and used them on the newly wounded. They too had been without food for four days and were approaching that level of exhaustion where the body simply stops functioning.

Holderman was among the helpless now, three times wounded, the last time by a sniper. His old wounds were bordering on gangrenous, he could tell by the rotten stench and by the pain that flared in dying nerves. Lionel Bendheim's smashed leg was also going bad. Whittlesey knelt by him and gave him a small piece of chocolate he had saved out of his ration. "Just imagine," he told him, "you'll be down on the Riviera while we're still soaking through these woods." The message was not just that Bendheim was going to get out of this: they all were, for better and for worse.[22]

Every now and then Whittlesey would hear a machine gun ripping off in the fog, killing men who slipped out of the perimeter to try to get water from Charlevaux Brook. If that went on half the force might wander off looking for water. The major posted a couple of riflemen with orders to shoot anyone else who tried to get to the brook. Then he turned the job over to Zip Cepaglia, who had a knack for getting down there and back without starting a firefight.

The *Minenwerfer* and machine guns began working them over again in the early morning, but at 10 A.M. they heard artillery firing from their own guns over the hills to the south. There was a horrible moment of doubt as the shelling walked up on them—were they going to be hit by their own guns again?—but this time the guns had the right coordinates. The men in the Pocket cheered as their shells tore into the woods and hills around them, and at the shrieks of the German wounded. Then, beginning at about 1 P.M., they heard heavy firing from beyond Hill 198, the unmistakable cough of the Chauchats indicating their own men were trying to break through to them.

The Germans started their regular attack on the Pocket punctually at three: twenty minutes of grazing fire from the machine guns and a pounding by the *Minenwerfer*. Whittlesey and McMurtry were flat out on the ground, face to face, as the bullets zipped overhead. "*Most* un-pleasant," Whittlesey remarked, "as though he were criticizing the flavor of a cup of tea." For the moment his spirits were on the rise: the sup-porting bombardment, the sounds of infantry coming to their aid, and the prospect of imminent action—of being able to hit back at the enemy who had been tormenting and killing his men—provided the lift. From his funk hole fronting the brook, Private John saw Germans dashing from tree to tree, trying to get behind his position. He cut loose, encour-aged by the sound of firing from other holes along the line, firing his rifle so fast the barrel became too hot to touch.

The attack on Company A's position was a feint. The real assault was aimed at the vulnerable right flank, below the promontory. As soon as they heard the first *crump* of the usual potato-masher barrage, Whittle-sey, McMurtry, and Lieutenant Revnes of the machine-gun section scut-tled over there. All three had been wounded, Whittlesey only scratched, but the others limping on damaged legs.

The Germans tried a new wrinkle: tying their grenades together in batches of five or six, to produce a bang equivalent to a mortar shell. In the middle of the attack one of these landed directly in a funk hole and tore off the legs of the soldier manning it. They could hear him yelling "Mama—Mama—Mama" all through the crack and wham of the fire-fight, and then at the end, "Good-bye everybody. I forgive all." Mc-Murtry directed the defense and beat the attack back, but Lieutenant Pool—Holderman's second—took a sniper's bullet in the back as he stood next to McMurtry. A grenade went off behind them and the ex-plosion drove its wooden handle into McMurtry's back. Between the adrenaline rush of combat and the pain of his earlier wounds he never felt it. Back at headquarters Whittlesey reached over and yanked it out, Mc-Murtry yelping with surprise and pain, "If you do that again I'll wring your neck."

Later, in the dark, with the brief exhilaration of combat going cold, Whittlesey and McMurtry assessed their situation. They could still hear shooting beyond Hill 198; if it was no closer it was at least continuing. There was a relief operation afoot, and it was their job to help it work ef-fectively. They needed to get a runner through to headquarters, to let them know the situation in the Pocket and guide the relief to them. Whit-tlesey turned to Corporal Botelle, who had been serving as his runner within the position, carrying messages under fire from one section to another. Would Botelle try? It wasn't an order, but if someone didn't go, the men in the battalion would die where they were. He praised Botelle for having set an example before this—didn't he want to keep himself up to that mark? He appealed to the two things for which a soldier might take such a fool's chance: the needs of his buddies and his pride of service, his standing among his peers, his manhood. Botelle said he'd go, and Private Friel with him.

At about that time there was a momentary upsurge in the firing from beyond Hill 198. Whittlesey told them to listen, it was "like the pipes at Lucknow." McMurtry and Peabody probably got the allusion to the Whittier poem about the relief of British troops besieged during India's Sepoy Rebellion (1857): the Plattsburghers loved the romance of empire, doing the World's Work, and the literature of the White Man's Burden. Then a practical suggestion: we ought to fire a few bursts to let them know we're still here. McMurtry went down to an auto-rifle team and ordered them to fire a series of short bursts with a fixed interval between. The sound of the Chauchat was like nothing in the German arsenal, and the odd firing pattern should be easily recognized as a signal. They managed three or four bursts before the Germans got the idea and began blazing away from all points, covering the signal bursts with noise. Botelle and Friel slipped out after the shooting stopped.

IT WAS THE 307th they had heard. The battalion led by Crawford Blagden had begun its supreme effort to take Hill 198 at about 1 P.M. that afternoon. As they crossed the open ground below the hills they were hit with German artillery firing from both flanks—they had no artillery support of their own. The three companies surged up the wooded slopes of the hill, one after another, officers and men stripped away by successive lines of machine-gun posts and by German artillery firing in close support. At the end of two hours "They had only made a hundred yards, losing a man for every yard." Blagden went down with a wound, Rainsford and his other company commanders were wounded or killed, and so were their seconds.

Captain Eddie Grant, alumnus of Harvard and Plattsburgh and ex-third baseman of the New York Giants, was commanding the reserve company. He had been leading them under fire for four days without a rest. His striker handed him a tin cup of hot coffee. He was so exhausted. It took him three tries to lift it to his mouth. He had just managed it when the runner came to tell him he was now in command of the battalion. He got up, went forward to take charge. He had to cross a railroad embankment exposed to enemy shell fire, and as he and his headquarters team were stumbling across it a German shell dropped alongside and killed him. Colonel Houghton told Grant's successor to give it up: there was no breaking through that line. His troops dug in on the slope and spent the night being periodically raked by German artillery. No one in the command heard the Chauchat signal from the Pocket.[23]

That night it rained again. In the Pocket "they were too exhausted even to bury the dead, and those who had given their lives lay with clotted blood on their faces and their clothes on the ground near by, glowing phosphorescently under a sky devoid of moon and stars, while their companions looked on with breaking hearts, but even the wounded did not cry aloud." True. But one who slept next to Whittlesey remembered that the major cried in his sleep.[24]

A New Approach: October 5–6

The *Amerikanernest* had been contained for four days on the night of October 5, but its existence had altered the plans of both American and German commanders. Pershing was anxious to restart his stalled offensive. His staff was working hard to bring order out of logistical chaos. The green divisions that had wrecked or discredited themselves in the first attack had been pulled out of line and replaced by some of the elite and veteran formations that had been recovering after St. Mihiel. While this was going on, Whittlesey had achieved his breakthrough and established a strong position behind the German front. His defense, and the desperate attempts of the 77th Division to relieve him, had effectively pinned the enemy forces in the Argonne. Now if Pershing's main force could advance in the center they might be able to flank the German units in the forest and compel a retreat that (with proper exploitation) might enable them to break and roll up the German line.[25]

There is some disagreement about how much of this tactical plan was made in response to the plight of Whittlesey's command, and/or the opportunity presented by his breakthrough. Pershing had no choice but to resume the offensive within the narrow sector of relatively open ground between the eastern edge of the forest and the Meuse River. The strength of the German position on the heights of the Meuse dictated an axis of attack closer to the Argonne. The original plan of the offensive had envisioned an advance in the Argonne as one that merely kept pace with the decisive thrusts up the Aire valley and across Montfaucon. Whittlesey's advance had created an unforeseen opportunity to do something decisive in the Argonne itself.

There was also, as always, the factor of morale to consider. Although it was sometimes impossible for headquarters to communicate with its own artillery, rumors could run through the whole army with astonishing speed. By October 4 practically everyone in the AEF had heard of the units cut off in the Argonne. Army morale, and the AEF's supposed moral ascendancy over the Germans, would be heavily compromised if so large a group of Americans should be wiped out or forced to surrender. Alexander was enraged by the prospect of a defeat that would discredit his division and himself, and drove his brigadiers hard to effect the relief. The exhausted soldiers in his rifle companies had spent what little strength they had, not because they feared Alexander but because their highest moral imperative was to come to the aid of comrades in grave peril. Both of these factors—fear of disgrace and the imperative of rescue—might restore to Pershing's tired and shot-up forces their zeal to close with the enemy.

There was also the home front to consider. What was rumor in the army would soon be blazing headlines across America, and what those headlines said could affect civilian support of the Liberty Loans, Selective Service, war appropriations, things that would determine the future strength or weakness of the AEF and the careers of its commanders. The connection between battlefield action and home-front publicity was not as swift in 1918 as it would be in later wars. There was a considerable time lag between a reporter's writing of his story and its transmission (via cable) to the States, and a further delay while stateside editors tried to fit the dispatch into its proper place in the deluge of information coming from the AEF, the Allied governments, and the War Department. Censors read and delayed all stories of current action. Reporters could not phone or radio their stories from headquarters; they had to leave the scene and travel on jammed roads to reach a transmission station; and since there were relatively few correspondents (as compared with World War II), good reporters preferred to stay through an action and file later.

In the meantime, the dispatches they filed with the censors, and the conversation among reporters about how events and their stories were developing, could make everyone involved aware that huge headlines were impending. That was what happened with the story of Whittlesey's stand at Charlevaux Mill.

The war correspondents accredited to GHQ and the various corps had been aware of the story for some time. Lieutenant Kidder Mead, press officer of the 77th Division, had been following the course of the battle on the headquarters map and recognized early on September 29 that the leading elements of the 154th Brigade—Whittlesey's command—were in danger of being cut off at L'Homme Mort. Mead was an ex-newspaperman who saw this as an appealing news story that might bring fame to his division, and he alerted the correspondents. But the bloody fight for Montfaucon pushed the Argonne into the background. While attention was elsewhere, Whittlesey's command was relieved at L'Homme Mort, broke through the German lines, and was surrounded *again* at Charlevaux Mill. When that news reached GHQ on October 3, the correspondents remembered Mead's earlier heads-up. In ones and twos reporters disengaged from the stalled divisions in Pershing's center and checked in at Alexander's headquarters to learn what was happening to Whittlesey.

The first stories on the fighting at Charlevaux Mill were transmitted on October 3 by Fred Ferguson of United Press. It was Harold Jacobs, cable editor of United Press, who recognized the situation as a modern analogue of "Custer and the Sioux on the Little Big Horn," and potentially a Big Story. He cabled Ferguson to "send more on Lost Battalion," his use of that name suggesting they were faced with imminent destruction, not "lost" in the sense of having gone astray. His phrase was picked up by the correspondents, press officers, and ultimately the field commanders in France, and became current there before it ever appeared in any American newspaper. However, stories *were* printed about Whittlesey's earlier cutoff, which Jacobs and others confused with the fighting at Charlevaux Mill: the *New York Herald*'s version appeared on October 3, "Desperate Fighting by Whittlesey Unit." It would have been read at GHQ a day or two later, as the siege at Charlevaux Mill was reaching its crisis. Thus feedback from the States reinforced the feeling of reporters and generals alike that this was an extraordinary story. The full story of the Lost Battalion would not be published until much later, on October 9 or 10, and readers in the States hearing of the battle for the first time might have thought it odd that they referred to "the famous Lost Battalion." The reporters described it that way because they and most of the AEF had been obsessed with Whittlesey's fate for days before their dispatches were filed.[26]

For all these reasons, then, Pershing's plan of attack for October 4 and the ensuing days called for strenuous efforts by the 77th Division to break through to Whittlesey and for a powerful offensive drive, spearheaded by the elite First Division, northward up the Aire valley along the eastern edge of the Argonne. On October 4—while the Pocket was being hit by its own artillery—the "Big Red One" advanced behind a well-timed and well-aimed barrage, took the heights of Montrefagne in one of the few true hand-to-hand fights of the war, dug in, and brought its artillery forward without a hitch to cover the next day's thrust. The German command called up a Prussian Guards division from their reserve and met the American attack on October 5 head to head. Once again the American artillery was used effectively, and these American troops were nearly as experienced as their German counterparts and a good deal fresher. The Germans were pushed back, and the AEF had intruded a broad blunt-headed salient into their lines from which it might outflank German forces in the Argonne.

General Liggett, commanding I Corps, and his chief of staff, Malin Craig, had a plan for doing just that. They would bring up the fresh 82nd Division behind the First, then swing it to the left to strike the German flank in the Argonne. The plan had risks. The 82nd could itself be flanked if the Germans had sufficient reserves in the northern Argonne. But Liggett and Craig thought the Germans there were worn out with fending off the 77th Division and dealing with Whittlesey, and the 82nd would be given the use of the First Division's superb artillery as an equalizer. The flank attack would jump off on October 6.

IN THE ARGONNE, the 154th Brigade had not given up its efforts to reach their trapped comrades. Their force had never been adequate to achieve the breakthrough, and every attack diminished it still further. Over four days of fighting the 308th alone would lose 766 men trying to relieve Whittlesey, more than half of the regiment's reserves. Paul Knight tried desperately to keep his word to Whittlesey, kept trying to work his men around the Germans on La Palette, but the French troops who were supposed to support him on the left were not to be found. Part of D Company under Lieutenant Turner probing out toward the French got so far separated from the rest that the Germans were able to close in and surround them, snipers and machine guns shooting his command to pieces. A German officer ordered a cease-fire and called out for Turner to surrender. He refused, and when he was killed the surviving leader of the unit, Private William Zapke, also rejected a chance to give up. The unit was killed to the last man.[27]

The 308th was obviously too decimated to make headway. The power in any attack would have to come from the 307th Infantry. So early on the morning of the sixth, Alexander met with Colonel Eugene Houghton. He was the only regimental commander in the division who was not regular army and was debilitated by an illness that would force his relief within the week. But Alexander respected him as a tough and competent officer, who had learned his trade fighting with the Canadians in Flanders and (like Alexander himself) had come up from the ranks. Houghton was against a frontal assault, but one of his companies under Lieutenant Tillman had found a gap between two sections of German wire. Tillman was holding the gap and had patrols out finding and marking other paths through the wire. If, under cover of darkness, small gangs could be systematically infiltrated through these breaks, a strong force could be accumulated inside the German wire, sufficient in numbers to storm the position by a surprise attack at first light. But Alexander would have to be patient. As the Germans had shown, attack by infiltration had to be done carefully. Otherwise the defenders could stage a preemptive attack while the infiltrators were still few in number. Houghton did not think he could make his assault until late the following day, October 7.

Alexander accepted the plan as the only one workable under the circumstances. In the meantime he would use the 50th Aero Squadron to drop supplies to Whittlesey. He also had his chief of staff, Colonel Hannay, draft an order to be dropped along with the supplies. The order was oddly conceived and would become controversial. It commanded Whittlesey to abandon the Pocket and "retire with your forces to Regimental P.C." (that is, to his original starting point). There was no possibility of coordinating the breakout with Houghton's planned attack, only the slim chance of a fortunate coincidence in timing. The only purpose of such an attempt would be to avoid the disgrace of a mass surrender, at the cost of abandoning the wounded. However, the order also called on Whittlesey to patrol aggressively out of the Pocket and attempt to link up with supporting elements—which contradicted the sense of the first order by implying that Whittlesey should hold his position and attempt to reestablish liaison with the Division, as called for in his original orders. Perhaps the new orders were badly written, appearing to make contradictory demands when they were supposed to offer Whittlesey a choice. The other possibility is that they were not written to be obeyed, but to provide Division with a paper record proving its orders had covered all contingencies if the battle ended in the surrender or destruction of Whittlesey's command.

Alexander had reason to think about covering himself. That same day Captain Albert Rich, assistant inspector general at Pershing's headquarters, arrived to investigate the cutting off of Whittlesey's command. All of the principal commanders were interviewed, except for Colonel Stacey (who had been relieved the day before) and Whittlesey. Alexander was defensive about his orders to Whittlesey and the vigor with which he had tried to relieve him. He made no mention of the friendly-fire bombardment on October 4, referred to in Whittlesey's pigeon dispatch, but blamed the French for making such an error on October 5. General Johnson's interview exposed his sharp disagreements with Alexander over the supposed advance by the French. If the battle ended in disaster, these issues might become critical in a court of inquiry. But for now the failures were laid off on Colonel Stacey, the only officer criticized in the report. If their battle went badly, Alexander and Johnson might face similar disgrace.[28]

On the German side, Whittlesey's stubborn holdout and the First Division's rapid advance had imposed an unpleasant tactical decision. German forces in the Argonne, and those opposing the French to the west of it, would have to pull back to their next line of defense. The general commanding in the Argonne protested the abandonment of such strong positions, but the orders were firm. Still, he regretted the lost opportunity to damage the Americans by destroying the *Amerikanernest*; and besides, the presence of that force would make it difficult for him to extricate the units he had infiltrated to cut off the Americans. So on the night of

October 5 headquarters granted him a battalion of the specially trained elite *Stosstruppen*, and a flamethrower section, and thirty-six hours' grace in which to wipe the Americans out.

IN THE EARLY hours of October 6, Whittlesey made his morning tour of the position, which the men recognized as one of life's routines in a place that had become, in a literal sense, terribly familiar. He exchanged the same questions and answers with the men in their funk holes, they asking in various ways if there was anything new, he answering that things were still the same. They were hungrier and thirstier, but otherwise no worse off than they had been last night. He had the burial detail heap leaves over the men who'd died last night, to spare his men the sight.

He reminded them to use the latrines, or else. There was something absurd about it. Within their small perimeter, even well-placed and properly used latrines still contributed their stink to the dense and complex stenches of the Pocket—their bodily filth, their gangrenous wounds, the rotting bodies of their dead. But his strictures told the men the unit was still intact, still under discipline. It still belonged to the army, and so the army would have to come and rescue it.

Whittlesey could detect no sign of slackening in his men's will to hang on and keep fighting. But he was terribly worried about their physical weakness. A soldier offered him some black bread he had filched from the body of a dead German, but Whittlesey told the boy he should eat it himself. Most had been without food for three days, and despite Cepaglia's canteen runs they had had to drink the filthy water from mud holes. They had slept in the mud and rain without blankets or shelter halves, with almost no chance to make a small fire to warm themselves. He ordered out a larger than usual number of combat patrols that morning and told them to probe as strongly as they could to see if there were any breaks in the encirclement.

Before the Argonne, as a staff and operations officer, he had been a more distant figure to the men than a Holderman or a McMurtry, who earned affection and respect through long and close association. His "Yankee" manner was against him: a snappish strictness in giving orders that suggested intolerance of anything less than prompt effective obedience. But he had won respect and even admiration for his leadership after September 26, and especially for having brought them through the German lines and up to Charlevaux Brook without any murderous charging of trench lines over open ground. That showed care for the lives of his men. They knew he had refused orders to break out because he was unwilling to leave his wounded behind. On October 3 and 4, when they had come under heavy attack, they had looked up to see him striding awkwardly about the position on his long stiff "stilt-like" legs, nobody's idea of a hero, but he didn't seem to mind bullets or shrapnel as he went from hole to hole "like the worried president of a corporation" checking to see how the workers were doing. If anyone asked him what he thought of their chances, he would answer, "Remember, there are two million Americans pushing up to relieve us." It was, under the circumstances, a joke: one million of Pershing's vaunted two millions were still stateside drilling with broomsticks. It was, in fact, a *soldier's* joke, and it made the men, for the first time, put "Galloping Charlie" in the same class with McMurtry as a "regular guy."[29]

As for how he felt about them, he told McMurtry, one night as the two lay side by side in their funk hole, "George, as long as you and I live we will never be in finer company." He would repeat those words afterward, back in New York, telling close friends around a fire at the Williams or the Harvard Club that the working-class men from the slums of the Lower East Side who served with him in the Pocket were "finer than anyone can say." He was not one of them, nor were they "his" in the sense that Pruyn and Brooks and Miles and McMurtry were. But their connection, based on what they had shared in that close-pent perimeter under continual peril of death and wounds, was as close as any relationship in his life.

There was only one story he would tell of his time in the Pocket, as if it symbolized for him the meaning of that experience. He told how his command post was set among the wounded, and the officers helped the medical detachment care for and comfort the hurt and dying. He had gone to sleep one night next to a wounded boy for whom he was particularly anxious, had slept restlessly, waking repeatedly to see how the boy was. At last "he awoke in the middle of the night to find his cheek touching the soldier's, which was cold in death."[30] His men were not mistaken in thinking he cared about them. For Whittlesey the story of the Lost Battalion was not in the end about orders proper or improper, glory whether earned or not, but also about an obscure and—for him as a man, a gentleman, an officer—a necessarily distanced tenderness.

Last Stand: October 6–7

All combat is an ordeal, a test of various kinds of strength, but the nature of the test differs from one situation to another. Assault troops have to overcome the terror of standing up and walking forward, breast and belly naked to an iron wind of bullets and shrapnel. But once started, if they sense they can actually reach and destroy the power that threatens to kill them they can be carried forward by the rage and adrenaline rush. Troops under intense bombardment must resist the maddening sense of utter helplessness and isolation and the wracking effect of noise and concussion, but the shelter of the trench is some comfort, as is the knowledge that the storm will have to end.

Prolonged immersion in combat produces a psychological and emotional numbness that can enable soldiers to endure and to continue functioning. Private John remembered his own reaction. In the intervals between attacks, when the men could move about the position, "such a mess you never did see. Some of our men were dead, other[s] dying and moaning for help. Some were already buried and some just in pieces."

> The most terrible thing of all, it seemed to me, was the fact that we could do next to nothing for the wounded. We had no first aid. . . . What little supplies each of us had carried, had long since been used, even shirts socks and underwear had been torn into rags for bandages. Everybody living was like a living scarecrow. It didn't seem so terrible then, as it was a sight before our eyes every minute of the day and to each of us it seemed so evident that it would only be a short time until we would take our place along side of them, that we almost became reconciled to it.

The troops in the Pocket had to maintain their will to resist—and more, their will to fight, to counterattack—in an environment of inescapable disgusting filth and deepening and unsatisfiable hunger and thirst, where they were continually sniped and pinned down by machine-gun crossfire, subjected to periodic murderous assaults, enduring a swarm of forces ranging from the trivial to the catastrophic that combined to kill, maim, debilitate, dishearten, and demoralize them. The guns that were supposed to support and protect them had instead raked them with high explosive that tore up their position and made casualties of one man in every eight, and to the horrors of their situation was added the understanding that they could be destroyed by mere blundering, by the sort of stupidity they laughed at every day of their lives.

At ten in the morning on October 6 they heard the drone of airplanes, and ten two-seater Allied machines dropped out of the overcast and roared along the Charlevaux valley, the observers in each craft pushing over the side long bundles swung on parachutes. Though the men in the Pocket waved and shouted, and signalman Larney raced to set out his white identification panels, the pilots never saw them and all of the bundles drifted into the trees on the German side of the valley. To the physical torment of their hunger there was now added the Tantalus torture of hearing enemy soldiers rejoice as they tore open bundles of rations, chocolate, cigarettes. Another joke on them. Another proof that their own army was blind and blundering. How could it rescue them if it couldn't tell where they were?

In one of those lost bundles was Hannay's order for Whittlesey to abandon his wounded and attempt a breakout.

Another day of *Minenwerfer* bombardment, machine-gun fire pinning them to their foul nests. The cover of trees and brush that had protected them at the start was being gradually stripped away by shell fire and bullets. Now the funk holes that sheltered the wounded came under fire. One shell found the hole Lieutenant Peabody was lying in, weak from loss of blood, infection, and the constant pain of a shattered leg, and blew him right out of it, rolling his dead body down a little slope into another funk hole. His men had given him the only overcoat in the company. The three privates in the hole—Cepaglia was one and Richards the pigeon specialist another—debated whether it was bad luck to wear a dead man's coat. They decided their luck was already as bad as it could get and shared it in turn.

At 3 P.M. a burst of firing and grenade explosions heralded the usual afternoon infantry probe of their positions. Except this time it would be worse. The attack came against Holderman's position on the right again. There were more bombs this time, one of which blew up Lieutenant Noon, one of the two machine-gun officers. Then the outposts came running in yelling "Liquid fire!" and long plumes of lava trailing thick black smoke arced up and out of the brush, reeking of petrol, dropping splashes that made little puddles of flame. The men were firing blindly, hysterical with fear of sudden horrible incineration, but McMurtry was there, and Whittlesey brought up some supports from C Company. The flamethrowers were terrifying, but not very effective if kept at a distance. Aimed rifle fire was the answer, and systematic use of the penetrating power of the Chauchats. Sergeant Carroll shot the *Flammenwerfer* squad leader between the eyes, McMurtry got the Chauchat gunners to concentrate their fire, and the attackers broke and scuttled back into the brush.

The runners Botelle and Friel struggled back to the Pocket later in the day. Both were wounded, Friel mortally, and they had not found a break in the encirclement.

As night shut down and the rain began again the officers had new information to consider. That afternoon's assault was the heaviest infantry attack they had yet faced, and the Germans who made it were not the reserve infantry they had faced so far, but *Stosstruppen*, the elite "storm troopers" who had led the Ludendorff offensives. Up to now it had seemed that the Germans lacked the infantry strength to take the position by assault. If the Pocket held out long enough, relief was bound to get through. But this last attack might indicate that the Germans were determined to wipe them out and had built up their strength to do it. Such an effort might be designed to cover a retreat; but it could indicate the enemy was determined to hold its present line at any cost. Cut off from contact with headquarters, there was no way to be sure which of these was most likely.

Their own strength was much reduced. The last attack had wrecked another machine gun—they had lost five of the nine weapons they had brought into the Pocket, and their ammunition was depleted. They had fewer than two hundred men still capable of fighting and an equal number of completely helpless wounded men. Those still manning the perimeter were debilitated by lack of food and many had become sick from drinking filthy water and the general squalor in which they lived and breathed. At a time when the role of officers and seasoned noncoms was more vital than ever, their complement of both had been severely reduced. Lieutenants Peabody, Noon, and Rogers and battalion Sergeant Major Gaedeke were dead; Lieutenants Griffin, Pool, Williamson, badly wounded; Leak and Harrington missing, presumably captured. Holderman was still hobbling around, but his wounds had become gangrenous and he was nearly done. McMurtry was limping from a shrapnel wound on October 3, and there was a hole in his back where he had been speared by the handle of the potato masher.

The choices before them were grim. They would certainly have to contract the perimeter, which would make every part of the position more vulnerable to German gunnery. In the middle of the conference a note was handed to Whittlesey from Lieutenant Revnes, the last surviving machine-gun officer, who was having his wounded ankle treated at the dressing station. Revnes was a "dark, handsome" man who had been an actor in civilian life. Despite a wound received early on, he had played an active and courageous role in the defense, moving about the perimeter to organize the troops and repel infantry attacks. His note mentioned the unmentionable: surrender. He used the word only to dismiss it—Whittlesey and McMurtry had made it clear that neither surrender nor retreat were acceptable. But he thought the enemy might allow the evacuation of the wounded if approached by a flag of truce.[31]

As practical advice the proposal was absurd. Why would the Germans permit evacuation when the presence of the wounded made the *Amerikanernest* less defensible, more prone to demoralization, and—in the event of a successful German assault—a substantial addition to their haul of prisoners? Despite Revnes's disavowal, his proposal made no sense except as a prelude to surrender. At best the note indicated resignation to impending defeat. An uncharitable reader might have suspected Revnes of seeking evacuation for himself, since he was one of the wounded. He had done his duty well and bravely so far, but every man has a breaking point.

Whittlesey went over to the aid station and spoke with Revnes. The conversation seeemed to buck up the lieutenant, but Whittlesey was more depressed and troubled when he returned. That one of his officers should need the cheer-up treatment was a sign of the command's weakening morale. They would have to do something to hasten their relief. The German lines were not continuous. If runners from the Pocket could work their way through a gap they could tell headquarters just what their situation was and guide reinforcements, resupply, even a relief column back through whatever holes in the wall they might have found.

McMurtry went to ask for volunteers, and eight men from his battalion and Holderman's company agreed: among them Jeremiah Healey who ran a New York perfume shop in civilian life, Newcom the Nebraska rancher,

Bob Yoder the Minnesota sharpshooter, Bill Begley from Brooklyn, and Frank Lipasti, usually identified as a "Wop" from New York but in fact one of the ex-miners from Butte. They crawled out into the flat swampy ground alongside Charlevaux Brook, a dark night and rain coming down. Suddenly a German rocket flare went up, caught Begley and Lipasti in the sudden blitz of light, and before they could hit the dirt machine gunners tore them up. The remaining six spread out and crawled down to the creek. German patrols stamped past overhead but missed them in the rain and dark. By blind chance four of them managed to take shelter in the same shell hole. Dawn was coming and they had not found a way through. They gave it up and crawled back to the Pocket.[32]

When Whittlesey made his morning inspection on October 7, he noticed that many of the men were using the early light and the absence of rain to write notes. They were necessarily brief because written on odd scraps of paper or torn-off shirttails, and not everybody had a pencil or pen and ink—some used a little blood from a pricked finger or a picked scab. They were mostly farewells, meant for parents or wives and children, and entrusted to an officer or to a buddy to be delivered just in case. It gave Whittlesey a mixed message: these men were not giving up, but they were not betting on their chances of survival either. Some did seem ready to surrender: Lieutenant Cullen reported nine of his men had deserted in the night. Then Healey and the others came in to report the failure of their attempt to slip by the Germans in the dark.

Whittlesey and McMurtry conferred: it might be easier to get a couple of men through by daylight than in the dark. The brush would provide cover enough, and the men could move faster if they could see where they were going. The major went to Holderman to see if he had any runners to recommend. Holderman told him Abe Krotoshinsky was the best possible man for the job.

To men like Whittlesey and Holderman Abe Krotoshinsky was the perfect physical embodiment of the eastern European Jewish racial type: "a little, stoop-shouldered Polish Jew . . . his uniform more than usually untidy. Pale, a long, hooked nose, not very erect posture." All of the physical and moral training of the Upton regime had been devoted to transforming such "slack-shouldered" alien specimens into proud, clean, upstanding Sons of Roosevelt. Apparently Krotoshinsky was a less apt pupil than some.

But Holderman trusted him as a runner, which meant that he had had the courage, the physical dexterity, and the brains to carry vital messages under fire—not only to deliver written messages, but to relay information by word of mouth, which required intelligence, the ability to understand, interpret, and accurately relay information given in few words under extreme stress. It is doubtful his officers knew much else about him: that he was not yet a citizen, but that his adopted country was "precious" to him; that he had a proud sense of himself as a Jewish man, as an American, and (if dreams come true) as a pioneer in a Jewish homeland. He had qualities shared by many of those who left the ghettos of Poland and Russia: the kind of self-respect, not easy for a Jew in those lands to have or preserve, that made him think he was entitled to live the life he desired. He would also have had the kind of courage and determination that enables a man to abandon all ties of family and culture, to commit himself to a life among strangers, to take whatever work comes his way, and to persist in his labors despite deep poverty, discrimination, an imperfect understanding of the language and customs. These qualities had gotten Krotoshinsky out of Plotzk ghetto, across the ocean to the Lower East Side, through Camp Upton, and into Captain Holderman's confidence.[33]

Whittlesey gave Krotoshinsky his instructions: get through to headquarters, tell them our condition, and guide them to us through the German lines. Two other men joined Krotoshinsky, and the three slanted off through the brush. A German machine gun seemed to pick up their movement almost immediately, but they were lost to view from the Pocket. Twenty minutes later the other two were back, one badly wounded. They didn't know if Krotoshinsky was alive or dead.

WHITTLESEY NOW TURNED to Lieutenant Gordon Schenck, Yale '13, one of the most active and effective of his officers. Could Schenck find more volunteers? Stanislaw Kozikowski, a Polish immigrant, and Clifford Brown, native-born and a devout Christian, agreed to go. Schenck told them to leave everything behind except their pistols, move cautiously, don't stop to fight, just keep moving and try to get through. He gave them his compass and told them to head north at first, cross the stream when they were nearly past Hill 198, then work their way across to where the 307th was supposed to be. Whittlesey told them: "Boys . . . you know our condition as well as I do. Tell them we have not surrendered and they are to reach us as soon as possible." Schenck escorted them out beyond the perimeter and got them started right. On his way back a trench mortar looped a shell into the position and Schenck took a steel splinter in the face. His loss hit Whittlesey and McMurtry hard: he had been one of the mainstays of the defense.[34]

Brown and Kozikowski were working their way forward when a noise from behind froze them. It was two men from C Company, who thought they were trying to sneak back to their own lines and wanted to go along. Kozikowski told them they'd have to follow at a distance, four men together was too much of a target. But the C Company men were too panicked, kept rushing to catch up, making noise enough to get them all killed. Finally the two messengers crawled aside and hid, let the others rush past and get themselves lost in the woods. Neither Kozikowski nor Brown ever saw them again, and they claimed not to have known their names.

SO LIEUTENANT CULLEN had been right in thinking some of the men were ready to desert. But the problem was not as widespread as he imagined. Of the nine men who had left his company in the night, none had deliberately surrendered themselves to the Germans or attempted to make their way back to the regiment. They were starving, there were dead Germans beyond the perimeter, and some might have rations on them or even a canteen of clean water. If you crawled off to search for them you weren't deserting, just trying to resupply so as to keep going, and if you got lucky you might even have enough to share with your platoon. Some of these men did get lucky and brought their finds back to the perimeter. Others found horrors: the burned bodies of two men in an outpost caught by the flamethrowers. Some were killed, like Private Henry Chinn, the lone Chinese-American in the command. Others were taken prisoner by the Germans, bandaged and fed, and taken to an intelligence officer, Leutnant Prinz, for interrogation.

German intelligence had been interrogating prisoners from the Pocket since October 4, but the captives had deliberately misled them. Lieutenant Harrington had told them there were two battalions in the Pocket, which was true, and added that they were at nearly full strength and well supplied with food and ammunition, which was a lie. When his interrogator remarked that most American troops were not that tough, Harrington agreed, but said that this outfit was from New York City and full of "gangster types," hard as nails. Leutnant Prinz thought he might have an easier time with the enlisted men. One of those "deserters" captured the night of October 6–7 was Lowell Hollingshead, who had been wounded in the leg before his capture. Prinz—who had worked for a time in Seattle—had the wounded American fed, bandaged, and brought to his warm bunker. After some polite conversation, to impress the private with the democratic manners of German officers, Prinz made a proposal. The Americans had done everything that could be asked of good soldiers and brave men, but their position was hopeless. The encircling forces now had been joined by a battalion of storm troopers with flamethrowers enough to incinerate the entire *Amerikanernest*. Prinz wanted to propose an honorable surrender to the American commander. Would Hollingshead take it? It was not dishonorable to do so: he would be saving lives, and medals were given to men who saved their comrades' lives, *nicht wahr*?

Hollingshead was a raw eighteen-year-old whose traditions of honor owed more to the schoolyard than the code of military honor to which Prinz referred. But he had also been imbued with the code of unit loyalty that held platoon and company together. His choice, as he thought it through, was between refusing the German's offer and going off to a POW camp where Germans would feed and protect him instead of trying to kill him or accepting the offer and going back to his buddies. Nothing was said about his having to return to the Germans once the message was delivered. Whether or not to accept the surrender offer was a problem for Whittlesey.

BACK IN THE Pocket Whittlesey and McMurtry redistributed their dwindling forces in anticipation of the afternoon attack, which always occurred punctually at 3 P.M. They were down to two machine guns and their last half-dozen or so boxes of ammunition. So many officers were dead or disabled they had to draw on noncoms to command companies and sectors, and felt fortunate that so many had shown themselves competent to command over the past few days. Among those who took charge of their units were Sergeants Roesch, Johnson, and Mynard, Corporal Klein of A Company, and Private Pollinger.[35] While they were at it, an outpost gave warning of a flag of truce out of the German position to the north, and here came Private Hollingshead, limping and leaning on the cane Leutnant Prinz had given him. He had a letter for the major, but McMurtry took it from him and grilled him on why he had left the perimeter. He was not pleased to hear that Hollingshead and several others had crawled out to try for one of those misdirected airplane parcels, but Whittlesey interrupted the dressing down: "George, let's look at the letter."

Prinz's spelling and grammar were a bit off the mark, but the letter was well designed. He first declared that the bearer had refused to answer questions after his capture, was bringing the letter against his will, "and is quite an honourable fellow, doing honour to his fatherland in the strictest sense of the word." It was important that it be understood that all parties here were men of honor, because Prinz needed to assure the Americans that their defense had fulfilled the requirements of honor. He informed the American commander that "it would be quite useless to resist any more in wiew [sic] of the present conditions." He appealed "to your human sentiments" to end the needless suffering of the men in the Pocket and averred that "your wounded man [i.e., men] can be heared over here in the German lines." Display of a white flag would be sufficient to show acceptance of the proposal. He closed by asking that Private Hollingshead be treated "as an honourable man. He is quite a soldier we envy you."

McMurtry and Holderman read the letter. The ex-Rough Rider grinned and said what all three were thinking: "We've got 'em licked! . . . Or they wouldn't have sent this!" If the Germans had the strength to simply overrun them, they would have done it. The talk of honor and humanity was guff, and the flattery of Hollingshead silly—as if the Americans did not know the quality of their own men. Yet there was a real choice here, and they all knew it. As Lieutenant Tom Pool, the Texan, would put it, this was *not* the Alamo or Little Big Horn, they did not face Crockett's or Custer's necessity of fighting to the death. This enemy would grant them mercy, and even a measure of honor. But there was never any discussion of surrender.[36]

The note did give them time to make final preparations. Read with the eye of a New York lawyer, it did not require the Americans to make a formal refusal, and Whittlesey would take full advantage of the loophole. He immediately ordered Corporal Baldwin to take in the white panels that had been set out (uselessly) to identify their position for the aircraft, then made his final dispositions for the attack.

Hollingshead went back to the funk hole he had abandoned the previous night, and rumor about the letter ran around the perimeter. In just about every one of the wet, malodorous funk holes the response was one of rage at the Germans. By proposing surrender—by presuming the Americans were the kind of men who would surrender—the Germans were mocking and ridiculing all the proof they had given, for nearly six mortal days and nights (not to mention the weeks and months before) of their valor, skill, loyalty to one another, and pride in the outfit. They might rationally have been angry at Whittlesey for getting them into this mess and keeping them in it when a word from him now could stop it. But there was no time for rational thought, and in any case it was nearly impossible under those conditions—days of fighting side by side to keep each other alive—to stand apart from the commander on whom they had come to depend. Perhaps later there would be second thoughts, but not now. Now the enemy was the man who had killed their comrades and tortured them with wounds and hunger and filth, then ridiculed their sacrifice, their suffering, and their small, hard-won triumphs.

Before the tonic of rage had worn off the Germans made their afternoon attack, an hour or so behind schedule. It was the heaviest yet, the storm trooper units as usual driving down through the trees and brush from the high ground to hit the right end of the perimeter front and flank, and now additional *Stosstruppen* were massed against the left flank, on the low ground south of the Roman road. They came in behind a barrage from the *Minenwerfer*, volleys of grenades, and flamethrowers. The Americans had only one machine gun at each end of the line and a clutch of Chauchat teams. On the right some of the storm troopers broke into Holderman's position; he was shot a third time but stayed on his feet and rallied his men, blazing away with his automatic pistol when the fighting came to close quarters. On the left, where McMurtry had charge of Companies B, C, and H, the German assault was driven to ground by gunfire, and while the enemy were in the open, caught between advance and retreat, the American troops heaved themselves out of their funk holes and staged a counterattack that killed the German commander and drove his troops back across the road in disorder.

It was a moment of inspiriting victory. But it was just a moment. Victory notwithstanding, they were still stuck in the mud with more dead and more wounded, and two hours hungrier than they were before. The overcast sky dimmed toward night, and the perennial chilling rain came with it. The men in the command post were exhausted. They had lost more officers and noncoms, even some of the newly made squad leaders. Holderman had another wound to be treated, and his old ones were rotten with gangrene; another day of heroism like the last might be beyond him. The medics Bragg, Sirota, and Gehris had collapsed from utter exhaustion. McMurtry was hurt. Teichmoller, the artillery observer, had terrible headaches from the concussion of a near miss—he was going deaf. A soldier crouched up to the Command Post and told McMurtry there was a Captain Somebody out on the road that wanted to talk with him.

Whittlesey was alert enough to guess what that must mean, but the others were too tired. The major took Cepaglia with him to see what it was about. Cepaglia wanted to know if it was safe to go out on the road, and Whittlesey said he supposed it was. They left.

It took McMurtry a couple of minutes to run through the conversation in his mind and figure out what was happening. Then he got up and limped as fast as he could the way Whittlesey and Cepaglia had gone. He found them out in the road, Whittlesey munching a sandwich with a lieutenant he had never seen before in an unbelievably clean uniform. But the sandwich! "For God's sake," cried McMurtry, "Give me a bite of that!"

The astonishingly clean lieutenant was Tillman of the 307th, leader of a relieving force from Houghton's command, and not far from him was the small, stoop-shouldered, long-nosed shape of Abe Krotoshinsky.

"You just step on my buddy again and I'll kill you": October 7–8

He had left the Pocket shortly after noon with his two companions, and almost immediately they had been fired at by a machine-gun nest. Krotoshinsky dived one way, the other men another—one of the latter was hit and they both returned to the Pocket. Krotoshinsky waited, gave the gunners time to calm down, congratulate themselves, begin to rest on their laurels. Then he began crawling, very low to the ground, very slowly, "an inch at a time," till he was clear of the zone the machine gun was likely to be covering. Then he went to a crouch and moved forward in zigzag dashes from cover to cover, pausing in each covert to listen to the whole landscape and then scan all around in quick stolen looks. It took hours for him to actually come up level with the machine-gun post, which he located by hearing the voices of the German soldiers chatting: it was so covered in heavy brush camouflage that the men in it could not see him off to the flank.

Another spell of crawling "an inch at a time," and then he went into the woods, crouching and dashing from cover to cover, there could be Germans anywhere, every other man who had tried to get through was dead, wounded, or a prisoner. "I remember crawling, lying under bushes, digging myself into holes." It was getting dark and starting to drizzle. Crawling blind through the brush, he suddenly found himself in a German post, enemy soldiers squatting on the ground in the dark smoking cigarettes. Krotoshinsky "hid under some bushes, lying prone and acting dead. A German, who, judging from the pressure, never knew anything about a reducing diet, stepped on one of my fingers, but I kept myself from making an outcry." He eased back into the woods and crawled on.

It was full dark now; he was no woodsman but his sense of direction was sound enough, and he went faster toward where the American lines must be. As he crouched in another empty German trench he heard voices, speaking American. "No music ever sounded better." Krotoshinsky hollered, and in a moment they were all around him, who was he, what was he doing out here, Krotoshinsky himself gabbling a little, hysterical with having somehow made it through to this impossible, this unreachable place from which they had been cut off it seemed forever. And he was dizzy with hunger; he hadn't eaten for four days and then the nightmare run through the woods—finally Bill Bergen, a Brooklyn boy, recognized him as "Abe Krotoshinsky from Company K."[37] They gave him coffee, which he gulped, and "corned willie," which he bolted down. The officer they had summoned came up while he was eating, and Krotoshinsky told him the situation briefly between gulps and bites: they had lost plenty of men, no food or water, Germans all around, "You should come right away."

"Can you lead us back?" the lieutenant wanted to know.

"Sure," said Krotoshinsky, "I feel good now." He grabbed up some extra rations and then led the way back into the woods.

The outfit he had contacted belonged to Houghton's 307th Infantry, part of the force under Lieutenant Tillman that had spent a night and most of the following day infiltrating small groups through the German wire on Hill 198. They made their move in the early evening of October 7, and this time the Germans on Hill 198 did not hold hard. Major Hünicken knew that the opportunity for overrunning the *Amerikanernest* had passed, that their whole force in the Argonne would be retreating, and he must extricate his men from between the Pocket and the main American forces.

But to the west La Palette was the anchor of the positions that covered

their retreat, and the Germans here refused to give ground to the supporting attacks made by the remnants of Knight's command and the Third
Battalion of the 308th. These troops ran into a line of enemy machine
guns that shot their advance into the ground. Sergeant Arthur Norwat,
the man who had taken over for the wounded Miles and held the captured
line at Revillon, tried to break the deadlock. "Norwat sprang to his feet in
full view of the enemy and opened fire with his automatic rifle. He continued to fire until he fell mortally wounded by many German bullets."
He had been Miles's top sergeant, "a very remarkable man. I have been
told he was of a strongly religious character. . . . He was posthumously
awarded the Distinguished Service Cross. He deserved more."[38]

The 308th was too weak to break through. But after dark Tillman and
his men from the 307th had only snipers to deal with as they felt their
way over Hill 198 and down to the road. They found Krotoshinsky as a
guide and on the way picked up Kozikowski and Brown as well. As they
reached the valley floor Tillman smelled something horrible, and it got
worse the farther he went, "a frightful odor of corruption, wounds and
death," the shit of sick and frightened men heaped six days deep in the latrines, the rotting bodies of men four, five, six days dead, the stench of
wounds going rotten with gangrene. In the dark and rain Tillman blundered into a funk hole and was nearly bayoneted by an American soldier.
"What's the matter with you?" Tillman wanted to know. They were on
the same side, weren't they? "I'm looking for Major Whittlesey."

"I don't give a damn who you are and what you want," the soldier
shot back, "You just step on my buddy again and I'll kill you."[39]

It was the definitive statement of what the defense of Charlevaux Mill
meant to the men who lived it. It wasn't about Foch's Grand Offensive,
or Pershing's determination that an independent American army make its
power felt, or the tactics that won the Meuse-Argonne. It wasn't about
the Fourteen Points, the World Safe for Democracy, and surely not "one
nation, one flag, one language." Once the fight began it was about the
loyalty of the men to one another, and to the units that through the long
days of training and combat had become their community, their tribe,
their family. Doesn't matter what uniform you're wearing or if you have
officers' bars on your shoulders: "You just step on my buddy again and
I'll kill you."

Behind Tillman came the relieving force from the 307th, and behind
them the detail carrying rations, and the medical units. Krotoshinsky

took a can of corned willie right over to the aid station and spoon-fed some to his buddy Fein. Then he went looking for the rest of his company, which was "certainly surprised to see me."

> I have been asked, just exactly what did they do? In the first place, let me say, they didn't cheer, despite what men may do in the movies under similar circumstances. In the war hardly anybody ever cheered. If they escaped death today, they figured they might not be so fortunate tomorrow. But to say the boys weren't happy was also not true. Their faces lit up; there was good spirit and optimism in the air.

Now that the crisis was over, "I had time to take stock of my disabilities. I discovered I was gassed and wounded, something to which I didn't pay attention before."[40]

It took all night to gather the wounded, there were hurt men hiding all over the place, it was hard for the medical details to ferret them out. Sick and wounded were carried out by stretcher details to where ambulances could pick them up, then to the narrow-gauge railroad that supplied the front, where they were loaded on open flatcars, still in the rain, waiting to be hauled off to the field hospitals. Rations came up, and the starving men bolted their corned willie, bread, butter, and syrup, then puked it all up again. Private John wolfed down a "big white onion," then some molasses and bread, then "prunes, tomatoes, spuds, rice and coffee a banquet if ever I looked at one. I would eat a few bites or rather gobble it down, then . . . run aside and I'd vomit it all up." They were billeted out of the rain, but he spent the night running to the latrine, "both ends operating." When he took his clothes off he snowed skin scales—the healed scabs of his measles. "Our underclothes were as stiff from dirt as if they had been starched."

By the chill light of another drizzly dawn the relievers could see what the battlefield looked like. It had been heavy second-growth woods when the battalions dug in on October 2. The forest "had been beaten into a perfect lumberyard, with trees hewn down and shivered to splinters by artillery fire." A marine captain's description of the aftermath of Belleau Wood approximates what Tillman would have seen in the Pocket:

> Day and night . . . men fought in its corpse-choked thickets, killing with bayonet and bomb and machine-gun. It was gassed and shelled and shot into the semblance of nothing earthly. The great trees were

down; the leaves were blasted off or hung sere and blackened. It was pockmocked with shell craters and shallow dugouts and hasty trenches. It was strewn with all the debris of war, Mauser rifles and Springfields, helmets, German and American, unexploded grenades, letters, knapsacks, packs, blanket, boots.

Later that morning Paul Knight and his scratch battalion from the 308th found their way to the Pocket by following the line of Whittlesey's runner-posts. The men he had left to man them were still there, their dead bodies "piled in threes, one across the other, with their shoes removed and their broken rifles beside them." Knight felt guilty for having failed to keep his promise to relieve Whittlesey, although he had done all that was possible. "We didn't do our job—didn't come up with them." They came to bury the dead, but were rewarded with the chance to do more. Knight heard a weak cry from among the heaps of bodies and found Private Lionel Bendheim, one leg smashed by a shell and rotten with gangrene, missed by the stretcher details as he lay unconscious. The medical corps would make good on Whittlesey's promise that he'd be enjoying the sun in the south of France while the rest of them were out in the cold rain, fighting their way through the Argonne toward the next line of German entrenchments. [41]

Whittlesey, McMurtry, and the men of the battalions who could still walk marched out of the Pocket and back to the reserve position, carrying their weapons. Only two of their original nine machine guns were left. Nearly three-quarters of the 675 men who had jumped off under Whittlesey and McMurtry on October 2 and Holderman on the third were either killed, wounded, or captured—a casualty rate of 72 percent. Fewer than two hundred of the survivors were still able to walk, and many of these would be invalided out to base hospitals as soon as the medical teams got a look at them.

They marched through the relieving troops and the medical and engineer details looking "neither right nor left. . . . 'When I looked into those eyes there was nothing I could say to them.' "[42]

Twenty-five years later, in another war, Ernie Pyle would have a similar reaction to the sight of troops coming off the line after several days in combat. "There is an agony in your heart and you almost feel ashamed to look at them. They are just guys from Broadway and Main Street, but you wouldn't remember them. They are too far away now.

They are too tired."[43] He understood that what they had been through had estranged them from everyone who had not been through it, estranged them even from the persons they had been before.

But Broadway and Main Street believed they *did* know these men and understood both their suffering and the meaning of their victory. The New York papers had already begun to transform their fight into a legend worthy of comparison with the Alamo, Custer's Last Stand, Gettysburg, and San Juan Hill. Like all such legends, the tale of the "Lost Battalion" would reflect a complex mixture of intentions and beliefs, of truth, speculation, and falsehood. It would become, in time, a significant addition to the lexicon of American national myths and mass culture fables; and it would make subtle but important differences in the heterogeneous culture of New York City. It would also help to destroy the peace of mind, and ultimately the life, of its greatest hero.

11

Print the Legend:

The "Lost Battalion" as Public Myth

> He climbed through darkness to the twilight air,
> Unloading hell behind him step by step.
>
> *—Siegfried Sassoon, "The Rear-Guard" (1917)*

For Whittlesey the battle survivor's estrangement of mind and personality began at the moment of relief. He and his men had been utterly immersed in the life and death struggle that filled the circumscribed world of the Pocket. The abrupt recovery of safety, the return of the larger world of the army and the war, was disorienting. Some were stunned, others giddy. Whittlesey's mood was precarious. An officer gave him a glass flask of whiskey and in his exhaustion he dropped and broke it—a comic accident, but it grieved him beyond all reason.

At that moment General Alexander appeared, tailed by a clutch of correspondents. The zone south of the Pocket was still under fire from the German rear guard on La Palette. Around them the survivors were being tended by medical personnel. Alexander's appearance was cause for uneasiness, but the presence of the correspondents was mystifying. Whittlesey could have no idea that his five-day battle had become a major news story and that he himself was on the verge of national celebrity.

There was an odd tension between Whittlesey and Alexander. The general had driven his subordinates ruthlessly for days, bawled out and relieved commanders who disappointed him. Perhaps he had come to interrogate Whittlesey and find fault with his conduct of an advance that had ended in near disaster. The major was also undoubtedly experiencing a wave of second thoughts about the decisions he had been making over the last six days. Even if he believed that they had won a victory—and he could not have been certain of that on October 8—he would have wondered whether it might have been won at lighter cost.

Alexander tried to put him at ease, informing him that he was promoted to lieutenant colonel. Damon Runyon, on the scene as a reporter for Hearst's *New York American*, heard Alexander tell him: "You are certainly a great anchor man for the division"—then add, somewhat ambiguously, that Whittlesey had had to fight them "where you were caught," which implied he had walked into a trap. Whittlesey made no answer beyond a "funny little smile." Alexander then looked around at the forest and quipped that he could see why the airplanes couldn't find the command. Zip Cepaglia, a city kid not in awe of shoulder straps, couldn't resist needling: "General, the artillery certainly found it."

"Oh no," Alexander responded, "that was French artillery." The remark told Whittlesey that Alexander did not want to admit that the Pocket had been fired on by the division's own artillery.

Alexander then left Whittlesey to tend his survivors and to deal with the reporters who were demanding interviews with the commander of the Lost Battalion. Whittlesey was extremely reticent, a quality most reporters accurately attributed to modesty. But his constraint also masked considerable stress. He was feeling the aftereffects of his ordeal and the growing awareness that the reality of his experience could never be fully communicated to those who had not shared it. All the survivors would have that feeling, but the implicit pressure to conceal the friendly-fire bombardment made it particularly painful for Whittlesey. He owed it to his men to tell the truth of their experience to the army and the public; but for the reputation of their division, and the good of the service to which Whittlesey had dedicated himself, he would have to repress or distort a significant element of that truth. He would also have to deny, implicitly or explicitly, the validity of that desperate dispatch he had sent with his last remaining pigeon: "Our own artillery is dropping a barrage directly on us." In his official report of the "Lost Battalion" (as even the army's investigators were now calling it), Whittlesey would declare his conviction that friendly fire had hit his position on October 4. But in public statements he made no mention of it, and he told those of his men who complained about Alexander's denial to let the matter go.[1]

The psychological strain was augmented by Whittlesey's own inevitable second-guessing of his command decisions. Although each choice had been based upon his best understanding of his orders and conditions on the field, the net result had been the isolation of his command and the loss of three-quarters of his men. Alexander had endorsed his actions by promoting him to lieutenant colonel. But then Alexander had suppressed the truth about the barrage to protect the division's reputation. Perhaps the promotion was just more whitewash, or a respectable cover for removing him from a front-line command.[2]

Whittlesey must have been aware that the regulars at corps and army headquarters were critical of his actions. Matters much more secret had been broadcast by rumor throughout the AEF. Reporter Thomas Johnson believed the staff at GHQ were disposed to "regard the siege as an unpleasant matter, to hush it up, gloss it over." An advance had been made, but in such a way that it could not be effectively supported. A large number of U.S. troops had been in imminent danger of destruction or surrender. The tactical plan for the second phase of the offensive had had to be altered to rescue them; and if the new plan produced a success, it had *not* yielded that decisive breakthrough Pershing had aimed for.

Some of the regulars' reaction reflected jealousy for Whittlesey's having received "Homeric honors for a grade of heroism not uncommon in the army." After all, he had not stormed a fortified line under fire, merely held on. It was hard to accept that a National Army officer, a Plattsburgh amateur, had conducted the advance and the defense with skill, good judgment, and proper notification of his position to headquarters— though that was precisely what Whittlesey had done. No formal criticism was ever levied, "it was merely in the air, existing as impalpably as an odor whose source cannot be traced." Under ordinary circumstances a court of inquiry would have examined the actions of all the participants, and many questions would have been settled by the reading of Alexander's orders. Alexander himself would have stated that Whittlesey had carried out his orders faithfully and correctly, and that if any blame attached to the cutoff it belonged to Alexander himself. That is what he said and wrote after the war, when interviewed about the Lost Battalion, but the words would have had more authority given under oath before a court of inquiry. However, no such court could have been convened in the closing months of 1918. The publicity given to the Lost Battalion made Whittlesey and his men heroes, and at a time when the

Meuse-Argonne campaign was getting nowhere at great cost, the army needed heroes. A court of inquiry would cause the public to question the legend of the Lost Battalion, even if in the end it exonerated Whittlesey. But the failure to hold a court left Whittlesey's own misgivings unresolved, with no way to defend himself against that "odor" of doubt that clung to his heroism.

Alexander's duplicity made questionable the honors that ought to have validated his sense of achievement, and the honors themselves estranged him from his comrades. On November 1 the same orders that returned the 308th to the front relieved Whittlesey and ordered him back to the States. He was going to receive the Medal of Honor, and the army wanted him to campaign for the Liberty Loan. Those orders separated him from the officers and men who knew and understood him best, who readily declared what they had already proved in action: that they would follow him anywhere. He was being sent away just as his men were returning to combat, which suggested that the army valued his celebrity more than his skill as a commander of troops.

But he would do for duty's sake what he did not want to do. First he had to stand awkwardly, smiling a small nervous smile, in front of the Signal Corps' still and movie cameras, posing with McMurtry and Alexander and one or two enlisted men—part of the publicity campaign that was already beyond his control. Then he shipped out for home. He would be accompanied by wounded officers from the division, including Captain Edward Harrigan, son of the famous Broadway entertainer. But Harrigan and the others had been relieved on account of wounds suffered in battle. Whittlesey was leaving the regiment because of an achievement whose value he questioned, to face a fame he did not want and a public celebrity for which he was temperamentally unsuited, bearing with him the survivor's guilt and unresolved doubts of a man who had led hundreds of his comrades to maiming or death.[3]

Politics Is (Not) Adjourned: The Lost Battalion Story and the Politics of Peacemaking, October–December 1918

The newspaper version of the story that would become known as "The Lost Battalion" began with a few brief and somewhat obscure bulletins published on October 1, followed over the next four weeks by a crescendo of news stories, features, interviews, and editorials that transformed Charlevaux Mill into a "last stand" worthy of inclusion in national mythology, alongside the Alamo, Little Big Horn, Pickett's Charge, and San Juan Hill. In November stories of greater importance pushed the Lost Battalion off the front pages: the surrender of Germany's allies, the decisive British breakthrough in Flanders, the bloody northward slog of the AEF through the Meuse-Argonne to Sedan. But the story of Charlevaux Mill periodically revived as new anecdotes of heroism and suffering were uncovered by reporters. The remarkable impact of the story, and its staying power—especially in the New York papers—derived from its combination of an extraordinary military episode with elements symbolic of some of the deepest concerns of contemporary politics. The performance of Whittlesey's men spoke directly to the issue of Americanism, proving that the hyphenates of the city slums were not "unfit spawn," slackers, or proto-Bolsheviki, but "100% Americans," as fit as any Sons of Roosevelt. But in October 1918 its chief interest was Whittlesey's display of uncompromising toughness, which seemed to many a symbolic answer to the central questions of the hour: How should the war be prosecuted, and what form should a peace settlement take?

Earlier in the war President Wilson had appealed for bipartisan support by declaring "politics is adjourned" for the duration, and Republicans in Congress had responded with support for his war measures. But the "adjournment" masked real disagreements about the conduct of the war and Wilson's design for peace, as set forth in the Fourteen Points. These offered an ambitious and idealistic vision of a future international order, based on a League of Nations; but they ignored, and in some cases contradicted, the stated policy of the Allies. Although they called for German withdrawal from all occupied territory, they made no reference to reparations and offered no plan for preventing a revival of German militarism. Wilson's support for the national rights of subject peoples and small nations was explicitly aimed at Austria-Hungary and Turkey, but also threatened the territorial and colonial ambitions of the British, French, and Italians. Roosevelt and the congressional Republicans were opposed to Wilson's policies for achieving and ordering the peace, but masked their criticism as support by advocating war more sternly than the president. Where Wilson could legitimately be suspected of wanting a negotiated "peace without victory," they demanded a "victory peace," imposed after a conclusive triumph on the battlefield and German surrender on the Western Front. Roosevelt and Lodge were both on record supporting the idea of a League of Nations. But where Wilson envisioned an organization with supranational powers founded on international law, Lodge and Roosevelt preferred something like a perpetual "entente" of the existing Great Powers. These would divide the world by agreement into spheres of influence, within which each power would protect commerce and maintain order. However, the ultimate guarantor of peace would be the "perpetual preparedness" of each power to defend itself against any other.

In August it was assumed that Germany could not be defeated before the summer of 1919, so the political contest over peace terms did not seem urgent. But the opening of Foch's grand offensive on September 26 was followed by a rapid sequence of events that showed victory was imminent. On September 29 Bulgaria broke with the Central Powers and withdrew from the war. Austria-Hungary, faced with mass starvation and the political defection of its constituent nationalities, opened negotiations on October 2. With the defeat of its armies in Mesopotamia and the Levant, Turkey also sued for peace. There was a political overturn in Germany as well: on October 4 the Kaiser appointed Prince Max of Baden to head a new liberal cabinet, signaling a willingness to "democratize" the imperial government—one of the preconditions for peace set by President Wilson. Prince Max immediately sent a secret note to Wilson, asking for a negotiated peace on the basis of the Fourteen Points—an admission that German leaders believed themselves on the brink of defeat and an invitation to the American president to assert his primacy in the alliance. For Roosevelt, the fact that "the Central Powers show a greedy eagerness to accept the so-called fourteen points" was a sign that its principles must be inimical to true Americanism, and "every decent American ought to be against it."[4]

It was in the midst of the burgeoning controversy over Wilson's plans for peace that news of the Lost Battalion reached the States. Prince Max's dispatch was received on October 4 while Whittlesey was scrawling his last pigeon message, "For heaven's sake, stop it." The papers got hold of the "German note" on October 8, the day the Pocket was relieved; and the first big wave of Lost Battalion stories coincided with the beginning of Roosevelt's campaign against the Fourteen Points. Reporters, editorialists, and politicians would find in this dramatic episode a storehouse of useful symbols for interpreting the political choices before them.

The scene was set by a first wave of stories that were published October 1–3. Wilbur Forrest of the *Tribune* described the Argonne Forest fighting as a "Duel in a Dark Room." Edwin James's page-one story in the *Times* said Argonne was the "toughest slice of the toughest job" faced by the AEF and told how "New York Boys Cut Their Way Through Miles of Wire in Night Battle in Woods . . . plugging [through] wire, stone, [and] wood" to get at the enemy. Don Martin of Pulitzer's *World* said the Upton men were fighting against the best of the German troops, in an "Argonne Jungle" sown with mines and booby traps.[5]

Martin was ill, perhaps with the influenza that had already reached epidemic levels in the States, but he got close enough to the front to get himself gassed. The troops he interviewed had been fighting in the lead-up to Whittlesey's cutoff at L'Homme Mort. His story was probably sent on September 29 or 30 and published on October 2. The Americanization of immigrant soldiers was his theme. Private Isidor Berkowitz told Martin how he and his buddies worked an ambush. Martin highlighted this welcome evidence of Jewish patriotism and soldierly virtue by the contrasting portrayal of "a negro from Virginia," met at a field hospital, who was glad to be out of the fighting because "I'm jes natu'lly a peaceful nigger." Martin's ridicule reminds the reader of the racial bottom line against which any ethnic group's Americanism will be measured. Martin also wanted to show that melting pot soldiers preferred Roosevelt's ruthlessness to Wilson's moderation in making war and concluding peace. In interviews, he elicited their endorsement of the principles expressed in General Alexander's General Orders No. 27 and likened them to Roosevelt's demand that people who indulge in "peace talk" or refuse to subscribe to the Liberty Loan be treated as traitors.[6]

Martin's major contribution to the Lost Battalion legend was the subsection of his story headlined "Desperate Fighting by Whittlesey Unit." He got the story at Division from press liaison Captain Ernest Dupuy, probably on September 30, before the relief of Whittlesey's command at L'Homme Mort. Since the story would appear on October 3, while Whittlesey's command was digging in at Charlevaux Mill, this became (for the reading public) the first episode in the saga of the Lost Battalion. Dupuy was a writer himself, and he gave Martin the kind of copy a New York paper would want. Whittlesey's men "went over in a dash that was a race, and in that race were men of Irish, Italian and of Jewish blood. They plunged into the forest just as our forefathers did when they won our land from the red men, and they fought Indian fashion." His description not only praises the "races" of the melting pot as loyal Americans and good soldiers, it links them to the primal myth of American nationality, the myth of the frontier, and to heroes of wilderness race war like Boone, Crockett, Custer, Cody, and Roosevelt.

That was Martin's last contribution. His illness exacerbated by the poison gas he inhaled, he was evacuated to a hospital and died a few days later. By then other reporters were on the story. Wilbur Forrest of the *Tribune* extended Martin's frontier metaphor: "New Yorkers Hack [Their] Way Into Forest of Wire" that is "worse than was ever faced by America's earliest pioneers who, armed with axes, hewed their way through the dense forests of the West against the Redskins." The hyphenates of New York's mean streets become, through the transforming effect of war, legitimate descendants of the pioneer settlers who reclaimed the West from savagery. However, their leaders are not frontier plebians, but capitalists, "men who occupied stools in brokers' offices," who had followed the prescription of the Strenuous Life and recovered the heroism of "pioneer" ancestors by reenacting their deeds.[7]

The first detailed stories about Charlevaux Mill began to appear on October 9 and 10, as reporters at division HQ filed dispatches on the successful relief: "American Battalion, Lost 5 Days, Rescued" (*American*); "Rescue U.S. Troops Lost for Five Days in Argonne Forest" (*Herald*); "Battalion, Cut Off in Woods, Rescued" (*World*); "Americans Exhausted After Four-Day Siege" (*Times*); " 'Lost Unit' Lived on Leaves" (*Tribune*). The *Times* called their fight "one of the classics of the war," the *Tribune* said the men were "infinitely proud of their gallant stand," and other stories referred to the battalion as "famous." That was certainly true in France, where rumors about its fate had made Whittlesey's command the focus of concern throughout the AEF. Most civilian readers in the United State had had little preparation for such an announcement, though "famous" would have whetted their appetites for a great story to come.[8]

These initial stories withheld the name of the division involved, in obedience to censorship. But on October 10 the *World* identified Whittlesey as commander of the unit, which "Leads Many to Believe Troops Belonged to the 77th New York." Thus without violating censorship the paper was able to claim the heroic stand for the hometown boys.

However, the *World* editorialists seem not to have read their own news story. They attributed the success of the Lost Battalion to its being composed of "ignorant farm boys" who felt at home in the woods. Without hard information it still seemed natural to assume that a typical American outfit would be manned by native-born farmers rather than hyphenates out of the mean streets.[9]

As the truth became clear there was a sudden enthusiastic turn toward celebration of the melting pot principle. That was the theme of the most colorful and influential account of the Lost Battalion, written by Damon Runyon and published in the *New York American* on October 13. Runyon was Hearst's most popular columnist, a Colorado-born newspaperman and short-story writer who was already renowned as the quintessential New Yorker, connoisseur of the city's varied high and low life, its style, its vernacular. Hearst sent him to France as a special correspondent, and Runyon's celebrity won him privileged access to cable facilities and general officers—General Alexander for one, who took Runyon along when he went up to meet Whittlesey's survivors. "Out of the fog of fighting that hangs over the Forest of the Argonne came limping to-day Whittlesey's battered battalion which made the epic defense in the dark glades beyond." Runyon reminds his readers how hapless these men appeared back in the summer of 1917 as they made their "straggling" parade up Fifth Avenue to catch the train for Camp Upton. He admits having had some fun at their expense. But the Lost Battalion changed all that. "The big town's polyglot population" had provided the "heroes of one of the Homeric fights of the war." They had fought the "Modern Battle of the Wilderness" and proved themselves worthy heirs of the men who had fought for the Union. The Argonne Forest would be forever known as the place "where Whittlesey's lost legion made its immortal battle. . . . Out of this scullery of war the American infantryman is emerging as the greatest fighter the world has ever seen."[10]

The Lost Battalion had vindicated the Americanism of the immigrants in general, and of easten European Jews in particular. The *New York Globe* identified the 77th not only as "a Yaphank division," but as "an eastside division, and to be even more explicit a Yiddish division." It embellished the legend by asserting that Whittlesey (like Travis at the Alamo) had consulted his men on their response to the German surrender note. "Major Whittlesey read the message to his men, and they shouted their rejection so loudly that the Germans thought they must be welcoming succoring reinforcements." This proved that "the division was a democratic one," a perfect embodiment of civic nationalism. As a result of living in such a republic, and serving in such a division, the Yiddish immigrants had been transformed into proud, virile Sons of Roosevelt:

> In less than a generation the Russian Jew has got out of his soul the consequences of centuries of tyranny and oppression. He went into the melting pot with many fears clouding his spirit; he emerges a full-grown man, who looks with level and unlowered eyes at the arrogant Prussian. No more satisfying proof of the essential soundness of American political and social institutions was ever given than is furnished by the behavior of this east-side battalion. America makes men. . . . By a clever alchemy America transmutes blighted raw material into men. Herein is our true glory, and to save the foundations of this glory men of every known race and accent are on the battle line of liberty on the frontiers of freedom.

The tale of the Lost Battalion is therefore a rebuke to the prejudices that would have excluded Jews as a race incapable of Americanization:

> If it had been said a year ago that the rather undersized tailors, factory workers, pushcart men, clerks, etc., then crowding the east side's streets would be capable of such a feat smiles of incredulity would have spread over many countenances. The Yiddishers fight like wildcats? Nonsense! It was not in them. But they did. Belittlers will please pass out by all exits.

The *American Hebrew* demanded to know "Who, ever again, would dare hold up to scorn the fighting capacity of the downtown New York Jew. . . . The Yiddish Battalion is showing the spiritual stuff of which the erstwhile needleworkers, peddlers, and ghetto dreamers are made. . . . The East Side Jews are fighters, no mistake about it."[11]

Lower East Side Jews had been treated as symbolic surrogates for the supposed defects of the new immigrants, so the heroism of the Yiddish Battalion redeemed the reputation of the whole melting pot. The *Times* editorial of October 14, "The Red Badge of Courage," declares that the 77th Division has answered the questions about the immigrant "races." We knew we could count on the "old American stock" for valorous performance in the field. Now the army's list of recipients of the DSC shows many "names [that] come out of the melting pot," proving the new "stocks" equal to the old.

The redemption of the East Side Jew in the court of public opinion was seemingly clinched by the emergence of a hero to symbolize the valor of the "race." Private Abraham Krotoshinsky would be remembered fifty years later as the city's greatest hero of the First World War. Whittlesey and Holderman recommended him for the DSC, and the text of his citation made the press aware that the "little stoop-shouldered Polish Jew" had brought rescue to the Lost Battalion. The *Times* devoted a whole editorial to him. Krotoshinsky "volunteered for a service which seemed certain death," as runner after runner had been killed. The editorial associates him with heroes of the War for the Union, but its highest praise is to compare him with a pair of Rough Riders at San Juan Hill, cited by Colonel Roosevelt for carrying messages under fire less intense and deadly than that faced by the little Jewish barber. "The private from the Bronx is now numbered among the bravest of the brave, who was captain of his soul and dared all for love of his comrades." British officers found that the war had undone the premises of their class system, by revealing superb officer material among the lower classes. In the United States race and ethnicity are the equivalent of class, and Krotoshinsky's heroism is a similar rebuke to prejudice. "So you never know . . . about the stock and names of heroes-to-be . . . especially when fifty nationalities leap from the melting pot at the call to arms. If the great war has proved anything, it is that men of all races and from all climes are brave to a fault, and that heroes may wear unfamiliar names: the name of Abraham Krotoshinsky, for instance."[12]

But the real hero of the Lost Battalion was Major Whittlesey, whose "Coolness Saved Surrounded Troops." He was the man in command, he belonged to a prominent old family, and as a lawyer-turned-soldier embodied the citizen-soldier ideal. An interview with his uncle, also named Charles Whittlesey, began the process of setting before the public his personality, with all its fascinating paradoxes: "He is the last man in the world we expected to do something heroic in this war . . . a very quiet fellow—shy you would call him—and he detested any form of publicity." Uncle Charles added that Whittlesey "often said he did not believe in war," yet had been among the first to enlist for Plattsburgh. Damon Runyon presented the commander of the Lost Battalion as a candidate as unlikely for heroism as any of his men, "a man who only a short time ago was a New York lawyer . . . a tall, lean-flanked fellow, around forty years old." (He was in fact just thirty-seven.) What struck Runyon was his "funny, little smile." He saw it first in the immediate aftermath of the relief, when General Alexander greeted "the New Yorker" with soldierly praise: " 'You are certainly a great anchor man for the division.' " In Runyon's telling, that smile becomes the silent signature of a will so adamant it needs no words to make itself plain.

That image of a modest peace-loving hero was transformed when reporters found out about his rejection of the German note carried by Private Hollingshead. As the *World* had it, when the Germans asked his surrender, " 'Go to Hell,' Replies Major Whittlesey" and the rest of the "Lost Battalion Jeers Germans Who Tried to Induce them to Surrender." The *Tribune* headlined the story, " 'Go to Hell!' Lost Battalions [*sic*] Answer to Huns' 'Surrender!' " Its reporter thought Whittlesey's answer was "the brightest spot in the heroic and amazing story, as yet untold, of the now famous 'lost battalion.' " The *Herald* used the same AP text as the *Tribune*, but its editor transforms Whittlesey's answer into a battle cry: " 'Go to Hell!' Shouts Major of 'Lost Battalion,' " and the words reflect his "grim determination to hold out to the last man." The *Herald* version had Whittlesey pausing briefly, perhaps for dramatic effect, before answering; but the *American* preferred to think "Major Whittlesey did not hesitate a fraction of a second" before telling the Germans to go to hell.[13]

It was a wonderful story that had no basis in fact. The reporters who told it had not spoken to Whittlesey himself, nor to anyone who was with him in the Pocket. The source seems to have been Alexander. When asked how Whittlesey had replied to the surrender demand, he answered offhandedly that the major had told them to go to hell. The reporters mistook figurative for literal and reported it in good faith. Its effect was to make Whittlesey's role in the battle more dramatic, even as it falsified both his actual response and the personality behind it. Only Damon Runyon got the story right. "It would make this story more dramatic to say that Whittlesey sent back some stirring phrase" in response to the German note. But "as a matter of fact he merely smiled his funny little smile . . . tucked the paper away in his pocket," and answered the Germans with bullets. When Runyon asked whether he had told them go to hell, Whittlesey said no, but allowed that "it covered his thoughts at the time."

The "Go to hell" scene was too good to be undone by mere truth. Despite the popularity of Runyon's work, despite Whittlesey's own denials, "Go to hell!" became the signature quotation of the Lost Battalion. Thus the *Times* on October 12 editorialized that the tale of "The Lost Battalion . . . touches the pride of the people of this city" and added that "the bit of profanity in the story not even the most pious American would have deleted." Newspapers across the country picked up the moment and the phrase, and played it according to their sense of the occasion. Most agreed with the *New York Globe*, which predicted that "the young major's classic reply . . . will go down into history as one of the most picturesque incidents of the war." The glorification of the episode went so far that a number of Christian newspapers and journals expressed concern that wartime emotions were creating "a state of mind that will make profanity popular." Though most agreed that the crimes of the Kaiser could not be properly characterized without resort to strong language, they hoped that with peace such "war expletives" would disappear from usage: "Swearing at the Kaiser is not the ultimate exemplification of loyalty, and profanity is not a synonym for patriotism. The wide prevalence of this vicious habit may reveal commendable intensity of conviction, but it also reveals a reprehensible forgetfulness of fundamental religious principles." A Boston religious paper asserted that the hard language of soldiers in past ages reflected a lower stage of moral evolution: "He who swears, even mildly, is at war with humanity. Any first-class psychology will tell you this. . . . General Pershing does not swear; he used to in moderation, but he quit it." But the *Literary Digest* found Whittlesey innocent of any impropriety. Their reporter interviewed his Irish landlady, who said that in ordinary life the major "never was a swearing man."

> "Not a single oath have I heard from him in the seven years he lived here," she declares, "and I've seen him looking for a collar-button at that. But you wouldn't call his remark to the Germans swearing exactly— would you, now? It was just what I would call very good advice."[14]

The concerns of Christians notwithstanding, most commentators praised the tone of Whittlesey's profane defiance, because "Go to Hell" Whittlesey symbolized the "hard war, hard peace" values for which Theodore Roosevelt and his allies had been contending. Even Willis J. Abbot, whose weekly analysis of strategy appeared in the *American*, contrasts Whittlesey's response to Leutnant Prinz's "German note" with Wilson's response to Prince Max. Where Wilson temporized, Whittlesey's response was instinctive and immediate: " 'Go to hell!' he shouted . . . with cheers his men took up again that seemingly hopeless defense. . . . 'Go to hell!' . . . In such spirit the American people are inclined to treat the German overtures."[15]

Whittlesey's apocryphal reply chimed perfectly with the hardening of the public mood. The passions roused by the administration's own propaganda, by its toleration and sometimes active promotion of vigilantism against critics and opponents, could not be held within the limits the president preferred. The vision of a negotiated "peace without victory" was becoming more impossible, as each day of stubborn German resistance brought longer and longer casualty lists to the pages of newspapers across the country. If Wilson articulated the reasoned hopes of American liberals, Roosevelt voiced the angry passions of a nation absorbed by strife. On October 15 Roosevelt made a major address, asserting that "Permanent Preparedness" for war was preferable to a League of Nations as the basis of a postwar order. There was, said Roosevelt, "very grave danger that this country will be cheated out of the right kind of peace if our people remain fatuously content to accept high-sounding phrases of muddy meaning." Of the Fourteen Points he declared, "I gravely doubt whether a more silly or more mischievous plan was ever seriously proposed by the ruler of a great nation." It would allow German militarism to survive, and by resting the peace on a "scrap of paper" rather than preparedness would allow any sufficiently "ruthless and efficient nation" to trample the rights of weaker powers with impunity. The only way to avert a pro-German peace was to elect a Senate willing to reject a Wilsonian peace treaty. On October 22 he called on the public to treat the midterm election as a referendum on Wilson and his policies, and "send to Washington public servants who will be self-respecting Americans and not rubber stamps" in the president's hands.

Wilson rose to the bait. In addition to concern over Republican opposition, he had begun to appreciate the difficulties he would have with Allied leaders in settling terms of peace. He believed he needed a stronger and more explicit popular mandate in order to maintain his control of events. On October 25 he called upon "My Fellow Countrymen" to endorse his leadership by "returning a Democratic majority to both the Senate and the House of Representatives." Although the Republican minority had been "unquestionably . . . pro-war" they had also been "anti-administration." If Wilson was to "continue to be your unembarrassed spokesman in affairs at home and abroad" he needed the "unmistakable" endorsement of a Democratic sweep in the 1918 elections.[16]

Wilson's abrogation of his own adjournment of politics proved a serious mistake. It freed elected Republicans to join Roosevelt in open attacks on the administration and allowed them to blame Wilson himself for the reversion to partisan politics in wartime. TR led the attack and the front page of the *Times* treated it as the opening of a second front: "Roosevelt Bitter in Beginning War on the President." He told a cheering audience in Omaha that he didn't want this fight to end on a decision: he wanted a "knockout," so that no other nation would dare to "look cross-eyed at us."[17]

The election results were a stunning rebuke to Wilson. Both houses returned Republican majorities. Roosevelt was once again a power within his party and a possible contender for the Republican nomination in 1920. But Wilson refused to read the result as repudiation. Encouraged by the celebrations that followed the Armistice on November 11, he showed his determination to control events by taking personal charge of the negotiations at Versailles and refusing to work with the incoming Republican leadership. Thus the partisan contest between advocates of Wilson's Fourteen Points and of Roosevelt's "victory peace" continued beyond the election.

Lieutenant Colonel Charles Whittlesey stepped into the middle of that debate when he landed in New York on November 14, 1918, one week after the election and three days after the Armistice.[18] Although he missed the raucous street celebrations, he was one of the first heroes of the AEF to return, and since the hometown whose name he had glorified was New York City he suddenly found himself one of the most famous men in the country. Of all the Plattsburgh alums he would seem to have come the closest to fulfilling the Rooseveltian ideal: the man of thought and moral conviction becoming the effective man of action. But the positions he espoused differed in tone and content from Roosevelt's strident advocacy of a hard peace, a nationalist foreign policy, and "100% Americanism." He had been a Socialist in 1912, an antiwar Wilsonian in 1916, a soldier because his sense of duty outweighed the personal morality that rejected war. Like Wilson he thought the only justification for war was to create a world order that would make war impossible. Yet a phrase he had never spoken had made him a symbol of Roosevelt's "hard war, hard peace" platform.

He was besieged by interviewers, but few of their questions solicited information about the fighting. His interlocutors had read so many reports of the battle they were confident they knew the whole story: how the men had hacked their way through barbed-wire thickets, circumvented ambushes that would have daunted Hawkeye, dashed recklessly headlong into the midst of their enemies, lived on dead leaves and puddle water, fought to the last bullet. What they most wanted to hear was how Whittlesey had felt when he answered the German demand for surrender by shouting, murmuring, or hissing through clenched teeth, "Go to hell!"

He did not realize at first how those words would haunt him. The week after his return he was honored in a ceremony at the Williams College Club in New York. In his first public appearance he wanted to praise the "Upton men." It had been an "honor" to command them; they were "the souls of honor and courage." He spoke of them not as immigrants or hyphenates, but as Americans: they "went to France as plain Americans, but after a few months of active service they gained a new outlook on life." The army had given them a deeper understanding of their nation's ideals; but it had also *internationalized* them, given them a broader appreciation of their country's potential role among the nations. That was why he—and they—supported Wilson's League of Nations.

It was a serious discourse that addressed the two major issues of the moment, peace and the immigration question—but then an elderly alum jumped up and interrupted with a yell: "Did you really tell them to go to hell?" According to the reporter on the scene, "Whittlesey, with a smile, replied: 'You just bet I did!'"

It was the only public occasion on which he did not answer that question with a firm denial. In that collegiate setting he accepted it in the spirit of good fellows sharing a joke, a comic exaggeration. But the incident was symptomatic of his fate. The phrase and the heroic figure it evoked were too perfect a symbol to be discredited by mere fact. The *Times* rated the "Lost Battalion's Defiance Shouted by Whittlesey" as one of the signature phrases that would define the Great War, along with Wilson's "world made safe for democracy," Pétain's "They shall not pass," and Pershing's "Lafayette, we are here." Their reporter did not think Whittlesey had actually said those words, but did not see that as diminishing their value for the nation's memory of the world war.[19]

The story of that profane defiance lived on, and nothing he later said could convince the public he was *not* "Go to Hell" Whittlesey. Worse, nothing he said that was not in the militant go-to-hell vein would be attended to or remembered—which was too bad, because he had some valuable things to say about "racial" and class differences, and about the criminal absurdity of a politics based on war. He would have preferred some truer fame, or (best of all) no fame whatsoever. But not only was fame inescapable, it was his duty to make use of it on behalf of the causes in which he was enlisted: the support of the army and Liberty Loan, and winning public appreciation for the service and sufferings of his men.

Whittlesey's prominence also made him vulnerable to the sort of second-guessing that would play upon his own self-doubts. Within the large chorus of praise were strains that implied criticism of his leadership. The *American*'s first report on the incident asserted that "the 'lost battalion' pushed ahead" of its supports and was surrounded because its leaders "were not used to forest warfare." The *Times* said it was the "eagerness" of the major and his men that led them into the "trap the Germans had set for them." It praised them for a deed, which "touches the pride of the people of this city," but added that "the truth was that the 'lost battalion' had blundered . . . through excessive ardor." That suited the paper's desire to see the battle as vindication of the martial spirit of the city's immigrant sons: "Though the tactics of these men of the National Army may have been crude," their "heroic resistance" proved that "when they have had more experience . . . they will be invincible." The unintended consequence of this proof was to suggest that Whittlesey had shown a lack of judgment in leading them into the Pocket.[20]

Whittlesey was trapped in a false position, in which his public role was increasingly at odds with his private understanding of the truth. The "Go to hell!" legend falsified his temper and his words, but that was trivial compared with what he saw as the falsification of the battle and the war. He knew the defense of the Pocket had not been the heroic adventure the press made it out to be, but a terrible, perhaps unnecessary, and quite possibly pointless ordeal. The praise for his supposed headlong attack, which the public saw as heroism, was for Whittlesey an aspersion of his military judgment and food for his own doubts about his conduct of the battle. But his sense of duty, and of obligation to the men who had served and suffered with him, prevented his speaking the full truth. To expose the fatal error of the friendly-fire bombardment, and with it General Alexander's cover-up, would discredit the army to which he owed both loyalty and obedience. To voice his second thoughts about his own decisions, or about the military value of the losses his men incurred, would tarnish the glory his men had earned by their suffering—and tarnish it at a moment when, as Whittlesey had reason to know, the loyalty of their ethnic communities was still under suspicion. So he was isolated in his false position and unable to abandon it, a psychological equivalent of the Pocket to which no relieving force would ever come.

During November or December he probably went home to see his family in Pittsfield. In early December Congress voted him the Medal of Honor, which called up another reprise of the Lost Battalion/"Go to Hell" legend. The award was made on Boston Common just before Christmas 1918, the medal draped around his neck by the former commander of the 26th "Yankee" National Guard Division, who told him "your act thrilled the entire American Expeditionary Force." At that same ceremony he was formally mustered out of service. (The rest of the 77th Division were still overseas and would not return till May.)

Now a civilian, Whittlesey made a round of public appearances in which he spoke more openly of his political views. In January he gave a major speech to a packed house at New York's Church of the Ascension. Speaking as a combat veteran, he declared that the men who had actually served in France did not share the "radical" spirit of the home front—by which he meant the extreme hostility to all things German and the wish to impose a punitive peace on Germany. Whittlesey asserted that "however radical a man might have been when he first went over," however deeply he might have hated Germans and Germany, "his experiences in the war had given him a broader outlook." Battle had taught him to see the enemy soldier as a man like himself, perhaps the agent of a wicked government, but still a man whose rights and dignity deserved respect. It followed that the best peace would be a negotiated peace, of the kind Wilson had sought back in 1917: a peace maintained by a League of Nations in which Germany would participate, rather than a punitive peace imposed by the victors. Whittlesey warned that "anything said or done in malice against the German people would surely react against American civilization." That was a rebuke to the malicious anti-Germanism with which Roosevelt and his allies belabored Wilson's foreign policy.

It was perhaps in this speech, or another given at about the same time, that Whittlesey also addressed the "Americanization" issue, explicitly praising his Jewish soldiers for their courage and loyalty to their adopted nation. His intervention was timely, and much appreciated by Jewish-American leaders. That anti-German malice of which he had spoken had already reacted against American civilization, spreading to other groups suspected of dissidence or alienation from "100% Americanism:" first socialists, labor radicals, pacifists, then "hyphenated Americans" and immigrants in general. After December 1918 the primary targets of that malice were the eastern European Jews from the Lower East Side. Just as they had been identified with with "pro-Germanism" and Socialism in 1917, so now they were identified with Russian Bolshevism—and not merely as sympathizers, but as the primary instigators and agents of a revolution that aimed at the destruction of Western civilization.[21]

"Are Lenin and Trotsky Yiddish?": The Anti-Immigrant Reaction, December 1918–February 1919

> More than half the agitators in the so-called Bolshevik movement were Yiddish . . . standing on the benches and soap boxes . . . talking until their mouths frothed. . . . I do not want to be unfair to them, but I usually know a Jew when I see one.
>
> —*Testimony of Rev. George Simons, Senate Judiciary Subcommittee, February 12, 1919*

American participation in the Great War had demonstrated the nation's ability to contend in a world of Great Powers, but destroyed the nation's sense of immunity to threats from beyond the oceans. The events that forced us into the conflict were proof of our vulnerability to foreign powers, and victory did not diminish that sense of exposure. Kaiserism had transmogrified into the greater menace of Communism—Lenin was seen as a German agent and Marxism as the offspring of German *Kultur*. The Russian Soviets could deploy against the West both the conventional resources of a Great Power and the unconventional weapon of revolutionary agitation. With their socialist credentials and record of opposition to the war, Communists seemed likelier than the Kaiser's secret agents to succeed in "subverting" American industrial workers, Negroes, and the hyphenates of the urban slums. It was a moment of precarious social balance. There was widespread concern that the transition from war to peace would derange the economy. Labor militancy was on the increase, driven by price inflation and fear of unemployment, as war industries closed and millions of doughboys came home looking for work. But some labor agitation took a radical and even revolutionary line, as the apparent triumph of socialism in Russia aroused unrealistic expectations of a successful workers' movement in the United States.[22]

In November 1918 the *Literary Digest* had been sure that America was immune to the Bolshevik virus, because nearly all Americans belonged to the decent, literate, property-loving classes. By January 1919 it saw Bolshevism as "without exaggeration . . . the end of civilization," and the United States as vulnerable to infection because of the large percentage of poor, uneducated, and incompletely Americanized workers. The editors were alarmed by the report of the U.S. Army's IQ tests, which revealed that a large percentage of "American soldiers . . . cannot read or write." The *Digest* put part of the blame on poor support for public education, but most of it on the toleration of teaching in languages other than English, which fostered "the rank growth of separatism . . . hyphenism, disloyalty."

> It is in this illiterate, ill-formed element, especially in that part of it which comes from foreign lands and herd together in this country, clinging to their Old World ideas and customs, that there is danger to the Republic. Such unassimilated and ignorant masses are the ideal breeding-places for the Bolsheviki, the anarchists, and the I.W.W.'s, and our American ideal of free speech has given their missionaries abundant opportunity to preach their pernicious doctrine without let or hindrance. It may yet be necessary to curb the tongues of these professional agitators in the interest of the safety of the Republic.[23]

Of all the "alien" racial or ethnic elements in the American population, the eastern European Jews were most perfectly suited to symbolize the dangerous tendencies that threatened America. They were the only immigrant group whose national origins linked them to *both* the Central Powers and Soviet Russia. Of all the new immigrants they were most strongly marked as belonging to a distinct "race," maintaining a distinct bloodline along with their cultural identity. They were also the only non-Christian element in the new immigration. A. C. Ratshesky, writing in the *Times* on November 24, asserted that Communist and Socialist organizations were mainly supported by aliens "saturated with the ignorance and anarchism of eastern Europe," who had not even learned English, let alone the principles of Americanism.[24]

Ratshesky's article was one of the first public expressions of a doctrine that had been developing in the councils of the Military Intelligence Division of the General Staff since the summer of 1918. MID's operations included areas that would today be divided among the intelligence branches of the several armed services, the Defense Department, the CIA, and the FBI. It processed information from the battlefield and from espionage and counterespionage operations, and also conducted surveillance of domestic "subversives," including labor unions, war protesters, dissidents of all sorts. For intelligence on eastern Europe, MID drew on defeated czarists and anti-Bolshevik nationalists from Poland and Ukraine. These men belonged to groups and movements with a tradition of virulent anti-Semitism, predisposed to blame the Jews for whatever was wrong in their homelands. Eastern Europe was being swept by waves of violence, both military and civil, as nationalist forces battled Soviet invaders and Reds battled Whites in civil war. Jewish communities were victimized by all sides in the conflict, subjected to pogroms and massacres, and Jewish organizations were lobbying the Wilson administration and the treaty makers at Versailles for measures to protect them. MID's nationalist and anti-Communist informants were eager to exonerate their countrymen from complicitity in pogroms, because they needed Wilson's support for their nationalist aspirations in the negotiations at Versailles. They therefore minimized the role of their people in anti-Jewish violence and excused undeniable cases on the ground that the Jews were responsible for Bolshevism, a barbaric and sacrilegious movement that their own peoples quite naturally detested.

The U.S. Army's prewar culture of anti-Semitism prepared MID to see Bolshevism as Jewish antipatriotism and materialism writ large. Their professional bias was to seek unifying patterns in the intelligence and an explanation that linked Bolshevism with Jewishness allowed them to see the domestic problems of immigration and labor dissidence as organically related to the international menace of Kaiserism-as-Communism. In June 1918 MID was telling the president and attorney general that it was "Jewish-German-Bolshevik collusion" that had taken Russia out of the war. In July an MID officer submitted as an intelligence find a copy of the *Protocols of the Elders of Zion*, an anti-Semitic fabrication that czarist police had cribbed from a German novel some fifty years earlier. The document had been supplied by Boris Brasol, a former officer and leader of the White opposition to the Bolsheviks, a fanatical anti-Semite of a type common in the czarist army and police, now an informant for MID. Brasol buttressed the *Protocols* with his own intelligence analysis, "Bolshevism and Judaism," which "discovered" a Jewish plot to achieve "world domination" through the strange alliance of international bankers with Bolshevik revolutionaries. The fund-raising and welfare activities of Jewish bankers and philanthropists, which appeared to support the American war effort, were supposedly cover for the conspiracy. Although some at MID were skeptical of the *Protocols*, they believed the document indicated "possible or probable fields of Jewish activity." In January 1919 they speculated that in the United States the conspiracy would involve Jewish Socialists and Bolsheviks (and perhaps the Freemasons), but also bankers like Jacob Schiff and a "Jewish International" masquerading as Zionism fronted by Supreme Court Justice Louis D. Brandeis.

MID's evaluation assumed that Jews as a group were hostile to American values and that their antipathy was not intellectual, but racial:

> Once a Jew always a Jew. Neither conversion nor naturalization will change him; Judaism and Socialism are different expressions of the same movement, which in the case of the Poale [leftist] Zionists amounts to sheer Bolshevism. . . . [The] coming of a world war; the chaos of Bolshevism . . . the red terror; and the breaking down of all religions save their own . . . are all predicted . . . by the Jews as a step toward their world domination.

As Americans, MID officers were prepared to accept the idea that racial conflicts inevitably provoke extraordinary and exterminating violence. That was the premise at the heart of Jim Crow that rationalized lynching. They therefore agreed with their informants that opposition to Bolshevism would culminate in a retaliatory pogrom.[25]

That thought became public just at the time of the Armistice, when the Reverend George Simons, a Methodist missionary driven out of Russia, told a reporter from the *Times* that if the Bolshevik reign of terror were not stopped, the revolution would end in "the greatest pogrom the world has ever seen." Simons would become the star witness in the Senate hearings that gave an official imprimatur to the linkage of Lower East Side Jews and Russian Bolshevism.[26]

Senator Overman's Subcommittee on the Judiciary had convened in September 1918 to investigate connections between "Brewing and Liquor Interests and German Propaganda." The subcommittee used the antiliquor premise as leverage to investigate a range of supposedly "pro-German" activities by newspapers, cultural associations, and advocacy groups. The bullying and humiliation of German-American witnesses, the evident bias and frequent editorial asides by the senators, showed that their primary purpose was to dramatize hyphenate disloyalty.[27] But the surprising turn of events that produced German defeat in November deprived the subcommittee of its original reason for being. At the turn of the year it therefore shifted its focus to the Bolshevik menace. Although the subcommittee's motives were suspect, its procedures biased, and its sources dubious, the subsequent history of the Soviet Union would validate many of the nightmarish prophecies the subcommittee entertained. However, it was not really interested in analyzing the character of the Soviet regime or U.S. policy toward Russia. Its real concern was domestic subversion, and its mission was to promote legislation to curtail the civil rights of Bolsheviks (real and imagined) and to reduce hyphenate communities through compulsory Americanization, forced deportation, and the radical restriction of immigration.

The Overman Subcommittee sought to build public support for these policies by publicizing the stunning revelation that Jews from New York had masterminded the Bolshevik Revolution. Its most important witness, the Reverend George Simons, testified on February 12, Lincoln's Birthday. He described himself as a "Christian socialist" who believed in the gospel call to charity and sharing of wealth. He denied any anti-Semitic bias and frequently made the claim that "some of my best friends are Jews," which may have been the first public use of that classic apology for bigotry. But he was compelled to report not only that the Bolshevik leadership was predominantly Jewish, but that its cadres and coffers were filled by Jews from New York's Lower East Side.[28]

Simons had been "impressed with the strong Yiddish element in this thing [the revolution] from the start, and it soon became evident that more than half the agitators in the so-called Bolshevik movement were Yiddish." When Kerensky, the premier of the liberal postczarist regime, went to the front to rally the army against the Germans, his work was undone by "hundreds of agitators who had followed in the trail of Trotsky-Bronstein, these men having come over from the lower East Side of New York." Simons knew they were from New York because several had approached him, "pleased" by the chance to talk to another American. But "their broken English showed that they had not qualified as being real Americans." As for how he knew they were Jews: he saw scores of them "standing on the benches and soap boxes, and what not, talking until their mouths frothed, and I often remarked to my sister, 'Well, what are we coming to, anyway? This all looks so Yiddish.' . . . I do not want to be unfair to them, but I usually know a Jew when I see one."

The word *Yiddish* puzzled Senator Nelson: "Hebrews?" he asked, using the term usually used to identify "racial" Jews, as distinguished from believers in Judaism. He had not heard Jews identified as "Yiddish" before. Simons confirmed the racial identification: "They were Hebrews, apostate Jews." At this point, Simons felt it necessary to declare himself an opponent of anti-Semitism: "I do not want to say anything against the Jews, as such. I am not in sympathy with the anti-Semitic movement, never have been, and do not ever expect to be. . . . I abhor all pogroms of whatever kind. But I have a firm conviction that this thing is Yiddish, and that one of its bases is to be found in the East Side of New York." "Decent" Russians had told him that the Bolshevik regime " 'is first of all German, and second, we know that it is Jewish. . . . This is not a Russian Government: this is a German and a Hebrew Government. . . . And very soon there is going to be a big pogrom.' "

Simons had taught the senators a new word, and as his testimony unfolded they made greater use of "Yiddish" to identify the suspect Jews, mostly from Poland, Austrian Galicia, Byelorussia, and Ukraine, who lived on the Lower East Side. Senator King asked, "Are Lenine [*sic*] and Trotsky Yiddish?" Senator Overman wanted to know, "Is [Trotsky] one of these Yiddish Jews? You call them Yiddish instead of Jews, and I want to distinguish." It was now possible to ask, "Is Such-a-person Yiddish?"— or perhaps "Is So-and-so a Yid?"—in the same way one might ask if he were a Negro or an Italian. In the idiom of the committee the word acquired the ambiguously dual quality of a racial and a cultural reference. Yiddish Jews can be spoken of as a "unique people" or separate "race," with special and ineradicable traits of character that are inborn. This distinction between "Yiddish" and "Jewish" was not unprecedented. It had been anticipated by prewar race theorists, who had speculated that eastern European Jews had an "Asiatic" Khazar ancestry, while the Jews of western Europe might be some subset of "White" ("Alpine" or "Latin," depending on which racial taxonomy is invoked). In 1918 Henry Fairfield Osborn had adapted that same theory to argue for a racial difference between Prussian "Huns" and true Teutons. Now that the Hun was the less-feared enemy the idea was being restored to its original function.[29]

The senators' surprise at their expert's use of this word, and the awkward earnestness with which they sought the distinction between

"Yiddish," "Hebrew," and "Jew" indicates that the usage was foreign to American English. Where did Simons learn it? There is a clue in testimony given later by a Colonel Hurban, formerly of the Czech Legion that had fought against the Bolsheviks. In explaining the Jews' support of the revolution, Hurban pointed to their mistreatment under the czarist regime. Among other abuses, "Whenever a Russian spoke to a Jew he always . . . [used] some insulting epithet which I cannot translate into English." The word he had in mind was *Zhid*. The literal English equivalent is "Yid," but that translation does not convey the insulting force of the Russian, which is closer in feeling to "kike"—or perhaps more precisely to "nigger," since it identifies a person whose humanity is dubious, who deserves to be despised, insulted, mocked, and abused by right-thinking people. Reverend Simons, eleven years in Russia and fluent in the language, used an English variant of *Zhid* to identify the sort of Jew it is right to hate.[30]

Senator Wolcott was deeply troubled by the idea that *American* Jews were responsible for Bolshevism. Most Americans thought Bolshevism a "passing fad," of no interest or danger. "But, of course, if the success of this monstrous thing in Russia is due to men who came out of New York City," then America herself is in peril. Simons answered with some double hearsay: "The latest startling information, given me by someone who says there is good authority for it" is that in the Petrograd Soviet only 16 of 388 delegates were "real Russians, and all the rest Jews, with the exception possibly of one man, who is a Negro from America, who calls himself Prof. Gordon." Of the 372 Jews, 265 "came from the lower East Side of New York." Later in his testimony he would offer a list of some twenty men with Jewish surnames, who had adopted Russian names when assuming roles in the Bolshevik government because "among the real Russians there would be an antipathy against the Jews." However, Simons admitted that he didn't know which, if any, of the listed individuals were from America.

The presence of Professor Gordon, the "Negro from America," sounds another subtheme of Simons's characterization of Bolshevism. This is a regime that depends on the lowest order of "real Russians" and on inauthentic Russian nationals, outright aliens, and non-Whites. According to Simons, the core of the Red Army, led by the Yiddish Jew Trotsky, was comprised of Letts and "Chinese coolies." The United States had its own underclass ethnic and racial minorities. What the

Overman Subcommittee wanted to know was whether the East Side Jews were the source of a revolutionary propaganda that (like the abortive Plan of San Diego) might rouse our hyphenates, Negroes, Mexicans, and Asians to rebellion. "I am very much impressed with this, that moving around here I find that certain Bolsheviki propagandists are nearly all Jews—apostate Jews. . . . I have no doubt in my mind that the predominant element in this Bolsheviki movement in America is, as you may call it, the Yiddish of the East Side." There had been a massive failure of Americanization among the Yiddish. "It seems strange to me, but when you talk with the average man from the lower East Side he is not going to speak English or Russian, but he is going to speak Yiddish."

Simons's morning testimony concluded with a reference to the most sensational evidence the government had in hand: *The Protocols of the Elders of Zion*, a summary of which had been provided to the subcommittee by MID. Senator King wanted to know why the Bolsheviks were so "bitter toward religion, especially the Christian religion." Simons referred them to Dr. Harrison Houghton, whom he identified as pastor of a church and a captain in the army and MID. It was Houghton who gave Simons "the so-called Jewish protocols," and it was Simons's view that "that book reflects a real organization." So explosive are its revelations that "the average person in official life here in Washington and elsewhere is afraid to handle it. Houghton says that even in his intelligence bureau they were afraid of it." The subcommittee registered horror: *A conspiracy so potent even great men in Washington fear to name it!* Senator King urged Simons, "Tell us about the book. What is so bad about it? Is it anti-Christian?" Of course, "it is anti-Christian," Simon answered, but more than that "it shows what this secret Jewish society has been doing" to achieve "a conquest of the world . . . to have the whole world, if you please, in their grip." Compare its design for world domination with the Bolshevik program of world revolution, and "it just looks as if it is connected in some way." It was imperative that the government investigate, let the consequences be what they may: "I have no animus against the Jews, but I have a great passion for the truth."[31]

Simons's testimony was a national sensation. His charges were made at a moment when there seemed to be a rising tide of anarchist and Bolshevik agitation and violence. Jewish spokesmen immediately came forward to rebut the accusations, and they were joined by some mainstream politicians. On February 17 a group of prominent New York politicians, including Governor Smith and Mayor Hylan, joined Marshall to "praise [the] Patriotism of East Side Jews" and express their "resentment" of Simons's testimony, and they were joined by Secretary of War McAdoo. On the Republican side, former presidential candidate (and future Supreme Court Justice) Charles Evans Hughes declared, "I greatly regret the broadcast aspersions [upon] the Jews of the east side. . . . They performed splendid service for their country." But however gratifying such expressions might be, they did not erase the impact of Simons's testimony. The *Times* put Simons's "Former East Siders Largely Responsible for Bolshevism" and "Atrocities to Young Girls" on page one—Louis Marshall's response on page sixteen.[32]

"Roosevelt and I": Defending the Lower East Side

> *Eyn got un azoy fil soynim.* (One god and so many enemies.)
>
> —*Yiddish Proverb*

Jewish leaders demanded a chance to rebut Simons's charges before the Overman Subcommittee, and statements were submitted by Louis Marshall of the American Jewish Committee (AJC) and Simon Wolf, chairman of the Board of Delegates of the Union of American Hebrew Congregations and a director of B'nai B'rith. Marshall was Jewish America's most influential spokesman, "the closest thing American Jews had to a *shtadlan*, the European court Jew, who pleaded the Jews' case to those in power." He defended the East Siders as solid, decent, bourgeois Americans, "reputable, honorable, and patriotic." Statistics showed that Jews had contributed disproportionately to the Liberty Loan. But the best proof that East Side Jews are true Americans is the valor of Jewish soldiers, and especially of the Lost Battalion. An AJC pamphlet edited by Simon Wolf "Point[ed] in Pride" to the record of Jews in the AEF and the fact that there was a "Larger Proportion of [the Jewish] Race in Service than in [the] Population." It cited the casualties suffered and the medals won, and pointed especially to the "exceptional heroism, [of] the men who fought in the Argonne Forest . . . who constituted part of the Lost Battalion" and were mostly from the East Side.[33]

Simon Wolf's response was more defiant than Marshall's, his English imperfect but catching the colloquial tone of the Jewish streets, mixing ethnic jokes that reflected the disillusioned wisdom of Yiddish folk culture with impassioned polemic. Wolf was the man who had, literally, written the book on Jewish-American valor and patriotism, *The American Jew as Soldier, Patriot, and Citizen,* excerpts from which had been appearing in the *American Hebrew.* He had the statistics to show that Jews had done more than their share for both the Liberty Loan and the AEF. To clinch his claim he quoted the *Times* editorial on Abe Krotoshinsky and a more recently published editorial from the Christian magazine the *Outlook,* "The Valor of the East Side." Based on a letter from a staff officer of the 77th Division, the article "glories in the splendid mettle and loyal Americanism of the men drafted from the motley foreign-born population of New York's east side," as exemplified in the heroism of the "lost battalion" and the 77th Division:

> This division is made up of the puny east siders, who a New York dud thought could never hold their own against the sturdy sons of the West. We have got something to be proud of in this, the great melting pot of New York typified and glorified. Our burial lists show the names of the Jew, the Italian, the Russian, the Polack, the Irishman, the German, fighting for the free Government which has aided and protected each. . . . In so doing [they] have become real Americans—no matter where they come from and how they spell their names, as good Americans as those of us whose ancestors fought in all our wars [the writer is one of these].

Although his purpose was defensive, Wolf dares to voice his anger at the subcommittee, quoting Shylock's threat, "the evil that you teach me I will repay, and it will go hard but I will better the exchange." Wolf felt *entitled* to his rage; the deeds of the Lost Battalion had proved that Jews were true Americans and had given him the right to challenge unjust proceedings by the national government. He answers the accusation of racial perfidy with a vindication of Jewish racial virtues. The racial qualities that enabled the Jew to "survive through the centuries—his capacity to endure, without breaking, prolonged and intense nervous strain; his initiative, his elasticity of mind, his faculty for organization, and, above all, his idealism"—have given Jews a special aptitude for Americanization. The ease with which the Jewish soldier "fit himself into a democratic army" proves racial difference is no bar to the achievement of true Americanism.

The danger in making such a defense was that race, by definition, was a fixed marker of difference between nationalities. Even if Jews were a uniquely virtuous race, it could be argued that their difference from racial Americans would make them incapable of complete amalgamation.

Wolf deals with the problem by suggesting that Americanization is a two-way street. The integration of Jews into the AEF made them into "real Americans," but at the same time transformed the nation itself, producing a new type of equality and nationality, even a kind of spiritual regeneration, a "new birth of freedom" like that which had been won at Gettysburg:

> War is the great equalizer, the real melting pot. It has welded for us a great people, united by the common bond of sacrifice and devotion, courage and suffering in a common cause. It is our regeneration, our rebirth, a revolution such as we have never experienced in all our history.[34]

Wolf thus makes the radical suggestion that the American democratic ideal requires a hybridization of national culture, rather than "one flag, one language, one people." As the Jew is Americanized, America too is "regenerated" or transformed by incorporating Jews *as Jews*, Yiddishers *as Yiddishers*, in a pluralistic American nationality.

But for the Immigration Restriction League and its allies on the subcommittee, Wolf's vision was simply a proposal for mongrelizing American culture and the American race. Given their commitment to a racial nationalism that identified America as Nordic, the racial intelligence and energy Wolf claimed for Jews simply increased their danger to the body politic. Simons continued to push the theory of a Jewish-Bolshevik world conspiracy. In a *Times* interview on February 17 he warned that "highly educated Russians, generals, intellectuals, and people of that class . . . believed that there is a secret society—made up of apostate Jews—aiming at domination of the world by Bolshevik methods." His purpose, he said, was to follow the line taken by Theodore Roosevelt and issue a stern warning to all those who sympathized in any way with the Reds that the nation would deal harshly with attempts to overthrow its civilization. He was not singling out Jews: "Dr. Simons explained carefully in his statement that he was not anti-Semitic, that many of his best friends were Jews." His warning applied to all Bolshevik sympathizers, whether socialist or progressive, and he accused the *New Republic*, the *Dial*, and the *Nation* of Bolshevik sympathies. Nevertheless, the city's Jewish community was directly responsible for the menace. "Right here in New York—let my Jewish friends know it—we have scores of restaurants where they are talking that stuff. . . . I want to make it dangerous to conduct revolutionary propaganda in a restaurant, or any other place." If Simons was right, Bolshevism was as native to the character of Yiddish Jews as *Kultur* was to Germans, and he hoped Wilson would deal with the Bolsheviks as Roosevelt had advocated dealing with Germans and pro-Germans. If Yiddish Jews did not purge themselves of their cultural heritage, their native disposition, perhaps America too would resort to something like a pogrom. The innocent would perish with the guilty, but the fault would lie in the refusal of Jews to control their own dissidents.[35]

It is a measure of the ambiguity and even ambivalence of Theodore Roosevelt's record on immigration and "racial" equality that both sides in the debate appealed to his words and symbolism. Simons invoked Roosevelt's call for draconian laws and vigilante reprisals against pro-Germans as a model for the repression of the supposed Jewish-Bolshevik conspiracy. The AJC countered by appealing to the Roosevelt of the "Square Deal" and the Great Rule of Righteousness. *American Hebrew*'s "Homage of American Jews to Our Great Ex-President, Theodore Roosevelt" is accompanied by a letter from Sergeant Major Irving Liner of the Lost Battalion, "Five Days Yom Kippur in the Argonne," in which patriotic service actually makes Liner a better Jew as well as a worthy American:

> Do you remember how hard it used to be for me to go without food for twenty-four hours on Yom Kippur? Well, I had to go without food for five days, and it didn't affect me in the least. I stuck it out with the Major . . . and became good pals with him. He himself . . . wrote my recommendation [for the DSC].

In a later article the bond between Liner and Whittlesey is imaginatively expanded into a vision of comradeship between the immigrant and the spirit of Roosevelt:

> I picture myself and many, many other immigrants, all of us eager and anxious to work for the common weal of our new fatherland, and I invariably picture Theodore Roosevelt on horseback in his Rough Rider's

hat leading the way. . . . I hear a voice whisper, 'America of the future is Roosevelt . . . and I think that each of us immigrants feels deep in his heart something which could best be expressed by three words, "Roosevelt and I."[36]

Roosevelt himself might have settled matters by endorsing one side or the other. Or he might have been able to perform his old trick of overriding contradictory moral and political impulses with the magic of his heroic persona. But the Republican victory in the 1918 midterm elections was his last political triumph. Physically and emotionally exhausted, debilitated by injuries and illness, depressed by his son Quentin's death in battle, Roosevelt had died in his sleep at Sagamore Hill on January 6.[37]

Failing a rebuke from Roosevelt, and against occasional objections by liberals and Progressives, Simons's views won a wide national following. The Literary Digest's editorial positions registered the effect of the Senate hearings. In December 1918 the question "Are Bolsheviki Mainly Jewish?" was treated as open to debate. By the end of February 1919, the Digest had its answer, paraphrased from Simons's testimony: "We know [the Soviet] is not a Russian government. It is German first and Jewish next." And "the Bolshevism of Russia is largely a transplant from America."[38]

On February 12—the day of Simons's testimony before the Overman Subcommittee—New York received notice that "Our Negro Soldiers" were coming home in glory. As the ships carrying them steamed into New York harbor, they passed the Statue of Liberty and Ellis Island, those landmarks of the White immigrants' passage through the Golden Door. Watching their arrival from barred detention rooms on Ellis Island were dozens of men and women, "Defiant Reds" accused of "Bolshevism, anarchy, and terrorism, and [being] members of the I.W.W." They had been rounded up by the Justice Department and by "Red squads" of local police, and imprisoned to await deportation—perhaps on those very ships, now thronged with Black men in khaki uniform, waving to the happy shore.[39]

12

"No Man's Land Is Ours": The Hell Fighters and the Lost Battalion Return, February–May 1919

> Vict'ry's won, the war is over,
> The whole wide world is wreathed in clover . . .
> All of No Man's Land is ours!
>
> —*James Reese Europe, "All of No Man's Land Is Ours" (1919)*

Colonel Hayward was determined that his regiment's homecoming be a triumph for his men, for "the race," and for Harlem. He wanted a public acknowledgment that his men had kept their promise and proved themselves, and their people, worthy of equality. A grand parade was also something he had promised his men after the Armistice, when bad treatment by the American army threatened to wreck their morale.

They had ended their service with the French on the highest possible note, rejoining the Fourth Army after the Armistice and becoming the first American regiment to cross the Rhine. On December 13, 1918, they assembled with their French comrades of the 161st Division for a grand review. General Lebouc read their citation of valor:

Under the command of Colonel Hayward, who, though injured, insisted on leading his regiment in the battle, of Lieutenant Colonel Pickering, admirably cool and brave, of Major Cobb (killed), of Major Spencer (grievously wounded), of Major Little, a true leader of men, the

> 369th R.I.U.S. engaging in an offensive for the first time . . . stormed
> powerful enemy positions energetically defended, took, after heavy
> fighting, the town of Sechault, captured prisoners and brought back six
> cannon and a great number of machine guns.

He pinned the Croix de Guerre on each of the field officers and on the
regimental flag. Subsequently every man in the regiment received his own
Croix de Guerre, and 170 medals were awarded for individual acts of
heroism.

Then they were returned to the American army, ordered to Le Mans
for delousing and reequipping, and things began to go badly. They had
been enlisted since the beginning of the war, and in all that time the army
had never sent them a single instructor. Now, when the war was over, after they had been under fire for 191 days and won a unit citation of the
Croix de Guerre, the U.S. Army sent a green lieutenant with no combat
experience to instruct them in the use of the rifle. It may simply have
been a case of bureaucratic stupidity, but the whole regiment, officers included, took it as an insult.

From Le Mans they entrained for Brest to await embarkation for
home. At every whistle stop they would lean out of the boxcars and hoot
at the support units on the platform, "Who won the war?" And before
the objects of derision could answer they'd holler that "the Bakers!"
won it, or the Quartermasters, the Red Cross, the MPs. They "laughed
their way through France," cocky and self-assured. They knew it was
themselves who had won the war, and that entitled them to razz the rear
echelon, White though most of them were. It was beginning to dawn on
them that they had not only survived battle, but had achieved that larger
mission that had been held out to them at the start of their service.

> Here were . . . men of the colored race, a race which had suffered
> wrongs of humanity for centuries; a race which had been classed by
> some almost as one of the lower animal kingdoms, not quite human be-
> ings; a race still suffering, and bound to suffer for a long time still to
> come, from prejudice in the hearts of white men. . . . And these men . . .
> were going home as heroes.

But within an hour of their arrival in Brest a private in the regiment
"had his head split open by a blow from the club of a [White] 'MP.' "
The private's offense had been to interrupt a conversation between two

MPs to ask directions to the latrine. His comrades instantly came to his aid and liberated the injured man from arrest: they knew what to expect from White troops, wanted to serve notice as they had since Spartanburg that they would resist insult or assault. Captain MacClinton of the 369th calmed the situation, and the men had begun to disperse when the MP spoke "with insolence" to MacClinton—which brought them back in a bunch to defend their officer. Little now came running. He knew the temper of his men: "I hate to think of what might have occurred if the thing had gone on a minute or two longer." He snapped everyone to attention and gave the MP a dressing down that satisfied the troops' anger. But the man's apology, which only Little heard, was dismaying. The MPs "had been warned that our 'Niggers' were feeling their oats a bit and that instructions had been given to 'take it out of them quickly, just as soon as they arrived, so as not to have any trouble later on.'"

Little soon discovered that White MPs had been instructed not to salute or obey orders given by officers—White or Black—commanding Negro troops. GHQ treated them as pariahs, refusing them permission to participate in the grand parade of French and American forces in Paris, holding back their pay, and denying them the Thanksgiving and Christmas rations distributed to White outfits. They were continually harassed by "the front-dodging MPs, the pampered pets of the war." Each act of "petty fault-finding was coupled with a threat of disciplinary action against the entire regiment." The danger was that any breach of discipline might be exploited by a high command eager to discredit Negro soldiers, destroying at a stroke the reputation it had cost them so much to build. As in Spartanburg, they had to maintain the precarious balance between prideful resentment of abuse and obedience to authority. Then it had been the hope of getting into combat that kept them in line. Now it was Hayward's promise that when they returned their achievements would be fully recognized by their city.

Their transports docked in New York on February 12, Lincoln's Birthday, and while the men were being ferried to the Long Island City depot for trains to Camp Upton, Hayward went to talk with the mayor and other officials about staging a parade. There were obstacles. The War Department had forbidden the parading of returning regiments until all troops had been brought home (that would take most of a year), after which there might be a grand review. It was the sort of directive that revealed just how out of touch with popular sentiment the Wilson administration was, and it would soon be rescinded, but the ban was in effect when the Old Fifteenth returned. In addition, workers with the city's community service organization, which provided refreshments for public events, refused to serve Negroes.[1]

But Hayward used all his political influence, aided by the united and enthusiastic support of the city's African-American political leaders, and by all the major city papers except Hearst's *American*, and the parade was scheduled for February 17.

"Oh, you Black Death!": The Hell Fighters' Triumph, February 17, 1919

Early that morning the Hell Fighters put on dress uniforms and climbed aboard special trains that carried them to Long Island City, where they boarded ferries for lower Manhattan. They assembled with the head of their column at Madison and Twenty-third, and at 11 A.M. stepped off for Fifth Avenue and the start of a parade that would take them through Midtown and up Lenox Avenue to Harlem.

Hayward and master showman James Europe had designed a parade that would astonish and impress a city used to grand spectacles. They remembered all too well the jokes about the regiment's first public drills, when straggling troops armed with broomsticks had marched in what one wag called a "Column of Bunches." For the march up Fifth Avenue Hayward formed them "in phalanx by company," a formation they had learned under Gouraud's command. Each company formed in a block, sixteen ranks across and twelve deep, with wide intervals between the companies—Hayward's headquarters command on horseback in the lead, followed by Lieutenant Europe's world-famous band, then the troops with bayonets fixed and glittering in the winter sun, and the convalescent wounded riding motor cars in the rear. It was, as the French designed it to be, an imposing formation, unusual in breadth, and the crowds that lined Fifth Avenue were astonished and impressed. The *Times* reporter said the sight made him feel sudden pity for the Germans who had had to face these men.

Europe had designed a musical progam that would define each stage of the march, building to a climax in Harlem. The band started off with "Sambre et Meuse," the French war song that had played the poilus into battle in 1914, then shifted to sprightlier, jazzier marches as they moved north. The crowds through Midtown, mostly White, were wild with enthusiasm. Hayward said he thought their "reception was certainly the greatest that returning soldiers ever got." As they passed the reviewing stand at 60th Street, they took the salute of Governor Smith, former Governor Whitman, who had authorized their formation in 1916, and a crowd of dignitaries including Emmett Scott as representative of the War Department. At 65th Street Mrs. Astor, wrapped in Old Glory, saluted from a window of her mansion, at 73rd Henry Clay Frick waved a flag from his. The onlookers had heard the stories of how soldiers missed their sweets and smokes, and they showered the passing ranks with packets of cigarettes and candy. Little, marching behind the band, could scarcely hear a note for the noise from the crowd.

The *Times* praised the regiment for its display of manhood, "swinging up the avenue, keeping a step springy with the swagger of men proud of themselves and their organization. . . . They had that peculiar sort of half-careless, yet wholly perfect, step that the French display . . . the jaunty ease . . . that comes only to men who have hiked far and frequently." They had amassed "one of the bravest records achieved by any organization during the war" and could hold their heads up in any company. Reporters and editorialists made it a point to contrast the present glory of the regiment with the suspicion and prejudice that had surrounded its organization. They thought it was much to the credit of White New Yorkers that now they democratically cheered the Black phalanx. The *World* reporter boasted that "New York is not race-proud nor race-prejudiced. That this 369th Regiment . . . was composed entirely of Negroes, made no difference in the shouts and flagwaving and handshakes that were bestowed upon it." He predicted the Old Fifteenth would become a permanent part of "this city's memory, archives, and in the folk lore of the descendants of the men who made up its straight, smartly-stepping ranks." The hope that the Hell Fighters' achievements would alter the way White people saw the race was realized for one reporter, who thought that the martial spirit of the men had somehow infused the bodies of the Black children who swarmed around them: "there seemed to be a little military swank even to the youngsters, as platoons of them stepped along with faces that had been scrubbed until they shone."[2]

But New York *was* divided by a color line, and the parade made it visible. As the regiment marched north it passed "through scores of thousands

of cheering white citizens," and when it crossed into Harlem it was surrounded by "a greater multitude of its own color." The cheers of Midtown had been, as Little put it, "impersonal"—cheers for a patriotic
symbol. Harlem took the regiment personally and knew its members in-
dividually. Hayward understood the situation completely, and as they
crossed 110th Street and turned west onto Lenox Avenue he ordered a
change in formation that broke the large company blocks into longer
narrower columns, so that the people lining the street could "see and
recognize . . . the face and figure of each soldier boy." The sidewalks of
the "Black Belt" were jammed, and from the windows, fire escapes, and
rooftops flowers rained down on the ranks. Europe's band swung into
"Won't You Come Home, Bill Bailey." "Mothers, and wives, and sisters,
and sweethearts . . . rushed right out through the ranks to embrace
them," crying out, " 'Oh, honey!' . . . 'Oh, you Charlie!' 'There's my
boy!' 'There's daddie!' 'How soon you comin' home, son?' " "For the final mile or more of our parade about every fourth soldier of the ranks
had a girl upon his arm—and we marched through Harlem singing and
laughing."

There were also intimations of the racial tension that lay just under
the surface of city life. The *Times* reported that the NYPD seemed
friendly and that it had been "trained to handle all races without friction." Nonetheless, the reporter heard one woman break off hugging her
just-returned husband with the remark that they "might be arrested if
they stayed too long in one spot." The soldier grinned and told her, "Not
today!"—meaning, perhaps, not on a day when we are being honored;
but also, perhaps, not in the presence of 3,000 armed Black veterans.
This was a community that knew itself to be still beleaguered by the hostility of Whites.

The edge of the community's deflected anger glinted in the cheers for
Henry Johnson. He rode alone in an open-topped touring car, bowing
side to side, his "tin hat" in his left hand and in his right "a bunch of red
and white lilies which some admirer had pressed upon him." In the immediate aftermath of his great battle, news reports had described Johnson as a "mulatto" with a significant share of White blood. Now the
World man remarked that he was "about as black as any man in the outfit, if not a trifle blacker," and he "grinned from ear to ear" as people ran
up to throw gifts and tokens into the car. As in that *Herald* cartoon that
had appeared back in June, this evocation of the "grinning darky" image

is linked to an exaggerated tale of his bloody-handedness: how the "mild mannered chauffeur" had "waded into a whole patrol of 'bush Germans'" and left "four dead foemen in front of him, thirty-four others done up so badly they couldn't even crawl away, and heaven knows how many more . . . put to flight." The "chauffeur" reference suggests that (one Black man being like every other) the reporter had confused Johnson with Sergeant Butler, the "indoor chauffeur" who had also won the Croix de Guerre.

But for the crowd, Henry Johnson's blackness had nothing comic about it. It was the sign of his capacity for deadliness in defense of himself and his people. "Looks like a funeral, Henry, them lilies!"

"'Funeral for them bush Germans, boy! Sure a funeral for them bushes,' shouted Henry." The *World* man heard "one particular cry" passed northward from block to block all the way up Lenox Avenue, "O-oh, you wick-ed Hen-nery Johnson! You wick-ed ma-an!"—at which "Henry the Boche Killer . . . grinned more widely than ever." As he passed down the street the *Times* reporter heard cries of "Oh, you Henry Johnson! Oh, you Black Death!"

The march ended at the 71st Regiment armory, where a huge feast of fried chicken and other delights had been laid on. Dance bands played into the night, there were speeches and boxing matches, celebrations spread through the streets in the wake of home-bound soldiers. Most of the regiment managed to reassemble next morning to return to Upton for formal mustering out. Only Henry Johnson was AWOL. He had been carried off to a succession of Fifth Avenue clubs and hotels by "a group of gentlemen" (race not specified), who "entertained him with food and drink, and rewarded him with money." When he returned to Upton, one day late, he told Little he could not have refused them without impairing the regiment's reputation for courtesy. "Of course, Johnson was forgiven."[3]

In the weeks that followed that glorious homecoming there were signs that the Old Fifteenth had achieved its mission of convincing White America that Negroes could meet the Roosevelt standard of "manhood, intelligence, and cooperation." James Weldon Johnson was proud that the Old Fifteenth was the first of New York's regiments to pass under the city's "Victory Arch." They had "saved the world for civilization" by repelling the German attacks on July 15. There was also satisfaction in noting that the regiment had won more battlefield honors than any of the state's White National Guard units—a nice rejoinder to General Ryan for refusing to include them in the 27th Division. And no other regiment had a hero like Henry Johnson or a bandleader like James Europe. Who could doubt that these achievements would make a difference in the struggle for equality? "We wonder how many people who are opposed to giving the Negro his full citizenship rights could watch the Fifteenth . . . and not feel either shame or alarm?" "Shame" for having abused so good a people—"alarm" for the militant potential symbolized by Henry Johnson and the cries of "Black Death!"[4]

Locally there were signs that the Hell Fighters had won new respect for Black New Yorkers. On February 26 the *Times* reported that Assemblyman Healy of Manhattan had introduced a bill that called for a National Guard regiment officered entirely by Negroes. He praised the "hell fighters" of the Old Fifteenth for having routed "thousands of Huns in the Argonne" and called attention to the injustice that had deprived them of well-earned commissions as officers. His bill would make it possible for any man who had served for any time in the regiment to obtain a Guard commission. Locally, there was a new sense that Blacks could respond from a position of moral strength when White prejudice reared its head. Two weeks after the parade the commander of Camp Upton, General Nicholson, decided to "draw the color line" at the hospitality center, forbidding Black soldiers or female visitors from entering when "large numbers of White women" were present. Harlem leaders protested, and the policy was reversed. The city now agreed to build an armory for the 15th and hired Vertner Tandy, one of the regiment's original Black officers, as architect for the project. There was talk of reorganizing the regiment with Black officers from colonel to second lieutenant. Colonel Hayward resigned shortly after the regiment was mustered out of federal service, followed by his second in command and successor Arthur Little, each man making clear his belief that a Negro officer ought to be placed in command.[5]

On May 5 the NAACP opened its national campaign for a federal antilynching bill by convening a National Conference on Lynching at Carnegie Hall. Charles Evans Hughes, once and perhaps future candidate for president, was the leading speaker, joined on the podium by such notables as Moorfield Storey (archfoe of TR's Philippine policy), Rabbi Stephen Wise, a Southern governor known for his opposition to lynching, and the artillery commander of the 92nd Division. Hughes characterized lynching as the "Essence of Hun Spirit" and demanded that "Killings Cease in Justice to Black Soldiers." He thus framed the antilynching campaign as, in effect, the carrying on of the war effort by other means. It was essential to his polemic that the achievements of Black soldiers be recognized and that the legislation be seen as fulfillment of the nation's part of the social bargain. So it was important for the artillery commander of the much maligned 92nd Division to assure the audience that this generation of Black men had proved as adept with modern artillery as prior ones had proved with rifle and cavalry saber. To clinch the case, the final resolution offered praise for the unquestioned heroism of the 369th Infantry. The conference called on Congress to pass antilynching legislation, and Representative Dyer of Missouri was asked to draft a bill for presentation to the House.[6]

It was a fortuitous juxtaposition that linked the grand pageant of Black patriotism with the squalid bickering of unions and employers, the fulminations of radicals, and the controversy over Simons's charge that Bolshevism was "Yiddish." But these events reinforced the *Age's* argument that White America had been mistaken in showing greater openness to immigrants than to American Negroes. The prospect of an "exodus of Italians and other southern Europeans from the United States, the imminent restriction of immigration by Congress, and the great need of labor arising during the reconstruction period" even seemed to have made organized labor willing to end its systematic exclusion of Black people. Samuel Gompers had gone on record favoring the idea, and a delegate to the AFL convention asked, "If you can take in immigrants who cannot speak the English language, why can't you take the negro, who has been loyal to you from Washington to the battlefields of France?" Some delegates to the AFL convention endorsed the principle that Johnson and DuBois had long contended: "With equal opportunity and equal wages and membership in the Federation, the colored man will not lend himself to strike-breaking."[7]

Although no African-American leader discounted the difficulties and dangers, there seemed good grounds for hoping that at least the "most deserving" Negroes, or the "Talented Tenth," might have won some access to political power through their wartime service. Certainly James Europe was primed for an unprecedented national role. He joined a heroic military record and an international musical triumph to his original celebrity as a composer, performer, and theatrical entrepreneur. He was an articulate spokesman for civil rights. A national concert tour would spread his fame and provide him with an incomparable platform for his ideas on Black music, culture, and civil rights.

Immediately after demobilization, "Lieut. James Reese Europe and His Famous 369th Infantry Band" began a ten-week tour of the Northeast and Midwest. Advertisements invited the public to hear the "Big Ragtime Soldier Band" play "the songs that the Doughboys of the Fighting Old 15th sang as they went 'over the top' and put the Huns to run!" Their opening performance was at Hammerstein's Opera House in New York, a venue whose high-culture associations made Sissle feel that jazz had been elevated among the arts. The band played some covers of popular songs, but the feature pieces were martial airs and marches, especially Europe's own compositions, "All of No Man's Land Is Ours" and "On Patrol in No Man's Land," with its jagged rhythms and explosive bursts of percussion mimicking the sound and sense of battle, "Obey my orders and you won't go wrong." Reviewers praised the "gorgeous racket of syncopation and jazzing," but also reverted to type with their praise of those "echoes of . . . the traditional darkey life that seems almost to have disappeared . . . [and] the gayety with which the colored brother takes his religion." Although Europe played to the White audience's expectations with a medley of "Plantation Echoes," he thought jazz treatment brought out the musical quality and the African spirit of the songs. He was not pleased when Herbert Wright, one of the band's "Percussion Twins," reinforced the minstrel show associations by clowning during the set.

James Weldon Johnson saw Europe's celebrity as a victory in the larger contest between Negroes and immigrants for a place in the American sun. In his view, Jewish musicians had "put the colored man out of the field" of ragtime, and James Europe was leading a " 'Comeback' of Negro Music and Musicians." Europe took a larger view. He told an interviewer for the *New York Tribune* that jazz is at once the most American of musics and essentially a "Negro American" music, and that its acceptance in the wider musical world was both a national triumph for American culture and a vindication of the cultural capacity of the Negro race. It was important to him that jazz be recognized as an art music by the keepers of high culture. But more important than acceptance by Whites was the value of Europe's achievement for African-Americans. In *Souls of Black Folk*, DuBois had seen "the Negro folk song—the rhythmic cry of the slave . . . not simply as the sole American music, but as the most beautiful expression of human experience born this side of the seas." Europe presents jazz as the development of that race music into an art form that is at once "modern" and "high," a credit to America, but achieved by the Negro race. He saw in the conjunction of jazz with wartime service a clue to the role of music in shaping a new, proud, dynamic, and militant American Negro culture—one which looked to itself for value and not to the imitation of White culture:

> I have come back from France more firmly convinced than ever that negroes should write negro music. We have our own racial feeling and if we try to copy whites we will make bad copies. . . . We won France by playing music which was ours and not a pale imitation of others.

His proud assertion, "We won France," refers literally to the band's phenomenal popularity with French audiences. More broadly, it equates that musical conquest with the AEF's victory. As Europe continually reminds the interviewer, he and his bandsmen "are all fighters as well as musicians, for they have all seen service in the trenches." The playbill for the national tour identified Sissle as "Young Black Joe," an allusion to the title of Irvin Cobb's famous article about the Battle of Henry Johnson.[8]

The racialization of cultural achievement and the desire that Blacks take pride in the race *as* a race, were concessions to the system of racialist thought that falsely divided humankind into subspecies. But in an America that believed devoutly in the importance of racial difference, only achievements that could be seen as racial would be accepted as proof of equality. Jews were discovering what African-Americans already knew, that pride in the race as a race offered the readiest antidote to that "double consciousness" that distorted the despised minority's understanding of itself. How that doubleness worked is illustrated by the February 15 edition of the *Age*. An article quotes Hayward's boast, "Our colored soldiers cared less for shell fire than any white man that ever breathed," and an accompanying piece reminds readers that Theodore Roosevelt himself "Believed in Negro Leadership"—the ability of Black men to manage a modern company or battle. But right next to the Roosevelt article is an ad for creams to "Lighten Your Dark Skin."[9] The idea that Blacks must *prove* their equality, which was the core of the social bargain made in 1917, assumes that "White" is the standard by which all things are measured. Inherent in Europe's campaign for a Black music was the idea that the culture and appearance of Black people were beautiful in their own terms.

Henry Johnson was going "national" as well. Like Whittlesey, Colonel Hayward had been asked to undertake a speaking tour for the Liberty Loan, and Henry Johnson was slated to go with him. They were a striking pair, as glimpsed in the double interview published in the *Literary Digest*. Hayward had been an important political figure before the war and was now being considered as a candidate for governor of New York, with higher office not out of the question. Johnson was one of the few enlisted men whose deeds had been celebrated in the national press, his symbolic stature acknowledged by the New York legislature, which invited him to testify on a bill offering preferential treatment to veterans applying for civil service jobs. (Johnson was for it: the country ought to "take care of the boys who did their bit.") Hayward appears as an idealized hero of the Roosevelt type: an athlete and a soldier, "the handsomest man in Nebraska," tall and dark-haired, "romantic, shadowy eyes that can blaze or brood . . . a type for a soldier or a hero of the movies." Johnson, described as a "big good-natured negro," comes forward limping from his many wounds, but wearing "a big smile" and acting like "a typical bashful negro doughboy." Reporters are "amazed at his ability to quote military terms and mix French with his typical negro English." He pays tribute to his "kunnel" for teaching him how to soldier. But when asked why he had fought so hard and returned to the regiment with unhealed wounds, Johnson answered: "Ah'll tell you, boss. We all said Company C was the best in the regiment, and Ah was jest out there a upholdin' old Company C and her reputation." It was his pride as a soldier and his loyalty to Company C that kept him up to the mark, not just the noble example of his White colonel.[10]

"The boys simply smiled their way through the war"

James Europe and Henry Johnson symbolized a new version of Negro character. "[The] masses have lost their fool and 'tricky darky' . . . [who] showed the whites of their eyes and turned a fool's somersault at the mere mention of watermelon and chittlings." They had proved they could measure up to the Roosevelt standard of "manliness, intelligence, cooperation" and seemed likely to show that, in peace as in war, they could "fear God, and take their own part." But that other, more traditional idea of the Negro—Sambo, Rastus, "Mr. Johnston the Darktown Coon"—was still prepotent in American culture. It peeked out at times in the description of the great parade, in the observation that "of course" there was lots of fried chicken at the homecoming celebration, and the image of the "ear to ear" grin in Henry Johnson's blacker-than-usual black face. The *American* hailed "New York Negroes Home Again Laden with War Honors" and quoted a French general who called them "the crack fighting unit of the Western Front." It noted that a battalion of the 369th had gone into action on September 26 with 700 men and twenty officers and come out with 150 men, seven officers, and the Croix de Guerre. But the accompanying photo layout shows a Black soldier identified as "Rastus, of the 370th Inft." a classic "grinning darkey" who played the cymbals and "clapped all the way to France and back again."[11]

In the aftermath of the parade the image of the ridiculous Negro resurfaced, undercutting the symbolic achievement of the Harlem Hell Fighters. Hayward himself appeared to encourage that view of his men when he said, "The boys simply smiled their way through the war." The line may have been meant as praise for their high morale, but in the context of the interview it reads as the setup for a "grinning darkey" riff, and that is how the reporters took it. Hayward wanted his men taken seriously and laid great stress on the regiment's valiant stand on July 15, which turned back the last German offensive and "saved civilization." Though many were killed or wounded, "Not One of the Famous 369th Was Taken Alive." But reporters wanted more funny stories about Black soldiers, and Hayward obliged, giving the *Times* a pageful of "Comic Anecdotes Brought Back by Negro Soldiers." Above the headline is a large-scale cartoon of a White doughboy flexing his muscle, asking Uncle Sam, "Anybody looking for trouble, Uncle?" The White veteran stands ready to continue the war against the country's enemies, foreign or domestic. The Black soldiers in the story below make comic display of their ignorance, incompetence, and disinclination to fight. A Black soldier is asked what he would do if Germans were to suddenly jump them. "Dey ain't gwine to know whar I is," answers the soldier. "How's that, Sam?" asks the sergeant. "Well you see, dey might know whar I wuz, but not whar I is." With his regiment holding an advanced line in front of ten thousand White troops, a Black rookie named "Henery" is asked what he would do if the Germans were to attack. "I ain't a-tellin' whut I'd do . . . but I know whut de rest o' you niggahs would do, an' I know whut de papers back home would be sayin' de nex' mawnin'. . . . 'Ten thousand white folks trampled to death.' " Hayward's soldiers are "insulted" when the French give them safety razors instead of the straight razors that are the Negro's supposed weapon of choice.

For a month or two Negro-soldier jokes were the rage. The *Sun* published a collection of similar stories, as did the *American,* retailed by Leon Cadore, who had been a replacement officer with the 369th at Bellevue and Sechault and was going back to his prewar job pitching baseballs for the Brooklyn Robins. Like Hayward he had praise for his men, who "put the fear of the Almighty in the hearts of the Boches." But he also has stories like the one about the crap-shooting Black private who "actually turned pale" when a dud shell hit near him: "Believe me, from now on, dis nigger's goin' to lead a different life." The *Literary Digest* reprinted most of these collections, under titles like "These Colored Fighters Never Lost Their Sense of Humor." Not all of the comic anecdotes were discreditable. Several reflect the high morale and self-confidence of Hayward's men. A nurse complains that Black soldiers make more trouble than all the rest of the AEF put together. "Yassum," the Black soldier answers, "dat's jes' whut de Germans is a-sayin' about us." Comic stories were often juxtaposed with more serious appreciations of Black valor, like the article that praises the gallant attack on Sechault as "typical of the way all our colored troops measured up to the demands of the war." But the piece is titled "Rare Praise for American Negro Troops" and ridicule infiltrates the praise. In one anecdote a Negro is killed in a "mad attempt to take revenge" using "a good old Southern shaving implement." A newspaper cartoon shows a Black soldier, armed with a razor, frightening German troops by asking, "Haircut or shave?" "It was seldom the German troops would hold out when the yelling, sweating negroes jumped into their trenches." All troops yell and sweat, but White soldiers are never described in these terms.[12]

DuBois's rigorous and eloquent defense of Black troops would be seconded by many others, who would publish their own histories of African-American participation in the war effort. But the "plastic moment" in which the pattern of race relations might have been altered was already passing. Hopes for the reform or abolition of Jim Crow rested on acceptance of the Black veterans, and by May 1919 it was clear that White veterans were not going to recognize Black fellow soldiers as comrades-in-arms. Moton and Scott, James Weldon Johnson and the *Age*, Spingarn and DuBois of the NAACP all appealed to the organizers of the American Legion and Veterans of Foreign Wars to open their ranks to Black veterans. They expected strong advocacy for their cause at the inaugural caucus of the American Legion, meeting in St. Louis May 8–10, where Theodore Roosevelt Jr. and Hamilton Fish were among the organizers. But despite public acclaim of the Old Fifteenth, and Fish's efforts behind the scenes, Roosevelt and the leadership of the American Legion decided that the organization's battle for "Americanism" should not be complicated by engagement with the race problem. On May 10 the American Legion caucus closed, leaving the question of Negro membership to local chapters, thus guaranteeing a Jim Crow Legion in the South. That same day, James Weldon Johnson noted the army's rejection of a Negro officer candidate on the stated grounds that he was "unqualified by reason of qualities inherent in the Negro race. . . . Negroes are deficient in moral fibre and force of character rendering them unfit as officers and leaders of men."[13]

Although Johnson could not have known it when he wrote his editorial, one of the men who might have made a difference in the coming struggle had just been eliminated. On the morning of that same May 10 newsboys in Harlem were crying "Extra! Jim Europe Killed in Boston Quarrel."

"He was the Roosevelt of the Negro musicians"

The Hell Fighters Band was in Boston, in the middle of its tour. The concerts had been received with tremendous enthusiasm, but the cold, miserable weather, the days of travel and nights in second-rate hotels, and the stress of performance were wearing on their physical health and their nerves. They had an open date on May 9, but Governor Coolidge invited them to a special ceremony on the tenth: Coolidge would present Europe with a wreath to be placed at the base of the Shaw Monument on the Common, which honored the Black veterans of the Civil War 54th Massachusetts. The gesture marked Europe as, in a sense, Shaw's successor. At the dawn of emancipation a White officer had led Black heroes in the battle that proved the race's entitlement to freedom; now a Black man would be honored for his leadership in this new phase of African-American liberation. It was a signal honor, but required them to play an extra performance on the night of the ninth. Their preferred venue, the Boston Opera House, had previously scheduled Al Jolson, the Jewish "jazz" singer who often performed in blackface, so the Hell Fighters had to play drafty old Mechanics' Hall.[14]

Europe was out of sorts, suffering from a heavy cold, perhaps complicated by the effects of the gassing he had suffered less than a year before. During intermission Noble Sissle saw him in his office, arguing with the "Percussion Twins," Steve and Herbert Wright. Europe was doing his best for them, keeping up the tour despite his illness so the band could get its money, but their performance and behavior were unprofessional. "[You] two boys, above anybody else in the band, should cause me the least worry. I have at all times tried to be a father to both of you, and there is nothing I wouldn't do to help both of you, and I don't want either one to worry me anymore." Steve was agreeable, but Herbert was angry: "I work hard for you. Look at my hands, they're all swollen where I have been drumming, trying to hold the time and yet, Steve, he makes all kinds of mistakes and you never say anything to him." To break up the quarrel Sissle sent in the Harmony Kings, the band's singing quartet, and eased the Wrights out. But Herbert Wright turned and burst back into the room, a small pocketknife open in his fist, yelling, "I'll kill anybody that takes advantage of me . . . !" Europe picked up a chair to fend off the attack. Then, on impulse, set it down and "relax[ed] his whole body": he wouldn't dignify this tantrum by taking it seriously. Wright abruptly "hurled himself" across the chair and struck at Europe with the knife. They tangled, the Kings swarmed on Wright and pulled him away, Sissle pushed him out of the room—when someone called out that Wright had stabbed Europe. Sissle saw Europe with his collar unbuttoned, "a stream of blood" pulsing from a small wound in his neck. An ambulance was called, but there was no sense of emergency, the knife was a small one and the wound did not look dangerous. They used a towel to stanch the blood. Sissle left to finish the concert, and Europe reminded him to have the band at the State House promptly at 9 A.M.

After the concert they went to the police station to give their statements. The hospital called: Europe was in serious condition. Sissle and the others drove to City Hospital as fast as they could and were preparing to give blood for transfusion when a group of doctors and the hospital chaplain came down the stairs, and an orderly told them "Lieutenant Europe is dead." The little knife had nicked an artery, a wound so small none of the band members, some of whom had seen men wounded in combat, recognized it for what it was. James Europe had bled to death.

The news hit Harlem on the morning of May 10. Bluesman W. C. Handy had been fighting a bout of insomnia by riding the subways all night, and as he came up to the street he heard the newsboys crying "Extra! Extra! All about the murder of Jim Europe." "The sun was in the sky. The new day promised peace. But all the suns had gone down for Jim Europe, and Harlem didn't seem the same."

The *New York Times* said his death was a loss to American music and a blow to our nation's attempt to establish itself as the Old World's equal in the high arts.

> Those who think that contemporary ragtime, however imperfect, is a stage in the evolution of a different sort of music which may eventually possess considerable merit will regret the untimely death of a man who ranked as one of the greatest ragtime conductors, perhaps the greatest we have had. And nobody can deny that JAMES REESE EUROPE and his band did something to enhance American prestige in a field where we were likely to lag behind.

Even so, the fact that Europe and his music were African-American makes the *Times* somewhat defensive about his achievement. "Ragtime may be negro music, but it is American negro music, more alive than much other American music; and Europe was one of the Americans . . . contributing most to its development." His was "a creditable artistic accomplishment, if a small one." The Hearst newspapers ignored Europe's death, as they had ignored the Battle of Henry Johnson the year before. But Damon Runyon's sports-page column noted, "Dempsey Will Not Draw Color Line If He Wins. / Considers Negroes Easier to Defeat than White Men."[15]

For the African-American press Europe's triumph was not subject to fussy qualifications, and there was no palliating his loss. The *Age* described the procession that wound its way through Harlem from the funeral parlor at 131st Street, up Seventh Avenue to 140th, east to Lenox and south to 125th Street. The two men who had commanded the Old Fifteenth were there: Charles Fillmore, the "Father of the Regiment," and the man who displaced him, William Hayward. At 125th Street mourners boarded a special train carrying the coffin to Europe's other world, the theater district. From Grand Central Station the cortège passed the Clef Club, filled with mourning Black musicians, the men and women for whom Europe had created the club as their showcase and employment agency. Then down Broadway to Penn Station and the train that would carry Lieutenant Europe's body to Arlington, for burial among the dead of the AEF.

The *Age* obituary honored him for bravery in war, for his efforts to "elevate" jazz as an art music, for his labors to "dignify the colored musician" and "the race of which he was proud to be a member," and for "fighting race prejudice with music." It praised him also for his success as a businessman, that essential measure of a man's fitness for the conditions of modern life: "Jim Europe's business success in life was chiefly due to the fact that he was a thinker and a hustler." And it compared him to the one man who above all others embodied the spirit of progress and Americanism: "He was the Roosevelt of the Negro musicians—a dynamic force that did things—big things."[16]

On the same page was an ad for the "70 Black Devils of the 350th Field Arty Band," which claimed it was the best jazz band in the army and had played for General Pershing and President Poincaré. The band's logo was a leering Sambo face, with thick lips and goggling eyes.

"Roses and Bayonets": The 77th Division Comes Home, May 1–7, 1919

The double image of Black soldiers as heroic Hell Fighters and ridiculous Sambos was mirrored in the bipolar image of Jewish-Americans as loyal members of the Lost Battalion and sinister agents of Yiddish Bolshevism. The homecoming of the 77th Division would bring those contradictory views into immediate confrontation, because it would coincide with May Day, the annual holiday observed by Socialists and Communists to celebrate and demonstrate for the cause of the working class.

May Day 1919 would be particularly significant, with Bolsheviks and revolutionary socialists striving for mastery in half of Europe and a rising tide of labor militancy at home. Each day's newspaper contained at least half a dozen accounts of strikes imminent or declared, IWW plots achieved or thwarted, radicals arrested, leftist speakers attacked by veterans and "workingmen," Bolshevik atrocities in Russia and Red uprisings across Europe. In the interlude between the homecoming parade of the 369th and the arrival of the 77th Division, the government's campaign against radicals and aliens intensified. On March 10 the Post Office Department reported that "the Industrial Workers of the World, anarchists, Socialists—in fact, all dissatisfied elements, particularly the foreign elements—are perfecting an amalgamation with one object . . . namely, the overthrow of the Government of the United States by means of a bloody revolution and the establishment of a Bolshevik republic." On the eve of May Day, the Post Office discovered what appeared to be a nationwide plot to murder leading political, corporate, and judicial figures by bombs sent through the mail. A. Mitchell Palmer, Wilson's attorney general, would use that plot as grounds for a wholesale round-up and deportation of supposed "radicals." News of the "bomb plot" hit the newsstands as May Day paraders were assembling in many large cities, and provided a perfect justification for vigilante violence against leftist marchers.[17]

In New York City police battled organized mobs led by ex-soldiers, who tried to storm the gathering of moderate Socialists at Madison Square Garden. Elsewhere in the city a mob ransacked the offices of the *Call,* newspaper of the Debs wing of the Socialists, and forced party workers to "Display [the] Flag and Sing [the] National Anthem." Meetings in lower Manhattan were broken up, including a concert held by the Clothing Workers' Union, and participants chased through the streets, beaten up, and clubbed. One of the mob leaders told a *Times* reporter, "We are Arthur Guy Empey's men, and we are going to treat 'em rough." Empey was the best-selling American writer wounded while serving with the British, who had been advocating a war of extermination against Germans and pro-Germans in the United States, to "make this America for Americans." Hearst's *American* implied its approval of the mobs by reminding its readers that Lord Bryce, the distinguished British diplomat and commentator on U.S. politics, had praised "vigilance committees" as a uniquely American invention for using "terrorism against would-be provokers of terror."[18]

But in a city like New York vigilante violence by "Guy Empey's men" was only half the problem. What if the Lower East Side and Little Italy decided to fight back and were joined by Jewish and Italian veterans of the 77th Division? War-hardened soldiers had been prominent on both sides of the violent street battles that led to revolutions in Germany and eastern Europe. Across the United States, veterans in uniform had appeared in Red-flag parades as well as in the mobs that attacked them. As a class veterans certainly had economic grievances: their only guaranteed benefit was a $60 "bonus" on demobilization, which was about $40 short of the retail price of a set of civilian clothes, and the city had 200,000 unemployed.[19]

So it was important that the Melting Pot Division be lionized for its patriotism. A massive display of public gratitude might inoculate the returning troops against the dissident tendencies of the East Side. The papers heightened public anticipation with a steady stream of reports on the preparations and the accolades the returning heroes would receive. Stories repeatedly cited the division's achievements: first National Army division to be sent overseas, first to see combat, the only division to have fought every day of the Meuse-Argonne campaign—and, of course, parent division of the now-legendary Lost Battalion, which was mentioned in nearly every article. The local Liberty Loan campaign was kicked off with a mass meeting at the "Argonne Forest Theater," a brand new auditorium that had been "constructed to resemble the Argonne Forest front through which . . . New York City's own division, the 77th, fought fiercely, foot by foot." The lobbies were decorated with replicas of tangled undergrowth and barbed wire, and the roof crowned with the wreckage of an airplane. "The scene called to mind the stories that have come back . . . of the 'lost battalion' . . . which have already become part of the lore of the American Army."[20]

Like Hayward and his colleagues, the officers of the 77th Division believed their outfit symbolized an important principle of Americanism, and they wanted to be sure that the public understood it. Division staff therefore authorized preparation of an official history while they were still in France. Major Julius Adler was put in charge because of his experience at the Times, and his team produced a beautifully designed book, well-bound and printed on fine rag paper, with decorative borders, maps, drawings, and photographs. It was immediately adopted by the newspapers as the primary source of information, and large excerpts were published in the Times and reprinted in other papers before the parade. The book was organized as a theme with variations: the war had transformed the nation and its constituent peoples, enabling them to realize the vision of Progressive nationalists like Theodore Roosevelt, and of all these things the 77th Division was the symbol. Although the division's foreign soldiers had no ancestral tie to the pioneers who had conquered the continent for Americanism, in the Argonne they were transformed into true Sons of Roosevelt: "The East-siders and West-siders of New York, the soldiers from Third Avenue and from Central Park West, were becoming adept woodsmen and learning the craft of the forest hunter." Men of diverse classes, interests, faiths, races, and ethnicities had set aside selfish individualism and "emerg[ed] from the melting pot of training, an amalgamated mass of clear-thinking, clean-living men of whom America might well be proud."

The parade itself, on May 6, was a colossal success: "A Million Cheer 77th In Final Hike . . . Bring Tears to Many Eyes . . . Miles of Cheers from Tremendous Throng . . . Soldiers Present Splendid Appearance as They Stride Along Crowd-Lined Avenue." The crowds showered them with "smokes and sweets," by now a traditional way of greeting returning troops. The *American* reminded its readers that these new-made sons of Roosevelt were also underpaid sons of the working class. "Until every one of these lads is given six months pay, until every one of them has as good or a better place than he left, this country will have little to be proud of." But the parade itself was a ceremony of class reconciliation, "the rich man's son was marching with the ice man's nephew," Bolsheviks please take note. Society reporter Virginia Terhune Van de Water described the occupants of Fifth Avenue mansions tossing bouquets onto the ranks of soldiers, making their march a festival of "Bayonets and Roses." The *Times* too dismissed fears of Bolshevik discontent among the veterans. They were "full of pep, full of ambition, with a valuable experience of things accomplished," ready for whatever the economy might throw at them.

Every paper published its own variation on the Americanization theme: although the soldiers came "from nearly every race on earth," they had come home true Americans. Their racial difference was celebrated in a variety of ways. Sing Kee was the "star exotic" of the occasion, but the *Times* reporter noted that he was "highly Americanized." The *New York American* affirmed the idea that war service had transformed men of alien race into *racial* Americans:

> In this parade to-day there is a lesson for all Americans. Here are men of many nationalities, many of them born across the water, but all ready to fight and die for liberty, and all able in a very short time to learn how to fight. For there is something in the air of this land of ours—something that the American imbibes, whether born on the soil

or coming to it to gain freedom—that makes a race which is and must always be unconquerable.

But in imagining this new American race, the paper figuratively transforms the division's Jews and Italians, Polacks and Irishmen into Vikings: the history of the 77th Division is "A modern Saga . . . in which the part if the Vikings was played by Mickey McCune and Pasquale Amato, Solly Rosenbaum and Ignace Podeiski." The Nordic "race" is still the standard against which all would-be Americans are to be measured.[21]

At a dinner given by the city for the officers of the 77th, Mayor Hylan praised "the gallant stand of the detachment of the 307th and 308th Infantry," and General Alexander drew laughs when he praised "these hardy backwoodsmen from Hester Street, the Bowery, and the East Side." There was still something comical about the idea of Yiddisher pants-pressers stalking Huns, like Hawkeye hunting Mingoes.

Alexander was a little put out by the continual harping on the phrase "Lost Battalion." *He* certainly had not "lost" Whittlesey's command: they were exactly where he had told them to go, holding their ground. A *Times* editorial twitted Alexander for taking the phrase so much to heart. It was a nickname given "by the American people" to mark a mythic moment in American history, and it would "last as long as the story of the war itself lasts."

What was it that set Alexander's teeth on edge? Perhaps those persistent rumors that suggested the whole fight was a series of blunders. The *Times* had just published the statement of a recently returned aviator, who "Blames Major Whittlesey for the Plight of the 'Lost Battalion' " and claimed Whittlesey "failed to coordinate his position with the remainder of the division and adjoining colored troops of the 92nd Division." There was no truth to the accusation. But there it was.[22]

Whittlesey himself took no part in the festivities. His last public statement before the parade was a letter to the *Times*, expressing his grief for the death of Major James A. Roosevelt, TR's cousin and commander of the 308th's supply train. Major Roosevelt had run the train with great efficiency, often going forward under fire to see that ammunition and food were delivered, surviving battle to die of "cerebrospinal meningitis" on the ship home. Whittlesey remembered Roosevelt as one who lived up to "the fine traditions of his family . . . a man to whom war was a bright and fine adventure," and a "kindly human spirit." After that, Whittlesey avoided interviews and public appearances. The name of the man who, more than any other, symbolized the Lost Battalion does not appear in the list of officers marching in the parade, nor the list of grandees and celebrities on the reviewing stand, nor at the various special appearances by battalion members. There is no evidence he even witnessed the event as a spectator, although he was in the city at the time.[23]

" 'East Side Jew' . . . ought not to be a term of contempt"

Sanitation workers cleaned up the detritus of celebration and the soldiers returned to Upton for muster out. There would be other parades, but none with quite so personal a meaning to New Yorkers.

The fame of the Lost Battalion would be periodically renewed over the next year, as hitherto hidden or unknown episodes of battle came to light, as newspapers and magazines attempted their summing up of America's Great War, as the generals explained themselves and the first unit histories began to appear. In July Edward A. McManus released a feature film titled *The Lost Battalion*. It was said to have been produced "under the personal supervision of General Alexander," and it made use of Signal Corps footage of Whittlesey, McMurtry, Krotoshinsky, and others of the battalion taken shortly after the battle. The film blended these images with fictional scenes shot in the studio to produce the illusion that "Lieut. Colonel Whittlesey . . . was one of the 'stars' who acted in the picture." The film takes an odd approach to the "Americanization" theme now inextricably bound up with the story. Instead of featuring a representative of one of the larger immigrant groups—an Italian or a Jew—the protagonists are two Chinese brothers, one middle class and the other a burglar in a Chinatown tong. The good brother loves a stenographer who dreams of becoming the "world's greatest actress." The conflicts are somehow carried over into the war, the brothers end up in the Lost Battalion, the burglar dies, and the good brother returns as a hero to marry the girl and (presumably) realize their American dreams. McManus's choice of hero may have been affected by the celebrity of Sing Kee.[24] But the effect, and perhaps the motive, of featuring a Chinese hero was to emphasize the *racial* difference of the immigrants.

For the soldiers themselves, such reminders of their fame were in increasingly ironic contrast to the difficulty of their circumstances. Not only were there no substantial benefits to be expected, for most of the veterans pay was well in arrears. Some disabled veterans were unable to support their families or pay their rent. Even the able-bodied had difficulty finding jobs. Fear of unemployment had been the ghost at the victory banquet all winter and spring. Newspaper coverage of the parades and the tales of returning veterans were accompanied by stories reflecting the rising tide of unemployment, the diminished job prospects for veterans, and the need for some institution—government, a consortium of businessmen—to do something about it. On the eve of the 77th Division's return, a city official told the *Times* that at least 6,000 men from the demobilized 27th Division still needed jobs and that the soldiers were not being cared for. The 77th Division Club, successor to the wartime civilian auxiliary, sponsored an employment agency and made plans to buy a building for use as a shelter for veterans unable to find or pay for decent housing. At the end of July the club reported placing 7,647 veterans in jobs, but was still seeking work for 3,200 others. Fully one-third of the division's veterans had had to make use of its services.[25]

Jewish organizations in the city were particularly concerned to show support for the Liberty Loan and provide jobs for the returning veterans. The community had a tradition of taking care of its own. But there was a special urgency to their efforts as they sought to counteract Simons's accusations and the rising hostility toward immigrants in general, and "Yiddish Jews" in particular. It was important to show the public that the Jewish veteran would not be a burden on the state, important to ensure full employment for East Side veterans so they would not become more radical in their politics.

On May 18, two weeks after the parade, Jewish groups organized a public event at the YMHA on 92nd Street. An impressive panel of speakers affirmed the patriotic and heroic services of Jewish soldiers and defended American Jews against accusations of Bolshevik sympathies. Despite his distaste for public appearances, Whittlesey joined the panel to speak in defense of his Jewish soldiers. His statement was brief but unambiguous in recognizing the essential point: whether the "hyphenates" were distinct races, religious sects, or national or language minorities, all had proved their Americanism in the only way that mattered, by standing for their country on the day of battle. Whittlesey praised "the splendid fighting qualities the Jewish boys of the east side had displayed" and added; "If I am ever pessimistic of the future of this country . . . I would always feel assured that I could go to the crowded quarters of the city and pick out Herschkowitz, Ciriglio, and O'Brien, and know that in them I could find the kind of men that were needed." Trotsky might be an "apostate Jew," Russian Bolshevik agitators might be "Yiddish," but Abe Krotoshinsky and most of the men who fought with Whittlesey's Lost Battalion were " 'Jew boys,' of whom the world had once said that they would not fight." They were American heroes, "recruited from the pants-makers, pressers, and buttonhole makers of the East Side, [who] have become super-fighting men."[26]

Association with the Lost Battalion improved the public image of Yiddish Jews, but only to a certain point. A colleague of the Reverend Simons offered "A Methodist Tribute to the Jew," moved by the thought that "Colonel Whittlesey's heroic 'Lost Battalion' . . . was so full of the little clothing workers that some called it a 'Yiddish Battalion.' " He declared that in future, " 'East-side Jew' . . . ought not to be a term of contempt," then added, "even though Russian Bolshevism recruited its forces in that populous section and revolutionary propaganda finds fertile soil among these waifs from lands which never knew such liberties as America offers to all." Praise for the Yiddish Battalion did not negate the assumption that Jews were a natural constituency for Bolshevism.

Jewish writers associated with the American Jewish Committee praised the Americanization of their people in similarly equivocal terms. Louis Popkin, writing in the *American Hebrew*, celebrated "The 'Melting Pot' Division" as "A National Ideal."

> Into the crucible of war, the hungry-eyed, rebellious shop-keepers and pants-pressers of Grand Street; the stolid chop-suey makers of Mott and Pell; the Scandinavian dock-hand, the law-breaking, crap-shooting boy of the streets, and the thoughtful professional Jew, were poured and melted into pure gold—true Americans. . . . Representing every country . . . speaking every language, living down alien customs and traditions, these men were yet Americans—true citizens of democracy.[27]

Yet even within these terms of praise is the suggestion that Americanization requires the hyphenates not simply to adapt to American ways but to "liv[e] down" their alien customs and traditions"—as if those traditions were a mark of shame.

The *Literary Digest*'s weekly compendium of press opinion reflected the ambivalence with which the 77th Division's proofs of Americanism were received. The May 24 issue offered a sampling of the honors paid to "'The Melting-Pot Division' That Pierced the Argonne Forest." But its chosen quotations emphasize the alien and even repellent aspects of the immigrant soldiers. It describes many of the Jews and Italians as "gunmen and gangsters" who could not speak English and identifies them by the use of ridiculing nicknames—in the case of the Jews the somewhat nasty moniker "Izzy Yidinski." Like the Negroes, hyphenates *are* Americans—but their Americanism is second-class, a legitimate object of ridicule and contempt.

The contradictions in these glorifications of the Lost Battalion reflected the unresolved conflicts in American society between civic nationality and cultural pluralism on one side, racial nationalism and "100% Americanism" on the other. Was the goal of Americanization to achieve perfect amalgamation and a nation homogeneous in culture and/or racial type? Or was ethnic difference compatible with American nationality? For the White and native-born the question was immediately political and social: On what terms (if any) ought they accept ethnic strangers as Americans? For Jews and other ethnic minorities the question was partly one of political strategy: whether to seek acceptance *with* difference, in *spite* of difference, or with difference *eradicated*. But on a deeper level, there was also a question of how Jewish- or Italian- or Polish- or Chinese-Americans ought to think of themselves: Should they despise their origins and seek to bury them, or proudly assert their cultural difference in the public spaces of politics and the popular arts? Their problem mirrored the dilemma of double-consciousness faced by African-Americans—whether to judge themselves by the standards of a majority that despised them, or affirm *both* sides of their hyphenate identity.[28]

The complexity of the problem is displayed in the ambivalent reaction of Jewish editorialists to Captain Edward Harrigan's praise of Jewish soldiers. Harrigan was the Irish vaudevillian's son who was reputed to have been "in command of the force which rescued Col. Whittlesey's famous 'Lost Battalion.'" Since his return he had been giving interviews and making speeches defending the heroism and Americanism of immigrant soldiers, especially Jews. The *Times* gave special prominence to his long article, "City Boys as Soldiers," publishing it in the parade issue of the Sunday magazine together with an extended excerpt from Adler's history of the division.

Harrigan said it was a mistake to think that city boys were inferior to the sons of rural America when it came to soldiering. In fact, whatever their comparative deficits in physique or diet, the "quick wittedness and adaptability" born of life in the streets gave them an edge in facing the disorder and disruption of modern war. Of all city boys, Jews make the *best* soldiers—not in spite of their racial propensities, but because of them. "[To] those who know the Jew, his psychology and mode of reasoning," their heroism at Charlevaux Mill was not surprising.

> [There is] no better soldier anywhere than the Jewish boy. About 40 per cent of the division were Jews; and what fighters they were! They put into their fighting the same quality that the Jew puts into business or professional work, and that make him successful; in other words, they use their keen Jewish intelligence in the business of fighting just as they would use it in any other business. The Jew is esssentially intelligent, keen, determined to make good; the Jewish boys of the 77th fought that way.

The *American Hebrew* was glad to seize on Harrigan's encomiums and link them to praises voiced by an even more heroic figure: "This praise comes on the heels of the enthusiastic laudation of the heroic behavior of the Jews of the 'Lost Battalion' by their commander, Lieut. Col. Whittlesey himself." But the editor is uneasy with the terms of praise. The traits for which Harrigan congratulates Jewish soldiers—sharpness of mind, extreme diligence in all forms of business—are those that belong to the "Shylock" stereotype, which the editor deplores. The editor even apologizes for citing Whittlesey's praise, because it reinforces the mistaken and harmful tendency of Americans to think of Jews as a race. If not compelled to defend his people against unjust and dangerous accusations, the editor would have preferred to speak only of *American* soldiers.[29]

The AJC and the German-Jewish leadership had accepted the terms of a social bargain that required Jews to prove their Americanism by transforming themselves into Sons of Roosevelt. In its most genial and optimistic form, this version of Americanization seemed to suggest that inside every ghetto-born Jew there was an American just waiting for the chance to get out. In "When the Jewish Doughboy Returns," Private H. L. Sternfeld described the AEF as a school of Americanization, which had transformed the sons of East Side rabbis and socialist pants-pressers into 100% Americans fit for the Strenuous Life. They had learned to do their duty without "kicking" all the time and to "display courage and fear nobody"—in Roosevelt's words, to fear God and take their own part. "The returning Jewish soldier will undoubtedly bring to the East Side the legend of the great, vast, and free America" and like a Jewish Daniel Boone show his people the way from the mean streets to the broad free ranges of the West.

But there was a darker side to this acceptance of 100% Americanism, a hostility to anything too distinctively Jewish that borders on self-hatred and takes the form of hostility toward the Yiddish-speaking component of the community. Joel Blau, a Jewish "Four-Minute Man," made an invidious comparison between the the patriotic Maccabees (the name means "hammer") of ancient Israel with the *knockers* (a Yiddish word meaning "big shot") of the East Side. The Maccabees lived by "this virile idea of hammering," of confronting one's enemies openly and fighting or working hard to overcome them, and their struggle is memorialized in Chanukah, the "most virile of our festivals." The "present-day Jewish life" of the East Side is characterized instead by "hypocrisy and effeminacy," qualities Roosevelt identified with the despised Chinese.[30]

By defending Jews *only* as 100% Americans, Marshall and the AJC failed to defend American Jews as they actually were. They also contributed to the development of a Jewish equivalent to the double-consciousness that afflicted African-Americans. By implicitly accepting the notion of native-born racialists that Jews could become American only by achieving a total "amalgamation," they had effectively agreed to consider the most distinctive elements of Jewish culture as "alien." From that perspective the culture and appearance of "Yiddish Jews" was equivalent to the iconic Sambo face, whose appearance mocked all assertions of Black equality. The Lost Battalion then becomes the "whitening cream," which palliates the difference between the old stock White American and the racial interloper.

But even the assimilationists of the AJC had to acknowledge that Jews were considered to be a race and had to defend themselves as such. For all its insistence on the primacy of Americanism, *American Hebrew* honors the Jewish veterans for having "served the Jewish cause even more than that of America"—disregarding what a believer in the *Protocols* might make of such words. Within a six-month period *American Hebrew* published two nearly identical works of short fiction based on the Lost Battalion, which translated the idea into fable. In both stories a Jewish draftee is subjected to anti-Semitic abuse by fellow soldiers and is treated with distant sympathy by a platoon commander who is a Jew passing as a "regular American." Once the unit goes into battle, the Jewish soldier fights like a hero and dies a hero's death. In one version he becomes a Jewish Sergeant York, single-handedly killing or capturing carloads of Germans before he is killed; in the other he kills his own brother (who is serving in the German army). In both stories his lieutenant is so overwhelmed by this display of Americanism that he regrets having "passed" and wishes he looked "more Jewish" so that he could not have evaded his identity. Thus heroism in battle transforms the significance of the "racial" qualities attributed to Jews and makes it possible to imagine an America willing to embrace Jews as Jews—perhaps even to mutually mix identities and cultures with them. As *American Hebrew*'s correspondent watched "New York's Own" marching up Fifth Avenue, with "Jewish faces fill[ing] the ranks," he imagined that for this day at least "even non-Jews caught the Jewish spirit."[31]

For the Lower East Siders themselves, the identification of the Lost Battalion as a Yiddish Battalion was an affirmation that, just as they were, they had *earned* acceptance as Americans. For many in the community, the headiness of that affirmation awakened a desire for full assimilation, the wish to escape "greenhorn" status and become unexceptionably American. But most first- and second-generation immigrants resisted the repudiation of Yiddish culture that such an escape implied and resented the German-Jewish leadership for disparaging that culture. It was not that they wanted to live in a linguistic ghetto. The Lower East Side dialect was a hybrid of Yiddish and American that became more American every year; and no one doubted that English would become, if it was not already, the community's primary language. What bound the community together was the culture of *Yiddishkeit*: a set of values that had served them well in the face of persecution, poverty, and exile; an attitude toward experience, a style rooted in the language but transferable to English—ironic, earthy, rich in sarcasm, skeptical of pretension and authority, dismissive of fine illusions, willing to hope but discounting the prospects:

> *Eyn got un azoy fil soynim.* (One god and so many enemies.)
> *Abi gezunt, dos lebn ken men zikh ale mol nemen.* (As long as you're healthy you can always kill yourself.)
> *Me zol zikh kenen oyskoyfn fun toyt, voltn di oreme layt gehat parnose.* (If the rich could hire others to die for them, the poor could make a living.)

They would cling to the cultural associations and styles of *Yiddishkeit* even as Yiddish itself descended from *mamaloshen* (mother tongue), to second language, to *bubbe-loshen*—the language of grandmothers.[32]

On the Lower East Side, *Yiddishkeit* was also linked to socialist politics. By the winter of 1918 the ideological terms of Americanism were understood to exclude all forms of socialism, from the American or Debsian variety to Bolshevism, and even the more militant forms of trade unionism. The *American Hebrew* cited the November electoral defeat of Morris Hillquit and Meyer London as a sign that the Lower East Side had finally become American. But the East Siders had not abandoned their identification with the cause of labor or the socialism of Debs and Cahan and London and Hillquit. They thought victory in war should be the prelude to the triumph of labor, and acted accordingly, marching for socialism and organizing a wave of strikes in the garment district. Nor did the vast majority see any inconsistency between their politics and Americanism. They had taken to heart the liberal promises of 1917, which represented a patriotic socialism as not at all incompatible with Americanism, as they remembered those phrases in CPI propaganda that approved the immigrants' wish to blend the "best of his old traditions" with Americanization.

The liberal propaganda of 1917 had prepared some native-born Americans to be receptive to that idea. Edward Harrigan, for one, was ready to defend a different kind of Americanization. He agreed that war had made the hyphenates into "100 per cent American, everyone speaking English" and that the 77th Division was "living proof that we can assimilate the foreigner." But Harrigan's understanding of "assimilation" is different from Roosevelt's: he is, after all, the son of the vaudevillian best remembered as "proud of all the Irish blood that's in me." He understands that what his men want to show the world is not only "that they were Americans, but that they represented the races they came from too." Reporter Gerald Breitgam of the *Globe* took Harrigan's notion one step further. He describes the relationship between the native-born White Plattsburgh officers and the hyphenate soldiers as a dialogue, an "interchange of thoughts" in which each learns something from the other. The net result is not just the Americanizing of the immigrant but "Americanizing America," moving the nation closer to realizing the ideal of civil democracy. Isidore Singer, writing in the *American Hebrew*, was moved to think that Jewish culture could provide Americans with a model of the pluralistic community to which America might aspire: "We Jews, in [the diversity of] our racial, national and religious makeup, form, in the true sense of the word, an ethno-religious Rainbow Division in the *Grand Armée* of mankind."[33]

But the current of public and political opinion was set against any compromise with the exclusive principle of 100% Americanism. Since the turn of the year, the *Literary Digest*'s editorials and compilations of press opinion had been moving away from the more liberal concepts of melting pot Americanism toward a more draconian insistence on the kind of Americanism espoused by Roosevelt in his Vigilante mode. It favored proposals for restructuring American education along nationalist lines: the "liberal arts," which foster ideological pluralism, must be replaced by a curriculum that would teach Americans to think of duties rather than rights and to see "loyalty" to the state as the paramount virtue. For immigrants, Americanization was not to be considered an option but an obligation; if necessary the state should compel them to attend the proper classes or face deportation. By summer the *Digest* was definitively in the anti-immigration camp. It was high time "to Clap the Lid on the Melting-Pot."

> The "Far-Famed Melting-Pot" has proved . . . a delusion and a snare. . . . It is impossible to keep out revolutionists and Bolshevists without keeping out substantially everybody. . . . No pot can melt its contents when more is being shovelled in all the time, so it is now proposed to clap on the lid and give it a chance to fuse.

The *Digest* also began to publicize the new "scientific" studies of racial differences that were being published by theoreticians and ideologists of the Immigration Restriction League and the eugenics movement. These studies, based on tendentious readings of the mass IQ tests administered by the War Department, contradicted the belief that military service had proved all races equally apt for Americanization. An article reprinted from the *Journal of Heredity* framed the question in Roosevelt's terms: "Are there 'fighting races'" with a special aptitude for success in a modern war? "That idiotic 'melting-pot' idea is blown to the devil by this war if they tell the truth about the thing. . . . Blood will tell": the more "real Americans" a division had, the better it fought. The question for postwar American policy makers was whether to adopt a laissez-faire approach, allowing the "survival of the fittest" to play itself out, or to promote the development of the racially superior "Nordic" type of American and restrain population growth among non-Whites and non-Nordic hyphenates.[34]

Among African- and Jewish-Americans there were signs of a tentative and limited understanding that they shared enemies and were being similarly victimized by racialist ideology and politics. The socialist Yiddish-language *Forverts* actively supported Black civil rights initiatives and drew parallels between anti-Jewish pogroms and anti-Black race riots. The *American Hebrew* included the KKK in its anathema against the "Soviet of Brawlers," the mobs who attacked socialist parades on the East Side. DuBois and the Black socialists Randolph and Owen rejected anti-Semitic red-baiting and emphasized the similarities in the race-based oppression directed at Jews and Blacks. They too noted the parallel between lynching and pogroms and used it to argue that socialism could resolve race conflict by uniting workers as a class.[35]

However, leadership elements in each community were still willing to defend their own people at the other's expense. How that could work is indicated by the last big Lost Battalion story of the year. *Washington Post* correspondent Herbert Bailey praises the Lost Battalion for its heroism and for demonstrating that "endurance and bravery were no monopoly of any one race." But he adds an element that had hitherto passed without mention: "The Real Story of the 'Lost Battalion' . . . Explains How the Germans 'Broke' Our Colored Troops by Playing on Their Superstitious Fears." Bailey falsely implies that the whole 92nd Division was involved and that the units engaged consisted of "negroes commanded by negroes." He claims that the Blacks thought the forest was haunted and were frightened because they did not believe Black officers could deal with supernatural powers. The Germans "merely lit up the forest with Very flares and lights," and "soon had the negroes contemplating the murkiness of the forest with staring eyes and gaping mouths," like the "darkies" in *Birth of a Nation*, terrified by the spectral appearance and magical sleight-of-hand of KKK horsemen.[36]

Bailey's article, and others like it, advanced the standing of White immigrants by contrasting the soldierly virtues of the Lost Battalion with the racial failings of a Black regiment. Jewish organizations of every kind supported the NAACP's antilynching campaign. But faced with the necessity of defending their communities against charges of un-Americanism, some Jewish community leaders and representatives would try to win allies or mollify enemies by compromising with or even appealing to color-line racism. For their part, there were Black leaders more than willing to exploit anti-immigrant feeling to maintain African-Americans' foothold in industrial employment. Instead of joining forces, the two groups remained competitors in a zero-sum game. They would face the political reaction of 1919–24 as rivals rather than allies.

13

The Black and the Red: Race Riots, Red Scares, and the Triumph of Reaction, 1919–1924

> [It] has taken us fifty years to learn that speaking English and wearing good clothes and going to school does not transform a Negro into a white man. . . . Americans will have a similar experience with the Polish Jew, whose dwarf stature, peculiar mentality, and ruthless concentration on self-interest are being engrafted upon the stock of the nation.
>
> —*Madison Grant*, The Passing of the Great Race *(1918)*

Woodrow Wilson had taken the nation into a war for which he had failed to prepare, and his soldiers paid the price. He hoped to be better prepared for the peace. In June of 1918 he organized the Reconstruction Research Division (RRD), a brain trust of experts to develop a plan for the transition from a war to a peace economy.

But the Great War ended with surprising suddenness. When Wilson received Prince Max's peace overture on October 4 the Lost Battalion was still trapped in the Pocket, the Meuse-Argonne was a bloody stalemate, and most Allied leaders expected the war to continue well into 1919. Just one month later the Kaiser abdicated, his armed forces were demoralized, and a new German government sued for peace. The machinery of mobilization, not quite complete but nonetheless running at top speed, had suddenly to be thrown into reverse. Nearly two million doughboys, who had expected to be fighting for the Rhine crossings, were instead preparing to ship out of France, and two million draftees training in the States had to be rapidly demobilized to clear the camps for their return. It was generally presumed that the transition to peace would produce a serious economic crisis, though experts disagreed on its timing and the form it would take. It seemed likely that the closing of war industries and the lag in restarting peacetime production would raise unemployment just when three to four million demobilized soldiers would be thrown upon the labor market. The fear that Bolsheviks might use the crisis to foment revolution added a terrifying aspect to a situation that would have been deeply troubling in any circumstances.

Demobilization would compel the United States to deal with four major problems, each of which was aggravated by fear of economic collapse.[1]

1. *What ought to be done about the returning veterans?* Should the state guarantee them employment, either by giving them favored treatment for civil service jobs or requiring employers to hire them—and fire the workers already on the job? Should they be paid a pension or only a token bonus on their army pay? Four million veterans, more than a million combat-trained, constituted a potentially powerful and dangerous political constituency. European revolutions had been made and suppressed by self-organized gangs of demobilized soldiers and sailors.

2. *How should the nation deal with its racial minorities and with future immigration?* The wartime rage against hyphenates and immigrant Bolsheviks generated pressure for a radical curtailment of immigration. On the other hand, the wartime celebration of hyphenate heroism in the Lost Battalion and other outfits argued for a more liberal policy. The issues were parallel for African-Americans: Should the government recognize the loyal and heroic service of Black troops by taking action to end lynching and reform (if not abolish) Jim Crow? Or should it continue prewar understandings of the limits of federal power and the right of communities to preserve their "customary relations"?

3. *Organized labor and organized capital were preparing for a major confrontation once wartime regulations were lifted.* Government regulators had kept production lines rolling during the war by mediating between labor and capital, which enhanced the power of unions by compelling managers to recognize them as negotiating partners. The unions hoped to build on these wartime gains; corporate owners and

managers intended to roll them back. There would be a wave of strikes and displays of labor militancy that fed into fears of Bolshevism, and lockouts that exacerbated fears of unemployment. The number, scale, and range of strikes in 1919 was alarming: 3,600 businesses were struck at one time or another, and four million workers (20 percent of the workforce) went out during the year.

4. *There was a default of national leadership and no ideological consensus on the proper role of the state in regulating the transition.* The "War Progressives" who led the RRD wanted to preserve the regulatory powers assumed by the government during the war and use them to manage demobilization and economic transition. But Wilson and his leading cabinet officers were committed to the economic philosophy of the New Freedom, which required speedy deregulation. The president himself was disengaged from domestic policy making, wholly concentrated on shaping the peace settlement. He was in Europe from December 1918 to June 1919, except for a brief return to the States in February and March, and even after his return devoted all his energies to winning support for the League of Nations. In the absence of any overarching presidential vision of postwar order, let alone executive management of readjustment, the conflicts among labor and capital, minorities and majorities, immigrants and native-born, White and Black played out in a series of violent confrontations:

- In June there was a second round of terrorist bomb attacks. Attorney General Palmer began the program of official denunciations, raids, arrests, and deportations known as the "Red Scare."
- In July there were massive and bloody race riots in Washington, D.C., and Chicago. At the same time a wave of anti-Jewish pogroms in eastern Europe intensified the controversy over immigration and the "racial" status of Jews.
- In September the steel strike brought the confrontation of labor and capital to a head. It was broken by a combination of propaganda, violence, and intimidation, and the use of Negro strikebreakers. The strike discredited labor and reinforced the Red Scare, the movement for immigration restriction, and opposition to Black demands for civil rights.

By the end of the year the political and ideological conflicts over the status of labor, returning veterans, Negroes, and immigrants had been resolved, and the more liberal options defeated. The social bargain that had structured the wartime role of African-Americans and "hyphenates" would be repudiated, and Congress would officially endorse a racial standard of Americanism that excluded racial and ethnic minorities.

In the atmosphere of impending economic and social crisis, the condition and temper of the returning veterans was perhaps the most troubling uncertainty. They had a unique moral authority as spokesmen for the democratic ideals that had shaped the nation's war aims and for the social bargains that were agreed at the outset. Yet they were also particularly vulnerable to the economic disruptions that threatened the transition to peace. There was no plan for reintegrating them with the civilian economy, no system of veterans' benefits or pensions, and only the most rudimentary support system to provide for veterans incapacitated by wounds or illness.

The veterans' psychology was volatile, their anger equally liable to turn against "Reds" or against business and government. During the Seattle general strike in February, the Soldiers and Sailors Council, a chapter of the radical World War Veterans (WWV) had split: a majority joined the strike, but another faction armed itself and joined the vigilantes who suppressed it. MID noted that some veterans who had served in the anti-Soviet Archangel expedition were planning to battle Red unionists in Detroit, while others were reaffiliating with militant labor: "After being up here fighting these people I will be ashamed to look a union man in the face. . . . I am 3/10ths Bolo [Bolshevik] myself." Many veterans, "disappointed with their treatment or progress in the army, have become very active Bolshevists." The army IQ tests had revealed that between a quarter and a third of enlisted men were illiterate, and as the *Literary Digest* noted, "American soldiers who cannot read or write" were liable to fall under the spell of radical agitators. Negroes and the foreign-born made up a disproportionate share of "this illiterate, ill-formed element," but the virus of radicalism, thriving among the aliens, could easily spread to ignorant, poor, discontented White veterans.[2]

In fact, few enlisted veterans were ready for radical political engagement. The speed with which they were demobilized, the disorder of the society to which they returned, prevented their thinking or acting as an organized body. They had jobs to find, relationships to restore. They had survivor's guilt to deal with, bad memories, the lingering effects of wounds too minor to get them out of the line (that "whiff of gas" so many talked about) but seriously degrading of their health and strength. The civilian roles to which they reverted broke up wartime comradeship and reestablished the old social and racial divisions. Negro veterans were niggers in the Jim Crow South, "Rastus" in the disdainful North. At Charlevaux Mill "Simon" the pants-presser and "Mick" the Irish cop had forged a bond as close as any either would ever experience. But of what use was it, how could it be *lived* when the pants-pressers' union was going on strike and the cop's bosses wanted him to keep his eye on the Reds?

On the other hand, the Plattsburgh alums who had commanded them *were* prepared for postwar politics. They were Sons of Roosevelt still, believers in the nationalist principles for which the war had been fought. TR's son and namesake, Theodore Jr., had come out of the war with a superb combat record in the elite First Division, several wounds, and the rank of colonel. The Roosevelt name and his own reputation made him immensely popular with enlisted men as well as officers. He shared his father's dream of building a new nationalism on the patriotism evoked by the war and had been thinking about organizing a veteran-based movement from the moment of his own enlistment. In February 1919, shortly after his father's death, he joined with three fellow officers to plan a veterans' organization that would work for the Rooseveltian goals of "permanent preparedness," universal military service, and "100% Americanism." This was the beginning of the American Legion, which would emerge after a year of struggle as the dominant veterans' organization in the country.[3]

The Legion's ideology and program were extrapolations from the New Nationalism and the Gospel of Preparedness. And though attempts were made to include enlisted men, it was initially an officers' club, a continuation of the Plattsburgh movement: the four founders were all Plattsburgh alums, as were most of those officers who were handpicked as delegates to the founding caucus of the Legion. Thus the Legion's program is an index to the ways in which the war had altered the ideology of Progressive nationalism. The old passion for economic and social reform was replaced by an anxiety-driven zeal for national security; the liberal and democratic side of Progressivism diminished as its authoritarian side, its racialism and class bias came to the fore.

The Legion caucus in St. Louis on May 8–10 established an administrative structure, authorized an annual convention, and framed a statement of principles. For Roosevelt and the leadership that statement was the critical task, because they believed the Legion's primary role was to promote "Americanism." Hamilton Fish, ex-captain in the Old Fifteenth and former disciple of Roosevelt Sr., headed the resolutions committee and wrote the preamble, a resounding but nonspecific paean to patriotism, service, and Americanism. There was broad agreement that anyone who had opposed the war was by definition un-American, including conscientious objectors, socialists, Bolsheviks, anarchists, and pro-Germans. The Legion opposed the granting of pardons or appeals that would shorten the sentences of those jailed under the Espionage and Sedition Acts; demanded the deportation of noncitizens who had availed themselves of their legal right to refuse conscription; and refused to take a stand against Jim Crow.[4]

Surprisingly, veterans' benefits were the most divisive issue at the caucus. Many delegates assumed the Legion would be for Great War veterans what the GAR had been for Civil War veterans: a permanent lobby to win government benefits for ex-servicemen and their families. There was a real and immediate need for government relief. Soldiers had been paid "a dollar a day," $30 a month, from which the government deducted allotments for dependents and an $8 premium for War Risk Insurance. For many even that meager pay was months in arrears, and civilian employment difficult to get. The bonus of $60 paid on demobilization was rightly regarded as inadequate, since prices had nearly tripled since 1915. The War Risk Insurance Board failed to properly inform enlisted men about the nature and value of their government insurance policies. An estimated 90 percent were allowing their policies to lapse, depriving their families of the only lifetime benefit provided for servicemen. Bureaucratic inefficiency also made it hard for beneficiaries of slain or disabled soldiers to collect on their policies.

Several proposals were put forward for increasing the bonus or "adjusted compensation" paid to demobilized soldiers. Some delegates cited the hardships of poor and working-class soldiers; but the strongest argument on behalf of the bonus was that many soldiers had "left lucrative employments" to enlist, a plea that reflected the middle-class bias of the membership. The wealthiest members *opposed* the bonus on a mixture of economic and ideological grounds. The few hundred dollars of the bonus was meaningless to them, and the requirement to pay the bonus would force the government to raise their taxes. Roosevelt Jr. put his immense prestige on the line to oppose any adjusted compensation as a violation of his father's principles. The bonus idea seemed to "place a cash value" on patriotic service, demeaning and commercializing it. The Legion caucus gave in to "the worthy son of a worthy sire" and stood in silent tribute to "the greatest statesman that this nation has ever produced—the president who defied Wall Street and every other combination—Theodore Roosevelt."[5]

But it was not Wall Street that the Sons of Roosevelt targeted. They were aware of the real hardships faced by veterans, aware of the resentment they felt against both capitalists and union workers who had prospered through the war years. The Legion's policy was to turn that resentment away from capital and toward socialists and unionists. The caucus went on record in favor of "immediately deporting every one of those Bolsheviks or IWWs." It blamed "alien slackers" for holding on to jobs that ought to go to returning veterans and called for their deportation as well. The Legion's newspaper, and the speakers it sent across the country, asked the public and government officials to look on the Legion as a representative of "100% Americanism" and a "bulwark against Bolshevism and anarchy." The Legion had found in the Red Scare its "moral equivalent of war," and the resentment its leaders fomented against "slackers," aliens, and Reds soon leached out into broader categories: immigrants of all sorts, Negroes, labor unions. Years later a legionnaire recalled his anger against striking workers. He admitted that the demand for a higher veterans' bonus "was probably unsound from a national point of view. But by God, settling every strike in a war plant during *war* by raising wages of home stayers . . . had been a damned sight unsounder. Maybe two wrongs don't make a right. But that was the way most of us came to feel about it." Another indignantly recalled that "Southern Negroes getting from eighty cents to a dollar a day working in the fields were suddenly raised to $3.30," while soldiers and their families struggled to get by on $22 a month (when they could get it). The May Day assaults on socialist meetings and marches indicated that "radicals" had been identified as the first legitimate targets. In July it became evident that African-Americans would be the next.

"Negroes Shoot Back": Race Riots in
Washington and Chicago, July–August 1919

> If we must die—let it not be like hogs
> Hunted and penned in an inglorious spot,
> While round us bark the mad and hungry dogs,
> Making their mock at our accursed lot. . . .
> What though before us lies the open grave?
> Like men we'll face the murderous, cowardly pack,
> Pressed to the wall, dying but fighting back!
>
> —*Claude McKay, "If We Must Die" (1919)*

The war years had seen a rise in levels of violence against African-Americans, reflecting the resistance of working-class Whites to the encroachment of Blacks on their jobs and neighborhoods. There had been major race riots in East St. Louis, Waco, and Houston in 1917. Lynchings had increased every year since the war began: 48 in 1917, 63 in 1918, and there would be 78 in 1919, 11 involving burning at the stake.

At the same time there was a rising temper of self-confident militancy among African-American leaders and at the grass roots, especially in urban centers like Chicago, Washington, and New York. Political prospects for civil rights had been enhanced by the government's outreach to the Black community, and the combat service of Black troops convinced African-Americans that they had earned better treatment. Northern factory jobs and higher pay for fieldwork in the South had improved the economic situation of Blacks. The government's on-again off-again prediction that former immigrants would be returning to Europe was "on-again" in June 1919, and African-American leaders were gratified by the AFL's pledge to end segregation in its member unions, "A New Emancipation." James Weldon Johnson declared his belief that the very concept of "race" was out of date. "Once it was popular, and it still is among some backward people, to discuss theoretically whether the Negro is capable of advancement." The performance of Blacks during the war had proved their capability; what remained to be seen was whether White America would permit the race to realize its potential. With rising expectations and race pride came a sharper sense of grievance for past wrongs—and for the persistence of prejudice and discrimination. June also saw the publication of DuBois's "Essay Towards a History of the Black Man in the Great War," with its explosive revelations about the U.S. Army's mistreatment of Negro officers and men.[6]

In the summer of 1919 the ascending lines of White resentment and Black militancy crossed, with explosive consequences. A series of bloody race riots began, which over a two-year period killed hundreds in cities and towns across the South and Midwest—Washington, D.C., Chicago, Omaha, Charleston, Elaine (Arkansas), Knoxville, and Tulsa. African-Americans not only suffered most of the casualties and property loss, they were blamed for the violence, and identified as a class dangerously open to the insurrectionary appeal of Bolshevism.[7]

Washington, D.C., and its suburbs had had a large Black population before the war, including a substantial middle class. After 1914 that population was augmented by migrants from the South, taking jobs in the area's war industries and supply depots. The nation's capital was also filled with soldiers, sailors, and marines—ill-paid, impatient for demobilization, resentful of well-paid and comfortable civilians in general, doubly resentful if the well-paid and comfortable were Black. Add in stifling summer heat and the inevitable rumors about Black men attacking White women and you have the materials for a race riot. As the *New York Times* had it, "Service Men Beat Negroes in Race Riot at Capital. Civilians Join to Avenge Attacks on White Women."

What was different this time was that African-Americans fought back. The traditional pattern of interracial violence since 1880 had all but precluded self-defense, since even minor resistance brought catastrophic vengeance on whole communities. That tradition was thrown to the winds by armed groups of young Black men and women, veterans among them. They showed a determination not only to defend their persons and neighborhoods but to "take the war to the enemy." They did not represent the whole community: the middle class stayed out of the violence and disapproved of it, recognizing that the whole race would be blamed, as indeed it was. But even moderates like James Weldon Johnson and the editor of the *Age* saw the counterviolence as proof that the manhood achieved by the Black doughboys had now been incorporated in the character of the race. African-Americans would no longer submit to being "terrorized by the cracker class." White America must understand that the violence would now flow in two directions: "Hereafter race wars are going to be race *wars*."[8]

Unfortunately, that was exactly the message White newspapers took from the event; and in any conflict structured and perceived as a "race war," their choice was always, immediately, and uncompromisingly to favor the Whites. Even the *New York Times*, which had been supportive of civil rights, blamed Negroes for causing (if not literally starting) the riot. It published as fact the assertions of White officials that Blacks had become unruly and defiant of law because the disciplines of Jim Crow had been allowed to lapse. It treated as valid the rumors of attacks on White women, and its editorial, "Race War in Washington," blamed Blacks for having "exasperated" White men into taking the law into their own hands—the standard excuse for lynching, here echoed by a paper formally opposed to mob justice.[9]

Less than a week later there was a more massive race riot in Chicago (July 27–31), which left 38 dead (23 Black), 537 wounded (342 Black), and scores of homes and businesses wrecked or burned. The Chicago riot was the result of twenty-five years of tension and conflict between the city's heavily unionized, predominantly White working class, and Black migrants from the South who had been used as strikebreakers. A vicious circle had been established, whereby the use of Blacks as scabs justified unions in remaining segregated, and union segregation left Blacks dependent on strikebreaking for employment. In the summer of 1919 unemployment rates were high, there had been hundreds of small strikes and lockouts, and the anticipated confrontation between the unions and Big Steel would be centered in the Chicago region. The explosion came when a Black youth, swimming at the border between segregated beaches on Lake Michigan, was stoned by Whites, struck on the head and drowned. Rumors of retaliation and atrocity ran through both communities and were believed: hateful violence was what each expected of the other. For five days organized White gangs attacked Black neighborhoods, mobbed individuals in the street, stopped streetcars, and hauled men and women off to beat them. In an effort to kill two birds with one stone, some burned down an immigrant housing district by the stockyards and tried to blame it on Blacks. Blacks responded with acts of individual and collective self-defense, and small groups of armed men sought out and battled gangs of Whites. The police stood by, especially when Blacks were the victims. Most of those arrested were Black.

The governor called out five White National Guard regiments. The Eighth Illinois, more recently the 370th Infantry, was not mustered, though its armory and much of its manpower were in the city and it was combat-tested. The implication was that Black troops could not be trusted. Newspapers reported as fact rumors that Black veterans were organizing and leading the mobs, and fears were expressed in the U.S. Senate that the "Negroes are arming" *en masse*. Some ex-soldiers may have been active rioters, but there was no organized violence by Black veterans. Haywood Hall and some of his comrades from the Eighth assembled at their armory to guard the weapons and plan "a defensive action" against a rumored invasion by Irish toughs from the other side of Wentworth Avenue. That invasion never materialized, nor did the feared confrontation between White Guardsmen and Black veterans. Despite their evident dislike for Negroes, the Guardsmen were more evenhanded than the police and succeeded in restoring order.

The riot was terrible enough, but the fears it aroused were more terrible still. The *New York Times* headlined "Negroes Storm Armory" to suggest the outbreak of a full-blown race war. Its editorial saw the uprising as proto-revolutionary: "Bolshevist agitation among the negroes, especially those in the South . . . is bearing its natural and inevitable fruit." The uprising is "not sporadic" but showed "intelligent direction and management" of a kind that presumably could not come from the Negro community. The proofs of Black loyalty so recently hailed by the *Times* are forgotten:

> There is no use in shutting our eyes to the facts: and we know that in the early days of the war there was a pro-German and pacifist propaganda among the negroes, which may well have turned into a Bolshevist, or at least a Socialist propaganda. . . . How far the original German propaganda among the negroes may have been utilized subsequently by the I.W.W. we do not yet know. . . . We stand at present amid the outburst of social forces of which we know little.[10]

Such fears received confirmation from "government agents" (the Justice Department and MID) who had "evidence that radical elements in this country are taking advantage of discontent among certain parts of the negro population to intensify ill-feeling between the races." The *Times* reported that "one of the most important negro publications" in New York was advising "all negroes" to join the IWW because it "draws no race, color, sex, or creed line." If their design was fulfilled, the IWW—whose membership the *Times* estimated at 800,000—would have a national membership of three million, and would "fairly rival" the AFL. Mass enrollment of Blacks would transform the IWW into a predominantly Black organization, raising the nightmarish vision of a revolutionary movement that aimed at both class war and race war. It was therefore ominous that the article advising Blacks to join the IWW was written by an unnamed "negro officer of the 367th Infantry"—in fact, by Osceola McKaine, whose 1917 article in the *Literary Digest* had so eloquently defended the "Buffaloes" from ridicule. McKaine now wrote that the mistreatment of Black troops had transformed patriotism into disaffection. "When black officers taught black men bayonet practice . . . they usually substituted the picture of the white Southerner for that of the Hun." They now regarded the American pretense of "making the world safe for democracy [as] a mockery." Black officers have had occasion to "curse . . . the flag and the country for which it stands a thousand times. . . . Intelligent negroes have all reached the point where their loyalty to the country is conditional." In the present crisis, "thousands" of Black veterans "now possess weapons to demonstrate, if need be, their legal right to self-defense against Southern encroachments and lynch law."[11]

The increased militancy of the Black press and political leadership fed the crisis atmosphere. James Weldon Johnson wrote that if lynchers intended "teaching the 'niggers' a lesson [in] 'Anglo-Saxon superiority'" they would be taught that "the mere thought of death" did not frighten a race whose "colored men died in France fighting for liberty." A contemporary survey of riot coverage in Negro newspapers showed an almost perfect consensus in favor of armed self-defense. Editorials urged "An Eye for an Eye" as a legitimate response to lynching and exhorted "Colored men" to fight the lynch mobs "till the last man falls and then let the women take up the fight! . . . Protect your homes. Don't start anything but when something is started make it hot for them and finish it!" "The NEW NEGRO, unlike the old time Negro, 'does not fear the face of clay,' and the white man will learn in time that he has in this new type of Negro a foeman worthy of his steel." A New York magazine called for resistance in Roosevelt's own words: "Let Us Stand at Armageddon and Battle for the Lord."[12]

But African-American organizations were in no position to follow the logic of armed resistance to a revolutionary conclusion. Most still had hopes of winning White support for important measures of benefit to the race. The NAACP would make passage of a federal antilynching bill the centerpiece of its postwar campaign and was lobbying to win congressional support. A broad consortium of African-American organizations remained interested in promoting the cause of decolonization at Versailles and winning passage of a declaration of human rights that would ban (or at least disapprove) race discrimination. There was deep satisfaction in expressions of pride and anger in warnings that veterans steeled by service in France would take arms against White oppression, but in the wake of the Washington and Chicago riots, in a nation made paranoid by fear of Bolshevism, this rhetoric proved disastrous. The iconic "gorilla" image or ape-man that had been used to link the Hun with Negroes and Asians was now being used by editorial cartoonists to symbolize Bolshevism.[13]

Is Bolshevism coming to America?

A new spirit is spreading through industry to turn it aside

Anxiety over the possibility of a domestic race/class war merged with international concerns. The *Times* cited Lenin's call for liberation of the colored peoples colonized by Europeans as evidence that America's troubles were part of a worldwide movement. It regarded as definitive the Justice Department's assertion that "Russian Reds and I.W.W." were behind the riots and that Russian money was financing "propaganda among negroes." Nor were the Soviets the only power attempting to stir what IRL propagandist T. L. Stoddard called "The Rising Tide of Color Against White World Supremacy." At Versailles, Japan had sponsored a controversial human rights proposal forbidding racial discrimination in the admission and naturalization of immigrants. It was aimed explicitly at the United States, whose exclusion laws affected the largest share of Japanese emigrants and travelers; and it forced Americans to face those aspects of the "so-called race problem," which had been postponed for the duration of the war. The Japanese proposal was supported by

African- and Jewish-American delegations at Versailles, who saw it as a way of undermining the moral and legal authority of Jim Crow, anti-Semitism, and the anti-immigration movement. During the war American editorialists had supported the principle of civic equality in summoning all races and creeds to the colors. Those same newspapers and magazines now reverted to the defense of social inequality and race-based nationality. The *Literary Digest* acknowledged the moral force of Japan's demand for "equal and just treatment of aliens." However, it affirmed the principle that "all nations reserve the right to practice some inequalities which other nations regard as unjust. Spain does not, and Russia did not, grant religious equality. America recognizes race distinctions in its internal policy," and where race difference is concerned the key issues are not political but "biological." But if the existence of Jim Crow is sufficient justification for excluding immigrants by color, it is but a small step to the corollary that the "racial" distinctions between Americans and certain European peoples are legitimate ground for the "practice [of] inequalities" against them.[14]

For conservative nationalists like William Randolph Hearst, the defense of Jim Crow and immigration restriction could now be heightened by invocations of the "Yellow Peril." In the August 2 issue of the *American* he warned President Wilson:

> The great problem before the white races is not whether the boundaries of white nations in Europe shall run this way or that way, but whether Japan shall absorb Asia for the conquest of the World. . . . Who shall say that the stupidities and jealousies of the white peoples . . . shall not some day . . . arouse the yellow races to succeed? . . . The Japanese situation is a genuine danger, more immediately to America, but ultimately to the whole white world. Upon us will fall the first burden of the battle for white civilization.

The riots allowed Hearst to link the present menace of a familiar racial "alien"—the Negro—with the prospective menace of the Japanese; and to associate the League of Nations and its sponsors with the liberals who had catered to the desires of a lower race. Riot stories were juxtaposed with a report on Japan's immigration initiative under the headline "Hold to Racial Equality, Ishii Urges Japan." The *American* played the riots themselves as classic "lynching" stories: Whites were avenging "repeated outrages . . . perpetrated by colored men against white women." A "Racial Clash" had escalated to "Racial War," with out-numbered and "helpless" policemen overwhelmed by "2,000 Negroes," and "15,000 Negroes in One Army" streaming through the city, where telegraph wires had been cut to prevent the National Guard from responding.[15]

There was little substance to fears of a Bolshevik-inspired race war. Genuine Bolsheviks were a small minority of American socialists, and the *Times* estimate of 800,000 IWW members was an absurd and frantic exaggeration. Though socialists and the IWW had made sporadic attempts to organize Black workers and had taken strong positions against racial discrimination, African-Americans as a group had been marginalized by the labor movement. The Chicago riot killed hopes of a rapprochement between Blacks and the AFL. In June the *Age* had hailed Gompers for offering Blacks a "New Emancipation," and on August 8 pointed proudly to the AFL's admission of the Red Caps union—the union Henry Johnson would have belonged to. But on August 16 it had to report that union leaders were defending the White rioters, and that Chicago union men had been prominent among the attackers.[16]

The *Times* and the Hearst papers agreed that the danger of a Black uprising arose from the "unwarranted" raising of Negro expectations by White liberals and Black civic leaders. Since those heightened expectations arose from the wartime social bargain, this position amounted to a repudiation of the implied promise of racial "fair play" made in 1917. Indeed, it threatened a reversion to a still more reactionary position, which would insist that the North adopt Jim Crow standards of racial subordination and separation. Hearst's *American* approved Senator Mc-Cormick's "justification" of White retaliation as a needed rebuke to Black presumption:

> That's the way with darkies that come from the north now. Unless they are compelled to comply with customs they will not do so. . . . Thousands of these negro boys came to Chicago from the South . . . and when they came to Chicago they had a kind of idea they could sit in your lap or do anything they pleased.

Give them an inch and they'll take an ell. "Negroes have been arming for months . . . to obtain what they regard as complete social equality, by force if necessary."[17]

Carried to its logical conclusion, this view made all agitation for civil rights tantamount to an incitement to riot if not revolution. The *Times* reported at length the charges made by Senator Byrne of South Carolina, blaming the race riots on the moderate leadership of the Negro community and demanding they be prosecuted under the Espionage Act. For African-Americans the emergence of a "New Negro" was the symbol of wartime progress. The *Literary Digest* saw the "New Negro" as a menace, whose repression might require the exemplary justice of a "hanging bee . . . [a] legal wholesale hanging." It quotes with tacit approval the words of Senator Williams of Mississippi, which rationalize lynching as a social and biological necessity: "Not only is blood thicker than water, but race is greater than law."[18]

American Race Riots and European Pogroms

The only White journals to take an entirely sympathetic view of Black self-defense were some socialist publications and Yiddish newspapers. Some of the latter went further than the *Age* in hailing Black self-defense. One quoted with approval a warning poster: "WHITES! WE ARE WARNING YOU! DO NOT GO OUT OF YOUR HOMES TONIGHT!" The *Forverts* praised Black self-defense for having "thrown great fear upon the capitalistic parties and the capitalistic press."

There were close parallels, in timing and significance, between the U.S. race riots of July and August and a new wave of anti-Jewish pogroms in eastern Europe. They came at a time when Jewish and Black leaders were trying to relate the defense of equality at home to the creation of a more democratic world order through the League of Nations. The Black engagement with the cause of African decolonization was paralleled by Jewish efforts on behalf of the persecuted Jews of eastern Europe. The old Pale of Settlement, where the czars had settled and segregated the Jewish population, was overrun by the armies and partisans of Bolshevik, anti-Bolshevik, Polish, Lithuanian, and Ukrainian forces. From the first there were reports of massacres, but not until late spring were Western reporters able to confirm them. In May, while New York was still celebrating the Yiddishers of the Lost Battalion, Jewish-American leaders began a maximum effort to raise funds for eastern European relief and to convince the victorious powers (or perhaps the

League) to rescue Jewish communities by direct intervention. Many in the AJC hoped that such measures would forestall a new large-scale immigration of eastern European Jews, which might undo their efforts at Americanizing the Yiddish-speaking community and make good propaganda for the IRL. But as the scale of the catastrophe in the Pale became clear, even the AJC recognized the necessity of seeking admission for large numbers of Jewish refugees.[19]

There was considerable sympathy in the United States for the Jewish victims. American Jews had been organizing protests against Russian pogroms since 1903, when they had won a hearing, though not support, from President Roosevelt. The achievements of the "Yiddish Battalion" had their effect. Politicians in New York City and State were particularly vocal on behalf of the co-religionists of their brave doughboys, and Congress considered several resolutions on the subject. To counter this tendency, the Immigration Restriction League and its allies appealed to the analysis offered earlier in the year by MID and the Reverend Simons, which rationalized the pogroms as the excessive but understandable—and politically desirable—response of Poles and other nationalities to the threat of domination by Yiddish Bolsheviks. Now their position was supported by journals that had earlier sympathized with Jewish victims of the eastern fighting. Cameron McKenzie, writing in the *New York Times*, described an orgy of slaughter, rape, and mutilation that attended the Polish recapture of the city. But he explained the violence as a response to atrocities committed by the "the Bolsheviki who came to Vilna . . . shrewd, keen, alert Jews—who were not without a certain amount of education; [and] Russian peasants of the lowest order." The *Literary Digest*'s June 7 article on the "Danger of Jewish Massacres" expressed a similar view of the causes and agreed with Polish diplomats that the pogroms were part of the suppression of Bolshevism. The *Digest* also agreed with Poland's opposition to any declaration by the League of Nations on the rights of racial minorities, on the ground that every nation has the right to resent the creation in its territory of a class with "special privileges." Implicit in this rationale for massacre was an understanding of racial animosity derived from Black-White relations. If (as Senator Williams of Mississippi had said) blood is thicker than water, and race more important than law, then pogroms, like lynchings, could be understood as natural—albeit excessive—acts of national self-preservation.

The administration sent a delegation to the region to investigate and report on the situation. It included General Edgar Jadwin, who worked closely with MID, and Henry Morgenthau, a Jewish-American who, as U.S. ambassador to Turkey, had labored heroically to halt the Turkish genocide against the Armenians in 1915. Jadwin espoused MID's view that Bolshevism was essentially a Jewish movement and that the Jews were therefore culpable for their own victimization. Morgenthau rejected that idea. But he shared the concerns of the AJC leadership about the potential conflict between "100% Americanism" and Jewish ethnic or racial self-assertion—especially when the latter took the form of Zionism or demands for special legislation to protect Jewish rights. So in a statement printed in the *Washington Post* on July 29, he averred that Polish Jews sometimes "Exaggerate Pogrom Tales," and warned them against crying wolf too often. He also admonished the Polish Jews for "sometimes overlook[ing] the fact that equal rights involve . . . equal duties" and urged them to "follow the example of their American co-religionists, who consider themselves above all things patriotic Americans." Although these words affirmed the primacy of Americanism for Jews in the United States, as applied to Polish Jewry they were tantamount to acceptance of the accusation that Polish Jews had been seeking to carve an autonomous enclave out of the national body of Poland.[20]

Morgenthau's rhetorical compromises, like those of the AJC, were not accepted on the Lower East Side. At street level, Jewish-Americans were no more willing than Blacks to forget their own grievances, or those of their kinsmen, or to forgo the social and political rewards they had earned by military service. Morgenthau's admonition against "exaggerating" the extent of the pogroms was swept aside by a wave of news stories out of Poland that verified the worst of the rumors. At the end of November a hundred thousand Jews, most from the Lower East Side, demonstrated in New York against the pogroms. Among them were "25,000 Ex-Yanks in Line"—veterans of the Lost Battalion and 77th Division in their uniforms. It was in every respect the counterpart to that "Silent Parade" of July 1917, in which Black Harlem had protested lynching and mass murder in East St. Louis, and it had the same result. Though statements of outrage and protest were issued, no special measures were adopted to rescue the Jews or admit them to the United States. Those who did manage to escape to America worked their way through the net with the help of wealthy *landsleit* and hometown organizations.[21]

The Steel Strike: "There must be only one class and all must bear true allegiance to it."

The steel strike of September–October 1919 was the culminating crisis of the year. It resolved the ideological standoff between labor and capital in favor of capital and provided the rationale for the Red Scare that decimated and marginalized the American Left. The strike itself has been studied in some detail by labor and social historians. What concerns us here is how the strike contributed to the turn of public opinion against the wartime social bargain and toward measures to restrict immigration and preserve racial segregation and subordination.[22]

The AFL authorized a strike at its June convention. In late August Judge Gary of the Steel Trust declared his commitment to the open shop and refused to negotiate with unions. President Wilson called for a national conference "to discuss fundamental means of bettering the whole relationship of labor and capital." He envisioned a domestic equivalent of Versailles and would have no better luck with one than with the other. Union and business leaders accepted the president's call, but neither was willing to compromise. However, Gary's refusal took a passive form—he simply refused to talk. That left the unions with no choices but surrender or strike. They struck, and were therefore blamed for interrupting production and fomenting class conflict at a time when the economy was slack and the nation menaced by enemies foreign and domestic.

The employers' goals were not simply to break the strike but to break the labor movement. In place of independent unions they would set up company unions to ensure the cooperation of labor and management on management's terms. They prepared for "war" by hiring armed guards and ordering police in their cities to take on special deputies. In western Pennsylvania there were as many as 25,000 of these under arms. They would police picket lines and the communities in which strikers lived, making arrests, conducting raids, beating up "agitators." Management confidently expected their overzealous and provocative actions would lead to retaliatory violence, which would discredit union men with the public. To make violence more certain the companies hired large numbers of Blacks as strikebreakers. It was barely two months since the Chicago riot, and obvious that steelworkers in Chicago and nearby Gary, Indiana, would be maddened by the sight of Negroes taking their jobs. The companies also hired provocateurs and instructed them to instigate violence and "stir up as much bad feeling as you can," especially against Negroes and foreign workers. Their success was reflected in recurrent headlines of shooting incidents between Black strikebreakers and White strikers, usually identified as "foreigners."[23]

AFL president Samuel Gompers tried to link labor's cause to the liberal principles of the Fourteen Points. The nation had won a war to make the world safe for democracy. Now "the workers of the world," like the nations in the League, "are determined to have a voice in settling reconstruction problems that affect them. . . . Tyranny, whether it be in political or industrial life, shall be no more." But the war had poisoned the moral well from which Progressivism drew its authority. Patriotism was now equated with 100% Americanism; "cooperation" implied submission to the overriding need of the national economy for continuous production. Just as *any* sort of opposition to the war qualified the dissident as "pro-German," so now in a time of economic "warfare" any party threatening to disrupt industrial production for its own ends could be identified as "Hun-like" or "Bolshevik" and made eligible for destruction by the power of the state.[24]

A stream of antilabor stories was generated by steel trust publicists and dutifully picked up and reported by the press, which rarely spotted or bothered to correct even obvious fabrications. The attempt to organize steelworkers was condemned as "nothing less than Bolshevism." Even if the public took these tales at a discount, there was so much smoke it was hard not to believe a radical fire was burning somewhere. The *New York Times* endorsed Judge Gary's testimony that " 'the minority [i.e., union workers] must not be allowed to control the majority.' " (This without irony from the president of a trust that controlled all steel production in America.) It supported Gary's contention that collective bargaining was an invasion of the "zone of contract and free will" between individual workers and corporations, and a threat to "Russianiz[e]" American industry. It endorsed the speculation of Senator Kellogg, late of the Overman Subcommittee, that strikers were "un-American," mainly foreigners, who had never contributed to the Liberty Loan or Red Cross. Hearst's *American* represented itself as a workingman's newspaper and often supported Gompers, but in major industrial disputes Hearst sided with the employers. His headlines claimed the strikers wanted to set up a "soviet" and noted that a mob of "500 foreigners" had blocked the mill gates until a vigilante group of "returned soldiers took charge."[25]

On October 4 a large number of Negro strikebreakers, escorted by police and deputies, crossed picket lines in Gary. They were attacked by White strikers, and two days of rioting ensued. When state forces were unable to restore order, federal troops were sent in and General Leonard Wood—who had just reestablished civil order in Omaha after a major race riot—took command. Wood moved a thousand regulars into Gary, declared martial law, and cleared the streets.

H. L. Mencken thought Wood a "glorified gendarme [whose] remedy for all ills and evil is force." In fact his approach to the steel strike was based on the best wisdom of Progressive sociologists, as filtered through the practical minds at MID. In 1917 the Army War College had developed "War Plans White" to guide the army in suppressing a revolutionary uprising in the United States during or after the war. It drew on the work of social scientists like Commons, Ely, and Ross, which pinpointed industrial cities as the locus of instability and identified Negroes and immigrant races as the destabilizing elements. MID extrapolated from their findings a two-part list: on one side those ethnic groups and organizations that could be expected to support the state; on the other those likely to subvert or rebel against it. Jews were singled out as the most suspect. Of African-Americans "War Plans White" declared: "Their class consciousness, racial instincts, poverty, instinctive hostility to the white race and susceptibility to propaganda, makes [sic] this group a fruitful recruiting field for radical agitators."

Though Wood professed neutrality, his policies worked against the strike. Workers were disarmed, but police and special deputies retained their guns and their freedom to disrupt strike meetings. He believed foreign agitators and Bolsheviks were behind the strike and turned MID loose to prove it. A series of raids on October 15 turned up bales of Bolshevist literature and produced scores of arrests. Hardly any of these were of union men, but the fact that the strike had attracted Bolsheviks in such numbers seemed ominous. With Wood taking Gary's place as the opponent of the strikers, the issue was changed from a conflict between workingmen and monopoly capitalists to a war between the legitimate heirs of the AEF and a mob of "foreign" workmen. It helped that

Wood's uniformed troops were augmented by veterans and American Legionnaires, acting as deputies and vigilantes. The government stood aside. At Wilson's "Peace Conference of Industry" Vice President Marshall, speaking for the president, declared that the principles of the New Freedom required a "government of discretion," acting "not [as] a lawgiver, but an evangelist." That left him nothing to offer but pious homilies and a reprise of wartime slogans—the "Country Needs a Rebaptism of Americanism"—which had no effect whatever.

The discrediting of the steel unions of course played into the burgeoning Red Scare. But it also fed back into the campaign against immigrants and Blacks. Hostile accounts of the strike emphasized the role of alien agitators and foreign-born workmen in fomenting the strike and the violence associated with it. The *New York Tribune* declared it was "industrial alienism for a disruptive purpose; and its purpose is un-American." A Cleveland paper noted that the strike call had been printed in a number of languages other than English and reminded its readers that war had taught the necessity of having "one country, one language, one flag." The *Times* reported "50,000 Aliens Here Spread Radicalism," calling for "confiscation of property and the overthrow of the American system of Constitutional government." To end radical agitation and disorder in the steel mills, alien workers should be forcibly Americanized or fired.[26]

Coverage of the steel strike linked the labor struggle with the race riots. The *New York Times*, the *World*, and the *Literary Digest*, all of which had hailed the Old Fifteenth as proof of the Negro's patriotism, now stressed the danger of Negro radicalism. "Evidence is in possession of the Government of the efforts of agitators of the I.W.W., Bolshevist, and radical Socialist groups to stir up discontent among the negroes, paralleling the agitation that is being carried on in industrial centres of the North and West, where there are many alien laborers." Blacks were now identified as the race most likely to go Bolshevik, just as the East Side Jews had been after Simons's accusations in February. Economic advancement had not solved the race problem, but exacerbated it. Charles A. Seldes's "Unrest in Prosperous Chicago" pointed out that support for Black "rioters" came from the regular Negro leadership, largely middle-class and educated. To White men used to the complaisant rhetoric of the Tuskegee Machine, the self-assertiveness and confidence of the "New Negro" seemed an intolerable breach of manners and the signal of a dire threat. Attorney General Palmer thought the political manners of Negro leaders were now "marked throughout by a spirit of insolent bravado." Their reaction to race rioting is "ill-governed," because they blame the violence on White mobs and officials rather than their own Black criminal classes and because they advocated "retaliatory violence in connection with lynching." They had even defied the primary structures and assumptions of racial separation, by making a "more open demand for social equality" and making light of the taboo against interracial sex. Palmer saw grave danger in the fact that Negroes have dared to "assume . . . [a] political stand toward the present Federal Administration, the South in general, and incidentally, toward the Peace Treaty and the League of Nations." This amounted to a finding that the articulation of any distinctive *political* position by Black leaders was by its nature inappropriate and menacing.

In February and March the achievements of the Old Fifteenth and its brother outfits had been hailed as proof of Negro patriotism and capability for citizenship. Now the Justice Department described that experience as the source of a corrupting desire for "social equality" among Negroes. Their social acceptance among White French men and women had made Black veterans determined to seek the same acceptance back home. Black soldiers had been allowed to marry French women, even of the better classes. They had seen Negro deputies at work in the French parliament, Black officers commanding racially mixed units, "in short, a country characterized by the fullest social, religious, and political equality for every class and race and nationality."[27] That a representative of the president who had gone to war "to make the world safe for democracy" could condemn the French, because their society granted full political and social equality to all citizens, was an indication of the extent to which the concept of democracy itself had been degraded by the war.

By the end of 1919 the tide of public and political opinion had set against the hopes and expectations of African-Americans and the White hyphenates. America had found another "moral equivalent of war" in a thoroughgoing crusade against radicalism and cultural difference. The nation required "a rewriting of the definition of treason" to proscribe any "group which gets hold of the throat of society and then squeezes. . . . Mankind can not get along if split into fighting class groups." Just as the foreign war had demanded that Americans see themselves as one people, with one nation, one flag, and one language, so now, in a time of "economic warfare . . . there must be only one class and all must bear true allegiance to it."[28]

When the long-delayed postwar recession hit in the spring of 1920, the fears and resentments generated by the Red Scare and the race riots led to the adoption of an explicitly racialist rationale for the making of social policy. The Harding administration and a majority of the Congress now assumed that immigration must be radically restricted, and Congress embarked on a series of hearings and legislative debates to decide what form restriction would take. As in the case of the Overman Subcommittee, the hearings were comparable in importance to the actual legislation, because they publicized and gave an official imprimatur to the idea that the racial character of certain immigrants made them dangerous to American society. At the same time, Congress failed to pass the Dyer antilynching bill, which would have engaged the federal government against the worst excesses of Jim Crow. Taken together, the effect of these congressional actions was to affirm racialism as an official ideology and a basis for the exclusion of certain peoples from full participation in the civil life of the nation.

The Bargain Betrayed: The Dyer Anti-Lynching Bill and the Johnson-Reed Immigration Act, 1920–1924

Representative Dyer's bill defined lynching as the killing of a U.S. citizen by three or more persons. In addition to criminal penalties for the perpetrators, it made law officers who made no effort to prevent a lynching liable for punishment as felons. When the bill came before the House in January 1922, Dyer defended it in a long well-argued speech. He cited the published opinions of Southern newspapers, declaring lynching a shame and a disgrace. He offered statistics to show it was "far from the truth" that most lynchings resulted from "rape" or "attacks upon women." He quoted in its entirety President Wilson's speech condemning lynching as a blot on the nation's honor and a detriment to the war effort, and concluded: "I appeal for justice; I appeal to you because it is right," and because lynching is a "disgrace [to] our republic."

Representative Sumners (D-Texas) immediately rose to offer the Southern response. He had constitutional arguments to offer, but his primary plea was an affirmative defense of the racial premises of Jim Crow. "God Almighty" had drawn "these lines of racial cleavage . . . [and] put the instinct of racial preservation there to protect them."

> When men respond to that call, they respond to a call which is higher than the law of self-preservation. It is the call to the preservation of the race. . . . When that call comes every man who is not a racial degenerate will answer it. [Applause.] It is the call of the blood.

It followed that those who supported the bill were racial degenerates, "Negro agitators and white negroettes." Instead of answering Dyer's arguments and crime statistics, Sumners regaled the House with fables of Black rape and White vengeance: "Suppose . . . a black man takes a little white child and drags her off into seclusion where no voice can hear and no hand can help, and rapes that child, and the father of that child and the brothers of the child come up on him and kill him. . . ."[29] While the bill was under consideration lynchings continued at prewar levels, and Tulsa experienced a race riot that killed more people than Chicago and Washington combined.

The strongest rhetorical counter to the rape fables of Southern congressmen was the appeal to the war record of Black regiments like the Old Fifteenth. But that appeal was vitiated by the series of investigations and reports that condemned and even ridiculed the combat performance of Black officers and enlisted men. The burden of their findings is summarized in Major General Hanson Ely's report to the general staff on "Employment of Negro Man Power in War":

> The negro does not perform his civil duties in times of peace in proportion to his population. He has no leaders in industrial or commercial life. He takes no part in government. Compared to the white man he is of admittedly inferior mentality. He is inherently weak in character. . . . As a fighter he has been inferior to the white man even when led by white officers.[30]

The Republican majority in the House guaranteed passage of the Dyer bill, but their Senate leadership had neither the numbers nor the political will to challenge the inevitable Southern filibuster. The quality of Republican support for the bill is suggested by the fact that President Harding, who was on record favoring it, accepted an honorary membership in the Ku Klux Klan while the bill was being debated in the Senate. The Klan had grown into a national organization since its revival in 1915, with five million members in the South and Midwest. In addition to the old passions of Jim Crow, it drew on the spirit of Protestant revanchism that had produced Prohibition and the immigration restriction movement. As such, it was a potentially strong constituency for Republicans as well as Southern Democrats. So when the Dyer bill passed the House, the Senate leadership held it over until after the midterm elections, depriving its supporters of the chance to campaign for it. At the end of November 1922, majority leader Henry Cabot Lodge withdrew the bill after a perfunctory attempt to halt the filibuster. The GOP would follow the same pattern for the next thirty years, sponsoring antilynching bills to embarrass the Democrats, but declining to make the end of Jim Crow a central plank in their platform.[31]

The core of the Jim Crow system was the belief expressed by Senator Williams of Mississippi in his response to the Chicago riot: "Not only is blood thicker than water, but race is greater than law." The case for immigration restriction would be made by mustering scientific proof that Jews and other "new immigrants" belonged to races that were nearly as different from White Americans as Negroes.

By the end of 1919 there was a broad consensus in favor of immigration restriction, though there remained differences about the kind, stringency, and duration of a restrictive policy. In 1920 Congress passed emergency legislation easing the rules for deportation of undesirables and limiting immigration for a three-year period. The House Committee on Immigration and Naturalization then began work on a long-term solution. The case for immigration restriction had, in a sense, already been made before the Johnson committee began its work. The committee's task was to harden this drift of thought into a clear set of ideological principles, which would support the immediate demand for immigration restriction and (over the longer term) educate the public mind to accept a more stringent segregation regime for "hyphenates" who were already here. The committee recognized that a radical restriction of immigration ran counter to the nation's legal and political traditions, to the symbol of the melting pot, and to the myth of a nation built by frontiersmen. Its argument was that the racial character of the new immigrants made them parasites rather than pioneers: they are a "beaten folk" with "twisted . . . mentality" and "perverted ideas. . . . They have no desire to form and build. They will exist on what has been prepared for them by a better people."[32]

The committee was chaired by Albert Johnson, a former captain in the AEF, author of a bill to bar from immigration the "hordes of Reds gathering on European and Asiatic shores ready to invade this country . . . this evil brood, who . . . look upon the United States as the land of the red rainbow of promise." Johnson was not simply anti-Communist. He was president of the Eugenics Research Association, which advocated radical means for keeping Nordic bloodlines pure: an absolute cutoff of all immigration from "inferior" racial stocks and measures to prevent social integration and biological mixing between those "inferior" stocks and "old-stock" Whites.

To ensure that new immigration standards would have a racial basis, Johnson hired Harry Laughlin, supervisor of the Eugenics Records Office, as the committee's expert on race biology. Laughlin testified, "The character of a nation is determined primarily by its racial qualities; that is, by the hereditary physical, mental, and moral or temperamental traits of its people." He provided the Johnson Committee with "An Analysis of America's Modern Melting Pot," which used statistics on criminality, "feeble-mindedness," and "social ineptitude" to show that immigrants from eastern and southern Europe were marked by "degeneracy and [social] inadequacy," were physically and mentally unfit, and racially unsuited for Americanization. "We in this country have been so imbued with the idea of democracy, or the equality of all men, that we have left out of consideration the matter of blood or natural inborn hereditary mental and moral differences." The case for inequality rested on the results of the IQ tests administered to drafted men in stateside army camps in 1918. The press accepted the assumption that the IQ differences revealed by the tests were due to *racial* heredity and touted them as the basis of a "Human Rating Scale," which explained the social success or failure of racial groups. Robert Yerkes, who had presided over the IQ tests and was now head of the Surgeon General's Division of Psychology, and his colleague Lewis Terman told the committee that the test results justified a cutoff of immigration by undesirable groups.[33]

Johnson and Laughlin maintained close contact with the IRL, now led by their friend Madison Grant, and solicited expert testimony from

IRL notables.[34] Grant did not testify in person, but the hearings are filled with references to his best-selling book, *The Passing of the Great Race*. Like Roosevelt in *Winning of the West*, Grant claimed that the United States had been conquered and settled by a great fighting race, which he called "Nordic" rather than Teutonic. The Nordic bloodstream had then been vitiated by interbreeding with lesser races, which was an inevitable consequence of combining open immigration with a fatuous democratic ideology that declared all men equal. "If the melting pot is allowed to boil without control and we continue to follow our national motto and deliberately blind ourselves to 'all distinctions of race, creed, or color," the "Great Race" of Nordic pioneers will become extinct in this country.

The crux of Grant's argument was the likeness between the Negro and the Indian, already recognized as racially incompatible with Whites, and immigrant groups previously accepted as White.

> [It] has taken us fifty years to learn that speaking English and wearing good clothes and going to school does not transform a Negro into a white man. . . . Americans will have a similar experience with the Polish Jew, whose dwarf stature, peculiar mentality, and ruthless concentration on self-interest are being engrafted upon the stock of the nation.

The "one drop" rule, by which any degree of Black ancestry made one a Negro, applies to Jews as well:

> Whether we like to admit it or not, the result of the mixture of two races . . . gives us a race reverting to the more ancient, generalized, and lower type. The cross between a white man and an Indian is an Indian; the cross between a white man and a Negro is a Negro; . . . the cross between any of the three European races and a Jew is a Jew."

The committee summoned Grant's disciple T. L. Stoddard to set the Jewish threat in a larger context. He had recently published two popular books extrapolating Grant's vision of racial apocalypse to the world historical scale. *The Rising Tide of Color Against White World Supremacy* (1920) argued that the Great War had weakened the hold of White nations over the colonized colored peoples, and that Asian powers would soon challenge Euro-American hegemony. But the committee was most interested in *The Revolt Against Civilization: The Menace of the Under-Man*

(1922), because it explained the connection between racial difference, class difference, and the rise of Bolshevism. The book fleshed out the conclusion of the Overman Subcommittee's report, which saw Bolshevism as "the pulling-down of the progressive rather than the lifting up of the retrogressive." The Bolshevik Revolution was led by intelligent but amoral "half-breeds" of mixed European and Jewish bloods, who won a war of extermination against the Russian aristocracy and now envisioned a similar war against White world supremacy. In Russia, their clever exploitation of democratic dogma appealed to the base instincts and low intelligence of a quasi-Asiatic Slavic peasantry. Though the American masses are White, army IQ tests revealed that a majority are "backward," and hence susceptible to the appeals of Jewish Bolshevism. Democracy is therefore *not* a safe thing for America. The doctrine of equality leads in the end to a "cacocracy," in which the "fecal classes," the "ordure of humanity," will constitute political society. To prevent this requires both a cutoff of new immigration and restrictive legislation in the spirit of Jim Crow to limit the political and social influence of non-Nordics.

A small minority of dissenters, led by two Jewish congressmen, Siegel of New York and Sabath of Illinois, struggled in vain to resist or ameliorate the Johnson Committee's foregone conclusions. At their request, testimony was taken from scholars who had worked with Franz Boas developing his scientific critique of Laughlin, Grant, Stoddard, and the rest. They provided the committee with detailed analyses exposing the logical fallacies in the racialist argument, the methodological and analytical flaws in Laughlin's statistics and in the IQ results of Yerkes and Terman.[35]

The dissenters also solicited testimony from leaders of the Jewish and Italian communities to defend their record of civic adaptation, social success, and patriotic service. As always, Louis Marshall of the AJC was foremost among the Jewish spokesmen. He mocked the pseudoscience of Grant and Stoddard and condemned the proposed quota system as un-American, because its clear purpose was to mark certain classes of Americans as inherently inferior and despicable. He reminded senators and congressmen that in 1917, "in the hour of stress" the foreign-born had met their country's need. "Did you ask any questions when the war was going on and we were seeking to enlist an army, or to conscript an army, as to whether the men you called were born abroad or here?" The war had proved their Americanism, and the Lost Battalion symbolized their heroism:

> I passed through the Argonne Forest a year ago . . . and my heart thrilled when I stood upon the ground where the Lost Battalion burrowed into the hillside. That Lost Battalion consisted largely of Jewish young men, practically all of them born abroad, immigrants, quite a number of them not yet naturalized, and they performed a feat that will live in American history.

He reminded the Johnson Committee of Abraham Krotoshinsky, "the little barber [from] the East Side who had not taken out his first papers," whose physique was exactly that of the stereotype Polish Jew, stooped and (in Grant's words) "dwarfish." Yet he was the man who had "saved the 'Lost Battalion.' "

> And now it is proposed to tell these people, who fought and bled for this country . . . "You are an inferior race. You are not the equal of the people who came from northern and western Europe. We consider you the dregs of humanity."

Rabbi Stephen Wise, the head of Reform Judaism, testified that the proposed law implied "contempt and degradation" on a racial basis for naturalized citizens and their children. He appealed to the memory of his old friend Theodore Roosevelt, asking that each man be judged as an individual. Gedalia Bublick, editor of the *New York Jewish Daily News*, warned that adoption of the quota would give official license to a "wave of hatred of man against man." Instead of inviting every person to pursue the American Dream, it would "teach people who came from certain stocks . . . to hate themselves. . . . Once America enters upon this way of telling a man that in his veins runs the blood of a low race, I say America is not America anymore."

But of course America had traditionally done exactly that, identifying non-Whites as people of "low race" unfit for equality. Jewish leaders (at least the non-Socialists) were themselves imbued with that kind of Americanism. When pressed by members of the committee to say whether they favored an end to *all* restrictions on immigration, Wise and Joshua Kantrowitz of B'nai B'rith endorsed the continued barring of Chinese and Japanese, because there was "a great gulf fixed" between Asians and Europeans (Wise) and "because . . . our law has always put them on a different basis from those representing European civilization" (Kantrowitz). By accepting the validity of color-based racism they not only undermined the principle they defended, they endorsed a principle the Johnson Committee would use against them, for the core of the racialist argument for Jewish exclusion was their likeness to Asians and Negroes.[36]

When the Johnson-Reed bill was reported to the House, Representatives Siegel and Sabath were joined by an Irish colleague in a minority report, which included the complete text of an article, "Eight American Soldiers," praising Jewish, Italian, and other foreign-born soldiers who had won the Medal of Honor. The people of Siegel's district had made clothing for the AEF and sent 13,000 men into the army—"How much more do you want?" Sabath reminded the House that Jews had provided 5 to 6 percent of the armed forces, though constituting only 3 percent of the population. They had "proved their mettle" in battle: "The famous 77th Division, of which Col. Whittlesey commanded a battalion, was largely Jewish," and Jewish soldiers fought on with Whittlesey after he answered the German note with "Go to hell."

Useless. Invoking the Lost Battalion had no more effect than the stack of school compositions Siegel tendered to the House: essays on Theodore Roosevelt by grammar school pupils, proof that immigrant children were learning Americanism. The scientific criticism that challenged the premises and methods of Laughlin, Grant, and Yerkes was simply ignored. The appeals of Marshall and his colleagues were dismissed as expressions of ethnic self-regard, and the support given them by sympathizers in Congress dismissed, because it behooves a man "10 per cent of whose constituencies are Jews to defend them." The National Association of Manufacturers and the National Industrial Conference Board, which had favored large immigration to keep labor cheap, now endorsed the view that immigration was essentially a "race question." Organized labor did not demur. In 1919 the Christian-Progressive journal *Outlook* had opposed restriction by national quota because it "would insult our war casualty lists, which show that many men of foreign extraction, because America *has* been a melting-pot, have gladly fought side-by-side with the native-born, and have made the supreme sacrifice for her." In 1923 the editors thought it was time to "Choose

Citizens, Not 'Let Them In' " and dismissed objections to the Johnson-Reed bill as "Alien Protests" that were "not in the interest of America, but in the interest of alien groups . . . who think, not simply as Americans, but as Italian-Americans, or Jewish-Americans, or some other kind of Americans" and "vote in more or less solid blocks." In 1919 George Creel of the CPI had rebuked the anti-immigrant prejudice that had led to abuse and discrimination against loyal hyphenates. In 1921 Creel thought the "Melting Pot" had become a "Dumping Ground," and urged Congress to "Close the Gates! The Way to Shut a Door Is to Shut It."[37]

World's Work, which had followed Roosevelt's line on nationalism and race theory, endorsed the secretary of labor's report that Polish and Russian Jews "did not know the meaning of the word truthfulness, and were carriers of disease caused by their extreme bodily filth" and have "very low mentality and moral fiber." It favored "a quota system that would frankly . . . encourage the entrance of northwestern Europeans" and bar all others. Americans were wrong to have "pinned our faith on the existence of some wonder-working alchemy in the American atmosphere which could transmute an inferior race into a superior one." The most important human traits are "innate in the germ plasm." While "the idea that one people can become as good as another . . . may satisfy the zeal of the political sentimentalist, [it] will never appeal to the practical statesman."[38]

To be identified as a racial enemy was, according to the American code, to be a legitimate target of mob or vigilante violence. For Blacks the threat of violence remained literal, and it was extended to Jews and other "foreigners" in some parts of the country. Between 1920 and 1925 the KKK, revived by *Birth of a Nation* in 1915, spread into the Midwest and West, rising to a peak membership estimated as high as five million, parading in Washington in their white robes a hundred thousand strong. Its name was now said to reference its hatred of "Katholics, Kikes, and Koloreds." Its political influence in the Democratic Party shaped presidential politics from 1920 to 1928, and its influence among Republicans was also considerable. President Harding became a member while in office; the Klan backed Hoover against Catholic Al Smith in 1928.

But the "vigilantism" experienced by Jews and Italians in the 1920s and 1930s more typically took the form of discrimination and insult: housing covenants that prevented their moving into certain neighborhoods, parks with signs reading "No Jews or Dogs Allowed," exclusion from certain civil service jobs, from employment in certain corporations (Ford refused to hire Jewish engineers). It was not possible to impose Jim Crow on white-skinned immigrants. (The Johnson Committee's proposal to require naturalized immigrants to carry identity cards was rejected as an undesirable extension of state power.) But individual institutions, such as universities, could take measures to prevent Negroes, Jews, Italians, and others from mingling freely with native stock. The logic of eugenics, and of the racial interpretation of IQ, required not only the exclusion of new immigrants but the social segregation of those already here. As a 1922 article in the *Atlantic Monthly* put it, "It is not only the individual [immigrant] whom we exclude, but . . . his descendants, whose blood may be destined to mingle with and deteriorate the best we have."

One of the most significant measures of exclusion was the adoption by Harvard University of a quota limiting the number of Jewish students it would admit. The policy was initiated by president Lawrence Lowell, a charter member of the IRL, and it would make America's leading university the exemplar of his long-held view that it was impossible for Jews, Negroes, and Whites to live as equals in one free society. The measure was controversial. It was opposed by Lowell's predecessor, Charles William Eliot, and by liberals among the trustees and faculty. But Lowell ultimately carried the issue, and other elite institutions across the country followed Harvard's example. The press acknowledged that such bans were ethically problematic in a society nominally committed to fair play and civil equality. But once again democratic principles were trumped by the felt need for national unity in a dangerous world, and for cultural "like-mindedness" to ensure that unity. If Yiddish Jews were allowed to compete freely, their racial intelligence and competitiveness would enable them to dominate the great universities. Instead of training an American elite, they would be "given up largely to educating the sons of a particular racial element. . . . Harvard would become, to a great extent, a Jewish institution . . . [and] will lose its national character." To save Harvard as an American institution, a strict Jewish quota was necessary.[39]

The imposition of a university admissions quota confirmed the prediction of Louis Marshall that passage of race-based immigration quotas would legitimate discrimination against Jews in a broad range of civil activities. The blow to Jewish morale was significant: the *numerus clausus* had been one of the most hated features of czarist anti-Semitism, and now America had adopted it. In material terms, university quotas were a serious setback to Jewish hopes of assimilation into the mainstream of American life. As the doughboys of the Lost Battalion had reason to know, Harvard and its kindred institutions produced the men who would lead and command in business, politics, and war. To be cut off from the opportunity symbolized by Harvard was to be denied the chance to prove yourself and your people equal to the Roosevelt standard, capable of management and command.

It was symbolic of the racialization of American Jews that Lowell also tried to ban, and succeeded in restricting, the admission of Negroes. Blacks and Jews had the same enemies and found themselves enmeshed in the same false categories and twisted logic of racialist ideology. But like the Hell Fighters and the Lost Battalion they continued to fight the same war on separate battlefields.

14

Unknown Soldiers: Charles Whittlesey
and Henry Johnson, 1919–1929

> At first Krebs, who had been at Belleau Wood, Soissons, the
> Champagne, St. Mihiel and in the Argonne did not want to talk
> about the war at all. Later he felt the need to talk but no one wanted
> to hear about it. . . . Krebs found that to be listened to at all he had to
> lie, and after he had done this twice he, too, had a reaction against
> the war and against talking about it. A distaste for everything that
> had happened to him in the war set in because of the lies he had
> told. . . . In this way he lost everything.
>
> —*Ernest Hemingway, "Soldier's Home"*

The American troops who returned in the winter and spring of
1919 rode home on a wave of public euphoria and high expectations. To
the civilians who lined Fifth or Michigan or Pennsylvania Avenue to
cheer the parading veterans and shower them with cigarettes and candy
and confetti, the returning soldiers were living symbols of the fulfillment
of American war aims and the achievement of national purpose.

Within a year events had rendered their prospects dubious and their
victory questionable. Wilson's Fourteen Points, which had defined U.S.
war aims, had been dismissed by the Allies at Versailles. The League of
Nations, for which Wilson had sacrificed his diplomatic and political
capital, was rejected by the Senate in November 1919, though the president drove himself to physical collapse in a vain attempt to rally public
support. There would be no new international order to ensure that the
Great War would be "the war to end all wars." Nor had victory made the

world "safe for democracy." Overseas the British, French, Italians, and Japanese carved up the spoils of the German and Turkish empires, while Bolshevism was triumphant in Russia. In the United States the ambitious reform program of the "War Progressives" had been overridden by the rage for order and security. The social violence and political hysteria of 1919, the race riots and displays of labor militancy, suggested that "victory" had left the United States more vulnerable than ever to the dangers of foreign subversion and social revolution. Democracy was not even safe in America, let alone the world, and it had become a serious question whether democracy was safe for America.

The speed with which the euphoria of victory degenerated into the paranoia of the Red Scare complicated a readjustment to civilian life that would have been difficult under any circumstances. The returned doughboys were, in a way, like immigrants from an alien culture, experiencing a peculiar form of double-consciousness. They were "natives" of this homeplace to which they had returned, but the experience of combat had alienated them from civilian America, immersed them in a world whose fundamental conditions, language, temporal rhythms, functions of life were utterly foreign to "normal" life. No one who had not shared their experience could possibly understand it, and there was no common language in which the whole truth of their experience could be communicated.

The combat soldier's relation to the meanings of his war is problematic. He is himself the instrument of the will and intentions of his government, the agent of its war aims. Yet he has no power to shape the meaning of his own war. He is too intensely engaged with the problem of day-to-day survival, the all-environing fear of personal death or wounding balanced only by the powerful demand of solidarity with the other men in his unit. On the personal level, means and ends in war are always incommensurate. In the abstract we can accept the sacrifice of life to protect some vital interest or principle; but it is extraordinarily difficult, for most people impossible, to accept that sacrifice face-to-face. For what idea would you consent to see your child or lover or dearest friend, or even a stranger named at random, deliberately torn apart by a blast of shrapnel, disemboweled by knives, blinded or castrated or paralyzed? In the isolated world of battle, preservation of the unit and one's buddies is a self-evident and sufficient value; it provides an authentic standard of meaning. A man who, in action, "had done the one thing, the only thing for a man to do . . . when he might have done something else" has a sense of self-worth that requires no confirmation by headquarters. Likewise the shame of having responded in ways that failed to meet the needs of the unit or the demands of the occasion could not be erased by the justifications and apologies of an after-action report. And all combat soldiers, no matter what their achievements, have experienced such moments of failure. With demobilization the unit is dissolved, the buddies dispersed, and the veteran no longer has access to the unit culture that gave his experience acceptable meaning. In the larger world of civilian life, exposed to the concerns and values of the nation, his need to find a higher value in what he has done and suffered becomes a psychological necessity.[1]

The brevity of U.S. engagement in the war made the gap between the veteran's knowledge and civilian understanding particularly difficult to bridge. In Europe the jaunty optimism of 1914 had been unlearned in four years of futility and unbearable loss on the battlefield. American civilians had seen success achieved relatively rapidly, and at an incomparably lower cost in blood and treasure. America's war had not lasted long enough nor cut deep enough to destroy that optimism about the future, that unyielding belief in personal and social progress, that had been the characterizing feature of American national culture since the founding of the Republic. But the forces of fear and hatred mobilized for the war effort had given a nasty twist to that congenital hopefulness. In the poisonous atmosphere created by wartime propaganda, and under the shadow of a lingering German/Bolshevik threat of subversion, to speak critically of the way the war was conducted, express doubts about its outcome or its value, or to show a lack of faith in America's postwar future was to risk an accusation of disloyalty or outright Bolshevism. That proved to be nearly as true for the returning veterans as for any so-called slacker, and its psychological effect on veterans could be severe. There were hard truths they needed to tell about the supposed glory of victory and the fabled idealism and efficiency of their commanders, but talk of that kind was disapproved.

The message was mixed in material ways as well. The homecoming troops were greeted with promises of swift and prosperous reintegration with the civilian economy, a chance to fulfill the high expectations generated about them. But the nation's political and business leaders had a very different set of priorities, which called for immediately dismantling all of the agencies through which the government had regulated the economy. Among the first to go was the U.S. Employment Service, which was to have coordinated the reemployment of demobilized soldiers. Private charities took up some of the slack, but most veterans were left to their own devices and the normal operations of the labor market. As a result the first wave of demobilized men faced rising prices and high unemployment, which contributed to the political and racial violence of the "Red Summer" of 1919. After a brief revival of production, a serious two-year recession that began in the spring of 1920 threw large numbers out of work.

The American Legion, the largest and most influential veterans' organization, did little to address the needs of unemployed ex-soldiers. Theodore Roosevelt Jr., echoing the ideas of his father, rejected any substantial program of veterans' benefits, on the grounds that for the true patriot military service was no different in principle from any useful labor. But then, as the steel strike of 1919 showed, this was a moment when all labor was being sharply devalued, both ideologically and financially. If the work of the battlefield was not to be valued differently from that of the blast furnace, soldiers were no more *entitled* to a higher bonus and medical benefits than unionized steelworkers were *entitled* to higher wages and better working conditions. The veterans' demands for an adjusted bonus would be partially met in 1924 after years of political wrangling, but no money would be paid until 1945. The implicit message of the process was that the ex-doughboys were simply another selfish interest group angling for government handouts, like a fired steel striker or a laid-off Negro strikebreaker.

Unable to live up to the American standard of self-reliance, most veterans were caught in a painful psychological bind: proud enough of their service to resent the way their country had treated them, but American enough to wonder if their problems were not their own fault. Their sense of grievance found expression in the social violence of 1919, with veterans appearing on both sides of the racial and ideological divide. In 1920 groups of veterans broke up army recruiting drives in several cities, reflecting "a general feeling that the government had broken some implicit promise to them."

While the living veterans were left to enjoy the neglect of a grateful nation, Washington decided to honor a dead "Unknown Soldier" as the chief symbol of the war and an object of public veneration. The irony was not lost on the veterans. In a popular song written in 1926 the Unknown Soldier asks:

Are my buddies taken care of? Was their victory so sweet?
Is that big reward you promised selling pencils in the street?
Did they really win the freedom that they battled to achieve?
Do you still respect the Croix de Guerre above that empty sleeve?
I wonder if the profiteers have satisfied their greed?
I wonder if the soldier's mother ever is in need?[2]

The ceremonial interment of the Unknown at Arlington in November 1921 was intended as a grand, solemn, and fitting closure to the story of America in the Great War. Representative Hamilton Fish Jr. (R-NY), ex-captain in the 369th Infantry, author of the American Legion statement of principles, had sponsored the movement to pay homage to an Unknown and was the chief organizer of the event. Among the honored guests was Charles Whittlesey, who stood through the speech making and band music with his friend George McMurtry and other Medal of Honor winners.

Whittlesey's postwar career traced the arc of Progressivism in decline. He was personally touched by the disappointment of Roosevelt's vision of political and economic reform and by the failure of Wilson's vision of the League of Nations. More than any of his colleagues, he sympathized with the enlisted men's struggle to recover physical and mental health and find a place in civilian life. He too was crippled by the unpurged trauma of combat and vulnerable to the extreme depression that comes to the veteran who fears that the terror he has suffered and the harm he has inflicted have been without good purpose or meaning. As a man and as an officer of the Red Cross he would exhaust his own physical and emotional reserves trying to help veterans in general, and Lost Battalion survivors in particular. There was no one to do the same for him.

Warrior and Wound-Dresser: Charles Whittlesey and the Failure of War Progressivism

In bitter safety I awake, unfriended,
And while the dawn begins with slashing rain
I think of the Battalion in the mud.
"When are you going out to them again?
Are they not still your brothers through our blood?"

—*Siegfried Sassoon, "Sick Leave" (1917)*

Charles Whittlesey came home from the war to find he had become "a national idol." His name and picture were in every newspaper and magazine, he was billed as a "star" in a movie about his "Lost Battalion." The defiant "Go to hell!" that was falsely attributed to him, and which no denial could erase, had entered the lexicon of American phrases along with "Remember the Alamo" and "Lafayette, we are here!" General Pershing had named Whittlesey one of the AEF's three outstanding heroes, and he was the only one of them living in New York City, then as now the center of mass media and national publicity. He could have made a fortune lecturing, but rejected the offers of eager booking agencies, saying he wished to put the war behind him.

He tried to disappear into the routines of law work and the privacy of his small circle of close friends and family. He frequently dined at the home of his law partner and best friend, John Pruyn, and was close to his younger brother Melzar, an Air Corps veteran who lived in the city with his new wife. Pruyn's sister-in-law noticed that "he never talked about the war, and we never dared ask him about it." He made them feel that to raise the subject was hurtful to "his modesty," but they were also aware that it aggravated "his sensitiveness for the horror of war." The war "preyed on his mind." The Pruyns thought he was haunted by a sense of guilt. "He was the sort of man who would say, 'Look at that poor fellow,' and think of all the poor boys who were killed and say, 'What right have I to be alive?' " Even with Melzar he did his best to make the subject taboo. "He was a man of finely wrought nerves, which he always kept under control. It was his suppressed, nervous temperament that made him stand out among men." The combination of an "extremely sensitive nature," balanced by courage and strength of will, made him attractive as a friend, and as a commander. But the traumatic stress of long combat, and especially of his command in the Pocket, rendered this balance of elements precarious.[3]

Success on the battlefield had not altered his fundamental belief that war was the worst possible means of resolving human disputes. His cheerful and businesslike manner with fellow officers, the confident words and manner that so encouraged the men in the Pocket, were skillful performances, undertaken because maintaining morale was one of those duties he disliked but would not evade. He had hoped that the war might justify itself, after all, by enabling the realization of President Wilson's vision of a new world order based on international law rather than military force. But at Charlevaux Mill he had led his own men, men he knew and with whom he had developed strong emotional ties, into a trap in which three-quarters of them had been killed or maimed. The experience made him doubt whether the achievement of *any* great purpose or ideal—national greatness, progress, a League of Nations—could be worth such a price.[4]

For Whittlesey, putting the war behind him meant escape from the double-bind by which his heart would blame him for killing his own men in a battle of dubious value and his conscience would damn him if he had failed to do his duty. He hoped to escape that false position by establishing a regime of silence with respect to the war. But his celebrity made that impossible, because it gave him the power to accomplish good works, and therefore another set of duties to fulfill. In October 1918 General O'Ryan, commander of the New York National Guard and of the 27th Division in France, asked Whittlesey to be his assistant in running the Red Cross Roll Call, which was tasked to raise funds for American hospitals, for sick or disabled veterans, and for victims of war in Europe: "Whittlesey to Aid O'Ryan / 'Lost Battalion' Leader Will Assist in Red Cross Campaign." Other charities also made their claims, but it was Whittlesey's famous name that was wanted, not his executive skills. When the Wall Street brokers staged their annual Christmas charity, when Harvard inaugurated a major capital campaign, when Williams College honored its founder, when decorated veterans of the 308th formed their own American Legion Post, they proudly announced that Colonel Charles Whittlesey of the Lost Battalion was among the honored guests.

With the honor such public appearances conferred came some of the more uncomfortable aspects of celebrity. When the *Times* announced his brother Melzar's wedding, the headline reduced the groom to "Brother of Commander of the Lost Battalion." A story on his Medal of Honor was accompanied by an alert from the American Legion, which warned that a "red-faced" man claiming to be an agent of Colonel Whittlesey had been trying to con money out of Legion members.[5]

His college chum Max Eastman took an ironic view of Whittlesey's position. "I felt as though destiny had outwitted him. For he had seemed more than the rest of us, in the lightning speed and intemperate force of his judgments, designed for fame. And yet he was contemptuous of it . . . [and] of all those values that loom so large to the ambitious." Their relationship was more distant now that Whittlesey no longer shared Eastman's socialism. He remained, as Eastman remembered, fond of

"speculation and friendship; classic beauty; a jest; an argument; a convivial evening," yet also "sharp-edged, impersonal, and unsentimental."
But the complexity of his experience had filled him with serious doubts
about the value of his own and his country's actions. His moral judgments could no longer be quick and "intemperate." Perhaps he had been
contemptuous of fame as a boy in college, but contempt implies a sense
of superiority and perhaps immunity. Now, though he might find fame
distasteful, he also understood it as a reality beyond his power to escape
or control, entailing responsibilities as grave in their way as those of the
line officer, dangerous rather than contemptible.

The commander of the Lost Battalion was uniquely privileged to challenge public prejudice with impunity. For Whittlesey, it followed that he
had an obligation to speak out. If the war was to have any meaning or
value at all, it must produce a more peaceful and equitable world order
and guarantee justice for the men who had borne the battle. As a famous
man, a public figure, it was Whittlesey's obligation not only to support
the proper political measures, but to use his position to win a hearing for
the principles he supported—especially since the causes he supported
were increasingly unpopular. In January 1919 he spoke against what he
called the "radical" spirit of hatred and contempt for all things German
and against the harsh and punitive "victory peace" advocated by Roosevelt and Lodge. The experience of war had taught him and (he believed)
most of his comrades to look beyond the ideological screen and see the
humanity of the enemy. To illustrate his point, Whittlesey declared that if
at some muddy crossroads one of his men had happened to meet the
Kaiser—probably the single most hated figure in the United States—"he
would have offered him a cigarette." In the audience, Bishop Greer of
the Episcopal Church, a pacifist who had suffered abuse and ostracism
for his opposition to the war, remarked to his companion: "He can say
that; if I had said it, they would have hissed."[6]

There was clearly a movement afoot to discredit and defame the immigrant groups whose sons had served under Whittlesey in France. The
testimony of the Reverend Simons, the reports of the Overman Subcommittee, the burgeoning propaganda in favor of excluding certain "races"
from future immigration, were selling the public the idea that East Side
Jews and Italians were disloyal, prone to Bolshevism, deficient in manhood or intelligence, incapable of Americanization. So Whittlesey did
not refuse invitations to speak in defense of his men: he did so at the

Williams Club just after his return, and again in January when he advocated Christian charity for the Hun, and most emphatically in May 1919, in his speech at the YMHA in New York:

> If I am ever pessimistic of the future of this country . . . I would always feel assured that I could go to the crowded quarters of the city and pick out Herschkowitz, Ciriglio, and O'Brien, and know that in them I could find the kind of men that were needed.

He was willing to go beyond speech making to engage the issue personally. In September 1920, Saul Marshall, a Jewish veteran of the Lost Battalion, sought Whittlesey's help in averting the deportation of a relative, Herman Ehrinberg, who had arrived at Ellis Island as a stowaway. Ehrinberg's was precisely the sort of case that was being held up as a scandal and a public menace by Johnson's Committee on Immigration. He had been held in confinement because immigration agents thought he was German. In fact he was something only slightly less suspect, a Polish Jew, a refugee from those pogroms whose existence the United States was not prepared to recognize, one of a group already accused of Bolshevist tendencies, racial insufficiencies, uncleanness, and proneness to disease; and he was an illegal entrant, trying to take advantage of the leniency of American law and the sentimental susceptibility of American hearts. Whittlesey immediately accepted responsibility for the case, spoke to the man, initiated an appeal on his behalf. But Ehrinberg despaired, and on the evening of Labor Day, while "aliens and guards were watching a sinuous dancer" hired for their entertainment by Immigration Commissioner Wallis, Ehrinberg and two companions escaped from Ellis Island and disappeared into the streets of Hoboken.[7] It was an embarrassing case with which to be associated, but Whittlesey seems not to have been deterred from involving himself closely in the difficulties faced by veterans of the Lost Battalion.

The price of being listened to on the League of Nations or the patriotism of immigrant soldiers was that he had to affirm that Charlevaux Mill had been an important and necessary victory in a war whose aims and outcomes were noble and good. On both of these points he felt grave doubts, which grew over time into a conviction that "the episode for which he was being honored [was] . . . fortuitous and futile" and the war "a bloody and unnecessary business." But to express his antiwar views "would have caused a violent scandal and made people think him insane." The good he was attempting to achieve would be discredited. Worse, it would undermine the belief of his surviving comrades that their ordeal had made a meaningful contribution to a worthwhile cause. He understood how important it was for the veterans to believe that their suffering and sacrifice had had positive meaning, and would not deprive his men of that comfort.

One detail in particular obsessed him: the friendly-fire barrage by American guns on October 4. It symbolized the most critical questions about his responsibility for what happened to his command. Had he given the wrong coordinates and thus caused the disaster? Had he misunderstood or somehow botched his mission, and thus led his men into a trap that nearly destroyed them all? There was no way for him to dispel his doubts without discrediting General Alexander and the memory of achievement that sustained his surviving comrades. When a former colleague asked him to expose the lie, Whittlesey told him, "Forget it; the war's over." But the unanswered questions kept eating at him: "We have the word of one of [his] old comrades that half a dozen times on lecture platforms he seemed on the edge of speaking of that deadly barrage of October 4, but always bit his lip." His silence also left unresolved the question whether Alexander's praise of Whittlesey's conduct was not also a cover story, concealing a truth it would embarrass Alexander to reveal. "It never occurred to [Whittlesey] that the official version might be fundamentally correct," at least with regard to the tactical merit of his actions.

Perhaps one reason why he "saw the deaths without seeing the triumph they bought" was that, in the three years following the Armistice, he came to see the triumph itself as an illusion. He had thought the creation of a League of Nations was the one result of the war that might be of permanent benefit to humanity. Wilson's cross-country campaign had failed to win the popular support that would carry the League through the Republican Senate, but Whittlesey hoped the 1920 presidential and congressional elections might reverse the verdict. In October he announced his support for Democratic candidate James M. Cox, who supported resubmission and ratification of the League treaty. But the League issue never caught fire, Cox's support for it was pro forma, and in any case the Republicans, led by Warren G. Harding, swept into office on a platform calling for a return to "normalcy" or "business as usual."[8]

The defeat of his political causes did not diminish Whittlesey's standing as a public man. An organization of Lost Battalion veterans asked him to appear at a fund-raiser for a residence for veterans who were homeless, out of work, or ill. Corporal Demaree asked him to write a preface to his *History of Company A, 308th Infantry*. Characteristically, the incident he chose to remember was the mortal wounding of his friend, Lieutenant Whiting, whose last words to Whittlesey were: "Oh, Whit, I don't want to leave the men." Individual veterans of his old regiment and division, or their relatives, would contact him to ask his help finding a job, to beg or borrow money for some emergency, or simply to hear him tell what had really happened to a lost son or brother. Some of these probably blamed and berated him for causing their death or wounding. His position as second in command of the New York Red Cross made him more eligible for personal appeals than fellow officers like George McMurtry. After the postwar depression hit in the spring of 1920 thousands of veterans were out of work. "His office became a rendezvous for job-hunting ex-soldiers—'Not a day but I hear from some of them,' he said once."[9]

If he could not redeem the horror of the war in the large, perhaps he could do something toward ameliorating its human consequences. The possibility of useful service brought out his skill and energy. He was very good at running the Red Cross Roll Call, but the service he had chosen also forced him to look again and again at the horrible effects of war and revisit that sense of helplessness in the face of overwhelming catastrophe that war produces. Once again, he had to remain positive about the possibilities for veterans, keep up morale for their sake and that of the organization—can't raise funds if you think the case is hopeless. Once again he found himself having to publicly espouse an optimism that, in his heart, he could not feel.

At around the time of Harding's election he broke up his partnership with John Pruyn, though the two remained close friends. He said he wanted to focus his practice on the technical intricacies of banking law, rather than the litigation and estate matters covered by Pruyn and Whittlesey. At White & Case he was "not a partner" but "one of our most promising assistants"—no longer an owner, merely a valued employee. His work was intellectually demanding and he was good at it, handling several complicated cases for his firm. Perhaps the impersonal nature of the work economized the emotional reserves he would spend on the Red Cross and the veterans of the Lost Battalion.

In his personal life he remained convivial and sociable. He was fond of sports, "never liked to miss a football game of importance, if it were within a reasonable distance," especially the annual Army-Navy game. "When he was not at home he would usually be found at the Williams or the Harvard Club, reading or studying or talking with some friends," among whom were several veterans of the 77th Division, including his close friend George McMurtry. It was not necessary to speak of the war with these men; they understood it all already. But given their code and manners it would have been hard for Whittlesey to discuss his doubts, his afterthoughts, his disillusionment, his anguish.

If his life was sociable, it was also without intimacy. Friends and family called him "a confirmed bachelor." He would occasionally squire a woman friend to the theater, but was never "married or engaged to be married." His sexual inclinations were expressed as a negation: he was not interested in women. As far as one can tell, he had no intimate companion, either male or female—no one with whom the necessary pose of strength could be abandoned, no one to whom the false position could be confessed. The closest he would come was a cryptic confession in his last letter to John Pruyn, that he had always felt himself to be a "misfit," one whose inner life was somehow out of phase with that of the sociable world he inhabited.

In August 1921 the 308th Infantry was chosen as one of the new Army Reserve regiments, and Whittlesey was asked to assume command with the rank of full colonel. It was just the sort of honor he could not decline, despite his antiwar sentiments—a tribute by the regular army to his old regiment. Perhaps the honor would remind the veterans that their country did value their achievements; it might help him in his efforts on their behalf. Yet there was a corrosive irony in the contrast between such honors and the real neglect of the veterans and their families that he saw firsthand. The depression ran on through the winter and into the new year. His colleagues at White & Case noticed that he received "constant calls from mothers who had lost sons" in the war and requests that he do "relief work for the bereaved relatives of the 77th Division men who had served in his battalion." Whatever satisfaction he felt in doing the right thing for his men or their families was offset by the depressing evidence that nothing he could do could alter their bereaved and often desperate situations.[10]

One particularly depressing incident was the death, in July 1921, of Jack Monson. He had been part of McKeogh's patrol, which brought relief to the troops at L'Homme Mort. He had received the DSC, the

French Croix de Guerre, and the Belgian Médaille Militaire, but could not find a place in civilian life. He had reenlisted in the army—then began to suffer from tuberculosis, attributed to the gas he had inhaled. He was ill and depressed when he went out on a pass from Governor's Island and failed to return. The army listed him AWOL while he was dying in Bellevue Hospital. His body lay unclaimed in the morgue for three days and was slated for burial among the nameless paupers in Potter's Field. Whittlesey found out about it and set about trying to have Monson buried with military honors. Among other things, he had to appeal to the army to set aside the technicality of Monson's having been AWOL when he died. On the day of the funeral Whittlesey himself was very sick, but came "to testify by his presence of his high regard for Monson." He had also to respond to an unseemly controversy in the press over whether Monson or Abe Krotoshinsky deserved to be called the savior of the Lost Battalion.[11]

A committee of the New York legislature invited him to testify on the proposal to give veterans preference for civil service jobs—the same bill that had first been proposed in the spring of 1919 and endorsed by Henry Johnson of the 369th. Two years later it was still hanging fire and accumulating amendments. Whittlesey was a Progressive, who valued the integrity of the civil service merit system and objected in principle to any wholesale grant of privilege. But he believed as strongly as Johnson that justice and humanity required that something be done for veterans, who had indeed been economically disadvantaged by their absence from the labor force while in the service. His response, in its style and its content, shows just those qualities that Max Eastman had admired in him: "sharp-edged, impersonal, and unsentimental," making difficult distinctions according to an exacting moral economy:

> I am opposed to this amendment . . . because it does not provide a preference for the soldiers who are entitled to a special consideration—the disabled men. . . . Such a preference would meet one's sense of justice. But the present amendment containing no limitation as to the class of veterans to be benefited . . . seems to be only a gesture intended to make a moment's emotional appeal; and for such ill-considered enactment I am unwilling to see the principles of merit in the civil service be set aside.[12]

But of course the consequence was that the entire measure failed.

For more than a year he had been working on an overhaul of fund-raising for the Red Cross Roll Call. Instead of buttonholing individuals for contributions, agents would work through the city's clubs, corporations, and civic organizations. That was where the wealthy gathered, and perhaps an appeal to their pride as members of the Harvard or the Racquet Club, Rotary or the Elks, would bring out their generosity. In October 1921 he was appointed chair of the national organization, and after a review of operations was satisfied that the changes had been effective, that the annual goal would be met.[13]

But all his efforts, charitable and political, seemed inadequate when measured against the unanswered needs and unrelieved misery of the veterans and their families, who continued to appeal to him. "Not a day goes by but I hear from some of my old outfit, usually about some sort of sorrow or misfortune." In November, as the winter of 1921 approached, his colleagues at White & Case saw him "besieged by wounded soldiers and widows of soldiers seeking aid," whose "appeals made him anxious and worried." The economic depression had been going on for a year and a half, the sick and unemployed, the widows and orphans were at the end of their resources, and Congress had still not acted on the bonus. A colleague thought him "sentimental" because "these appeals made him anxious and worried," as if these were strangers playing upon his tender sympathies. But Whittlesey had no patience with sentimentality. To him these were not supplicant strangers but a sort of kindred, bound to him by a blood-tie—the blood they had shed and spilled together. He had marched them into a valley of death and they had fought it out under his command, and when it was over had said that they loved him for what he had been and what he had done. As they had fulfilled their duty by following him then, so he must fulfill his by meeting their needs now.

"His . . . work as Chairman of the Red Cross Roll Call this month was all based on the suffering of the wounded. He would go to two or three funerals every week, visit the wounded in the hospitals, and try to comfort the relatives of the dead." At one such event he told a companion, "Raking over the ashes like this revives all the horrible memories. I'll hear the wounded screaming again. I have nightmares about them; I can't remember when I last had a good night's sleep." In dreams he relived the horror of the Pocket, expressed in vivid images of intimacy and loss: he was lying among the wounded in the shallow trench they had dug for them, lying side by side with a badly wounded boy; he fell into a brief exhausted sleep and "awoke in the middle of the night to find his cheek touching the wounded soldier's, which was cold in death."

His helplessness to relieve the misery of the war came home to him in the most intimate terms. His younger brother Elisha was a poet and an idealist who had joined the war for civilization before American entry, serving in France as a volunteer ambulance driver, fighting without shedding blood. He had contracted a mysterious illness in the trenches, a lingering infection that affected his lungs and disabled him with recurrent bouts of fever. Whittlesey could do nothing for him. His own health was poor, the aftereffects of the gassing he had got on the Vesle complicated by nervous strain. He had a "racking cough for weeks" that fall, so loud it was "heard by the other young men who lived with him" in the bachelor's boardinghouse at 136 East 44th Street.

He had no use for sentimentality, for strong useless feeling. These were an indulgence that went against his understanding of manhood and his moral code. It was his duty to see clearly and act strenuously to bring something positive out of all the misery and injustice. The task was beyond his strength, yet he couldn't wash his hands of it, had above all to do that which he could not bear to do. "They're always after me about the war," he told a friend. "I've got to help some soldier or make some speech or something. I used to think I was a lawyer; now I don't know what I am."

That November he was accorded another of those honors that were embittered for him by their evocation of the war's horror, death, and failure: an invitation from Hamilton Fish to join the phalanx of Medal of Honor winners at the ceremonies honoring the Unknown Soldier.

The contrast between Whittlesey and Fish, as men and as veterans, was striking. Fish stood out even among the mass of dignitaries, high officials, and legislative leaders attending the ceremonies at Arlington: tall and powerfully built, in robust good health, obviously at home in the public eye. He had been one of the chief organizers of the first national convention of the American Legion, had easily won election to Congress in 1920, and immediately emerged as a strong party leader. He had led the movement to honor an Unknown and taken charge of the ceremonies. His position on the bonus was equivocal, but he was not the sort of man to be depressed by a conflict between his ideal of what was right and his understanding of what his career and his party required.

The body of the Unknown Soldier lay in state in the Capitol Rotunda. On the morning of November 11 the coffin was placed on a gun carriage and the "Solemn Journey of [the] Dead" to Arlington began. The Medal of Honor winners marched as a battalion eight abreast, at the front the old men in the faded blue uniforms of the Civil War, Indian Wars, Cuba, and the Philippines, behind them Whittlesey and his good friend George McMurtry with the other Great War veterans in khaki. Behind them came the solitary black carriage carrying President Wilson, "his once strong body broken by ill-health," too ill to march or even to sit through the ceremonies, barely acknowledging the respectful cheers of the crowd—a melancholy embodiment of the failed ideals of his "war to end all war." On the platform at the burial site were President Harding and other high dignitaries, including General Pershing, Marshal Foch, Admiral Beatty, former prime ministers Balfour and Briand. There were addresses by representatives of the Allies, a tribute by Chief Plenty Coups of the Crow tribe in "full war dress." The Marine Band played Christian hymns—"God Our Help in Ages Past," "Nearer My God to Thee"—then, after a two-minute silence, played "America," while a choir sang, "Oh beautiful for spacious skies . . ." The song was taken up by audiences in New York City's Madison Square Garden, and in other halls around the country, connected to the Washington ceremony by wireless.

President Harding gave the chief address, his rhetoric an unconscious parody of Wilson's idealistic eloquence, a "series of platitudes . . . terrifically repeated," marred by errors in English usage. "Mr. Secretary of War, and Ladies and Gentlemen," he began, "We are met here today to pay the impersonal tribute." He meant, of course, that they had come to honor *every* fallen soldier by honoring one whose personal identity had been obliterated. But his way of putting it was dismally suggestive of other ideas: that it was the *impersonality* of war and death to which they were paying tribute, honoring not the man but the Thing that had obliterated his individual humanity. Or was it that the tribute itself was "impersonal," an official gesture with no personal feeling behind it?

"We know not whence he came, but only that his death marks him with the everlasting glory of an American dying for his Country." For Whittlesey such a phrase would have been a hateful distortion of everything he knew about combat, everything he believed about the war. Every day he confronted the gap between the "everlasting glory" his comrades had won and the shameful neglect of their health and their hopes. Harding thought the Unknown had died "perhaps believing his to be a service destined to change the tide of human affairs." The *New York*

Times editorial on the event asked rhetorically, "Would the immense audience . . . have joined the President in prayer over the body, or have caught up the strains of 'America' . . . and sung the words in unison . . . if they had not in their hearts a fully dared belief that his service was destined to bring a better world[?]"Amid that chorus of affirmation Whittlesey was alone, doubting whether the war had achieved anything of enduring value to balance its terrible costs. To his companion George McMurtry he said, "I keep wondering if the Unknown Soldier is one of my men. . . . I should not have come here."[14]

Friends who saw him in the succeeding weeks thought he was more grim than usual. He dined with his brother Melzar's family, but "he never talked about his experiences in the war and, with characteristic silence, said nothing about the burial of the unknown soldier." After dinner was cleared away, Melzar dared to ask "how he had been impressed by the ceremonies." All he would say was that it had made "a profoundly deep impression," though it was evident to Melzar's wife that he had been deeply upset.

His work load at White & Case was increasing as his skill in analyzing complex cases became evident. But that month he found time to complete his highly successful reorganization of Red Cross fund-raising. On Sunday, November 20, he attended a large fund-raiser at the New York Hippodrome, where he shared the honors with Field Marshal Foch and Napoleon Marshall of the 369th. They sat on the stage surrounded by "wounded men, some of them armless and legless," objects of pity to win contributions from the prosperous audience. A colleague thought the evening "added to a weight of horror he was unable to shake from his mind," the cumulative effects of the Unknown Soldier ceremony and months under "siege" by disabled comrades and bereaved families. The next day, Monday, he bought a ticket for a voyage to Havana on the United Fruit liner *Toloa*, departing the following Saturday.

That week the firm entrusted him with a particularly difficult case, whose details he set about mastering. Thursday the twenty-fourth was Thanksgiving, and he took time out to visit the Pruyns. It was their baby's first birthday, and he brought a present of "baby pins for the little one." Mrs. Pruyn's sister was there—she had been maid of honor to his best man at the Pruyns' wedding—and she thought he was "in very gay spirits." Friday was a workday again. He mentioned to his landlady Mrs.

Sullivan that he was leaving for a holiday—he had been feeling tired. He told several colleagues that he planned to go away that weekend. They assumed he was going to the Army-Navy game at West Point, since he rarely missed an "important game." But he told one friend that he and his brother Elisha would be taking the train to their parents' home in Pittsfield. The prospect seemed to cheer him; he was in a "carefree mood." That night he went to the theater with his "oldest woman friend"—not anyone he was "involved" with, "simply an old friend."[15]

On Saturday he put Elisha on the train to Pittsfield. His parents would take care of the invalid while Whittlesey was on his holiday. He boarded the *Toloa* and sailed that afternoon. That evening he dined with the captain and a few other guests, and fell into conversation with a Mr. Maloret, a Puerto Rican gentleman who had served in uniform but not gone overseas. For once he spoke freely about the war, the talk was easy and pleasant, wreathed in cigar smoke. He had always enjoyed good conversation, lingering for hours in his club caught up in the play of wit and anecdote. Then quite abruptly he caught himself, took notice of the time—nearly midnight!—rose, said his good nights, and left the salon. It was dark outside, the ship's deck lights dimmed by fog.

The steward who came to clean his room the next morning found eight sealed envelopes on his desk, one addressed to the captain, which made it plain that Whittlesey had gone over the side, probably within a few minutes of leaving the salon. The captain put the ship about and cruised over his course for half a day in the forlorn hope of finding him. Then he cabled New York, and the *Times* got the news on November 29: "Lieut. Col. Charles W. Whittlesey, Commander of the 'Lost Battalion,' holder of the Congressional Medal of Honor and one of the outstanding heroes of the World War, is believed to have committed suicide by jumping from the United Fruit liner *Toloa*." Two pages of interviews and tributes followed. More details were released next day and over the following week as his former comrades organized a memorial service.

William Cullen, the red-haired giant who had been so vital to the defense of the Pocket, declared that "Citizen Whittlesey, helping a deceased soldier's family, visiting a wounded buddy in a hospital, hurrying to the assistance of a man in trouble, or conducting a drive for some auxiliary" was still as much "in the service" as when he led "his comrades in an imperishable exploit." He believed that "the grim determination that

scorned an enemy's insolent request quailed in contemplation of neglected comrades. . . . No shell-racked towns . . . nor late patrols, but
empty sleeves and missing limbs or steel-braced members tautly held,
and the sturdy heart of America's son cracks in the presence of a greater
price." Perhaps Whittlesey was even "envious of their plight and disappointed in that he was not permitted to pay an equal price." At the memorial service on December 4 in the 71st Regiment Armory, there was
an empty caisson to signify that Whittlesey would be listed as "Missing
in Action." His former commander, Colonel Averill, said that though he
was "stunned" by the news of his death, "yet the more I think . . . the
more I am convinced that his death was in reality a battle casualty and
that he met his end in the line of duty as if he had fallen by a German bullet." The *Times* saw him as the epitome of the citizen-soldier, his death as
testimony that "there is still a great deal to be done for those who have
suffered for us all."[16]

His letters were returned to the United States by diplomatic pouch, addressed to his parents, his brother Melzar, his friend John Pruyn, and his
colleagues at White & Case. To his "dear Bayard" he had written: "Just a
note to say good bye. I'm a misfit by nature and by training, and there's an
end of it." The rest of the letter dealt briefly with Whittlesey's estate, of
which Pruyn was to be executor. Neither his parents nor his brother ever
revealed what he had written to them. Melzar told an interviewer more
than a dozen years later that he had never opened the letter, did not want to
read what his brother had not been able to say to his face. His colleagues
were told they would find the paperwork on the difficult case in his desk at
136 East 44th Street, complete in every detail. By coincidence, on the day
he committed suicide the *Times* announced that Colonel Whittlesey's new
method of funding the Red Cross Roll Call had proved entirely successful,
the annual goal would be met or exceeded.[17] He had fulfilled all his obligations before the indulgence of doing, for once, a thing he *did* want to do.

Black Death: The Fame of Henry Johnson, 1919–1929

Henry Johnson had nothing in common with Charles Whittlesey, except
that both were heroes to a significant section of the American public. A
hero has privileges, but the accolade carries a heavy weight of expecta-

tion and, for Henry Johnson as much as for Charles Whittlesey, it entailed serious responsibilities. Whittlesey's fame was national; he was a White man of "old American stock" and a hero of the AEF. His fame and his conscience made him feel responsible to a class that was both very large and very singular: veterans in general, and Lost Battalion survivors in particular. It was a task for which he was temperamentally and psychologically unsuited, and though he had the security of an established social position, the resources of a fine education, and the support of strong and well-placed friends, it broke him.

Johnson's fame was not as broad, but it was intensely felt within his embattled community. His task was in some ways heavier than Whittlesey's. He was asked to represent his people to a White American public sitting in unfriendly judgment on the Negro race, and to compel that public to recognize in him the proof that Black people were valiant, patriotic, and fit for citizenship in modern America. It was a powerful symbolic role at a moment of crisis, with the future of the race seeming to hang in the balance. He had none of Whittlesey's social and educational resources, but he did have a powerful sense of the worth of his achievement, and the unit culture that had shaped the Old Fifteenth had taught him to see his personal triumph as vindication of his race. He would represent that truth in the only way he could: by plain speaking about what Black men had had to endure to earn the right to die for their country. His fame would be briefer than Whittlesey's, but no less destructive to him.

Johnson came home a genuine hero, the first U.S. soldier to win a major decoration for valor, the first to win the Croix de Guerre. Theodore Roosevelt praised him as "one of the five bravest" to have fought in the war. He was famous on both sides of the color line, hailed as "Black Death" by his own people and interviewed by reporters for the great White daily papers and magazines, sitting by the side of Colonel Hayward, the self-respecting Black man equal in fame and interest to his high-born White commander.[18]

Relations between Johnson and the officers of the regiment had not always had that quality of mutual respect. Hayward and Little regarded Black enlisted men like Johnson—poor, ill-educated—with a mixture of sympathy and condescension. Little speaks of him in diminutives as a "sweet, unassuming boy, ready and eager to do whatever he could."

After his famous battle, Little calls him a "little hero," who became "one of the great pets of the regiment" after he returned from hospital.

> Colonel Hayward expressed the affectionate feeling of many of us when he said . . . the least we could do for [Johnson], after all he had done for us, was to treat him as the old 7th Cavalry had treated Custer's horse—let him nibble grass around Headquarters, and when company came call him in and show him off.

However, after receiving his medal Johnson showed a different side of his nature, a proud self-awareness, which Little perceived as uppitiness or unearned *vanity*. Little makes a mildly invidious comparison between Johnson and his own ideal of American manhood: "While democratic in his bearing, just as the late Colonel Roosevelt was democratic, still he never forgot that he wore the purple." Johnson was not "lacking in full appreciation of his own greatness. . . . And he never let anyone else forget it." That same mix of respect and condescension permeates the story Little tells of his farewell to Johnson, which is also the anecdote that closes his history of the Old Fifteenth. Sergeant Johnson, "the little homicidal king," knocks on Little's door to say good-bye. Little shakes his hand and asks Johnson not to forget him. " 'Furgit yer! Suh Major, Sur,' answered Henry Johnson—his eyes opening wider and wider. 'Furgit yer! Suh? Why, Suh Major Sur, yer made a man of me!' "[19]

It is hard to know just how much of this scene is remembered, misremembered, or invented. It is so precisely what Little and his colleagues wished to hear that it seems suspect. While granting the Negro's capacity to be uplifted, it emphasizes his dependence on the paternal guidance of his White benefactor. Yet this patronizing concession of "equality" represented the *best* response Johnson could hope for from any White figure or audience. The officers of the 369th had proved their commitment to civil rights, and to Henry Johnson, at the risk of lives and reputations. Yet when Johnson asserted his equality, claiming as if by right the place and privileges he had earned in battle, they were annoyed, felt he was getting above himself. With other White men, not of his regiment, the reaction would be far more severe.

There is no doubt the war had given Johnson a new sense of himself. He felt he had earned, in the hardest way possible, the right to be treated with respect by White people, and also the right to get ahead, to prosper financially. There was no possibility of getting his old redcap job back.

His wounds were crippling and kept him in continual pain. "One of Johnson's feet had had most of the bones removed, so that he had to walk in a manner that might be described as 'slap-foot.' " But his fame gave him other prospects. Back home in Albany, Governor Al Smith hosted a dinner for him, promised to name a street for him, and give him a financial reward as a token of the state's appreciation. A local philanthropist promised to build the Johnsons a house.

In March 1919 he was asked to address the state legislature on the bill to give preference to veterans in hiring for the civil service. He was for it: the government was obliged to "take care of the boys who did their bit." It seemed possible that he might become a respected spokesman for his buddies and his race. Colonel Hayward invited Johnson to share the platform in a tour on behalf of the new Liberty Loan. A New York booking agent offered Johnson $10,000 for a speaking tour; his buddy Needham Roberts had already signed up for one. But Johnson preferred to pick his own manager—suspicious, perhaps, of all these White people eager to do him good.[20]

There was reason to be suspicious. In the spring of 1919 the papers told of Black veterans beaten or lynched in the South for wearing their uniforms. Black newspapers acknowledged frustration in trying to win support for measures to moderate Jim Crow. The systematic defamation of the 92nd Division cast aspersions on all Black veterans, even those who belonged to a regiment whose battle honors set them among the elite of the AEF. As it had been a symbol of pride in the bargain fulfilled, so now the Old Fifteenth symbolized the bargain betrayed. In April 1919 the *Crusader*, a Negro magazine published in New Orleans, printed a piece titled "Fighting the Savage Hun and Treacherous Cracker," which revealed that "the hardest fight of all" for the "black warriors of the 369th and other Negro units" was the fight against the prejudice of their White fellow soldiers, who did not scruple to abuse men who were defending their "hides and homes and families." White officers gave them the filthiest and most dangerous assignments; the YMCA saved their candy and cigarettes for Whites; White nurses treated Germans before wounded Black doughboys. White staff officers told the French the Negroes would rape and murder their women. "[The] 'Hell Fighters' might as well have been fighting the AEF for all the support they received from it. It was only after they had been placed with the French that they began to make their fighting qualities tell upon the Hun."[21]

Henry Johnson remembered his army experience in just that way. The warm words he had spoken about Hayward and Little were sincere, but the officers of the Old Fifteenth were exceptional White men who had proved their friendship to the limits allowed by the color line. The U.S. Army was no better than any other White institution. Johnson remembered all the slights and abuse he and his comrades had had to suffer in Spartanburg and Camp Mills, in the labor battalions at Saint-Nazaire, and every time they were billeted in an American rest area. He had not fought for Colonel Hayward or Hayward's version of American democracy, but for his own people: who were, first of all, "Company C . . . the best in the regiment"; and now that the war was over, his people were the people from whom Company C had sprung. He was "Black Death"—why should he be afraid to speak the truth to power?[22]

After his appearance before the New York legislature in March, he was invited to speak in St Louis as the star attraction of a program celebrating Negro contributions to the war effort. He demanded a fee of $1,500 and refused to leave the greenroom until it was paid—determined that others recognize him as worthy of his hire. His stubbornness delayed the festivities, but when he appeared onstage, his chest ablaze with medals, the crowd went wild. The speakers before him, mainly "Colored preachers," had spoken hopefully of a new age of "equanimity" (not equality!) between the races. Johnson stepped up and delivered a "barrage" that "broke up" the facade of equanimity. There had been no racial comradeship at the front. White marines had refused to fight alongside Blacks, not only because they were bigots but because they were cowards. The marines knew that "when it came to real fighting the negroes were sent in," and the battle would be desperate. Maybe that proved Negroes were brave and good soldiers, but that wasn't *why* they were sent into the worst situations; he had heard a White officer say, "Send the niggers to the front and there won't be so many around New York." The war made Henry Johnson a hero, but it wasn't his war, and it wasn't a Black man's war. Look at what White men made out of it, and see what little was conceded to Black men for their service. Perhaps he was thinking of Hayward and putting himself on the colonel's level, when he added, "If I was a white man I would be the next governor of New York."

The anger of a lifetime had found expression, and it came from his Jim Crow youth in North Carolina and from redcapping in Albany as much as from Saint-Nazaire or Combat Group 29. But in the midst of his tirade he also said a true and vivid thing about his actual experience: "Yes, I saw dead people. In fact, I have seen so many dead bodies piled up that when I saw a live one I didn't think it was natural." What he had suffered as a Black man merged with what he had suffered as a soldier, the psychological damage that comes of intense immersion in a world pervaded by death—that comes of having killed a man, especially at quarters so close that his breath is in your face.

The reaction on the stage and in the crowd was fierce. Some of the other dignitaries, preachers and military officers, apologized for Johnson's "bitter and vindictive" speech. But Lieutenant Charles Fearing of the 92nd Division, who was still in service and in uniform, defended Johnson, asserting that when they went into action "the negroes were hit more from behind than they were in front"—that is, they were sniped at by their White "comrades." Fearing "brought the crowd to its feet when he attacked the white soldiers" as back-shooters. As a White reporter for the *St. Louis Republic* put it, "More than 5,000 negroes cheered, kissed, and fairly carried . . . Sergt. Henry Johnson, negro hero, around the Coliseum last night. . . . Women became hysterical and strewed flowers around him," although when they tried to kiss him he broke free and made his way out down a fire escape.

The *Republic* condemned Johnson for inflaming racial passions, for claiming all White soldiers were "cowards" and that "the only soldiers in France were negroes." It debunked his claim to have been decorated by King George and President Poincaré and criticized him for keeping the dignitaries waiting while he collected his $1,500 fee. One Henry O'Hara of St. Louis saw the story and sent it with an irate letter to Secretary of War Newton Baker:

> If this Sergeant Henry Johnson is still within the War Department's jurisdiction may we not look for some relief from this highly inflammatory tirade. . . . He openly degrades all efforts made by the white soldiers of this country. . . . The fertile mind of the weak and vacillating brother of his race will accept . . . the unbelievable lies he has uttered against the decency of all manhood.

Baker forwarded the letter and clipping to the "Negro Subversion" section of MID. The section head, Major Loving, looked into the New York end, heard about Johnson turning down $10,000 from the big booking firm, and concluded that "Johnson is densely ignorant and is suffering from a severe case of 'swelled head.'" In St. Louis a local MID operative discovered that after the speech Johnson had been threatened by some marines for slandering the corps. Six or eight had knocked on the door of his hotel room and been greeted by a "little" Negro man in a dressing gown, who told them Sergeant Johnson was out. They took his word and left—though it was Johnson they had spoken to. They returned later; this time they saw Johnson in uniform, but on the wrong side (for them) of a glass door, which he refused to open. Foiled twice in their attempts at vigilante justice, the marines complained to the local office of the Justice Department. But Johnson had already taken the train back home to Albany.[23]

MID took the matter seriously. For more than a year they had been receiving warnings of imminent racial insurrection, often in the form of letters from wealthy Southerners about vague threats uttered by disgruntled chauffeurs, but also in the writings and speeches of Black radicals and socialists. They were seriously concerned that Black veterans might use their soldierly skills in an uprising. In March Major Loving had set a surveillance team on the heels of two other veterans of the 369th, Sergeant Anthony Buckner and Corporal George Thomas, who were canvassing for the radical Equal Rights League. Johnson was not part of any organization, but he was a national celebrity, and the story of his attack on White soldiers had been covered by papers throughout the Midwest. A federal warrant was issued charging Johnson with wearing his uniform beyond the permitted time of three months following discharge, but since Johnson was actually within that limit, the warrant was voided. The director of MID thought he should be charged with inciting to riot if he persisted in speaking out. According to one account, Johnson did make another controversial appearance, with Colonel Hayward in Texas, but was forced to flee the state after calling a White man a "cracker." In the end the only action taken against him by MID was a symbolic humiliation: he was ordered to stop wearing his uniform, although the privilege still had another month to run.[24]

Despite this personal disaster, Henry Johnson remained the personification of Black military achievement, and the most potent symbol in the community's rhetoric of self-defense. In June, with the AFL appearing ready to admit Negroes, James Weldon Johnson used him to symbolize the possibility that Blacks could win admission to full citizenship by proving their worth. He reminded his readers that Henry Johnson,

"Black Death" of the Old Fifteenth, had been a redcap; that unlike the IWWs, Blacks had been willing to fight for their country. After the riots in July, other Black journalists invoked Henry Johnson as a symbol of militant opposition to Whites. A Negro paper in Richmond reprinted a sermon that likened the "Battle of Henry Johnson" to the Revelation of John as a vision of the world redeemed:

> Old things passed away when Roberts and Johnson on the field of No Man's Land shed their blood in the cause of Liberty. Old things began to pass away when four hundred thousand black men joined the other race on No Man's Land—and when they return this nation must understand that "old things have passed away."

Among those old things was the " 'old type' of Negro," who tamely submitted to the will of Whites. An article reprinted in many papers that summer asked, "ARE YOU AWARE that a Negro [Henry Johnson] was the First American to Receive the Croix de Guerre with Palm and Gold Star? . . . That Negroes [the 369th Infantry] established a record for continuous service in the trenches—191 days?" The lesson learned from that fight is that liberty must be fought for, and so the "New Negro" has concluded that "the preservation of the Negro's liberty . . . must be a negro's individual fight." DuBois's "Essay Towards a History of the Black Man in the Great War" invoked Henry Johnson and other Black soldiers as race heroes rather than national heroes, representative of moral and political positions *opposed* to those of the national government for which they had fought.[25]

Johnson symbolized heroism and defiance, but to what end? Was he proof of the Negro's Americanism, or proof that the Black race is brave and strong enough to cut its own way to freedom? If it was difficult for Black leaders to reconcile the conflicting demands of anger and politic accommodation, it was impossible for Henry Johnson to bear the strain of symbolizing Black manhood under such conditions. His power as a symbol was unquestionable, and it made him for a while one of the most famous Black men in America. But the symbolism was ambiguous, offered no real guidance as to how he should think of himself, how he should behave, what he should say. He could neither escape it nor live with it.

After St. Louis, things went bad for him with terrible speed. In the best of times his wounds would have made it impossible for him to work at any job that required walking, let alone lifting and hauling, which eliminated his old redcap job and most other semiskilled work. After the postwar slump hit in the spring of 1920 a Black man with his disabilities would have had few chances of finding employment. His son Herman (born in 1917) remembers that "like most of the returning veterans" he found little "if any acceptable employment. His life was one of employment below his abilities." The promised house was never provided, no street was named for him. The measure he had advocated, for giving veterans privileged access to civil service jobs, was rejected by the legislature. His controversial performance in St. Louis, and perhaps interference by MID (which kept him under surveillance for a year), killed his prospects as a platform speaker. He had to support wife and child on whatever he could make from occasional employment, supplemented by a very small disability payment. His health deteriorated, his wounds continued to plague him; he numbed the pain with drink and sank into alcoholism and possibly drug use. In 1923 his wife divorced him. For a while he kept in touch. Herman Johnson remembers that his father spent time with the family, "and I enjoyed being with him." In the late 1920s they lost contact with him.

In 1936 Major Little published his reminiscence of the Old Fifteenth, *From Harlem to the Rhine.* The book concludes with the scene of Johnson shaking Little's hand and thanking him for having "made a man of me." When the book appeared Johnson was seven years dead. He had died in 1929, in an Albany VA hospital, thirty-two years old and utterly alone. As late as 2001, Herman Johnson believed his father had died in 1937 and been buried in an unmarked grave in the Albany potter's field. In fact, the army had buried him in Arlington, presumably with appropriate honors, but had never notified his family.

In a sense his death confirmed the symbolic status he had earned in France. It signaled the defeat of the hopes raised by the victories of the Harlem Hell Fighters.[26]

15

"Say, Don't You Remember . . . ?":
Public Memory, Public Myth, and the
Meaning of the War, 1919–1930

> Once in khaki suits—gee we looked swell
> Full of that Yankee-doodle-y dum.
> A half a million boots went slogging through hell,
> And I was the kid with the drum.
> Say don't you remember, they called me Al?
> It was Al all the time.
> Say don't you remember, I'm your pal,
> Brother, can you spare a dime?
>
> *—Jay Gorney and E. Y. Harburg,*
> *"Brother, Can You Spare a Dime?" (1932)*

Most veterans of the Lost Battalion and the Harlem Hell Fighters were neither destroyed by their experience nor exalted to celebrity
status. The regulars remained in the service, though with the army reduced to peacetime levels, opportunities for advancement were limited.
Robert Alexander held a number of staff and administrative appointments, but received no further promotions. Nelson Holderman won the
Medal of Honor, stayed in the army, and attended Staff College, where
he wrote a well-received monograph on the Lost Battalion, but never
fully recovered from his wounds. He commanded the California Veterans
Home from 1926 until his death in 1953.

Eugene Houghton, the soldier of fortune who had commanded the

307th and developed the tactical plan for the relief of the Lost Battalion, went back to Canada where he had been in business before the war. In June 1919 Winnipeg was hit by a general strike, characterized as "an attempt at revolution and an imitation of Soviet autocracy." Houghton commanded a force of special police and vigilantes, financed by area businessmen, which employed "extremely direct action" to suppress the strike.[1]

The Plattsburgh officers returned to their careers, though for some that return was delayed by recovery from wounds or illness. It took Wardlaw Miles a year to recover from the amputation of his leg and his numerous bullet wounds. Princeton did not restore the professorship he had resigned in 1917. He taught at a prep school, then at Johns Hopkins, where he would have a distinguished career and be remembered with affection by the students with whom he shared his love of English poetry. His history of the 308th Infantry was published in 1927. Kerr Rainsford also wrote his regiment's history, and resumed a successful career as an architect, enjoying the life of an avid sportsman—horseback riding, canoeing, mountain climbing, swimming. He would shock a Memorial Day reunion of the 307th Infantry with a speech blaming the American Legion for refusing to support the League of Nations and so making another world war inescapable.

Julius Adler came out of the war with a reputation for heroism that ranked just behind Whittlesey's. He won his DSC in spectacular fashion, riding into the strategic town of St. Juvin on a motorcycle with only his batman and a Chauchat gunner, and bluffing the Germans into surrender. But his expectation that he would succeed Adolph Ochs as publisher of the *Times* would be disappointed. Ochs chose his son-in-law, Cyrus Sulzberger, and Julius was relegated to a supporting role. Like Whittlesey, he took a commission in the reserves and by 1944 had risen to major general. He served as a deputy division commander in New Guinea and after the war commanded the 77th Division in the reserves.

Other Plattsburgh alums returned to the Wall Street law or brokerage firms they had left in 1917. Many would continue to meet at the Harvard Club, where the Plattsburgh idea had been conceived back in 1915. The 369th's Napoleon Marshall was frequently in attendance, though his law practice was uptown. Hamilton Fish would have been there when not in Washington. Frank Tiebout was a member, and he showed his ongoing commitment to the Plattsburgh doctrine of preparedness by staying with the reserves, rising to the rank of colonel. Crawford Blagden, one of the founding fathers of Plattsburgh, coached football at Harvard, went back to his brokerage business, stayed solvent through the crash of 1929, but died of the flu in 1937 at age fifty-five. George McMurtry succeeded his father as a corporate director and was prominent in local sporting circles as a tennis and polo player. He often met Whittlesey at the club, and his friend's suicide touched him deeply. He had seconded Whittlesey through the five days of fighting at Charlevaux Mill and would replace him as patron of Lost Battalion survivors down on their luck. He organized and paid for the series of reunions of battalion survivors, which met annually from 1938 until McMurtry's death in 1958.[2]

William Hayward was greeted as a star by New York society and the Republican Party. His second marriage in June 1919 to wealthy heiress and socialite Mae Plant confirmed his position among the city's social elite. His sterling war record and classic good looks, coupled with a solid record of public service as a judge in Nebraska and public service commissioner in New York, made him an obvious candidate for higher office. In 1921 he was appointed U.S. attorney for the Southern District and busied himself prosecuting violators of Prohibition. But he lost the 1924 gubernatorial nomination to Theodore Roosevelt Jr. (who lost the election to Al Smith) and withdrew from politics. Like Theodore Roosevelt, he marked the break by embarking on adventures, hunting big game in Africa and exploring the Arctic. Unlike Roosevelt, he never attempted a political comeback. He continued to appear at reunions and reviews of the 369th, was interviewed from time to time on racial issues, but was not especially prominent in the struggle for civil rights. Nonetheless he was remembered with real affection by the enlisted men who served under him, and they turned out to say good-bye when he died in October 1944 at the age of sixty-seven.[3]

Arthur Little of the 369th returned to his printing business, but remained active in politics as a pro–New Deal Republican. He worked for two agencies under the National Recovery Administration, which was tantamount to socialism in the eyes of conservatives. In 1936 he was briefly considered for the vice presidential nomination and as "fusion" candidate for mayor. He became a staunch supporter of Fiorello La Guardia and served as the mayor's military advisor in 1941. He was also active in civil rights organizations and often called on to advise government agencies and panels on racial matters. When he died in 1943 his obituary in the *Times* called him a "Champion of Negroes' Rights," which does justice to his goodwill and diligence in that cause.[4]

Leon "Josh" Cadore, who had started the war as a draftee in the 77th Division and ended it as a lieutenant in the 369th, returned to his prewar job pitching baseball games for the Brooklyn Robins (later the Dodgers). In 1917 he had been a promising rookie on a pennant-contending team. In May 1919 he went from demobilization at Camp Upton to Ebbets Field, where his greatest days as a ballplayer were ahead of him. He won fourteen games and lost twelve in 1919 and in 1920 went 15–12 for a pennant-winning team. That year Cadore earned baseball immortality by pitching all twenty-six innings of a 0–0 tie against the Boston Braves, the longest game ever played, then pitching all thirteen innings of the game played to break the tie. That epic achievement, rather than war injuries, shortened his career. He retired as a player in 1924, but married the daughter of the owner of Ebbets Field and enjoyed a long and successful career in management.[5]

Organized baseball also remembered Eddie Grant, who had played for Brooklyn's archrival New York Giants, not for his deeds on the playing field (his lifetime batting average was .249), but for his death leading the 307th's attempt to reach the Lost Battalion. At a ceremony on May 31, 1920, he was honored with a bronze plaque at the Polo Grounds, which praised him as "Soldier Scholar Athlete."

Most of the enlisted men returned to the neighborhoods and the work they had left in 1917, some in good health, some showing the effects of bullet or shrapnel wounds and "whiffs" of poison gas. Of those who sang "The Democratic Army" at Camp Upton, Private Goldberg had been captured, Sergeant Kessler gassed, Sergeants Leumann, Ginsberg, and Del Duca, and Privates Patrissi and Sargeant (of Erin and the NYPD) severely wounded. Also among the wounded was Raymond Flynn, the vaudevillian who had staged those Upton entertainments, "Bachi Galoop" in blackface, "The Jews and Wops, the Dutch and Irish cops." He recalled all those good times, as well as the loss of so many friends, in his *History of Company E* (1919). Then he went back to vaudeville, trying out various ethnic personae with varied success, until in 1932 he and his partner hit upon "Joe and Bateese," a pair of comical French-Canadians. Flynn enjoyed a three-year run as "Joe LaFlamme," then moved to Hollywood to work as a bit player. There he might have run into Harold Neptune, a replacement who had joined before the Argonne. Neptune had proved up his 320-acre Montana homestead, but left it in the 1930s for Hollywood, where he was one of the "Gower Gulch" cowboys who worked as horseback-riding extras.

Of the other Westerners, Clarence Roberts went home to a small stock ranch thirty-four miles out of Hardin, Montana, mail twice a week, and "on a clear day you can see three ranges of mountains." Ruben Ahlstedt returned to work as an engineer on the Chicago, Rock Island and Pacific, running freight between Herington and Kansas City. Clyde Hintz bought a ten-acre farm near Hutchinson, Minnesota, ran the popcorn wagon on Main Street every summer. Lowell Hollingshead, the POW who carried the surrender demand to Whittlesey, made a career in the Ohio Department of Corrections, rising to captain of guards. Lieutenant Eager became a college professor at Stillwater Agricultural and Mining College. A. O. Kaemper, the Butte miner, did not fare so well. When reporter Thomas Johnson found him in 1937 he was in the Veterans Hospital in Fort Harrison, whether suffering from wounds or a miner's lung complaint is not stated. Olaf Johnson, the Minnesota Swede, was also in chronic ill health, working at the state hospital in St. Paul when he was not a patient. Still, he managed to raise a family, and two of his sons would serve in World War II. Of the Native Americans, Frank Martinez was killed in the Pocket and James Rainwater returned to work as a coal miner in Butte, where he died in 1936 or '37. Robert Dodd, a Paiute from Nevada, was wounded in the ankle and shoulder and went back to the reservation after the war.

The New Yorkers returned to their trades. James Carroll went back to selling draperies for the same house that employed him before the war. Jeremiah Healy, the perfume salesman, hooked on with Coty, Inc., tops in his line of work. Bernard Sweeney was a plumber; John Scanlon would serve twenty-six years as a New York City fireman. Isadore Willinger and Arthur Fein (who had been left for dead on the battlefield) got jobs in the post office. Pistoria Bonaventura lost a leg, but wrote his buddies to say he was married and doing all right. Manny Zwerling went back to his beat as a New York City cop, despite the shrapnel in his legs picked up at Ville Savoye. In 1925 he was a founding member of the Shomrim Society, the fraternal organization of Jewish policemen. Jack Voorheis lived in Rochester, where he was "associated with a manufacturer of tailored fur garments." Phil Kornelly would make a career at the New York Trust Company: three of his sons served in World War II and in Korea, one of them killed in action.[6]

Jack Herschkowitz had won the DSC for valor as one of Lieutenant McKeogh's party, sent to bring relief to Whittlesey's men at L'Homme Mort. His heroism was usually and erroneously associated with Charlevaux Mill, and the army and newspapers rarely spelled his name the same way twice. On first view, Whittlesey had thought him "the worst possible material for soldier-stuff . . . thick-set, stupid looking, extremely foreign." In the end he singled Herschkowitz out as the prime example of the Lower East Side Jews' capacity for heroism. In 1919 Herschkowitz went back to the Lower East Side and got into the grocery business, married, raised a family, built a successful wholesale company, moved to Brooklyn then to Long Island. When Thomas Johnson interviewed him in 1936 or '37 he was in "robust health." He lived until 1985.[7]

James Deahan had been a barman before the war. Johnson did not ask how he had made his living during Prohibition, but in 1937 Deahan was the proprietor of his own tavern in Brooklyn. He didn't go out of his way to tell his own war stories, but thought an article about the Lost Battalion "might be good for business."

For some the trauma had lasting effects. Lionel Bendheim was still having trouble with the stump of his amputated leg when Johnson visited: "nerve pains—and he has to go to bed." Patrick D'Amato, back at his trade of barbering, told Johnson "he does not like to remember [the Pocket] now, or any war experience. He does not even like to see war movies." Dakota cowboy Ralph John was haunted by terrible memories of "marching on and marching on, I didn't think anything of stepping over dead bodies of men with whom I had started out or wading through a pool of blood, but now something comes up in my throat." He remembered the helpless wounded in the Pocket with their rotting wounds, the "unbearable" smell, some men dead, "other[s] dying and moaning for help."

> Some were already buried and others just in pieces. You may think it is an easy job to write about it all, but I write awhile and my eyes get so filled with tears . . . that I just have to quit. Then something big comes up in my throat and chokes me. I try to lie down and rest but I can't rest nor sleep. If, after exhaustion, I do sleep it is only to live it all over again in dreams, seemingly more real than when I'm awake.

He still thought his war was a "just cause," but twenty years later was "heartsick" at the thought that a new generation might be called to the horrors of a second world war.

Philip "Zip" Cepaglia also had trouble getting his name spelled right. He was one of those remembered most fondly and vividly by other survivors, the "little fellow" who ran the gauntlet of German machine guns to get water for them. When Johnson interviewed him, he tried to explain why he had been able to risk his life again and again, and come up smiling every time. Cepaglia shrugged. "After the first day we were surrounded, I got used to it. . . . Didn't get all worked up—just took things as they came. So did Whittlesey." The major's way of displaying courage invited you to feel you could be equally brave: you look at the man and see not only his heroic qualities but your own best possibilities. That was why Whittlesey's suicide was so troubling to Cepaglia: "I don't know why he disappeared afterward, but it wasn't because he was afraid of anything. He was the bravest man in the A.E.F." Evidently there were things too dark for even the bravest man to face.[8]

For others there was an abiding sense of grievance, whose specifics they could not articulate. When reporter Thomas Johnson found Stanislaw Kozikowski, the Polish-American veteran was a machinist in the Brooklyn Navy Yard. It was a good job and he had gotten it (presumably after some bouncing around) just as the Depression hit in 1929. He was a big man, 225 pounds, but not one to look for trouble, didn't like talking about the Pocket, "fight[ing] the war over." The war was history, his wife and two children and the job were what mattered. When he retired in the early 1950s his supervisors and coworkers would praise him as one of the best machinists in the navy yard: "No job is too difficult for Stan. . . . The man is extremely cooperative and never complains about any assignment." As he talked with Johnson the intensity of his repressed feeling showed, "he strode the floor, fists clenching and unclenching, eyes flashing." On the morning of October 7 he had volunteered for the same mission as Krotoshinsky, to carry word of the battalion's plight through the German lines. Every man who had tried it before had been killed. Suddenly he quieted and sat down, back in the present. " 'Well, it's only history now,' he said."[9]

The Defense of Memory: Unit Histories and the Myth of the Failed War

The war was *only* history now, but in 1917–18 it had seemed a plastic moment, when Americans had the power to reshape their lives, their nation, and the world. Roosevelt and Wilson in their different ways had envisioned American participation in the Great War as the fulfillment of national destiny, the culminating episode of the national myth. But the real results of all that strenuous striving, all that expense of lives and dollars, did not measure up to the mythic promise. Instead of a just and rational world order, Versailles produced an unseemly quarrel over spoils, perpetuating an international order based on greed, imperial ambition, and threats of war. The War Progressives had promised social justice at home, reconciliation between classes and races; they had delivered the Red Scare, race riots, and the sanctimonious hypocrisy of Prohibition. Any lingering belief that the war had been a great patriotic adventure, overriding personal greed and self-interest, was stripped away by the memoirs and novels of veterans who had lived the horror of the Western Front, by journalistic exposés and congressional investigations that revealed how the propaganda of Britain and the Committee on Public Information had falsified German atrocities and Allied virtues or unmasked profiteering by financiers, munitions makers, and military suppliers.

The veterans had to cope with their memories in solitude and in whatever conversations were possible with family and friends. But their processing of war memory was also affected by the way in which their society chose to memorialize the war, and especially by the public myths that developed in the 1920s to explain what had happened and what the experience meant. One of the promises made to those who served had been the transfiguration of their experience by its translation into the symbolism of national myth, so that the Argonne would join Bunker Hill, Gettysburg, and Custer's Last Stand as symbols of the character and mileposts in the historical progress of the American nation. By 1922 a new "myth" of the Great War was emerging in the United States, which saw it as a tragedy without point or purpose, a colossal sham, and saw the men who fought it as a "Lost Generation."

The moral effects of that sardonic denigration of the "war to save democracy" were felt by the Plattsburgh alums. Those who published their memoirs or unit histories in the immediate aftermath of victory were confident that their sufferings had enabled the nation to fulfill the glorious promises of 1917. Those who published later in the 1920s felt the need to defend their achievements. Wardlaw Miles's wounds and his search for academic employment delayed completion of his *History of the 308th Infantry* until 1927. In the interim, postwar triumphalism had given way to dark second thoughts about the war and the men who fought it. Describing the moment when the regiment's transport ship passes the Statue of Liberty outward bound, his words reflect the hindsight of 1927 rather than the martial enthusiasm of 1918:

> How many crimes—how many blunders worse than crimes—are committed in her name! Yet however faulty our purpose and our preparation, it was not altogether either crime or blunder that was sending these thousands so widely differing in race, fortune, and desires on one common journey for one common end.

The emotional distance Miles had traveled between Plattsburgh and Prohibition is registered in the difference between "We stand at Armageddon" and "not altogether either crime or blunder." But Miles was unwilling to see his own suffering and the sacrifices of his men as wholly vain. He still "believed that it was right for America to fight Germany in 1917," still believed that "the world is 'essentially a theater for heroism'" and just war a proper expression of the human spirit. He would pass that faith on to his children. His son Samuel served as a field surgeon with the marines and was killed on Guadalcanal in 1942. Corporal Russell Whittlesey, USMC, the son of Charles Whittlesey's brother Melzar, was killed in that same campaign.[10]

All of the veterans suffered in one way or another from the public conviction that theirs had been a "bad war," a waste of blood and treasure, a sucker's game. But the racially/ethnically marked veterans had grievances that went beyond the inadequacy of their benefits and job opportunities. Their country had given them a two-faced welcome, hailing them as American heroes one day and on the next reminding them that they were still considered strangers.

A 1926 article about Robert Dodd, published in *American Indian* (a journal devoted to Native American affairs), illustrates the ambivalent way in which racialized soldiers were remembered in the White press. Author O'Hara Smith intended the article as a reminder to Whites of the good service done by Native Americans in the war. But its title, "Chief Lo Was with the Lost Battalion in France," invokes an old and derisory stereotype of Native Americans. During the Plains Indian wars of 1865–90, racial "realists" who favored the dispossession of the tribes used the imaginary personification, "Lo, the Poor Indian," to mock as maudlin the sympathy expressed by "philanthropists" for Indian rights. Although Dodd graduated from a "prominent Indian college," his real identity is entirely absorbed in the derisory ethnic sobriquet given by his comrades: "Somewhere between the 'awkward squad' and his promotion to first-class private the 'Lo' was added. As Chief Lo . . . his real honest-to-goodness name was forgotten," and he became simply "a representative member of his race," who fought the nation's battles "with the same enthusiasm that marked the buffalo hunts of his forefathers." Captured by the Germans, he defeats his interrogator by answering with "a gutteral 'Ugh!'" Smith extends the same ambivalent mix of praise and denigration to the hyphenate Whites of the 77th Division, appropriate comrades for the descendant of savage Indians because they are urban savages:

> [They] came from the East Side, or the "Melting Pot" of New York, [and could] slit a German's gullet with as little compunction as though preparing a chicken for dumplings, and, while not as bloodthirsty as his forefathers were reputed to have been, Chief Lo found their company just to his liking.

Thus praise for the service rendered by the Native American and the immigrant is subsumed in the politics of ridicule.[11]

In these circumstances, minority veterans might well have wanted to forget the war, forget the memory of trauma and of disappointed hopes. But they also had good reason to defend what they remembered. The experience itself, traumatic as it was, had given them a consciousness of achievement, a confidence in their own powers and in the moral justice of their demands; and the appeal to their war record still offered the most persuasive argument in behalf of their claims. They answered the White majority's double-edged praise with their own ambivalent mix of self-assertion and sharp-edged irony. During the division's parade a reporter asked Sing Kee "what on earth a 'Chinaman' could do to . . . earn such recognition."

> Sergeant Kee (who is originally from California and speaks perfect English) looks at him slyly and replies, "Me no savee Inglis," and then turns smartly and joins the victory parade, receiving the accolades of New Yorkers as he marches with his unit up Fifth Avenue.

He refuses to explain himself, mocks the reporter in terms his own community will savor, confident in his identity as Chinese and American.

That confidence was only partly justified. The people of Chinatown would become more fully integrated with the life of the larger city, but the development of their community would be stunted by the discriminatory provisions of the 1924 immigration acts, which prevented wives or marriageable women from entering the country, deepening the sexual imbalance of Chinatown and the consequent distortion of community and family life. Sing Kee himself would find opportunities in Chinatown too restricted. He moved back to California, where he appears to have prospered.[12]

New York's Jewish community was stunned by the sudden reversal that transformed Yiddish Jews from Lost Battalion heroes to racial Bolsheviki, and its organizations responded with an ambivalent mixture of defensiveness and defiance. The conservative German-Jewish leadership hoped to accommodate the demand for "100% Americanism" by repudiating both Zionism and Yiddish culture: the former because it implied that Jews were a distinct "people," race, or nationality, the latter because it made Jews culturally distinctive. Congressman Julius Kahn, a stalwart supporter of liberal immigration policies, reminded his constituents that the world war taught Americans to "put . . . [the] United States first":

> We have just eliminated hyphenism in the United States. . . . Thank God for it! We no longer have the German-American, the Irish-American . . . or any other diluted form of American. And what is Zionism trying to do? Create a new form of hyphenism, the Jewish-American.

The editors of *American Hebrew* looked forward to the day when Jewish-Americans would simply be 100% Americans of the Jewish faith, their difference no more striking than that between Baptist Americans and Methodist Americans. With that principle in mind, the editors exultingly announced, "Zionism Is Dead; Long Live Judaism!"[13]

But that defense failed, first because it could not persuade those nativists for whom Jews were by definition an alien race, second because it refused to acknowledge the complex character of the community being defended. The hyphen was not a disposable component of Jewish-American identity, it was the essence of that identity. The social bargain of 1917 had seemed to promise the immigrant soldier acceptance and respect for "the traditions of his race and the land of his nativity" in exchange for loyal service in war. For Lower East Siders, those traditions included an ethical and political attraction to a socialism that, until the Red Scare put the whole Left under a ban, had seemed compatible with the normal workings of American electoral politics and trade unionism. They were committed to making new lives as Americans, but were passionately attracted to the Zionist project as an assertion of community pride and a refuge for persecuted brethren in eastern Europe. In 1917 it had been possible for Elias Lieberman of the *American Hebrew* to see no contradiction in the sight of a little Jewish boy waving a Zionist flag while singing the " 'Star-Spangled Banner' . . . blend[ing] the dualities of his affections and his loyalty with childish naivete and directness," proving "that a man can be simultaneously a good Zionist and a good American." That was how Abe Krotoshinsky had described himself: as an "ardent [American] patriot," eager to fight for his adopted country, and as a Zionist daydreaming of life in a Jewish country. But in an America that had decided to treat the hyphen as a mark of racial difference, that dual identity seemed no longer sustainable.[14]

War Memories and Ethnic Self-Defense:
Abe Krotoshinsky and Meyer Siegel

Abe Krotoshinsky was the Henry Johnson of American Jewry, the man chosen to represent his race in the pantheon of American heroes. Like Johnson, his ability to sustain that role foundered on the growing recognition that American society would continue to treat his people as racial aliens and inferiors.

His return to America and civilian life began well. The New York papers had already made him a hero; he was toasted at a series of celebrations, interviewed by the press, and Mayor Hylan himself presided at the ceremony that granted him naturalized citizenship. He readily found work and had time and energy to give to social service. He was active in veterans' affairs, using his fame to win support for the 307th Infantry's American Legion Post, its job placement service, its aid association, and the home for indigent veterans of the 77th Division. "The movement to keep Company K together is headed by Private Abraham Krotoshinsky . . . wearer of the Distinguished Service Cross, the only despatch bearer to get through." He was particularly in demand as a representative of American Jews, which was at first gratifying, because it implied that his adopted country had accepted him *as a Jew,* with all of his differences from the standard model American. Asked by an interviewer how he had strength enough to complete his mission, he answered: "After five days of starving, I was stronger than many of my friends who were twice my size. A Jew finds strength to suffer." After his return from France, he was eager to become a citizen. He told an interviewer how General Pershing had pinned the DSC on his chest and told him, "I should try to be a good citizen—that that was as much as to be a good soldier. And now . . . won't you please tell me how I can, quick, get my citizen papers."

But the anti-Semitic propaganda fomented by the Overman and Johnson committees, the articles by racist eugenicists in the popular press and anti-Semitic journals like Henry Ford's *Dearborn Independent,* were a shocking rebuke to Jewish expectations of full acceptance. Krotoshinsky felt like an American, but had to wonder whether the country felt the same way about him. When Americans looked at him, did they say, "There goes a good man; and he is *our* man"? Or did they think, "There goes another one of those Yids," an incipient Bolshevik with the wrong clothes and the wrong nose and the wrong language on his tongue. He may also have begun to suffer the delayed reaction from wartime trauma that afflicted most of his buddies. Talking about those events "gets me all excited and doesn't do me any good."[15]

Through his work for Jewish charities in the city he met Nathan Straus, a supporter of the Henry Street Settlement and other philanthropies. Straus was particularly interested in the National Farm School in Bucks County, Pennsylvania, founded in 1894 by Dr. Joseph Krauskopf, a Jewish-American disciple of Tolstoy, to train immigrants in modern farming methods and help them purchase land. No life could be more American than that of a farmer on his own ground. Freed from the Yiddish ghetto and dispersed across the country they would Americanize more completely and win recognition for their people as just another subtype of American, no stranger than Germans or Scandinavians. But the prospect of establishing a Jewish homeland in Palestine opened the further possibility of training Zionist pioneers, and this was of particular interest to Nathan Straus. Within a year of demobilization Krotoshinsky had enrolled at the National Farm

School, with Straus providing tuition and capital for the purchase of a farm in *Eretz Yisroel*.

In the meantime Krotoshinsky could not escape his status as a public symbol, and as the ideological battles over the future status of Jews in America intensified he found himself in a unique and solitary exposure. The controversy that blew up over the funeral of poor Jack Monson was indicative of the pain and embarrassment to which he was now vulnerable. In its embattled condition, the Jewish community of New York could not allow anyone to share Krotoshinsky's preeminence. Jewish protests were included in the *Times* story on Monson's funeral, asserting that there "Can't Be Two Claimants" to be "the 'hero who reunited the Lost Battalion.'" Krotoshinsky had always insisted that what he had done was unremarkable, that others had shown equal bravery and had equal success breaking through the German lines. He shared Whittlesey's sense of obligation to honor Monson, but also understood the anxiety behind the protest. Perhaps it would be simpler to be a Jew in the land of Israel, with no need to reconcile love for America with resentment of the blind animosities Americans felt for him and his kindred.

On December 2, 1921, as the mourners gathered for Colonel Whittlesey's funeral, Abe Krotoshinsky, "the man who saved the Lost Battalion," was boarding the Greek ship *Themistocles,* bound for Palestine. To reporters "he spoke with deep feeling of [Whittlesey's] tragic fate, and said that he had been loved by the men of the battalion." He had seen the colonel at a recent gathering of veterans and "thought he was very much depressed." He said nothing of his own emotions at this turning point in his own life, when he was giving up his dream of a life in America—the "precious" country for which he had been willing to lay down his life— to live as a Jew in a Jewish nation.[16]

Krotoshinsky's choice was one with which many Lower East Siders sympathized, but for the vast majority an intense interest in the building of a Jewish state did not translate into a desire to adopt "100% Jewish" nationality. For better and worse, this was the country in which they would make their Jewish life and struggle to establish a viable identity. They had adopted America as their country, adapted to its life and language, and served it in war. They not only belonged in America, they had earned the right to assert their own interpretations of Americanism.[17]

When Meyer Siegel was drafted in 1917 he was working days in his father's remnants shop and going to Brooklyn Law School at night. He fought on the Vesle and in the Argonne with the 308th, marched in the grand parade through the cheering streets, and came home to the Lower East Side to find "a big 'Welcome Home, Meyer' sign and an American flag flying" from the window of his parents' Suffolk Street apartment. Combat awakened his sense of ultimate things, the imminence of death and crippling harm, the inability of reason and law to protect one from madness and malice. But he "was one of the lucky ones to come home in one piece," and that sense of being favored by fortune buoyed his confidence. His father expected him to work in the remnants shop, finish his studies, become a professional man. Siegel wanted to marry the girl next door and go into business for himself. Instead of a farm in Israel he dreamed of "a chain of stores like the A&P." In 1921 he took the risk of moving from the city to Amsterdam, New York, to work in his brother Sam's grocery, hoping to save enough to open his own store. "I didn't do so good," he admitted, and he "hated Amsterdam."

Then the Ku Klux Klan came to town, organizing in the Schenectady area, "selling its anti-Semitic merchandise to the Amsterdam population" as part of the national drive that would bring them to their peak membership in 1925. Siegel was outraged, not simply as a Jew but as a veteran: "For this my buddies died in France?" He called on the congregation of his synagogue to take action: "We boys had bled and fought the Germans for democracy and . . . for democracy's sake we must turn the Ku Klux Klan out." Faced by their vocal opposition, the Klan "moved elsewhere." Although the victory was a small one, Siegel's motives for engaging battle are significant: his identification with the 77th Division made him confident of his own Americanism and allowed him to invoke American values against the most virulent and racist proponents of "one hundred per cent-ism." Moreover, for Siegel politically engaged Americanism was compatible with Zionism. After the victory over the Klan, he helped to found two Jewish organizations in the Amsterdam-Schenectady area, "a strong Jewish War Veterans" post, and a "strong . . . Zionist Organization (ZOA)."[18]

Siegel's militancy was not unique. Pride in the achievements of immigrant soldiers lent confidence to their communities and a sense of moral authority to their demands for social and economic justice. Despite the threats of antisocialist mobs and the government's Red Scare, New

York's garment unions remained militant in practice and socialist in sympathy, conducted strikes, and made significant gains in 1919–20. Though the Left was increasingly divided after 1920, Jewish engagement in city politics became stronger, more self-conscious, and more influential in shaping policy. The postwar period saw the formation of new organizations, whose approach differed from the "100%-ism" of the American Jewish Committee. The American Jewish Congress, B'nai B'rith, and the Jewish War Veterans did not insist on the dissolution of a separate Jewish identity as a precondition for Americanization. Their approach accepted and reflected the cultural tendencies of the Jewish streets, which refused to cast away its socialist inclinations, its Zionist sympathies, and its pleasure in Americanized *Yiddishkeit*. It acknowledged that Jews themselves were unable to disentangle the purely cultural or religious element in their identity from their sense of belonging to a "tribe," a blood-kindred, a race. Instead of resolving the race/culture impasse, they sought to make it irrelevant by working for a redefinition of American nationality that would incorporate cultural *and* racial difference. They were working toward a *pluralist* concept of Americanism, which offered an ideological recipe for integrating all the various ethnic and racially marked communities, including the African-American, without devaluing their particular identities.

To change American culture it was necessary to revise the national mythology, the official and consensus version of the national past. Wartime propaganda and the civics classes at Upton had taught the immigrant soldiers the importance of schooling in the shaping of consciousness. So one of their earliest and most important campaigns was the effort to revise American history textbooks and school curricula.

The history curriculum in schools and colleges had been transformed after 1910 by the "new history," which brought greater rigor to the discipline by shifting focus from hero-centered myths to the analysis of underlying economic, political, and demographic forces. This approach dovetailed with the interests of Progressive reformers, whose program of corporate regulation drew authority from histories that criticized the increasing concentration of capital and its effects on American democracy. After the war the "new history" was attacked by pro-business conservatives for its reformist biases, and by nativists and Nordic supremacists who had always understood the American story as the tale of the "Great Race" and its heroic "Conquest of a Continent." But the attack was also joined by organizations representing immigrant and African-American constituencies in New York City (1922) and Chicago (1924), because in a history without heroes there was no narrative device for representing an ethnic group's contribution to the nation's development. In New York, a Jewish official who identified himself as "101 percent American" condemned history texts that tended to "belittle illustrious American patriots"; he was joined in his complaint by representatives of the Black community. The *American Hebrew* shared their concern: "There is no good reason why American histories should not be fair to the great men and women of the past who made America possible. . . . Justice should be done to all, regardless of race, creed, or color." German-Americans joined the struggle to repair the damage done to their historical reputation by wartime defamation. In Chicago the Knights of Columbus, speaking for the Irish and Italian communities, was openly alarmist:

> Americans, Wake Up! . . . Our history is being distorted and polluted and our children thereby de-Americanized. The achievements of many different races—Irish, German, Italian, French, Scandinavian, Slavik [*sic*], Polish, Spanish, etc. in founding, developing and maintaining the institutions of this country are treated with contempt to the glory of England—the age-long, implacable foe of America.

The movement for "integrating" American history texts carried over into the politics of public school staffing and curriculum, in which Jewish organizations and teachers played an increasingly important role, sometimes in alliance with the NAACP.

Opponents of immigration and "hyphenism" responded with accusations that such movements falsified history and threatened to disunite American culture. Progressive scholars like Carleton Hayes defended the "new history" as a scientific alternative to the "boastful, intolerant nationalism" of 100% Americanism on one side, and the demands of "special group–loyalties" on the other, which threatened to turn "the American melting-pot [into] a seething cauldron of fiery nonfusible nationalisms."[19]

Hayes had a point. A national myth-history that emphasizes the roles of race-representative heroes implicitly perpetuates a racialist view of human nature and risks vitiating the concept of American nationality by reducing national politics to identity politics. An alternative approach was already available in the work of Franz Boas, Horace Kallen, and other advocates of the *culturalist* (as opposed to the *racialist*) understanding of human development. Their theories did not deny the reality of genetic heredity, but exposed the contemporary taxonomy of "races" as a pseudoscientific rationalization of existing social and political differences. Boas and Kallen also rejected the premise that national societies could only cohere if they were monocultural—the view expressed in Lowell's dictum that Jews, Negroes, and Anglo-Saxons could not live as free men in the same society. They believed democracy in the modern world required *cultural pluralism*, the cooperative coexistence of different ethnic groups within a single frame of law and social order.[20]

But despite its conceptual liabilities, the creation of "race heroes" for minorities was a necessary rhetorical tool in a country that still saw race as the fundamental unit of social identity. The most useful affirmations of Jewish racial heroism were those that came from "old stock" Americans. One of the most significant was *Patriotism of the American Jew*, published in 1924 in rough coincidence with passage of the Johnson-Reed immigration bill. It was written by Samuel W. McCall, a former congressman and governor of Massachussetts, with a foreword by Charles W. Eliot, Lowell's predecessor as president of Harvard and the leading opponent of anti-Jewish (and anti-Black) admissions policies. These pillars of New England liberalism undertook a systematic defense of Jewish patriotism because, as the sad record of anti-Black sentiment had shown, "Before a settled race prejudice, constitutional guarantees are likely to shrink into mere paper rights." Eliot and McCall make it clear that Jews are to be defended *as a race*. After speculating as to whether "the Jew . . . is an ethnological [or] merely a theological being," they adopt a variation on the "one-drop" rule: despite all admixtures, age-long "segregation," religious faith, and racial "vitality" have "preserved unimpaired . . . [the] general physical and mental characteristics of the race." To a Madison Grant, such a statement is damning. To Eliot and McCall it is a term of praise, for it allows them to treat the deeds of converts and non-practicing Jews as evidence of the *race*'s value to civilization (e.g., as promulgators of Christianity).

In theory, McCall condemns the use of individuals as symbols of racial character as prejudicial: "Not the least of the wrongs inflicted upon the Jew is that he is judged as one of a mass and not as an individual." If a Jew commits treason, the whole race is charged with lack of patriotism; yet the "English race" is not condemned because of the treachery of Benedict Arnold. But in telling the tale of Jewish service to America, he continually and necessarily resorts to hero tales and to the rhetorical presumption that the individual's deeds reflect the virtues of the race. Here the most important demonstrations are provided by the Great War, especially by Abe Krotoshinsky, "a Jew stripling from a crowded tenement of New York. Less hopeful hero material is hardly imaginable; yet what that lad dared and did was enough to rouse the enthusiasm of all America." McCall describes Krotoshinsky as "a small, shy emaciated youth, with large limpid blue eyes set far apart in a face which suffering and privation have pinched very close to the contour of his skull." Though Jewish by race, his appearance is attractive by "American" standards. He also seems to be fluent in English.[21]

McCall's Krotoshinsky symbolizes the possibility, even the desirability, of the racial Jew as American. The problem with the symbol is that it does not sufficiently acknowledge the *difference* of the man himself—the features of his face and speech, not to mention the turn of mind that struck so many "old stock" Americans as alien.

In 1926 Abe Krotoshinsky returned to the United States. He had tried to run the farm in Palestine, had married there and fathered two daughters, but the farm was not a success. He remained a Zionist in principle, but could not make a life in Israel. So he returned to America, and to that odd double-consciousness that made him at once a "real American" and a racial Jew.

War heroes were no longer in vogue; there were no philanthropists eager to buy him a barbershop. He moved into an apartment in the Bronx, knocked about the city doing odd jobs, working occasionally as a barber. In 1927 he took the exam for a post office job, but heard nothing from the civil service board and assumed he had failed the test. He was in desperate circumstances, "without a job, faced [with] starvation, with no place for his family and himself to live."

In November a reporter for the *World* got wind of Krotoshinsky's situation: world war hero jobless and neglected in the Big City. The story jogged memories. Miles's *History of the 308th Infantry* had been published earlier that year, and a spate of reviews and excerpts from the book revived interest in the Lost Battalion. (Even Al Capone was claiming he had served with Whittlesey.) The American Legion's Thomas Mulcahy hired Krotoshinsky as a clerk while the Jewish War Veterans

(JWV) tried to find something permanent. Congressman La Guardia intervened, appealing to President Coolidge to help "the hero of the Lost Battalion." Krotoshinsky had "made every effort to rehabilitate himself" (from what illness or failing was not specified), was "without doubt one of the outstanding heroes of the World War," and wanted "work and not charity," which made him one of the *deserving* poor. In the meantime someone (perhaps at La Guardia's instigation) looked into the civil service exam. Krotoshinsky had actually passed "by a wide margin," but the notification had either been mislaid or deliberately buried. Such devices for getting around the merit system were often used to keep Jews, Italians, and African-Americans from getting civil service jobs. Coolidge made the issue moot by waiving the civil service exam, in recognition of Krotoshinsky's service as "the savior of the 'Lost Battalion.'" His fiat made Krotoshinsky eligible for "any government place . . . without examination," but modesty forbade his taking advantage of that blank check. He would work at the same Bronx substation until his death in 1953.[22]

He returned to his role as an active member of veterans' organizations, was an honored presence at the funerals of veterans from his old regiment and celebrations honoring the dead. Though he still found it upsetting to talk about the war, he was willing to tell his story at length when asked by a Jewish publication.[23] But the anti-Semitism inaugurated in the 1920s intensified in the 1930s, and his hero status still entailed the obligation to lend his name and voice to the defense of the Jewish people. In February 1940 he provided the occasion for a small but disturbing display of the ugly ideas and feelings that still attached to "Yiddish Jews."

Meyer Berger was a Jewish-American writer for the *New York Times*, then at the start of what would become a distinguished career. His "About New York" column would win a Pulitzer Prize, and his acute observations of New York life and characters would make him a beloved city legend. But his story on Krotoshinsky has a dark and even nasty edge to it. As he tells it, the "little barber [who] . . . saved the Lost Battalion" has been forgotten: "a little fella. Kroto—Krotoshy, or some such name." Berger goes to the "gloomy post-office" where Abe works. At his call "a little stoop-shouldered Polish Jew slithered from behind [a] pile [of mail]. His garb was more than usually untidy. Pale, a long, hooked nose. Not very exact posture . . . he squinted through gold-rimmed spectacles. He could have stood shaving." Despite his war experience, his body has not exchanged the Jewish stoop for the upright American stance. In all of Krotoshinsky's other interviews his speech is rendered in colloquial American English, suggesting that service and heroism had indeed Americanized him. Berger reproduces Krotoshinsky's broken English, which emphasizes his foreignness. He even misnames his own decorations: "Some clippings I still got . . . from Gen'ral Pershin' . . . I got a Conspicuous Service Cross." Of the war he says, "Mostly I forgot already." Berger's Krotoshinsky is not the appealing "Jewish stripling," the "small, shy emaciated youth, with large limpid blue eyes" and face pinched by "suffering and privation," described in Governor McCall's 1924 book; nor is he the "unlikely" Jewish hero that the AJC had put before the American people just three years earlier. He is at best a pitiable figure, at worst a repulsive one, who bears all the stigmata of the despised racial Jew: pathetic, unmanly, shabby, filthy, perhaps sinister if we pick up on "slithering," physically repulsive—as though he were a " 'nigger' . . . an ugly creature, a frog instead of a person."[24]

That a Jewish-American writer of some sophistication should offer such a portrayal in 1940, with Hitler on the march and Father Coughlin still issuing his anti-Semitic diatribes, is disturbing. But the repulsion and disdain in the gaze Berger turns on Krotoshinsky is symptomatic of a larger phenomenon, the distorting power of the double-consciousness that was an inescapable consequence of American racialism. If you attempted to work out your identity within the terms set by American concepts of race, you inevitably found yourself measuring the achievements, culture, character, and physical beauty of your "race" against a White Anglo-American standard—a standard you might approximate, but never equal. As editor Gedalia Bublick had prophesied in his testimony before the Johnson Committee, the official affirmation of "this race prejudice" was to "teach people who came from certain stocks . . . to hate themselves." Assimilated and middle-class Jews had learned from hard experience how important it was to placate the prejudices of the WASP elite, by separating themselves from anything that might remind them of the foreignness of Jews. They learned to anticipate prejudice by looking at other Jews as if through the eyes of a disdainful WASP, and so had internalized those prejudices, become part-sharer in them. That tendency was augmented by the traditional disdain of

German-Jewish Americans for their "primitive" co-religionists from Poland and eastern Europe.

The imperative of assimilation also produced an enduring strain of self-hatred among the Yiddish Jews, comparable to that experienced by African-Americans: the desire to shed all traces of Yiddish culture, to alter or conceal those aspects of speech, appearance, or family name that marked one as a Jew, were comparable to the motives behind those ads for skin-whitening cream in the *Age*, the mockery of "Mister Johnson the Darktown Coon" in the *Crisis*. This tendency was especially marked among the eastern European Jewish entrepreneurs who created the Hollywood studio system and made cinema the dominant medium of popular culture.[25]

Yet the racial approach to cultural pluralism was unavoidable. Even if, in a scientific and philosophical view, the idea of dividing mankind into races was false or wrong-headed, the fact was that Jews must expect always to be treated as a "race." Louis Marshall shared this confusion, despite his political commitment to a purely religious definition of Jewishness, as he showed when he told an NAACP meeting in 1926, "I belong to an ancient race which has had even longer experience of oppression than you have."[26] That he made the remark to a Black audience suggests the growing recognition that under the political and cultural conditions of the 1920s, American ethnic groups could only work toward *cultural* pluralism by insisting on *racial* pluralism, on their right as "racial" minorities to civic equality. The political alliance of Blacks and Jews in the pursuit of civil rights began with this recognition of likeness between a racialized Jewish community and the racially defined community of color.

"What Has That Uniform Ever Got You?": Remembering and Forgetting the Negro's War, 1919–1933

African-Americans already understood what Jewish-Americans were just beginning to learn about living as a racially marked minority in the United States. But they were no closer to resolving its central conundrum: democratic ideology often moved White Americans to offer equality to any race that could meet the tests of "Americanism," but no result was acceptable that did not annihilate the perceived racial difference, whether of color or of culture. Both groups had put their faith in the wartime social bargain, sending their young men to earn equality by fighting the nation's war; both had seen that bargain abrogated and betrayed by White Americans.

In the aftermath of war Harlem had to cope with the same ambivalent mix of pride and disappointment that afflicted the Lower East Side, Chinatown, and other ethnic communities. Its disappointment was, if anything, deeper and more embittered, because the fall from triumph back into the politics of ridicule was so abrupt and violent. Yet the memory of wartime hope and success could not be entirely obliterated. Though Whites had rejected the "proofs" made by outfits like the Old Fifteenth, African-Americans believed in their validity and concluded that the frustration of their hopes was not due to their own supposed failings, but to the prejudice and injustice of White society. That moral confidence would be buttressed in the 1920s by a growing cultural confidence, as Harlem became the capital of Black America, and jazz musicians and the artists and writers of the Harlem Renaissance began to exert real influence on American high and popular culture.

Politics in Harlem were as dynamic as the cultural scene. Most civic and political organizations still sought an accommodation with White America that would alleviate the worst features of Jim Crow. But the traditional methods of the "Tuskegee Machine" had been found wanting even before the war, and the militant variation DuBois espoused in 1917–18 was discredited by the racialist reaction of 1919–21. In a variety of ways, on a range of fronts, African-Americans in Harlem set themselves to gain control of the political apparatus that governed their district. Within the two major parties, the struggle focused on the office of district leader, which was the conduit for patronage and the gateway to municipal or state office. Through most of the 1920s, the leadership positions in Harlem were held by Whites—once the majority in the district, now a declining minority. In 1929 a combined effort by clergy, political leaders, and journalists (notably Fred Moore of the *Age*) forced Republican leader Abraham Grenthal out of the leadership and replaced him with Charles W. Fillmore, who had been working as an auditor for the state tax bureau. It must have been a gratifying triumph for the "father" of the Harlem Hell Fighters, who had had to give way to a White colonel in 1916.

The rise of working-class movements, of socialism and communism, suggested that Blacks see themselves as part of an oppressed class, not essentially different from White workers and peasants. A. Philip Randolph and others would spend the next twenty years trying to integrate the Socialist Party and the labor movement. The emergence of anticolonial independence movements in Africa and the Caribbean suggested that African-Americans see themselves as a repressed race-nationality, and they organize *as* a race to pursue political equality. For some, the logic of racial politics required a quest for nationality, perhaps a Black Zion in Africa or the Caribbean. That was the approach advocated by Marcus Garvey's Universal Negro Improvement Association (UNIA). For a brief time Hubert Harrison's Liberty League and the Equal Rights League emerged as radical alternatives to the NAACP. The ERL's leader, William Monroe Trotter, was "a superradical, left of DuBois on race," who stressed the racial basis of oppression, castigating "Whites" as a group for using politics and economics to maintain specifically racial privileges. The ERL had joined Randolph and Harrison in opposing the war, had ties to Garvey's UNIA, though it rejected Garvey's idea of a return to Africa or the establishment of an autonomous state, and joined DuBois in his anti-imperialist work at Versailles.[27]

DuBois had always conceived racial identity in the race-nationalist terms of Herder and Fichte, and his work with the Pan-African Congress at Versailles suggested the possibility of an international alliance of Black peoples against imperialism. Charles Young shared that belief, so he swallowed the injustice of his "medical" retirement in 1917, sought and won reinstatement on the active list so he could return to Liberia as military attaché to the American legation. In July 1919 he could still autograph a photo of himself with the words, "Yours for race and country." He hoped to influence American policy toward the anticolonial movements on the continent and perhaps induce those movements to pursue American forms of democracy. But his health had in fact been weakened by high blood pressure and earlier exposure to tropical illness, and he died in 1922 while on a journey through the Nigerian backcountry.

Napoleon Bonaparte Marshall was also drawn by the vision of establishing a bond of mutual support between African-Americans and anticolonial movements among Black peoples overseas. His efforts on behalf of Haiti would engage him in a bitter and trying eight-year battle with the U.S. legation and the State Department.

Marshall had returned to the States with the 365th Infantry of the 92nd Division, to which he had been transferred in July 1918. But he was greeted by the Harlem papers as a founding father of "Harlem's Hell Fighters," and though he was a loyal defender of the 365th, that was how he preferred to be remembered. He bore several bullet wounds, and his spine had been severely injured while he led a platoon in the capture of Xon Hill, a strongpoint from which the 92nd Division would mount an assault on Metz. The injury temporarily paralyzed him, but he stayed with his men (most of whom were rookies) to defend the hilltop, where they had orders to "Remain to the Last Man." He considered the Armistice that night an act of Providence that saved them from almost certain death.

His back injury made sitting upright for long periods extremely painful, but he resumed his successful law practice and became a leading figure in city politics. He was on the platform with Whittlesey at the ceremonies honoring Marshal Foch—Foch shook Marshall's hand and called him "*bon soldat.*" His opposition to imperialism and dislike of Theodore Roosevelt had made him a Wilson Democrat, a supporter of the League of Nations and self-determination for small nations. He agreed with Hubert Harrison's Liberty League, whose platform demanded for "every people the right to rule their own ancestral lands free from domination." So in 1922, when Senator McCormick of Illinois offered him the opportunity to serve race and country, he abandoned his practice and accepted a clerkship with the U.S. legation in Haiti.[28]

Haiti had always been an important symbol for African-Americans, as the first independent state established by formerly enslaved people of African descent. In 1920 it remained, with Ethiopia and Liberia, one of only three Black nations not directly ruled by European powers. But its government and society were unstable, and since 1915 it had been occupied by U.S. Marines and run by an American High Commission. In 1920 there was a scandal over mistreatment of captives taken in a "bush war," and Republican candidate Warren Harding capitalized on it to win Black votes in the North. In return, Negro organizations wanted him to appoint two or more Black men to the High Commission to see that Haiti's people were treated fairly. Harding passed the buck to Senator McCormick, who conciliated Black opinion by placing Marshall in the legation.

There was strong opposition to the appointment of any Negroes to the commission, particularly from the new high commissioner, Georgia-born Colonel Russell. But McCormick assured Marshall that whatever his nominal position he would be part of Russell's "official family," able to work independently as both a watchdog of the occupation and an unofficial emissary from African-Americans to the people of Haiti. At a mass meeting of his Black supporters in Chicago, McCormick "made a most stirring speech about the efforts of the United States to improve the situation in Haiti and the part that American negroes should play there, and . . . then said dramatically that he 'passed on the gauge of battle' to Captain Marshall who was about to leave for his post."

With that gesture McCormick went into retirement, leaving Marshall to the mercy of an employer who had no wish for his services and resented his presence. His position was anomalous. Regulations required that a clerk be no older than thirty-five, fluent in French, and a skilled typist. Marshall was fifty-six, only moderately skilled in translation, and could hardly type. His official salary was $2,000 a year, with no expenses allowed for travel or the purchase of a residence—this for an older man in impaired health, with a wife to support, who had had an annual income of between $10,000 and $30,000. Marshall believed the palpable and unconcealed irregularity of his appointment was proof that he was expected to act as an extraordinary agent. At first officials at the legation had the same impression and left him to his own devices. Marshall and his wife involved themselves heavily in charity work among the island's poor. He used his membership in various gentleman's clubs in Port-au-Prince to make influential friends among Haiti's political leaders and among businessmen, both local and international, who were considering investment in Haitian development.

But Marshall aligned himself with factions opposed to president Louis Borno, the high commissioner's preferred instrument. Abetted by Commissioner Russell, his supervisors at the legation began a campaign to force his resignation. They could not simply dismiss him, because the administration was worried about the reaction among Negro leaders, some of whom visited Haiti and expressed concern about Marshall's position. So they tried to drive him out by humiliating him and damaging him financially. Rumors were circulated that Haitian gentlemen had "refused to receive an American negro." His disability benefits were denied and part of his army pay withheld. Marshall was a gentleman in the traditional sense, compelled for the sake of his mission to remain among men who disdained his society and wished him gone. The duties of his clerkship were menial, beneath his gifts, education, and dignity; and however he might perform them, his efforts were certain to be disapproved. His health was declining and it was costing him money to maintain his position, but he fought for seven years to retain it, asking Harvard chums in the administration to intervene on his behalf, resisting their appeals that he spare himself (and them) "humiliation" by resigning. He had undertaken an international mission on behalf of his race and would not voluntarily give it up. In the end the State Department had to declare its intention to fire him to force his resignation.

He returned to New York in January 1929, to his practice and the Harvard Club, where he was the perennial choice as official toastmaster. He campaigned in Harlem for Democratic candidates from 1930 to 1932, wrote several articles critical of the American regime in Haiti, but like Charles Young refused to complain about the personal treatment he had received. In his memoir of military service, published by Hubert Harrison's Liberty League, he recalled the question a Black man had asked him shortly after his return from France: " 'What Has That Uniform Ever Got You?' " He was still willing to reaffirm his old opinion that "any man who is not willing to fight for his country is not worthy to be one of its citizens." He had no "misgivings or remorse" about his wartime "adventure in patriotism," and if he regretted his failure to change U.S. policy in Haiti he did not regret having made the effort.

He lived to see Franklin D. Roosevelt defeat Hoover for the presidency in 1932, and died on June 5, 1933, "of bullet wounds received in the World War." His body lay in state in the new armory that had been built to house the 369th Infantry. Later that year FDR signed a treaty ending the U.S. occupation of Haiti, and on August 14, 1934, the marines were withdrawn from Port-au-Prince.[29]

Marshall's experience is indicative of the political limitations inherent in the attempt to reform American race relations by appealing to international anticolonial movements or attempting to build a transnational movement unifying Africans with the Black diaspora. DuBois would persist in trying to link the civil rights movement with communism and anticolonial nationalism, developing ideas that profoundly influenced the history and sociology of colonialism, but failing in the end to unite the Black diaspora behind a political program. It was nevertheless clear that African-Americans could make no progress toward civil equality unless they could somehow transform White America's understanding of racial difference. Even A. Philip Randolph, who saw racial oppression as a by-product of capitalism, recognized the necessity of organizing Black Americans around specifically racial issues. In his editorial, "A New Negro—A New Crowd" (1919), he demanded that "young [Black] men who are educated, radical, and fearless" take the political reins from the "Old Crowd," which compromised with Jim Crow to fight a White man's war. There must be "no armistice with lynch-law; no truce with Jim-Crowism and disfranchisement; no peace until the Negro receives complete social, economic, and political justice." He also found it useful to relate the situation of Black Americans to that of Jews—considered as a race, not a religion:

> The Jewish people are virile, vigorous, and progressive. They stand at the extreme wings of both capitalism and Radicalism. They have a quickness and efficiency for organization that puts to shame almost every other racial group. This efficiency is largely directed towards labor and Socialist organizations . . . fairer and squarer in their treatment of Negroes, than any other people in the world.

DuBois expressed similar views, drawing parallels between the Zionist projects of the Jewish diaspora and the interest of Black Americans in Africa: both reflect the aspirations of races seeking the national identity to which all peoples are entitled.[30]

Set aside the fact that Randolph's praise echoes the racial stereotypes that Madison Grant and his friends were invoking as proof that Jews were dangerous aliens. Set aside as well the corresponding elements of stereotype in the praise offered by Jewish spokesmen for the militancy of Blacks and what they took to be Black culture. Both groups were working through the given language of American racism to overcome the evil effects of that language. For Jews, acknowledgment of their likeness to Blacks entailed abandonment of the presumption that becoming American meant being treated "like white people ought to be."[31] The gain was that their quest for civil equality was no longer a parochial pursuit of Jewish special interests, but part of a movement for human rights in general. For Blacks, recognition of likeness to the Jewish "race" was a way

"Say, Don't You Remember . . . ?" 517

of breaking the conceptual limitations of American racial categories, reducing "Blackness" from the sole and primary basis of difference to merely a single distinction among many—and linking the fight against Jim Crow to universal principles.

Still, it is worth noting that the terms in which Randolph praises the Jews are identical with the Roosevelt ideal of American manhood, which he accepts as a national standard. The war had provided ample proof that Black men were capable of that kind of heroic virility, but the memory of their heroism was deliberately and systematically overwritten and erased by an officially sponsored campaign of defamation.[32]

The tone had been set by the army boards whose findings ignored the achievements of the 369th and other fighting regiments and ridiculed Blacks as incompetent officers and cowardly soldiers. It was popularized through the unremitting production of jokes and ridiculing anecdotes that appeared in newspaper and magazine articles, the memoirs of White officers, and in fiction and film. The nadir was reached in 1928 with the publication of Charles E. Mack's *Two Black Crows in the A.E.F.* Mack was part of the blackface vaudeville team of Moran and Mack, whose stage characters were Willie and Amos, a pair of "darkies" devoted to stealing watermelons, playing dice, and cheating on their wives. Mack turned their routines into a series of pulp novels, some of which were made into movies. In this war novel the two Black Crows enlist to escape female and legal complications at home, rather than for patriotism or race betterment. Being naturally cowardly, they try to evade combat and finally go AWOL. Being ignorant and incompetent, they run straight into the front lines where they are captured by the Germans. Instead of feeling shame, they are relieved to find "they were once again among white folk . . . [who] recognized obligations to the colored race. Most of the time you could depend on them to take good care of you." On their return to the States Amos claims he won a medal "for taking a battery of artillery and slaughtering boo-coo men wid a butcher knife"—a mockery of the Battle of Henry Johnson.[33]

The White officers of the Old Fifteenth (and others who commanded Black troops) did what they could to counter the myth of Negro failure and remind the public of what their troops had accomplished. But their efforts were unpersuasive, because they were, in the end, unable to truly imagine the "equality" of the men they praised. Hayward expressed fierce pride in his soldiers, but could not help playing to the hankering of

White reporters for comic "darkie" anecdotes. Arthur Little's commitment to civil rights is unquestionable, and his regimental history, *From Harlem to the Rhine* (1936), leaves the reader in no doubt about the heroism of the men of the Old Fifteenth. But every scene reaffirms the assumption that Negroes require systematic and continual tutelage by White men to keep them up to the American standard.[34]

Of all the officers, Hamilton Fish Jr. was best situated to defend both the memory and the civil rights of Black and ethnic soldiers. As a member of his party's congressional leadership and an official of the American Legion, he was an influential spokesman for veterans' issues and civil rights measures. Yet he made little effort to align the Legion with opposition to Jim Crow. He spoke eloquently in defense of Negro infantrymen and rejected General Robert Bullard's accusation that Blacks are racial cowards as "a gross calumny against fearless soldiers." Yet he accepted Bullard's judgment that Black men were racially unfit to serve as officers.[35]

Though the Harlem Renaissance was rich in novelists and poets, African-American writers made no systematic attempt to redeem from shame and obscurity the memory of Black service on the Western Front. The Harlem Renaissance was mainly the work of civilians, some with prewar reputations like James Weldon Johnson, Paul Lawrence Dunbar, and Claude McKay, and many new younger artists like Langston Hughes, who had not served in uniform. Their subject was not war or history, but contemporary Black life amid the social and cultural flux of the twenties. They too were affected by the public mood of disillusionment with Mr. Wilson's War, and the ideals that begot it. They had more reason than most to reject the subject, since the war had proved more of a sucker's game for Blacks than for any other group. Of the Black officers, only Napoleon Marshall published a memoir, and it was only a dozen pages long. The better-educated enlisted men, like Sergeant Cheatham, had been embittered by their experience and preferred simply to get on with their lives. After July 1919 no one came around to ask the corporals and privates to tell their war stories. Horace Pippin had a story to tell, but he had lost his war diaries and sketchbooks, and his right arm was so crippled that for some time he could neither write nor draw.

Veterans of the 369th and of other New York outfits like the 367th probably participated in all of Harlem's various political movements, though none were prominent as leaders. In 1919 MID had a file and some surveillance on Sergeant Anthony Buckner and Corporal George Thomas of the Old Fifteenth, who were canvassing Harlem as recruiters for the Equal Rights League.[36] Marcus Garvey's United Negro Improvement Association adopted a military-style uniform and drill, and its parades were designed to remind Harlem of the triumphal march of the Hell Fighters. However, veterans in AEF uniform seem not to have played the same large symbolic role that (for example) Jewish veterans played in political demonstrations in 1919–22.

As with the veterans of the 77th, most of the men returned to their former employment and dealt with the hard economic times and the physical and psychological effects of their service as best they could. William Layton of the 369th found work as a painter, becoming in time the owner of a painting and interior decorating business; he joined the American Legion, the VFW, and was active in the regimental association. He suffered from persistent migraines and the eruption of "brown spots" on the skin of his chest and neck. He would have twelve children, five of whom would serve in the military.[37]

Needham Roberts shared Henry Johnson's celebrity, was given a parade when he returned to Trenton, and tried to capitalize by making a speaking tour through Ohio in the summer of 1919, sponsored by the YMCA. But he too was crippled by wounds and had to scrabble for odd jobs. Trenton was still a segregated town, and opportunities were limited. Roberts tried to remind people of his war service, with humiliating results: in 1924 he was sent to federal prison for wearing his old army uniform more than three months after demobilization. In 1928 he was convicted of "sexual abuse" and served a brief sentence, but the Black community seems not to have thought his crime a serious one. For a Black man "sexual abuse" might involve nothing more than making a pass at a White woman. In 1932 the community held a benefit for Roberts and published a short pamphlet containing his reminiscence of the fight and a poem by Mary Kennard, which praised him as the symbol of African-America's history of unrequited patriotic service.

Roberts moved to Newark, found work as a messenger and later as "sound man" for a New York radio station, married and fathered a daughter. The family lived in a modest apartment, and after the daughter married they rented out her room to a Miss Claggett. In 1949 a "complaint was made against him when [an eight-year-old] girl sitting next to him in a Market Street theater told a spectator Roberts was bothering her." Roberts was arrested and charged with "molesting" the girl, then released on bail. At midnight Miss Claggett saw Roberts and his wife, Idia, at the kitchen table, discussing the case. The next morning she found them hanged by clothesline nooses in their small bathroom. Mrs. Roberts had left a note: "This is a very hard letter to write. Neadham and I are going together. It is best that way. He is innocent of any charge against him." In light of his earlier conviction, they may have despaired of proving his innocence. Whether Roberts bothering the child amounted to molestation was never resolved.[38]

The Old Fifteenth had been famous for its band, and its musicians made the most successful transition to civilian life. But the murder of James Europe eliminated the one Black veteran who understood the political potential of cultural achievements and had the public standing to guarantee him a hearing. His colleagues in the band were fine musicians, not political activists. The most notable of Europe's followers was Lieutenant Noble Sissle, star of Europe's "Hell Fighters" tour, "The Greatest Singer of His Race." After Europe's death he teamed with pianist-composer Eubie Blake and enjoyed great success in vaudeville. In 1921 Blake and Sissle combined with Miller and Lyles, an African-American blackface dance team, to develop a musical comedy for Broadway, "to realize Jim Europe's dream: to restore the Negro to the American stage." *Shuffle Along* was cobbled together from vaudeville skits, a thin plot premise frequently interrupted for singing and dancing. But the script challenged convention by presenting a "serious" romantic relationship between a Black man and woman. *Shuffle Along* would be one of the few shows of the period to have more than 500 performances. The song "I'm Just Wild About Harry" became a national hit and a pop standard, and helped win Blake and Sissle membership in ASCAP, the organization that protected the rights and royalties of music composers—and "rarely admitted Negroes."

Sissle and Blake built on the show's success—as stage performers, in early sound movies, as songwriters, and as creators of other shows and revues. Their careers lasted into the 1970s. Measured by its long run and its influence on other shows, *Shuffle Along* may have been "the most successful, influential, and widely disseminated work of musical theater ever written and performed by American blacks." The show provided jobs for dozens of Black performers, including Josephine Baker and Paul Robeson. But Sissle and Blake had defined "success" as winning popularity with a White audience, and they achieved that success by pushing only slightly (and in largely nonthreatening ways) beyond the racial stereotypes of the blackface tradition. Their achievement left unsolved the artistic problem of how to integrate the reality of African-American experience—the bitter memories of Jim Crow, trench warfare, and unrewarded sacrifice—with the mythic narratives that composed the main stream of American national consciousness.[39]

16

The New Deal and the Renewal
of American Nationalism, 1930–1941

> I have fought for what I believed in for a year now. If we win here
> we will win everywhere. The world is a fine place and worth the
> fighting for.
>
> —*Ernest Hemingway*, For Whom the Bell Tolls *(1940)*

The onset of the Great Depression in 1929–30 hit veterans with disproportionate severity. A special census taken in 1931 found 11.7 percent of men thirty to fifty-four years old were unemployed, but 20 percent of the four million who had served in 1917–19 were out of work—roughly 805,000 men. Ex-doughboys petitioned the government for early payment of the additional bonus granted in 1924. The Hoover administration refused on the ground that it would unbalance the budget and that it was wrong in principle to treat veterans as a "special class," a position supported by a bipartisan majority in Congress and by the leadership of the American Legion.

The veterans answered that they had been treated as a "special class" when the government conscripted them and left other workers in place. As current unemployment statistics suggested, this had given the stay-at-homes an edge in postwar competition. Veterans had also suffered the physical and psychological damage that distinguishes war service from wage work. But the devaluation of victory also diminished the moral standing of the victors. Congress rejected their plea, instead passing a law that allowed veterans to borrow up to 50 percent of the face value of their bonus certificates at 4.5 percent interest—a rate that would effectively devour the long-term value of the bonus, leaving elderly veterans or their survivors unprovided for. Nevertheless, within five months over half of the 4.4 million eligible veterans had applied for loans, and 65 percent used the money for basic living expenses.

A grassroots movement of unaffiliated veterans and dissident Legionnaires organized the so-called Bonus Expeditionary Force to march on Washington to back a renewed lobbying effort. The administration was fearful of what such a large demonstration might portend. Governments in Italy and Germany had been threatened or actually overthrown by veterans marching on the capital. Although Communist and IWW "agitators" were active on the fringes of the movement, the administration's fear of subversion was exaggerated. The encampment was orderly and at times had the festive quality of a reunion. But neither administration nor Congress were willing to negotiate early payment. Congress lowered the interest rate on the loan to 3.5 percent (which made little practical difference), then adjourned. When the "Bonus Army" refused to leave its tents, President Hoover ordered the U.S. Army to drive them out. General MacArthur sent in horse cavalry and armored cars, troops combing the shantytown with bayoneted rifles behind clouds of tear gas. General Peyton March, who had been Pershing's chief of staff, was appalled at how far esteem for the doughboys had fallen since the Armistice of 1918:

> It would have taken a long vision to have looked forward . . . to see the difficulties these men would have in the race of life with other men who stayed at home when they went to war. It would have been impossible . . . to have convinced me that there would ever come a time when the American people would view such sacrifice with indifference.[1]

Indifference to the plight of the veterans was symptomatic of a larger phenomenon: the discrediting of American nationalism. The core idea of the nationalist vision had been the creation of a strong central government, which would engage energetically in the worldwide competition of the Great Powers, and within the borders assert the public and national interest through active oversight and regulation of economic and social life. The failure of War Progressivism to deliver a world safe for democracy produced a powerful cultural reaction, against the war and against the idealization of state power that the war encouraged. With Progressive nationalism a dead letter, the ideology of corporate laissez-faire reasserted itself. Freed of meaningful regulation, and with organized labor virtually powerless, American capitalists generated a speculative boom that ended with the crash of 1929.

The intensity and national scale of the Depression created demand for a national response. Franklin Roosevelt's New Deal met that demand with a series of initiatives by the central government, ranging from emergency measures to halt the banking panic and provide relief to longer-term measures intended to stabilize and reenergize the economy. Although these measures varied in effectiveness, they began the process of restoring public confidence in the ability of the state to relieve distress and restore public order and economic health. As it developed, the New Deal rehabilitated and updated the ideology of Theodore Roosevelt's New Nationalism, with its vision of a strong national government regulating the economy in the public interest, intervening to make an equitable peace between labor and capital and guaranteeing a social security "safety net" for disabled and elderly workers.[2]

A full appreciation of the intellectual roots of the New Deal, of its history, and of its influence on American development is beyond the scope of this book. What concerns us here is that one of its effects was to complete that "nationalization of American life," which had begun with the Civil War, and to set the terms in which a revival of American political nationalism could occur. Where in 1865 the federal presence in most counties was restricted to the post office, by 1940 Washington was engaged in every region with land management, relief, public works, workplace regulation, and law enforcement. Other streams of nationalization reached maturity independently of the New Deal, but augmented its power. The transportation and communication networks begun in the 1860s had been elaborated into a web of rails, roads, and wires that bound even small isolated communities to the rest of the nation. Mass print media expanded their audience nationally and were supplemented now by the powerful and prevalent new form of radio and by movies distributed nationally from a centralized production site.

The New Deal used the rhetoric and publicity devices pioneered by the Committee on Public Information to dramatize the struggle against the Depression as that "moral equivalent of war" for which Progressives had yearned. The centerpiece of the First New Deal, the National Recovery Administration (NRA), was promoted with the same kind of parades and pageants that had been used to mobilize the doughboys and sell the Liberty Loan. The "Blue Eagle" emblem displayed by cooperating companies, stores, and unions was a counterpart of the blue or gold stars hung in the windows of families with boys in the service. The regulatory regime of NRA was "enforced" by moral appeals to the public interest and national patriotism, backed by the distant threat of federal intervention.

The administration fostered national consciousness through programs that gave employment to teachers, writers, and artists, most notably the WPA (Works Project Administration) Federal Writers Project. They produced stage plays, radio dramas, and mural paintings, often with historical themes, not only in the big urban centers but in small cities across the country. A series of state-by-state tourist guidebooks invited Americans to get to know the different regions of the country; and each guidebook included a history, sometimes written by first-rate scholars or novelists, which placed the locality in the frame of national history. It was part and parcel of the New Deal's democratic ideology to praise the "common man" and to show how ordinary folk can shape history even more effectively than the heroes of Theodore Roosevelt's mythology. So researchers went out to discover, record, and publicize the folk culture of the American people. They brought the stories and music of marginalized peoples, especially rural Whites, African-Americans, and White ethnics, into the mass media and central discourses of national culture. For the first time, American culture was being systematically represented as a confederacy of different—but equally *American—* racial, linguistic, and ethnic traditions.

Political crises and threats from the Communist Left and Fascist Right sharpened these cultural tendencies into a nascent ideology of liberal or pluralist nationalism. The 1936 presidential campaign resembled the watershed election of 1912 in representing a broad range of political tendencies, from conservative to revolutionary. The New Deal was challenged by Republican conservatives seeking a return to the unregulated corporate economy of the 1920s, and by a reenergized Left of Communists and Socialists. There was also a stirring of third-party and factional movements, from the aggravated populism of Huey Long to the protofascist, anti-Semitic anticapitalism of Father Coughlin. Roosevelt's landslide electoral victory affirmed the fundamentals of New Deal liberalism as an approach to domestic problems and began the recuperation of the national myth of perpetual economic progress. However, after 1936 it was the mounting threat posed by the aggressive expansionism of Japan and Nazi Germany that transformed what had been a reform program into a new, liberal version of American nationalism.

The same ideological divisions that had shaped the "Preparedness" debate of 1915–17 reappeared in 1937–39, but in a radically altered political and cultural setting. As in 1915, the nationalist reformers favored preparedness and, in the event of war, intervention; and where TR's Progressive war hawks had been in opposition, in 1937 liberal proponents of preparedness controlled the White House. But the cultural traditions to which the war hawks had successfully appealed had been disrupted and discredited by the failure of Mr. Wilson's War. To complete the liberal nationalist program and forge an ideological and political link between domestic reform and an activist international agenda, American culture would have to overcome the twin legacies of the Bad War: the fear of hyphenism and the despair of heroism.

As in 1917, opponents of preparedness feared that the nation might be tricked into a war by the machinations of pro-British interests and/or political lobbying by German-Americans. Memories of the postwar Red Scare gave Jews a new prominence among dangerous hyphenates. To overcome that legacy and unite a multiethnic society behind a nationalist program, it would be necessary to counteract the antipathies that fostered racial exclusion and to recover the allegiance of racial groups whose good faith had been betrayed by White America's abrogation of the wartime social bargain.

But developing a pluralist patriotism was only half the battle. Before Americans would accept the necessity of preparing for war, they would have to be able to imagine war as a necessary and useful way of protecting and enabling progress, democracy, the Good American Life. Both Theodore Roosevelt and Wilson had advocated war, not simply to further national interests but as the fulfillment of the nation's destiny, the culmination of the national myth, a demonstration of the heroic possibilities in our national character. Americans had gone willingly to war in 1917 because they believed that "the world is 'essentially a theater for heroism.'" The Bad War myth that shaped public memories of 1917–18 made heroism seem impossible or absurd. Whether opposition to preparedness came from the isolationist Right or (after Stalin's 1939 nonaggression pact with Hitler) the Communist Left, antiwar polemics gained a powerful emotional charge by invoking the images of the Great War's cruel absurdity from the novels and poems of the Lost Generation and from movies like *What Price Glory?* (1927) and *All Quiet on the Western Front* (1930).[3]

Once the balance of political and public opinion had accepted the likelihood and necessity of war, Hollywood would deliberately take up the task of transforming the Bad War myth into a fable of patriotic heroism. But the struggle to recover and reinterpret the legacy of the war had begun earlier, among veterans whose only agenda was to make sense of what they had experienced in battle and what had happened to them in the long aftermath of public neglect and economic hardship.

Remembrance and Reunion:
Thomas Johnson and the Lost Battalion Veterans

Thomas Johnson had covered the Argonne fighting as war correspondent for the *New York Sun* and interviewed Whittlesey and some of the enlisted men just after the battle. In 1928 he had written a chapter on the Lost Battalion in his history of the Meuse-Argonne campaign, *Without Censor: New Light on Our Greatest World War Battles*, which he intended as a summing up of the war experience. But Whittlesey's suicide troubled him with the suggestion of some vital thing left undeciphered and unsaid. Nine years later he returned to the story; he went back to study the battlefield, investigated German as well as American sources, clarified most of the questions about timing and tactics. He also interviewed many of the survivors, refreshing his memory of what the doughboys were like, contrasting their postwar lot with their wartime heroism and loyalty to each other.

Johnson designed *The Lost Battalion* as a tribute to the heroism of Whittlesey and his men and an implicit rebuke to the society that had neglected and forgotten them. *The Lost Battalion* would not be a "history," but a close study of a detail clipped from the big picture. However, despite the modesty of the book's stated aims and avoidance of historical grandiosity, Johnson intended his narrative of small-unit action to be suggestive of larger political and cultural significance. It was with that end in mind that he collaborated with Fletcher Pratt, author of a critically acclaimed and highly popular history of the Civil War.

The tight focus allowed Johnson and Pratt to develop the individuality of a number of enlisted men and show something of the dynamics
that hold the unit together. This kind of detail work was all but impossible in broad-scope histories of the war. Here it had the effect of making
the unit culture central to our understanding of what the events might
mean. We cease to measure the significance of events on a Wilsonian
scale—the scale that, after all, shows the war to have been a failure. Instead, we judge their meaning by the importance they have for the men
in the unit. The Great War might or might not have been a failure, but
the Lost Battalion's story is the tale of a moral victory for the unit, whose
true cost is registered in the classically tragic fate of its hero.

Seen from the ranks, it is also a fable of successful Americanization
and the triumph of pluralism. Under the stress of combat the varied
constituents of the American population come together in perfect solidarity. Johnson and Pratt often make use of derogatory slang to refer to
the ethnic soldiers, as in "Lipasti the Wop," "Andrews the Boston Jew-
boy," Krotoshinsky the "little, stoop-shouldered Polish Jew." But this
usage is usually framed as an echo of the slang used by the men themselves, their own way of recognizing and reconciling differences—as in
their performance of "The Democratic Army" back in Camp Upton.
The epithets also serve as ironic reminders to the "American" reader
that the wops and Jew-boys who fought so heroically for their country
were marked after the war as objects of racial prejudice and discrimination.

For hyphenated Americans much had changed since 1924. The para-
doxical effect of immigration restriction and ethnic discrimination had
been to speed up both the Americanization and the politicization of the
hyphenate communities. The Johnson-Reed Act of 1924 cut off the in-
flux of new immigrants from the old country and made it much harder
for older immigrants to go back and forth between Europe and America.
The rate of naturalization consequently increased, and once they had become citizens, immigrants naturally turned to politics for redress of grievances and the pursuit of advantage. Despite the power of anti-immigrant
and racialist movements in the 1920s, their political influence grew. In the
eastern cities and in the Midwest, Catholics and Jews joined in resenting
the nativist Protestantism of the KKK. The nomination of Al Smith, a
Catholic, as Democratic candidate for president in 1928 was a sign of
their growing strength; and though Smith was defeated, the election

returns showed that the "hyphenate" vote was capable of breaking the GOP's hold on key midwestern states.

The children of the greenhorns became Americanized, entered the mainstream of politics and industry, became major contributors to the nation's culture through scholarship, literature, mass media, film, and the arts. Their communities had learned how to organize effectively, to protect their political and economic interests, and to preserve, as far as possible, what was most precious and distinctive in their cultural traditions. Having been denied the tolerance they had earned in 1917–18, they had chosen to compel respect by displays of political strength. In the 1930s, all three of the major Jewish organizations—the American Jewish Committee, the American Jewish Congress, and B'nai B'rith—increased their membership and their effectiveness in lobbying and propaganda. For the first time they were able to employ permanent staff, instead of relying on volunteers. The Jewish War Veterans also emerged as a presence in national politics, addressing political concerns that went beyond veterans' issues. They were no longer dependent on the disdainful patronage of establishment figures like Theodore Roosevelt or Hamilton Fish. They had become vital elements of the coalition that sustained the New Deal and the preparedness campaign of 1939–41.[4]

Still, their struggle was far from complete. Their influence was limited by the Democratic Party's institutional structure (which privileged supporters from the Solid South) and by the biases of FDR and his closest advisors. The intellectual leaders of the eugenics and anti-immigrant movement retained their influence in the business community and in the U.S. Department of State. There were popular anti-Semitic movements that had large followings among working-class Whites, including those led by Father Coughlin and Gerald L. K. Smith. Though never able to form a successful political party, these organizations won a wide hearing in the volatile political atmosphere, and their claims resonated with the commonplace prejudices of native-born White Protestants. A 1939 public opinion poll indicated that most Americans thought Jews and Italians "made the worst American citizens." FDR himself told a Catholic aide that he expected Catholics and Jews to "go along with anything I want," because "you know this is a Protestant country, and the Catholics and Jews are here under sufferance."[5]

Before that kind of sneering tolerance could be transformed into genuine pluralism, the United States would have to recognize and repudiate the likeness between American racialism and the repellent doctrines and practices of Nazi Germany. Despite its influence in intellectual and government circles, "Nordic" had never replaced "White" as the defining expression of racial Americanism. After 1934 it was discredited by association with a dictatorial and anti-Christian regime, which seemed bent on starting another world war. Even Americans who thought Yiddish Jews alien and objectionable were disgusted by the unseemly violence with which all German Jews (not just "objectionable" ones) were persecuted. As the threat of war became more palpable, dislike for Nazi behavior was augmented by recognition of Germany as an enemy. Under these circumstances, it was galling to be reminded, by Hitler on one side and American liberals on the other, of the close resemblance between Germany's racial laws and Southern Jim Crow statutes, between concentration camps and Indian reservations, between pogroms like *Kristallnacht* and American lynchings and race riots.

The outbreak of war in 1939 compelled Americans to make critical choices between what they feared and what they hoped and desired to achieve. Nazi victories in Europe, and the Japanese advance in Asia, brought to a head the conflict between those who saw a second world war as the repetition of a catastrophic historical error and those who saw it as a "plastic moment" that required the application of force to give it the necessary shape. The debate between preparedness and antiwar forces also brought to the surface the unresolved issues of "hyphenism," of the proper place of racial and ethnic minorities in the American body politic. Both controversies would find expression in the battle between the Roosevelt administration and the antiwar movement, which ultimately organized as "America First." Among the leaders of the latter movement was Hamilton Fish Jr., Republican congressman from New York, who had once been a captain in the Harlem Hell Fighters.

America First: Hamilton Fish
and the Decadence of Progressivism

Fish had begun his career as a Roosevelt Progressive, backing the Bull Moose Party and the New Nationalism in 1912, supporting the movement for preparedness and intervention in the Great War. Twenty years later he was a leader of the conservative opposition to the New Deal and an isolationist in foreign policy, opposed to any U.S. cooperation with Britain and France to resist the aggression of Nazi Germany. It is tempting to see his political development as a betrayal of Roosevelt Progressivism. In fact, Fish's opposition to the New Deal and a second world war was based on rigid fidelity to the racial-nationalist strain in Progressive thought, as modified by the war and by the anti-Bolshevik hysteria of 1919–24.

Fish's opposition to the regulatory regime of the New Deal did represent a break with the strong-government ideology of the New Nationalism. However, Fish's postwar political career began amid the Red Scare (which Roosevelt had helped to foment), and he followed the logic of militant anti-Communism into unquestioning support of corporate and business interests. On ethnic and racial issues Fish maintained the same ambiguous positions that had been considered progressive in TR's heyday. He was a supporter of African-American causes, especially the antilynching bill, throughout his career; and before his association with America First poisoned relations, was considered an ally of Jewish-Americans because of his support for the homeland in Palestine. However, his backing of Zionism was perfectly consistent with the ideology of racial nationalism and with immigration restriction—which Fish also supported. While he supported fair treatment for Black enlisted men and equal standing for the race under Selective Service, he accepted the army's judgment that Negroes were not fit for field command or service in elite units. He was outspoken in support of antilynching bills, but by the late 1930s Republican backing for such legislation had degenerated into a political ploy for embarrassing liberal Democrats. He showed little interest in more ambitious programs for using federal power to dismantle Jim Crow.

Fish's "America First" neutralism was a recidivist version of TR's "nationalist-internationalist" principles, but his opposition to war was also rooted in experience and reflected the disaffection with foreign wars and former allies prevalent in the American Legion and VFW. A 1930 poll of Legion members found that 44 percent believed the war had been a failure and blamed our former allies for the barrenness of good results. "With smiles and smirks our associates accepted our childish enthusiasm. Then they took our money and our lives. We were the world's prize fat boy with the bag of candy among a horde of hungry urchins. . . . Hello, suckers."[6]

The antiwar movement that would culminate in the organization of America First began to take definite political form after the failure of the Munich agreement of 1938 to check German expansionism by appeasement. The outbreak of war in 1939, the division of Poland between Hitler and Stalin, and the fall of France in 1940 led to the formation of the America First Committee in September 1940. It would oppose any measure likely to embroil the United States in the conflict, including aid to help Great Britain hold out against the Nazis, and to that end would appeal for the support of every antiwar organization, from Socialists to the Nazi sympathizers in the German-American *Bund*.

Fish was a founding member and leading congressional spokesman for America First. But the organization's most important leader was Charles Lindbergh, who had been a national hero since his solo transatlantic flight in 1927. He was the son of a Minnesota Progressive, thoroughly grounded in the mythology of the Strenuous Life. His worldview was drawn straight from the pages of Madison Grant and T. L. Stoddard: the "Nordic" nations of the West are confronted by a rising tide of color, especially of "Mongolians" led by the Japanese and by quasi-Asiatic Russian Communists under Jewish leadership. In 1939 Lindbergh warned that a new European war would repeat the error of 1914–18, igniting a civil war among the White races that would leave the West vulnerable to a new "Genghis Khan" and to the "infiltration of inferior blood," either by conquest or a breakdown of immigration restrictions. He called for the maintenance of "White ramparts" of military force and immigration restriction to "guard our heritage from Mongol, Persian and Moor." Before 1939 he hoped for a White alliance to oppose the rising tide with the combined powers of the British navy, the German Luftwaffe, French infantry, and "an American nation." The outbreak of war made such an alliance impossible, but he continued to work for American neutrality and a compromise peace with Hitler, especially after the defeat of France in June 1940.

When Hitler attacked Soviet Russia in June 1941 Britain allied with the Communists, creating what was for Lindbergh the nightmare combination of English imperial and banking interests with Stalin's Asiatic hordes. For America to support such a combination would be to risk both subordination and racial pollution. In September 1941 Lindbergh told a large crowd in Des Moines that the country was being driven into war, against its interest and the public will, by a conspiracy of three groups, "the British, the Jewish, and the Roosevelt administration." The British were desperate, unable to defeat Germany alone. The Roosevelt people had used the crisis to win a third term for the president. As for the Jews, "the persecution they suffered in Germany would be sufficient to make bitter enemies of any race." He added, "No person with a sense of the dignity of mankind can condone the persecution of the Jewish race in Germany." But he went on to accuse the Jews of seeking war "for reasons which are not American." Without using the word *pogrom*, Lindbergh followed the same line of argument as the Reverend Simons, who had predicted that because Bolshevism was "Yiddish" it would be overthrown in a massive race riot. He warned "the Jewish groups in this country" to stop "agitating for war" and begin "opposing it in every way," for if they succeeded in getting America into a war "they will be among the first to feel the consequences."

But where Simons's testimony had received respectful treatment in mainstream newspapers and magazines and in the halls of Congress, Lindbergh's speech brought widespread condemnation even from some who shared his opposition to war. Moderate and liberal Republicans, like Fiorello La Guardia and presidential hopefuls Wendell Willkie and Thomas E. Dewey, denounced Lindbergh's speech as an incitement to race hatred. This response bewildered and enraged Lindbergh, who considered himself a 100% American in the Progressive tradition. His warning to the Jews was no more dire than the explicit threats of expulsion and vigilante justice Theodore Roosevelt had made to "hyphenate" Americans in 1917–18. But instead of recognizing him as a belated disciple of Theodore Roosevelt, the *New York Times* scored Lindbergh as a would-be American Hitler, whose "un-American" speech is "a clear echo, if ever there was one, of the early days of Nazi propaganda in Germany."[7]

The change in attitude was reflected in political action as well as public rhetoric. The administration promoted a "Nazi scare," analogous in some ways to the anti-German campaign of 1917 and the Red Scare of 1919–20. It accused America First of acting in the interest of the Nazis, and identified individual members, including Lindbergh, as Nazi sympathizers. Even MID "for the first time . . . began to regard anti-Semitism as a manifestation of un-American and possibly subversive trends." One investigation uncovered a Nazi sympathizer working for Father Coughlin's Christian Front. By a rather sweet irony, he was one of those MID officers who had told the Overman Subcommittee that the Russian Revolution was masterminded by "New York Jews."[8]

Hamilton Fish was hit by the backlash when—headstrong as ever—he carried his opposition to extremes by addressing a meeting of the German-American Bund with a swastika flag at his back. The gesture hurt his cause and eventually doomed him in politics. Fish professed himself bewildered by the response: he had spoken to antiwar Socialist audiences as well, and no one could possibly think him a Socialist. Theodore Roosevelt had addressed German-American audiences with his appeal to patriotism and national interest, without being suspected of "pro-Germanism."

What made the difference in public reception of Fish and Lindbergh was an inchoate but nonetheless palpable cultural shift away from racialism and toward a more liberal and pluralist understanding of American nationality. The *Times* scored Lindbergh as "un-American" not for his opposition to war, but for his racialism, for assaulting "the tolerance and brotherhood without which our liberties will not survive." Lindbergh's 100%-ism "exposed to derision and contempt . . . Americanism itself." In reaction against Lindbergh, the *Times* editorial even questions the validity of the *concept* of race, at least as that concept applies to Jews. How could "a religious group whose members come from almost every civilized country and speak almost every Western language . . . be called a 'race' "?[9]

But if Jews, with their long history of tribal solidarity and exclusiveness, were *not* a race, then neither were any of the new immigrant groups (Italians, Poles, Ruthenians, etc.) named in the famous *Dictionary of Races* used by immigration officers since 1910. If followed to its logical conclusion, the de-racialization of the Jews could bring down the whole structure of racialist categories on which so much of immigration policy, IQ evaluation systems, and sociological analysis had been based. Perhaps the color line itself might become untenable.

In the same month that Lindbergh spoke in Des Moines, Ben Kaufman, who had won the Medal of Honor trying to fight through to Whittlesey on October 4, was elected National Commander of the Jewish War

Veterans. He would become both a symbol and an agent of the movement to make the United States a genuinely multiracial democracy.

"Why Hate Ben Kaufman?": The Jewish War Veterans and Liberal Americanism

The organizational nucleus of the Jewish War Veterans was formed in New York after the great demonstrations of May and November 1919, in which uniformed veterans led mass marches calling for the rescue of Jews imperiled by Polish and Ukrainian pogroms. Ex-doughboys in large numbers affiliated with an existing organization of Civil War and Spanish-American War veterans, the Hebrew Veterans of the Republic, took it over and adopted a new name and charter in 1927. The JWV shared with other veterans' groups the task of working for public recognition of the service done by the veterans and for public policies to meet their needs. But its special mission was to defend the patriotism and effective service of Jewish soldiers and to work—through agitation, publicity, and political action—for the elimination of ethnic and religious discrimination against Jews. Through the 1920s the JWV organized demonstrations and engaged in active lobbying of public officials for American intervention against pogroms, for diplomatic protests to foreign governments guilty of mistreating Jews, for the relaxation of immigration quotas to permit family reunification. They mounted publicity campaigns against the use of racial slurs in theatrical performances and the telling of "Jew jokes" by public officials; they demanded that the public school curriculum make a formal place for the teaching of tolerance. They protested discrimination against Jewish doctors in city hospitals, raised money for a statue to Revolutionary War patriot-financier Haym Salomon, and set publicists to work on challenging the anti-Semitic propaganda disseminated by Henry Ford's *Dearborn Independent*. In their magazine, *The Jewish Veteran*, they retold the story of Jewish valor in wartime. It was their special mission to put the hero, and specifically the Jewish hero, into American history. The motto they adopted in 1927 was "Fight Back."

They were the most pro–New Deal of all the mainstream veterans organizations and spoke for Jews *as a race*: "It is a byword that Jews as a race are always leaders in philanthropic undertakings." In 1933 they supported early payment of the bonus and uniform pensions for disabled vets and their families or survivors—policies opposed by the American Legion. Their 1935 platform showed the persistence of Teddy Roosevelt–style Progressivism. Along with demands for veterans' benefits they called for the deportation of "Anti-U.S. Aliens" and for radical preparedness measures, including a federal takeover of munitions making and the "Draft[ing of] Capital and Industry, with Men, in Time of War." However, their antialien plank was not aimed at immigrants in general, but at Bolsheviks and agents of the Hitler regime who were organizing among German-Americans. They favored extending the immigration quotas to reunite families and admit Jewish refugees. With other veterans' organizations, the JWV protested unsuccessfully when, in deference to Nazi policies, the Amateur Athletic Union refused to let Jewish athletes compete in the 1936 Berlin Olympic Games. After the games they succeeded in forcing the resignation of part of the AAU's leadership. They publicized the atrocious results of Nazi race doctrines and thus contributed to the undermining of American Nordicist racialism. Jewish veterans turned out for counterdemonstrations when pro-Nazi organizations paraded in major cities. Groups of Jewish veterans showed up at Bund rallies and fought with the toughs in swastika armbands. In March 1933, shortly after Hitler took power, they organized a boycott of German goods and promoted the campaign with publicity and parades led by Jewish veterans. Endorsement by the Congress of Industrial Organizations (CIO) in 1937 made the boycott a success, sharply cutting American trade with Germany and provoking strong reaction from the Nazi government and its American sympathizers.[10]

Ben Kaufman became national commander of the JWV at the very moment that Lindbergh was attacking the Jews as an un-American race seeking to drive the American people into an unnecessary war. He would use the tale of his own heroism to symbolize the valor and patriotism of Jewish-Americans and, by implication, the positive value of the victory they had helped the United States win in 1918. His recognition and acceptance as an American hero by mainstream media was one of the signs that the old TR standard of racial Americanism was giving way to the more generous standard of ethnic pluralism.

Kaufman had come home from the war to find his prospects less promising than they had been in 1917. His wounds left him with some disability, but he did not apply for compensation. After demobilization he moved from Brooklyn (where his parents still lived) to Trenton, worked as a paper salesman, married, had one child, a daughter. He saved money to buy his own business, but it "went to pieces"; he tried selling insurance, but the Depression ruined that business as well. His father had died in 1929, and Ben and his siblings shared the support of their mother. Despite hard times, Kaufman was active in the JWV, Disabled American Veterans, and American Legion. He was also a celebrity in the Jewish community, where his legendary exploits were sometimes confused with those of Sergeant York. His civic work and standing as a local hero got him a job as inspector in the state motor vehicle department.

In 1936 Harold G. Hoffman was elected governor of New Jersey. He was a reformer of sorts, who (in the words of a contemporary) "did away with the spoils system that did not include Jews, Italians or blacks." Hoffman appointed Kaufman director of the Trenton subdivision of the U.S. Employment Service—namesake of the agency whose sudden dissolution in 1919 had doomed so many veterans to joblessness. Kaufman would serve effectively in that office through the war years. As a liberal he did not fare well in Trenton politics, was defeated as candidate for city commissioner and for mayor. The city was no longer the northern outpost of the Confederacy that Needham Roberts remembered, but its schools were racially segregated. It took the war, and the new embarrassment at likenesses between American and Nazi racism, to change that.[11]

Kaufman also increased his work for veterans' groups, serving as state commander of the DAV, national vice commander of the Legion of Valor, and for three years chief national aide to successive national commanders of the JWV. Kaufman was elected national commander in 1941 and reelected in 1942 after the outbreak of the war. This was a breach of the JWV's one-term rule, motivated in part by the need to preserve managerial continuity through a period of crisis. But even before the war, the JWV recognized that in Kaufman they had the perfect symbol of Jewish Americanism with which to combat the anti-Semitic propaganda of the Nazis, American nativists, and America First.

JWV press releases coupled reminders of Kaufman's Medal of Honor and links to the Lost Battalion with accounts of his career in public service to identify him as the perfect blend of martial valor with New Deal humanitarianism. In 1942 a half-hour radio play, "Ben Kaufman—The Story of a Hero," dramatized him as a Jewish variation on the all-American boy heroes of Mark Twain and Horatio Alger. He begins as a country boy, milking cows and churning butter; then, when the farm is lost, he holds his own among Brooklyn's Dead End Kids. The play dramatizes his near-blinding on the Vesle, his noble "desertion" from the hospital to return to his unit in the Argonne, and his heroism in the attempt to rescue the Lost Battalion.

In January 1942 *Look* magazine did a four-page spread on anti-Semitism. The top half of the first two pages carried an article by the Irish-American writer Vincent Sheean, "Anti-Semitism Is a Danger to the Nation." Sheean had been "startled" by the anti-Semitic character of Lindbergh's 1941 speech in Des Moines. Those "vague feelings" of dislike for Jews or Catholics or Negroes that Americans took for granted could no longer be tolerated. They threatened to "crystallize into business or 'social' discrimination" and become "a reactionary force in our national life." In wartime, when perfect solidarity is a life-and-death matter, prejudice and discrimination become intolerable.

To dramatize Sheean's arguments and put a human face on his polemic, the bottom half of his two pages (and all of a third and fourth page) are devoted to "Why Hate Ben Kaufman?" a story illustrated with a dozen captioned photographs.[12] The subtitle tells us that the "target of Nazi-style anti-Semitism is a mythical Jew created by propaganda. *Look* here presents a flesh-and-blood Jew: citizen, father, friend of man."

> Wherever you go in Trenton you hear about Ben Kaufman. He's not brilliant or rich or powerful. He just happens to like people and to enjoy giving them a helping hand. And he feels a little more keenly than most of us his obligations as an American citizen.

Look's juxtaposition of Kaufman's biography with Sheean's article frames Kaufman as the perfect symbolic answer to Lindbergh's attack on the Jews. Kaufman is not rich, does not have "large ownership" of media outlets. He is a product of a melting pot culture who has succeeded as an individual, by his own efforts, not seeking sympathy or special treatment. He is not only tolerant, he works with and for the benefit of people of all races and creeds. Though as a Jew he has experienced prejudice he is not "bitter," forgives those who injure him, and loves his country. Like any good American, "Ben speaks out when there's something on his mind. There's plenty on it these days," but no specifically Jewish concerns. The concluding triptych of pictures, "Here's Ben Kaufman in a Nutshell," shows him primarily concerned about national unity. He worries that race prejudice will divide Americans in the face of the enemy. But the lesson of wartime comradeship will save us: "Americans are fighting and dying side by side to preserve this country. Surely we'll be able to live together peaceably at home." He insists on "loyalty" in the most conventional terms: "In these times of emergency, let's not indulge in uninformed criticism of our leaders." Finally, he tacitly acknowledges that as a Jew he has been the beneficiary of a social bargain granted by Americans of older stock: "It's not a duty but a privilege to serve our country. It's our chance to pay back a little for all we have received."

As national commander, Kaufman systematically associated the JWV with liberal causes and celebrations. His first act was to send a telegram to President Roosevelt, expressing "the unanimous sentiment of our membership who are in accord with your program of national preparedness and foreign policy." On the outbreak of war he immediately issued an emergency call to "mobilize 250,000 Jewish veterans" to join the war effort, either by enlistment or some other form of service. The JWV promoted purchases of war bonds and raised money to buy fighter planes for the air force. Kaufman himself attempted to enlist, though at age forty-seven and with a disabled arm he was inevitably rejected. By word and gesture he insisted on recognition of Jewish Americanism. In May 1942 he helped organize a large public meeting at which a series of political and military leaders praised the record of Jews in all of America's wars and condemned as "fifth columnists" those who defamed Jews by claiming they let "others do the fighting for them." In 1943, as Kaufman passed the commandership to his successor, the JWV called for an end to the ban on Jewish immigration to Palestine, a direct challenge to the U.S. State Department and British Foreign Office.[13]

Kaufman's influence did not end with his second term as national commander. He continued to work for passage of the GI Bill of Rights, a program of veterans benefits that would make it possible for millions of working-class soldiers to go to college or get specialized training, buy a home, and receive medical benefits. In 1947 the JWV appointed Kaufman national executive director, a position created (in part) to keep him in a leadership role. He served until 1959, and after his retirement remained a major force in the organization. He was one of the leaders who engaged the JWV in a range of postwar liberal causes, including support for racial integration in the armed forces and antidiscrimination legislation. The

JWV also supported the African-American civil rights movement, especially in the period of intense struggle preceding the passage of the Public Accommodations and Voting Rights Acts of 1964 and 1965. The Vietnam War challenged the patriotism Kaufman had espoused all his life. His first reaction to the sight of protesters burning their draft cards was to want to incinerate the protesters. But as the war began to seem mistaken, as it began to tear the country apart, his views shifted. In 1968 Kaufman sponsored Jerome Cohen, a navy veteran of World War II who wanted U.S. forces withdrawn from Vietnam, for national commander. Cohen was defeated in 1968, but won election two years later and persuaded the JWV to become the first veterans' organization to call for prompt withdrawal of American troops.[14] Kaufman died in 1981.

Implicit in Kaufman's legend and explicit in the agenda of the JWV and other Jewish organizations, was the insistence that the social bargain of 1917 must now at last be fulfilled. Kaufman was living proof that the Jews had kept their part of the original bargain. Nazism was a demonstration of what could happen to a nation that could not overcome race prejudice. Jews were ready to fight in a second world war—even Kaufman, a survivor of the first, was willing to fight again—but acceptance of their Americanism could not be conditional on the quality of their performance. Their Americanism must be assumed and recognized at the start.

African-American leaders wanted to make the same claim and insist upon the same recognition. But they would have a harder time winning the kind of public recognition Kaufman enjoyed, because the memory of their soldiers' deeds in 1918 had been erased and overwritten by the legend of Negro cowardice and incompetence.

Horace Pippin: The Art of Historical Memory, 1920–1946

The nationalizing work of the New Deal raised African-American hopes and also disappointed them. FDR's dependence on the support of southern Democrats foreclosed the possibility of federal action against lynching or the legal essentials of Jim Crow. (FDR actually appointed Thomas Dixon, the notoriously Negrophobic author of *The Clansman*, to a federal court clerkship.) Blacks benefited to some degree from the public works and relief programs in the South, but the Southern Democrats who controlled appropriations and federal appointments in their region discriminated in favor of Whites and saw to it that Black rural workers remained tied to the tenant and sharecrop system. On the other hand, the nationalization of communications and tourism exposed Southern communities to the shaming glare of publicity, depriving them of the cultural insulation from national and world opinion that had made lynching and the protection of lynch mobs tolerable. Southern opposition to lynching rose throughout the period, and by the end of the 1930s the frequency, geographical range, and cruelty of lynching had significantly diminished.

For African-Americans, the New Deal created "a revolution only in their expectations," but that revolution energized political movements and suggested a new approach to effective action. The prominence of First Lady Eleanor Roosevelt as an advocate of civil rights contributed to the impression of an administration open to Black initiatives. A. Philip Randolph believed that "though the New Deal had not altered fundamentally the plight of black Americans, there was a feeling among them that here, for the first time in the present century, was an administration whose liberal rhetoric and whose liberal philosophy suggested a genuine concern for their problems." The *Crisis* found that "the most important contribution of the Roosevelt administration to the age-old color-line problem has been its doctrine that Negroes are part of the country as a whole. The inevitable discriminations notwithstanding, this thought has been driven home . . . [and] for the first time in their lives the government has taken on meaning for the Negro masses."[15]

African-Americans also had a greatly enhanced role in national mass culture. Film and radio gave Black performers a cultural presence and influence that could not be diminished by segregation of seating in movie palaces. The work of Black artists, musicians, and writers was promoted by White scholars and critics influenced by the neonationalist search for the native roots of culture and by leftists searching for authentic voices of an American proletariat. Among the artists they discovered was Horace Pippin, formerly a corporal in the 369th Infantry.

Pippin had been badly wounded when the 369th began the series of assaults that culminated in the taking of Sechault. Though he would recover sufficiently to be able to march with the regiment on its return to New York, he was permanently disabled, could not raise his right arm to shoulder height. He was living on his disability checks ($22.50 a month) in 1920 when he married Jennie Giles, a widow four years his senior, mother of a six-year-old son. They moved into the home she owned in West Chester, outside of Philadelphia, where they could raise some of their own food and live on her wages as a laundress plus his government check.

While rehabilitating in the hospital Pippin began drawing charcoal designs on cigar boxes as therapy for his injured arm. As his strength and dexterity improved he tried other media, wood-burning, whittling, making decorative boxes and picture frames. His recovery *from* the war also involved a recovery *of* the war, through memories he translated into images. In 1928, at age forty, he took up oil painting for the first time, using his left arm as a prop for his right forearm. In 1930 he completed *The End of the War: Starting Home*: a dark picture of German soldiers raising their arms in surrender or fleeing through tangles of barbed wire, as shells burst behind them and a burning plane falls from a gray sky. Over the next two years he produced several paintings on the war theme, small in size because of the restricted range of movement in his wounded arm.[16]

When he began painting it was in order to address the recovered memory of the war, and this project extended to the three "journals" he worked on after his marriage. A small notebook dated October 4, 1920, begins an account of his first experiences in the line, but breaks off abruptly. Two other undated notebooks survive, which represent two different attempts to recover the experience. One begins with a letter to "Dear Friends," to whom he explains that the war "brought out all the art in me." This was true in a double sense. He had begun systematic sketching as a soldier, using his art to understand and control the experience of war, "made some seens of france, something like a truckload of them yet at last I hatto birn them up." Now those images returned with recovered memories of the war. He thought in pictures, comparing the vividness with which he could recall the agony and suffering to the memory of the beautiful sunsets that all too rarely illuminated the murk of the battlefield: "I can never forget suffering, and I never forget sun set. that is when you could see it, so I came home with all of it in my mind, and I Paint from it to Day. . . . it came the hard way with me; I thank you."[17]

He never completed any of these attempted narratives. At some point words failed him. He was more eloquent with his paintbrush in the series of war paintings he made between 1928 and 1931, which show a rapid and remarkable growth in sophistication of design and emotional suggestiveness. Almost all the paintings refer to specific moments in the regiment's history. Pippin's "primitive" style, the flat perspective, the high contrast between simply drawn objects and blocks of color, pushes each scene toward abstraction. He juxtaposes visual elements and motifs in ways that surprise and trouble the viewer. *Gas Alarm Outpost: Argonne* (1931) pictures one of the most terrible aspects of combat in a scene whose leafy stylized shrubbery and fluffy clouds recall the serene jungles of Henri Rousseau rather than the trenches of *All Quiet on the Western Front*. *Dog Fight Over the Trenches* is a beautifully designed composition that rises in layers: a green gravesite and cross at the bottom, then a snowy-white band of earth turned out of the trench in which soldiers are sheltering; beyond that darkening gray bands of barbed wire and torn ground, rising to the gray sky in which planes fight and fall. Perhaps the most striking image is *Shell Holes and Observation Balloon: Champagne Sector*. The shell holes torn out of the dark earth look like monstrous flowers, the wrecked house behind them is all fractured geometry, and in the gray sky above floats the small bean-shape of the balloon. A soldier viewing the image knows that it is the smallest and least alarming element in the picture that has actually caused all the destruction in the foreground.[18]

Until 1937 Pippin was simply a local craftsman who painted for a hobby and sold or gave his work to neighbors. Then his painting was noticed by the president of the Chester County Art Association, who invited Pippin to exhibit at the annual show. The CCAA was not an ordinary local art society. Its members included several noted artists, among them the famous painter and illustrator N. C. Wyeth. The judges awarded Pippin a prize and also introduced his work to art dealers and museum curators in New York. It was a propitious moment. The modernists had always been drawn to the abstraction, the convention-annihilating "naïveté" of so-called primitive art. The idea of a Negro painter with strong folkloric roots also appealed to the artistic Left, with its yearning for a genuine popular or proletarian source of national art. Pippin's work was shown at the Museum of Modern Art's "Masters of Popular Painting" exhibition, then sent on a national tour. His work began to sell, and he formed a close and profitable connection with a gallery in Philadelphia run by Robert Carlen, who introduced him to a circle of Jewish artists and intellectuals that included the leftist playwright Clifford Odets.

From then until his death in 1946 Pippin pursued a modestly successful career as a painter. Having addressed the war and his memories he reached for other themes, some symbolic, others purely formal: a series on biblical subjects and another on episodes from African-American history, still lifes and nature paintings, a beautiful series of houses that verge on pure abstraction, paintings of Southern Negro life. During the Second World War he produced political posters and paintings, commissioned by his acquaintances in Popular Front circles. His most important works in this vein were two symbolic paintings, *Tribute to Stalingrad* and *Mr. Prejudice* (1943)—the latter a visualization of the Left's insistence that victory in war required the elimination of racial prejudice and discrimination at home. Alain Locke, the exacting philosopher and critic who was one of the leaders of the Harlem Renaissance, thought Pippin "very original; and in some canvases a startlingly original painter." Pippin was also, inevitably, the victim of the kind of success he enjoyed. A friend thought "Pippin was really exploited to the hilt in many ways. . . . I don't think he was ever fully treated as a human being." The "primitive" category in which the critics placed him concealed a man who "though not the scholar . . . was certainly a thinker and he did more research than most people realize." The art world valued him for the supposed naïveté of his technique and his intellect. As the technique became more sophisticated and the complexities of his point of view developed on canvas, he was criticized for compromising and commercializing his authenticity as a folk artist.

But Pippin had an independent turn of mind and was not awed by the educated and wealthy Whites with whom he often had to deal. A patron of his, having taken Pippin to see an exhibition of classic Western art at a Philadelphia museum, suggested that Pippin try to follow the old masters in technique and subject matter. Pippin answered, "Do I tell you how to run your foundation? Don't tell me how to paint." A younger African-American artist admired Pippin for the confident self-respect that seemed integral to him, a quality he thought was common among Black men who had served in the Great War:

> They had self respect and [Pippin] had lots of self respect. He knew he was strong. To me he was the kind of black man who wouldn't take too much smart alecky stuff from other people. Other people knew that . . . so they didn't try it with him.[19]

The pride that had been embodied in the Hell Fighters had not been *entirely* forgotten in Harlem. A tradition of militancy was still associated with the regiment. In 1937 Walter Garland and Vaughn Love, both Socialists, enlisted in the International Brigades to fight Fascism in the Spanish Civil War. As a boy Garland had seen the Old Fifteenth return in triumph and had enlisted for peacetime service in the unit, where he learned how to operate a machine gun. Vaughn Love was Henry Johnson's godson. Henry Johnson's son Herman would serve in the all-Black 332nd Fighter Group, the "Tuskegee Airmen," during the Second World War. Raised by his mother after the divorce, he worked his way through college and won a commission in 1942.[20] But before Black Americans agreed to a second wartime social bargain, they would demand a better deal than the New Deal had so far offered.

"Negro America must bring its power and pressure to bear": A. Philip Randolph's March on Washington, 1941–1942

The threat of a new world war strengthened the hand of Black civil rights leaders, just as it had in 1917. It had been possible, then, to convince

Blacks to enlist on the vague promise that their interests might be con-sulted at some future time. The betrayal of that promise in 1919–24 was too well and rawly remembered for the same indefinite promise to work again. After 1937, the NAACP and other organizations intensified their efforts to open all branches of the armed services (especially the elite Air Corps) to Blacks and to end the ban on admitting African-Americans to the service academies. But there was unremitting resistance to all these initiatives from the several armed services, the academies, and the secretaries of war and the navy. The NAACP's power of persuasion was weakened, with both the public and White officials, by the distorted heritage of 1917–18. Unlike the Jewish and White ethnic communities, African-Americans could not refute accusations of disloyalty or incompe-tence by appealing to symbolic heroes like Ben Kaufman. Public memory of the heroism of Henry Johnson and the 369th had been overwritten by the defamatory myth that labeled the Black doughboys unreliable, disor-derly, and cowardly. Charles Houston of the NAACP tried to recover the history lost in the myth. Testifying before the congressional committee on Selective Service in 1939, he cited his own and his family's tradition of military service:

> We are a generation of men in our forties and I come from three gener-ations of soldiers. I served in the late World War. . . . When you come from three generations of fighting men, four generations of which are lying in one Ohio churchyard, you are an American, and you know your salvation rises or falls with this country and that you have got to defend it.

He had been a combat soldier and a loyal patriot, but the treatment he received in 1918 was "so bitter that I never even applied for a service medal." Yet if the nation would keep its promise of fair treatment he would serve again.

Far from being convinced, let alone shamed by such testimony, Sena-tor Thomas Connally (D-Tex.) negated its effect by reminding the Senate of the Houston "riot" of 1917 and Theodore Roosevelt's punishment of the "Brownsville raid." Connally could not recall *any* details of either incident—he got the date of the Houston riot wrong by a year, exagger-ated the violence committed by the Black troops in both cases, and blamed the riots on "agitators" and "social climbers" who stirred up "colored people" to further their own political interests. In his view, any advocacy of political or civil rights constituted an appeal to the race's "sordid instincts," and those who "continually . . . agitate, disturb, stir up dissension and raise the devil about what they speak of as their political and social rights" thereby make Black soldiers "a terrible danger." Connally was "ready to fight for the rights of the colored man under the laws and the Constitution." However, he reminded his colleagues that "constitutional and legal rights are one thing," but "there is something in the Anglo-Saxon[,] written in the Constitution of the race, there is something written in the statutes of our blood" that rejects any demand for acceptance of "any man, whether he is white or black or yellow or red, as my social companion and equal, if I do not want to accept him." The laughter from the Senate galleries, and the final vote of his colleagues, confirmed Connally's view that the constitution of the race trumped "the Constitution and the laws." Congress and the administration repelled all requests for the integration of the armed forces and for the adoption of formal antidiscrimination clauses in military contracts.[21]

Nonetheless the lobbying campaign persisted, aided by the active participation of Eleanor Roosevelt. These efforts finally led to the authorization of a training program for Black pilots in March 1939, which would eventually produce the Tuskegee Airmen. The outbreak of war in Europe, and the acceleration of U.S. preparedness measures, strengthened the case of the NAACP and its allies. It was obvious that neither military recruitment nor the manning of war industries could succeed without the willing engagement of more than "ten percent" of the population. But the critical initiative was taken by A. Philip Randolph, who took the risk Black leaders had been afraid to take in 1917: he organized a movement that threatened to withhold Black support from the war effort if reform was not forthcoming.

Randolph recognized Nazi Germany as, in a way, a perfect enemy, because its ideology developed the premises of racialism in the most uncompromising and repellent terms. The triumph of Nazi principles would worsen the condition of Black people everywhere; but if Americans could be brought to an understanding, and a repudiation, of the core values of Nazism, they would have taken a step toward the recognition and repudiation of their own racialism. Randolph also guessed that a second war against Germany would reconstitute the opportunity for advancing the African-American cause that had been thwarted in 1917–19. He stood now where DuBois had stood in 1917, but with the advantage of knowing how DuBois's volunteer spirit had been betrayed.[22]

As a union leader, with twenty years of experience as president of the Brotherhood of Sleeping-Car Porters (the largest all-Black union in the United States), he believed that the strategic goal must be to bring the president to the bargaining table. Traditional approaches—"public statements, strongly worded telegrams to Washington, and conferences with White House officials"—had failed. Civil equality could never be won by agreement between the White elite and the colored Talented Tenth. "Only power can effect the enforcement and adoption of a given policy," and power flows "from the masses . . . the organized masses, the masses united for a definite purpose." Only an organization centered in and uniting the African-American community behind a *racial* agenda could compel the White political classes to pay attention. "Negro America must bring its power and pressure to bear upon the agencies and representatives of the Federal Government to exact their rights in National Defense Employment and the armed forces." Only by showing their political power *as a race* could they compel recognition of racial injustice. Therefore, "We shall not call upon our white friends to march with us. There are some things we must do alone."

In December 1940 he began agitating for and planning a mass march. It would demand federal action to ensure equal treatment for Black draftees, equal opportunity for Black officers, and nondiscrimination in war industries. Marchers were to present themselves as loyal citizens demanding the "right to work and fight for our country," just as they had in 1917. Then they had settled for a conditional agreement, which required them not only to serve but to prove their fitness to serve. This time they would insist they be allowed to work and fight as equals: "WE MUST FIGHT FOR IT AND FIGHT FOR IT WITH GLOVES OFF." The idea was not uniformly accepted by African-American leaders or by antiracist forces on the Left. Some objected to the militant tone, others to the danger that, should Randolph fail to bring the promised thousands to the capital, the movement as a whole would be discredited. The antiwar Left opposed his pro-war stance. The Communists accused Randolph of race chauvinism because of his insistence that only African-Americans participate. Even such staunch allies as Eleanor Roosevelt and Fiorello La Guardia tried and failed to dissuade him.

The Roosevelt administration took the threat seriously. A demonstration of any size would embarrass the government by reminding the world and the American people of the likenesses between Jim Crow and Nazi racialism. In a tough negotiation, Randolph won limited but significant concessions: an executive order banning discrimination "because of race, creed, color, or national origin" in government service or defense industries and establishment of the Fair Employment Practices Commission (FEPC) to enforce the order.

Randolph's "march on Washington" was one of several wartime events that would rouse the African-American community for a renewed drive for civil rights. The success of the Tuskegee Airmen as fighter pilots and bomber escorts would become a symbol of what African-Americans could achieve. A tank battalion of Black troopers with White officers (the 761st) would be similarly cited as a demonstration case to prove Black men made good combat soldiers. The 92nd Division was reconstituted and sent into battle in northern Italy in the last months of the war. In the manpower emergency that arose during the Battle of the Bulge, volunteer platoons of Black riflemen were drawn from labor battalions and sent as replacements to fight in White infantry units. Propaganda and press coverage periodically took notice of the role being played by Black servicemen, and an effort was even made to restore the Black doughboys to the place they had briefly held in the national mythology. In his 1943 book, *New World A-Coming: Inside Black America,* noted Black journalist, historian, and activist Roi Ottley reminded his readers of the military achievements of Henry Johnson and his comrades, and of the silent protests against discrimination made by the troops in France, which were precedents for the present and promising struggle for equality.[23]

These successes were gratifying, but limited to the scale of tokenism. The presence of Henry Johnson's son Herman in the Tuskegee Airmen is an ironic reminder that the "proof" of valor offered by the Tuskegee Airmen and the 761st had been made twenty-odd years before in the Battle of Henry Johnson and at Sechault. For that matter, it had been made at Fort Wagner during the Civil War, in the Indian wars, at San Juan Hill in 1898 and Parral in 1916. In the past that proof had been rejected, because the imperative of maintaining White supremacy overrode all other considerations. To a considerable degree that remained true in 1941–45. The army's determination to restrict Black troops to labor and service battalions meant that African-Americans would constitute a smaller proportion of combat troops than in any war since 1863.

Nonetheless, there were differences that ensured that this time the "proof" would not be entirely erased. The most significant factor was the politicization of the Black community and the development (by Randolph and others) of a movement based on grassroots organizing. Units like the Tuskegee Airmen used their standing as combat troops to challenge discrimination and segregation on the bases at which they were stationed. Lieutenant Jackie Robinson, who would break baseball's color line in 1947, risked a court-martial in 1945 by refusing to sit in the back of a segregated bus on his Southern army base. Black leaders pressed the demand for equal treatment in the military and in defense jobs throughout the war. Their "Double V" slogan demanded that the war produce a "Double Victory," over Nazism abroad and Jim Crow at home. This slogan found increasing acceptance among New Deal liberals who had not hitherto put the race issue high on the list of national priorities. It was not simply that Jim Crow undermined their propaganda for the war against Germany and Japan. The war itself, and the revelation of what Nazi and Japanese racism were capable of, convinced them that putting an end to racialist ideology and Jim Crow practices was a moral necessity. One of the key elements in that transformation was the role of Hollywood, whose films would shape the myth of World War II as "the Good War," in which a multiracial American democracy defeated two evil empires based on racist fanaticism. By a kind of poetic justice, the movie that would inaugurate that mythmaking process would link Black soldiers with the "ghosts" of the Lost Battalion.

17

The Bargain Renewed: The Myth
of the "Good War" and the Memory
of the Lost Battalions, 1938–1965

> They are just guys from Broadway and Main Street, but you wouldn't
> remember them. They are too far away now. They are too tired.
>
> —*Ernie Pyle*, Here Is Your War *(1943)*

It required the total immersion of the United States in the violence of World War II to compel the nation's leadership to embrace a pluralist vision of American nationality and make antiracialism a formal tenet of Americanism. Neither of these ideological developments should be confused with acceptance of the principle of racial equality. While it forbids explicit expressions of prejudice and acts of discrimination, "antiracialism" permits the believer to go on thinking that Black people tend to be good dancers and poor scholars, that Jews are too clever, that Italians make bad soldiers.

Nonetheless, the change in official rhetoric and policy lent new authority to the ideas of those antiracialist social scientists who had been fighting the Grant/Stoddard/Laughlin school of White supremacy since 1920. Ruth Benedict's *Race, Science, and Politics* and Ashley Montagu's *Man's Most Dangerous Myth* were bestsellers in 1942–43. Benedict's work was picked up by the government's Public Affairs Committee (a less powerful version of the old CPI) and adapted for its pamphlet

"Races of Mankind." This strong appeal for racial tolerance, with its denial of all theories of racial inferiority, was distributed to schools and
army bases and went through five printings in six months. In 1944 the
government asked the Swedish sociologist Gunnar Myrdal to undertake
a systematic study of race and race relations in America. One of the moving spirits behind Myrdal's project was Newton Baker, who as Wilson's
secretary of war had told Emmett Scott that the administration would
not allow the war to become an occasion for addressing "the so-called
race problem." Now he was ready to acknowledge the necessity of resolving it. Myrdal's *An American Dilemma* would provide the underpin-
ning for much of the legal work and policy planning of the postwar civil
rights movement.[1]

At the level of popular culture, the transformation of American racialism required a transformation of national mythology. Since 1918 the
movie business, eventually centered in Hollywood, had become the most
important medium for recalling and retailing mythic renderings of American society and the national past. Through the 1920s and 1930s, genres
like the western, the biographical film, and the historical costume epic
had translated historical mythology into powerful visual fables, sometimes reproducing traditional versions of Americanism, sometimes promoting revisionist views of the national past. As war became more
imminent, Hollywood took up the task of reconsidering and refurbishing
the myth of the "Bad War." In so doing it also rediscovered, and revalued,
the role of Black and "hyphenate" Americans in shaping national history.

The Hollywood Combat Film and the
Myth of the Good War, 1940–1946

In 1940 and 1941 Warner Brothers produced two films that offered a revised and upbeat version of infantry combat on the Western Front. *The
Fighting 69th* was based on the memoirs of regimental chaplain Francis
Duffy, about the famous Irish regiment that became the 165th Infantry
of the Rainbow Division. *Sergeant York* told the story of the Tennessee
mountaineer and conscientious objector whose single-handed capture of
a company of Germans was one of the legendary episodes of the war.
Both represent the fight against Germany as a democratic and Christian

crusade. They also link their positive attitude toward war with the symbolism of a melting pot America.[2]

Fighting 69th echoes "The Strenuous Life" vision of war as a proper proving ground for spiritual regeneration and for the affirmation of religious, ethnic, racial, and national identity. The main plot concerns the conflict between a selfish and cowardly street kid (played by James Cagney) and Father Duffy (Pat O'Brien), the regimental chaplain, who sees war as a religious mission and soldierly self-sacrifice as service to Christ. But the choice of the Irish 69th highlights the specifically *ethnic* element in American national identity; and that theme is emphasized by the appearance of a single Jewish soldier in their ranks. His presence is an ethnic joke with a serious point. The Jewish soldier identifies himself in a ridiculous brogue as "Michael Murphy," though his long hooked nose and Yiddish-inflected speech give away the secret of his "race." The enmity of the Jews and the Irish was proverbial, but "Murphy" insists on serving in the Fighting 69th. The Jewish soldier imagines his "Americanization" as requiring the chrysalis stage of passing for an Irishman, and the Fighting 69th, with its Irishness intact, becomes a metaphor for America. It is worth noting that this imaginative ploy is a faithful echo of the memoirs and unit histories written by Miles, Rainsford, and Tiebout, all of which saw the Irish as the model minority for Jews, Italians, and Chinese to emulate. Thus the film takes up the Americanization theme where Progressives dropped it in 1919.

Sergeant York is far more explicit in its justification of war, as befits a film released after Lend-Lease and on the eve of Pearl Harbor. It was extraordinarily successful, both commercially and critically, winning two Oscars and nine nominations. York was played by Gary Cooper, a major Hollywood star long identified as the quintessential American "uncommon common man" by his performances in western movies and in Frank Capra's *Meet John Doe* and *Mr. Deeds Goes to Town*. The first part of the film deals with York's life as a whiskey-drinking, rifle-toting, blood-feuding Tennessee mountaineer—a life transfigured when divine grace, in the form of a lightning bolt, prevents York from committing murder. After he is drafted he vindicates his faith by refusing to take up arms; but when York's preacher justifies the war in patriotic and Christian terms, York experiences a second "conversion," from simple Christian to Christian Soldier. But there is more to York's second conversion than theology.

The unit in which he finds himself is a "melting pot" mix, in which a Jewish soldier from Brooklyn ("Pusher") is most prominent. These hyphenated Americans have already accepted the patriotic duty to which York must be converted. When York agrees to fight he rises to a standard they have already met, and earns a comradeship that is valued as highly as the bonds that unite his congregation. The parties to the social bargain of 1917 have reversed positions: the melting pot city has become America, the WASP from the hinterland must prove *his* Americanism to "the Jews and the Wops."

Both *Fighting 69th* and *Sergeant York* use thematic and structural elements associated with the legend of the Lost Battalion. However, the Lost Battalion story itself was not turned into a film. Perhaps the "last stand" quality of the battle diminished its appeal for filmmakers looking for something positive from the last war to take into the next. But the destruction of the battleship fleet at Pearl Harbor, and the defeat and surrender of American forces on Wake Island and in the Philippines, made the question of whether or not to intervene purely academic. The fact that the war began with a series of major defeats meant that any films made during the first year of fighting would have to deal with "last stands," and turn these doomed defenses into prophecies of triumph. Under these circumstances, the legend of the Lost Battalion offered the perfect model for a war film scenario.

The movie that would establish the combat film as a major addition to Hollywood's repertoire of genres was *Bataan*, made and released in 1943. Its producers canvassed the repertoire of existing war films and the studio's research library for possible story lines, and rediscovered the Lost Battalion. Edward McManus's 1919 film was of less interest than John Ford's *Lost Patrol* (1934), not a literal retelling but a concise and visually striking realization of the kind of ordeal suffered by Whittlesey's command. The literary account by Johnson and Pratt was a fresher source, and its narrative was well designed and easily adapted to film, tightly focused on combat, with minimal but highly effective allusions to the civilian identities of the men.[3]

The filmmakers would also have found a number of suggestive analogies between the Lost Battalion and the last stand at Bataan. Nearly everyone who wrote about the Argonne described the forest as a "jungle," which compelled troops to fight like "Indians." The Philippine jungle is of course different from the Argonne, but the analogy is close enough. Uniforms, helmets, and weaponry were essentially the same as those used in 1918, and in depicting battle action the filmmakers replicated the tactics of 1918—trench-line defense anchored on heavy machine guns, and fixed-bayonet counterattacks "over the top." The mission of the *Bataan* unit is initially clearer than the orders that carried Whittlesey into the Pocket. They are to prevent the enemy from rebuilding and crossing a bridge, delaying the Japanese advance so American forces can regroup. But like the Lost Battalion, the breakdown in communications with headquarters compels them to make their own moral decision to stay and fight.

The story as told by Johnson and Pratt was positive in its representation of the heroism of ordinary Americans and the success of the melting pot. Those same ethnic types could be used in *Bataan*, since there had been little change in either the constituents of the melting pot or in ethnic and racial stereotypes. The unit is technically an infantry squad, with three air corps supernumeraries attached. However, as the combat film genre developed it became idiomatic to refer to all such small units as "platoons," and infantry combat movies are often referred to as "platoon movies."

A roll call early in the film establishes the unit as a microcosm of the American people. It includes six White Anglo-Saxon Protestants and six racial/ethnic characters. Captain Lassiter is a WASP West Pointer, as is the pilot Lieutenant Bentley. The tough top sergeant is Bill Dane, whose name vaguely suggests Viking or Nordic derivation. Corporal Todd is a kind of gangster figure. Purckett is the small-town, Tom Sawyer/Andy Hardy type, naive, eager, versatile. The medic is a conscientious objector who will die fighting. The ethnic characters are a Jew (Feingold), an Irishman (Malloy), a Pole (Matowski), a Hispanic (Ramirez), an African-American (Eeps, pronounced "Epps"), and two representatives of the American empire, the Filipinos Salazar (a Moro) and Katigbak. As Asians, the Filipinos reproduce the roles originally played by the Chinese in the Lost Battalion, but they also hold the place of Native Americans like Rainwater and Dodd. In the original screenplay, the unit was to have contained a Native American whose grandfather had fought against Custer at Little Big Horn. The character was replaced by Salazar, whose Moro people supposedly have the same "savage" qualities as Native Americans: an inordinate love of battle, "wildness" or lack of discipline, and filial love of the Great White Father (in Salazar's case, General MacArthur).

The racial and ethnic types are represented favorably, but their difference from the WASP standard is marked by the use of patronizing stereotypes. The Irishman is coarse and feisty, the Jew has bad feet (a traditional anti-Semitic stereotype), the Hispanic is addicted to jazz and dance music, the Moro is distinctly more "savage" than the other Filipino. Eeps is brave and dignified, but still comfortably within the range of accepted racial stereotypes: he sings blues and spirituals, is a would-be preacher, and does all the grave-digging.[4] Nonetheless, all behave heroically in combat.

The squad in *Bataan* mirrors the melting pot qualities of the legendary Lost Battalion. Ethnic and city types are blended with native-born Whites from the country, just as the 77th Division mixed its western replacements with the original city boys. The Jewish character is the most prominent of the ethnics, which corresponds to the identification of Whittlesey's command as a "Yiddisher Battalion." General Alexander had urged the melting pot troops to fight like the "gangsters" some of them presumably had been. Corporal Todd is a gangster type, who calls a samurai sword a "shiv." There may even be an ironic allusion to the race and labor troubles of 1919 in the plot device that has the Pole Matowski and the Black man Eeps as friends: the 1919 steel strike pitted Negro strikebreakers against workers often identified as Slavic. The only significant ethnicity of the original Lost Battalion that is entirely omitted is the Italian-American—replaced by the Hispanic Ramirez, who widens the geographical reference.

The studio's most radical innovation was the decision to include an African-American in *Bataan*'s symbolic unit. The segregation of Blacks in separate military units was still the rule in the U.S. Army and Marine Corps, and Blacks were segregated by assignment on navy ships. Hollywood's fictive vision of an idealized America ran well ahead of real-world practice.

The inclusion was deliberate and consciously political. The makers of *Bataan* seized the premise that the breakup of segregated regular units made integration possible. As the combat film developed, the studios persisted in placing African-Americans in their war stories even when the premise for inclusion was rather thin. Hollywood had implicitly accepted the "Double Victory" principle, which linked victory over Nazism to the destruction of race prejudice.

Eeps's role is an appropriate amendment to the myth of the Lost Battalion. Literally and figuratively, Whittlesey's men and the Harlem Hell Fighters had come from the same place and had fought the same battles.

The epic last stands for which they are remembered were fought on different parts of the same battlefield, and the last day's fighting at Sechault was followed directly by the first day's fighting in the Pocket. Yet they fought their battles separately and remembered them differently, divided in war and peace by the racialism each struggled to overcome. It was more than time for them and for their children to see that those separate wars were really the same war—time for Henry Johnson and Horace Pippin to be counted with the Lost Battalion.

Since 1943 the "ethnic platoon" has become a cliché of American war movies, a standard formula for the representation of the nation and the American people. We see it now not only in combat films, but in other genres that dramatize the activities of the state, ranging from police precinct dramas to science-fiction fantasies: a uniformed unit representing the significant racial, ethnic, class, and now gender differences must put differences aside to save the unit, and the nation it represents, from an enemy who threatens annihilation or enslavement. But in 1943 it was a radical innovation in the way war stories were conceived and in the way American society was to be represented.[5]

Fulfilling the Social Bargain:
Cold War Liberalism, 1949–1965

The *Bataan* formula proved extraordinarily successful. By 1946 so many war films had been made on essentially the same plan that a new genre or form of moviemaking was established, with a distinct and well-understood set of conventions. The form proved extremely flexible, allowing filmmakers to address a wide range of wartime issues and concerns simply by altering the mix of characters or slightly modifying the politics of command or the combat mission. These films made the realization of "melting pot" values *at home* the symbolic equivalent of a war aim, a domestic analogue of FDR's Four Freedoms. From 1943 to 1965, whatever the divisions of local politics, when one looked to those media that mirror the life and ideal values of "America at war," what one saw was no longer the racial dualisms of *Birth of a Nation* (1915) or *They Died with Their Boots On* (1941), but the multiethnic platoon of *Bataan, Sahara, Guadalcanal Diary* (1943), *Objective Burma* (1945), *A Walk in the Sun* (1946), *Steel Helmet* (1951), *To Hell and Back* (1955), and *Pork Chop Hill* (1960).[6]

It is important not to overstate the nature of this shift. Despite Hollywood's glorification of racial and ethnic tolerance, World War II ended without the achievement of that "Double Victory" African-American civil rights leaders had called for. Until 1965 the government made only half-hearted attempts to modify Jim Crow. Racial segregation was maintained by law throughout the South, and the ideologies that sustained it prevailed outside the South as well. Manners and customs still permitted the attitudes, modes of speech, and behavior that marked certain groups for denigration and discrimination. The "racial" quotas for immigration and admission to the Ivy League were unaffected and would for the most part remain in place until the 1960s. The ideological stance reflected in the *New York Times* editorial against Lindbergh is not so much *for* a vision of racial equality as it is *against* racialism as a way of speaking about society and politics. It would take another twenty years of struggle to translate the platoon movie myth into reform of the social and political order.

However, the veterans of both world wars did win both a material triumph—successful entry to the American middle class—and an ideological victory, signaled by public acceptance of the "platoon myth" image of America as a multiethnic democracy. The passage of the GI Bill and the changes flowing from it went a long way toward fulfilling the material terms of the bargain that had been offered to the men of the Lost Battalions when they went to war, then snatched away after their return. It provided support for home purchases and college tuition to a huge number of eligible veterans. When coupled with the postwar economic expansion, these measures underwrote an unprecedented economic and social transformation. The middle class was greatly enlarged as industrial workers and their children earned higher wages and went to college in greater numbers. The huge enrollment of veterans drove an expansion in the size and number of colleges and universities and turned institutions reserved for the affluent and elite into resources for a wider public. The veterans altered the demography of college student bodies and eventually of faculties and administrations, challenged and ultimately overthrew the ethnic and racial quota systems that had been instituted in the 1920s to bar minorities from the top universities.

On the civil rights front, the work of Black organizations and their liberal allies was aided by the Cold War. The first great breakthrough in integration was President Truman's use of executive order to eliminate segregation in the armed forces. Though many military leaders resisted, heavy losses on Korean battlefields compelled them to follow through. Presidents from Truman to Lyndon Johnson recognized that Jim Crow was a real liability to the United States in the ideological struggle against Communism, within the United States and overseas in the decolonized new states of Asia and Africa.[7]

In 1964 and 1965 the social bargain of 1917 was finally fulfilled, by federal legislation that guaranteed Blacks equal access to public accommodations and the right to vote. The enforcement provisions allowed federal officers to prosecute violations of civil rights—including lynching. The legal change did not end race hatred, discrimination, social violence, or social injustice. It did make it possible for African-Americans to fight for their rights with a reasonable hope of success. In the same year Congress passed the Voting Rights Act (1965), it abolished the racial quota system that had been the basis of immigration restriction since 1924. The rationale behind the law was as significant for American culture as the law itself—race-based quotas had affirmed that America belonged to its native-born White people and legitimated the discriminatory use of racial identification in every phase of American civil life. The immigration reform of 1965 was an affirmation of the idea that America is "a nation of nations," able to take all comers as they are and win their allegiance. Had such laws been passed forty years earlier, when the Hell Fighters and the Lost Battalion were young, this would now be a better and happier country.

The legislation of 1964–65 did not purge the nation of racism or racial discrimination. The straightforward advocacy of racial equality as *both* an objective of social reform and a fact of human nature did not become a norm of liberal rhetoric until the 1970s and has not been fully embraced by conservatives even now. The strong racialist theory espoused by the intellectual descendants of Grant and Stoddard has remained influential among policy and opinion makers down to the present time, though it is no longer the dominant approach in the human sciences. Every decade or so some scandalous new study reignites the old debate over the validity of IQ tests as a measure of "racial mental aptitudes," in terms barely changed since the days of Osborn, Terman, Brigham, and Laughlin. The stresses of unemployment, and of social and cultural change, periodically revive immigration-restriction movements that seek to exclude groups by race. Geopolitical theorists periodically produce maps of international conflict that mirror Grant's and Stoddard's "Rising Tide of Color," pitting a red or yellow or brown Eurasia against the blue of the Western alliance.[8]

Nevertheless, it seems fair to say that the ideology of White and Nordic supremacy has been driven to the margins of national politics and public discourse. For more than three centuries the superiority of European Whites and the inferiority of Negroes, Asians, and Indians had been taken for granted by American settlers and citizens. From the founding of the Republic to the end of World War II that assumption had been reified by the work of our leading social and natural scientists. Theodore Roosevelt and Mississippi's Theodore Bilbo differed in their ideas about how the qualitative difference between Black and White should be managed, but both believed racial superiority and inferiority were inescapable fact. A belief that was once regarded as proven scientific fact is now seen as a prejudice—powerful in its effects, but without moral and intellectual legitimacy.

Coda: Nationality, Diversity, and Patriotism

In the fifteen years since the end of the Cold War we have seen both the global spread of transnational economic and cultural forces, and the violent recrudescence of racial nationalisms, attended by genocidal violence, ethnic cleansing, or the coercive imposition of religious uniformity. Much of this violence has occurred in states just emerging from colonization, but a great deal of it has also occurred in Europe. The creation of the European Union is a significant move toward a postnational world order, but the borders and governments of many of those peacefully partnered states were established little more than a generation ago by massive acts of ethnic cleansing. Most member nations have seen the rise of old-style nationalist parties, anti-"Europe" and anti-immigrant, sometimes espousing neo-Fascist or neo-Nazi ideologies; and the naturalization of immigrant workers is still severely restricted by law in most European states. The observation made by Timothy Garton Ash during the collapse of Yugoslavia still seems apt: "History suggests that a contemporary European state with a less than 80 percent ethnic majority is inherently unstable." In Europe generally, "people . . . prefer to be ruled by those they consider somehow 'of their own kind.'"

Even in the United States, where the vision of a pluralist melting pot society has been idealized for two or three generations, one of the main themes of the intense "culture wars" of the last dozen years has been the fear that our diversity has become dangerous to our national solidarity. In *The Disuniting of America* the liberal historian Arthur M. Schlesinger Jr. wondered if "the melting pot [would] give way to the Tower of Babel." Robert Kaplan's vision of "The Coming Anarchy" saw the breakup of Yugoslavia and Russia and secessionist movements in Canada and Spain as precedents of the fracturing of American society on ethnic lines:

> [It] is not clear that the United States will survive the next century in exactly its present form. Because America is a multiethnic society, the nation-state has always been more fragile here than it is in more homogeneous societies like Germany and Japan.

Kaplan's concern has been echoed by a large and influential school of thought that sees the social cohesion of the United States as imperiled by multiculturalist ideologies and ethnic particularism. Samuel Huntington's *Who Are We?: The Challenges to America's National Identity* sees Latinos as the gravest threat. Peter Brimelow's *Alien Nation* argues more generally for new restrictions on both the number and the color of new immigration, in order to preserve the existing "racial and ethnic balance" of the nation. Immigration inevitably changes the culture of the receiving nation. Brimelow asks the question that underlies the anxieties of Huntington, Schlesinger, and Kaplan: "*Why* does America have to be transformed?"[9]

The answer seems to be that transformation, whether gradual or accelerated, is the rule in human affairs. Events change us, but above all contact and exchange with other peoples change us. A living culture in contact with others is continually transforming, exchanging, hybridizing at all points of contact. The global reach of trade and communications, the global migration of labor, mean that contact with others is inescapable. That being the case, histories of successful adjustment and productive hybridization will be of more use to us than nostalgia for "homogeneous societies." Indeed, the historical record of the twentieth century refutes Robert Kaplan's idea that ethnically "homogeneous" states like Germany and Japan are inherently stronger and more sturdy politically than heterodox states like the United States. Ideologies of racial nationalism plunged both Germany and Japan into dictatorship and wars of conquest that proved ruinous to themselves and the world. A polyglot United States, riven by deep ethnic and racial divisions, managed to weather the Depression and world wars without resort either to dictatorship or to chauvinistic wars of conquest.

Americans in the 1920s resisted the transformation of their culture by the admixture of African-American, Jewish, and Italian cultures. Is the nation or its culture poorer or richer for having been altered by the jurisprudence of Brandeis and Thurgood Marshall, the music of Ellington and Armstrong, Copland and Gershwin, or the writing of Ralph Ellison and Toni Morrison, Norman Mailer and Adrienne Rich? Rational arguments can be made for limiting the number of immigrants admitted at a particular time, and there are legitimate reasons for denying admission to individuals. But racial or cultural difference *per se* is not a rational or legitimate reason for exclusion. Since the end of the Cold War the most radical movements aimed at the destruction of the American state have come not from immigrants or racial minorities but from "100% Americans" of the extreme right: terrorists like Timothy McVeigh, neo-Nazis like William Pierce and Richard Butler, antigovernment vigilantes and militias organized by the likes of Gordon Kahl and John Trochmann. The separation of church and state has been weakened, not as the Progressives feared by Irish and Italian papists, but by fundamentalist White evangelical Protestants from the South and Midwest.

The history of the Lost Battalions provides an answer to the question whether a "nation of nations" can maintain itself as a nation-state. In 1917 immigrants in every stage of assimilation from "fresh off the boat" to 100% Americanized, from Chinese deprived of families by the Exclusion Acts, to African-Americans subjected to the immiseration and humiliation of Jim Crow, all showed their willingness to serve the country in war and their desire to play a responsible role as political citizens in peace. It did not require ethnic homogeneity, cultural "amalgamation," or the imposition of a "one-language" standard for citizenship to make them effective patriots. To win their hearts and minds, their acceptance of the ultimate sacrifice, the nation had only to offer safety, a measure of dignity, a chance for material betterment, a credible promise of justice somewhere down the road, and a plausible claim that the war itself was just and necessary.

No more than that, and nothing less.

Abbreviations

AH	*American Hebrew*
AJC	American Jewish Committee
ALH	*American Literary History*
AMHI	American Military History Institute
ASEQ	Army Service Experience Questionnaires
CPI	(U.S.) Committee on Public Information
JWV	Jewish War Veterans
LD	*Literary Digest*
NA RG	National Archives Record Group
NAACP	National Association for the Advancement of Colored People
NMJAMH	National Museum of Jewish American Military History
NR	*New Republic*
NYAmer	*New York American*
NYH	*New York Herald*
NYS	*New York Sun*
NYT	*New York Times*
NYTrib	*New York Tribune*
NYW	*New York World*
SEP	*Saturday Evening Post*
WP	*Washington Post*
WW	*World's Work (Review of Reviews)*

1: Safe for Democracy

1. William James, "Moral Equivalent of War," *Memories and Studies*, chap. 11.

2. Quoted in Gifford Pinchot, "Roosevelt as President," in Theodore Roosevelt, *State Papers as Governor and President, Works,* 15: xxxiii. Donald Rumsfeld, secretary of defense and architect of the Iraq War, had a paperweight engraved with this quotation. Evan Thomas, "Rumsfeld's War," *Newsweek*, Sept. 16, 2002, p. 23.

3. Julius O. Adler, *History of the Seventy-seventh Division*, p. 8.

4. W. E. B. DuBois, *Souls of Black Folk*, in *Oxford W. E. B. DuBois Reader*, pp. 104–5.

5. Nancy G. Ford, *War and Ethnicity*, pp. 42–43; Walter Millis, *Road to War*, p. 445; Byron Farwell, *Over There*, p. 61.

2: "The Great Composite American"

1. Balibar and Wallerstein, pp. 83, 85, 96. On the creation of nation-state and the role of mythmaking see Etienne Balibar and Immanuel Wallerstein, *Race, Nation, Class*, pp. 83–92, 96; Benedict Anderson, *Imagined Communities*; Geoffrey Hosking and George Schopflin, eds., *Myths and Nationhood*, esp. chaps. 1, 6; Edmund S. Morgan, *Inventing the People*; Richard Slotkin, *Fatal Environment*, chap. 2; and *Gunfighter Nation*, "Introduction"; John Hutchinson and Anthony D. Smith, eds., *Ethnicity*; Anthony D. Smith, *Ethnic Origins of Nations*, pp. 177–86, 192ff; and *Myths and Memories of the Nation*, chaps. 2, 4, 5, 10; Wilbur Zelinsky, *Cultural Geography of the United States*, pts. 1, 2, 6.

2. On the conflict between racial and civic models of American citizenship see Alexander Saxton, *Rise and Fall of the White Republic*; Roger M. Smith, *Civic Ideals*.

3. Slotkin, *Fatal Environment*, chap. 19.

4. Tichenor, *Dividing Lines*, esp. pp. 79, 115; and on immigration see also Roger Daniels, *Coming to America*; Philip Taylor, *The Distant Magnet*.

5. Frederick Emory, "The Homogeneity of Our People," *WW* 6:3598–612; F.A. Walker, in Allan Chase, *Legacy of Malthus*, p. 110; Tichenor, pp. 71, 120.

6. On Progressivism see John W. Chambers II, *Tyranny of Change*; Herbert Croly, *Promise of American Life*, esp. chap. 9; Alan Dawley, *Changing the World*; Leon Fink, *Progressive Intellectuals and the Dilemmas of Democratic Commitment*. On corporate concentration, managerial rule, and the Gospel of Efficiency see Alfred D. Chandler, *Visible Hand*; Samuel Haber, *Efficiency and Uplift*; Samuel P. Hays, *Conservation and the Gospel of Efficiency*; Martin J. Sklar, *Corporate Reconstruction of American Capitalism*; James Weinstein, *Corporate Ideal in the Liberal State*. On the Social Gospel see Ruth Hutchinson Crocker, *Social Work and Social Order*; Rivka Shpak Lissak, *Pluralism and Progressives;* Lillian D. Wald, *Windows on Henry Street*; Robert A. Woods and Albert J. Kennedy, *Settlement Horizon*. On race and class see Robert L. Allen, with Pamela P. Allen, *Reluctant Reformers*; Richard Hofstader, *Social Darwinism in American Thought*.

7. On Roosevelt see John M. Blum, *Republican Roosevelt*; Lewis L. Gould, *Presidency of Theodore Roosevelt*; Edmund Morris, *Rise of Theodore Roosevelt*; and *Theodore Rex*; Slotkin, *Gunfighter Nation,* chap. 1; Hofstader, *American Political Tradition*, chap. 9; John Milton Cooper Jr., *Warrior and the Priest*. On Roosevelt's racial ideas see Thomas G. Dyer, *Theodore Roosevelt and the Idea of Race*, and esp. Gary Gerstle, *American Crucible*, chap. 1. On "manhood" and war in Progressive thought see Kristin L. Hoganson, *Fighting for American Manhood*; J. A. Mangan and James Walvin, eds, *Manliness and Morality*, esp. chap. 11; T. J. Jackson Lears, *No Place of Grace*, chap. 3; "Theodore Roosevelt—American," in *LD*, Jan. 18, 1919, 7–9.

8. Roosevelt, "Strenuous Life," pp. 3–8, 11, 19; and "Expansion and Peace," pp. 28–29, 35–36, in *Works*, vol. 12; and *Winning of the West*, vol. 3, p. 145.

9. The best discussion of Roosevelt's racial nationalism is Gerstle, chap. 1. A fascinating study of racial and nationalist thinking among New York intellectuals is Matthew P. Guterl, *Color of Race in America*, which notes commonalities as well as differences of thought between arrant White supremacists like Madison Grant and W. E. B. DuBois. On the fallacy of racialism see Allan Chase, *Legacy of Malthus*. See also Lears, pp. 107–17; Dyer, chap. 7; George Sinkler, *Racial Attitudes*, pp. 406–9; Gustav Le Bon, *The Crowd*, preface and chap. 1.

10. Quoted in Owen Wister, *Roosevelt*, pp. 253–54, 256; Roosevelt, *Writings*, p. 197.

11. Tichenor, pp. 121–22, 125, 128ff; Morris, *Rise*, pp. 285–88, 299, 384–87; Slotkin, *Gunfighter Nation*, pp. 37–38, 159–60.

12. John R. Commons, *Races and Immigrants in America* (1907, 1920), pp. 6–7.

13. Cooper, pp. 161, 174, 197, 201–27, 214; Roosevelt, *Social Justice and Popular Rule, Works*, vol. 17: pp. 265, 271, 292.

14. Millis, pp. 237–39; Farwell, p. 31. See also Gregor Dallas, *1918: War and Peace*; Patrick Devlin, *Too Proud to Fight*; Harvey A. DeWeerd, *President Wilson Fights His War*; Walter Karp, *Politics of War*.

15. Roosevelt, *America and the World War, Works*, vol. 18, pp. 200–1, 206, 358–59; *Writings*, pp. 379–80, 385; and *Theodore Roosevelt, An American Mind*, pp. 161–62; Cooper, pp. 280–81, 304, 317; Anthony C. Troncone, *Hamilton Fish*, pp. 36ff.; Millis, pp. 77, 93, 317.

16. Alan Seeger, *Poems*, pp. 144, 162, 165; Walter Lippmann, *Drift and Mastery*, p. 2.

17. John Gary Clifford, *The Citizen Soldiers*, pp. 1–4; Hermann Hagedorn, *Leonard Wood*, vol. 2, pp. 189–90.

18. On Plattsburgh see Clifford, esp. pp. 5, 18–23, 48–66, 78–79, 195, 200–3. On Progressive support for the war, esp. by the *New Republic*, see John A. Thompson, *Reformers and War*.

19. O. O. Ellis and E. B. Garey, *The Plattsburgh Manual*, pp. 145–48. Compare James A. Moss, *Manual of Military Training*.

20. Clifford, pp. 82–85, 216–20; Cooper, p. 317; Roosevelt, *America and the World War*, pp. 200–1, 359; and *Writings*, pp. 379–81; Farwell, p. 31.

21. Roosevelt, *America and the World War*, pp. 190, 198–205; Cooper, p. 325; "The Roosevelt Division," *Outlook*, May 16, 1917, pp. 92–93; *Outlook*, May 30, 1917, p. 175, and June 6, 1917, p. 209. The proposal has been dismissed as quixotic, but French premier Clemenceau, a notably hard-headed realist, thought it had real value. A division was too large for mere symbolism, but a smaller unit might have served the purpose.

22. Stallings, p. 118; S. L. A. Marshall, *World War I*, p. 295; "The Sammies Are Now Teddies," *NYT*, July 6, 1917, p. 8.

3: No Black in the Rainbow

1. "Don't Bite the Hand that's Feeding You," Thomas Hoier and Jimmie Morgan, 1915; Clifford, p. 85; Ford, p. 44; Millis, pp. 5–7, 56, 93, 106–7, 176, 238–40, 367; Roosevelt, *America and the World War*, pp. 201, 225, 359; and *Writings*, pp. 380–81; R. M. Brown, p. 127.

2. Slotkin, *Gunfighter*, p. 240; Chase, pp. 113, 140–43; Tichenor, pp. 76–81, 115–21. Thomas Dixon, whose novel *The Clansman* (1902) was the basis of Griffith's film, published *The Death of a Nation* (1915), a "prophetic" sequel to *Birth of a Nation*, in which German immigrants replace Blacks as the racial menace.

3. James A. Sandos, *Rebellion in the Borderlands* is the best study. See also Jose David Saldivar, "Americo Paredes and Decolonization," in *Border Matters*, chap. 2; Frank N. Samponaro and Paul J. Vanderwood, *War Scare on the Rio Grande*, chap. 3 and pp. 127–29; John D. Eisenhower, *Intervention!* Thanks to Julie Ruiz for her advice on sources. The fear of racial uprisings was longstanding in the border region. See for example Sutton Griggs, *Imperium in Imperio* (1899), a novel by a Black minister/ journalist that fantasizes a revolutionary plot to establish a Black republic in Texas; and see Weaver, *Brownsville Raid*.

4. Millis, pp. 11, 285, 343, 409. On *Patria* see Slotkin, *Gunfighter Nation*, pp. 412–43; David Nasaw, *Chief*, pp. 260–64; Louis Pizzitola, *Hearst Over Hollywood*, pp. 153–62.

5. Millis, p. 445; Farwell, p. 61; Ford, pp. 100–2; Bernard C. Nalty, *Strength for the Fight*, p. 108.

6. Farwell, p. 50; Ford, pp. 41–43, 49–54; Ronald Schaffer, *America in the Great War*, pp. 176–77; David M. Kennedy, *Over Here*, p. 49; Harries, pp. 282–83; James R. Mock and Cedric Larson, *Words That Won the War*, p. 3; H. C. Peterson and Gilbert C. Fite, *Opponents of War, 1917–1918*, pp. 27–28; Christopher M. Sterba, *Good Americans*, p. 64.

7. On "War Progressivism" see Schaffer, *America in the Great War*; Ellis W. Hawley, *Great War and the Search for a Modern Order*, pp. 21–23; Kennedy, *Over Here*, pp. 31, 47, 50, 60–63; Thompson, *Reformers and War*; Neil A. Wynn, *From Progressivism to Prosperity*. On war propaganda see Alfred E. Cornebise, *War as Advertised*, pp. 1–7, 26, 57, 76–77, 115, 121; Mock, pp. 3, 10–11, 162–71; Farwell, pp. 122–23; Harries, p. 171. CPI, *The Meaning of America*, no. 33 (June 29, 1918), pp. 5, 10, 16, 20, 25–26, 76–77. Broderick, *Progressivism at Risk*, pp. 37–38, 45; Richard T. Ely, *Suggestions for Speakers*, National Security League, 13:2; S. Stanwood Menken, *Knowledge by the People*, NSL, 1:1, 4–7; Arthur E. Bestor, *America and the Great War*, NSL 15:8; Shailer Mathews, *Democracy and World Politics*, NSL, 10.

8. Robert McNutt McElroy, *The Ideals of Our War*, NSL 5:3–6; Herbert Myrick, *Fifteen Little War Stories* NSL 28:[2–3]; Mead, p. 75.

9. Roosevelt, *America and the World War*, pp. 190, 198, 201, 204–5; Cooper, p. 325; DuBois, "Colonel Charles Young," p. 264; David P. Kilroy, *For Race and Country*, esp. pp. 71–73; Greene, *Charles Young*, pp. 64, 69–73, 79; Eisenhower, pp. 270–75; Charles Young, *Military Morale of Races and Nations*, pp. 4, 7, 11, 15–25, 75–76, 98–105, 208, 211, 219, 271, 273. For the validity of Young's analysis of the role of morale in the Great War see John Keegan, *First World War* (1998), pp. 411–12. Young was qualified for high command in the AEF, but many White officers refused to serve under a Negro (Greene, *Charles Young*, pp. 30–33, 40, 52, 133). To avoid the issue the army retired him for "medical" reasons. See correspondence between Young, Roosevelt, and F. S. Stover (May 8–30, 1917) in John Motley Collection.

10. James Weldon Johnson, *Black Manhattan*, pp. 153–57, 231; "Views and Reviews," *Age*, Oct. 5, 1916, pp. 4, 5; *Age*, Oct. 5, 1916, p. 5; "Labor from the Southland," *Age*, Apr. 5, 1917, p. 1; Gilbert Osofsky, *Harlem: The Making of a Ghetto, Negro New York, 1890–1930* (1996), pp. 13, 282.

11. For the founding of the regiment and Fillmore's controversial protest of a lynching while in the Ohio National Guard see Charles Johnson Jr., *African American Soldiers in the National Guard*, pp. 63, 78–81; Gail Buckley, *American Patriots*, p. 188; William Miles, *Men of Bronze* (documentary); Stephen L. Harris, *Harlem's Hell Fighters*, chap. 1; [J. A. Jamieson et al.], *Complete History*, frontispiece photo, misspelled "Filmore."

12. Troncone, pp. 34–36.

13. Ibid., pp. 44–45; Farwell, p. 152; Buckley, pp. 189–91; S. Harris, pp. 43–44, 81–84.

14. Coffman, p. 69, 233; S. Harris, p. 34; Jamieson, p. 19; C. Johnson, p. 81; Emmett Scott, *Scott's Official History*, chap. 15; Osofsky, pp. 165–66, 171–72; *Age*, Oct. 5, 1916, pp. 1, 4, 5, which confuses the action by Black troopers at Carrizal with the fight at Parral, at which Young's troop of Tenth Cavalry rescued White troops. See Eisenhower, pp. 270–75.

15. Reid Badger, *A Life in Ragtime*, is the definitive biography. On Europe's career before 1917 see chaps. 1–10, esp. pp. 26–27, 32–34, 141.

16. Ibid., pp. 51, 105; Europe's *Tribune* article reprinted in Robert Kimball and William Bolcom, *Reminiscing*, pp. 60–64.

17. Badger, chap. 11; Arthur W. Little, *From Harlem to the Rhine*, p. 122; Gary Mead, *Doughboys*, pp. 78–79.

18. Jervis Anderson, *This Was Harlem*, pp. 99–103; Little, p. 10.

19. DuBois, *Souls of Black Folk*, in *Oxford Reader*, p. 102.

20. J. W. Johnson, *Black Manhattan*, pp. 232–33; J. Anderson, *Harlem*, p. 102; Farwell, p. 150; J. Anderson, *A. Philip Randolph*, pp. 8–10; Hubert Harrison, *Hubert Harrison Reader*, pp. 86–96.

21. J. W. Johnson, *Black Manhattan*, pp. 232–33; J. Anderson, *Harlem*, p. 102–5; Farwell, p. 150; Anderson, *Randolph*, pp. 8–10; Hubert Harrison, *Hubert Harrison Reader*, pp. 86–96.

22. Nalty, *Strength*, p. 108; "Loyalty," *Age*, Apr. 5, 1917, p. 4; J. W. Johnson, "Duty

of the Hour," p. 4. An article in an adjoining column reports on the "Crawford lynching" in South Carolina: see below, chap. 8.

23. Farwell, pp. 149–50; Coffman, p. 70.

24. Scott, pp. 41–45. The approach was indirect, through a White member of the Tuskegee board. Baker quotes in Walter A. Jackson, *Gunnar Myrdal and America's Conscience*, p. 17; David Levering Lewis, *W. E. B. DuBois*, pp. 542–43; Cornebise, p. 23.

25. Nalty, *Strength,* pp. 109–10; Lewis, *DuBois*, pp. 528–34; Harries, p. 168.

26. Nalty, *Strength,* p. 61; Anderson, *Randolph*, pp. 10–11; Harrison, p. 143; Isaiah Butts, "Why a Government Jim Crow Camp?" *Age*, Apr. 5, 1917, p. 4; *Crisis* 14:2, pp. 59–62; *Crisis* 14:1, p. 1; Farwell, p. 149.

27. Charles Williams, *Sidelights on Colored Soldiers*, p. 23.

28. Little, chap. 3, 96–97; Scott, p. 197; Badger, p. 4.

29. "Roosevelt Planned to Form 2 Negro Regiments," *Age*, June 7, 1917, p. 1; Jamieson, *Complete History*, p. 62.

30. S. Harris, pp. 37, 82–83; Badger, p. 293n26; C. Johnson, p. 83.

31. Buckley, p. 189; S. Harris, pp. 85–86; *LD*, June 15, 1918, pp. 43–44.

32. Troncone, chap. 1, esp. pp. 8–10, 16, 18–23, 30–31.

33. Roosevelt approached Fish for help in recruiting Black troops for his abortive volunteer division. Hamilton Fish, *Memoir*, pp. 24–27; Troncone, pp. 44–47; Buckley, pp. 190, 196; Little, pp. 3, 13–14, 26–28.

34. S. Harris, pp. 94–96; Badger, pp. 141, 293n26; C. Johnson, p. 81; Buckley, p. 191; Stallings, p. 312.

35. Napoleon B. Marshall, *Providential Armistice*; S. Harris, pp. 3, 45–47, 82; C. Johnson, p. 81; Jamieson, pp. 38–39; Miles, *Men of Bronze*. On his father-in-law see Tom W. Dillard, " 'Golden Prospects and Fraternal Amenities,' " *Arkansas History Quarterly* 25:4, pp. 307–33. On Harriet Gibbs Marshall see Web site listing.

36. Willard B. Gatewood, *Black Americans and the White Man's Burden*, pp. 246–49; Marshall's speech is online: http://www.boondocksnet.com/ai/ailtexts/their_hope.html.

37. N. B. Marshall, pp. 3, 12; Arthur E. Barbeau and Florette Henri, *Unknown Soldiers*, pp. 7, 11, 16–17, 31–32, 206–207; Buckley, p. 191. A letter from Booker T. Washington, *Papers of*, vol. 2; pp. 379–80, refers to Marshall's break with Washington and the Republican Party.

38. Troncone, pp. 56–59; S. Harris, pp. 87–88.

39. Fillmore to Cmdg. Officer [Hayward], Aug. 23, 1917, and Little to Cmdg. Officer, Company B [Fillmore], Aug. 24, 1917, in NA RG 391, Box 4253, E2133, HM1999; Little, p. 239.

40. S. Harris, p. 83.

41. S. Harris, pp. 39, 83, 86, 92–93; Schaffer, pp. 182–85; Jamieson, pp. 137–39.

42. Little, pp. 40–41, 153.

43. Kimball and Bolcom, pp. 15–34.

44. S. Harris, pp. 91–92; Jamieson, pp. 138–39; Miles, *Men of Bronze*; Neadom Roberts, *Brief Adventures*, p. 3, collection of John Motley; and see www.capitalcentury.com/1918html.

45. Letter to the author from Herman Johnson; S. Harris, pp. 90–91; and see Web sites for Henry Johnson.

46. Buckley, p. 195; Miles, *Men of Bronze*.

47. Judith E. Stein, "An American Original," in *I Tell My Heart*, pp. 2–43; and Selden Rodman, *Horace Pippin*, pp. 6–7.

48. Little, pp. 4–6, 16, 31; see also "Negro Soldiers, Led by Zulu, Ask to Try Out New Gas Masks," *NYH*, Oct 2, 1917, p. 13.

49. CPI, *Home Reading Course*, pp. 48–49.

50. Little, pp. 13–14, 22; Ralph Ellison, *Invisible Man*, pp. 13–14.

51. S. Harris, p. 234.

52. Contrast the tone of the Fillmore/Little correspondence above with Fillmore's

friendly exchange (Aug. 22, 1917) with Sgt. H. C. Smith, in NA RG 391, Box 4265, Cos.
B & C Misc. Records.

53. Troncone, pp. 56–59; Harris, pp. 87–88.

54. Elliott Rudwick, *Race Riot at East St. Louis;* Lewis, *DuBois,* p. 537; McElroy,
p. 3; "The St. Louis Riots," *Outlook,* July 11, 1917, p. 392; "What Some Americans
Think of East St. Louis," *Outlook,* July 18, 1917, pp. 435–36.

55. Quoted in Troncone, pp. 47–48; Lewis, *DuBois,* p. 538.

56. "The Spoiled Child," *NYT,* July 8, 1917, II, 2:1. See *NYT* coverage of the riot,
July 3, 1917, p. 1.; July 7, 1917, p. 1; July 8, 1917, p. 1. For TR's subsequent support of
Black troops and popularity in Harlem, see Troncone, p. 47; and "Women's Auxiliary
Lauds Roosevelt," *Age,* July 19, 1917, p. 1.

57. Buckley, pp. 195–96; "Negro Guardsmen in San Juan [Hill] Riot," *NYT,* July 4,
1917, p. 9; "Army Begins Inquiry into Race Rioting," "Hayward Begins Inquiry Into
Riot," and "Urges Negroes to Get Arms," *NYT,* July 5, 1917, p. 9; "Hayward Defends
His Men," *NYT,* July 6, 1917, p. 9.

58. J. W. Johnson, *Black Manhattan,* pp. 236–37; *Age,* Aug. 2, 1917, p. 1; DuBois,
Oxford Reader, p. 379.

59. Little, chaps. 5–7, p. 19; Scott, p. 198; S. Harris, pp. 118–19; Jamieson, p. 140.

60. Troncone, pp. 49, 61, and 54n31, which cites publication in *NYW,* Oct. 28,
1917. Little, p. 150, erroneously suggests the idea arose after they arrived in France.

61. Troncone, p. 47; Buckley, p. 190.

62. Little, p. 46; S. Harris, chap. 7.

63. "Fighters at Upton Buy Liberty Bonds . . . Negro Battalion to Vanish," *NYS,* Oct.
4, 1917, p. 3; Norval Dwyer, Camp Upton Story, Longwood Web site.

4: *"The Jews and Wops . . ."*

1. Dwyer, Camp Upton, Longwood Web site; Farwell, p. 63; W. Kerr Rainsford,
From Upton to the Meuse, pp. 1–3, 7; Frank B. Tiebout, *History of the 305th Infantry,*
pp. 11, 13, 16–17; *NYAmer,* Oct. 13, 1918, p. 3.

2. Adler, *Seventy-seventh,* p. 8.

3. Cornebise, pp. 4, 64–66; Ford, pp. 88–92; Schaffer, pp. 177, 182–84; Farwell,
pp. 27, 37, 58; Mead, pp. 95–98; U.S. Army War College, *Order of Battle,* p. 445.

4. Adler, *Seventy-seventh,* pp. 8, 32.

5. Harries, p. 30; Ford, pp. 41, 49–54; Tiebout, pp. 78–79.

6. Irving Howe, *World of Our Fathers,* pp. 295–97; Melvyn Dubofsky, *When
Workers Organize;* Schaffer, chaps. 6–7.

7. Joseph W. Bendersky, *"Jewish Threat,"* pp. 5, 38.

8. Adler, *Seventy-Seventh Division,* pp. 161–62, 165; Stallings, pp. 182, 198;
Slotkin, *Gunfighter,* chap. 3.

9. Harries, p. 100.

10. Stallings, p. 200; L. Wardlaw Miles, *History of the 308th Infantry,* pp. 8–9,
19–20, 57–58; Rainsford, pp. x–xi, xiii–xvi, 1; Tiebout, p. 12; "Col. Blagden Dies,"
NYT, Jan. 13, 1937, p. 23; Clifford, p. 58; "George McMurtry," *National Cyclopedia,*
vol. 47, pp. 686–67; "George McMurtry," *NYT,* Nov. 24, 1958, p. 29; "77th Officer
Dies" (James A. Roosevelt), *NYT,* March 27, 1919, p. 4 and "Maj. J. A. Roosevelt Dies on
Transport," p. 13.

11. "Son of Actor Harrigan on Wounded List," *NYAmer,* Oct, 13, 1918; for
Harrigan Sr., see John Kenrick, *History of the Musical Stage,* http://www.musicals101
.com/1879to99.htm; Little, p. 10. On Eddie Grant see Stallings, p. 274, and *Baseball
Encyclopedia;* on Leon "Josh" Cadore see *Baseball Encyclopedia* and "High Jinks of
Motley Quota Off for Yaphank Amuse Spectators," *NYH,* Oct. 9, 1917, p. 12.

12. W. Kerr Rainsford, Architect," *NYT,* July 24, 1947, p. 23; Rainsford, pp. xiii–xiv,
xxv–xxvi; Miles, pp. 57–58, 68; "Dr. L. W. Miles," *NYT,* June 29, 1944, p. 23.

13. Susan Tifft and Alex Jones, *Trust*, pp. 5–25, 32, 86–87, 94–96, 102–9, 117–21.

14. "Charles White Whittlesey," *National Cyclopedia*, vol. 20, 396–97; Thomas M. Johnson and Fletcher Pratt, *Lost Battalion*, pp. 130, 289–314; Irving Werstein, *Lost Battalion*, pp. 25–27.

15. Max Eastman, *Enjoyment of Living*, pp. 215–16, 228–30; "Col. Whittlesey of the 'Lost Battalion' Vanishes from Ship," *NYT*, Nov. 29, 1921, pp. 1, 3.

16. Ibid., p. 3; Miles, p. 115; Eric Homberger, *Historical Atlas*, pp. 158–59, 303–4; George Chauncey, *Gay New York*, pp. 78–86, 104–7, 113–14, 134–37; Christine Stansell, *American Moderns*, chaps. 7–8; William L. O'Neill, *Last Romantic*; Whittlesey to Pruyn, Nov. 26, 1921, Whittlesey Papers, Williams College.

17. Eastman, pp. 330, 355, 396, 400–20, 579–81.

18. Werstein, p. 27; Stallings, p. 278.

19. Harries, p. 100; Adler, p. 8; Miles, pp. ix, 5, 8–9, 19–20; Johnson and Pratt, p. 128.

20. Rainsford, pp. xii, 7; Tiebout, p. 11.

21. For recruitment issues see Mead, esp. chap. 4; Sterba, chaps. 2–3; Ford, pp. 46–47, 98–100, 232, 246–47. For propaganda directed at alien draftees see CPI, *Meaning of America*, pp. 5, 45–47; Mock, pp. 164–65, 175; and compare Joseph Buffington, *Friendly Words to the Foreign-Born*, pp. 3–4, 6, 8, 46–47; CPI, *American Loyalty by Citizens of German Descent*, p. 3. For general studies of the relation of ethnicity and race to American nationality in this period see John Bodnar, *Remaking America*; Lawrence H. Fuchs, *American Kaleidoscope*; George M. Frederickson, *Black Image in the White Mind*; Gerstle, *American Crucible*; Jonathan M. Hansen, *The Lost Promise of Patriotism*; Kenneth L. Karst, *Belonging to America*; Desmond King, *Making Americans*; Leon F. Litwack, *Trouble in Mind*; Alessandra Lorini, *Rituals of Race*; Cecilia Elizabeth O'Leary, *To Die For*; Werner Sollors, *Beyond Ethnicity*.

22. Howe, chaps. 6, 7, 12; Arthur A. Goren, *New York Jews*, chaps. 2, 4, 5; Lydio F. Tomasi, ed., *Italian in America*, chaps. 12, 16, 18; M. Kaz, "Farewell America!" *AH*, Oct. 12, 1917, p. 23.

23. Wallace Foster, *A Patriotic Primer*, p. 11; Jacob Riis, *How the Other Half Lives*, pp. 80–81; Bruce Edward Hall, *Tea That Burns*, esp. pp. 184–85; Min Zhou, *Chinatown*, p. 39; Rose Hum Lee, *Chinese in the United States*, esp. chaps. 2, 4, 5, 7–12, 14.

24. Sterba, chap. 1; Howe, chap. 7, esp. p. 253; Goren, pp. 214–15; "Report of Dr. J. L. Magnes," *AH*, Nov. 10, 1916, and "Among Our Brethren Abroad," a regular column.

25. Howe, pp. 141–46, 230–35, 311–15; L. L. Lorwin, *Women's Garment Workers*, chaps. 25–29.

26. Howe, chap. 11, and pp. 134–35, 279–82, 311–18; "What It Means to Be a Gentile in N. Y." in *AH*, Jan. 19, 1917, p. 351.

27. Nick Salvatore, *Eugene V. Debs*, pp. 284–85; Sterba, p. 66; Emma Goldman, *Living My Life* (1977), pp. 633–34, 674; Goren, pp. 214–15, 228–31; Sterba, pp. 61, 69–71, 121; Schaffer, p. 183; Mark Slobin, *Tenement Songs*, p. 53. For contemporary responses to the Russian Revolution see the "Passover Issue," *AH*, Apr. 6, 1917. For coverage of Jews in English language press, see for example, "Jews Urged to Aid Pershing's Army," *NYW*, Oct. 8, 1917, p. 3, "First Army Camp Paper Out Today," p. 6, "Mobilize Morale Is Fighting Plan," p. 9 (and compare "Houston Rioters Face Gallows," same page); "God's Blessing Is Invoked for America's Armies" by Catholic, Protestant, and Jewish leaders, and "Jews of Nation Decide to Extend War Relief Work," *NYH*, Oct. 29, p. 12; "$1,000,000 Needed for Jews in Army" and "Jews Show Patriotism," *NYW*, Oct. 28, 1917, II, p. 2; "Jews to Aid Recruiting: But Patriotic League Will Not Form a Separate Regiment," *NYT*, April 6, 1917, p. 8; "Austrian Jews Would Aid [the War Effort]: Rabbi Buchler to Enlist Them for the Army and Navy," *NYT*, April 7, 1917, p. 6.

On Jewish Socialists' responses see Salvatore, p. 281–85; Howe, chap. 9. On Cahan see articles from the *Forward* (1917): "Horrible Pogrom Against Negroes in Saint Louis,"

July 3, p. 1, and "The Military Pogrom," p. 4. For criticism of TR and anti-Germanism see Hillel Rogoff, "A Cloud Hovers Over the Heads of the American-Germans," July 2, p. 3; and "Roosevelt's Fight Against the 'Foreign' Presses," July 6, p. 4. On the draft see "A Special Draft List," July 22, p. 1, which uses a Yiddish term for czarist conscription; "Who Is Eligible and Who Can Be Excused Now," July 4, p. 5; "Will a Whole Million Be Taken?" July 7, p. 1; "One Can Only Get Exemption Through Affidavits," July 11, p. 1; editorial, July 12, p. 4. On the war see B. Levitan, "Thoughts on Destruction," July 1, p. 3; "War Until the Bitter End," July 1, p. 6; "The Railroad Companies Are Profiting," July 2, p. 4; but note elements of "Americanism" in "A Sad Holiday," July 4, p. 1; "Wilson's Friendly Speech to the Workers," July 16, p. 4; H. Rogoff, "Wilson's Opportunity to Bring Peace to the World," July 23, p. 3; and "The First Encouraging Developments of Wilson's Diplomacy," p. 4.

28. Sterba, pp. 63, 66–67. Articles in *AH*, 1917: Joseph Silverman, "The Patriotism America Needs," Apr. 20, pp. 830–51; Milton Rubinstein, "A Jewish Boy's Tribute to America," May 25, p. 3; "From a Soldier Boy," June 20, p. 279; Louis Marshall, "New York Jewry's Duty," Dec. 7, pp. 124–25; "Jewish Regiments," Aug. 17, p. 376; "The War and American Jewry," and George Mason, "The Duty of American Jews," Aug. 24, pp. 398–99; Sarah V. Jacobs, "My Country" and "Registration Day," June 1, p. 102; Lieberman, "Melting Pot: In the Shadow of War," p. 132; editorial, "Jews in American Wars"; and Marie Trome, "Jews in American Wars," Aug. 3, pp. 319, 329–30. "Passover Issue," Apr. 6, contains "The War for Peace," p. 727; "The War for Democracy," p. 692; Fabius Schach, "Jewish War Heroes," p. 708.

29. Racial theory is esp. prominent in M. J. Woldis, "Is the Jewish Race Declining?" *AH*, Jan. 19, 1917, pp. 347–48, and Elisha M. Friedman, "Zionism and Hebrew Idealism," *AH*, June 29, 1917, p. 8. See also Samuel Shulman, "The Problem of American Judaism," *AH*, Feb. 23, 1917, pp. 491, 512; "Symposium on Zionism," *AH*, May 25, 1917, esp. Stephen S. Wise, "No Jews Need Apply," pp. 66–67; Ahad Ha'am, "A Proud Jew," *AH*, "Passover Issue," Apr. 6, 1917, p. 682; Harry Friedenwald, "Israel's Cause," *AH*, June 29, 1917, pp. 200–3; "In the Press," May 25, 1917, p. 99; and Elias Lieberman, "The Melting Pot: The Invisible Flag," p. 101.

30. The account that follows is from Abraham Krotoshinsky, "How the Lost Battalion Was Saved," *Jewish Veteran*, April 1937, pp. 5–6; clipping file, NMAJMH; picture in [L. C.] McCollum, *History and Rhymes*.

31. Sterba, pp. 28–29, 53–54; "Seditious Disorder Brings 30-Day Term" and "Will Defy Magistrates," *NYT*, Aug. 29, 1917, p. 8.

32. Farwell, chap. 4 and pp. 60–61, 97, 308; details on recruitment of AEF divisions are in U.S. Army War College, *Order of Battle*.

33. Farwell, pp. 96–97; Glenn Gray, *Warriors*, pp. 47–48.

34. Nancy K. Bristow, *Making Men Moral*, pp. xviii–xvix, 2, 18–19, 20, 31–37, 51, 55–56, 79–80, 127ff.; Coffman, pp. 20–23; Harries, p. 170; Farwell, p. 143; Ford, pp. 19, 31–36, 175–77; "Selective and Swift, Too," *NYS*, Oct. 2, 1917, p. 14; Francis F. Byers, "Camp Upton—The Melting Pot," *World Outlook* 4, Apr. 18, 1917, p. 15; Odell, "Making Democracy Safe for the Soldier," *Outlook*, Nov. 28, 1917, p. 516; and "The Spirit of the New Army," *Outlook*, Nov. 14, 1917, pp. 414–15.

35. Ford, pp. 48–54, 58–59, 70–71, 218, 268–69; Daniels, p. 223; Sterba, pp. 121, 193; Goren, p. 228. "$1,000,000 Needed for Jews in Army" and "Jews Show Patriotism," *NYW*, Oct. 28, 1917, II, p. 2, estimates 40 percent of those at Upton are Jews. See also American Jewish Committee, *War Record of American Jews*, pp. 10–12, 39; "Will Aid Jewish Soldiers," *AH*, Apr. 13, 1917, p. 812; "Welfare Work for Soldiers," *AH*, Nov. 30, 1917, p. 89, and "Jews Named Officers," p. 91. On Voorsanger and other Jewish chaplains see Albert Isaac Slomovitz, *Fighting Rabbis*.

36. Ford, pp. 218–22, 232, 246–47, 260, 262–63, 266; "War Department Puts Ban On the Use of 'Nigger' and 'Coon' in United States Army," *Age*, Dec. 29, 1917, p. 1.

37. Ford, pp. 38–39, 61–67, 71–73, 235–38, chap. 6; U.S. War Department, *Home*

Reading Course for Citizen-Soldiers (1917), pp. 3, 6, 10, 12–14; 17–18, 22–24, 55, 57; Schaffer, pp. 177–78; Ford, pp. 3–10, 26, 39, 48, 51–55, 113–14, 245.

38. Farwell, p. 51; AJC, pp. 10–12; Ford, pp. xiv–xv; Sterba, p. 57. Figures on naturalization at Upton are from Suffolk County Naturalization Project Web site.

39. Thanks to Mitchell Yockelson at National Archives for suggesting this approach. RG 120, Box 6622, Records of the AEF, General HQ, Administrative Staff, JAG, General Correspondence, 77th Division, Mar. 1, 1919, "Statistical Report of Courts Martial"; 27th Division, July 1, 1918, "Annual Report"; 26th Division, July 1, 1918, "Annual Report." See also RG 120, Box 209, 330.14. Criticisms. H. G. Learnard, AG, War Dept. to all Dept. Commanders. Memorandum 145, EE Booth, Lt. Col. and Chief of Staff; F. I. Brower to Gov. Whitman, Sept. 30, 1917; Ford, pp. 298–302.

40. Young, p. 4.; Roosevelt, *Roosevelt in the Kansas City Star*, pp. 13–14.

41. Adler, *Seventy-seventh*, pp. 11, 17; Tiebout, p. 13; Herbert Kaufman in *NYAmer*, Oct 1, 1917, p. 18; "U.S. Troops to Rely on Rifle As of Old," *NYW*, Oct. 5, 1917, p. 2.

42. Adler, *Seventy-seventh*, pp. 8, 13; Ford, chap. 1; Slotkin, *Fatal Environment*, chaps. 13–14, and *Gunfighter Nation*, pp. 88–101.

43. On problems of U.S. military organization see Mead; Coffman, *War to End All Wars;* Keegan, *First World War*; S. L. A. Marshall, *World War I*.

44. Farwell, p. 65.

45. Montague Glenn, "Potash and Perlmutter Discuss the Czar Business," *NYAmer*, Oct. 7, 1917, M:1; and "Potash and Perlmutter on 'Soap Boxers and Peace Fellers,'" Oct. 14, 1917, M:1; "Soldiers at Upton Sign for First Pay," *NYW*, Oct. 1, 1917, p. 7; "New York Sends 2,000 More Men to Camp Upton" and "Woman Trudges from New York," *NYTrib*, Oct. 1, 1917, p. 4; Frazier Hunt, "Yaphank Bennie Writes About This Army Stuff," *NYS*, Oct. 21, 1917, V, p. 2; "Old Orderly to Go Overseas," *NYS*, Oct 13, 1917, p. 1; "George Draftman Ready for his Job," *NYS*, Oct. 8, 1917, p. 3; "Missing Draft Soldier Found," *NYTrib*, Oct. 7, 1917, p. 8; *NYH*, Oct. 6, 1917, p. 12; "Amok, Head Hunter," *NYS*, Oct. 6, 1917, p. 3; and compare "Negro Soldiers, Led by Zulu, Ask to Try Out New Gas Masks," *NYH*, Oct. 2, 1917, p. 13.

46. Miles, p. 7; Adler, *History of the 306th Infantry*, chap. 1; Rabbi Lee J. Levinger, *Jewish Chaplain in France*, p. 117; Tiebout, p. 18; Rainsford, pp. 1, 7–10. Herschkowitz is spelled in a variety of ways in the AEF records and unit histories. This is the spelling used in his obituary, NMJAMH.

47. Miles, p. 68; "308th to Lose Its Only Bearded Man," *NYS*, Oct. 5, 1917, p. 2; "Bearded Soldier—Jew Can Eat Bread Only," *NYAmer*, Oct. 5, 1917, p. 3; "Recruit's Beard a Problem at Upton," *NYW*, Oct. 5, 1917, p. 4. It is not clear how the case was resolved. If Bednash was strictly Orthodox he might have been unable to use Mills's loophole, since Jewish law forbids trimming "the corners of the beard." Bednash was in fact overage and might have been dismissed for that reason, or on account of ill health. But the episode reflects the positive relations between Jewish draftees and their officers. See for example "One Train Cuts Joy," *NYW*, Oct. 9, 1917, p. 4; "479 Rejected Men," *NYTrib*, Oct. 2, 1917, p. 4.

48. Rainsford, pp. 10–11; Tiebout, p. 17.

49. Miles, p. 68; Ellis and Garey, pp. 145–48; Young, p. 69.

50. "George McMurtry," *National Cyclopedia*, vol. 47, pp. 686–87; obit., *NYT*, Nov. 24, 1958, p. 29. For McMurtry Sr., see "One of New York's 500 Millionaires," *NYT*, Aug. 7, 1915, p. 7; Anne E. Mosher, *Capital's Utopia*, pp. 130–31, 138, 147–48, 167.

51. Miles, pp. 7–9, 19–20, 140–41; Johnson and Pratt, pp. 214–15; Alexander T. Hussey and Raymond M. Flynn, *History of Company E,* esp. pp. 5–6, 83; Adler, *Seventy-Seventh*, p. 13. Compare Roosevelt's technique in Samuels, chap. 2.

52. Werstein, p. 29; Miles, pp. 37–38, 84, 115–18; Johnson and Pratt, pp. 130–31.

53. On the Liberty Loan see Harries, pp. 175–77; Ford, pp. 48–49; Cornebise, pp. 48, 68; Farwell, pp. 128–29. On use of racial and ethnic minorities as shaming devices and as scapegoats see Cornebise, pp. 1, 49–50, 70–73; Ford, pp. xiii, 68; "Socialist Machine German, Says T.R," *NYS*, Oct. 16, 1917, p. 2; "The Sergeant's Dream," *NYS*, Oct. 18, 1917, p. 1; Theodore Roosevelt, "Liberty Loan and Pro-Germans" and "German Plot Aimed to Kill Liberty Loan," *Roosevelt in the Kansas City Star*, p. 14; Farwell, p. 128; Peterson and Fite, pp. 142–43.

54. The men were paid $30 a month, from which was deducted $8 for insurance and varying "allotments" for the support of their families. "Boys at Yaphank Buy Liberty Bonds," and "Jews Urged to Aid Pershing's Army," *NYW*, Oct. 8, 1917, pp. 3, 6. See Roosevelt's linkage of "Hearst, Hylan, and the Hohenzollerns," in a treasonous triumvirate, *NYW*, Oct. 2, 1917, p. 1; "Vigilantes Support Mitchel," *NYTrib*, Oct. 1, 1917, p. 9. Hearst fired back, accusing Roosevelt of having aided the enemy by criticizing the country's lack of preparedness. See *NYAmer* of 1917: "Demagogy and Bravado," Oct. 1, p. 18; "Mitchel Branded 'Yellow,'" Oct. 27, p. 1; "German Charges Against TR," Oct. 3, p. 1; and "Says Colonel [Roosevelt] 'Aided Enemy,'" Oct. 6, p. 3. *NYTrib* published a regular front-page column titled "Who's Who Against America?" The first person so featured was Hearst (Sept. 30), the second Cahan (Oct. 7), the third Hillquit (Oct. 28). See also "Class Consciousness Behind Russian Revolution" and "Proletariat Gunning for Capitalism Rather than Autocracy," *NYW*, Oct. 4, 1917, p. 5; "Hillquit Wins Irish Cheers with Pacifist Appeal," *NYTrib*, Oct. 26, 1917, p. 1. However, the *Sun*, which supported Mitchel, praised Cahan as "an Americanizing institution" and saw no reason to suppress a paper merely for being socialist: "A Hearing for 'Forward,'" *NYS*, Oct. 9, 1917, p. 16.

55. "Fighters at Upton Buy Liberty Bonds," *NYS*, Oct. 4, 1917, p. 3; "The Hun Within Our Gates," p. 14.

56. Miles, pp. 115–16.

57. Stallings, p. 198; *NYH*, Oct. 9, 1917, p. 12.

58. Dwyer, Longwood Web site; Joseph Demaree, *History of Company A*, pp. 8–9; Werstein, p. 29; Hussey and Flynn, pp. 2–7; Krotoshinsky, pp. 5–6.

59. Tiebout, pp. 15, 17, 47–48.

60. Harries, p. 129; "Anti-Jewish Prejudice at Camps," *AH*, Nov. 23, 1917, p. 69; Lieberman, "The Jew as a Fighter," *AH*, Nov. 16, 1917, p. 39, and "Tribute to Jews in Army," p. 52; Z. Sher, "A Jewish Soldier," *Forward*, Aug. 7, 1919, p. 3.

61. Tiebout, p. 19.

62. This account of Kaufman's life is based on "Why Hate Ben Kaufman?" *Look*, Jan. 27, 1942, and "Meet Ben Kaufman, CMH" (both NMAJMH).

63. Adler, *306th Infantry*, chap. 1; Bristow, pp. 79, 89; Miles, p. 20; Hussey and Flynn, p. 5.

64. Morris Gutentag ASEQ, AMHI; Ford, p. 295; Miles, pp. 64–65, 135; Rainsford, pp. xxv–vi; Tiebout, p. 18; Adler, *Seventy-seventh*, p. 19; Farwell, p. 97.

65. Miles, p. 18; Demaree, p. 23.

66. Tiebout, p. 28; Adler, *Seventy-seventh*, p. 12; Scott, pp. 191–92. See NA RG 120, HQ 77th Div., Box 197, decimal file 253, Prisoners, July 22, 1918, attack on Black troops by Whites, and attachment, "Feeling Existing Between Black Soldiers and White Soldiers."

67. Young, pp. 215–16; Hasia R. Diner, *In the Almost Promised Land*, p. 50.

68. Ford, pp. 300–1.

5: The Politics of Ridicule

1. "Close African Dodger Booth in Buffalo," *Age*, June 7, 1917, p. 2; Prof. William L. Bulkley, "Fighting Ridicule," *Age*, May 3, 1917, p. 6; Odell, "The Spirit of the New Army," *Outlook*, Nov. 14, 1917, p. 496; *Crisis*, 14:3, July 17, 1917, pp. 112, 114; DuBois, *Oxford Reader*, pp. 104–5; Barbeau and Henri, p. 79; Chester D. Heywood, *Negro Combat Troops*, pp. 3, 5, 9; "Camp Dix Recruits will Miss Fifteenth Infantry" and

"When Europe Goes to Europe," *NYH*, Oct 7, 1917, I: pt. 2, p. 1; see also "Soldiers at Camp Upton the Minute Men of 1917," p. 6.

2. Little, pp. x–xi; Badger, p. 154; *Age*, Apr. 13, 1917, p. 4; *LD*, Apr. 21, 1917, p. 1153; Nalty, *Strength*, pp. 103–6, 108; Farwell, pp. 154–55.

3. "South Alarmed by Threat of Negro Uprising," *NYTrib*, Oct. 7, 1917, p. 9; "Pro-Germans Busy at Spartanburg," *NYT*, Sept. 17, 1917, p. 4; Little, pp. 49–51. See also Badger, pp. 154–55; Scott, p. 199.

4. NAACP, *Thirty Years of Lynching*, p. 91; Leon F. Litwack, *Trouble in Mind*, pp. 309–12; J. W. Johnson, "The Mask Thrown Off,"and "The Duty of the Hour," *Age*, Apr. 5, 1917, p. 4; "Staying in the Gutter," *Age*, Sept. 6, 1917, p. 4.

5. On Spartanburg see David L. Carlton, *Mill and Town*, pp. 2–6, 164–66, 223–29, 244–49, 266–67; NAACP, *Thirty Years*; Litwack, pp. 302–3.

6. Bristow, p. 145; Badger, p. 155; Little, chap. 8; S. Harris, chap. 9.

7. Little, pp. 54–55; "Fifteenth Regiment," *Age*, Oct. 18, 1917, p. 1.

8. On racial incidents in Spartanburg see Badger, pp. 155–60; Troncone, p. 49; Fish, p. 26; Little, pp. 55–62, 63.

9. Little, p. 191.

10. Buckley, p. 198; Lester A. Walton, "Democracy at Spartanburg, S.C.," *Age*, Aug. 10, 1918, p. 5; "Soldier Hazed," *NYT*, Oct. 17, 1917, p. 1; Sterba, pp. 128–29; Coffman, p. 73.

11. Various accounts of the episode are given in S. Harris, pp. 111–12, 134–36; Buckley, pp. 196, 199; Troncone, pp. 40–41; Fish, pp. 26–27; Jon Guttman, "Regiment's Pride," *Military History* 8:36; Miles, *Men of Bronze*. Newspaper accounts are: "Alabama Troops Clash with Negro Soldiers," *NYW*, Oct. 27, 1917, p. 1; "Race Riot at Camp Mills," *NYS*, Oct. 27, 1917, p. 3; "Negroes Moved at Camp Mills / Troops Withdrawn Following Threatened Clash with Men of Alabama Regiment," *NYAmer*, Oct. 29, 1917, p. 3; and *NYT*, Oct. 28, 1917, p. 18.

12. Badger, pp. 161–63; Little, chaps. 12–13; Horace Pippin, "Autobiography," p. 1, Horace Pippin Papers.

13. Rodman, p. 8; Buckley, p. 200; Edgerton, pp. 107–8; Barbeau and Henri, pp. 169–70.

14. Troncone, pp. 57, 61–62; letter in *NYT*, May 5, 1918, p. 2, reprinted from *Age*.

15. Buckley, p. 201; Little, chap. 19; Badger, p. 163.

16. Mead, p. 169; N. B. Marshall, p. 4.

17. For overall understanding of military strategy and tactics on the Western Front, and conditions facing U.S. troops, I have used Coffman, *War to End All Wars*; Keegan, *First World War*; Farwell, *Over There*; Harries, *Last Days of Innocence*; S. L. A. Marshall, *World War I*; and Stallings, *Doughboys*.

18. Badger, pp. 175–77; Buckley, pp. 202–3; Pippin, "Autobiography," p. 4, and small notebook, pp. 4–5.

19. Barbeau and Henri, pp. 113–14; S. Harris, pp. 179–82; Keegan, pp. 329–30, 422; David Miller, *Guns of the 20th Century*, pp. 414–15; Heywood, pp. 88–89; N. B. Marshall, pp. 4–5.

20. Badger, pp. 180–33.

21. Scott, p. 204; Badger, pp. 174–75; S. Harris, pp. 182–84; Barbeau and Henri, chap. 7, pp. 113–14.

22. Pippin, small notebook, p. 14; N. B. Marshall, p. 5.

23. Badger, p. 175.

24. Lt. O[sceola] E. McKaine, " 'The Buffaloes' A First-Class Colored Fighting Regiment," introduction by Col. James A. Moss, *Outlook*, May 22, 1918, pp. 144–47. For general views on race in *Outlook* see "No Race Segregation By Law," Dec. 5, 1917, pp. 548–49; Lyman Abbott, "Can the Negro Be Educated?" Dec. 12, 1917, pp. 602–4; "Lynching a National Offense," June 26, 1918, p. 339, and "Negroes Under War Conditions," pp. 334–36; Lt. Charles C. Lynde, "Mobilizing 'Rastus,' " *Outlook*, March 13, 1918, pp. 412–17. See also John W. Thomason Jr., *Fix Bayonets!*, pp. 105–6.

25. Pippin, "Autobiography," pp. 1, 7–8, 11–12; small notebook, pp. 21–27; Rodman, pp. 8–9.

26. There are variant versions of the "Battle of Henry Johnson." See S. Harris, chap. 14; Little, chap. 30; Roberts, *Brief Adventures*, pp. 4–6; "Col. Bill Hayward and His 'Black Watch,'" *LD*, Mar. 8, 1919, p. 59; Jamieson, p. 24; John H. Patton, *History of the American Negro*, p. 147. This account follows Johnson's interview in Patton, but checks his account of event and sequence against Roberts, Hayward, and Little.

27. Little, pp. 197–200.

28. Troncone, p. 61; Fish letter in *NYT*, May 5, 1918, p. 2; "Fighting 15th in Front Line Trench," *Age*, May 11, 1918, p. 1; *Crisis* 16:2, June 18, 1918, p. 68; "Negro Regiment in Action," and "Negro and Wife Lynched," *NYT*, May 20, 1918, p. 6.

29. *LD*, June 15, 1918, pp. 43–44; Scott, p. 22; "Bravery of Negroes Told By Pershing," *NYT*, May 21, 1918, p. 6; editorial, *NYT*, May 22, 1918, p. 12; Barbeau and Henri, pp. 117, 232; *Age*, May 25, 1918, pp. 1, 2; Ellen Yan, "'Harlem Hellfighter' Honored," *Newsday* Online, Jan. 11, 2002 ; "Honor Negro War Heroes," *NYT*, June 28, 1918, p. 8; Little, pp. 194–201; "New York Police Looking for Counterfeit War Hero," *Age*, July 13, 1918, p. 1. I examined every issue of the *American* from May 20 to July 15, and found no mention of Henry Johnson.

30. "The Two War Crosses," *Age*, June 1, 1918, p. 4; "Two Negroes Whip 24 Germans" and "Mob Lynches Negro and His Wife," *Age*, May 25, 1918, p. 4; Philip Dray, *At the Hands of Persons Unknown*, pp. 245–46; "Lynching," *Outlook*, June 5, 1918, pp. 215–16; "Lynching a National Offense," June 26, 1918, p. 339.

31. *Crisis*, 16:2, June 1918, pp. 58, 62, 68; 16:3, July 1918, pp. 130–32; 16:4, Aug. 1918, pp. 164, 179, 187.

32. R. M. Brown, p. 127. His novel, *Old Judge Priest*, was filmed as *Judge Priest* (1934), dir. John Ford, with Will Rogers as the crafty country judge and Hattie McDaniel and Stepin Fetchit as comic Negroes.

33. Badger, pp. 184–85.

34. Irvin Cobb, *Glory of the Coming*, pp. x, xv, 169–72.

35. Scott, p. 231; Cobb, *Glory*, pp. 187–88, 287–89; and "Young Black Joe," *SEP*, Aug. 24, 1918, pp. 7–8, 77–78, esp. pp. 8, 77.

36. Ibid., pp. 294–307; Barbeau and Henri, p. 117.

37. "War Department Puts Ban On the Use of 'Nigger' and 'Coon' in United States Army," *Age*, Dec. 29 1917, p. 1; Ford, p. 266. J. W. Johnson was pleased but skeptical: "A New Meaning for an Old Term," *Age*, Aug. 31, 1918, p. 4.

38. *Age*, Nov. 8, 1917, editorial, p. 4; *Crisis* 16:4, Aug. 1918, p. 179.

39. "Evolution of a Superior Race," *LD*, Sept. 29, 1917, pp. 24–25; T. M. Johnson, *LD*, June 15, 1918, pp. 43–44; compare Edgerton, pp. 105–6, and *NYT*, Feb. 18, 1919, pp. 1, 6. On the "bolo" see Cobb, *Glory*, p. 23; Hayward letter in Patton, p. 147.

40. "Bill and Needham," *NYT*, May 22, 1918, p. 12; Jordan, *Old Eph*, p. 29; Little, pp. 206–7.

41. "Two First-Class Americans," *NYH* cartoon in Scott, p. 22.

42. Buckley, p. 203; Sidney Mitchell and Archie Gottler, "Mammy's Chocolate Soldier," 1918.

6: The Slamming of Great Doors

1. Cobb, *Glory,* pp. xv, 462–63.

2. Miles, pp. ix, 23, 50; Pinchot, p. xxxiii.

3. For conditions of battle and the experience of combat I have referred to works (fiction and nonfiction) dealing with WW II as well as WW I: Mead, *Doughboys*; Stallings, *Doughboys*; Gray, *Warriors*; Coffman, *War to End All Wars*; S. L. A. Marshall, *World War I*; Keegan, *First World War;* Hervey Allen, *Toward the Flame;* Paul Fussell, *Great War and Modern Memory* and *Wartime*; Robert Kotlowitz, *Before Their Time;*

Samuel Hynes, *The Soldiers' Tale*; John C. McManus, *Deadly Brotherhood*; Ernie Pyle, *Brave Men* and *Here Is Your War*; Erich Maria Remarque, *All Quiet on the Western Front*; Thomason, *Fix Bayonets!*

4. U.S. Army War College, *Order of Battle*, p. 297; Robert Lloyd, "Good Morning, Mr. Zip-Zip-Zip!" 1918.

5. Adler, *Seventy-seventh*, p. 27; Demaree, p. 37.

6. "New York Troops on Flanders Front," *NYS*, May 18, 1918, p. 1.

7. Miles, pp. 32–39; Tiebout, p. 40.

8. John A. Lomax and Alan Lomax, *American Ballads and Folk Songs*, pp. 557–60, and http://www.acronet.net/~robokopp/english/armentir.htm.

9. Miles, pp. 36, 41–44, 68–69; Hussey and Flynn, p. 19; Tiebout, pp. 40, 50, 76–77.

10. Miles, pp. 45–50; Hussey, p. 22.

11. The account that follows is from Miles, chap. 4, esp. pp. 59, 300.

12. Tiebout, p. 99, and also pp. 44, 113; Cobb, *Glory*, pp. 190–91.

13. Miles, p. 68.

14. Rainsford, p. 61; Julius Klausner, *Company B 307th Infantry*, pp. 8 (photo), 15; Gray, pp. 51–52.

15. Miles, pp. 138, 143; Web sites for Ben Kaufman; and files in NMJAMH.

16. On the arrival of the 77th see "New York's National Army Troops Rouse London," *NYW*, May 12, 1918, p. 1; "308's Crossing Ocean Like Picnic," *NYAmer*, May 14, 1918, p. 4. On fighting see "Americans in Hardest Fighting of War," *NYTrib*, Oct. 4, 1918, p. 3; "Upton Men in Hard Test," *NYT*, Oct. 3, 1918, p. 2; "Major Jay Wounded," *NYAmer*, Oct. 1, 1918, p. 4; "New York's Own Division," *NYT*, July 1, 1918, p. 10; Stallings, pp. 110–11.

17. Gray, p. 31; Ernie Pyle, *Brave Men* (1944), p. 103.

18. Gray, pp. 52–54.

19. Adler, *Seventy-seventh*, p. 39; Howard Johnson and Percy Wenrich, "Where do we go from here?" 1917.

20. S. Harris, pp. 205–7; Badger, pp. 186–87; Jamieson, pp. 21–22. Little, p. 227, dates "Let's go!" later, but S. Harris, p. 184, cites reference *Age*, June 1, 1918.

21. Pippin, "Autobiography," p. 13.

22. S. Harris, pp. 204–10; Fish to Hershey, 78th Div., July 2, 1918, NA RG 391, Box 4267, Records of Co. K ; Badger, p. 190; Barbeau and Henri, pp. 121–22.

23. Ibid., pp. 77–81; S. Harris, pp. 209–10, 232.

24. Badger, pp. 190–91.

25. Little, pp. 213–20, 226; Patton, p. 141; Harris, p. 207; Fish, p. 30.

26. Fish, pp. 35, 42; Barbeau and Henri, p. 233; Harris, pp. 223–26, 232–33; "American Negro Troops Put Germans to Flight Near Verdun," *Age*, July 6, 1918, p. 1, reprinting report from the *Sun*. Barbeau and Henri, pp. 117–18, and Badger, pp. 186–87, place them near Chateau Thierry, as does Pippin, "Autobiography," pp. 14-17, 29. However, official accounts place them east of Rheims. See U.S. Army War College, *Order of Battle*, p. 438; U.S., American Battle Monuments Commission, *93rd Division*, p. 5.

27. "For Colored Officers," *NYT*, Feb. 26, 1919, p. 4; Pippin, notebook fragment, p. 1.

28. Pippin, "Autobiography," pp. 43–44.

29. U.S. American Battle Monuments Commission, *American Armies*, p. 5 and maps; Jamieson, pp. 131–36.

30. Little, pp. 237–39.

31. Pippin, "Autobiography," pp. 12, 15–17; small notebook, pp. 40–41.

32. Jamieson, pp. 50–52.

33. Rodman, p. 79; Pippin, "Notebook," pp. 7–19, 23–24; notebook fragment, p. 4; and "Autobiography," p. 46. The last page of his notebook reads: "FEAR/DEATH/MINUTES/VOICES/SQUAD."

34. Barbeau and Henri, p. 117; Badger, 186–87; "Member of Old Fifteenth Wins French Cross of War," *Age*, Aug. 31, 1918, p. 1, reprints story by Lincoln Eyre in *NYW*.

35. The account of the raid that follows is pieced together from passages in Pippin's autobiography, notebook, small notebook, and the notebook fragment. The passages may refer to two different raids, but recurrence of certain details suggest he may have made three attempts to recall a single episode. I've treated these as a single incident to give a sense of how this kind of operation worked and how Pippin reacted to such expeditions. Pippin, "Autobiography," pp. 25–28; notebook, pp. 11–15; small notebook, pp. 41–42, 46, 48; notebook fragment, p. 3.

36. Buckley, p. 203; Badger, pp. 187–88; Tim Gracyk and Brad Kay, *Lieut. Jim Europe's 369th U. S. Infantry "Hell Fighters" Band: The Complete Recordings.*

37. Barbeau and Henri, p. 121; N. B. Marshall, p. 6; S. Harris, pp. 190, 232.

38. Ibid., pp. 118–19; Little, pp. 242–43; Jamieson, pp. 138–39.

39. Buckley, p. 203.

40. John Jacob Niles, *Singing Soldiers* (1927), p. 17; Miles, pp. 74–75; Tiebout, p. 90.

41. For the fighting along the Vesle see Miles, chap. 5.

42. Tiebout, pp. 92–95; Hussey, pp. 29–30.

43. Rainsford, chap. 4; Miles, pp. 79–83, 95, and photo opposite p. 93; Adler, *306th,* chap. 4.

44. Mead, p. 191; Tiebout, p. 94.

45. Mason and Furr, p. 86; Miles, p. 98; Thomason, p. 200; James Tobin, *Ernie Pyle's War,* p. 109.

46. Tobin, pp. 199–200; Miles, pp. 97–98; Pyle, *Brave Men,* p. 58.

47. Remarque, pp. 273–74; Pyle, *Brave Men,* p. 241.

48. Adler, *Seventy-seventh,* pp. 43–44; and *306th,* chap. 4.

49. Adler, *Seventy-seventh,* pp. 8, 55–57; Miles, pp. ix, 8–9, 19–20, 83–84.

50. The account that follows is from Miles, pp. 83–97, except where noted.

51. Adler, *Seventy-seventh,* p. 44.

52. Louis Popkin, "The 'Melting Pot' Division, A National Ideal," *AH,* Apr. 11, 1919, pp. 520–21, 603.

53. Miles, p. 143.

54. Tiebout, p. 107, U.S. American Battle Monuments Commission, *American Armies,* p. 104.

55. Tiebout, pp. 119–20; Adler, *306th,* chap. 4.

56. Pyle, *Brave Men,* pp. 241–42.

57. Gray, pp. 47, 62.

58. Miles, pp. 57–58, 106. The poetry quote is from a reminiscence by Louis Forster, John Hopkins University class of '41, and was at http://www.alumni.jhu.edu/memories .html but has since been removed.

59. Miles, pp. 103–10, 281–82; "Captain Miles Fell Leading His Company," *NYAmer,* Oct 15, 1918, p. 4.

60. Pippin, "Autobiography," pp. 47–51; Little, chap. 39.

61. Pyle, *Here Is Your War,* pp. 247–48; Gray, p. 124.

62. U.S. American Battle Monuments Commission, *American Armies and Battlefields,* pp. 104, 369.

63. Miles, p. 95; Lomax, p. 559. The 77th appears to have been the only American division so honored.

7: Home Fires Burning

1. Wilson, *Political Thought,* p. 343; Millis, p. 454.

2. Peterson and Fite, pp. 11, 14–18, 195; Kennedy, pp. 46, 49, 54–55, 67, 75; Harries, pp. 282–83; Cooper, pp. 308, 322–23; Peterson and Fite, pp. 14–18; Robert K. Murray, *Red Scare,* p. 13; Stéphane Audoin-Rouzeau and Annette Becker, *14–18,* pp. 151ff.

3. Arthur Guy Empey, "Our Real Enemy," *McClure's,* July 1918, pp. 21, 46.

4. Peterson and Fite, p. 149; Frederick Tupper, "The Awful German Language," *Nation*, Sept. 7, 1918, pp. 248–50.

5. Roosevelt, *Writings*, p. 376; *America in the World War*, pp. 223, 225; Gerstle, pp. 46–59; Millis, p. 70; Osborn quoted in Chase, *Legacy of Malthus*, p. 185. H. L. Mencken noted the irony that Roosevelt was forced to condemn "militarism . . . in terms of militarism," and arraign "the Kaiser . . . in unmistakably *kaiserliche* tones." H. L. Mencken, *Mencken Chrestomathy*, p. 236.

6. Harries, pp. 294–96; Cobb, "Thrice Is He Armed," *SEP*, Apr. 21, 1917, pp. 7, 133–37; Cobb, "The Prussian Paranoia," *SEP*, May 5, 1917, pp. 3–4. For the supposed Asiatic or "Khazar" ancestry of eastern European Jews see Chase, p. 359, and Bendersky, pp. 41–43, 406–8. Poster, "Destroy This Mad Brute," http://www.examinghistory.tripod .com/id8.html/; line-cut version in Ross, *Propaganda*, frontispiece; Harding, "He Shall Not Pass" in "Cartoons of the Week," *Outlook*, June 19, 1918, p. 303.

7. Peterson and Fite, chaps. 18 and 23.

8. William Hard, "Traitors," *NR*, Nov. 24, 1917; Alvin Johnson, "To a Slacker," *NR*, May 4, 1918, pp. 18–19; Roosevelt, *Foes*, p. xxv; "La Follette Is Hun's Ghost Dancer," *NYTrib*, Oct. 1, 1917, p. 7; "Four I.W.W. Heads / Seized in Raid," *NYW*, Oct. 1, 1917, pp. 1, 2, and "Russian Pendulum," p. 3; "The Shadow Huns," *NYS*, Oct. 2, 1917, p. 14; "The Hun Within Our Gates," *NYS*, Oct. 4, 1917, p. 14; "Says Liberty Rail Cures Seditionists," *NYS*, May 17, 1918, p. 7; *NYTrib*, Oct. 28, 1917, III:3. On Lafollette and Hearst see Nasaw, pp. 268, 630; Peterson and Fite, pp. 69–71.

9. Roosevelt, *Kansas City Star*, pp. 177, 180–81, 221–23.

10. Roosevelt's enthusiasm for vigilantism is a by-product of his preference for a racially homogeneous society, in which law is needless because all men act on the same instinctive moral principles. See Peggy and Harold Samuels, *Teddy Roosevelt at San Juan*, p. 59; R. M. Brown, *Strain of Violence*; Slotkin, *Gunfighter*, chap. 5; and Slotkin, "Equalizers."

11. Peterson and Fite, pp. 8–9, 56–67; Kennedy, p. 73. Roosevelt, "Bolshevism and Applied Anti-Bolshevism," *Outlook*, Sept. 18, 1918, pp. 92–93; and *Kansas City Star*, p. 215. The IWW was considered the most radical antiwar organization, but its official position was nonresistant, and 95 percent of members registered for the draft. Dubofsky, *We Shall Be All*, pp. 356–71, 380–91, 410.

12. Peterson and Fite, p. 18; "Mob Violence and War Psychology," *NR*, Aug. 3, 1918, pp. 5–7. Zane Grey, the popular writer of pulp westerns, treated the IWW's class war as a species of race war in the novel *Desert of Wheat*. See Slotkin, *Gunfighter*, pp. 216–17.

13. Hawley, p. 79; Murray, chap. 3; Peterson and Fite, pp. 9, 18–19, 142; "Fighting Germany's Spies: The American Protective League," *WW*, Aug. 1918, pp. 393–401; Kennedy, pp. 81–82; *LD*, June 9, 1917, p. 1765; Emerson Hough, *The Web*.

14. Peterson and Fite, pp. 141, 212, 216–20; Dubofsky, *We Shall*, pp. 393–94; Murray, p. 13; Kennedy, pp. 78, 80–83; *LD*, Apr. 20, 1918, pp. 16–17.

15. *NR*, Sept. 8, 1917, pp. 194, 207; Brown, *Strain*, pp. 126–27; Peterson and Fite, pp. 14, 81; Roosevelt, *Foes*, p. xxv.

16. William D. Miller, *Pretty Bubbles in the Air*, p. 14; Empey, "Our Real Enemy," *McClure's*, July 1918, pp. 21, 46.

17. Peterson and Fite, pp. 14, 26–27, 31–36, 40–48, 64, 83–86, 143, 149–55, 170–74, 199–204.

18. Alfred M. Brooks, *Converted and Secret Americans*, National Security League no. 30, pp. 2–8.

19. Roosevelt, quoted in Gregor Dallas, *1918: War and Peace*, pp. 85–86 ; Roosevelt, "Bolshevism and Applied Anti-Bolshevism," *Outlook*, Sept. 1918, pp. 92–93; and *Kansas City Star*, p. 215. For TR's response to racial lynchings see Sinkler, p. 432; Dyer, pp. 110–17; Slotkin, *Gunfighter*, p. 185.

20. Judge Charles F. Amidon, "A Judicial Definition of Allegiance," *Outlook*, Sept. 1918, pp. 88, 90.

21. Clarence Stone Yoakum and Robert M.Yerkes, *Army Mental Tests*, pp.viii–xi, 12; Chase, *Legacy*, pp.232–35, 241–52; Dr. Frederick Peterson, "The Reconstruction of the Race," *LD*, Oct. 12, 1918, pp.20–21.

22. Spencer quoted in Cornebise, p.135.

23. Harries, pp.301–8; Peterson and Fite, pp.28, 73–74; "Education in Americanism" series, "Columbus Day," *LD*, Oct. 12, 1918, p.32.

24. Kennedy, pp.53, 60, 69; Ford, pp.270–90; Lillian Faderman, "Social House-keeping Becomes a Profession: Frances Kellor," in *To Believe in Women*; Frances Kellor, *Straight America: A Call to National Service* and *Immigration and the Future*.

25. Peterson and Fite, pp.159, 165–66; A.A. Roback, "Yiddish Books and Their Readers," *Nation*, Sept. 12, 1918, pp.408–9, 412; David Philipson, "The American Jew," *Nation*, Nov. 2, 1918, p.517; Roback, "The Jews and Yiddish," *Nation*, Dec. 21, 1918, p.774.

26. "New York's Own Division," *NYT*, July 1, 1918, p.10; "Kavanagh Killed 8 in Bayonet Duels," *NYS*, Sept. 4, 1918, p.3; "Belvedere Brooks Killed Near Fismes," *NYT*, Sept. 4, 1918, p.4; "New York Boys Win Honors on Vesle," *NYS*, Sept. 6, 1918, p.2; "New Yorkers Lead Chase from Vesle," *NYS*, Sept. 7, 1918, p.2; "Yankees Make Brilliant Coup," *NYS*, Sept. 8, 1918, p.1.

27. Sinkler, p.125.

28. "Billion Fund to Help Jews," *NYAmer*, Oct. 18, 1918, p.9; Slobin, pp.138–39, 141.

29. Walter White, *Rope and Faggot*; Peterson and Fite, p.200; NAACP, pp.19, 26–27, 30; Lewis, *DuBois*, p.579; United States Congress, *Congressional Record, 67th Cong., 2nd sess.*, p.787; Peterson and Fite, chap. 8; Harries, p.296; Wilson quoted in "Why the Negro Appeals to Violence," *LD*, Aug. 9, 1919, p.11.

30. *NYT*, July 21, 1918, p.1; "Back from Trenches," *Age*, Aug. 17, 1918, p.1.

31. "Member of Old Fifteenth Wins French Cross of War," *Age*, Aug. 31, 1918, p.1.

32. "A New Meaning for an Old Term," and J.W. Johnson, "Irvin Cobb on the Negro Soldiers," *Age*, Aug. 31, 1918, p.4.

33. "Sedition," *Outlook*, May 1, 1918, pp.10–11; "Lynching," *Outlook*, June 5, 1918, pp.214–16. A related article by William Miller of Hampton Institute assured readers that "the Negro at heart loves the South," would stay if treated fairly and allowed to "make a decent living." The *Outlook* also published a series by Tuskegee's Robert Moton on Negro contributions to the war, as soldiers, workers, and subscribers to the Liberty Loan: "Negroes Under War Conditions," *Outlook*, June 26, 1918, pp.334–36; Robert R. Moton and Kate M. Herring, "The Patriotism of the Negro Citizen," *Outlook*, Nov. 20, 1918, pp.452–53; "The Mob Spirit and Lynching," *Outlook*, Aug. 7, 1918, p.542.

34. Buckley, p.184; "Old Fifteenth to Be Seen on Screen,"*Age*, Aug. 3, 1918, p.1; J.W. Johnson, "Why the Negro Should Fight," *Age*, Aug. 3, 1918, p.4; Walton, "The Colored Soldier on the Screen," *Age*, Aug. 24, 1918, p.5; Walton, "Democracy at Spartanburg, S.C.," *Age*, Aug. 10, 1918, p.5; "Wasted Fighting Spirit," *NYW*, Oct 14, 1918, p.10; "Germany 'Offers' Peace to the Ku-Klux Kaiser's Enemies," *NYH*, Oct. 12, 1918, I:12.

35. Lewis, *DuBois*, pp.543–44, 552–56.

36. Buckley, pp.178–79.

37. See Mark Ellis, *Race, War, and Surveillance*; Peterson and Fite, p. 90; Harries, pp.283–84; J. Anderson, *A. Philip Randolph*, pp.87–92, 98–110.

38. Lewis, *DuBois*, pp.552–60; Bendersky, pp.54, 62–64.

8: *"Tout le Monde à la Bataille!"*

1. Keegan, p.409; S.L.A. Marshall, pp.423–44. My account of the Meuse-Argonne campaign is based primarily on Paul F. Braim, *Test of Battle*, pp.50, 67–68, 81–85, 93, 123, 164–66, 187. See also Harries, pp.331–35, 349–51; Stallings, pp.125–26, 225.

2. Ralph E. John, "A Personal Memory," Longwood Web site; Nell, pp. 61–63.

3. Johnson and Pratt, pp. 24, 39, 45, 146–47; O'Hara Smith, " 'Chief Lo' Was with the 'Lost Battalion' in France," *American Indian*, Nov. 1926, p. 9; Peterson and Fite, pp. 53–56; Dubofsky, *We Shall*, pp. 366–75.

4. Miles, p. 120; Demaree, p. 69; Johnson and Pratt, pp. 24, 147; Braim, pp. 111–12; Nell, p. 69; John, "A Personal Memory."

5. Braim, p. 90; Johnson and Pratt, p. 272; Pippin, "Autobiography," p. 10.

6. Miles, pp. 117–18, 137–38, 318.

7. Johnson and Pratt, pp. 130–31; "As We Know Them: The Major," *NYTrib*, May 12, 1918, V:1.

8. Miles, pp. 120–21, 139.

9. Barbeau and Henri, p. 128; Badger, pp. 175, 191; Coffman, p. 231; J. W. Johnson, *Black Manhattan*, pp. 244–45; Barbeau and Henri, pp. 114–15; Buckley, p. 163.

10. Barbeau and Henri, pp. 133, 136.

11. Barbeau and Henri, pp. 79–81, 133; Heywood, pp. 3–5, 9; Mason and Furr, pp. 9–10, 19.

12. Buckley, p. 187; William S. Bradden, *Under Three Banners*, pp. 113–14, 125–26, 182, 185; Barbeau and Henri, p. 123; Marvin, "Report on the 370th Infantry (Colored) Brigade in 73rd Division (French)," June 14, 1918, in Historical Section, Army War College, "The Colored Soldier in the United States Army," 1942. Appendix 16, World War, AGO, GHQ, AEF G-1, C-9, D-2, File 211.39, Folder 63, p. 53, AMHI.

13. Buckley, p. 189; T. A. Roberts to Col. Fox Connor, in Historical Section, Army War College, "The Colored Soldier in the United States Army," GHQ, G-3, GHQ, 590, pp. 54–55, AMHI. See Bradden's response to Charles Lynde, "Mobilizing Rastus," in the *Outlook*, above, chap. 5, fn. 23; Bradden, pp. 125–27.

14. Mason and Furr, pp. 20, 22, 26, 43–44, 75–76, 99–102; Barbeau and Henri, pp. 80, 100–2, 109, 128–29.

15. Nalty, *Strength*, pp. 118–19; Little, p. 252.

16. Bradden, p. 199; "Horace Pippin," in Jessie Carney Smith, ed., *Notable Black American Men*, pp. 941–42.

17. "Col. Hayward Home with his Fighting 15th," *NYH*, Feb. 13, 1918, II:1, 5.

18. S. Harris, pp. 232–37.

19. Coffman, pp. 318–20; Nalty, *Strength*, pp. 113–19; S. Harris, p. 44.

20. Moss quoted in Scott, pp. 194–96. An example of how a competent and well-disposed officer could deal with anti-Black prejudice is in Nell, *Lost Battalion*, pp. 7–8.

21. Charles Williams, p. 21; NA, RG 120, HQ 77th Div, Box 197, decimal file 253, Prisoners; Barbeau and Henri, pp. 58–65, 79–81; Heywood, pp. 3, 5, 9; Mason and Furr, preface, pp. 9–20; Buckley, pp. 178–79; Coffman, p. 72; Nalty, *Strength*, pp. 113–14; Charles Young, letter, *Crisis*, June 1918, p. 58, and letter from General Ballou, p. 62.

22. Mead, p. 76.

23. Braim, p. 80.

24. Nell, pp. 68–69.

25. Miles, pp. 119–20.

26. S. Harris, pp. 240, 245; Little, p. 269.

27. John, "A Personal Memory."

28. Braim, p. 86; Miles, pp. 121–26.

29. Rainsford, p. 167.

30. Ibid., p. 164; Miles, p. 127.

31. Braim, p. 87.

32. U.S. Army War College, *Order of Battle*, pp. 321, 318; Braim, pp. 87, 91–98; Stallings, p. 236; Harries, pp. 357, 363, 368.

33. Rainsford, pp. 158–59.

34. John, "A Personal Memory"; Miles, pp. 123–29; Braim, pp. 111–12.

9: The Last Long Mile

1. Mason and Furr, p. 118; U.S. American Battle Monuments Commission, *93rd Division*, p. 11, and maps.
2. S. Harris, *Hell Fighters*, pp. 244–46; Badger, p. 189; Mason and Furr, p. 118.
3. Pippin, "Autobiography," pp. 51–52; Nalty, *Strength*, p. 119; Morris J. MacGregor Jr., and Bernard C. Nalty, eds., *Blacks in the United States Armed Forces*, vol. 4, pp. 253–55
4. Pippin, "Autobiography," pp. 52–54.
5. S. Harris, pp. 248–49; Little, pp. 270–71, 310–11; Barbeau and Henri, pp. 119–20; Jamieson, p. 35; Braim, p. 101.
6. Pippin, "Autobiography," pp. 54–57.
7. Little, p. 271.
8. Stallings, p. 105; Little, p. 273.
9. S. Harris, pp. 250–51; Little, pp. 272, 281.
10. Braim, pp. 98, 159–60.
11. Gray, p. 50.
12. Rainsford, chap. 9; Braim, p. 104; Stallings, p. 126.
13. Coffman, pp. 315–17; U.S. American Battle Monuments Commission, *92nd Division*, pp. 12–19.
14. Miles, pp. 131–32, Demaree, pp. 7, 63, 70.
15. Arthur McKeogh, *Victorious 77th Division*, pp. 4–6.
16. The account of the action at L'Homme Mort is from Miles, pp. 133–39.
17. Miles, p. 291; McKeogh, " 'The Lost Battalion,' " *Collier's*, Nov. 16, 1918, pp. 5–6, 18–26.
18. Johnson and Pratt, p. 105; Miles, p. 139.
19. The account of the fighting at Sechault is from Little, chap. 41 and S. Harris, chap. 18; U.S. American Battle Monuments Commission, *93rd Division: Summary*, pp. 11–22.
20. "Col. Hayward Home with his Fighting 15th," *NYH*, Feb. 13, 1918, II:1, 5; Nalty, *Strength*, p. 119; Hayward to Commander in Chief, GHQ, Oct. 9, 1918, in MacGregor and Nalty, vol. 4, pp. 253–55.
21. Casualty estimates assume that most of Third Battalion's 550 casualties fell Sept. 26–28, when it led the attack. The regiment went into action with less than 3,000 effectives; and after deducting 400+ for supply and rear echelon assignments I assume the regiment could have taken 2,200–2,500 riflemen into action. Aggregate losses are listed in U.S. American Battle Monuments Commission, *American Armies*, p. 369.
22. Mason and Furr, pp. 122–23; Little, pp. 293–95; Badger, p. 189; Guttman, "Regiment's Pride," pp. 35–41; http:www.snowbizz.com/HWRepublican/George_Robb/georgerobb.htm.
23. Buckley, pp. 208–9; Badger, p. 189; Little, pp. 306–10; S. Harris, *Hell Fighters*, says Clark and Second Battalion were relieved that morning, but I have preferred Little's account, since he was in command at the time.
24. Little, pp. 310–11.

10: The Lost Battalion

1. My account of the action at Charlevaux Mill follows Johnson and Pratt, *Lost Battalion*; Miles, chap. 7; Whittlesey's official report in Hugh A. Drum, "Papers Relating to Lost Battalion, 77th Division," AMHI; and Nelson M. Holderman, " 'The Lost Battalion' 77th Division," U.S. Army War College (1926), NA RG 77th Division AEF, RG 120, decimal file 277–18.2.
2. Miles, pp. 272–78; Hussey, p. 51.
3. Johnson and Pratt, pp. 30–31, 290.

4. Adler, *Seventy-seventh*, pp. 161–62; Stallings, pp. 182, 198–200.

5. Johnson and Pratt, pp. 92–93, identifies this as Gen. Orders 28; Adler, *Seventy-seventh*, p. 169, says same text is Gen. Orders 27; Stallings, p. 278.

6. Ibid., p. 31.

7. Rainsford, chap. 9. The initial strength of Whittlesey's command was probably about 600 men. The Lost Battalion roster in Miles, pp. 270–78 lists only the men who fought the whole battle in the Pocket, of whom 455 are from the 308th. However, that figure excludes the 88 men lost fighting their way into the Pocket and 20–30 men left in the runner-posts. It also excludes 33 men in E Company, who spent one night in the Pocket but were lost outside it, trying to contact Knight's command. In assessing the impact of losses on Whittlesey and the battalion, it makes more sense to consider the casualties suffered by his whole command from the beginning of the action on Oct. 2.

8. Miles, pp. 115, 150; Johnson and Pratt, p. 24; Hussey, pp. 51–52.

9. Rainsford, chap. 9 is the best source for the 307th's attack on Hill 198; Johnson and Pratt, p. 36.

10. Hussey, p. 51; Johnson and Pratt, p. 54.

11. Ibid., pp. 48–49. The possibility for a major tactical breakthrough may have seemed real to Alexander and others on the scene, but Braim, pp. 112, 116, is probably correct in seeing the potential as minimal, because of the terrain and the 77th's lack of reserves. However, our concern is not with the tactical reality, but with Alexander's belief (and insistence) that a breakthrough was expected.

12. Johnson and Pratt, pp. 49–52, 106.

13. Miles, pp. 140–41.

14. Johnson and Pratt, pp. 70–74.

15. Drum, p. 73; Hussey, pp. 51–52; Johnson and Pratt, p. 79.

16. Ibid., pp. 90–96; Ralph John, "Personal Memory."

17. Johnson and Pratt, p. 103.

18. Ibid., pp. 113–15.

19. http://www.us-israel.org/jsource/biography/kaufman.html; Miles, p. 143.

20. Johnson and Pratt, p. 125; Robert Manson, "Through Six Days of Heroism with the 'Lost Battalion,' " *LD*, Mar. 29, 1919, pp. 46–47.

21. Johnson and Pratt, pp. 78–79, 139–40, 147, 160; Miles, p. 160.

22. Ralph John, "Personal Memory"; Johnson and Pratt, p. 183.

23. Ibid., pp. 178–80; Rainsford, chap. 10; Stallings, p. 274; Damon Runyon, "Eddie Grant Died Leading His Battalion," *NYAmer*, Oct. 23, 1918, p. 3.

24. Hussey, p. 56; Johnson and Pratt, p. 276.

25. Ibid., p. 189. Rainsford, pp. 223–24, thought that the Germans held their lines longer in hopes of wiping out or capturing the Lost Battalion.

26. Werstein, pp. 131–32; Johnson and Pratt, pp. 182, 208, 309; Emmet Crozier, *American Reporters on the Western Front*, pp. 254–55; *NYH*, Oct. 3, 1918, pp. 1, 4.

27. Johnson and Pratt, pp. 126, 298, 303, 144, which cites a total of 1,003 casualties for the whole regiment in fighting related to Charlevaux Mill. Of these, 237 were in Whittlesey's command. The forces attempting to relieve Whittlesey lost 450 men on Oct. 4–6, and 315 on Oct. 7—the equivalent of a battalion.

28. Johnson and Pratt, p. 268; Drum, "Reports," pp. 82–84, 89.

29. Johnson and Pratt, pp. 74, 130–32.

30. Lost Battalion Reunion Newsletter, no. 4, p. 2; Johnson and Pratt, p. vii; "Col. Whittlesey," *NYT*, Nov. 30, 1921, p. 5.

31. Johnson and Pratt, p. 210; Miles spells the name "Revnis."

32. Johnson and Pratt, p. 216; Adler, *Seventy-seventh*, p. 121.

33. Johnson and Pratt, p. 223; Krotoshinsky, "How the Lost Battalion Was Saved," *Jewish Veteran*, pp. 5–6; "Krotoshinsky, 60 / World War I Hero," *NYT* obituary, Nov. 5, 1953, p. 31. The name is spelled various ways in newspaper accounts and Adler's divisional history: Kretoshinsky, Kratoshinsky, Kretoshchinsky, etc.

34. Johnson and Pratt, pp. 231–32. Miles says he was killed repelling the next German assault.

35. Johnson and Pratt, pp. 244, 283; see the entries for these men in "Decorations and Citations," Miles, pp. 279ff.

36. Johnson and Pratt, pp. 245, 313.

37. Krotoshinsky, p. 6; Johnson and Pratt, pp. 250–51.

38. Miles, pp. 142–43.

39. Ibid., p. 253.

40. Krotoshinsky, p. 6. Johnson and Pratt do not mention the use of gas against the Pocket, but Krotoshinsky may have inhaled gas lingering close to the ground from earlier fighting.

41. John, "Personal Memory"; Johnson and Pratt, pp. 256, 285, 308; Thomason, p. 58.

42. Pratt and Johnson, p. 308. To assess the real losses of the command, we need to consider the total numbers engaged. The initial strength of Whittlesey's command on Oct. 2 was 575 (see note 7 above); and 99 were added when Company K of the 307th reached the Pocket on Oct. 3, for a total strength of 674. Of these, 194 were able to walk out of the Pocket, though some were so debilitated as to be useless for further combat. Add to this total Lt. Wilhelm and the four men who made it through the lines with him, and the total of ambulatory survivors reaches 199. By this tabulation Whittlesey's command lost 574 dead, wounded, or captured, a 70 percent casualty rate. Miles's estimate for the rest of the 308th during this period is 766 casualties, excluding those with Whittlesey, perhaps 40 percent of its infantry strength. Like the 369th, the 308th was destroyed as a combat command while winning its greatest victory. For the remaining month of the war the 308th would be "less actively engaged" than the rest of the Division.

43. Ernie Pyle, *Here Is Your War*, p. 248; Gray, p. 124; Tobin, p. 113.

11: Print the Legend

1. Johnson and Pratt, pp. 262–80; Runyon, "Runyon Sees Return of Lost New York Battalion," *NYAmer*, Oct. 13, 1918, p. 3; Drum, pp. 12, 24, 34, 46, 56, 73–74, 79, 85; Johnson and Pratt, pp. 276–77.

2. Miles, chap. 8, esp. pp. 173–75; Stallings, p. 330; Lincoln Eyre, "St. Juvin," *NYW*, Oct. 18, 1918, p. 1.

3. Johnson and Pratt, pp. 264–68; "Son of Actor Harrigan on Wounded List," *NYAmer*, Oct. 13, 1918, p. 4. Doubts about Whittlesey's performance were reinforced by the court of inquiry held to look into Lt. Revnes's suggestion that Whittlesey open negotiations with the enemy. Revnes's defense criticized the conduct of the engagement, and Whittlesey was not present to defend himself.

4. Roosevelt, *Kansas City Star*, pp. 189–93, 226–27.

5. "Americans Clearing the Argonne Forest," *NYT*, Oct. 1, 1918, pp. 1, 6; "Yanks Advance Despite Bitter Hun Attacks," *NYTrib*, Oct. 1, 1918, p. 1; "Argonne Forest Battle Is Like a Duel in a Dark Room," *NYTrib*, Oct. 1, 1918, p. 9; "Upton Men in Hard Test," *NYT*, Oct. 3, 1918, pp. 1, 2; Edwin James, "Americans Clearing the Argonne Forest," *NYT* Oct. 1, 1918, pp. 1, 6; and "Foe Quits On Our Front," *NYT*, Oct. 3, 1918, pp. 1, 2. See also *NYAmer*, Oct. 1, 1918, p. 3.

6. Don Martin, "New York Troops Are Fighting in Argonne Jungle," *NYH*, Oct. 2, 1918, pp. 1–2; "New York Boys Describe Bitter Argonne Fighting," *NYH*, Oct. 3, 1918, p. 1; and "Desperate Fighting by Whittlesey Unit," *NYH*, Oct. 3, 1918, p. 4. Other papers similarly contrasted the loyalty of U.S. hyphenates with the treachery of Germans and pro-Germans. "New York Troops Take Big Toll of Treacherous Hun," *NYH*, Oct. 8, 1918, p. 4; "New York Men Slay Garrison," *NYAmer*, Oct. 4, 1918, p. 1, and "Our Troops on Dead Man's Hill Shelled," p. 4 (a reference to L'Homme Mort); "Canada Joins Attack

Upon Democracy's Internal Enemy," *NYAmer*, Oct. 3, 1918, p. 18; "German Blood No Bar to Our Men at the Front . . . Fighting Qualities of Adopted Sons Proved Time and Again," *NYAmer*, Oct. 5, 1918, p. 4-L; "Pvt Isaac Hotgard," *NYAmer*, Oct. 1, 1918, p. 4.

7. Editorial tribute to Martin, *NYH*, Oct. 8, 1918, p. 12. "New Yorkers Hack Way Into Forest of Wire," *NYTrib*, Oct. 4, 1918, pp. 1, 3; "New York Troops Take Big Toll of Treacherous Hun," *NYH*, Oct. 8, 1918, p. 4.

8. James, "Americans Rescued from Enemy Trap," *NYT*, Oct. 9, 1918, p. 8; "Rescue U.S. Troops Lost for Five Days in Argonne Forest," *NYH*, Oct. 9, 1918, pp. 1, 3; "Battalion, Cut Off in Woods, Rescued," *NYW*, Oct. 9, 1918, p. 1; "Americans Exhausted After Four-Day Siege," *NYT*, Oct. 10, 1918, p. 2; " 'Lost Unit' Lived on Leaves," *NYTrib*, Oct. 10, 1918, p. 2; "American Battalion, Lost 5 Days, Rescued," *NY Amer*, Oct. 9, 1918, p. 1. The priority given to initial notices of Charlevaux Mill meant that the first reports about the Pocket overlapped with older stories about L'Homme Mort. Since all of the commanders and units were identical, and since the "hook" for the story was the same, it was easy for reporters, editors, and readers to blend the two. Johnson and Pratt, pp. 182, 208, 265; Werstein, pp. 131–32; James, "Americans Break Through the Kriemhilde Line," *NYT*, Oct. 5, 1918, p. 1; "Furious Fighting," *NYT*, Oct. 6, 1918, pp. 1, 4; "New York Men Slay Garrison," *NYAmer*, Oct. 4, 1918, p. 1, and "Our Troops on Dead Man's Hill Shelled," p. 4. The confusion was reinforced by an odd coincidence. Arthur McKeogh had been recalled to the States for duty as a press officer, after his daring sneak through enemy lines from L'Homme Mort. He arrived in New York as the Lost Battalion story was breaking, and accounts of his adventures were inevitably (though erroneously) attached to the Lost Battalion. McKeogh tried to straighten out the confusion, to no avail: even the subtitle given to his own article in *Collier's* identified his story with " 'The Lost Battalion.' " "Daring M'Keogh Saved Battalion Foe Surrounded," *NYW*, Oct. 17, 1918, p. 3; Miles, pp. 134–35; McKeogh, " 'The Lost Battalion,' " pp. 5–6, 18–26.

9. "Battalion Lost in Argonne Was Exhausted, Now Happy," *NYW*, Oct. 10, 1918, p. 3, and "The Lost Battalion," p. 12.

10. Runyon, "Runyon Sees Return of Lost New York Battalion," *NYAmer*, Oct. 13, 1918, p. 3; " 'Three Weeks in Hell,' Says Runyon of Argonne Fight," *NYAmer*, Oct. 20, 1918, p. 3; "Eddie Grant Died Leading His Battalion," *NYAmer*, Oct. 23, 1918, p. 3; "Notable New Yorkers at 'Old Home Week' in Argonne Reviewed by Damon Runyon," *NYAmer*, Oct. 16, 1918, p. 3; "Our Gunners, Fit and Cheery, Fight," *NYAmer*, Oct. 19, 1918, p. 2.

11. Reprinted in AJC, *War Record*, pp. 39–40; "The Yiddish Division," *AH*, Oct. 18, 1918, p. 610; "The Yiddish Battalion," *AH*, Oct. 25, 1918, p. 630.

12. "The Private from the Bronx," *NYT*, Dec. 19, 1918, p. 24; "Krotoshinsky, 60 / World War I Hero," *NYT*, Nov. 5, 1953, p. 31

13. Runyon, "Battalion Lost in Argonne," *NYW*, Oct. 10, 1918, p. 3; " 'Go to Hell,' Replies Major Whittlesey," *NYW*, Oct. 11, 1918, p. 2; " 'Go to Hell!' Lost Battalions [*sic*] Answer to Huns' 'Surrender!' " *NYTrib*, Oct. 11, 1918, p. 2; " 'Go to Hell!' Shouts Major of 'Lost Battalion,' " *NYH*, Oct. 11, 1918, p. 2 ; "Our Men Jeer Foe's Demand To Surrender," *NYAmer*, Oct. 11, 1918, p. 3. Stallings, p. 277, attributes the "Go to hell" story to Runyon. In fact, Runyon is the only reporter who got it right.

14. "Are we growing profane?" *LD*, Oct. 26, 1918, pp. 33–34; "The Gray Man of Christ" and "A Call," *LD*, Nov. 30, 1918, pp. 29–31.

15. Willis J Abbot, [headline missing], *NYAmer*, Oct. 13, 1918, II:4; H. Warner Allen, "Heroic Stand by Americans Makes New War History," *NYH*, Oct. 13, 1918, II:2.

16. Roosevelt, *Kansas City Star*, pp. 229–36; "The Colonel's Fourteen Points and the President's," *NYT*, Oct. 30, 1918, p. 10; Wilson, *Political Thought*, p. 486.

17. L.F.A[bbott], "Making America Safe for Autocracy," *Outlook*, Nov. 6, 1918, pp. 349–50; " 'Fight It Out Now' " Says TR," *NYT*, Oct. 13, 1918, p. 6; "TR Calls Wilson a Partisan," *NYT*, Oct. 26, 1918, p. 2; "Roosevelt Bitter in Beginning War on the

President," *NYT*, Oct. 29, 1918, pp. 1–2; "Look Cross-eyed at Us," *NYT*, Oct. 5, 1918, p. 5; "Hunt Presidential Timber in West," *NYT*, Oct. 13, 1918, p. 6. In contrast see "Roosevelt in Mad Attack Upon Wilson," *NYAmer*, Oct. 29, 1918, p. 3.

18. "Two Who Won Fame in France Get Home," *NYT*, Nov. 15, 1918, p. 24; "Whittlesey to Get Highest Decoration," *NYT*, Dec. 6, 1918, p. 7; "To Decorate Whittlesey," *NYT*, Dec. 24, 1918, p. 8.

19. "Honor Col. Whittlesey," *NYT*, Nov. 22, 1918, p. 11; "Stirring Words Born of the War," *NYT*, Jan. 27, 1919, p. 5.

20. "American Battalion, Lost 5 Days, Rescued," *NYAmer*, Oct. 9, 1918, p. 1; "Battalion Spurned Offer of Safety/"Go to Hell!" Shouted Whittlesey," *NYT*, Oct. 11, 1918, p. 5; "The Lost Battalion," *NYT*, Oct. 12, 1918, p. 12; "General Led Hunt for Lost Battalion," *NYT*, Nov. 10, 1918, II:1.

21. "Says War Broadened Army," *NYT*, Jan. 27, 1919, p. 7; *AH*, Jan. 31, 1919, pp. 293–94; "Are the Jews Responsible for the Russian Revolution?" *AH*, Nov. 29, 1918, p. 71.

22. Burl Noggle, *Into the Twenties*, p. 67; Wynn, p. 203; Murray, pp. 92–93; W. Miller, p. 72; David Montgomery, *Fall of the House of Labor*, pp. 390–94; "Chicago Socialists Cheer Bolsheviki," *NYT*, Nov. 18, 1918, p. 24.

23. "Bolshevism Threatening the World," *LD*, Nov. 23, 1918, pp. 9–12; "Bolshevik Mutterings Here,"*LD*, Dec. 7, 1918, pp. 17–18; "Bolshevism, The End of Civilization," *LD*, Jan. 11, 1919, p. 17, and "American Soldiers Who Cannot Read or Write," pp. 27–28; "Why the Nation Went Dry," *LD*, Jan. 25, 1919, pp. 9–11; "The Danger of Reducing Prices," and "Not Enough Jobs," p. 15.

24. Ratshesky, "Americanization the Cure for Bolshevism," *NYT*, Nov. 24, 1918, pp. 45–46.

25. Bendersky, pp. 50, 54, 62–64, 71.

26. "Declares Terrorism Reigns in Russia," *NYT*, Nov. 11, 1918, p. 4; "Are the Jews Responsible for the Russian Revolution?" *AH*, Nov. 29, 1918, p. 71.

27. U.S. Congress, 66th Cong., 1st sess., Senate, doc. no. 62, *Brewing and Liquor Interests and German and Bolshevik Propaganda* 1:iii–viii, xvi–xvii, 99, 117–18, 568, 616–18, 732–35, 743–44, 756–57; "Why the Nation Went Dry," *LD*, Jan. 25, 1919, pp. 9–11. U.S. Congress, *Brewing and Liquor*, 1:v–viii,

28. U.S. Congress, *Brewing and Liquor*, 1:xxix–xxx; 3:6–8, 11–13, 14, 16–19, 69, and 109ff. For "some of my best friends," see pp. 120 and 141. A posting by Fred R. Shapiro to George Thompson, American Dialect Society, since taken down, offered 1934 as the earliest use. Bendersky, pp. 62–63.

29. U.S. Congress, *Brewing and Liquor*, 3:112,114, 116, 135, 140, 143; Chase, *Legacy*, p. 359 and Bendersky, pp. 41–43, 406–8.

30. U.S. Congress, *Brewing and Liquor*, 3:116, 444.

31. Ibid., pp. 113–15, 127–29, 135–36, 142–43; Bendersky, pp. 63, 137, 141.

32. *AH*, Feb. 22, 1919, pp. 11–12; "East Side Named as Birthplace of Bolshevism," and "Trotzky Regime Installed with New York Fund," *NYH*, Feb. 13, 1919, II:1; "Praise Patriotism of East Side Jews," *NYT*, Feb. 17, 1919, p. 4, but see same page, "Dr. Simons Stands by Senate Words"; Zelda Feinberg, "The East Side Emerges," *AH*, Nov. 15, 1918, p. 36; *AH*, Jan. 17, 1919, pp. 256, 262; *NYT*, Feb. 15, 1919, p. 16; "Stop-Press News," *AH*, Mar. 7, 1919, pp. 397–400; "Jews Point in Pride to Record in War," *NYT*, Feb. 24, 1919, p. 6; "A. J. Sack Corrects Idea that Jews Foster Bolshevism," and "Soviets Composed of 'Riffraff,' Say Senate Witnesses," *NYH*, Feb. 14, 1919, II:3.

33. H. Diner, p. 123; "Tell of Jews' Part in Conduct of the War," *NYT*, Nov. 11, 1918, p. 24; *NYT*, Feb. 15, 1919, p. 16; "Stop-Press News," *AH*, Mar. 7, 1919, pp. 397–400; "Praise Patriotism of East Side Jews," *NYT*, Feb. 17, 1919, p. 4; U.S. Congress, *Brewing and Liquor*, 3:178–79, 181, 268–69, 275, 378–79, 383–86. Articles in AH systematically associate Lost Battalion stories with rebuttals of Simons. See "Week in Review," *AH*, Feb. 19, 1919, pp. 360–61; *LD*, Feb. 22, 1919, pp. 11–13; "Stop-Press News," *AH*, Mar. 7, 1919, pp. 397–400; and Robert Manson, "Through Six Days of

Heroism with the 'Lost Battalion,'" p.411. See in same issue "Lesson of Americanism," *AH*, Jan. 24, 1919, pp.273–74, and Otto Kahn, "When the Tide Turned," pp.274, 281, which contrasts patriotic soldiers with "the slimy brood of the Bolshevik-Socialists, of the Boloists, Caillouxists and pacifists."

34. U.S. Congress, *Brewing and Liquor* 3:381–82; "The Valor of the East Side," *Outlook*, Feb. 19, 1919, p.320; "Jews Point in Pride to Record in War," *NYT*, Feb. 24, 1919, p.6.

35. "Praise Patriotism of East Side Jews" and "Dr. Simons Stands By Senate Words," *NYT*, Feb. 17, 1919, p.4; "Jews from America in the Bolshevik Oligarchy," *LD*, Mar. 1, 1919, p.32; *LD*, Feb. 22, 1919, pp.11–13.

36. "The Homage of American Jews to Our Great Ex-President, Theodore Roosevelt," *AH*, Jan. 3, 1919, pp.232–33, and Irving Liner, "Five Days Yom Kippur in the Argonne," p.251; "Roosevelt and I," *AH*, Jan. 17, 1919, pp.256, 260; "The War Record of American Jews," photo of Krotoshinsky, "The Man Who Brought Aid to the Lost Battalion," p.262.

37. "Theodore Roosevelt—American," *LD*, Jan. 18, 1919, pp.7–9; *LD*, Jan. 25, 1919, pp.46–47, 50, 56; "A Many-Sided Man," *Outlook*, Jan. 22, 1919, p.133.

38. *LD*, Feb. 22, 1919, pp.12–13; Reuben Fink, "Japanese Demands and the Jewish Clause," *AH*, Apr. 4, 1919, p.21; *AH*, Jan. 31, 1919, pp.294–95; "What Japan Asks," *LD*, Mar. 8, 1919, p.22; "Trying to Tame the Bolsheviki" and "President Wilson's Russian Program," *LD*, Feb. 8, 1919, pp.16–17; "British-American Discord," *LD*, Jan. 4, 1919, p.9; "What is back of the bombs?" *LD*, June 14, 1919, pp.9–11.

39. "Our Negro Soldiers," *NYT*, Feb. 12, 191, p.12; "Bring Defiant Reds Here to Deport," *NYT*, Feb. 12, 1919, p.9.

12: "No Man's Land Is Ours"

1. Little, pp.340, 349–54, 358; Barbeau and Henri, pp.166–68; Buckley, pp.164, 219; "Baker Greets Old 15th," *NYT*, Feb. 23, 1919, I:5.

2. "New York and Illinois Fighters Are Cited," *Age*, Feb. 1, 1919, pp.1, 3; Little, pp.358–62; "Fifth Av. Cheers Negro Veterans," *NYT*, Feb. 18, 1919, p.1; "Our Negro Soldiers," *NYT*, Feb. 12, 1919, p.12; Edgerton, pp.102, 104–6.

3. "Fifth Av. Cheers," *NYT*, Feb. 18, 1919, p.6; *NYW*, quoted in Edgerton, pp.105–6; and see "Evolution of a Superior Race," *LD*, Sept. 29, 1917, pp.24–25, and description of Henry Johnson as a mulatto, *LD*, June 15, 1918, pp.43–44; Little, pp.365–66.

4. "Old 15th Regiment Given Rousing Reception," *Age*, Feb. 22, 1919, p.1; and J.W. Johnson, "First Under the Victory Arch," p.3; "Old Fifteenth Regiment Helped Smother Last German Offensive," *Age*, Mar. 15, 1919, p.2.

5. "For Colored Officers," *NYT*, Feb. 26, 1919, p.4; "Would Draw Color Line at Camp Upton," "City Officials Join in Plan to Build Armory for Old 15th," and "N.Y. City Regiment with Colored Officers," *Age*, Mar. 1, 1919, 1; Barbeau and Henri, p.244n35; C. Johnson, p.127.

6. Dray, pp.245, 254–57; NAACP, pp.19, 29–30, 63; Lewis, *DuBois*, p.579; note stories on facing pages, *Age*, Jan. 11, 1919, "The Soul of a Lyncher," p.3, and Ralph W Tyler, "Honor Decorations for 92nd Division," p.4; "Hughes Condemns Lynching," *NYT*, May 6, 1919, p.15; "[Rabbi Wise] Sees the End of Lynching," *NYT*, May 7, 1919; "Launch Movement to Stop Lynching," *Age*, May 10, 1919, p.1, and "Conference on Lynching," J.W. Johnson, "The Fight on Lynching," p.4; *Selected Writings*, 2:30–31.

7. "Restriction of Immigration," *Age*, Feb. 8, 1919, p.3; J.W. Johnson, "One Question of the War Answered," *Age*, Apr. 26, 1919, p.4; "Roosevelt Lauds Our Negro Troops," *NYT*, Nov. 3, 1918, p.12; "The Health of Colored Troops," *LD*, June 14, 1919, p.23; "The Negro Enters the Labor-Union," *LD*, June 28, 1919, p.12; Lewis, *DuBois*, pp.565–66; Buckley, p.228; Scott, pp.17ff.; Edgerton, p.102. There is a

consistent paralleling of stories about the loyalty of Black troops and the disloyalty of immigrants. See for example "Fifth Av. Cheers" and "I.W.W. Beaten," *NYT*, Feb. 18, 1919, p. 1; "City's Negro Fighters Parade 5th Av. Today," *NYT*, Feb. 17, 1919, p. 1, and "Dr. Simons Stands By Senate Words," p. 4; "Col. Hayward Home with his Fighting 15th," *NYAmer*, Feb 13, 1919, II:1, 5, and "East Side Named as Birthplace of Bolshevism" and "Trotzky Regime Installed with New York Fund," II:1; "New York Gives Ovation to Its Black Fighters," and W. B. Wilson, "All Aliens Found Preaching," *NYAmer*, Feb. 18, 1919, pp. 2, 4. For African-American responses see *Age*, Feb. 15, 1919: "Pay Tribute to the Memory of Theodore Roosevelt" and "Old Fifteenth Back in the United States," p. 1; "Return of Our Fighters," p. 4; "[TR] Believed in Negro Leadership," p. 7. See also J. W. Johnson, *Selected*, 2:33.

8. J. W. Johnson, "First Under the Victory Arch," "Colored Military Bands to Delight American Audiences," and "70 Black Devils," *Age*, Feb. 22, 1919, pp. 3, 5; Walton, "92nd Division Made Good," and J. W. Johnson, "The 'Comeback' of Negro Music and Musicians," *Age*, Mar. 22, 1919, pp. 1, 3; Buckley, p. 203; Badger, pp. 204–6; James R. Europe, "A Negro Explains 'Jazz,'" *LD*, Apr. 26, 1919, pp. 28–29; Kimball and Bolcom, pp. 73ff; *NYT*, Feb. 13, 1919, p. 5.

9. "Hayward Returns," "Pay Tribute to the Memory of Theodore Roosevelt," and, "Lighten Your Dark Skin," *Age*, Feb. 15, 1919, pp. 1, 7.

10. "Col. Bill Hayward and His 'Black Watch,'" *LD*, Mar. 8, 1919, p. 59. "Whitman Prepared to Support Hayward," *NYT*, Mar. 24, 1919, p. 6; "Decorated Negro Argues for Civil Service Preference," *NYT*, Mar. 6, 1919, p. 7; *Age*, Feb. 15, 1919, item on movement to buy home for Henry Johnson, p. 2; Buckley, p. 220.

11. Walker H. Jordan, *With "Old Eph,"* p. 11; "New York Negroes Home," *NYAmer*, Feb. 10, 1919, 2:1, 4; "Col. Bill Hayward and His 'Black Watch,'" *LD*, Mar. 8, 1919, p. 59. Compare *NYT Magazine*, Feb. 23, 1919, multipage spread of photographs of the march, and front page of the theater section, which features actor George Marion in blackface.

12. "Some Wartime Humor of the Negro soldier," *LD*, Apr. 12, 1919, p. 88; "Comic Anecdotes," *NYT*, Mar. 23, 1919, p. 74; "These Colored Fighters Never Lost Their Sense of Humor," *LD*, May 10, 1919, pp. 63–64; "Col. Hayward Home with his Fighting 15th," *NYAmer*, Feb. 13, II, pp. 1, 5; "*Croix de Guerre* and Rare Praise for American Negro Troops," *LD*, Jan. 18, 1919, pp. 55–57, 60 (gets regimental number wrong but clearly refers to attack on Sechault); W. Jordan, pp. 11, 29, 48; Adler, *Seventy-seventh*, p. 223. For Black reactions see J. W. Johnson, "Offensive Nicknames," *Age*, Jan. 18, 1919, p. 3; review of Cobb, *Age*, Apr. 5, 1919, p. 4.

13. "Advocates Jim Crowing of Colored Soldier," *Age*, Apr. 26, 1919, p. 1; "Two Nations Honor Heroes of the Old Fifteenth," *Age*, May 3, 1919, p. 1; J. W. Johnson, "Soldiers' Organizations," *Age*, May 24, 1919, p. 4; "The Fight on Lynching" and "Army Qualifications," *Age*, May 10, 1919, p. 4; *Selected* 1:38; William Pencak, *For God and Country*, pp. 68–69; Ellis, *Race, War and Surveillance*, pp. 214, 217ff; Buckley, p. 222; Harries, p. 440.

14. Badger, pp. 213–18; "Jim Europe Killed in Boston Quarrel," *NYT*, May 10, 1919, p. 1; "Lt. James Reese Europe Buried with Honors," *Age*, May 17, 1919, p. 1.

15. "Loss of an American Musician," *NYT*, May 12, 1919, p. 12. I examined every *American* for May and June and found no mention of Europe's death; Runyon, "Dempsey Will Not Draw Color Line," *NYAmer*, May 11, 1919, 2:7. On Hearst's racial attitudes see Lundberg, p. 124.

16. "Lt. James Reese Europe," *Age*, May 17, 1919, pp. 1, 5.

17. W. Miller, pp. 69–70; Murray, pp. 69–73; *LD*, Mar. 8, 1919, pp. 45–50, Mar. 29, 1919, pp. 11–14, 17–18; *NYT*, Mar. 11, 1919, pp. 1–2; "Discover Plot, Nation Wide, to Kill with Bombs," *NYT*, May 1, 1919, p. 1, and similar in all New York dailies; Thompson, *Reformers*, pp. 10–11. Only the *American* considers possibility of agents provocateurs, "Gerber Calls Bombs a Detective Cache," May 1, 1919, p. 2.

18. "Hylan Assails Alien 'Fanatics,'" *NYT*, Apr. 3, 1919, p. 1; "1,700 Police Guard Mooney Meeting," *NYT*, May 2, 1919, p. 1; "1 Dead, Many Hurt in Cleveland Riot,"

p. 3; "Soldiers and Sailors Break Up Meetings," *NYT*, May 2, 1919, p. 3; "May Day in New York," *NR*, May 17, 1919, p. 89; "1,000 Service Men" and "Police Beat Soldiers in May Day Riot," *NYAmer*, May 2, 1919, pp. 1, 7; "Why Terrorism Will Not Thrive on the Soil of Free America," *NYAmer*, May 3, 1919, p. 18; Empey, "Our Real Enemy," *McClure's*, July 1918, pp. 21, 46.

19. Murray, pp. 74–76; "A Division of New Yorkers," *NYAmer*, May 1, 1919, p. 18. "Our Returned Fighters Need an Even Break" and "Nearly 200,000 Jobless in City,"*NYAmer*, May 3, 1919, p. 5; "Soldiers Service Bureau," *NYAmer*, May 2, 1919, p. 13. "The Spirit of the Soldiers," *NYT*, Apr. 2, 1919, p. 10; "Storm of Protest May Save Parade," *NYT*, Apr. 5, 1919, pp. 1, 4; and "The Seventy-Seventh's Parade," p. 14.

20. "Gov. Smith Buys First Loan Note," *NYT*, Apr. 21, 1919, pp. 1, 2; stories from *NYT*, 1919: "'Lost Battalion' Warmly Welcomed," Apr. 29, p. 6; "'Lost Battalion' Unit to Parade for Loan," May 1, p. 4; "Gen. Alexander Makes Plea," May 2, p. 6; "77th Parade in Six Days After Return," Apr. 2, p. 5.

21. Adler, *Seventy-seventh*, pp. 8, 13, 17, 69; "History of the 77th . . . the 'Lost Battalion,' " *NYT Magazine*, May 4, 1919, pp. 3–6, 73–74; "Heartfelt Ovation," *NYT*, May 7, 1919, pp. 1, 5; "77th's Argonne Campaign Unique in Annals of War," *NYAmer*, May 4, 1919, 2:3; "Millions Hail Marching Men of Argonne," *NYAmer*, May 7, 1919, pp. 1, 7; "New York Ready to Pay Homage," *NYAmer*, May 6, 1919, p. 1; Gene Fowler, "The Cosmopolitans March," *NYAmer*, May 7, 1919, p. 1, and "Millions Hail," cont'd p. 7; "Re-Employment and Wages," *NYT*, May 11, 1919, 2:7.

22. "City Today Pays Honor," *NYT*, May 6, 1919, p. 1; "The 77th On Parade," p. 14; Charles Grasty, "Americans Abroad Take Pride," *NYT*, May 5, 1919, p. 6; "Alexander Denies Battalion Was Lost," p. 4; and "77th Will Arrive," p. 5; "Millions Hail," *NYAmer*, May 6, 1919, pp. 1, 7, and "Tribute to 77th Officers," May 7, 1919, p. 6; "A Million Cheer," *NYT*, May 7, 1919, pp. 1, 5; "City Gives Dinner," p. 6, and "Lost Battalion," p. 14; "77th Parade," Picture Section, *NYT*, May 11, 1919, 5:1, 4–5; "Troopship Carries," *NYT*, May 9, 1919, p. 15.

23. "77th Officer Dies," *NYT*, Mar. 27, 1919, p. 4, and "Maj. J. A. Roosevelt Dies," p. 13; "Vanguard of 77th Comes to NY," Mar. 28, 1919, p. 5; Charles W. Whittlesey, "Major Roosevelt," *NYT*, Apr. 6, 1919, 3:1. "Order of the 77th Parade," *NYT*, May 4, 1919, p. 49, lists all on reviewing stands. A database search of *NYT* does not indicate Whittlesey attended any of the dinners, etc., related to the event.

24. Alan Gevinson, ed., *Within Our Gates*, pp. 611–12; "Lost Battalion on Screen," *NYT*, July 3, 1919, p. 15; review of D. W. Griffith's *Broken Blossoms*, *LD*, June 14, 1919, pp. 28–29. Clips can be seen at http://homestead.com/prositesjohnrcotter/lost_battalion.html. In addition to Adler's division history, unit histories by Tiebout, Demaree, Hussey, and Flynn appeared in 1919, and Rainsford in 1920. Among the odd follow-ups was a spate of stories about Cher Ami. See for example "Wounded Hero Birds," *NYT*, May 25, 1919, p. 7 and "Lost Battalion Pigeon," May 28, 1919, p. 7.

25. "Say 27th Men Need Jobs," *NYT*, Mar. 28, 1919, p. 5; "77th Division Club Plans to Buy Home," *NYT*, July 27, 1919, p. 1; "Justice for Returning Soldiers," *LD*, Jan. 18, 1919, pp. 10–11; "Still Withholding Soldiers' Pay," *LD*, May 10, 1919, p. 78.

26. "Plans for a Jewish Welcome," *AH*, May 2, 1919, p. 25; "Jobs for the Men," *AH*, May 2, 1919, p. 25; *NYT*, Apr. 2, 1919, p. 5; Reuben Fink, "Possibilities of Immigration Restriction" and "Again the Immigration Problem," *AH*, Apr. 18, 1919, p. 611, Kaufman's MOH award, p. 620, and "Liberty Division Returns in Triumph," p. 659; "To Our Boys in the 77th," *AH*, May 2, 1919, p. 654; "Praise Jewish Boys Who Served in War," *NYT*, May 19, 1919, p. 32; Louis Popkin, "The 'Melting Pot' Division, A National Ideal," *AH*, Apr. 11, 1919, pp. 520–21, 603, "How They Fought—and Died," p. 524, and "Melting Pot Division," p. 572.

27. "A Methodist Tribute to the Jew," *LD*, Apr. 19, 1919, p. 32; Popkin, "'Melting Pot' Division," p. 520. Compare George Creel, "How we abused the loyalty of our 'Foreign-Born,' " *LD*, Mar. 8, 1919, pp. 92, 94, 96. Creel laments the mistreatment of hyphenates, but omits Jews from his list of nationalities improperly singled out for persecution.

28. "The Melting-Pot Division," *LD*, May 24, 1919, pp. 70, 74, 89–90; M. Glass, "Potash and Perlmutter at the Peace Conference," *NYAmer*, May 4, 1919, p. 10. Contrast statements by Adler and Lehman in "Praise Jewish Boys," *NYT*, May 19, 1919, p. 32.

29. Edward Harrigan, "City Boys as Soldiers," *NYT Magazine*, May 4, 1919, p. 82; *AH*, Jan. 31, 1919, pp. 293–94. McKeogh, " 'Lost Battalion,' " pp. 5–6, 18–26, praises Herschkowitz as a "shrewd little Jewish-German" who tried to "bargain [the Germans], as it were, into a surrender."

30. Pvt. H. L. Sternfeld, "When the Jewish Doughboy Returns," *AH*, Feb. 7, 1919, p. 320; "Week in Review," *AH*, May 2, 1919, p. 653; Joel Blau, "4 Minute Talks: The Hammerers" and "Are the Jews Responsible for the Russian Revolution?" *AH*, Nov. 29, 1918, p. 71. Isidore Singer, "The God of the Trenches," *AH*, Dec. 6, 1918, p. 90, recommends Winthrop Talbott, *Principles of Americanism*, which represents Jews as a "race" especially adapted for Americanization.

31. "Soviet of Brawlers," *AH*, May 9, 1919, p. 681; E. Lieberman, "In the Day's Work," *AH*, Nov. 15, 1918, pp. 29ff.; I. Kaufman, "Private Silverman," *AH*, May 2, 1919, pp. 670–71, 677, 680; and Zelda Feinberg, "The East Side Emerges," p. 27.

32. Herman Galvin and Stan Tamarkin, *Yiddish Dictionary Sourcebook*, pp. 305ff; and see *AH*, Feb. 14, 1919, pp. 338–39.

33. Harrigan, "City Boys as Soldiers," p. 82; see also *NYT Magazine*, May 4, 1919, pp. 6–7; Breitgam quoted in "Melting Pot Division," *LD*, May 24, 1919, p. 89; Singer, "God of the Trenches," *AH*, Dec. 6, 1918, p. 125.

34. William McAndrew, "Americanism at Its Source," *LD*, May 17, 1919, pp. 36, 113–21; "Aliens Leaving Our Shores," *LD*, June 26, 1919, pp. 96–99; "To Clap the Lid on the Melting-Pot," *LD*, July 5, 1919, pp. 28–29; "Millions of War-Weary Europeans," *LD*, May 24, 1919, pp. 66, 70; "Are there 'fighting races'?" *LD*, May 17, 1919, pp. 122–25, 127. Compare Overman Subcommittee report, issued May 28, which sees Bolshevism as a reversal of evolution, U.S. Congress, *Brewing and Liquor*, 1:xli, xlvi–xlviii, 36.

35. "Soviet of Brawlers," *AH*, May 9, 1919, p. 681; H. Diner, chaps. 2–3, esp. p. 151; "Jewish Pogroms," *Messenger*, July, 5, 1919, p. 6; Ellis, p. 197.

36. Herbert Bailey, "The Real Story of the 'Lost Battalion,' " *WPost*, Nov. 2, 1919, p. AU6; compare "Restriction of Immigration," *Age*, Feb. 8, 1919, p. 3; J. W. Johnson, "One Question of the War Answered," *Age*, Apr. 26, 1919, p. 4.

13: The Black and the Red

1. This analysis of the postwar transition is based on: Kennedy, pp. 248–49; Noggle, pp. 8–9, 37, 50–53, 67, 200; Wynn, pp. 197–203; Murray, pp. 34–38, 43, 48, 73, 78–81, 106–12; Montgomery, pp. 388–94; "After Our Civil War and After the World War," *LD*, June 26, 1919, pp. 98–99; "Labor's Bill of Rights," *LD*, May 24, 1919, pp. 13–15; "Labor's Voice at the Peace Table," *LD*, Feb. 8, 1919, pp. 11–13; "Moral Gains and Losses of the War," *LD*, Jan. 11, 1919, p. 29; "What is back of the bombs?" *LD*, June 14, 1919, pp. 9–11; "Meaning of the Western Strikes," *LD*, Mar. 1, 1919, pp. 14–15; *Outlook*, July 31, 1918, pp. 508–10.

2. Jennifer D. Keene, *Doughboys, the Great War, and the Remaking of America*, p. 165; Thomas A. Rumer, *American Legion*, pp. 44–45; "American Soldiers Who Cannot Read or Write," *LD*, Jan. 11, 1919, pp. 27–28.

3. The American Legion was the only organization open to anyone who had served in uniform. Veterans of Foreign Wars required overseas service; Disabled War Veterans was condition-limited; "Military Order of the World War" was for officers; Jewish and Catholic War Veterans were faith-based. Its original competitor, "Comrades in Service," was sponsored by Wilson and Pershing and operated under the auspices of the military chaplains and the CTCA, but disbanded after accusations Wilson was using it for political ends. Rumer, pp. 9–10. 22, 34, 44–45, 52–55; Pencak, pp. 49–53.

4. Pencak, pp. 13, 39, 51–59, 61, 69.

5. Rumer, pp. 41, 53, 56, 60–64, 77; Pencak, pp. 83, 173, 177; Theda Skocpol, *Protecting Soldiers and Mothers*, pp. 272–78; "Still Withholding Soldiers' Pay," *LD*, May 10, 1919, p. 78; "Justice for Returning Soldiers," *LD*, Jan. 18, 1919, pp. 10–11; "Soldiers Who Return," *LD*, May 31, 1919, pp. 50–51.

6. NAACP, p. 29; Rep. Dyer cites 83 in 1919, U.S. Congress, *Congressional Record*, 67th Cong., 2nd sess., 1919, p. 787. "Federation of Labor Wipes Out the Color Line," *Age*, June 21, 1919, p. 1, and J. W. Johnson, "A New Emancipation," p. 4; "Economic Opportunity for the Negro," *Age*, June 28, 1919, p. 4; *Selected*, 2:30–31, 33–34; "The Negro Enters the Labor Union," *LD*, June 28, 1919, p. 61; DuBois, "An Essay . . . the Black Man in the Great War," *Crisis*, June 1919, pp. 63–87; *Crisis*, July 1919, pp. 127–30.

7. Dray, chap. 8; Shapiro, *White Violence, Black Response*, chap. 8.

8. "Service Men Beat Negroes," *NYT*, July 21, 1919, p. 1; "Race Riot at Capital," "Our Own Subject Race," and "Mob Law at Capital," *Age*, July 26, 1919, pp. 1, 4 (emphasis added), and Claude McKay, "If We Must Die," p. 4; William M. Tuttle Jr., *Race Riot*, pp. 22–29, 216.

9. "4 Dead, 5 Dying," *NYT*, July 22, 1919, pp. 1, 2; "Negroes Again Riot," *NYT*, July 23, 1919, p. 1, and "Race War in Washington," p. 8.

10. "Race Riots," *NYT*, July 28, 1919, p. 10; "Negroes Storm Armory," *NYT*, July 29, 1919, p. 1. The best analysis of the riot is Tuttle, pp. 8–10, 15, 33, 49, 55, 61, 64, 112–19, 121, 209–10; also Buckley, p. 224.

11. "Radicals Inciting Negroes to Violence," *NYT*, Aug. 4, 1919, p. 1.

12. Robert T. Kerlin, *Voice of the Negro 1919*, pp. 1, 15–19, 23, 77; "Chicago Is in the Grip," "Negroes of Washington," and "The Press on Race Wars," *Age*, Aug. 2, 1919, pp. 1, 4; J. W. Johnson, *Selected*, vol. 1. p. 70; "More of the Fruits of Lawlessness," *Age*, Sept. 6, p. 4; "The IWW Bogy in Congress," *Age*, Aug. 30, 1919, p. 4; "Psychology of the Present Racial Situation," *Age*, Aug. 2, 1919, p. 1; also notes " 'Red Caps' Join American Federation of Labor," mentions Henry Johnson. " 'Our Own Subject Race' Rebels," *LD*, Aug. 2, 1919, p. 25 is sympathetic to Blacks, cites Old Fifteenth.

13. Buckley, p. 228; "Is Bolshevism coming to America?" *NYT*, Mar. 24, 1919, p. 24.

14. "Negroes of World Prey of Agitators," *NYT*, Aug. 24, 1919, p. 1; "Russian Reds and I.W.W. Blamed for Race Riot," *NYT*, Aug. 27, 1919, p. 11; "For Action on Race Riot Peril," *NYT*, Oct. 5, 1919, p. 112; "What Japan Asks," *LD*, Mar. 8, 1919, pp. 11–13; "Nation-wide Press-Poll on the League of Nations," *LD*, Apr. 5, 1919, pp. 13–16, 120, "Japan Alarms Our Pacific Coast," pp. 20–21, and "The Murders and Mysteries of Kansas City's 'Little Italy,' " pp. 51–53, 55.

15. Swanberg, pp. 295–98; Nasaw, pp. 261–63, 270–71; "Constant Preparedness is America's Only Guarantee Against Japanese Danger," *NYAmer*, May 7, 1919, p. 18; "Mexican Butchering of Americans," *NYAmer*, July 19, 1919, p. 16; "Chicago Police Quell Race Riot" and "Hold to Racial Equality, Ishii Urges Japan," *NYAmer*, July 26, 1919, pp. 1, 2; *NYAmer*, July 23, 1919, "Racial War Rages," "Suburb Reports Crowd of Colored is Marching on Washington," pp. 1, 2; "What Do You Good Church People Think of the Japanese Now?" *NYAmer*, July 21, 1919, p. 20; "State Attorney Blames Black Belt Politics," *NYAmer*, July 31, 1919, p. 1.

16. Tuttle, pp. 21, 214–29; Ellis, pp. 214, 217–25; Dray, pp. 257–59; E. K. Jones, "Union Labor Leaders Foment Trouble in Chicago," *Age*, Aug. 16, 1919, p. 1; " 'Our Own Subject Race' Rebels," *LD*, Aug. 2, 1919, p. 25; "Why the Negro Appeals to Violence," *LD*, Aug. 9, 1919, p. 11; "What the South thinks of Northern Race-Riots," *LD*, Aug. 16, 1919, pp. 17–18, and "Religious Papers on the Negro Problem," p. 34.

17. "Vice and Politics as Factors in Chicago Riots," *NYT*, Aug. 3, 1919, p. 41; "Chicago Riot Spreads," and "Sen. McCormick Sees Justification," *NYAmer*, July 30, 1919, p. 1. *The American* pointedly contrasts the AFL's moderate requests for economic change with the Blacks' attempt to compel change by force: "Labor Demands Profiteering Cease," "Troops Battle Rioters as Chicago Race Ware Rages," and "State Attorney Blames Black Belt Politics," *NYAmer*, July 31, 1919, p. 1.

18. "Blames Race Riots on Negro Leaders," *NYT*, Aug. 26, 1919, p. 14; "State Attorney Blames Black Belt Politics," *NYAmer*, July 31, 1919, p. 1; Swanberg, pp. 211–12; Nasaw, p. 106; "Negroes May Rise, Senate Is Warned," *NYT*, Aug. 29, 1919, p. 2; "Seek Black Colonies," *WP*, Aug. 29, 1919, p. 1; "Mob-Rule as a National Menace," *LD*, Oct. 18, 1919, pp. 9–11.

19. H. Diner, pp. 52–53; "Billion Fund to Help Jews," *NYAmer*, Oct 18, 1918, p. 9; "Says Jews' Fate Lies with America, Race Must be Saved by Members Here," *NYAmer*, May 18, 1919, p. A5.

20. Bendersky, pp. 56–58, 71, 79–89. For sympathetic response see "Terror Ruled Vilna," *NYT*, June 15, 1919, p. E3; "Danger of Jewish Massacres," *LD*, June 7, 1919, pp. 21–22; Herman Bernstein, "Poles Murder Jews," *WP*, Aug. 24, 1919, p. 1; "Kill Jews for Loot," *WP*, Aug. 29, 1919, p. 9; "Sees Vilna," *WP*, Aug. 30, 1919, p. 5. For negative response see "Exaggerate Pogrom Tales," *WP*, July 29, 1919, p. 1. Note parallel articles, "The Case Against Zionism" and "The Case Against Lynching," *LD*, June 14, 1919, pp. 30–31, which argue that efforts by the victims to assert "racial" rights will only cause them to be still more hated and persecuted in the future. See also Henry Morgenthau, "The Jews in Poland," *WW*, Apr. 1922, pp. 617–30, which blames agitation by nationalist Zionists for keeping anti-Semitism alive.

21. "100,000 Jews Parade," *WP*, Nov. 25, 1919, p. 5.

22. See esp. David Brody, *Labor in Crisis*, and Cliff Brown, *Racial Conflict and Violence*; Murray, pp. 124–29, 138, 142.

23. Gary quoted in *LD*, Oct. 11, 1919, pp. 11–13; "Labor's Duty to the Public," *LD*, Sept. 6, 1919, pp. 13–15; "Labor Chiefs Open Crusade for Treaty," *NYAmer*, July 19, 1919, p. 2; see also Murray, pp. 139–46; "Negro Workers Shoot Picket," *NYT*, Oct. 4, 1919, p. 2; "Negroes Open Fire on Donora Strikers," *NYT*, Oct. 10, 1919, p. 4; "Negroes Shoot Two Pickets," *NYT*, Oct. 11, 1919, p. 2.

24. "American Labor and Bolshevism," *LD*, June 21, 1919, pp. 9–11; "The Socialist Party Split," *LD*, June 28, 1919, pp. 16–7; "Hughes Condemns Lynching of Negro," *NYT*, May 6, 1919, p. 15; "Treaty Dooms 'Prussianism,'" *NYAmer*, May 8, 1919, p. 2.

25. Montgomery, pp. 392–95; Murray, pp. 92–93, 146; "Senators Hear Gary," *NYT*, Oct. 2, 1919, pp. 1–2; "Steel Strike Facts and Issues," *NYT*, Oct. 2, 1919, p. 16; "'Open Shop the Issue; No Reason for Strike," *NYAmer*, Oct. 2, 1919, p. 1; "Soviets Aim of Strikers, Millmen Say," *NYAmer*, Oct. 5, 1919, p. 1; "Police and 5,000 Russians in Fifth Avenue Riot," *NYAmer*, Oct. 9, 1919, p. 1.

26. "Gen. Wood Orders Arrest," *NYT*, Oct. 1, 1919, p. 1; Murray, pp. 147–48; Shapiro, p. 152; Hagedorn, vol. 2, pp. 326–36; Mencken, *On Politics*, pp. 11, 14; Dawley, p. 249; Joan M. Jensen, *Army Surveillance*, pp. 178–204; "Red Literature Seized," *NYAmer*, Oct. 8, 1919, p. 1; "Lane Neads Industrial Conference," *NYAmer*, Oct. 7, 1919, p. 1; "Capital in Accords with Gary in Stand for the 'Open Shop,'" *NYAmer*, Oct. 11, 1919, p. 1; "Industrial Conference Dooms Gompers's Steel Plan," *NYAmer*, Oct. 15, 1919, p. 1, and "Army Men Lay Steel Strike to Anarchists," p. 2; "Labor-Capital Again at Odds," *NYAmer*, Oct. 20, 1919, p. 2; "Industrial Conference Wrecked," *NYAmer*, Oct. 24, 1919, p. 1, and "'Peace Patriotism' Is Marshall's Remedy," p. 2; *LD*, Oct. 11, 1919, pp. 11–13; "Army Men Lay Steel Strike to Anarchists," *NYAmer*, Oct. 15, 1919, p. 2; "Americanize Steel Plants," *NYAmer*, Oct. 14, 1919, p. 2; "Fifty Thousand Aliens," *NYT*, Oct. 17, 1919, p. 1.

27. A. Mitchell Palmer, *Investigation Activities of the Department of Justice*, 66th Cong., 1st sess., Senate doc. no. 153, vol. 12, 1919, esp. pp. 180–87; Kerlin, p. 153; "Reds Are Working Among Negroes," *NYT*, Oct. 19, 1919, p. 6; Sidney D. Frissell, "Meeting the Negro Problem," *NYT*, Dec. 14, 1919, p. 10; Charles A. Seldes, "Unrest in Prosperous Chicago," *NYT*, Dec. 21, 1919, pp. 75–76. Compare headline for "Colored Bishop" who "Denies Negroes Are 'Reds'" (*NYT*, Nov. 23, 1919, p. xxi) with head for Marshall's denial of Simons's accusations, "Says Mass of Jews Oppose Bolsheviki . . . East Side Not a Hot Bed," *NYT*, Feb. 15, 1919, p. 16.

28. "How the Consumer Boosts Prices" and "The High Cost of Strikes," *LD*, Aug. 30, 1919, pp. 15–17.

29. The debate is in U. S. Congress, *Congressional Record*, 67th Cong., 2nd sess., 1922, pp. 786–807, esp. pp. 797–99; also *Congressional Record*, 66th Cong., 1st sess., pp. 8029–30. Dray, pp. 258–72 notes parallels between the arguments for the bill and the regulatory and surveillance rationales of the War Progressives.

30. Hanson Ely, "Employment of Negro Man Power in War," in MacGregor and Nalty, p. 4:322–25; Coffman, pp. 317–18.

31. Dray, pp. 266–71; Gerstle, pp. 105, 112–14; Wyn Craig Wade, *Fiery Cross*, p. 165.

32. "Mob-Rule as a National Menace," *LD*, Oct. 18, 1919, pp. 9–11; Dawley, p. 249; Emerson Hough, *The Web*, pp. 458–59, 461; articles by Prescott F. Hall and Henry P. Fairchild in Edith M. Phelps, *Selected Articles on Immigration*, pp. 114–17, 125–31, 138–42, 148–50; Harry H. Laughlin, "An Analysis of America's Modern Melting Pot," *Hearings Before the Committee on Immigration and Naturalization*, House of Representatives, 67th Cong., 3rd sess., serial 7-C, pp. 737, 756–57; "Barring Undesirables," *NYT*, Oct. 19, 1919, p. X8; "Nation-wide Press-Poll on the League of Nations," *LD*, Apr. 5, 1919, pp. 13–16, 120, "Japan Alarms Our Pacific Coast," pp. 20–21, and "The Murders and Mysteries of Kansas City's 'Little Italy,'" pp. 51–53, 55; U.S. Congress, *Congressional Record*, 67th Cong., 1st sess., 1921, pp. 497–99; and 68th Cong., 1st sess., p. 262; Gerstle, pp. 100–3; Tichenor, pp. 142–44; Chase, p. 289; Murray, p. 205.

33. Laughlin, "An Analysis," pp. 737, 755–57; Tichenor, p. 144; "Psychological Tests for College Entrance," *LD*, Feb. 22, 1919, pp. 26–27, and "Blondes, Brunettes, and Success in Life," pp. 70, 72, 74; Bruce Barton, "Measuring the Abilities of Men by Psychological Tests," *LD*, Mar. 8, 1919, pp. 66–74; "Personal Incompetence Is To-day's Greatest Cause of Failure," *LD*, May 24, 1919, pp. 44–45; William McAndrew, "Americanism at Its Source," *LD*, May 17, 1919, pp. 36, 113–21, and "Are There 'Fighting Races'?" pp. 122–25, 127; William McDougall, *Is America Safe for Democracy?* pp. 256–57; Lewis Terman, "We Were Born That Way," *WW*, Aug., 1922, pp. 655–60; Chase, p. 283.

34. Ross analyzed racial quality by studying facial features and body types, using standards that reified his personal prejudices: "To the practiced eye the physiognomy of certain groups unmistakeably proclaims inferiority of type. I have seen gatherings of the foreign-born in which . . . [in] every face there was something wrong." Edward A. Ross, "Racial Consequences of Immigration," *Century* Magazine 1914; Phelps, pp. 120–25.

35. A revised edition of Grant, *Passing of the Great Race* was issued in 1918; Rep. Raker, *Hearings on Immigration*, 68th Cong., 1st sess., pp. 540–42, 570–73, 608–16, and Laughlin, "Europe as an Emigrant-Exporting Continent," pp. 1237, 1254–58; Chase, pp. 166, 170–73, 252–85, 293–94; Slotkin, *Gunfighter*, pp. 198–202.

36. Statement of Louis Marshall, *Hearings on Immigration*, 68th Cong., 1st sess., pp. 289–315; "Emergency Immigration Legislation," *Hearing Before the Committee on Immigration of the United States Senate*, 66th Cong., 3rd sess., pt. 2, pp. 103, 316, 341–44, 350, 393; "The Week in Review," *AH*, Jan. 3, 1919, p. 8a; "The Jewish Bill of Rights," *LD*, Jan. 11, 1919, pp. 30–31; Gerstle, 120–21.

37. U. S. Congress, *Congressional Record*, 66th Cong., 1st sess., 58: 180–83, 506, 587, 4265–74; "View of the Minority," *Hearings on Immigration*, 68th Cong., 1st sess., pp. 42–46; "Hughes Asks Rigid Immigration Ban," *NYT*, Apr. 20, 1921, p. 1; "Hughes Sent Files Not Views on Races," *NYT*, Apr. 21, 1921, p. 2; "Is America a Melting-Pot?" *Outlook*, Feb. 12, 1919, p. 249; "Reducing Law to an Absurdity," *Outlook*, Oct. 24, 1923, p. 297; "Mental Tests for Immigrants," *Outlook*, Mar. 5, 1924, p. 376; "Choose Citizens, Not 'Let Them In,'" *Outlook*, Dec. 12, 1925, pp. 619–20; Raymond G. Fuller, "Immigration and Americanism," *NR*, June 4, 1924, p. 48. Compare Creel, "How We Abused the Loyalty of Our Foreign Born," *LD*, Mar. 8, 1919, pp. 92, 94, 96; "Melting Pot or Dumping Ground?" *Collier's*, Sept. 3, 1921, p. 9; and "Close the Gates! The Way to Shut a Door Is to Shut It," *Collier's*, May 6, 1922, p. 9.

38. Burton L. Hendrick, "The Jews in America," *WW*, Nov. 1922, pp. 144–61; "Do

the Jews Dominate American Finance?" *WW*, Jan. 1924, pp. 266–86; "The 'Menace' of the Polish Jew," *WW*, Apr. 1923, pp. 366–77; "Keep up the Bars Against Immigration," *WW*, Apr. 1922, pp. 127–28; "Three Per Cent. Immigration Biologically Considered," *WW*, Oct. 1922, pp. 580–81.

39. Dawley, pp. 292–93; Tichenor, pp. 143–44; Chase, pp. 262–63, 289, 390; Laughlin, "An Analysis," pp. 756–77; "The Jews and the Colleges," *WW*, Aug. 1922, pp. 351–52; Marcia G. Synnott, *Half-Opened Door*, chaps. 1–3.

14: *Unknown Soldiers*

1. Mead, pp. xii–xiii, 400, 406; Harries, pp. 429–32; "The Psychology of Victory," *LD*, Jan. 4, 1919, pp. 22–23; "Moral Gains and Losses of the War," *LD*, Jan. 11, 1919, p. 29; Ernest Hemingway, "Soldier's Home," *Complete Short Stories*, p. 111.

2. Pencak, p. 44; Keene, pp. 165–68, 173; "Unknown Soldier," http://www.thero mantic.com/patrioticlyrics/unknownsoldier.htm.

3. This account of Whittlesey's last years is based on Pratt and Johnson, pp. 275–81, 312; "Col. Whittlesey of the 'Lost Battalion' Vanishes from Ship," *NYT*, Nov. 29, 1921, pp. 1, 2; "Sought Whittlesey Half Day in Midsea," *NYT*, Nov. 30, 1921, p. 5.

4. Werstein, p. 24; "Comrades in Arms Honor Whittlesey," *NYT*, Dec. 4, 1921, p. 6.

5. "Whittlesey to Aid O'Ryan; 'Lost Battalion' Leader will Assist in Red Cross Campaign," *NYT*, Oct. 2, 1918, p. 17; "Brokers' Early Christmas," *NYT*, Dec. 21, 1918, p. 19; "Harvard Drive Nets," Sept. 30, 1919, p. 17; "Williams College to Honor Founder," *NYT*, June 13, 1920, p. 34; "Cited Men in Legion Post," *NYT*, July 31, 1919, p. 15; "Mrs. Ingram Weds M. M. Whittlesey," *NYT*, Sept. 28, 1920, p. 10; "War's Highest Role of Honor" and "Legion Warns Donors," *NYT*, Sept. 26, 1920, pp. 25, 47.

6. Eastman, pp. 215–16; "Says War Broadened Army . . . Lieut. Col. Whittlesey Warns Against Revenge on Germans," *NYT*, Jan. 27, 1919, p. 7; E. Clowes Chorley, "Dr. Slattery's Portrait of Bishop Greer," *NYT*, May 8, 1921, p. 48.

7. "Praise Jewish Boys Who Served in War," *NYT*, May 19, 1919, p. 32; "Stowaway Aided by Whittlesey Gone," *NYT*, Sept. 8, 1920, p. 11.

8. "Whittlesey Out for Cox," *NYT*, Oct. 12, 1920, p. 10.

9. "1,000 Attend Dance of the 'Lost Battalion,'" *NYT*, Feb. 12, 1921, p. 12; Demaree, p. 7.

10. "Whittlesey Talked About War on Ship," *NYT*, Dec. 1, 1921, p. 16; "Command for Whittlesey," *NYT*, Aug. 11, 1921, p. 9; "Many Applications for Citizens," *NYT*, June 27, 1921, p. 20.

11. "Lost Battalion's Messenger in Morgue," *NYT*, July 12, 1921, p. 13; "Last Honors," *NYT*, July 15, 1921, p. 10; "Bury Argonne Hero," *NYT*, July 16, 1921, p. 6. Monson was not in the "Lost Battalion." The confusion between Whittlesey's two "last stands" persisted.

12. "Col. Hits Preference," *NYT*, Oct. 17, 1921, p. 17; "Decorated Negro Argues for Civil Service Preference," *NYT*, Mar. 6, 1919, p. 7.

13. "Red Cross Roll Call," *NYT*, Oct. 24, 1921, p. 7; also Oct. 27, p. 18.

14. "Solemn Journey of Dead," *NYT*, Nov. 12, 1921, pp. 1–2, and "Why We Went to War," p. 12; Werstein, pp. 31–32; Mencken, *On Politics*, p. 43.

15. "Sought Whittlesey," Nov. 30, 1921, p. 5; "Whittlesey Talked About War on Ship," *NYT*, Dec. 1, 1921, p. 16.

16. "Comrades in Arms Honor Whittlesey," *NYT*, Dec. 4, 1921, p. 6; "Comrades in Arms Honor Whittlesey," *NYT*, Dec. 5, 1921, p. 17; "A Citizen Soldier," *NYT*, Dec. 6, 1921, p. 18.

17. Whittlesey Papers, Correspondence, Williams College; "Red Cross Roll Call," *NYT*, Nov. 27, 1921, p. E2.

18. Biographical information on Henry Johnson can be found on Web sites listed in Bibliography.

19. Little, pp. 363–67.
20. "Decorated Negro Argues," *NYT*, Mar. 6, 1919, p. 7; "Coming! Coming! Sergeant Neadom Roberts," YMCA poster, Aug 22, 1919, Collection of John Motley; Buckley, p. 220; Maj. W. H. Loving to Dir. MID, Apr. 6, 1919, NA RG 165, M1440 Roll 5, War Dept., General and Special Staffs, "Correspondence . . . Relating to 'Negro Subversion,' " 1917–41.
21. Barbeau and Henri, p. 172; *Crisis*, Dec. 1918, pp. 66–67; Harries, p. 439; "Jobs for Soldiers," *Age*, Mar. 8, 1919, p. 3.
22. "Col. Bill Hayward and his 'Black Watch,' " *LD*, Mar. 8, 1919, p. 59.
23. "Negroes Did Heavy Fighting," *St. Louis Republic*, Mar. 29, 1919, p. 1; Henry O'Hara to Newton Baker, Mar. 29, 1919, Loving to Dir. MID, Apr. 6, 1919, and Maffitt to Dir. MID, Apr. 15, 1919, in NA RG 165, 5. Poincaré did review the regiment, and the King may have done so as well. A clipping in this file from *Chicago Defender*, a black newspaper, "White Soldiers Accuse Sergt. Johnson of Slander," Apr. 4, confirms and adds some details.
24. Charges vs. Johnson in NA RG 165, M. Churchill, Dir. of MID, to Capt. T. S. Maffitt, Apr. 10, 1919. NA RG 165, M1194, Rel 109, War Dept. General and Special Staffs, Name Index to Correspondence of MID. Dunn/Loving, March 3 and Mar. 8, 1919, reports of Negro soldiers from 15th New York canvassing for Equal Rights League; Loving to Dunn; and a report that soldiers of the 370th Infantry, led by their Black ex-colonel, were forming a "secret society" to fight for "social equality," GHQ, AEF from Asst. Chief of Staff, G-2; to Acting Dir. of MID, Jan. 30, 1919; D. E. Nolan, G2, Feb. 18, 1919; J. M. Dunn to MID, Mar. 4, 1919, in NA RG 165, M1440 Roll 5, "Correspondence . . . Relating to 'Negro Subversion,' " 1917–41.
25. "The Press on Race Wars" and " 'Red Caps' Join American Federation of Labor," *Age*, Aug. 2, 1919, p. 4; Kerlin, pp. 31–34; DuBois, *Oxford/Reader*, p. 500.
26. Herman Johnson to author, Oct. 1, 2001; Buckley, p. 220; Rumer, pp. 97–98.

15: *"Say, Don't You Remember . . . ?"*

1. "Capt. N. Holderman of 'Lost Battalion,' " *NYT*, Sept. 4, 1953, p. 34; "Eugene H. Houghton, Rescuer of Troops," *NYT*, Jan. 20, 1949, p. 28. On the strike see David J. Bercuson, *Confrontation at Winnipeg*, pp. 121–25, 167–69, 187; "The Canadian Strike," *NYT*, May 28, 1919, p. 14; "Canada's Labor War," *LD*, June 14, 1919, pp. 18–19; Johnson and Pratt, p. 292.
2. Rainsford may have trusted too much his strength as a swimmer, for he died by drowning in 1947 at age sixty-three: "W. Kerr Rainsford, Architect, Drowns," *NYT*, July 24, 1947, p. 23. His Memorial Day speech is described in "World War Dead Honored in City," *NYT*, May 25, 1942, p. 17. On Adler see Stallings, p. 330; Lincoln Eyre, "St. Juvin," *NYW*, Oct. 18, 1918, p. 1; Tifft and Jones, pp. 121–22, 233; "Funeral Is Held for Gen. Adler," *NYT*, Oct. 7, 1955, p. 18. "Frank B. Tiebout," *NYT*, Feb. 25, 1959, p. 31; "Col. Blagden Dies," *NYT*, Jan. 13, 1937, p. 23; on McMurtry, "George McMurtry," *National Cyclopedia*, vol. 47, pp. 686–87; "George McMurtry," *NYT*, Nov. 24, 1858, p. 29; LB Newsletters, Longwood Web site; Johnson and Pratt, pp. 214–15, 266. For the reunions see the Newsletters, Longwood Web site, esp. 1:2; 3:1–5; 2:1, 4–5, 8–9. LB Newsletter 3, 2; 4:1.
3. "Col. Hayward Dies, Commanded 369th," *NYT*, Oct. 14, 1944, p. 13; "Hayward Marries," *NYT*, June 22, 1919, p. 22; "City Officials Join" and "N.Y. City Regiment with Colored Officers," *Age*, Mar. 1, 1919, p. 1; C. Johnson, p. 127; Barbeau and Henri, p. 244n35; Osofsky, pp. 172, 175–76.
4. "Col. A. W. Little, 69, War Hero, Is Dead," *NYT*, July 19, 1943, p. 15.
5. "Leon Cadore, 66, Former Dodger," *NYT*, Mar. 7, 1948, p. 29.
6. Johnson and Pratt, pp. 284, 301, 304; Britten, p. 80; Hussey and Flynn, p. 5; Adler, *Seventy-seventh*, pp. 138–44; JWV, *Routes to Roots* 2:2 (Aug. 1982), p. 28 (NMJAMH); and see LB Newsletters, Longwood Web site, for individuals named.

7. Levinger, p. 117; "Jack Herschkowitz, World War I Hero," *Newsday*, Aug. 1985, clipping from NMJAMH.

8. Johnson and Pratt, pp. 301–7; John, "Personal Memory," Longwood Web site.

9. Johnson and Pratt, pp. 231, 301–5.

10. Miles, pp. vii–ix, 23. His regimental history stirred interest in the Lost Battalion, esp. when *NYT Magazine* published an excerpt, Sept. 30, 1928, pp. 80–83. For his life see "Dr. L. W. Miles, 71, Soldier, Educator," *NYT*, June 29, 1944, p. 23. Russell Whittlesey's death is in Andrew Carroll, *War Letters*, pp. 197–98.

11. Smith, "Chief Lo," *American Indian*, Sept. 1926, p. 9; Britten, p. 80. The epithet refers to a verse by Alexander Pope, "Lo, the poor Indian, where he stands . . ." which treats the Indian as an object of sentimental pity.

12. Hall, *Tea*, pp. 185, 194, 202–3. He is identified as Lau Sing Kee on a Web site that has been discontinued, http://www.weservedwithpride.com. "Lau" may be an honorific.

13. Gus J. Karger, "New Hyphenism in Zionism," *WPost*, Feb. 16, 1919, p. ES12; Morris R. Cohen, "Zionism: Tribalism or Liberalism?" *NR*, Mar. 8, 1919, pp. 182–83; Simon W. Rosendale to Rollin Sanford (R-NY), "Zionism vs Americanism," U.S. Congress, *Congressional Record*, 65th Cong., 3rd sess., 57:78–79; Henry S. Hendricks, "Americanism *Versus* Nationalism," *AH*, Jan. 31, 1919, pp. 296–97, and "Just Where We Stand," p. 295; "Zionism Is Dead; Long Live Judaism!" *AH*, Feb. 7, 1919, p. 317; "Super-Zionism," *WPost*, Mar. 18, 1919, p. 6.

14. Ford, pp. 38–39, 214, 235–38, chap. 6; Lieberman, "Melting Pot: A Good American," *AH*, Oct. 18, 1918, p. 629.

15. "The Hero of the Lost Battalion," *AH*, Dec. 27, 1918, 104:8; "Co. B of 307th Infantry Dance," *NYT*, Dec. 11, 1918, p. 13; "Macy's Honors War Veterans," *NYT*, Dec. 8, 1918, p. 15; "Legion to Aid Job Seekers," *NYT*, Sept. 24, 1919, p. 8; see his entry in JWV, *1919 Year Book of the Jewish Valor Legion*, NMJAMH; Krotoshinsky, "How the Lost Battalion Was Saved," *Jewish Veteran*, Apr. 1937, pp. 5–6 (NMJAMH); Johnson and Pratt, pp. 311–12.

16. William W. H. Davis, *History of Bucks County*, 3:276–77; "Last Honors Today for Argonne Hero," *NYT*, July 15, 1921, p. 10; "Nathan Straus Sends War Hero Abroad," *NYT*, Dec. 3, 1921, p. 13.

17. Slobin, pp. 139–40.

18. Meyer Siegel, "A Measure of Life," typescript. Jacob Rader Marcus Center of the American Jewish Archives, Hebrew Union College, pp. 8–11, 22, 26–28; Sterba, pp. 53, 181, 183, 209–11; Howe, chaps. 9–11, 13, 15–16.

19. Jonathan Zimmerman, *Whose America?* pp. 16–17, 20–30; Stewart Svonkin, *Jews Against Prejudice*, pp. 21–22; Gino Speranza, "Playing Horse with American History," *WW*, Apr. 1923, pp. 602–10; "Would Limit Immigration," *NYT*, Dec. 10, 1923, p. 29; "Immigration Restriction," *NYT*, Jan. 13, 1924, p. XX8; "Jews Offended by Mr. Sargent's 'Synagogue,'" *LD*, Nov. 1, 1919, pp. 30–31.

20. H. Diner, pp. 101–5, 147–49; Lawrence A. Fuchs, *American Kaleidoscope*, chaps. 1, 3.

21. McCall, chaps. 1–2, pp. 7–12, 134–41, 241–42; see review by John Corbin, "McCall Interpreting Jewish Records in America," *NYT*, Book Review, May 25, 1924, p. 19, which also dwells on Krotoshinsky.

22. "Argonne Hero Gets Job," *NYT*, Nov. 27, 1927, p. 7; "Pleads for Krotoshinsky," *NYT*, Dec. 10, 1927, p. 16; "Lost Battalion Hero Gets Postal Job Here," *NYT*, Dec. 18, 1927, p. 21; "Krotoshinsky, 60, World War I Hero," *NYT*, Nov. 5, 1953, p. 31; Johnson and Pratt, p. 283; William Mathews, *Our Soldiers Speak*, p. 310; Richards, *Italian-American*, pp. 194–95; Herbert Asbury, "The Emperor of Gangland," *McClure's*, Feb. 1929, pp. 54–62; Kate Sargent, "Chicago, Hands Up!" *Forum*, Oct. 1927, pp. 522–32.

23. "Arthur C. Sanders, World War Hero, *NYT*, Apr. 11, 1938, p. 15; "War Dead to be Honored," May 17, 1939, p. 15; Johnson and Pratt, pp. 312–13; Krotoshinsky, "How

the Lost Battalion Was Saved," *Jewish Veteran*, Apr. 1937, pp. 5–6." *Jewish Veteran* also published an excerpt about Krotoshinsky from Johnson and Pratt, NMJAMH.

24. H. Diner, pp. 50–52; Meyer Berger, "About New York," *NYT*, Feb. 2, 1940, p. 20. Ellipses in original. The *Times* would name an award after Berger, for the best "New York Story" of the year.

25. See Neal Gabler, *An Empire of Their Own*.

26. H. Diner, p. 151.

27. See Nathan Huggins, *Harlem Renaissance*, and D. L. Lewis, *When Harlem Was in Vogue*; Osofsky, pp. 174–76; Ellis, pp. 190–92.

28. N. B. Marshall, pp. 7, 9–11; Barbeau and Henri, pp. 157–58; Jamieson, pp. 38–39, differs in some details of his wounding; H. Harrison, p. 88. On Haiti see Max Boot, *Savage Wars of Peace*, pp. 156–77; and Hans Schmidt, *United States Occupation of Haiti 1915–1934*. This account of Marshall's experience in Haiti is based on the extensive correspondence and other material relating to Marshall's tenure at the Legation in Haiti in NA RG 59, Dept. of State, Decimal File, 1910–1929, Box 1526. Munro to White, April 24, 1924, Re: "Call of Mr. Claude A. Barnett, re Haiti," is especially valuable for the light it sheds on the details of Marshall's appointment, and the concern among Black leaders about his situation.

29. N. B. Marshall, pp. 11–12; "Keating Rally in Harlem," *NYT*, Sept. 15, 1931, p. 2; "Capt. N. B. Marshall," *NYT*, June 8, 1933, p. 19.

30. "A New Negro—A New Crowd,"*Messenger*, June 1919, p. 9; "Jewish Pogroms," *Messenger*, July 1919, p. 6; J. Anderson, *A. Philip Randolph*, pp. 26–27; Ellis, p. 197.

31. H. Diner, pp. 58–60, 102, 151; Ford, pp. 300–1.

32. See for example, Scott, *Official History;* Jamieson, *Complete History;* Kelly Miller, *Negro Soldier in Our War*, all published in 1919.

33. Coffman, pp. 317–18; MacGregor and Nalty, pp. 322–25; Mead, pp. 415–16; Little, p. xi; Niles, *Singing Soldiers*; Charles E. Mack, *Two Black Crows in the A.E.F.*, pp. 281, 338; W. Irwin MacIntyre, *The Colored Soldier* contains dialect tales of comic soldiers, with names like "Corporal Shoe-Blacken." The only offsetting fictional portrayal of Black soldiers is *Wings on My Feet: Black Ulysses at the Wars* (1929) by Howard W. Odum, a Southern-born White sociologist who learned to abhor Jim Crow and developed an abiding interest in Southern Black culture. The novel is cruelly realistic, and experimental in form, rendering the hero's consciousness in a bluesy style. As a war novel it bears comparison with the work of William March and John Dos Passos. It had (and has) no critical following, and no imitators—a sign of the oblivion to which the Black military experience was consigned.

34. Chester Heywood's *Negro Combat Troops* is better written than Odum's book, with a harder edge in its account of racial discrimination and combat, but has some of the same flaws. See the letter from Francis Leigh, Dec. 11, 1933, attached to the copy of the book in the Collection of John Motley.

35. For Fish's political record see U.S. Congress, *Congressional Record*, 67th Cong., 2nd sess., pp. 1359–60; 68th Cong., 2nd sess., pp. 3344; American Battlefield Monuments Commission, *American Armies*, p. 361; Edgerton, pp. 120, 128, 140; Nalty, *Strength*, p. 138.

36. Dunn to Major Loving, Mar. 3, 1919, and Loving to Dunn, Mar. 8, 1919, NA RG 165, M1440 Roll 5, War Dept. General and Special Staffs, "Correspondence . . . Relating to 'Negro Subversion,' 1917–41."

37. Buckley, pp. 209–10.

38. Neadom Roberts, *Brief Adventures*, p. 7; Trenton High School, "Couple Die By Hanging," *Newark News*, Apr. 18, 1949, p. 13; John Blackwell, *The Trentonian*, June 13, 2003 online. "Coming! Coming! Sergeant Neadom Roberts," YMCA poster, Aug 22, 1919, http://dbs.ohiohistory.org/africanam/page.cfm?ID=4415.

39. Kimball and Bolcom, pp. 21, 75, 86, 93–95, 108, 116, 237; on Briggs, see Web site in Bibliography.

16: The New Deal and the Renewal of American Nationalism

1. Keene, chap. 8, pp. 181–85, 191; Pencak, pp. 202–3; Farwell, p. 294.
2. On the New Deal I have used esp. Gerstle, chaps. 1, 4; Richard H. Pells, *Radical Visions and American Dreams*, pp. 310–11; T. H. Watkins, *Hungry Years*, chaps. 8–11.
3. Miles, pp. viii–ix; Howard Mumford Jones, "Patriotism—But How?" *Atlantic Monthly* 162 (November 1938), pp. 585–92.
4. Montgomery, pp. 462–63; Svonkin, pp. 12–13.
5. Gerstle, pp. 158–61, 183–85. Laughlin, *Immigration and Conquest*, solicited by the NY State Chamber of Commerce. Laughlin had a position of considerable power as head of the Carnegie Institution.
6. Mead, p. xi; Pencak, p. 44. In his autobiography Fish would characterize himself as a lifelong "Jeffersonian democrat," devoted to small government and laissez-faire ideals. But he not only supported TR in 1912, he worked to get Public Works Administration aid for his district. See Harold Ickes, *Secret Diary*, pp. 685–86; Donald C. Bacon et. al., "Hamilton Fish," *Encyclopedia of the United States Congress,* vol. 2, pp. 845–46. For his positions on Blacks in the military see Buckley, pp. 262–65; Edgerton, p. 120, 128, 147; Nalty, *Strength*, p. 138. On immigration see U.S. Congress, *Congressional Record,* 67th Cong., 2nd sess., p. 4435; 66th Cong., 3rd sess., pp. 11, 4354; 67th Cong., 2nd sess., on Palestine, pp. 5693, 5035, 5759, 6289; on lynching, pp. 1359–60, 1373; on Bonus, p. 4435.
7. Bendersky, pp. 276, 283–85; "Lindbergh Sees a 'Plot' for War," *NYT*, Sept. 12, 1941, p. 2; "Lindbergh Accused of Inciting Race Hate," Sept. 14, 1941, p. 25; "Ask Lindbergh Debate" and Sept. 15, 1941, p. 2; "Dewey Denounces Lindbergh Talk," Sept. 15, 1941, p. 2; "Jewish New Year Begins," *NYT*, Sept. 21, 1941, p. 35.
8. Bendersky, pp. 279–82.
9. "The Un-American Way," *NYT*, Sept. 26, 1941, p. 22.
10. Mosesson, pp. 19–24, 32–55, 40–41, 51–56; Spivack, pp. 55–59.
11. Interview with Herbert B. Gross, Rutgers Oral History Archives of World War II, http://fas-history.rutgers.edu/oralhistory/Interviews/gross_herbert.html; Orvill "Ozzie" Zuckerman, "Newsman Heralded the Happenings of the Old Neighborhood," *New Jersey Jewish News*, online.html (1999); "Meet Ben Kaufman," *Jewish Veteran*, Sept. 1941, p. 3 (NMJAMH).
12. Vincent Sheean, "Anti-Semitism Is a Danger to the Nation" and "Why Hate Ben Kaufman?" *Look*, Jan. 1942, in clipping file, NMJAMH. Except where indicated, information on Kaufman is from *Look* article. See also "Meet Ben Kaufman," *Jewish Veteran*, p. 3.
13. "Mark 150th Year of Bill of Rights," *NYT*, Sept. 26, 1941, p. 25; "Let Veterans Use Church," *NYT*, Oct. 12, 1942, p. 14; "Would Mobilize Veterans," *NYT*, Dec. 11, 1941, p. 7; "Veterans to Sell Bonds," *NYT*, Dec. 22, 1941, p. 30; "Another War Plane Presented," *NYT*, July 11, 1941, p. 6; "Jews War Record Cited By Senator," *NYT*, May 18, 1942, p. 7; "Would Open Palestine / Jewish Veterans Demand End of Immigration Curbs," Sept. 23, 1943, p. 28.
14. Clipping file, Ben Kaufman, Trenton Historical Society; NMJAMH web site.
15. Dray, pp. 336–54, 363–64; Shapiro, chaps. 8–9; J. Anderson, *Randolph*, pp. 241–43.
16. Stephen May, "World War I Veteran Horace Pippin," *Military History*, February 1998, pp. 14, 16, 18, 80; Stein, pp. 3–5.
17. Horace Pippin Papers, notebook fragment, letter, and pp. 1–3. Stein, pp. 6–7, dates the drawings from these notebooks as 1917–18, but the letter indicates that the original notebooks were destroyed.
18. Stein, pp. 54, 60–62. All the paintings referred to are in Stein.
19. Ibid., pp. 3–4, 8, 11–15, 21, 29, 32, 65, 75–80, 156–58; "Horace Pippin," *Notable Black American Men*, pp. 941–42; Lewis Nichols, "Deep Are the Roots," *NYT*, Oct. 7, 1945, p. XI. After 1944 his situation deteriorated. His wife became mentally ill

and addicted to amphetamines; he was deeply worried about his stepson in the armed forces and began drinking to excess. He died in his sleep, of a stroke, on July 6, 1946.

20. Danny Duncan Collum et al., *African Americans in the Spanish Civil War*, pp. 18, 41, 245; Buckley, p. 248; Herman Johnson to author, Oct. 1, 2001.

21. MacGregor and Nalty, chap. 8, and pp. 469–70, esp. pp. 528, 535–36.

22. This account is from J. Anderson, *Randolph*, 236–59.

23. Roi Ottley, "Negroes are saying . . ." in *Reporting World War II*, vol. 1, pp. 442–43; see Motley, *Invisible Soldier*, for Blacks in World War II.

17: The Bargain Renewed

1. Gerstle, chap. 5, pp. 192–93; Fuchs, pp. 154–55; Walter A. Jackson, *Gunnar Myrdal and America's Conscience*, esp. chap. 1.

2. John M. Blum, *V Was for Victory*, pp. 21, 29, 37; Jeanine Basinger, *World War II Combat Film*, pp. 83–107; Slotkin, "Unit Pride: Ethnic Platoons and the Myths of American Nationality," *ALH* 13, no. 3, pp. 469–98.

3. Basinger, p. 340n9. Another likely source is the anthology of war stories edited by Ernest Hemingway, *Men at War* (1942). A major theme is the "last stand," and examples range from Thermopylae to the Alamo, Custer's Last Stand, a doomed British battalion in 1918, and the "Lost Battalion," an article-length abridgment of Johnson and Pratt. The film is officially listed as a remake of John Ford's *Lost Patrol* (1934).

4. Combat films were exceptional among Hollywood productions in their representation of Blacks as competent, dignified, and heroic. The industry resisted attempts by the NAACP and other organizations to modify those stereotypes in other contexts. See Koppes and Black, "Blacks, Loyalty, and Motion-Picture Propaganda in World War II," *Journal of American Historians* 73, no. 2 (1986), pp. 383–406, esp. pp. 400–1 and 405.

5. Dower, *War Without Mercy*, chaps. 4–7, pp. 181–90; Shapiro, chap. 12; Blum, *V Was for Victory*, chap. 5; Slotkin, "Unit Pride: Ethnic Platoons and the Myths of American Nationality," *ALH* 13, no. 3, pp. 469–98.

6. On the formula see Basinger, *World War II Combat Film*, chap. 1; on the myth see Slotkin, "Unit Pride"; Richard Rorty, *Achieving Our Country*, p. 100; Gerstle, pp. 42, 87, 204–10, 255, 340.

7. See Mary L. Dudziak, *Cold War Civil Rights*, esp. chaps. 1–3; MacGregor, *Integration of the Armed Forces 1940–1965*.

8. See for example Samuel Huntington, *The Clash of Civilizations* (1998).

9. T. G. Ash, "Cry the Dismembered Country," *New York Review of Books*, Jan. 14, 1999, pp. 29–33, esp. pp. 32–33; Arthur M. Schlesinger Jr., *Disuniting of America*, p. 18; Robert D. Kaplan, "The Coming Anarchy," *Atlantic Monthly* (1992), pp. 60, 68–69; Huntington, *Who Are We?*; Peter Brimelow, *Alien Nation*. See also Ash, "Anarchy & Madness," *New York Review of Books*, Feb. 10, 2000, pp. 48–53; Benjamin C. Schwarz, "The Diversity Myth: America's Leading Export," *Atlantic Monthly* (May 1995), pp. 57–58.

SELECTED BIBLIOGRAPHY

Newspapers and Magazines

I looked at microfilm copies for the following newspapers from January 1, 1917, to December 31, 1919, inclusive, except for the *Jewish Daily Forward* (read and translated by Chana Pollack): *The Age; Jewish Daily Forward (Forverts); New York American; New York Herald; New York Sun; New York Times; New York Tribune; New York World*. I used a keyword search for particular subjects on Proquest Database for the *New York Times* and *Washington Post*.

I looked at microfilm or bound copies for the following, January 1, 1917, to December 31, 1919, and January–March 1922 through December 1924: *American Hebrew; Collier's; Crisis; Literary Digest; McClure's Magazine; The New Republic; Outlook; Saturday Evening Post; World's Work (Review of Reviews)*.

Sound Recordings

Lieut. Jim Europe's 369th U. S. Infantry "Hell Fighters" Band: The Complete Recordings. Liner notes by Tim Gracyk and Brad Kay. Memphis Archives. 1996.

Films

Bataan, dir. Tay Garnett, 1943; *Birth of a Nation*, dir. D. W. Griffith, 1915; *The Lost Battalion*, dir. Edward McManus, 1919; *The Lost Battalion*, dir. Russell Mulcahy, 2001; *Men of Bronze*, dir. William Miles, 1977.

Archives and Manuscript Material

Collection of John Motley, African-American Military History. The collection is scheduled for transfer to the museum at Tredegar Iron Works, Richmond, Va.

National Archives

369th Infantry: RG 391, Boxes 4253, 4258, 4265, 4267; RG 120 Records of the American Expeditionary Forces, File 193; 93rd Division General Correspondence, Box 14990, File 293–11.4.

77th Division: Record Group 120, Records of the American Expeditionary Forces. Historical Files: Operations Reports, Unit Histories, Messages. Boxes 16–18, 52, 189, 197, 209, 253, 3821, 6622.

92nd Division: Record Group 165, Records of the War Dept. General and Special Staffs, Box 6623.

Military Intelligence Division: M1080 War Plans [White]. 212-E Box 241–13, Correspondence; M1440 Roll 5, RG 165 War Dept. General and Special Staffs, Correspondence . . . Relating to "Negro Subversion," 1917–41; M1194, Name Index, Rolls 37 (Cahan), 109 (Henry Johnson), 123 (Krotoshinsky), 145 (N.B. Marshall).

Department of State: RG 59 Decimal File, 1910–1929. Box 1526, 123: Napoleon B. Marshall.

National Museum of American Jewish Military History, Washington, D.C. File material on Benjamin Kaufman, Abraham Krotoshinsky, Jack Herschkowitz.

The Papers of Horace Pippin. Archives of American Art, Reel 138, 1972. Smithsonian.

Siegel, Meyer. "A Measure of Life," typescript. Jacob Rader Marcus Center of the American Jewish Archives, Cincinnati Campus, Hebrew Union College, Jewish Institute of Religion, 1978–79.

Trenton Historical Society: File materials on Ben Kaufman and Neadom (Needham) Roberts.

U.S. Army Military History Institute, Carlisle Barracks, Pa.:

Army Service Experiences Questionnaires, 1914–21 (ASEQ), for 77th Division Veterans (11 forms).

U.S. Army War College. "Replies to Army War College Questionnaires of 7 May 1924 Concerning Use of Black Manpower," AWC File 127–12; "The Colored Soldier in the United States Army," prepared in Historical Section, Army War College (1942); "The Use of Negro Manpower in War," November 10, 1925.

Wilfahrt, Jeffrey John, compiler. "Charles John Wilfahrt in World War I." Typescript.

Williams College, Williamstown, Mass., Whittlesey Papers, Correspondence.

Web Sites

The World Wide Web was a rich source of information on particular individuals, on the military history of World War I, and on some aspects of the social history of the units examined in this study. Some of the material cited in the footnotes is not permanently posted. Web sites that appear stable and are important sources are:

Longwood http://www.longwood.k12.ny.us/history/index.htm. Offers primary sources on the 77th Division, especially unit histories. Select "Camp Upton" from the Contents.

"Lost Battalion Website," created by John Cotter. http://www.homestead.com/prosites-johnrcotter/lost_battalion.html. Links to information about participants, stills from the 1919 movie *The Lost Battalion*.

"Doughboy Center, First Army." http://www.worldwar1.com/dbc/ghq1arm.htm. Links to information about all aspects of WW I. "Detached Segregated Regiments" page provides information on the 369th Infantry.

"Trenches on the Web." http://www.worldwar1.com/. Numerous links to sites dealing with the war, the 77th Division, and the 369th Infantry.

For Benjamin Kaufman, see http://www.us-israel.org/jsource/biography/kaufman.html.

For Henry Johnson, see http://www.arlingtoncemetery.net/henry-johnson.htm; http://www.albany.edu/cuyt/hjohnson.htm; http://www.gop.gov/Committeecentral/bills/hr480.asp; http://www.state.ny.us/governor/press/year02/jan8_3_02.htm.

Music. A good source for music of the period is http://mysongbook.de/msb/songs. Other Web sites, many of which can be accessed via a name-based search, were sources for information on song lyrics (by title or first line).

For Napoleon B. Marshall's 1900 anti-imperialist speech see http://www.boondocksnet .com/ai/ailtexts/their_hope.html. For Harriet Gibbs Marshall, http://www.aaregistry .com/african_american_history/1993/Harriett_GibbsMarshall.

Books and Articles

Adler, Julius Ochs. *History of the 306th Infantry* (1935), Longwood Web site.
[Adler, Julius Ochs.] *History of the Seventy-Seventh Division, August 25th 1917–November 11, 1918.* New York: W. H. Cranfer Co. for the 77th Division Association, 1919.
Alexander, Robert. *Memories of the World War, 1917–1918.* New York: Macmillan, 1931.
Allen, Robert L., with Pamela P. Allen. *Reluctant Reformers: Racism and Social Reform Movements in the United States.* Garden City, N.Y.: Anchor Books, 1975.
American Jewish Committee. *The War Record of American Jews: First Report of the Office of War Records, American Jewish Committee, January 1, 1919.* New York: American Jewish Committee, 1919.
Anderson, Benedict. *Imagined Communities: Reflections on the Origin and Spread of Nationalism.* London: Verso, 1983.
Anderson, Jervis. *A. Philip Randolph: A Biographical Portrait.* Berkeley: University of California, 1986.
———. *This Was Harlem: A Cultural Portrait, 1900–1950.* New York: Farrar Straus and Giroux, 1982.
Audoin-Rouzeau, Stéphane, and Annette Becker. *14–18: Understanding the Great War,* translated by Catherine Temerson. New York: Hill and Wang, 2002.
Badger, Reid. *A Life in Ragtime: A Biography of James Reese Europe.* New York: Oxford University Press, 1995.
Balibar, Etienne, and Immanuel Wallerstein. *Race, Nation, Class: Ambiguous Identities,* translated by Chris Turner. London: Verso, 1991.
Barbeau, Arthur E., and Florette Henri. *The Unknown Soldiers: Black American Troops in World War I.* Philadelphia: Temple University Press, 1974.
Basinger, Jeanine. *The World War II Combat Film: Anatomy of a Genre.* Rev. ed. Middletown, Conn.: Wesleyan University Press, 2003.
Bendersky, Joseph W. *The "Jewish Threat": Anti-Semitic Policies of the U.S. Army.* New York: Basic Books, 2000.
Bernheimer, Charles S., ed. *The Russian Jew in the United States: Studies of Social Conditions in New York, Philadelphia, and Chicago, with a Description of Rural Settlements.* Philadelphia: John C. Winston Co., 1905.
Bestor, Arthur E. *America and the Great War.* Patriotism Through Education Series, no. 15. New York: National Security League, 1917.
Binder, Frederick M., and David M. Reimers. *All the Nations Under Heaven: An Ethnic and Racial History of New York City.* New York: Columbia University Press, 1995.
Blum, John Morton. *The Republican Roosevelt.* New York: Atheneum, 1966.
———. *V Was for Victory: Politics and American Culture During World War II.* New York: Harcourt Brace Jovanovich, 1976.
Blumenstein, Christian. *Whiz Bang!* Buffalo, N.Y.: Christian Blumenstein, 1927. Buffalo and Erie County Library.
Boas, Franz. *Race, Language, and Culture.* Chicago: University of Chicago Press, 1982.

Bodnar, John. *Remaking America: Public Memory, Commemoration, and Patriotism in the Twentieth Century*. Princeton, N.J.: Princeton University Press, 1992.

Bogardus, Emory S. *Essentials of Americanization*. Los Angeles: University of Southern California Press, 1919.

———. *Immigration and Race Attitudes*. Boston: D. C. Heath & Co., 1928.

Boot, Max. *The Savage Wars of Peace: Small Wars and the Rise of American Power*. New York: Basic Books, 2002.

Bradden, William S. *Under Three Banners: An Autobiography*. Nashville, Tenn.: National Baptist Publishing Board, 1940.

Braim, Paul F. *The Test of Battle: The American Expeditionary Forces in the Meuse-Argonne Campaign*. 2nd ed. rev. Shippensburg, Pa.: White Mane Books, 1998.

Breen, William J. *Uncle Sam at Home: Civilian Mobilization, Wartime Federalism, and the Council of National Defense*. Westport, Conn.: Greenwood Press, 1984.

Briggs, John W. *An Italian Passage: Immigrants to Three American Cities, 1890–1930*. New Haven: Yale University Press, 1978.

Brigham, Carl C. *A Study of American Intelligence*. Foreword by Robert M. Yerkes. Princeton, N.J.: Princeton University Press, 1923.

Brimelow, Peter. *Alien Nation: Common Sense About America's Immigration Disaster*. New York: Random House, 1995.

Bristow, Nancy K. *Making Men Moral: Social Engineering During the Great War*. New York: New York University Press, 1996.

Britten, Thomas A. *American Indians in World War I: At War and at Home*. Albuquerque: University of New Mexico, 1997.

Broderick, Francis L. *Progressivism at Risk: Electing a President in 1912*. New York: Greenwood Press, 1989.

Brody, David. *Labor in Crisis: The Steel Strike of 1919*. Philadelphia: J.B. Lippincott Co., 1965.

Brooks, Alfred M. *Converted and Secret Americans*. Patriotism Through Education Series, no. 30. New York: National Security League, 1918.

Brown, Cliff. *Racial Conflict and Violence in the Labor Market: Roots in the 1919 Steel Strike*. New York: Garland Publishing, 1998.

Brown, Richard Maxwell. *Strain of Violence: Historical Studies of American Violence and Vigilantism*. New York: Oxford University Press, 1975.

Buckley, Gail. *American Patriots: The Story of Blacks in the Military from the Revolution to Desert Storm*. New York: Random House, 2001.

Buffington, Joseph. *Friendly Words to the Foreign Born*. Loyalty Leaflets no. 1. [Washington, D.C.]: Committee on Public Information, 1917.

Carlton, David L. *Mill and Town in South Carolina, 1880–1920*. Baton Rouge: Louisiana State University Press, 1982.

Chambers, John Whiteclay, II. *The Tyranny of Change: America in the Progressive Era, 1890–1920*. New Brunswick, N.J.: Rutgers University Press, 1992.

Chandler, Alfred D. *The Visible Hand: The Managerial Revolution in American Business*. Cambridge, Mass.: Belknap Press of Harvard University Press, 1977.

Chase, Allan. *The Legacy of Malthus: The Social Costs of the New Scientific Racism*. New York: Alfred A. Knopf, 1977.

Chauncey, George. *Gay New York: Gender, Urban Culture, and the Making of the Gay Male World, 1890–1940*. New York: Basic Books, 1994.

Clifford, John Gary. *The Citizen Soldiers: The Plattsburgh Training Camp Movement, 1913–1920*. Lexington: University of Kentucky Press, 1972.

Cobb, Irvin. *The Glory of the Coming: What Mine Eyes Have Seen of Americans in Action in the Year of Grace and Allied Endeavor*. New York: George H. Doran Co., 1918.

Coffman, Edward M. *The War to End All Wars: The American Experience in World War I*. New York: Oxford University Press, 1968.

Cohen, Miriam. *Workshop to Office: Two Generations of Italian Women in New York City, 1900–1950*. Ithaca, N.Y.: Cornell University Press, 1992.

Collum, Danny Duncan, ed., and Victor A. Berch, chief researcher. *African Americans in the Spanish Civil War: "This Ain't Ethiopia, But It'll Do."* New York: G. K. Hall & Co., 1992.

Commons, John R. *Races and Immigrants in America*. 2nd ed. New York: Macmillan, 1920.

Cooper, John Milton Jr. *The Warrior and the Priest: Woodrow Wilson and Theodore Roosevelt*. Cambridge, Mass.: Belknap of Harvard, 1983.

Cornebise, Alfred E. *War as Advertised: The Four-Minute Men and America's Crusade, 1917–1918*. Philadelphia: American Philosophical Society, 1984.

Cowan, Sam K. *Sergeant York and His People*. New York: Funk & Wagnalls Co., 1922.

Creel, George. *How We Advertised America*. New York: Arno Press, 1972.

———. *Rebel at Large: Recollections of Fifty Crowded Years*. New York: G. P. Putnam's Sons, 1947.

———. *The War, the World and Wilson*. New York: Harper & Bros., 1920.

Crocker, Ruth Hutchinson. *Social Work and Social Order: The Settlement Movement in Two Industrial Cities, 1889–1930*. Urbana: University of Illinois Press, 1992.

Croly, Herbert. *The Promise of American Life*. New York: Macmillan, 1912.

Crozier, Emmet. *American Reporters on the Western Front, 1914–1918*. New York: Oxford University Press, 1959.

Dallas, Gregor. *1918: War and Peace*. London: John Murray, 2000.

Daniels, Roger. *Coming to America: A History of Immigration and Ethnicity in American Life*. New York: HarperCollins, 1990.

Davis, Philip, ed. *Immigration and Americanization: Selected Readings*. Boston: Ginn and Co., 1920.

Dawley, Alan. *Changing the World: American Progressives in War and Revolution*. Princeton, N.J.: Princeton University Press, 2003.

DeBauche, Leslie Midkiff. *Reel Patriotism: The Movies and World War I*. Madison: University of Wisconsin Press, 1997.

Demaree, Joseph. *History of Company A (308th Infantry) of the Lost Battalion*. New York: Harvey Press, 1920.

Detweiler, Frederick G. *The Negro Press in the United States*. Chicago: University of Chicago Press, 1922.

Devlin, Patrick. *Too Proud to Fight: Woodrow Wilson's Neutrality*. New York: Oxford University Press, 1975.

DeWeerd, Harvey A. *President Wilson Fights His War: World War I and the American Intervention*. New York: Macmillan, 1968.

Diner, Hasia R. *In the Almost Promised Land: American Jews and Blacks, 1915–1935*. Westport, Conn.: Greenwood Press, 1977.

Diner, Steven J. *A Very Different Age: Americans of the Progressive Era*. New York: Hill and Wang, 1998.

Dixon, Thomas. *The Clansman*. Lexington: University of Kentucky Press, 1970.

———. *The Fall of a Nation: A Sequel to the Birth of a Nation*. New York: Arno Press, 1975.

Dollinger, Marc. *Quest for Inclusion: Jews and Liberalism in Modern America*. Princeton: Princeton University Press, 2000.

Dower, John W. *War Without Mercy: Race and Power in the Pacific War*. New York: Pantheon Books, 1986.

Dray, Philip. *At the Hands of Persons Unknown: The Lynching of Black America*. New York: Random House, 2002.

Drum, Hugh A. "Reports—Statements—Etc./Papers Relating to Lost Battalion, 77th Division." Typescript at AMHI.

Dubofsky, Melvyn. *We Shall Be All: A History of the IWW, the Industrial Workers of the World*. New York: Quadrangle Press, 1969.

————. *When Workers Organize: New York City in the Progressive Era*. Amherst: University of Massachusetts Press, 1968.

DuBois, W. E. B. *The Oxford W.E.B. DuBois Reader*, edited by Eric J. Sundquist. New York: Oxford University Press, 1996.

Dudziak, Mary L. *Cold War Civil Rights: Race and the Image of American Democracy*. Princeton, N.J.: Princeton University Press, 2000.

Duffy, Francis Patrick. *Father Duffy's Story*. Garden City, N.Y.: Doubleday, 1919.

Dyer, Thomas G. *Theodore Roosevelt and the Idea of Race*. Baton Rouge: Louisiana State University Press, 1980.

Early, Gerald. "Pulp and Circumstance: The Story of Jazz in High Places," in *The Jazz Cadence of American Culture*, edited by Robert G. O'Meally, 393–430. New York: Columbia University Press, 1998.

Eastman, Max. *Enjoyment of Living*. New York: Harper & Bros., 1948.

Edgerton, Robert B. *Hidden Heroism: Black Soldiers in America's Wars*. Cambridge, Mass.: Westview Books, 2002.

Eisenhower, John S. D. *Intervention! The United States and the Mexican Revolution, 1913–1917*. New York: W.W. Norton, 1993.

Ellis, Mark. *Race, War, and Surveillance: African Americans and the United States Government During World War I*. Bloomington: Indiana University Press, 2001.

Ellis, O. O., and E. B. Garey, *The Plattsburg Manual: A Hand Book for Federal Training Camps*. New York: Century Co., 1917.

Ely, Richard T. *Suggestions for Speakers*. Patriotism Through Education Series, no.13. New York: National Security League, 1917.

————. *The World War and Leadership in a Democracy*. New York: Macmillan, 1918.

Fairchild, Henry Pratt. *Immigration: A World Movement and Its American Significance*. New York: Macmillan, 1925.

————. *The Melting-Pot Mistake*. Boston: Little, Brown, 1926.

Farwell, Byron. *Over There: The United States in the Great War, 1917–1918*. New York: W. W. Norton, 1999.

Fielding, Raymond. *The American Newsreel, 1911–1967*. Norman: University of Oklahoma Press, 1972.

Fink, Leon. *Progressive Intellectuals and the Dilemmas of Democratic Commitment*. Cambridge, Mass.: Harvard University Press, 1997.

Fish, Hamilton. *Memoir of an American Patriot*. Epilogue by Brian Mitchell. Washington, D.C.: Regnery Gateway, 1991.

Fletcher, Marvin. *The Black Soldier and Officer in the United States Army, 1891–1917*. Columbia: University of Missouri Press, 1974.

Foley, Barbara. *Spectres of 1919: Class and Nation in the Making of the New Negro*. Urbana: University of Illinois Press, 2003.

Foner, Philip S. *Organized Labor and the Black Worker, 1619–1981*. New York: International Publishers, 1982.

Ford, Nancy Gentile. *War and Ethnicity: Foreign-Born Soldiers and United States*. Ph.D. diss., Temple University, 1994.

Foster, Wallace. *A Patriotic Primer for the Little Citizen*. Indianapolis: Levey Bros. and Co., 1898.

Frederickson, George M. *The Black Image in the White Mind: The Debate Over Afro-American Character and Destiny, 1817–1917*. New York: Harper Torchbooks, 1972.

Fuchs, Lawrence H. *The American Kaleidoscope: Race, Ethnicity, and the Civic Culture*. Middletown, Conn.: Wesleyan University Press, 1990.

Fussell, Paul. *The Great War and Modern Memory*. New York: Oxford University Press, 2000.

Gabler, Neal. *An Empire of Their Own: How the Jews Invented Hollywood*. New York: Doubleday, 1988.

Gatewood, Willard B. *Black Americans and the White Man's Burden, 1898–1903.* Urbana: University of Illinois Press, 1975.

Gerstle, Gary. *American Crucible: Race and Nation in the Twentieth Century.* Princeton, N.J.: Princeton University Press, 2001.

Gevinson, Alan, ed. *Within Our Gates: Ethnicity in American Feature Films, 1911–1960.* Berkeley: University of California Press, 1997.

Gold, Michael. *Jews Without Money.* New York: Horace Liveright, 1930.

Goldman, Emma. *Living My Life,* edited by Richard and Anna Maria Drinnon. New York: New American Library, 1977.

Goldstein, Yaacov N. *Jewish Socialists in the United States: The Cahan Debate, 1925–1926.* Sussex, U.K.: Academic Press, 1998.

Gompers, Samuel. *Address by Samuel Gompers, President of the American Federation of Labor.* Patriotism Through Education Series, no. 19. New York: National Security League, 1917.

Goren, Arthur A. *New York Jews and the Quest for Community: The Kehillah Experiment, 1908–1922.* New York: Columbia University Press, 1970.

Gould, Lewis L. *The Presidency of Theodore Roosevelt.* Lawrence: University Press of Kansas, 1991.

Gould, Stephen J. *The Mismeasure of Man.* New York: W. W. Norton, 1981.

Graham, Otis L. *An Encore for Reform: The Old Progressives and the New Deal.* New York: Oxford University Press, 1967.

Grant, Madison. *The Passing of the Great Race, or the Racial Basis of European History.* New York: Charles Scribner's Sons, 1916.

Gray, Glenn. *The Warriors: Reflections on Men in Battle.* New York: Harper & Row, 1959.

Greene, Robert E. *Black Defenders of America, 1775–1973.* Chicago: Johnson Publishers, 1974.

——. *Colonel Charles Young: Soldier and Diplomat.* Washington: R. E. Greene, 1985.

Guterl, Matthew Pratt. *The Color of Race in America, 1900–1940.* Cambridge, Mass.: Harvard University Press, 2001.

Guttman, Jon. "Regiment's Pride,"*Military History* 8 (October 1991): 35–41.

Haber, Samuel. *Efficiency and Uplift: Scientific Management in the Progressive Era, 1890–1920.* Chicago: University of Chicago Press, 1964.

Hagedorn, Hermann. *Leonard Wood: A Biography,* 2 vols. New York: Harper & Bros., 1931.

Hall, Bruce Edward. *Tea That Burns: A Family Memoir of Chinatown.* New York: Free Press, 1998.

Hanks, Richard Kay. *Hamilton Fish and American Isolationism, 1920–1944.* Ph.D. diss., University of California, Riverside, 1971.

Hansen, Jonathan M. *The Lost Promise of Patriotism: Debating American Identity, 1890–1920.* Chicago: University of Chicago Press, 2003.

Harries, Meirion, and Susie Harries. *The Last Days of Innocence: America at War, 1917–1918.* New York: Vintage Books, 1997.

Harris, Bill. *The Hellfighters of Harlem: African-American Soldiers Who Fought for the Right to Fight for Their Country.* New York: Carroll and Graf, 2002.

Harris, Stephen L. *Harlem's Hell Fighters: The African-American 369th Infantry in World War I.* Washington: Brassey's, Inc., 2003.

Harrison, Hubert. *A Hubert Harrison Reader,* edited by Jeffrey B. Perry. Middletown, Conn.: Wesleyan University Press, 2001.

Hart, Albert Bushnell, and Arthur O. Lovejoy. *Handbook of the War for Public Speakers.* New York: National Security League, 1917.

Hawley, Ellis W. *The Great War and the Search for a Modern Order: A History of the American People and Their Institutions, 1917–1933.* New York: St. Martin's Press, 1979.

Hays, Samuel P. *Conservation and the Gospel of Efficiency: The Progressive Conservation Movement, 1890–1920.* Cambridge, Mass.: Harvard University Press, 1959.

Hemingway, Ernest, ed. *Men in War.* New York: Bramhall House, 1942.

Henri, Florette. *Bitter Victory: A History of Black Soldiers in World War I.* Garden City, N.Y.: Doubleday & Co., 1970.

Hertzberg, Arthur. *The Jews in America.* New York: Columbia University Press, 1998.

Heywood, Chester D. *Negro Combat Troops in the World War: The Story of the 371st Infantry.* Worcester, Mass.: Commonwealth Press, 1928.

Higham, Robert. *Bayonets in the Streets: The Use of Troops in Civil Disturbances.* Lawrence: University Press of Kansas, 1969.

History of Company D, 308th U.S. Infantry, 77th Division. New York: Harvey Press, 1919.

Hofstader, Richard. *The American Political Tradition, and the Men Who Made It.* New York: Vintage, 1973.

———. *Social Darwinism in American Thought,* rev. ed. Boston: Beacon Press, 1955.

Hogan, William T. *Economic History of the Iron and Steel Industry in the United States,* vol. 1. Lexington, Ky.: D. C. Heath & Co., 1971.

Hoganson, Kristin L. *Fighting for American Manhood: How Gender Politics Provoked the Spanish-American and Philippine-American Wars.* New Haven: Yale University Press, 1998.

Holderman, Nelson M. " 'The Lost Battalion' 77th Division." Typescript of presentation to Army War College (1926), National Archives, Records of the 77th Division AEF, 277-18.2.

Homberger, Eric. *The Historical Atlas of New York City: A Visual Celebration of Nearly 400 Years of New York City's History.* New York: Henry Holt and Co., 1994.

Hornaday, William. *Awake! America: Object Lessons and Warnings.* New York: Moffat, Yard & Co., 1918.

Hosking, Geoffrey, and George Schopflin, eds., *Myths and Nationhood.* New York: Routledge, 1997.

Hough, Emerson. *The Web.* New York: Arno Press, 1969.

Howe, Irving. *World of Our Fathers.* New York: Harcourt Brace Jovanovich, 1976.

Huggins, Nathan Irvin. *Harlem Renaissance.* London: Oxford University Press, 1971.

Huntington, Samuel P. *The Clash of Civilizations and the Remaking of World Order.* New York: Simon & Schuster, 1998.

———. *Who Are We? The Challenges to America's National Identity.* New York: Simon & Schuster, 2004.

Hunton, Addie W., and Kathryn M. Johnson. *Two Colored Women with the American Expeditionary Forces.* New York: G. K. Hall & Co., 1997.

Hussey, Alexander T., and Raymond M. Flynn. *The History of Company E, 308th Infantry (1917–1919).* New York: Knickerbocker Press, 1919.

Hutchinson, John, and Anthony D. Smith, eds. *Ethnicity.* Oxford, U.K.: Oxford University Press, 1996.

Hynes, Samuel. *The Soldiers' Tale: Bearing Witness to Modern War.* New York: Penguin Books, 1997.

Iorizzo, Luciano J., and Salvatore Mondello. *The Italian Americans.* Boston: Twayne Publishers, 1980.

Isenberg, Michael T. *War On Film: American Cinema and World War I, 1914–1941.* London and Toronto: Associated University Presses, 1981.

Jackson, Walter A. *Gunnar Myrdal and America's Conscience: Social Engineering and Racial Liberalism, 1938–1987.* Chapel Hill: University of North Carolina Press, 1990.

Jacobson, Matthew Frye. *Special Sorrows: The Diasporic Imagination of Irish, Polish, and Jewish Immigrants in the United States.* Berkeley: University of California Press, 2002.

———. *Whiteness of a Different Color: European Immigrants and the Alchemy of Race,* Cambridge, Mass.: Harvard University Press, 1998.

James, William. *Memories and Studies*. London: Longmans, Green, and Co., 1911.

[Jamieson, J. A.] et al., *Complete History of the Colored Soldiers in the World War*. n.p.: Bennett and Churchill, 1919.

Jensen, Joan M. *Army Surveillance in America, 1775–1980*. New Haven: Yale University Press, 1991.

Johnson, Charles Jr. *African American Soldiers in the National Guard: Recruitment and Deployment During Peacetime and War*. Westport, Conn.: Greenwood Press, 1992.

Johnson, James Weldon. *Along This Way: The Autobiography of James Weldon Johnson*, edited by Sondra Kathryn Wilson. New York: Penguin Books, 1990.

———. *Black Manhattan*. New York: Arno Press, 1968.

———. *The Selected Writings of James Weldon Johnson*, 2 vols, edited by Sondra Kathryn Wilson. New York: Oxford University Press, 1995.

Johnson, Thomas M. *Without Censor: New Light on Our Greatest World War Battles*. Indianapolis: Bobbs-Merrill Co., 1928.

Johnson, Thomas M., and Fletcher Pratt. *The Lost Battalion*. Introduction by Edward Coffman. Lincoln: University of Nebraska Press, 2000.

Jordan, Walker H. *With "Old Eph" in the Army (Not a History): A Simple Treatise on the Human Side of the Colored Soldier*. Baltimore: H. E. Houck and Co, n.d.

Jordan, William G. *Black Newspapers and America's War for Democracy, 1914–1920*. Chapel Hill: University of North Carolina Press, 2001.

Karp, Abraham J., ed. *The Jewish Experience in America: Home in America*, vol. 5. New York: Ktav Publishing House, 1969.

Karp, Walter. *The Politics of War: The Story of Two Wars Which Altered Forever the Political Life of the American Republic (1890–1920)*. New York: Harper & Row, 1979.

Karst, Kennet L. *Belonging to America: Equal Citizenship and the Constitution*. New Haven: Yale University Press, 1989.

Keegan, John. *The First World War*. New York: Random House, 2000.

Keene, Jennifer D. *Doughboys, the Great War, and the Remaking of America*. Baltimore: Johns Hopkins University, 2001.

Kellor, Frances A. *Immigration and the Future*. New York: George H. Doran Co., 1920.

———. *Straight America: A Call to National Service*. New York: Macmillan, 1916.

Kennedy, David M. *Over Here: The First World War and American Society*. New York: Oxford University Press, 1980.

Kerlin, Robert T. *The Voice of the Negro 1919*. New York: Arno Press, 1968.

Kilroy, David P. *For Race and Country: The Life and Career of Colonel Charles Young*. Westport, Conn.: Praeger, 2003.

Kimball, Robert, and William Bolcom. *Reminiscing with Noble Sissle and Eubie Blake*. New York: Cooper Square Press, 1973.

King, Desmond. *Making Americans: Immigration, Race, and the Origins of the Diverse Democracy*. Cambridge, Mass.: Harvard University Press, 2000.

Kirkpatrick, Clifford. *Intelligence and Immigration*. Baltimore: Williams & Wilkins Co., 1926.

Klausner, Julius. *Company B 307th Infantry, Its History, Honor Roll, Company Roster*. n.p.: Pevensey Press, 1920.

Koppes, Clayton R., and Gregory D. Black. *Hollywood Goes to War: How Politics, Profits, and Propaganda Shaped World War II Movies*. Berkeley: University of California Press, 1990.

Kosak, Hadassah. *Cultures of Opposition: Jewish Immigrant Workers, New York City, 1885–1905*. Albany: State University of New York Press, 2000.

Kotlowitz, Robert. *Before Their Time*. Garden City, N.Y.: Anchor Books, 1998.

Krotoshinsky, Abraham. "How the Lost Battalion Was Saved." *Jewish Veteran* (April 1937): 5–6. NMAJMH.

Kryder, David. *Divided Arsenal: Race and the American State During World War II*. Cambridge: Cambridge University Press, 2000.

Laughlin, Harry H. *Analysis of America's Modern Melting Pot*, in *Hearings Before House Committee on Immigration and Naturalization*. 67th Congress, 3rd Session, Serial 7-C. Washington, D.C.: Government Printing Office, 1923.

———. *Immigration and Conquest: A Report of the Special Committee on Immigration and Naturalization of the Chamber of Commerce of the State of New York*. New York: Chamber of Commerce of the State of New York, 1939.

Lears, T. J. Jackson. *No Place of Grace: Antimodernism and the Transformation of American Culture, 1880–1920*. New York: Pantheon Books, 1981.

Le Bon, Gustav. *The Crowd: A Study of the Popular Mind*. 2nd ed. Dunwoody, Ga.: Norman S. Berg, 1968.

Lee, Rose Hum. *The Chinese in the United States of America*. Hong Kong: Hong Kong University Press, 1960.

Levinger, Rabbi Lee J. *A Jewish Chaplain in France*. New York: Macmillan, 1922.

Lewis, David Levering. *W. E. B. Du Bois: Biography of a Race, 1868–1919*. New York: Henry Holt and Co., 1993.

———. *When Harlem Was in Vogue*. New York: Penguin Books, 1997.

Link, Arthur S. *Woodrow Wilson and the Progressive Era, 1910–1917*. New York: Harper & Bros., 1954.

Lippmann, Walter. *Drift and Mastery: An Attempt to Diagnose the Current Unrest*, edited by William Leuchtenberg. Englewood Cliffs, N.J.: Prentice-Hall, 1961.

———. *Force and Ideas: The Early Writings*, edited by Arthur Schlesinger Jr. New Brunswick, N.J.: Transaction Publishers, 2000.

Lissak, Rivka Shpak. *Pluralism and Progressives: Hull House and the New Immigrants, 1890–1919*. Chicago: University of Chicago Press, 1989.

Little, Arthur W. *From Harlem to the Rhine: The Story of New York's Colored Volunteers*. New York: Covici Friede Publishers, 1936.

Litwack, Leon F. *Trouble in Mind: Black Southerners in the Age of Jim Crow*. New York: Vintage Books, 1999.

Lorini, Alessandra. *Rituals of Race: American Public Culture and the Search for Racial Democracy*. Charlottesville: University of Virginia Press, 1999.

Lorwin, Lewis Levitski, as Louis Levine. *The Women's Garment Workers: A History of the International Ladies' Garment Workers Union*. New York: B. W. Huebsch, 1924.

Luebke, Frederick C. *Bonds of Loyalty: German-Americans in World War I*. De Kalb: Northern Illinois University Press, 1974.

Lundberg, Ferdinand. *Imperial Hearst: A Social Biography*. New York: Equinox Cooperative Press, 1936.

Lynk, M. V. *Negro Pictorial Review of the Great War*. n.p.: By the author, 1919.

MacGregor, Morris J. Jr. *Integration of the Armed Forces 1940–1965*. Washington, D.C.: Center of Military History, 1981.

MacGregor, Morris J. Jr., and Bernard C. Nalty, eds. *Blacks in the United States Armed Forces: Basic Documents, Segregation Entrenched 1917–1940*, vol. 4. Wilmington, Del.: Scholarly Resources, 1981.

MacIntyre, W. Irwin. *The Colored Soldier*. Macon, Ga: G. J. W. Burke Co., 1927.

Mack, Charles E. *Two Black Crows in the A.E.F.* New York: Grossett & Dunlap, 1928.

MacLean, Nancy. *Behind the Mask of Chivalry: The Making of the Second Ku Klux Klan*. New York: Oxford University Press, 1994.

Madigan, Tim. *The Burning: Massacre, Destruction, and the Tulsa Race Riot of 1921*. New York: St. Martin's Griffin, 2001.

Mangan, J. A., and James Walvin, eds. *Manliness and Morality: Middle-Class Masculinity in Britain and America, 1800–1940*. New York: St. Martin's Press, 1987.

March, William. "Company K," in *A William March Omnibus*, edited by Alistair Cooke. New York: Rinehart and Co., 1956.

Marshall, Napoleon Bonaparte. *The Providential Armistice: A Volunteer's Story*. Washington, D.C.: Liberty League, 1930.

Marshall, S. L. A. *World War I*. Boston: Houghton Mifflin Co., 1961.

Mason, Monroe, and Arthur Furr, *The American Negro Soldier with the Red Hand of France.* Boston: Cornhill Co., 1921.

Mathews, Shailer. *Democracy and World Politics.* Patriotism Through Education Series, no. 10. New York: National Security League, 1917.

Mathews, William. *Our Soldiers Speak, 1775–1918.* Boston: Little, Brown, 1943.

May, Stephen. "World War I Veteran Horace Pippin Used Art to Purge Himself of the Horrors of the Trenches." *Military History* (February 1998): 14, 16, 18, 80.

McCall, Samuel Walker. *Patriotism of the American Jew.* Foreword by Charles W. Eliot. New York: Plymouth Press, 1924.

McCollum, [L.C.], ed. *History and Rhymes of the Lost Battalion.* n.p.: Bucklee Publishing, 1939.

McDougall, William. *Is America Safe for Democracy?* New York: Charles Scribner's Sons, 1921.

McElroy, Robert McNutt. *The Ideals of Our War.* Patriotism Through Education Series, no. 5. New York: National Security League, 1917.

McKeogh, Arthur. *The Victorious 77th Division (New York's Own) in the Argonne Fight.* New York: John H. Eggers Co., 1919.

———. "'The Lost Battalion,'" *Collier's: The National Weekly,* November 16, 1918, 5–6, 18–26.

McManus, John C. *The Deadly Brotherhood: The American Combat Soldier in World War II.* Novato, Calif.: Presidio Press, 2000.

Mead, Gary. *The Doughboys: America and the First World War.* Woodstock, N.Y.: Overlook Press, 2000.

Menken, S. Stanwood. *Knowledge by the People the True Basis of National Security.* Patriotism Through Education Series, no. 1. New York: National Security League, 1917.

Mershon, Sherrie, and Steven Schlossman. *Foxholes and Color Lines: Desegregating the U.S. Armed Forces.* Baltimore: Johns Hopkins University Press, 1998.

Metzger, Isaac, ed. *A Bintel Brief: Sixty Years of Letters from the Lower East Side to the Jewish Daily Forward.* Garden City, N.Y.: Doubleday and Co., 1971.

Miles, L. Wardlaw. *History of the 308th Infantry, 1917–1919.* New York: G. P. Putnam's Sons, 1927

Miller, Kelly. *Kelly Miller's History of the World War for Human Rights.* n.p.: A. Jenkins and O. Keller, 1919.

Miller, William D. *Pretty Bubbles in the Air: America in 1919.* Urbana: University of Illinois Press, 1991.

Millis, Walter. *The Road to War: America, 1914–1917.* New York: Houghton Mifflin, 1935.

Minder, Charles F. *This Man's War: The Day-by-Day Record of an American Private on the Western Front.* New York: Pevensey Press, 1931.

Mink, Gwendolyn. *Old Labor and New Immigrants in American Political Development: Union, Party, and State, 1875–1920.* Ithaca, N.Y.: Cornell University Press, 1986.

Mock, James R., and Cedric Larson. *Words That Won the War: The Story of the Committee on Public Information, 1917–1919.* Princeton, N.J.: Princeton University Press, 1939.

Montgomery, David. *The Fall of the House of Labor: The Workplace, the State, and American Labor Activism, 1865–1925.* Cambridge, Mass.: Harvard University Press, 1987.

Morgan, Edmund S. *Inventing the People: The Rise of Popular Sovereignty in England and America.* New York: W. W. Norton, 1988.

Morris, Edmund. *The Rise of Theodore Roosevelt.* New York: Coward McCann and Geoghegan, 1979.

Morris, Edmund. *Theodore Rex.* New York: Random House, 2001.

Mosesson, Gloria R. *The Jewish War Veterans Story.* Washington, D.C.: Jewish War Veterans, 1971.

Mosher, Anne E. *Capital's Utopia: Vandergrift, Pennsylvania, 1855–1916.* Baltimore: Johns Hopkins University Press, 2004.

Moss, James A. *Manual of Military Training*, Menasha, Wis.: George Banta, 1914.

Motley, Mary Penick, ed. *The Invisible Soldier: The Experience of the Black Soldier, World War II*. Detroit: Wayne State University Press, 1975.

Murray, Robert K. *Red Scare: A Study of National Hysteria, 1919–1920*. New York: McGraw Hill, 1955.

Myrick, Herbert. *Fifteen Little War Stories*. Patriotism Through Education Series, no. 28. New York: National Security League, 1918.

Nalty, Bernard C. *Strength for the Fight: A History of Black Americans in the Military*. New York: Free Press, 1986.

Nasaw, David. *The Chief: The Life of William Randolph Hearst*. Boston: Houghton Mifflin Co., 2000.

National Association for the Advancement of Colored People. *Thirty Years of Lynching in the United States, 1889–1918*. New York: NAACP, 1919.

National Cyclopedia of American Biography. 47 vols. New York: J.T. White, 1898–1971.

Nell, John W. *The Lost Battalion: A Private's Story*. San Antonio, Tex.: Historical Publishing Network, 2001.

Niles, John J. *Singing Soldiers*. New York: Charles Scribner's Sons, 1927.

Noggle, Burl. *Into the Twenties: The United States from Armistice to Normalcy*. Urbana: University of Illinois Press, 1974.

Odum, Howard W. *Wings on My Feet: Black Ulysses at the Wars*. Indianapolis: Bobbs-Merrill Co., 1929.

O'Leary, Cecilia Elizabeth. *To Die For: The Paradox of American Patriotism*. Princeton, N.J.: Princeton University Press, 1999.

O'Neill, William L. *The Last Romantic: A Life of Max Eastman*. New Brunswick, N.J.: Transaction Publishers, 1991.

Osofsky, Gilbert. *Harlem: The Making of a Ghetto: Negro New York, 1890–1930*. Chicago: Ivan R. Dee, 1996.

Painter, Nell Irvin. *Standing at Armageddon: The United States, 1877–1919*. New York: W.W. Norton, 1987.

Palmer, Frederick. *America in France*. New York: Dodd, Mead & Co., 1918.

Park, Robert E., and Herbert A. Miller. *Old World Traits Transplanted*. New York: Harper & Bros., 1921.

Park, Robert R. *The Immigrant Press and Its Control*. New York: Harper & Bros., 1922.

Patton, Gerald W. *War and Race: The Black Officer in the American Military, 1915–1941*. Westport, Conn.: Greenwood Press, 1981.

Patton, John H. *History of the American Negro in the Great World War*. [Chicago]: G.G. Sapp, 1919.

Pencak, William. *For God and Country: The American Legion, 1919–1941*. Boston: Northeastern University Press, 1989.

Perlman, Mark. *Labor Union Theories in America: Background and Development*. Evanston, Ill.: Row, Peterson and Co., 1958.

Peterson, H.C., and Gilbert C. Fite. *Opponents of War, 1917–1918*. Madison: University of Wisconsin Press, 1957.

———. *Propaganda for War: The Campaign Against American Neutrality, 1914–1917*. Norman: University of Oklahoma Press, 1939.

Phelps, Edith M., ed. *Selected Articles on Immigration*. New York: H.W. Wilson Co., 1920.

Phillips, Laughlin, et. al. *Horace Pippin, with an Essay by Romare Bearden*. Washington, D.C.: Phillips Collection, 1977.

Pinchot, Gifford. "Roosevelt as President" in *State Papers as Governor and President, 1899–1909, The Works of Theodore Roosevelt*, vol. 15, xxxiii. New York: Charles Scribner's Sons, 1926.

Pizzitola, Louis. *Hearst Over Hollywood: Power, Passion and Propaganda in the Movies*. New York: Columbia University Press, 2002.

Pyle, Ernie. *Brave Men*. New York: Henry Holt and Co., 1944.
———. *Here Is Your War*. New York: Henry Holt and Co., 1943.
Rainsford, W. Kerr. *From Upton to the Meuse with the Three Hundred and Seventh Infantry: A Brief History of Its Life and of the Part it Played in the Great War*. New York: D. Appleton & Co., 1920.
Ranlett, Louis F. *Let's Go! The Story of AS No. 2448602*. Boston: Houghton Mifflin, 1927.
Richards, David A. J. *Italian American: The Racializing of an Ethnic Identity*. New York: New York University Press, 1999.
Riis, Jacob. *How the Other Half Lives: Studies Among the Tenements of New York*, edited by Luc Sante. New York: Penguin Books, 1997.
Roberts, Kenneth L. *Why Europe Leaves Home*. n.p.: Bobbs-Merrill Co., 1922.
Roberts, Neadom. *Brief Adventures of the First American Soldiers Decorated in the World War, as told by Neadom Roberts*. [Trenton]: Collection of John Motley, [1933].
Rodman, Selden. *Horace Pippin: A Negro Painter in America*. New York: Quadrangle Press, 1947.
Rogin, Michael Paul. *Blackface, White Noise: Jewish Immigrants in the Hollywood Melting Pot*. Berkeley: University of California Press, 1998.
Roosevelt, Theodore. *The New Nationalism*, edited by William E. Leuchtenberg. Englewood Cliffs, N.J.: Prentice-Hall, 1961.
———. *Roosevelt in the Kansas City Star: War-Time Editorials by Theodore Roosevelt*, edited by Ralph Stout. Boston: Houghton Mifflin Co., 1921.
———. *The Rough Riders*. New York: Da Capo Press, 1990, repr. 1902 ed.
———. *Theodore Roosevelt, An American Mind: Selected Writings*, edited by Mario R. DiNunzio. New York: Penguin Books, 1994.
———. *Winning of the West*, 7 vols. New York: G. P. Putnam's Sons, 1907.
———. *The Works of Theodore Roosevelt*, vols. 12, 17–19. New York: Charles Scribner's Sons, 1926.
———. *The Writings of Theodore Roosevelt*, edited by William H. Harbaugh. Indianapolis: Bobbs Merrill, 1967.
Rorty, Richard. *Achieving Our Country: Leftist Thought in Twentieth-Century America*. Cambridge, Mass.: Harvard University Press, 1998.
Ross, Edward Alsworth. *The Old World in the New: The Significance of Past and Present Immigration to the American People*. New York: Century Co., 1913, 1914.
———. *What Is America?* New York: Century Co, 1919.
Ross, Stewart Halsey. *Propaganda for War: How the United States Was Conditioned to Fight the Great War of 1914–1918*. Jefferson, N.C.: Macfarland, 1996.
Ross, Warner Anthony. *My Colored Battalion*. Chicago: Warner A. Ross, 1920.
Rudwick, Elliott. *Race Riot at East St. Louis, July 2, 1917*. Foreword by William Julius Wilson. Urbana: University of Illinois Press, 1982.
Rumer, Thomas A. *The American Legion: An Official History, 1919–1989*. New York: M. Evans and Co., 1990.
Sachar, Howard M. *A History of the Jews in America*. New York: Alfred A. Knopf, 1992.
Salvatore, Nick. *Eugene V. Debs, Citizen and Socialist*. Urbana: University of Illinois Press, 1982.
Samponaro, Frank N., and Paul J. Vanderwood. *War Scare on the Rio Grande: Robert Runyon's Photographs of the Border Conflict, 1913–1916*. Austin: Texas State Historical Association, 1994.
Samuels, Peggy, and Harold Samuels. *Teddy Roosevelt at San Juan: The Making of a President*. College Station: Texas A & M University Press, 1997.
Sandos, James A. *Rebellion in the Borderlands: Anarchism and the Plan of San Diego, 1904–1923*. Norman: University of Oklahoma Press, 1992.
Sarna, Jonathan D. *The American Jewish Experience*. New York: Holmes and Meier, 1997.
Saxton, Alexander. *The Rise and Fall of the White Republic: Class Politics and Mass Culture in Nineteenth Century America*. London: Verso, 1990.

Schaffer, Ronald. *America in the Great War: The Rise of the War Welfare State*. New York: Oxford University Press, 1991.

Schlesinger, Arthur M. Jr. *The Disuniting of America: Reflections on a Multicultural Society*. New York: W. W. Norton, 1992.

Schmidt, Hans. *The United States Occupation of Haiti 1915–1934*. New Brunswick: Rutgers University Press, 1971.

Scott, Emmett J. *Scott's Official History of the American Negro in the World War*. New York: Arno Press, 1969.

Scott, Lawrence P., and William M. Womack Sr. *Double V: The Civil Rights Struggle of the Tuskegee Airmen*. East Lansing: Michigan State University Press, 1994.

Seeger, Alan. *Poems*, edited by Amanda Harlech. Paris: Edition 7L, 2001.

Shapiro, Herbert. *White Violence and Black Response from Reconstruction to Montgomery*. Amherst: University of Massachussetts Press, 1988.

Sinkler, George. *The Racial Attitudes of American Presidents from Abraham Lincoln to Theodore Roosevelt*. Garden City, N.Y.: Doubleday Anchor Books, 1972.

Skeyhill, Tom. *Sergeant York: Last of the Long Hunters*. Philadelphia: John C. Winston Co., 1930.

Sklar, Martin J. *The Corporate Reconstruction of American Capitalism, 1890–1916: The Market, the Law, and Politics*. New York: Cambridge University Press, 1988.

Skocpol, Theda. *Protecting Soldiers and Mothers: The Political Origins of Social Policy in the United States*. Cambridge, Mass.: Belknap Press of Harvard University, 1992.

Slobin, Mark. *Tenement Songs: The Popular Music of the Jewish Immigrants*. Urbana: University of Illinois Press, 1982.

Slomovitz, Albert Isaac. *The Fighting Rabbis: Jewish Military Chaplains and American History*. New York: New York University Press, 2001.

Slotkin, Richard. "Equalizers: The Cult of the Colt in American Culture," in *Guns, Crime, and Punishment*, edited by Bernard Harcourt. New York: New York University Press, 2003, chap. 3.

———. *The Fatal Environment: The Myth of the Frontier in the Age of Industrialization, 1800–1890*. New York: Atheneum, 1985.

———. *Gunfighter Nation: The Myth of the Frontier in Twentieth-Century America*. New York: Atheneum, 1992.

———. "Unit Pride: Ethnic Platoons and the Myths of American Nationality," *American Literary History* 13, no. 3 (2001): 469–98.

Smith, Anthony D. *The Ethnic Origins of Nations*. New York: Oxford University Press, 1987.

———. *Myths and Memories of the Nation*. London: Oxford University Press, 1999.

Smith, Jessie Carney, ed. "Horace Pippin," in *Notable Black American Men*, 941–42. Detroit: Gale Research, 1998.

———. *Notable Black American Men*. Detroit: Gale Research, 1998.

Smith, O'Hara. " 'Chief Lo' Was with the 'Lost Battalion' in France." *American Indian* (November 1926): 9.

Smith, Roger M. *Civic Ideals: Conflicting Visions of Citizenship in U.S. History*. New Haven: Yale University Press, 1997.

Sollors, Werner. *Beyond Ethnicity: Consent and Descent in American Culture*. New York: Oxford University Press, 1982.

Spivack, Michelle, et al., *The Jewish War Veterans of the USA: 100 Years of Service*. Paducah, Ky.: Turner, 1995.

Stallings, Laurence. *The Doughboys: The Story of the AEF, 1917–1918*. New York: Harper & Row, 1963.

Stansell, Christine. *American Moderns: Bohemian New York and the Creation of a New Century*. New York: Henry Holt and Co., 2000.

Stein, Judith. *I Tell My Heart: The Art of Horace Pippin*. Philadelphia: Pennsylvania Museum of Fine Arts, 1993.

Stein, Leon, ed. *Out of the Sweatshop: The Struggle for Industrial Democracy*. New York: Quadrangle Press, 1977.

Sterba, Christopher M. *Good Americans: Italian and Jewish Immigrants During the First World War*. New York: Oxford, 2003.

Stoddard, T[heodore] L[othrop]. *The Revolt Against Civilization: The Menace of the Under-Man*. New York: Charles Scribner's Sons, 1922.

———. *The Rising Tide of Color Against White World Supremacy*. New York: Charles Scribner's Sons, 1920.

Strauss, H. A. "Negro Agitation." National Archives, U.S. Department of Justice "Glasser File: Negroes 1917–1924" (1938).

Svonkin, Stewart. *Jews Against Prejudice: American Jews and the Fight for Civil Liberties*. New York: Columbia University Press, 1997.

Swanberg, W. A. *Citizen Hearst: A Biography of William Randolph Hearst*. New York: Charles Scribner's Sons, 1961.

Synott, Marcia Graham. *The Half-Opened Door: Discrimination and Admissions at Harvard, Yale, and Princeton, 1900–1970*. Westport, Conn.: Greenwood Press, 1979.

Takaki, Ronald. *Double Victory: A Multicultural History of America in World War II*. Boston: Little, Brown, 2000.

Taylor, Philip. *The Distant Magnet: European Immigration to the U.S.A.* New York: Harper & Row, 1971.

Thomason, John W. Jr. *Fix Bayonets!* New York: Charles Scribner's Sons, 1926.

Thompson, John A. *Reformers and War: American Progressive Publicists and the First World War*. Cambridge: Cambridge University Press, 1987.

Tichenor, Daniel J. *Dividing Lines: The Politics of Immigration Control in America*. Princeton, N.J.: Princeton University Press, 2002.

Tiebout, Frank B. *A History of the 305th Infantry*. New York: 305th Infantry Auxiliary, 1919.

Tifft, Susan E., amd Alex S. Jones. *The Trust: The Private and Powerful Family Behind the New York Times*. Boston: Little, Brown, 1999.

Tobin, James. *Ernie Pyle's War: America's Eyewitness to World War II*. Lawrence: University Press of Kansas, 1997.

Tolnay, Stewart E., and E. M. Beck. *A Festival of Violence: An Analysis of Southern Lynchings, 1882–1930*. Urbana: University of Illinois Press, 1992.

Tomasi, Lydio F., ed. *The Italian in America: The Progressive View, 1891–1914*. New York: Center for Migration Studies, 1972.

Troncone, Anthony C. *Hamilton Fish Senior and the Politics of American Nationalism, 1912–1945*. Ph.D. diss., Rutgers University, 1993.

Turkington, Grace A. *My Country: A Textbook in Civics and Patriotism for Young Americans*. Boston: Ginn and Co., 1918.

Tuttle, William M. Jr. *Race Riot: Chicago in the Red Summer of 1919*. Urbana: University of Illinois Press, 1996.

U.S. American Battle Monuments Commission. *77th Division: Summary of Operations in the World War*. Washington, D.C.: Government Printing Office, 1944.

———. *92nd Division: Summary of Operations in the World War*. Washington, D.C.: Government Printing Office, 1944.

———. *93rd Division: Summary of Operations in the World War*. Washington, D.C.: Government Printing Office, 1944.

———. *American Armies and Battlefields in Europe*. Washington, D.C.: Center for Military History, 1995.

U.S. Army War College. *Order of Battle of the United States Land Forces in the World War, American Expeditionary Forces*. Washington, D.C.: Government Printing Office, 1931.

U.S. Committee on Public Information. *American Loyalty by Citizens of German Descent*. Washington, D.C.: Committee on Public Information, 1917.

———. *Division of the Four-Minute Men. The Meaning of America.* Bulletin no. 33. Washington, D.C.: Committee on Public Information, June 29, 1918.

———. *Home Reading Course for Citizen-Soldiers.* War Information Series, no. 9. Washington, D.C.: Committee on Public Information, October 1917.

U.S. Congress. 61st Cong., 3rd sess., Senate Document no. 662. *Dictionary of Races or Peoples.* Washington, D.C.: Government Printing Office, 1911.

———. 61st Cong., 3rd sess., Senate Document no. 747. *Abstracts of Reports of the Immigration Commission.* 2 vols. Washington, D.C.: Government Printing Office, 1911.

———. 66th Cong., 1st sess., Senate Document no. 62, vol. 1. *Brewing and Liquor Interests and German and Bolshevik Propaganda. Reports and Hearings of the Subcommittee on the Judiciary, United States Senate.* 3 vols. Washington, D.C.: Government Printing Office, 1919.

———. 68th Cong., 1st sess. *Restriction of Immigration, Hearings before the Committee on Immigration and Naturalization of the House of Representatives.* Washington, D.C.: Government Printing Office, 1924.

———. *Congressional Record: Proceedings and Debates of the 1st Session of the 66th Congress.* Vol. 58. Washington, D.C.: Government Printing Office, 1920.

———. *Congressional Record: Proceedings and Debates of the 1st Session of the 67th Congress.* Washington, D.C.: Government Printing Office, 1921.

———. *Congressional Record: Proceedings and Debates of the 2nd Session of the 67th Congress.* Vol. 62, pt. 1. Washington, D.C.: Government Printing Office, 1921.

———. *Congressional Record: Proceedings and Debates of the 1st Session of the 68th Congress.* vol. 65, pt. 6. Washington, D.C.: Government Printing Office, 1924.

U.S. Department of the Army. *United States Army in the World War 1917–1919.* 9 vols. Washington, D.C.: Center of Military History United States Army, 1989.

U.S. Department of Justice. *Annual Report of the Attorney General of the United States for the Fiscal Year 1921.* Washington, D.C.: Government Printing Office, 1921.

Vaughn, Stephen. *Holding Fast the Inner Lines: Democracy, Nationalism, and the Committee on Public Information.* Chapel Hill: University of North Carolina Press, 1980.

Wade, Wyn Craig. *The Fiery Cross: The Ku Klux Klan in America.* New York: Simon & Schuster, 1987.

Wald, Lillian D. *Windows on Henry Street.* Boston: Little, Brown, 1934.

Waldrep, G.C. III. *Southern Workers and the Search for Community: Spartanburg County, South Carolina.* Urbana: University of Illinois Press, 2000.

Watkins, T.H. *The Hungry Years: A Narrative History of the Great Depression in America.* New York: Henry Holt and Co., 1999.

Weaver, John D. *The Brownsville Raid.* New York: W.W. Norton, 1970.

Weinstein, James. *The Corporate Ideal in the Liberal State, 1900–1918.* Boston: Beacon Press, 1968.

Werstein, Irving. *The Lost Battalion.* New York: W.W. Norton, 1966.

Wharton, James Blanton. *Squad.* New York: Grossett and Dunlap, 1929.

Whittlesey, Charles Barney, Willis Savage Whittelsey III, and Sarah Kimball Whittelsey. *Genealogy of the Whittlesey-Whittelsey Family.* 3rd ed. Salt Lake City: Artistic Printing Co., 1992.

Williams, Charles. *Sidelights on Colored Soldiers.* Boston: B.J. Brimmer Co., 1923.

Williamson, Joel. *The Crucible of Race: Black-White Relations in the American South Since Emancipation.* New York: Oxford University Press, 1984.

Wilson, Woodrow. *The New Democracy: Presidential Messages, Addresses, and Other Papers (1913–1917),* vol. 2, edited by Ray Stannard Baker and William E. Dodd. New York: Harper and Bros., 1926.

———. *The New Freedom: A Call for the Emancipation of the Generous Energies of a People.* New York: Doubleday, Page & Co., 1913.

———. *The Political Thought of Woodrow Wilson,* edited by E. David Cronon. Indianapolis: Bobbs-Merrill Co., Inc., 1965.

Winkler, John K. *William Randolph Hearst: A New Appraisal.* New York: Hastings House, 1955.

Wister, Owen. *Roosevelt: The Story of a Friendship.* New York: Macmillan, 1930.

Woods, Robert A., and Albert J. Kennedy. *The Settlement Horizon.* New Brunswick, N.J.: Transaction Publishers, 1990 (1922).

Wu, Cheng-Tsu, ed. *"Chink!" A Documentary History of Anti-Chinese Prejudice in America.* New York: Meridian Books, 1972.

Wynn, Neil A. *From Progressivism to Prosperity: World War I and American Society.* New York: Holmes and Meier, 1986.

Yoakum, Clarence Stone, and Robert M. Yerkes. *Army Mental Tests.* New York: Henry Holt and Co., 1920.

Young, Charles. *The Military Morale of Races and Nations.* Kansas City, Mo.: Franklin Hudson Publishing Co., 1912.

Zelinsky, Wilbur. *The Cultural Geography of the United States.* Englewood Cliffs, N.J.: Prentice-Hall, 1973.

Zhou, Min. *Chinatown: The Socioeconomic Potential of an Urban Enclave.* Philadelphia: Temple University Press, 1992.

Zimmerman, Jonathan. *Whose America? Culture Wars in the Public Schools.* Cambridge, Mass.: Harvard University Press, 2002.

ACKNOWLEDGMENTS

I want to thank my research assistants, Carolyn Lackey for her work at AMHI, and Chana Pollack for her careful examination of and translations from the *Forward*.

I am very grateful to John Motley, for allowing me to use his superb collection of books, letters, and other material relating to African-American military history; to Mitch Yockelson, Ed Barnes, Sally Kuisel, and the staff at National Archives II for their good and patient advice and their help in finding key documents; to Pamela Feltus at the National Museum of Jewish American Military History, for her help in finding information on Jewish soldiers; to Martin Langeveld, for information about the Whittlesey family; to John Cotter for maintaining the superb "Lost Battalion" Web site; to Gary Nigh of the Trenton Historical Society. I want also to thank Julie Ruiz for her helpful suggestions on the Mexican-American movement in the Rio Grande Valley, and Jeanine Basinger for her invaluable advice about movies.

Thanks also to all of those who answered my inquiries, especially Herman Johnson, Bill Miles, Michael Norman, Christine Stansell, Scott Wong, Marshall Peabody Hoke, Jeff Wilfahrt, Rich Wagner, Jack Fosmark, Daphne Kwok, and to Kate Wolfe and Erhard Konerding of Olin Library.

As always I'm grateful to my editor, Jack Macrae, for his excellent advice; my agent, Carl Brandt; and Iris, for love and editing.

Entries in *italics* refer to illustrations.

About the Author

RICHARD SLOTKIN is the Olin Professor and the former director of American studies at Wesleyan University. His previous titles include *Abe: A Novel of the Young Lincoln*, National Book Award finalist *Gunfighter Nation* and *Regeneration Through Violence,* also a National Book Award finalist and winner of the Albert J. Beveridge Prize. He lives in Middletown, Connecticut.